MW01011739

Fundamentals of Lawyer Leadership

EDITORIAL ADVISORS

Rachel E. Barkow
Segal Family Professor of Regulatory Law and Policy
Faculty Director, Center on the Administration of Criminal Law
New York University School of Law

Erwin Chemerinsky
Dean and Jesse H. Choper Distinguished Professor of Law
University of California, Berkeley School of Law

Richard A. Epstein
Laurence A. Tisch Professor of Law
New York University School of Law
Peter and Kirsten Bedford Senior Fellow
The Hoover Institution
Senior Lecturer in Law
The University of Chicago

Ronald J. Gilson
Charles J. Meyers Professor of Law and Business
Stanford University
Marc and Eva Stern Professor of Law and Business
Columbia Law School

James E. Krier
Earl Warren DeLano Professor of Law Emeritus
The University of Michigan Law School

Tracey L. Meares
Walton Hale Hamilton Professor of Law
Director, The Justice Collaboratory
Yale Law School

Richard K. Neumann, Jr.
Alexander Bickel Professor of Law
Maurice A. Deane School of Law at Hofstra University

Robert H. Sitkoff
John L. Gray Professor of Law
Harvard Law School

David Alan Sklansky
Stanley Morrison Professor of Law
Faculty Co-Director, Stanford Criminal Justice Center
Stanford Law School

ASPEN COURSEBOOK SERIES

Fundamentals of Lawyer Leadership

Leah W. Teague

Associate Dean and Professor of Law
Baylor University School of Law

Elizabeth M. Fraley

Associate Professor of Law
Baylor University School of Law

Stephen L. Rispoli

Assistant Dean of Student Affairs and *Pro Bono* Programs
Baylor University School of Law

Wolters Kluwer

Copyright © 2021 CCH Incorporated. All Rights Reserved.

Published by Wolters Kluwer in New York.

Wolters Kluwer Legal & Regulatory U.S. serves customers worldwide with CCH, Aspen Publishers, and Kluwer Law International products. (www.WKLegaledu.com)

No part of this publication may be reproduced or transmitted in any form or by any means, electronic or mechanical, including photocopy, recording, or utilized by any information storage or retrieval system, without written permission from the publisher. For information about permissions or to request permissions online, visit us at www.WKLegaledu.com, or a written request may be faxed to our permissions department at 212-771-0803.

Cover image: Larsen & Talbert Photography

To contact Customer Service, e-mail customer.service@wolterskluwer.com, call 1-800-234-1660, fax 1-800-901-9075, or mail correspondence to:

Wolters Kluwer
Attn: Order Department
PO Box 990
Frederick, MD 21705

Printed in the United States of America.

1 2 3 4 5 6 7 8 9 0

ISBN 978-1-5438-2525-1

Library of Congress Cataloging-in-Publication Data

Names: Teague, Leah W., author. | Fraley, Elizabeth M.,
   author. | Rispoli, Stephen L., author.
Title: Fundamentals of Lawyer Leadership / Leah W. Teague,
   Associate Dean and Professor of Law, Baylor University School of Law;
   Elizabeth M. Fraley, Associate Professor of Law, Baylor University
   School of Law; Stephen L. Rispoli, Assistant Dean of Student Affairs and
   Pro Bono Programs, Baylor University School of Law.
Description: New York : Wolters Kluwer, [2021] | Includes bibliographical
   references and index. | Summary: "This is a lawyer leadership
   development coursebook for law students"—Provided by publisher.
Identifiers: LCCN 2020048850 (print) | LCCN 2020048851 (ebook) | ISBN
   9781543825251 (paperback) | ISBN 9781543825268 (ebook)
Subjects: LCSH: Lawyers—Training of. | Practice of law. | Law—Study and
   teaching (Continuing education). | Leadership—Study and teaching
   (Continuing education).
Classification: LCC K120 .T43 2021 (print) | LCC K120 (ebook) | DDC
   340.068/4 — dc23
LC record available at https://lccn.loc.gov/2020048850
LC ebook record available at https://lccn.loc.gov/2020048851

About Wolters Kluwer Legal & Regulatory U.S.

Wolters Kluwer Legal & Regulatory U.S. delivers expert content and solutions in the areas of law, corporate compliance, health compliance, reimbursement, and legal education. Its practical solutions help customers successfully navigate the demands of a changing environment to drive their daily activities, enhance decision quality and inspire confident outcomes.

Serving customers worldwide, its legal and regulatory portfolio includes products under the Aspen Publishers, CCH Incorporated, Kluwer Law International, ftwilliam.com and MediRegs names. They are regarded as exceptional and trusted resources for general legal and practice-specific knowledge, compliance and risk management, dynamic workflow solutions, and expert commentary.

We dedicate this book to the lawyer leaders before us, those leading now, and those whose leadership journey is just beginning. May they all continue the tireless work of lawyers to make the world a better place.

-Leah, Liz, and Stephen

Summary of Contents

Contents

 ## Overview of Leadership Fundamentals

Leadership of Self: Growing Into Leadership

Chapter 4: Understanding Leadership Theory   43

Chapter 5: Character, Traits, and Characteristics of Leaders   69

Chapter 6: Skills, Competencies, and Leadership Style   95

Chapter 7: Fixed versus Growth Mindset: "I Can't" Meets "I Can't Yet"   117

Chapter 8: Grit and Resilience   137

Chapter 9: Setting Goals   155

Chapter 10: Giving and Receiving Feedback   167

Chapter 11: The Importance of Well-Being: Thriving in the Legal Profession   185

Chapter 12: Integrity and Character   201

Chapter 13: The Right Leader at the Right Time   227

Part III   Leadership with Others: Effective Group Dynamics

Chapter 14: Leadership and Emotional Intelligence   237

Chapter 15: Relationships and Influence   249

Chapter 16: Followership   273

Chapter 17: Diversity, Inclusion, and Cultural Intelligence   289

Chapter 18: Communication Styles, Public Relations, and Crisis Management   331

Chapter 19: How Organizational Structures Affect Leadership Roles   361

Chapter 20: How Leaders Manage Effectively   377

Part IV   Leadership Within Community: Service and Impact

Chapter 21: Lifelong Learning   393

Preface: Introduction to Lawyer Leadership

"You must be the change you want to see in the world."

Mahatma Gandhi[1]

NAVIGATING LEADERSHIP

"Leadership is a journey, not a destination. It is a marathon, not a sprint. It is a process, not an outcome."

Bill George[2]

We believe the study of leadership is a deeply personal journey. Becoming a leader is a voyage all lawyers take, whether consciously or unconsciously. Like many passages into the unknown, the leadership journey is full of unexpected detours, obstacles to overcome, and revelations about yourself. The experiences along the way teach much about leading and about your vision for change.

Our leadership journeys have been diverse. Each of us came to leadership from a different path but aligned at some point in our view of the importance leadership has for law students and lawyers. As we see it, a leadership journey is one of self-discovery. We hope that you, too, will learn truths about yourself, gain clarity about the way you perceive the world and others in it, and discover how to help grow others and your communities through your time, talent, and energy.

YOUR LEADERSHIP JOURNEY

"Before you are a leader, success is all about growing yourself. When you become a leader, success is all about growing others."

Jack Welch[3]

The desire to help others brings many to law school and leadership opportunities. What brought you to law school? Was it a desire to be part of something meaningful? Were you looking for a career where your work mattered? If you came to law school to make a difference, you are not alone. Admission essays suggest that the desire to help others brought most students to law school. They hoped to make a difference or serve a cause greater than themselves, and at some fundamental level, they realized that legal skills give power to do good. Beyond the technical aspects of being a lawyer, developing skills and training that can help someone in need makes pursuing a law degree worthwhile. The work is hard, but it prepares you for entry into this profession and equips you for a life of impact and significance. Being a lawyer is valuable; being a lawyer-leader is invaluable.

The extent to which students have been exposed to leadership theory and opportunities before law school varies. Some students have experienced leadership in business or the military. Other students may have led organizations in high school or college but not had formal leadership training. Whether you come to law school with much leadership knowledge or little, every law student can learn much from studying leadership as it intersects with the law.

Lawyers have a unique ability to lead others. They communicate well, they are willing to work hard, and they understand the need to inspire others. Wanting to make a difference, however, is not the same thing as knowing how to make that change. You need to spend time studying leadership to become an effective leader, and many of the competencies of leadership actually help you become a better lawyer. By the same token, the competencies you learn as a law student translate to leadership. Notably, formal leadership development has not been part of traditional law school curriculum. We believe the time for more intentional leadership training for lawyers is here. Investing time and effort in this leadership course will augment the other knowledge, skills, and professional competencies gained in law school. All these efforts will better prepare you for the opportunities that await. You will become part of a long line of lawyers who made a difference. It's a storied tradition, and one you will be glad to join.

LAWYERS AS LEADERS AND THE ROLE OF THE LAWYER IN SOCIETY

"We educated, privileged lawyers have a professional and moral duty to represent the underrepresented in our society, to ensure that justice exists for all, both legal and economic justice."

Justice Sonia Sotomayor[4]

Lawyers have been leaders in society since the profession began. They were creators and guardians of the rule of law, providing security to the vulnerable and defending against those who preferred a more lawless society. You may recall the line from Shakespeare's *Henry VI*, when Dick the Butcher exclaims, "The first thing we do, let's kill all the lawyers."[5] That line still gets a laugh 300 years later. Audiences assume it means ridding society of the kind of lawyers who give the profession a bad name and prompt lawyer jokes.[6] When Shakespeare wrote it, however, the line reflected more sober times. During that the period, lawyers stood as a bulwark against anarchy. In the play, rebel leader Jack Cade sought a kingdom where beer flowed freely, no one worked and those who could read were punished.[7] The way to create a world where anarchy ruled was to abolish the rule of law, and lawyers stood in their way. Killing all the lawyers, then, meant killing the fair and equal application of the law that protected a civilized society.

While lawyers have been leaders throughout history, Alexis de Tocqueville recognized the special status entrusted to American lawyers. de Tocqueville observed that American lawyers, as keepers of the rule of law and with their special training as problem solvers and advocates, occupied "a separate station in society."[8] He declared lawyers the "American Aristocracy," based on his experience with the European tradition from which he came.[9] The aristocracy in Europe entrusted the care and feeding of the charges to the lords, and that privilege of wealth and power carried with it a duty to protect.[10] Lawyers from Alexander Hamilton and Abraham Lincoln to Barack Obama continued that tradition and led the country through its formation, crises, and remodeling of our views of citizens and their rights. Lawyers have led in ways that mattered greatly.

Despite their significant leadership impact, lawyers are a statistically small group, representing less than one-half of one percent of the population.[11] This small a group, however, accounts for more governmental leaders than any other profession. Of the 55 men who signed the Declaration of Independence, 24 were lawyers.[12] Thirty-five of the 55 delegates to the 1787 Constitutional Convention were lawyers.[13] The majority of our presidents have been lawyers. The occupation with the largest representation in the U.S. Congress is the legal profession.[14]

Though small in number, lawyers are large in influence, impacting decisions made every day. Lawyers lead in every aspect of society,[15] in part because our professional obligations include service to society. The preamble to the ABA Model Rules of Professional Conduct: A Lawyer's Responsibilities, reminds us that "[a] lawyer is a representative of clients, an officer of the legal system, and a public citizen having special responsibility for the quality of justice."[16] Society looks to lawyers to be the guardians of our democracy, protectors of individual rights and liberties, advocates for the powerless, effective mediators, creative problem solvers, and wise leaders in our communities. As described by Harvard Professors Heineman, Lee, and Wilkins, the role of lawyers has traditionally been three-fold — that of *technical expert, wise counselor,* and *effective leader.*[17] These roles are intertwined with and informed by ethics, and through education, training, and experience build on one another. Work to develop each of these components and an understanding of a lawyer's ethical duties. Add to that curriculum a moral commitment to society, and you will be on your way to becoming a complete lawyer — a great lawyer.

LEADERSHIP DEVELOPMENT AS PART OF LEGAL EDUCATION

"Leadership and learning are indispensable to each other."

John F. Kennedy[18]

Given the important role of lawyers as leaders in society, you may be surprised to learn that formal courses and programs on leadership development are new to legal education. In 2007, Ben Heineman wrote about the low priority and presence of leadership training in legal education:

> The profession and the law schools should more candidly recognize the importance of leadership and should more directly prepare and inspire young lawyers to seek roles of ultimate responsibility and accountability than they do today. Why do I advance this thesis? First, our society is suffering from a leadership deficit in public, private, and non-profit spheres. The core competencies of law are as good a foundation for broad leadership as other training. Second, the legal profession, by many accounts, is suffering from a crisis of morale, from a disconnect between personal values and professional life. Providing leadership can affirm — and test — our vision and core values. Third, other professional schools — business and public policy — have as their explicit mission the training of leaders for the public, private, and non-profit sectors. The graduates of our law schools are at least as talented as those who enter other professional and graduate schools. And law schools should have a similar vision to enhance the careers of their outstanding students, thus serving society and addressing the values crisis that affects portions of the profession.[19]

Those words ring true. The intentional cultivation of lawyers as leaders has declined even as the bar recognizes a greater need for lawyers to lead.[20] Influential jurists and members of the Bar call on lawyers to reclaim the traditional role of lawyers as advocates, counselors, and community leaders.[21] A call to leadership is a common theme of law school commencement addresses, speeches, and remarks delivered in varied settings within the profession.[22] Leadership is explicitly mentioned in the mission statements of many law schools.[23] With all of these calls for leadership, why is there a relative dearth of lawyer-leaders? Law schools expect students to engage actively and civically in their communities in a variety of leadership capacities following graduation; should the same schools not be more intentional in providing the training to help graduates lead?

Even with scant classroom time devoted to answering the question "what makes lawyers good leaders," aspects of legal training help lawyers succeed as influencers and leaders. Law students graduate with skills that are crucial for gaining and succeeding in leadership roles. They become decisive, effective communicators who are able to see the big picture while honing in on specific issues, and efficiently solve problems. Lawyers, by training, are able to lead by strategizing, persuading, and ultimately commanding the room, whether a boardroom, courtroom, or arena of public opinion. These are foundational leadership skills developed in law schools.

Deborah Rhode noted in her book *Lawyers as Leaders* that "the legal profession attracts a large number of individuals with the ambition and analytic capabilities to be leaders but frequently fails to develop other qualities that are essential to effectiveness."[24] Being more intentional in our programming and training will ensure our students are better equipped to lead as those opportunities are presented.

We can start by reframing the way we think about leadership development training. While a simple internet search generates a wide variety of definitions and examples of what is "leadership," we suggest leadership is less about titles or positions and more about one individual influencing another. Our legal training, our law license, and our professional status afford us daily opportunities to influence those around us. Now more than ever, we need to recognize our obligation to society and better equip ourselves for the opportunities that will come our way because of our position and legal training. What a difference even a small band of inspired lawyers can make when ready, willing, and able to answer the call.[25] As Margaret Mead said, "Never doubt that a small group of thoughtful committed citizens can change the world. Indeed, it is the only thing that ever has."[26]

THE GREATER GOOD

"The way to achieve your own success is to be willing to help somebody else get it first."

Iyanla Vanzant[27]

Leadership development and training can help individuals thrive. We benefit from becoming more confident and accomplished versions of ourselves; this work improves as well the organizations in which we serve. Demonstrating a willingness to lead often creates opportunities to lead. In a law firm setting, showing initiative, taking point on an important project or case, or spending time developing new business shows leadership. In the community, leadership opportunities abound in helping an organization achieve its goals, protecting protesters' right to peaceful demonstrations, or being elected to office. A surprising benefit of leadership is the ability to serve. Through leadership opportunities we can use our resources (time, talents, and treasures) to better the world in which we live. While accolades and promotions may come from holding leadership positions, most leaders find deeper satisfaction and fulfillment by helping others and making a positive difference in their communities. We hope you will know both personal and professional achievement through leadership but also find significance through service to others.

Internationally acclaimed author Sheila Murray Bethel expressed it well when she wrote,

> If leadership serves only the leader, it will fail. Ego satisfaction, financial gain, and status can all be valuable tools for a leader, but if they become the only motivations, they will eventually destroy a leader. Only when service for a common good is the primary purpose are you truly leading.[28]

As you search for success through leadership, do not forget what significance through service will look like.

THE WAY FORWARD

Learning and honing your legal skills is a life-long pursuit; the same is true for leadership development. For some of you, this book marks the beginning of your leadership education. For others, you have been leading since middle school but want to sharpen the craft. For all of you, we will guide you through a process of self-discovery, self-reflection, and contemplation about your impact on the world around you. We want you to spend time getting to know yourself and to take care of yourself. Throughout the process and the book, you will notice themes of service, an emphasis on integrity and ethics, and the importance of building and nurturing relationships. We want you to use this time as an opportunity to be thoughtful about what is important to you and to be strategic about creating a future of fulfillment, impact, and influence.

In Part 1, we look at the underpinnings of leadership, what it means, and how history guides our view of it. We can learn much from leaders in the past, the challenges they faced, mistakes made, and their courageous choices. In Part 2, we examine Leadership of Self: Growing into Leadership. The leadership journey requires a look inward to examine who you are, what type of lawyer you want to be, and how you will lead. We introduce you to several tools and approaches for learning more about your character and your natural inclinations. Each unique leader brings different attributes to different scenarios, and understanding our strengths, characteristics, and capabilities allows us to be more adaptable and strategic leaders. We will also press you to look at weaknesses or areas where you are not naturally comfortable. We all have these areas, but accomplished leaders take an unflinching look at needed areas of growth, work to improve their skills, or learn to add team members who can fill those gaps.

In Parts 3 and 4, we focus on growing your influence on others and making an impact in the world. Leadership with Others: Effective Group Dynamics covers topics such as building and nurturing relationships, developing emotional and cultural intelligence, establishing effective teams, and inspiring others. We want you to be familiar with the dynamics of organizations where you will likely work, such as law firms and other legal employers, and organizations where you might serve and lead, such as professional associations and community organizations. We look finally at Leadership within Community: Service and Impact. Because you are a lawyer, people will look to you for input and guidance, allowing you to have influence even when you are not in charge. Time and effort spent participating in community activities and professional associations can build relationships that also benefit your practice. Contributing your energy to worthy causes about which you are passionate will bring purpose and satisfaction to your life. In the last chapter, we will encourage you to be thoughtful about your legacy and to be strategic in planning next steps. How you invest your resources in serving others, seeking justice, and protecting the rule of law will have an impact that lasts beyond your life. Moreover, your impact on your loved ones, your community, and our nation will be meaningful.

We wish for you a life of meaning and purpose, impact, and passion, and we hope to get you started on this journey.

Endnotes

1. Mahatma Gandhi, Biography.com, https://www.biography.com/activist/mahatma-gandhi (last visited Jul. 20, 2020). Mahatma Gandhi was the primary leader of India's independence movement and also the architect of a form of non-violent civil disobedience that would influence the world. Until Gandhi was assassinated in 1948, his life and teachings inspired activists including Martin Luther King Jr. and Nelson Mandela.
2. Quote attributed to John Donahoe, *in* Bill George, et al., True North: Discover Your Authentic Leadership (Jossey-Bass 2007).
3. Jack Welch & Suzy Welch, Winning: The Ultimate Business How-To Book (HarperCollins 2009).
4. Quote by Justice Sonia Sotomayor. *See e.g.,* Randy James, *Sonia Sotomayor: Obama's Supreme Court Nominee,* TIME (May 27, 2009), http://content.time.com/time/nation/article/0,8599,1900943,00.html.
5. Debbie Vogel, '*Kill the Lawyers,' A Line Misinterpreted,* The New York Times (Jun. 17, 1990). Shakespeare's exact line "The first thing we do, let's kill all the lawyers," was stated by Dick the Butcher in *Henry VI,* Part II, Act IV, Scene II, Line 73. Dick the Butcher was a follower of the rebel Jack Cade, who thought that if he disturbed law and order, he could become king. Some debate Shakespeare's intention but one can interpolate it as a compliment to attorneys and judges who instill justice in society.
6. One such joke: What is the difference between a lawyer and a catfish? One is a scum-sucking bottom-dweller and the other is a fish.
7. *See generally supra* note 5.
8. Alexis de Tocqueville, Democracy in America 302–09 (1835) (Henry Reeve trans., Pa. State U. 2002), http://seas3.elte.hu/coursematerial/LojkoMiklos/Alexis-de-Tocqueville-Democracy-in-America.pdf.
9. *Id.*
10. *Id.*
11. ABA National Lawyer Population Survey, A.B.A. (2020), available at https://www.americanbar.org/content/dam/aba/administrative/market_research/national-lawyer-population-by-state-2020.pdf.
12. America's Founding Fathers: Delegates to the Constitutional Convention, *available at* http://www.archives.gov/exhibits/charters/constitution_founding_fathers_overview.html (last visited Jul. 20, 2020).
13. *Id.*
14. Thirty-seven percent of the Members of the House and fifty-five percent of the Senators in the 116th Congress. Jennifer Manning, Membership of the 116th Congress: A Profile (Congressional Research Service, June 1, 2020) *available at* https://fas.org/sgp/crs/misc/R45583.pdf.
15. Deborah L. Rhode, Lawyers as Leaders 1 (Oxford Univ. Press 2013).
16. A.B.A. Mod. Rules Prof. Cond., Preamble and Scope.
17. *See* Ben W. Heineman, William F. Lee & David B. Wilkins, *Lawyers as Professionals and as Citizens: Key Roles and Responsibilities in the 21st Century,* Center on the Legal Profession at Harvard Law School (Oct. 20, 2014), https://clp.law.harvard.edu/assets/Professionalism-Project-Essay_11.20.14.pdf.
18. Remarks prepared for President John. F. Kennedy's speech at the Trade Mart in Dallas, Texas (undelivered) (Nov. 22, 1963), *available at https://www.jfklibrary.org/archives/other-resources/john-f-kennedy-speeches/dallas-tx-trade-mart-undelivered-19631122.*
19. Ben W. Heineman, *Lawyers as Leaders,* 116 Yale L. J. Pocket Part 266 (2007), http://yalelawjournal.org/forum/lawyers-as-leaders.
20. Leah Witcher Jackson Teague, *Lawyers as Leaders: Community Engagement and Leadership Benefit All,* State Bar of Tex., https://www.texasbar.com/AM/Template.cfm?Section=articles&Template=%2FCM%2FHTMLDisplay.cfm&ContentID=39075 (last visited Jul. 22, 2020).

21. Louis D. Brandeis, *The Opportunity in the Law, Address Before the Harvard Ethical Society* (May 4, 1905) *in* Business — A Profession 313, 321 (1914); The Texas Lawyer's Creed — A Mandate for Professionalism (adopted by the Supreme Court of Texas and the Court of Criminal Appeals Nov. 7, 1989), *reprinted in* Texas Rules of Court: Volume I — State 723 (ThomsonReuters 2017); Anthony T. Kronman, The Lost Lawyer: Failing Ideals of the Legal Profession (1993); Ben W. Heineman, Jr., Law and Leadership, Lecture as part of The Robert H. Prieskel and Leon Silverman Program on the Practicing Lawyer and the Public Interest (Nov. 27, 2006) [hereinafter "Heineman, *Law and Leadership*"].

22. Neil W. Hamilton, *Ethical Leadership in Professional Life*, 6 U. St. Thomas L. J. 358, 359–60 (2009); "Roscoe Pound and Chief Justice Burger understood that the best way for the profession to continue to resolve society's conflicts is to lead." (*see* Roscoe Pound, Speech at the Annual Meeting of the American Bar Association (1906) and Chief Justice Warren Burger, Speech at the Pound Conference (1976) *in Report on the Future of Legal Services in the United States,* ABA 8 (2016), http://www.americanbar.org/content/dam/aba/images/abanews/2016FLSReport_FNL_WEB.pdf (hereinafter ABA Report)..

23. Elizabeth M. Fraley & Leah Witcher Jackson Teague, *Where the Rubber Hits the Road: How Do Law Schools Demonstrate a Commitment to Training Leaders?*, U. Tenn. L. Rev. (forthcoming).

24. Rhode, *supra* note 15.

25. Joseph Jaworski, Synchronicity: The Inner Path of Leadership (Berrett-Koehler 2011).

26. Margaret Mead Quote, Intercultural Studies, http://www.interculturalstudies.org/faq.html#quote (last visited Jul. 20, 2020).

27. Iyanla Vanzant (@IyanlaVanzant), Twitter (Jan. 24, 2013, 3:23 PM), https://twitter.com/IyanlaVanzant/status/294556149729095681.

28. Shiela Murray Bethel, Making a Difference: 12 Qualities That Make You a Leader (Berkley Books 1990).

Acknowledgments

This book exists because of a talented and dedicated group of individuals who made this journey possible for us. We begin by thanking Justin Billing, Jordan Jepsen, and the team at Wolters Kluwer Legal & Regulatory U.S. We appreciate their partnership in advancing the work of leadership development for law students and lawyers. Their commitment to a textbook in this new area of formal study in legal education evidences their leadership in the publication world. Their confidence in us is appreciated. Our special thanks to Karen Hall at The Froebe Group. Her guidance and encouragement were invaluable.

We also recognize those who are the true pioneers in teaching leadership development to law students. Their work continues to inspire us. We pay special tribute to:

- Deborah L. Rhode, Ernest W. McFarland Professor of Law and the Director of the Center on the Legal Profession at Stanford Law School,
- Doug Blaze, Dean Emeritus, Professor of Law and Director of the Institute for Professional Leadership at the University of Tennessee College of Law,
- Donald J. Polden, Dean Emeritus and Professor of Law at Santa Clara University School of Law,
- Garry W. Jenkins, Dean and William S. Pattee Professor of Law at the University of Minnesota Law School, and
- David H. Gibbs, Visiting Leadership Fellow, University of Tennessee College of Law.

We thank them for their leadership in encouraging leadership development programming throughout legal education. We also want to acknowledge Neil Hamilton and Jerry Organ for their work at the Holloran Center for Ethical Leadership in the Professions. Their encouragement and efforts in the development of law students' professional formation edify our work. At the top of our list to acknowledge and thank is Deborah L. Rhode. Her persuasive scholarship and advocacy, as well as her legendary status in the academy, paved the way for the creation of the American Association of Law Schools Section on Leadership. Our work would not be possible without the investments made by these respected colleagues and so many others who believe in the mission of preparing our students for effective lawyering and leadership.

We are eternally grateful for the support received from our leader at Baylor Law. Dean Brad Toben's unwavering belief in the importance of this work has encouraged us and strengthened our resolve to pursue endeavors that will better equip law graduates for impact and significant in their future roles. We also thank our colleague, Professor Patricia A. Wilson, for her review and suggestions for vital aspects of this work.

To the following team of talented Baylor Law students, we cannot thank you enough for the many hours of tedious labor spent getting our boat in the water and to this point. We appreciate your insight, dedication and long hours of work:

Lanie Bennett
Shannon Black
Cody Branstetter
Chris Carbonaro
Kyli Cotten
James Fryer
Stefan Garcia
Kellsey Hansen
Blaine Hill
Molly Maier
Max Moran
Chele Naudin
Sarah Van Sciver
Juan Antonio Solis
Alli Szabo

We give special thanks to Max Moran and Chele Naudin for their steadfast efforts to finalize the book.

We appreciate the work of the following reviewers for their valuable contributions to the development of our work:

Doug Blaze
Dean Emeritus, Professor of Law & Director of the Institute for Professional Leadership
University of Tennessee College of Law

Melissa Essary
Dean Emeritus & Professor of Law
Norman Adrian Wiggins School of Law, Campbell University

B. Keith Faulkner
Dean & Professor of Law
Liberty University School of Law

Neil W. Hamilton
Holloran Professor of Law & Co-Director of the Holloran Center for Ethical Leadership in the Professions
University of St. Thomas

Susan R. Jones
Professor of Clinical Law
George Washington University Law School

Jerome M. Organ
Bakken Professor of Law & Co-Director of the Holloran Center for Ethical Leadership in the Professions
University of St. Thomas

Aric Short
Professor of Law & Director, Professionalism and Leadership Program
Texas A&M University School of Law
Dean Emeritus, Professor of Law & Director of the Institute for Professional Leadership
University of Tennessee College of Law

D. Gordon Smith
Dean & Woodruff J. Deem Professor of Law
Brigham Young University Law

Karen J. Sneddon
Professor of Law
Mercer University School of Law

Thomas Sneed
Associate Professor & Director of the Law Library
Washburn University School of Law

Special thanks to Nancy Cosby, who spent countless hours reviewing the book in the final stages. Her thorough consideration of the content and suggested revisions make this book better than ever. We are grateful for her help and support.

Finally, thank you to our friends and family who supported us through this journey, specifically, Ted Teague, Zach, Alex, and Katie Fraley, Jeanine Rispoli, Frank and Val Rispoli, and Matthew Rispoli and Melis Tekant. Your love and encouragement sustained us in this endeavor. For so many reasons, we are grateful to you.

— Leah Teague, Liz Fraley, and Stephen Rispoli

P.S. — We're continually impressed by Leah's leadership, grit, and resilience. Even though she fought Covid-19 during an important phase of this book, she powered through and continued to work as much as she could to make this book the best that it could be. She amazes us for many reasons, but this is just one more. -Liz and Stephen

The authors would also like to thank the following:

American Bar Association, excerpts from Model Rules of Professional Conduct ©2020 by the American Bar Association. Reprinted with permission. All rights reserved.

This information or any or portion thereof may not be copied or disseminated in any form or by any means or stored in an electronic database or retrieval system without the express written consent of the American Bar Association.

Lewis, Richard D., The Lewis Model, Courtesy of Richard D. Lewis.

Saucedo, Jennifer Hamlet. First published on Facebook. Reprinted with permission of the author.

Smith, Patrick Caleb. Timeline of Rebel Mascots. Reprinted with permission.

Fundamentals of Lawyer Leadership

Part I

Overview of Leadership Fundamentals

Chapter 1 — What Is Leadership?

We don't accomplish anything in the world alone and whatever happens is the result of the whole tapestry of one's life and all the weavings of individual threads from one to another that create something.

Sandra Day O'Connor[1]

Purpose

Encourage thought and discussion about leadership and its importance in the legal profession and our society.

Learning Objectives

At the end of this chapter, you should be able to:

- Define what it means to be a leader.
- Describe key aspects of leadership.
- Describe the difference between leadership and authority.
- Discuss the lawyer's role in society and how leadership development will assist lawyers in fulfilling that role.

Discussion

INTRODUCTION

What is leadership? This seems like such a simple question, but ask it of a hundred business executives, consultants, lawyers, and politicians, and each will give you a different answer. The answers share common elements, but each of these people sees leadership through a different lens, perhaps borne of personal experience, or perhaps simply seeing it as an overused buzzword associated with corporate CEOs. While one can then associate leadership with training CEOs on how to manage people, leadership means so much more than that. A transformative leadership experience, where a team brings to fruition an important goal and vision, captures the essence of good leadership.

Many leaders have tried to encapsulate the concept of leadership in a quote. We find these quotes everywhere — in books of all types, on people's walls, and in graduation speeches. When you look at quotes about leadership from excellent leaders, you may note a couple of important attributes of leaders. First, they share a common vision. Second, they may not fit a prototype of what we think a leader is. Third, they focus on the people whom they lead as much as the vision of where they are leading them:

> Fight for the things that you care about, but do it in a way that will lead others to join you. — *Ruth Bader Ginsburg*[2]

> The greatest leader is not necessarily the one who does the greatest things. He is the one that gets the people to do the greatest things. — *Ronald Reagan*[3]

> And in my own life, in my own small way, I've tried to give back to this country that has given me so much. That's why I left a job at a law firm for a career in public service, working to empower young people to volunteer in their communities. Because I believe that each of us — no matter what our age or background or walk of life — each of us has something to contribute to the life of this nation. — *Michelle Obama*[4]

> A true leader has the confidence to stand alone, the courage to make tough decisions and the compassion to listen to the needs of others. He does not set out to be a leader but becomes one by the equality of his actions and the integrity of his intent. — *Douglas MacArthur*[5]

> Leading in a complex world means recognizing the simple things you can do to make things better. — *Condoleezza Rice*[6]

> Leadership is not bullying and leadership is not aggression. Leadership is the expectation that you can use your voice for good. That you can make the world a better place. — *Sheryl Sandberg*[7]

A leader takes people where they want to go. A great leader takes people where they don't necessarily want to go, but ought to be. — *Rosalynn Carter*[8]

Defining leadership for all situations is a formidable task and one that warrants a lifetime of study. As you master one aspect of leadership, you will find a new challenge in leading, whether because of the nature of the goal, the composition of the team, or your maturity as a leader. We encourage you to study leadership not only in this course but as part of the lifelong learning that leadership in different roles will demand. In this chapter, we look at some aspects that are fundamental to forming your own understanding of leadership and the opportunities you will have to make a positive difference each day.

DEFINITIONS OF LEADERSHIP

Attributes of leadership and individual leaders have been the subjects of significant academic study for over a hundred years, with scholars providing more than two hundred different definitions of leadership.[9] Tens of thousands of books have been written about leadership.[10] Some define leadership by identifying the traits of leaders or describing behaviors. Some approach leadership as a process of sharing information and as a way to explain relationship. "Leadership has been studied using both qualitative and quantitative methods in many contexts, including small groups, therapeutic groups, and large organizations."[11] After studying the "multitude of ways in which leadership has been conceptualized," Peter Northouse defines leadership as "a process whereby an individual influences a group of individuals to achieve a common goal."[12] Popular leadership author John C. Maxwell notes that "[l]eadership is not about titles, positions, or flowcharts. It is about one life influencing another."[13]

The understanding of leadership has evolved and changed. In the early twentieth century, definitions of leadership focused on power and control.[14] At a leadership conference in 1927, leadership was defined as "the ability to impress the will of the leader on those led and induce obedience, respect, loyalty, and cooperation."[15] In the 1930s and 1940s, the emphasis shifted away from leadership by dominance to leadership by persuasion, influencing a group because of a leader's traits and behaviors.[16] By 1960, leadership was described as "acts by persons which influence other persons in a shared direction."[17] In the 1970s, the focus shifted to organizational behavior and interconnectedness, as shown in J.M. Burns's seminal definition:

> Leadership is the reciprocal process of mobilizing by persons with certain motives and values, various economic, political, and other resources, in a context of competition and conflict, in order to realize goals independently or mutually held by both leaders and followers.[18]

Scholarly and popular self-help works in the 1980s expanded the conversation about the nature of leadership.[19] Beginning in the 1960s, the study of leadership has focused on the process of leading. A number of approaches were identified and named, including authentic leadership, servant leadership, and adaptive leadership.[20] In the last 60 years, more than 65 different classification systems "have been developed to define the dimensions of leadership."[21] While there are various approaches to leadership,[22] the evolving nature of looking at leadership defies a rigid definition or structure:

> After decades of dissonance, leadership scholars agree on one thing: They can't come up with a common definition for leadership. Because of such factors as growing global influences and generational differences, leadership will continue to have different meanings for different people. The bottom line is that leadership is a complex concept for which a determined definition may long be in flux.[23]

Despite the breadth of scholarship on traits, behaviors, and processes, we agree with Northouse's definition of leadership as "a process whereby an individual influences a group of individuals to achieve a common goal."[24] There are some key aspects to the process of leadership. First, it is relational and involves a social interaction contract: The leader needs followers, owes them a responsibility, and motivates them to be better versions of themselves for the good of a common goal.[25] By the same token, followers follow, adhering to the vision and achieving the common goal. Second, leadership starts within the person through what may be called leadership of self. In the leadership of self, an individual develops the needed ethics, skills, vision, integrity, and courage to lead others effectively.[26] Third, leadership requires vision: a true sense of where the endeavor needs to go.[27] Fourth, leadership takes effective communication, in sharing the vision, motivating the individual, and being able to work cooperatively.[28] Finally, trusted leadership — the kind to which those in the legal profession should aspire — requires integrity. Integrity adheres to a moral core that allows people to trust the leader, her word, her goal, and her vision.[29]

As we frame what leadership is, it may be important to recognize what leadership is not. Leadership is a frame of mind, not a position.[30] Leadership is not tied to what position the person with a leadership mindset holds. A person with a leadership mindset thinks about how she will be most effective in whatever role she plays in the life of an individual, an organization, or the community. Men and women have been put in the C-suite[31] and given a team to run without ever becoming leaders. By the same token, many a private in the army has led men in battle when the situation called for it,[32] for example, when officers were scattered or injured or simply overwhelmed, such that the titular leader was wholly ineffective. The person who understood what needed to happen and convinced his platoon members to join him was the one who led to victory irrespective of rank.[33] Studying successful sports dynasties revealed that the common element in their success was not an inspirational coach, natural talent and athleticism, or an abundance of resources. The "secret sauce" was instead a special player on the team who led the team from the *inside*.[34] The same is true in our communities. While we elect officials to hold public office, they are not exclusively the leaders. Many leaders without an office or title nevertheless lead others in classrooms, businesses, neighborhoods, and community organizations.

Leadership, likewise, is not about personal attributes. The stereotypical picture of a leader as a charismatic extrovert does not define leadership.[35] Many lead quietly and calmly, without fanfare or flash. Introverts can make great leaders thanks to their willingness to think contemplatively and listen carefully to the input of others. While extroverts may be powerful leaders, they also can be so domineering that they overwhelm and alienate rather than unify. It is not the picture of the person that makes a leader, it is the measure of a person that does.

Similarly, leadership is not the same thing as management. As Peter F. Drucker put it, "Management is doing things right; leadership is doing the right thing."[36] Leadership is more about vision, while management is about execution of that vision.[37] "Management was created as a way to reduce chaos in organizations, to make them run more effectively and efficiently."[38] Many highly effective managers are not good leaders because they are too focused on the details of the work to see the big picture.[39] Similarly, not every good leader is a good manager because the leader is so focused on the big picture that the details needed for execution of that vision are ignored.[40] While many confuse management and leadership, they serve different roles and fill different needs.[41]

Leadership is also not about control or imposing the leader's will on the followers.[42] There are many situations in which we are compelled to follow rather than choose to follow. As Clay Scroggins describes it, some leaders mistake authority for leadership and "wield the gun of authority":

> When someone has to pull the gun of authority, something is broken. You only pull out the gun of authority when nothing else is working. The gun will get people moving, at least for a time.[43]

A middle school student punished for a rule infraction must follow the principal's direction to spend a day in detention, but one would not fairly describe the student as following a leader. By the same token, a robber who points a gun at his intended victim certainly controls but does not lead. Followers choose to pursue the directives of effective leaders not because they are forced to but because the leader has made the direction appealing.[44] As early scholars determined, leadership is not about dominance. Leadership is influence toward a common goal.

Common threads, then, emerge from situations showing what leadership is and what it is not. We next look at how leadership, a vital skill for a lawyer, is developed in law school.

LEADERSHIP DEVELOPMENT IN LAW SCHOOL

Leadership is especially important for lawyers because every aspect of client representation applies practical leadership. By advising, advocating, and working with others, lawyers can address an identified need and work to accomplish a greater good.[45] Not infrequently, this involves convincing others to work collaboratively toward a common goal, even when they are adversaries. Sometimes the common goal simply involves resolving a dispute or closing a deal. Lawyers must persuade and work collaboratively for their clients. Beyond individual representation, lawyers can utilize their talents and capabilities to have a tremendous impact on society.[46] Lawyers have contributed their leadership talents to impact pivotal historical events from the founding of our nation through the progressive era, the New Deal, and the civil rights movement.[47] As heads of nations, universities, foundations, companies, legislative committees, and public offices, lawyers have shaped our society and culture.[48]

Today, lawyers play a variety of key roles, whether advocating for important causes, counseling businesses, serving nonprofits, or through any of the other opportunities lawyers have to lead. Training on how to make an impact starts in law school, where lawyers learn strategy, persuasion, and ultimately how to command the room. While not overtly part of the traditional law school curriculum, leadership can be taught and leadership skills developed during the formative process of legal education. Law school provides an opportunity to study great legal leaders and to envision how to lead while also acquiring the foundational knowledge, skills, and competencies to prepare you for your journey. You may lead student organizations, teams, or community service projects in your first forays into lawyer leadership. Learning from these experiences helps prepare you to lead after graduation. Whether studying the theory and history of lawyer leaders or applying the lessons learned, leadership will be a valuable part of your legal practice.

The fundamental distinction between the study of leadership and many other aspects of law school is that leadership is personal to you. Unlike doctrinal classes where you can learn rules and apply them to fact patterns, some lessons of leadership are difficult to learn and even harder to apply without experience. Few written rules govern your interactions with others. The "rules" that are written prevent you from offending or hurting others, but people do not come with instruction manuals about the best way to work with them. Instead, you learn by doing.

While in law school, spend time studying yourself. Not only will that insight help you as you learn more about your own skills, you will get better perspective on how others view you and interpret information you try to convey. Second, study others so that you understand better what motivates them, how they hear and receive information, and how teams work together. Third, practice your problem-solving skills by assessing the issues and needs of people involved, developing a plan to achieve the goal, and assessing and overcoming barriers to the goal. Finally, understand and internalize the importance of living your life, leading and practicing law as a person of integrity and good moral character. Start the process of choosing the right thing to do, even when it is difficult or comes with unpleasant consequences. The challenges will likely be greater in practice than in law school, so testing your mettle and your willingness to choose ethical behavior now means you are more likely to make the right decision at the right time. Leading is a complex process, and studying its different facets can make you a better leader.

Our society needs effective leaders who can see things both as they are and as they should be. Inspirational leaders help us see and want to move in this new direction. We need their guidance and support to accomplish the targeted goal. We want to be better versions of ourselves and to make a difference in the world around us in a multitude of ways. We need to feel part of something bigger and more profound than simply going to the office and billing hours. As the world changes at an ever-increasing pace, we must be able to adapt and change. Leaders take us on that journey.

CONCLUSION

Lawyers serve as leaders in ways big and small. Leadership is more than a title or position — it is a lifelong commitment to being the best you can be while striving to also help others become the best versions of themselves. Understanding how to lead and what leadership involves — leadership of self, leadership of a team, and leadership of the community — helps distinguish law as a profession, not just a business. Leading is a skill as necessary as learning critical and analytical thinking, writing well, and providing sound counsel to a client. Lawyers lead every day in their homes, offices, and communities.

Hundreds of books try to define leadership and offer advice about how to be a leader. Dozens are devoted to lawyer leadership.[49] We encourage you to read some of these books and develop your knowledge base on how to lead. Start to develop your own list of attributes (character, skills, and competencies) needed to become a great leader. We look forward to exploring these aspects of leadership with you.

Exercises

What Does Leadership Mean to You?

In advance, find a quote about leadership and a definition of leadership. Bring both and be prepared to discuss them.

Discussion Questions:

1. What is it about the quote that resonates with you? Why did you choose it?
2. Why did you choose that definition of leadership? How can you make that definition better?

Influence for Positive Change

Break into small groups (groups of three or four are ideal). Discuss this prompt:

Thinking back to your immediate pre–law school experience (college or career), describe a time when you were facing a difficult decision and turned to a person (or persons) whose advice you value for guidance.

- What was your relationship with those people before you sought their advice?
- Why did you turn to them for help?
- How did they help you?
- How did that conversation or interaction affect your relationship (i.e., was your relationship stronger or closer after and what is your opinion of them now)?

Journal Prompts

1. Include the leadership quote and definition you found. What does each mean to you and why did you choose them?

2. Who have you known in your life that exemplified what you believe to be good leadership? What did that look like?

3. Who in your life has influenced you? What did you learn from that person? Was that leadership?

4. What do you hope to learn as you study leadership?

Endnotes

1. *See* Anusia Gillespie, *Should You Talk About What You Do, or What You Love?*, ABA Career Center (2020), https://www.americanbar.org/careercenter/blog/should-you-talk-about-what-you-do--or-what-you-love-/. Sandra Day O'Connor is an American attorney, politician, and jurist who served as an Associate Justice of the Supreme Court of the United States from 1981 until her retirement in 2006. She was the first woman to serve on the Court. *Sandra Day O'Connor*, Biography.com, https://www.biography.com/law-figure/sandra-day-oconnor (last visited July 8, 2020).
2. Ruth Bader Ginsburg in a speech at Harvard University on May 29, 2015. Ruth Bader Ginsburg was a Justice on the United States Supreme Court from 1993 until her death in 2020. *Ruth Bader Ginsburg*, Oyez, https://www.oyez.org/justices/ruth_bader_ginsburg (last visited July 20, 2020).
3. Interview by Mike Wallace with Ronald Reagan, President of the United States (Dec. 14, 1975). Ronald Wilson Reagan was an American politician who served as the 40th president of the United States from 1981 to 1989 and became a highly influential voice of modern conservatism. Prior to his presidency, he was a Hollywood actor and union leader before serving as the 33rd governor of California from 1967 to 1975. *Ronald Reagan*, The White House, https://www.whitehouse.gov/about-the-white-house/presidents/ronald-reagan/ (last visited July 8, 2020).
4. Michelle Obama, speech at the Democratic National Convention on Aug. 25, 2008. Michelle Obama is the former First Lady of the United States, a lawyer, a writer, and the wife of former President Barack Obama. *Michelle Obama*, Whitehouse.gov, https://www.whitehouse.gov/about-the-white-house/first-ladies/michelle-obama/ (last visited July 21, 2020).
5. *See Douglas MacArthur Quotes*, Goodreads, https://www.goodreads.com/quotes/359193-a-true-leader-has-the-confidence-to-stand-alone-the (last visited July 8, 2020). General of the Army Douglas MacArthur was an American five-star general and Field Marshal of the Philippine Army. He was Chief of Staff of the United States Army during the 1930s and played a prominent role in the Pacific theater during World War II.
6. *Condoleezza Rice Quotes*, AZ Quotes, https://www.azquotes.com/quote/998497 (last visited July 21, 2020). Condoleezza Rice is the first black woman to serve as the National Security Advisor and U.S. Secretary of State. *Condoleezza Rice*, Biography.com, https://www.biography.com/political-figure/condoleezza-rice (last revised Nov. 13, 2019).

7. Cynthia McFadden & Jake Whitman, *Sheryl Sandberg Launches "Ban Bossy" Campaign to Empower Girls to Lead*, ABC News (Mar. 10, 2014), https://abcnews.go.com/US/sheryl-sandberg-launches-ban-bossy-campaign-empower-girls/story?id=22819181. Sheryl Kara Sandberg is the chief operating officer of Facebook, the founder of LeanIn.Org, and a philanthropist. In June 2012, she was elected to Facebook's board of directors, becoming the first woman to serve on its board.

8. *See* Kara Goldin, *Great Leaders Take People Where They May Not Want to Go*, Forbes (Oct. 1, 2018), https://www.forbes.com/sites/karagoldin/2018/10/01/great-leaders-take-people-where-they-may-not-want-to-go/#6960995e1421. Eleanor Rosalynn Carter is an American who served as First Lady of the United States from 1977 to 1981 as the wife of President Jimmy Carter. For decades, she has been a leading advocate for numerous causes.

9. Peter G. Northouse, Leadership Theory and Practice 2 (8th ed. 2019).

10. At the time of the writing of this book, a search for "leadership" in Amazon books returned over 80,000 results, and "leadership for lawyers" returned over 600 results.

11. Northouse, *supra* note 9, at 1.

12. *Id.* at 2.

13. John C. Maxwell, The 5 Levels of Leadership: Proven Steps to Maximize Your Potential (Center Street 2011).

14. Northouse, *supra* note 9, at 2.

15. *Id.* (citing B.V. Moore, *The May Conference on Leadership,* Personal Journal 6, 124–28 (1927)).

16. *Id.* at 2–3.

17. *Id.* at 3 (citing M. Seeman, *Social Status and Leadership* 53, Columbus: Ohio State University, Bureau of Educational Research (1960)).

18. *Id.* (citing James Burns, Leadership (Harper Torchbooks 1978)).

19. *Id.*

20. *Id.* at 4.

21. *Id.* at 5 (citing E.A. Fleishman et al., *Taxonomic Efforts in the Description of Leader Behavior: A Synthesis and Functional Interpretation*, 2 Leadership Q. 245–87 (1991)).

22. *See* Chapter 2.

23. Northouse, *supra* note 9, at 4.

24. *Id.* at 5.

25. Reagan, *supra* note 3.

26. *See* Donna Brighton, *Secrets of Successful Leaders*, Brighton Leadership Group (Aug. 7, 2019), https://brightonleadership.com/2019/08/07/secrets-of-successful-leaders/.

27. Reagan, *supra* note 3.

28. *See The Art of Great Leadership*, Hardiman Williams (2020), http://www.hardimanwilliams.com/downloads/HW_The_Art_of_Leadership.pdf.

29. *See Douglas MacArthur Quotes*, *supra* note 5.

30. *See* Goldin, *supra* note 8.

31. "C-suite" is a term frequently used to lump together positions with "Chief" titles, such as Chief Executive Officer (CEO), Chief Financial Officer (CFO), Chief Operating Officer (COO), etc. *See* Boris Groysberg et al., *The New Path to the C-Suite*, Harv. Bus. Rev. (Mar. 2011), https://hbr.org/2011/03/the-new-path-to-the-c-suite.

32. Those such as Private Jacob Parrot, the first person to be awarded the Medal of Honor for his leadership during the Great Locomotive Chase, or Andrews' Raid, during the Civil War. Ben Brimelow, *13 Incredible Stories of American Servicemen Who Were Awarded the Medal of Honor*, Bus. Insider (Mar. 26, 2018), https://www.businessinsider.com/medal-of-honor-winners-incredible-stories-military-2018-3#jacob-parrott-civil-war-.

33. *Id.*

34. Sam Walker, The Captain Class (Random House 2017).

35. *See* Knowledge@Wharton Podcast, *Analyzing Effective Leaders: Why Extraverts Are Not Always the Most Successful Bosses*, Wharton Sch. of the U. Pa. (Nov. 23, 2010), https://knowledge.wharton.upenn.edu/article/analyzing-effective-leaders-why-extraverts-are-not-always-the-most-successful-bosses/.

36. Peter F. Drucker, The Effective Executive: The Definitive Guide to Getting the Right Things Done (HarperCollins 2006).

37. *Id.*

38. Northouse, *supra* note 9, at 12.

39. *Id.*

40. *Id.*

41. *Id.*

42. *See* Vineet Nayar, *Leadership Redefined*, Harv. Bus. Rev. (Sept. 23, 2008), https://hbr.org/2008/09/leadership-redefined (quoting Mahatma Gandhi).

43. Clay Scroggins, How to Lead When You're Not in Charge 30, 31 (Zondervan 2017).

44. *See, e.g.,* Robert Kelley, *In Praise of Followers*, Harv. Bus. Rev. (Nov. 1998), https://hbr.org/1988/11/in-praise-of-followers.

45. *See* A.H. Nishikawa, *10 Famous People Who Were Lawyers*, National Constitution Center (May 1, 2019), https://constitutioncenter.org/blog/law-day-2013-10-famous-people-who-were-lawyers.

46. *Id.*

47. *Id.*

48. *Id.*

49. *See supra* note 10.

Chapter 2

Why Lawyers Should Study Leadership

In periods where there is no leadership, society stands still. Progress occurs when courageous, skillful leaders seize the opportunity to change things for the better.

Harry Truman[1]

Purpose

Discuss the history of lawyers' roles as leaders in our society and the relevance of studying leadership lessons from history.

Learning Objectives

At the end of this chapter, you should be able to:

- Define the traditional role of lawyers in society.
- Describe the contemporary perception of lawyers in society.
- Explain leadership development as part of the traditional law school curriculum.
- Explain the benefits of studying leadership lessons from history.

Discussion

INTRODUCTION

You will recognize these names. Here are some facts you may not know about each of these people:

Alexander Hamilton, one of the country's Founding Fathers, was an illegitimate orphan from St. Croix in the Virgin Islands. His illegitimate status kept him from attending school, so he was educated at home. He attended Princeton University and ultimately became a lawyer in New York. In addition to his law practice, he served both in the military and in public office. He founded the *New York Post*,[2] a newspaper that continues in publication today. He wrote most of the Federalist Papers, died in a duel, and now lives on in the wildly popular Broadway musical bearing his name.

Abraham Lincoln studied to be a lawyer only after serving his first term in the Illinois General Assembly. From his legislative experience he learned that success in a legislative arena required the skills of a lawyer.[3] His abilities as a lawyer and a leader were legendary. His skill in reading juries and making oral arguments contributed to his leadership as President. During his tenure, he led the country through the great moral, constitutional, and political crisis that was the American Civil War. His Gettysburg address, one of the most memorable pieces of advocacy ever delivered, was only 272 words long but still moves the hearts and minds of all those who hear it.

Mahatma Gandhi is widely recognized as one of the twentieth century's greatest political and spiritual leaders. He studied law in London, briefly practiced in India, and then went to South Africa, originally as a legal adviser. His life changed when he became an advocate for the rights of the oppressed. Honored in India as the father of the nation, he is revered the world over for his nonviolent philosophy of passive resistance to tyranny through mass nonviolent civil disobedience. Gandhi was known to his many followers as Mahatma, or "the great-souled one."[4]

Thurgood Marshall, former U.S. Supreme Court Justice, had a stellar legal career before his legendary service as the first African American on the highest court in the land. He won his first Supreme Court case at the age of 32. Marshall won 29 out of the record 32 cases he argued in front of the Court, including *Brown v. Board of Education of Topeka*. He played an instrumental role in promoting racial equality during the civil rights movement.[5]

Sandra Day O'Connor graduated third in her law school class at Stanford in 1952 and then could not get a job in a legal position at a California law firm because of her gender. She was offered a position as a secretary instead. She began her legal career as a deputy county attorney for no salary and without an office. She served as a state senator for Arizona before she joined the Supreme Court in 1981 as its first female Justice.[6]

Nelson Mandela was a South African anti-apartheid revolutionary. While known as a lawyer, he was a terrible student who repeatedly left university without graduating.

He attempted an LL.B. but withdraw in 1952. He tried again in 1962, but it was not until the last months of his 27 years in prison (for his anti-apartheid efforts) that he finally completed his law degree. He served as the country's first Black head of state and the first elected in a fully representative democratic election. His government focused on dismantling the legacy of apartheid by tackling institutionalized racism and fostering racial reconciliation.[7]

These lawyers used their legal training and experience to achieve extraordinary results and to make a difference in the world in which they lived. Each is worthy of your consideration and study, not because they were always right or a paragon of virtue but because they were willing to work long and hard to become a lawyer and a leader. Each beat the odds in his or her own way and accomplished what would seem to some as improbable achievements.

An early expectation communicated in law school is the need for students to engage in their communities, especially in service and leadership roles. In fact, much of the law school curriculum is targeted toward making law students complete lawyers who combine technical expertise, wise counsel, and effective leadership with ethical behavior — in other words, the roles that lawyers play in society. While the majority of law students do not become world leaders or Supreme Court Justices, a significant number serve as leaders in government, business, and nonprofit organizations both nationally and internationally. Through their work, lawyers influence an array of clients, colleagues, and other leaders. Central to their calling in a service profession, lawyers have an obligation to protect the rule of law, which in itself is a form of leadership.[8]

An ongoing issue in the profession has been a lax attitude toward the broader societal responsibility of being a lawyer. It can become easy to focus on the business side of the law rather than addressing the larger responsibility. Influential jurists and scholars try to remind lawyers to reclaim the role of lawyer as leader.[9] Not surprisingly, calling lawyers to leadership is a common theme for law school commencement addresses and bar association speeches.[10] The need for lawyers to lead, however, is more urgent now than ever. The current lack of public trust in institutions, our inability to engage in civil discourse, and the polarizing nature of the news cycle and social media mean that those trained in the law are needed more than ever.[11] While the need is rising, the number of lawyers serving in key leadership roles is declining. For example, in the mid-nineteenth century, "almost 80% of members of Congress were lawyers. By the 1960s, this dropped to under 60%,"[12] and in the 116th Congress, the number of lawyer-members in Congress was slightly under 40 percent.[13] Congress struggles to agree on issues and struggles to find language to debate issues without personal attacks. The declining number of lawyers involved in politics could have a direct impact on the role that the legal profession has enjoyed as a prominent influencer in our society.

Lawyers have always been needed to play an influential role in society, and now is no different. In this chapter, we discuss the role of lawyers in society, and we make the case for why law students and lawyers should make it a habit to study leadership.

We encourage the study of leaders of the past to learn from their successes and their failures as well as their strengths and their flaws.

USING HISTORY TO STUDY LEADERSHIP

Those who fail to learn from history are condemned to repeat it.

George Santayana[14]

A common pedagogy in education is to study the past to learn from the successes and failures of others, and leadership is no exception. The study of historical leaders necessarily will embrace people who served as good examples and those who exhibited less stellar behavior. These are all human beings, with their flaws and foibles, from whom we can learn. Studying them does not mean embracing their character defects or questionable choices. It does, however, remind us that leadership is a process that takes place within a time frame, complete with its social mores, biases, and constraint. Our goal, though, as we examine history is to learn how we might incorporate the good and learn from the bad. Winston Churchill, even with his flaws, is a favorite and fascinating study.

Just 20 years after the end of World War I, Germany's leadership began solidifying military and political power. In the years leading up to 1938, Adolf Hitler, Germany's Nazi party leader, eliminated opposition in the German government and introduced military conscription in violation of the Treaty of Versailles. In a move signaling war in the making, Germany annexed Austria on March 13, 1938.

At the time, England's leadership wanted desperately to avoid another world war — at almost any cost. Prime Minister Neville Chamberlain hoped to appease Hitler by signing, along with France, Germany, and Italy, the Munich Agreement, which allowed Germany to annex the Czechoslovak Sudetenland area in return for the promise of "peace in our time." At the same time Chamberlain sought to appease, the First Lord of the Admiralty was Winston Churchill. Through his own personal military experience and study of history, Churchill recognized the threat that Hitler posed and that appeasement would fail. Churchill proved prescient in recognizing the danger Hitler presented and the negative effect of the tepid British reaction. On May 10, 1940, Chamberlain was ousted as Prime Minister, and Churchill took his place.[15] Through the dark and difficult years of World War II, Churchill proved to be the leader the free world needed most, and the rest, as they say, is history.

How did a contrarian admiralty lord become the right person to lead Great Britain? History has proven his brilliant leadership, but at the time, how did he know what the next right step was at each turn? What doubts did he have? Churchill became Prime Minister despite having suffered political and personal failures, and by any objective measure should have been very nervous about taking over as leader of Great Britain. After all, World War II was Churchill's second stint as Britain's Lord of the Admiralty. Early in World War I, as Lord of the Admiralty, Churchill made the disastrous decision to attack the Ottoman Empire at Gallipoli without consulting experts, seeking advice, and bringing their recommendations to the War Council. Churchill relied upon his own military experience and ignored warnings that the attack would fail. Nearly half a million of his own men died in an eight-and-a-half-month battle. As a result of his poor leadership, Churchill was dismissed from the War Council.[16]

So what changed? When he became Prime Minister in 1940, he had doubts about his decisions but had learned from his experience and background how to gauge the right next step. Churchill, perhaps unknowingly, had spent his life preparing for this moment both as a public servant in the military and the government, and as a master student of history. Churchill not only studied the lessons of history, in wartime and in peace, but he wrote prolifically to supplement his income. As a war correspondent during several military campaigns, Churchill saw firsthand the impact of military strategy and its relationship with history. He researched and wrote several history volumes, including semi-autobiographical books about himself and his family, and his six-volume *A History of the English Speaking Peoples*. His command of history and the English language as well as his personal failures positioned him perfectly to recognize the Hitler threat and know how to respond.[17]

Churchill was a lifelong learner who always found interesting people to learn from and new information and skills to absorb. This was one of the qualities that made him a great leader, and his love of language and history provided rich context for his assessment of current events. One way to continue to develop your leadership skills is to study history. As we learn about past events, we learn about the men and women who shaped history. We learn about the decisions those leaders made and the consequences of those decisions — each of which has an underlying principle that the reader can discern. Throughout this book, we use historical examples to give context and detail to principles of leadership, helping crystallize why a principle is important and how you can use it as a leader.

What can we learn from Winston Churchill and Neville Chamberlain? First, Chamberlain and Churchill had contrasting leadership styles. Chamberlain was as afraid of public opinion as he was of another world war should he make the unpopular decision to confront Hitler. With the horrors of World War I still fresh in the collective memory, Britons did not want war, and neither France nor the United States was willing to engage. Even President Franklin Roosevelt wrote to Hitler seeking peace. Churchill, on the other hand, chose the then-unpopular option of standing up to Hitler. Churchill was willing to lead based on what he knew to be right, not what he understood would be convenient. The enduring lesson is that leaders should make the right choice for the right reasons, even if it is unpopular in the moment.

Another leadership lesson is the need to learn from past failures. Rather than blame others or write off his disastrous first experience as Lord of the Admiralty, Churchill surrounded himself during World War II with experts and listened to their advice. Even if he disagreed and implemented his own designs, the disagreements with others allowed for the full development of ideas and plans.

We can also learn how to overcome failure. Rather than shrink from public life after failure, Churchill rebounded. Churchill returned to Parliament and military affairs after his expulsion from the War Council in World War I. In the early 1930s, he lost his seat in Parliament and turned to writing. By the end of the 1930s, he was again Lord of the Admiralty and poised to become Prime Minister. By 1945, he was swept out of his office as Prime Minister before World War II officially ended. He returned to power once more in the 1950s, again serving as Prime Minister. These ups and downs seemed to make Churchill stronger and more resilient, allowing him time to think, recover, and build again. He became a better leader after each setback.

Churchill provides countless lessons about leadership, although this is true of many historical leaders. By taking the time to read about his failures and triumphs, as well as those of other leaders, you can discern lessons and principles that help shape your leadership style, the way you approach problems, and the way you work with people.

Because history is often written by others and filtered through their own lens, you should consider several factors to determine whether a particular historical example is helpful. Some of the questions to ask include the following:

1. Do we have sufficient context to know whether the decisions made by the leader were correct? Given the sometimes secretive nature of statecraft, the public may not have a clear picture of the circumstances influencing a decision or event.
2. Has enough time passed that we can accurately assess the consequences? Closely related to context, time often allows us to gather all the relevant information surrounding an event or decision so as to accurately evaluate consequences. For that reason, recent events — within 20 or 30 years of the present — may not have had enough careful study by scholars and historians to allow us to understand fully the implications of an event.
3. What are we using the example to demonstrate — a broad leadership point or an analogy to a current event? Do the circumstances translate accurately to the circumstance we are studying?
4. Are we examining a success or a failure? Both can be instructive, but you certainly look at them differently.
5. What can we learn from historical leaders? As we seek to grow ourselves and our skill sets, it's helpful to look at the traits, characteristics, and styles of famous leaders.
6. How do we learn from history? We can do this by asking questions after studying a past historical event:
   - What decisions were made?
   - Were they good or bad decisions?
   - What were the results of those decisions?
   - Can I learn something from those decisions and apply it to my own life?

The study of historical leadership can guide lawyers as they strive to become effective and influential leaders. Great leadership books may not focus on lawyers per se, but they still help guide us in evaluating others in difficult positions, trying to make good decisions. Studying the history of those in high office reminds us of the people they were and what it took for them to lead. Similarly, by studying the history of the legal profession, and of those lawyers who had to make hard choices, you can learn more about the profession and yourself as you seek to lead. Ruth Bader Ginsburg's legal career before becoming a U.S. Supreme Court Justice provides an excellent example. In the pursuit of gender equality, she followed the path that Thurgood Marshall set during the civil rights era litigation.[18] While this skill is part of becoming an effective lawyer and leader, the real goal is to become a complete lawyer.

BECOMING A COMPLETE LAWYER

Lawyers have three distinct roles in society: technical expert, wise counselor, and effective leader.[19] Much of what you learn in law school helps you become a technical expert, including skills like "issue spotting, analytic power, ability to draft, negotiate, and advocate — but also an increasing degree of a highly sophisticated substantive and procedural expertise."[20] The law is not always clear, making it difficult to give your professor a definitive answer. The same will be true as you try to advise a client: You may have to give an answer that changes depending on the area of law or circumstances presented. Your duty as a lawyer is to advise the client about various options, possibilities, and outcomes so that the client can make an informed choice.[21] Developing technical expertise helps you answer the question, "Is it legal?"[22] While technical expertise is foundational to your duty to the client, your role does not end there.

The next role, wise counselor, allows you to answer the questions the client really wants answered: "Is it right?" and "What should we do?"[23] The lawyer must move beyond the theoretical question posed to the technical expert and provide realistic guidance on what the client can and should do. The wise counselor may offer a broad range of options for dealing

> **ABA Model Rule 1.1: Competence**
> A lawyer shall provide competent representation to a client. Competent representation requires the legal knowledge, skill, thoroughness and preparation reasonably necessary for the representation.

with the underlying issue. Some may involve judicial processes and others nonjudicial processes but all help the client think through the consequences of particular routes of action.[24] Business clients may need help with the ideal structure for a new venture, or to minimize risk or to preserve assets for a next opportunity. The holistic approach may include giving advice beyond merely the legal issues. Wise counsel can make the difference between bankruptcy and a lasting legacy.

Finally, in the role of "effective leader," lawyers occupy positions of responsibility and accountability as the final decision maker.[25] This may mean serving in traditional roles of legal leadership, such as being a judge or arbiter, head of a law firm, or an attorney general. Lawyers also find themselves in decision-making positions in government, the private sector, and nonprofit organizations.[26] Lawyers in these roles use their skills as technical experts and wise counselors to consider a wide array of legal, institutional, political, economic, ethical, reputational, and other factors to make decisions.[27] They must have the additional "require[d] organizational skills — vision, planning, budgeting, management, personnel," and so forth — to effectuate them.[28]

The roles of a complete lawyer overlap and build on each other. If you are not technically good at what you do, people will not turn to you for advice or leadership. A lawyer who is not a wise counselor may know the law, but his poor advice places clients in a worse position. Lawyers who are not effective leaders fail to achieve their potential and are unlikely to find meaningful purpose for their lives. "Effective leader" goes beyond the traditional view of the person at the decision-making apex of an organization. An effective leader can be in any position within a group if that person uses his abilities to add value to the position and uplift those around him, and strives to advance and improve the company, organization, or community.

Professional responsibility and ethics as essential components of leadership are particularly relevant for lawyers.[29] "[L]awyers have explicit and implicit obligations to protect the interests of clients, to promote the rule of law, and to generally provide services in the public interest."[30] Without adhering to a code of ethics, lawyers are uniquely able to take advantage of or harm others in our society, making it critical for lawyers to recognize their responsibilities and live up to them.[31]

These four aspects — technical expert, wise counselor, and effective leader, overlaid by adherence to ethics — are what it takes to be a complete lawyer. They provide a simple framework for your efforts at growth in the profession. All are important, deserve attention, and require effort, although you may choose to work on one aspect at a time. This book was written to help you become an effective leader and a complete lawyer.

THE LAWYER'S ROLE IN SOCIETY

Lawyers use their legal training in a variety of ways, both in practice and in leadership roles. Many lawyers begin in a law firm or government position, flexing their technical expertise and wise counsel muscles. This traditional path affords many opportunities to become better at the practice of law while under the tutelage of more experienced attorneys. But paid legal service is merely a beginning. Considering the abundant unmet legal needs in our communities, every lawyer should find a way to serve her community. Neglecting the responsibility to serve is akin to stunting your professional growth. Preparing for a life of service and leadership can take a variety of paths, but we look specifically

ABA Model Rules Preamble: A Lawyer's Responsibilities
[1] A lawyer, as a member of the legal profession, is a representative of clients, an officer of the legal system and a public citizen having special responsibility for the quality of justice.

to three: lawyers as seekers of justice, lawyers as community helpers, and lawyers as public servants. We encourage you to consider these or other areas of interest to use your time, talent, and treasure in service to others.

Lawyer as Seeker of Justice

In 1961, police arrested Clarence E. Gideon for allegedly robbing a pool hall. Possessed of an eighth-grade education and with no resources for a lawyer, he defended himself in a Florida state court. Not surprisingly, he was convicted. Florida's court of appeals and supreme court both denied his petitions for relief, but Gideon maintained his innocence. While imprisoned, he taught himself law and filed a writ of *habeas corpus* to the United States Supreme Court. With a handwritten letter on prison stationery, Gideon asked the Court to find that the Sixth Amendment guaranteed him a lawyer in a criminal case, even if he could not afford one.[32] After granting *certiorari*, the Court appointed renowned lawyer and future Supreme Court Justice Abe Fortis, who represented Mr. Gideon *pro bono*. The Court unanimously recognized Gideon's Sixth Amendment right to counsel and ordered a new trial in which Gideon would have the benefit of counsel. Gideon later won his freedom.[33]

Gideon v. Wainwright may be the most famous example of a lawyer doing *pro bono* work. Other than Clarence Darrow, Abe Fortis likely was the best known and most expensive lawyer of his generation. Fortis's decision to undertake representation at the Supreme Court without charging a fee cannot have been popular with his law partners, but it demonstrated Fortis's commitment to the service of justice. The principles that underpin *pro bono* work, such as access to justice, representing a good cause, and doing public service, are more than ideals; they actually shape the course of justice for individuals and for society. Each individual on death row deserves someone to ask the question whether the death will serve the interests of justice or violate the constitutional prohibition against cruel and unusual punishment. Without an effective advocate to protect the rights of an accused, we run the risk that we no longer have a constitution that matters.

Not every *pro bono* case will reach the United States Supreme Court, but even routine *pro bono* work makes an impact. In Milwaukee, a lawyer named Kathy Charlton helped her client, Helen, get a divorce *pro bono*. Helen returned to Charlton's office two years later with a friend who also needed a divorce. Helen related that she initially thought she needed help with a divorce (technical competence), but what she actually needed was to feel valuable and worthy of respect (wise counsel). Charlton's guiding Helen through the legal process helped the client feel like an agent of her own happiness. Empowered by that feeling and wanting to share it with a friend, Helen brought Charlton a referral. Handling Helen's divorce *pro bono* and doing it well, Charlton both helped Helen and landed new business.[34]

Reports reveal that the vast majority of Americans either cannot afford legal assistance,[35] do not believe they can afford a lawyer,[36] want a less expensive alternative,[37] or "do not recognize that their problems have a legal dimension."[38] Funding for those who cannot afford assistance is woefully insufficient and threatened.[39] We should be alarmed that in the last 30 years litigants in some categories of civil matters have gone from being almost 100 percent lawyer-represented to the vast majority now being self-represented.[40] "Without significant change, the profession cannot ensure that the justice system serves everyone and that the rule of law is preserved."[41]

Pro bono work benefits society most significantly by improving access to justice. Free legal services provide the client a day in court the client would not otherwise have had. Beyond that one day, however, the *pro bono* attorney gives the client access to the legal system as an avenue to resolve her dispute. This reinforces that the rule of law is for the people. In a day when many people feel that they do not have access to the judicial system or that the rule of law does not apply to them, *pro bono* efforts reconnect citizens to their courts.

A person with a dispute to resolve but no access to the courts often resorts to self-help, violence, or other dispute resolution methods with anti-social effects. *Pro bono* work defangs the temptation to use those negative dispute resolution methods by providing access to the judicial system. Lawyers who offer free service increase faith in the law as a system of dispute resolution. A person given *pro bono* access to the law is more likely to work within the system of those laws to retain that access. Put another way, people who experience justice trust it and believe it improves their lives. By promoting access to the legal system, the benefits of *pro bono* work ripple far beyond a single case for an individual client.

Lawyer as Community Helper

Some lawyers volunteer their time because they like the feeling of helping another person. Others are required to provide *pro bono* work by their firm. At the heart of the profession, lawyer leaders have a responsibility to use their skills and training to help others. *Pro bono* work may involve representing an individual or tackling issues on a systemic or organizational basis. Lawyers train to think critically, advocate fiercely, and analyze carefully. Those skills are valuable and in demand for organizations whose primary purpose is doing good rather than making money. Local food banks, charities, and shelters need leaders trained in those skills to be effective. Even if a lawyer cannot afford to take on *pro bono* work often, serving on a board or as a volunteer still provides benefit.

Another benefit to *pro bono* work is that it lets the lawyer match time to passion. Irrespective of where on the political spectrum an organization's agenda may fall, there is probably a lawyer who agrees with the cause and who wants to help it succeed. As such, some lawyers will lend talents to Planned Parenthood; others to the National Rifle Association. All who get involved with a cause promote a healthy civil society, which is the bedrock on which political democracy is built. In addition, promoting respectful civil discourse lessens the rancor and incivility that can polarize society.

To lead effectively, lawyers have a responsibility to use their training to promote those causes in which they believe.

Lawyer as Public Servant

Lawyers can deploy their training and skills through service in political office. Lawyers have a long history of government and political service going back to the founding of our country: Fifty-eight percent of the signers of the Constitution were lawyers.[42] During the 1800s, lawyers routinely comprised more than 75 percent of congressional membership.[43] While that number has declined, lawyers are still needed to serve in Congress. Lawyers constitute less than one-half of 1 percent of the overall population but comprise almost 40 percent of the U.S. congressional membership.[44] No other profession is so well represented in political leadership.[45]

Those trained in the law excel in the political realm. The critical thinking and analytical skills combined with advocacy training that make lawyers valuable to causes also translate to political leadership. Lawyers tend to be competitive and therefore are willing to put in the effort to win elections.[46] Lawyers are taught to disagree without being too disagreeable, or at least they should be. As professionals, lawyers can zealously defend their position in the courtroom during the day and congenially socialize with opposing counsel in the evening. In today's partisan landscape, more political bodies would benefit from members better trained in civil discourse.[47] Just as lawyers put their clients' needs ahead of their own, so too should political power be wielded to serve their constituents and their ideas.

LEADERSHIP TRAINING IN LEGAL EDUCATION

Much of law school education contains elements of leadership training that help prepare lawyers for leadership roles. In the first year, you begin with identifying issues, learning and researching the law, and analyzing cases to find the lessons for the future.[48] These are skills you will use in practice and in leadership. Identifying the legal issue is a top priority in a client interview. Identifying issues related to operations and the needs of employees is the job of a leader. Legal analysis is critical whether you are solving clients' problems or developing options for future transactions. The leader who can analyze the problem or identify the opportunities adds value to the organization. Law schools train students to be persuasive oral and written advocates so they can speak for the powerless and advocate for justice.[49] Time spent in legal writing and advocacy courses that teach students to convey ideas clearly and concisely prepares them to someday persuade audiences — whether that be an appellate court, a business client, a team they lead, or a community. Advocacy training and the practice of meticulously attending to detail make lawyers invaluable to an entity in the process of creating, articulating, and conveying organizational values to followers and outside parties.[50]

Law school is a training ground for taking an idea and turning it into a vision. Lawyers are trained to advocate by confidently communicating with intent to influence others. Advocacy training incorporates words, gestures, inflections, and emotions aimed at persuading the audience.[51] In law school, students learn that lawyers are bound to conduct their practice in accordance with the established ethical behaviors in professional codes of conduct. As leaders, lawyers can use those skills and values to inspire individuals to transcend their immediate self-interest in the service of the greater good of the organization, or society.[52]

Law schools provide excellent preparation for the important roles lawyers play as leaders in society.[53] Formal leadership training is relatively new in law school. While some law schools have had programs for a couple of decades, most programs have been started in the past decade.[54] Given the pervasive need for lawyers to be trained in leadership, every law school should have leadership training as a mandatory part of the law school experience. This model has proven effective for introducing professional responsibility in law schools and should be adopted for leadership training.[55]

CONCLUSION

You are at the beginning of your professional life now, but one day you will look back on what that has meant and what you have accomplished. One day you may have the chance to look back on your life and evaluate the expertise you gained through continual learning and practice. You may develop a thriving law practice and see much material success and recognition for your accomplishments. You may hold office in professional organizations and shape the future of the profession. But we hope you also are sought after as a wise counselor. And most of all, we hope that you have found a way to serve your individual clients, your community, and society as a whole. You follow in the footsteps of countless lawyers whose quiet work across their communities, the nation, and the world helps to serve justice. These men and women change the world daily by serving where needed, not for money or glory but to protect the rule of law, secure the dreams and aspirations of families, defend the rights of the accused, and seek justice on behalf of those wronged by others or by society. They do this because they have chosen to do what is right and honorable. They share the values you are learning. Attending law school means not only that you have seen the light of right and justice, but that you understand its source and have chosen to be guided by it.

Exercise

Lawyers in the Movies

This exercise is designed to facilitate group discussion around professional obligation and the role of the lawyer in society. Divide into small groups to discuss these prompts:

- Pick a legal movie where the attorney has agreed to represent someone *pro bono* because it was the right thing to do, even if it was unpopular at the time or created a significant risk for the lawyer (personal, professional, reputational, or financial).
  - Why was the lawyer's representation important?
  - What repercussions did the lawyer face for doing so?
  - Thinking about our system of justice, how was the lawyer's representation critical to its proper functioning?
- Pick a legal movie where the attorney took on a cause (environmental, financial, defective products, etc.) that made positive changes for future generations.
  - Why was the lawyer's representation important?
  - What repercussions did the lawyer face for doing so?
  - Thinking about our system of justice, how was the lawyer's representation critical to its proper functioning?

Journal Prompts

1. Reflect on your path to law school — other than financial security, what motivated you to attend law school? Did you want to gain new skills to help you solve problems for others? Did you want to become a person that others seek for counsel and advice? Was your goal to learn the competencies that would make you an effective leader in a variety of situations and settings? Was it some combination of these?

2. Do your own research on the reputation of lawyers in our society. What are some common perceptions of lawyers? Do you agree with these perceptions? Why or why not?

3. As discussed in this chapter, we believe that leadership development training is part of the non-explicit curriculum of law school. Looking back, what aspects of your law school education have allowed you to acquire or develop leadership skills?

4. Pick three of your favorite historical leaders. (Keep in mind that you should pick leaders from at least 20 years ago.)

   a. For each leader, write why that person is a favorite and what you have learned from him or her.

   b. What positive attributes about these leaders can you incorporate into your personality or leadership style?

   c. What negative attributes or facts about these leaders are significant to you? How will you avoid making similar mistakes?

5. Pick one memorable event resulting from a leader's decision(s). (Keep in mind that you should pick an event from at least 20 years ago.) Why is it instructive?

Endnotes

1. *See Truman Leadership Quote*, HARV. LEADERSHIP WEBLOG (June 5, 2011), https://blogs.harvard.edu/leadership/truman-leadership-quote/. Harry S. Truman, THE WHITE HOUSE, https://www.whitehouse.gov/about-the-white-house/presidents/harry-s-truman/ (last visited July 8, 2020).

2. At the time, it was known as the *New York Evening Post*.

3. TALMAGE BOSTON, RAISING THE BAR: THE CRUCIAL ROLE OF THE LAWYER IN SOCIETY (State Bar of Texas 2012).

4. Mahatma Gandhi, BIOGRAPHY.COM, https://www.biography.com/activist/mahatma-gandhi (last visited July 20, 2020). Mahatma Gandhi was the primary leader of India's independence movement and also the architect of a form of nonviolent civil disobedience that would influence the world. Although Gandhi was assassinated in 1948, his life and teachings continued to inspire activists including Martin Luther King, Jr. and Nelson Mandela.

5. *Thurgood Marshall*, HISTORY.COM, https://www.history.com/topics/black-history/thurgood-marshall (last visited July 20, 2020).

6. *Sandra Day O'Connor*, BIOGRAPHY.COM, https://www.biography.com/law-figure/sandra-day-oconnor (last visited July 21, 2020).

7. *Nelson Mandela*, SOCIAL JUSTICE RESOURCE CENTER, https://socialjusticeresourcecenter.org/biographies/mandela-nelson/ (last visited July 21, 2020).

8. HERB RUBENSTEIN, LEADERSHIP FOR LAWYERS 3 (2d ed. 2008).

9. Louis D. Brandeis, *The Opportunity in the Law*, Address Before the Harvard Ethical Society (May 4, 1905), *in* BUSINESS — A PROFESSION 313, 321 (1914); The Texas Lawyer's Creed — A Mandate for Professionalism (adopted by the Supreme Court of Texas and the Court of Criminal Appeals Nov. 7, 1989), *reprinted in* Texas Rules of Court: Volume I — State 723 (ThomsonReuters 2017); ANTHONY T. KRONMAN, THE LOST LAWYER: FAILING IDEALS OF THE LEGAL PROFESSION (1993); Ben W. Heineman, Jr., *Law and Leadership*, Lecture as part of the Robert H. Prieskel and Leon Silverman Program on the Practicing Lawyer and the Public Interest (Nov. 27, 2006).

10. Neil W. Hamilton, *Ethical Leadership in Professional Life*, 6 U. ST. THOMAS L.J. 358, 359–60 (2009); "Roscoe Pound and Chief Justice Burger understood that the best way for the profession to continue to resolve society's conflicts is to lead" (*see* Roscoe Pound, Speech at the Annual Meeting of the American Bar Association (1906) and Chief Justice Warren Burger, Speech at the Pound Conference (1976), *in* Report on the Future of Legal Services in the United States, AM. BAR ASS'N 8 (2016), http://www.americanbar.org/content/dam/aba/images/abanews/2016FLSReport_FNL_WEB.pdf_ [hereinafter ABA Report].

11. *See generally* Alfred S. Konefsky & Barry Sullivan, *In This, the Winter of Our Discontent: Legal Practice, Legal Education, and the Culture of Distrust*, 62 BUFF. L. REV. 659 (2014).

12. Nick Robinson, *The Decline of the Lawyer Politician*, 65 BUFF. L. REV. 657 (2017).

13. *Membership of the 116th Congress*, CONGRESSIONAL RESEARCH SERVICE, https://fas.org/sgp/crs/misc/R45583.pdf (last visited July 20, 2020).

14. GEORGE SANTAYANA, THE LIFE OF REASON (1905). Jorge Agustín Nicolás Ruiz de Santayana y Borrás, known in English as George Santayana, was a philosopher, essayist, poet, and novelist.

15. History.com Editors, *Winston Churchill Becomes Prime Minster of Britain*, HISTORY.COM (May 26, 2020), https://www.history.com/this-day-in-history/churchill-becomes-prime-minister.

16. Dean Williams, *Winston Churchill's Terrible Leadership Failure*, FORBES (2015), https://www.forbes.com/sites/forbesleadershipforum/2015/04/24/winston-churchills-terrible-leadership-failure/#3c7db7374dbe.

17. ANDREW ROBERTS, CHURCHILL: WALKING WITH DESTINY (Viking 2018).

18. Robert Cohen & Laura Dull, *Teaching About the Feminist Rights Revolution: Ruth Bader Ginsburg as "The Thurgood Marshall of Women's Rights,"* ORGANIZATION OF AMERICAN HISTORIANS (Nov. 2017), https://www.oah.org/tah/issues/2017/november/teaching-about-the-feminist-rights-revolution-ruth-bader-ginsburg-as-the-thurgood-marshall-of-womens-rights/.

19. Heineman, *supra* note 9, at 10.

20. *Id.* With the advent of technology and the increasingly available legal resources provided via the Internet, more and more people are seeking access to the law on their own. Lawyers are no longer the gatekeepers of the law, so we must adapt and grow in serving clients. This discussion, while important, is outside the scope of this book. *See, e.g.*, Thomas R. Moore, *The Upgraded Lawyer: Modern Technology and Its Impact on the Legal Profession*, 21 UDC/DCSL L. REV. 27, 33–36 (2019); *see also* Raymond H. Brescia, Walter McCarthy, Ashley McDonald, Kellan Potts & Cassandra Rivais, *Embracing Disruption: How Technological*

Change in the Delivery of Legal Services Can Improve Access to Justice, 78 Alb. L. Rev. 553 (2014); *see also* Michele R. Pistone & Michael B. Horn, Disrupting Law School: How Disruptive Innovation Will Revolutionize the Legal World (2016); *available at* https://www.christenseninstitute.org/publications/disrupting-law-school/.

21. *See* Heineman, *supra* note 9.
22. *Id.*
23. *Id.*
24. *Id.*
25. *Id.* at 10.
26. *Id.* Even though lawyers account for less than 1 percent of the population, nearly half of the signers of the Declaration of Independence were lawyers. Over half of the delegates at the Constitutional Convention of 1787 were lawyers. The majority of U.S. Presidents and members of the U.S. Congress have been lawyers. *See* America's Founding Fathers: Delegates to the Constitutional Convention, *available at* http://www.archives.gov/exhibits/charters/constitution_founding_fathers_overview.html.; *see also* Jennifer Manning, Membership of the 115rd Congress: A Profile 2 (Congressional Research Service, Apr. 12, 2018), *available at* https://www.senate.gov/CRSpubs/b8f6293e-c235-40fd-b895-6474d0f8e809.pdf (38 percent of the members of the House of Representatives and 55 percent of the Senators in the 115th Congress).
27. Heineman, *supra* note 9, at 10.
28. *Id.*
29. *Id.* at 12.
30. *Id.*
31. *See id.*
32. Story adapted from Victoria Sherrow, Gideon v. Wainwright: Free Legal Counsel (1995).
33. *Id.*
34. probonoweek, JUST Stories: Kathy Charlton, YouTube (June 26, 2012), https://youtu.be/PJZQHdkPhrw.
35. *Justice Gap Report: Measuring the Civil Legal Needs of Low-Income Americans,* Legal Services Corporation (2017), https://www.lsc.gov/media-center/publications/2017-justice-gap-report.
36. Rebecca Sandefur, *What We Know and Need to Know About the Legal Needs of the Public,* 67 S.C. L. Rev. 443, 450 (2016).
37. ABA Report, *supra* note 10.
38. *Id.*
39. *Id.* Nearly 5.3 million Texans qualify for legal aid. Only approximately 178,000 Texas families are assisted by legal aid organizations. *Access to Justice Facts,* Tex. Access to Justice Found., http://www.teajf.org/news/statistics.aspx (last visited Dec. 12, 2017).
40. Jessica K. Steinberg, *Demand Side Reform in the Poor People's Court,* 47 Conn. L. Rev. 741, 749 (2015).
41. ABA Report, *supra* note 10.
42. *Founding Fathers,* National Archives, https://www.archives.gov/founding-docs/founding-fathers (last visited July 20, 2020).
43. Adam Bonica, *Why Are There So Many Lawyers in Congress?* (Feb. 11, 2020), *available at* http://dx.doi.org/10.2139/ssrn.2898140.
44. *Id.*
45. *Id.*
46. *Id.*
47. *Id.*
48. *Id.*
49. *Id.*
50. *Id.*
51. *Id.*
52. *Id.*
53. Leary Davis, *Competence as Situationally Appropriate Conduct: An Overarching Concept for Lawyering, Leadership, and Professionalism,* 52 Santa Clara L. Rev. 725, 729 (2012).
54. Leah Teague, *Training Lawyers for Leadership,* 58 Santa Clara L. Rev. 633 (2018).
55. *See* Deborah L. Rhode, *Ethics by the Pervasive Method,* 42 J. Legal Ed. 31, 32 (1992).

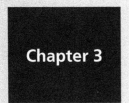

Chapter 3

Leading versus Managing

Managers light a fire under people; leaders light a fire in people.

Kathy Austin[1]

Purpose

To identify and understand the distinction between leadership and management and how to effectively manage tasks by leading people.

Learning Objectives

At the end of this chapter, you should be able to:

- Identify distinct attributes of leadership and management.
- Differentiate objectives of management from those of leadership.
- Describe the common attributes of leadership and management.

Discussion

INTRODUCTION

Distinguishing leadership and management is challenging. While each concept has attributes unique to it, they share common traits, and the lines can be blurry. Larger

29

organizations have the luxury of people who serve as exclusively as managers in a role distinct from those in leadership positions. In other organizations, individuals must both lead and manage, causing some to conflate the two concepts and use "leadership" and "management" interchangeably.[2] Lawyers struggle with this distinction, especially firms that use the term "managing partner" to denote the partner who is responsible for leading the firm. In learning how to understand the ways in which managing and leading are distinct but related concepts, we can look to Steven Covey who, in his book *The 7 Habits of Highly Effective People*, made the distinction this way: "Management is efficiency in climbing the ladder of success; leadership determines whether the ladder is leaning against the right wall."[3] Put another way, "leadership is about producing change, while management focuses on creating processes to produce predictable results."[4] The important difference is the functionality of the role and how each provides a framework for success in working with a team rather than a list of absolute and rigid criteria that must be followed depending on which role you fill.[5] Leadership and management, then, are best seen as a continuum of the functions of leaders.[6]

Leadership-Management Continuum[7]

Leadership	⬅➡	Management
Strategy		Policies and procedures
Articulates a vision		Executes plans
Creates values		Counts values
Influences		Controls
Creates change		Manages change
Has followers		Manages work
People-focused		Task-focused
Risk tolerant		Risk averse
Sets direction		Plans detail
Asks for feedback		Gives directions

While not an exhaustive list, this shows a flexible method of approaching leadership and management. For example, rather than using a binary focus on people *or* things, you may need to blend the two based upon your audience and the task at hand. By thinking of skills and professional competencies of leaders and managers as part of a continuum, you can balance the approach based on the situation and the context.

How, then, do you know if you are expected to lead versus manage? It can be easier if the individual or organization differentiates the two roles internally, so that the leader and manager have greater clarity about their function and can address specific situations effectively as either a leader or manager. Understanding the attributes and differences between managing and leading is important when deciding who plays what role in an organization, or how to shift between them if one person has to do both. In this chapter, we present distinctive aspects of each role as well as the areas in which overlap or shared responsibility exists.

LEADERSHIP

Leaders are visionary. Important aspects of leadership are "establishing a clear vision; sharing that vision with others so that they will follow willingly; providing the information, knowledge, and methods to realize that vision; and coordinating and balancing the conflicting interests of all members and stakeholders."[8] Innovative leadership sets the direction for a group or an organization and then effectively communicates that vision so that the team wants to invest in that vision. Leaders motivate the team to work toward the same goal and get everyone on the next page when it is time to make a transition. As essential as the vision is the need to keep the organization focused and on task.[9] Building coalitions and effective teams allows the leader to produce forward movement.[10]

Leaders also encourage and support employees' efforts to enhance their skills and develop new ones. They are optimistic about the future, and in turn, promote creativity and new ideas.[11] Leaders foster confidence in workers by acknowledging their contributions and value to the company and inspire a sense of accomplishment as they move the organization toward the vision or goal.[12]

MANAGEMENT

Management is defined as "the organization and coordination of the activities of a business in order to achieve defined objectives."[13] A good manager takes care of the administrative aspects of running an organization by creating policies and procedures that ensure tasks are completed timely and functions operate smoothly. Management skills involve setting expectations, planning out the details, and appealing to the employees by creating task-based incentives.[14]

Good management looks a lot like good leadership — creating trust, focusing on strengths, and instilling accountability. The managers' duties focus more on the orderly operation of tasks to create efficiencies and productivity. Managers get the work done within the parameters set by the leadership. Hiring the right talent, planning the work, creating the budget, establishing policies and procedures for conduct, and developing incentives are key to accomplishing the organizations' objectives.[15] A manager's experience can help with troubleshooting, providing creative problem solving to move a project forward.

Most companies understand the importance of having highly effective managers, but few invest heavily in training to help them manage well. In the law firm structure, large firms commonly have full administrative teams handling the administrative aspects of firm operations. This frees the lawyers to focus on meeting the clients' needs. Some medium and smaller firms have a firm administrator to manage staff and handle administrative tasks. The smaller the firm, the more likely that lawyers will have to shoulder both the leadership and management issues for the firm.

This is problematic because the managers whose employees are most involved are those who put their all into managing. The managers who worked hardest were more effective in achieving outcomes. Those same managers inspired their employees to go all in. A hard-working manager's employees worked up to 19 percent more hours than their colleagues who reported to less hard-working managers.[16] Though the busy managers worked more hours, their employees showed higher engagement rates with the busy manager. Employees of managers in the lowest 25 percent of utilization had lower than average engagement scores (2 to 4 percent lower). In short, people are more engaged when they work for a manager who works at least as much as they do.[17] Employees who work for less invested managers are less likely to be invested in the company. Bad management is estimated to cost the U.S. economy up to $398 billion annually.[18] If attorneys are trying to practice law and manage the firm, their attention is necessarily divided, and they may not be handling either job effectively.

Effective training in management and ongoing feedback can improve performance and result in a higher quality of life for workers. The most successful companies will continue to be the ones with the best managers, where the managers understand their role and look for opportunities to lead their employees as well.[19]

HOW LEADERSHIP AND MANAGEMENT INTERSECT

You do not lead by hitting people over the head. That's assault, not leadership.
Dwight D. Eisenhower[20]

Given that leadership and management each have distinct functions in some areas while sharing or overlapping in others, it can be challenging to understand your role. For the cleanest delineation of responsibility, however, leaders and managers should be clear about who handles vision and who handles implementation. Your company wants to be sure that the leader can see the forest while the manager is responsible for the trees.

Leading a team well involves skills that motivate people to accomplish goals and tasks. Managing a team well involves skills that ensure those tasks are completed by the people to whom they are assigned.[21] Individuals in both positions must be able to motivate and inspire team members to be part of the leader's vision for the organization.[22] When people are motivated to accomplish goals, the goals are more likely to be accomplished.[23] An effective leader can motivate and influence employees through the chain of command. When employees see their job as important, no matter how small or large the responsibility, they will believe in the mission of the organization and take ownership of their assigned duties to support that mission. Disney is famous for its employee culture of ownership and buy-in to the mission.

Walt Disney's organizational cultural focus can be summed up in one statement: *employees are the most important because they make dreams a reality. . . .*

Walt Disney knew in order to bring that dream to life, he needed employees who would share his values and carry out the magic of Disney in every nook and cranny of their daily deeds. From the moment they stepped on Disney grounds, he needed them to become part of the dream.[24]

While leaders hew to the vision, a good manager ensures that tasks are accomplished as well. The key is the *how*. A good manager with leadership skills can ensure that tasks are accomplished but in a more internally sustainable way that also ensures the employees are motivated to do an excellent job.[25] As soon as an organization grows beyond a small number of employees who interact with the leader on a daily basis, the role of managers becomes critical. Leaders need their managers to partner in the execution of the vision.

Leading

Strategy
Articulate a
vision
Creating values
Influence
Create change
Having followers
People-focused
Risk tolerant
Sets direction
Ask for feedback

Accomplish
a goal
Explain vision
Motivate others
Positions of
influence
Mobilize
resources
Communication

Managing

Policies and
procedures
Execute plans
Counting values
Control
Manage change
Managing work
Task-focused
Risk averse
Plans detail
Give directions

As the chart[26] depicts, leadership and management overlap. A leader may even switch between leadership and management within the same meeting or conversation. Take, for example, when the senior partner sits down with her team to discuss a large transactional deal for a client. She may spend a few minutes in a leadership role explaining the importance of the client, the goals of the client, and what she hopes the team will accomplish while representing the client. In other words, the senior partner is *creating value* and *influencing* the team by sharing the *vision* and *setting direction* for the matter. The senior partner will then likely shift into a management role, discussing the intricacies of the deal that need attention and assigning work to various team members. The partner may address time constraints and assign deadlines by which each person must submit his work so the deal can close on time. The partner may ask about other projects so she can manage work flow of other matters. By doing so, the partner is engaged in management of the team, the matter, and the firm's other business. She is *planning with detail*, *managing work*, *focusing on the task*, and *giving directions*. Toward the end of the meeting, the partner will likely shift back to a leadership role, inspiring the other team members to do a good job for the client.

Contrast the leader-manager hybrid example with a partner who only fills the leadership role. The partner explains the importance of the client, the value of the matter, and the goals for the team, and then leaves, expecting the team to figure out the "how." Even if a senior associate assigns tasks and makes sure all the work gets done, this strategy does not keep the partner engaged in the conversation and does not identify the timeline and the needed actions or allow time for feedback from the client or partner. It also does not ensure that the team integrates and collaborates when needed. Similar problems arise with a partner who does not share the vision or strategy with the team but simply assigns a list of tasks to the associates on the team. The work would get done, but without vision the associates may miss opportunities to make the end result better and buy into the vision. They may be less motivated because they do not understand the "why." The team has not been given the context of the deal or the importance of its work in the larger picture. The work will get done, but it may not get done with the same degree of quality or attention to detail that it might otherwise have received.

These examples are, of course, basic scenarios of how these roles interrelate and oversimplify the reactions and complexities of a team of lawyers. However, the principle remains the same. By learning how to be competent in both leadership and management roles, you will be more effective at both. Further, the cumulative effect of combining these talents will be greater than the sum of your efforts.

KEY DISTINCTIONS BETWEEN LEADERSHIP AND MANAGEMENT

The following discussion focuses on several dichotomies that illustrate the differences between leaders and managers. These guardrails represent extremes of each role and are provided to help you navigate which role to slip into for different situations. It is rare that a situation will demand an extreme of one role over the other. Instead, you will likely need a blend of these skills for each situation.

1. **Leadership inspires change, management manages transformation.**

   A leader must set direction and inspire people to follow them. The process of following often requires great change. This is where strong management comes in. It's the manager's job to oversee the work needed to implement the necessary changes and realize the organizational transformation set forth by the leadership.

2. **Leadership requires vision, management requires tenacity.**

   A leader needs to envision what the business is to become. A great manager must have the willingness to do whatever it takes to achieve the goals set forth by the leader.

3. **Leadership requires imagination, management requires specifics.**

   A great leader can cultivate their imagination to inform their vision. It helps them to "see" what can be. Managers must understand that vision and drive their teams to do the specific work necessary to accomplish what has been expressed.

4. **Leadership requires abstract thinking, management requires concrete data.**

   By definition, abstract thinking enables a person to make connections among, and see patterns within, seemingly unrelated information. The ability to think abstractly comes in very handy when reimaging what an organization can become. Conversely, a manager must be able to work with, and analyze, concrete data in order to ensure optimal results.

5. **Leadership requires ability to articulate, management requires ability to interpret.**

   A good leader can describe their vision in vivid detail so to engage and inspire their organization to pursue it. A good manager must interpret that stated vision and recast it in terms that their teams can understand and embrace it.

6. **Leadership requires an aptitude to sell, management requires an aptitude to teach.**

   A leader must sell their vision to their organization and its stakeholders. They must convince all concerned parties that what is envisioned is achievable and provides greater value than what is created by the business today. In keeping, a manager must be able to teach their teams what must be learned and adapted to attain the stated vision.

7. **Leadership requires understanding of the external environment, management requires understanding of how work gets done inside the organization.**

   A leader must understand the business environment in which the enterprise operates so to better anticipate opportunities and evade misfortune, while a manager is relied on to figure out how to get things done using the resources available to the business.

8. **Leadership requires risk-taking, management requires self-discipline.**

   A leader will take educated risks when setting a strategic direction for a business. Managers must have the self-discipline to stick to the plan for realizing that strategic direction so to ensure that the strategy comes together as planned.

9. **Leadership requires confidence in the face of uncertainty, management requires blind commitment to completing the task at hand.**

   A leader's life is filled with uncertainty. They're setting a course for their company in unchartered waters. Once the course is set, managers are duty-bound to follow the stated direction and commit to delivering the results expected.

10. **Leadership is accountable to the entire organization, management is accountable to the team.**

    Finally, leaders must consider the impact of their decisions on the whole organization. A misstep can bring an entire business to its knees. It's a huge responsibility. Accordingly, managers are responsible for their teams. They must ensure that their teams are prepared to deliver and that each member is equipped to do what is required for success.[27]

Both leadership and management are necessary for any organization to succeed, whether it is a business, law firm, agency, or nonprofit. Even when different people are filling different roles, leaders and managers who know their areas of responsibility, who understand the mission, and who work well together will help an organization operate and endure. An organization with well-defined roles filled with capable people who are inspired by, and believe in, the vision has a chance to thrive and reach the vision.

LEADERSHIP TRAINING IN LAW FIRMS

As noted above, "managing partners" are often the lawyers charged with leading the firm, but that routinely includes managerial responsibilities as well. In the "management" role, these lawyers supervise the day-to-day operations of the law firm through the law firm staff.[28] They also likely maintain their own client representation workload.[29] Many law firms are still siloed, meaning that the partners within the firm more or less have their own specialties and run their own files.[30] As a result, the individual partners may not be aware of changes occurring in the profession or be keeping an eye on innovative developments in the practice of law.[31] Thus, the managing partners are also usually responsible for looking for ways to lead the firm through turbulent times or difficult situations.[32]

Young lawyers move through different roles as they climb the firm hierarchy. Along the leadership-management continuum, they often manage first before moving toward leadership as they gain experience and expertise. Commonly, young lawyers initially are given assignments. As they become more proficient, they can anticipate and generate work, ultimately leading the team. Knowing when and how that transition takes place, however, can be challenging. One young lawyer talked about the difficulty she faced when she left a large firm where she was a senior associate and became a partner in a new firm. She was accustomed to asking more senior colleagues for assistance in her trust and estate planning practice, but suddenly found herself the most senior person in the practice area. She struggled to develop confidence in her own abilities but eventually was able to assume the role of partner. Owning the progression along these different points in practice can be a challenge but is crucial to developing as a leader.

Some firms have a formal structure or program to address the training needs of young associates. Those programs focus more on the associates' growth as technical experts in their field and may assign young associates to research a topic and deliver a presentation to the department, division, or firm. These sessions may help young lawyers grow their legal knowledge and skill, but they do not address the other aspects of advancing within the firm. Ideally, firms provide professional development programs that will include aspects of leadership development in recognition of the need to help young lawyers develop competencies beyond legal knowledge and skills. Programs aimed at helping women and lawyers of color develop as leaders recognize that additional barriers to success and advancement stymie opportunity for those individuals. These programs have mixed results. Firms with training efforts that go beyond education may assign mentors to young lawyers, again with mixed results. Most senior lawyers who are willing to make the time can be good coaches, and when the mentoring relationship between the two is strong and the mentoring is lively, both parties can benefit.

Unfortunately, many firms spend no specific time at all on leadership training or strategic planning. If formal programs are not available, look for training opportunities through another source. Leadership development programs abound, and if leading is important to you, find the resources to help you meet that goal.

CONCLUSION

Make sure you're not just waiting for someone else to fix things, or hoping that things will improve. . . . Figure out what's going on and make a plan to improve things.

Kenneth Thomas[33]

Strong leaders are not necessarily good managers and strong managers are not always good leaders, but an organization needs both. Leaders set the direction of the organization, represent the organization externally, and inspire others to buy into the vision for the organization. Managers also are responsible for motivating employees and helping them understand the vision, but they focus on how to execute the steps to achieve the vision. Managers are charged with overseeing the effective and efficient execution of the operation or strategy. The concepts of leadership and management should work together to create a culture that inspires each member of the organization to take ownership not only in their assigned areas but in the overall success of the organization.

Exercises

Completing Tasks for Law Student Organization Speaking Event

A law student organization is planning an event with an invited outside speaker. You are the vice president of the organization and are tasked with ensuring that the event goes smoothly. You have a committee of other officers, but not the president, helping you with the event. While the speaker and date, time, and location have been confirmed, you know that a successful event needs to be heavily publicized, and that members need to attend and encourage their friends to attend. It is about two weeks before the event, and your committee has not created any flyers or social media posts and has not included a message in the student announcements. Further, food for the event has not been ordered. Unfortunately, all of these things (flyers, posts, food, etc.) must be approved by the law school administration before the final step can be taken (food ordered for delivery, flyers posted, etc.), which delays your timeline even more. After checking with the officers on your committee, you learn that the people assigned to do these things have not begun their work.

Discussion Questions:

- As a manager, you are responsible for ensuring the tasks are completed and you need to decide how to do this.
  - One option is to become a drill sergeant or overbearing taskmaster to coerce your committee members to get the job done. What are the positives and negatives of this option?
  - Another option is to step in and do the work yourself. What are the positives and negatives of this option?
  - With these options in mind, what course of action would you pursue?
  - Are there other options?
- Where is there an overlap between your duties as manager and as leader?
- How do you accomplish the goals of both roles (leader and manager) while not alienating members of the organization?
- As a leader, you must be concerned about the future of the organization. How might the approach you take positively or negatively impact the future of the student organization?

ABA Grit Project: Struggling with Your Workload

Watch the ABA Grit Project's "Struggling with Your Workload" video but disregard the prompted questions at the end of the video. Instead, answer the following questions:

- If John is Jane's supervising partner (and thus charged with helping her grow as an attorney and contributing member of the firm), how well did he manage the flow of work coming to his associate?
- Assume that John is Jane's supervising partner. He believes that the IP work that they are taking on will be a growth area for the firm and that she is capable of becoming the right member for team leadership in the future.
  - In his capacity as a leader in the firm, what further conversations should John plan to have with Jane in the future?
  - As a leader, what further conversations should John have with Bill, Lisa, and others to ensure that Jane achieves her full potential?
  - As a manager, what further conversations should John have with others in the firm to ensure effective and efficient management of client matters? In answering this question, assume that resources are limited and the firm does not have the ability to simply hire more lawyers.

Journal Prompts

1. List the past leadership positions you have held and what you did for the organization.

   a. What aspects of your work related to leadership?

   b. Which tasks that you performed were related to management?

   c. Did you know at the time you were managing rather than leading or vice versa?

2. Thinking back to the leadership-management continuum, are you more task- or vision-oriented? No matter which orientation is your natural preference, developing both skills will help ensure success in your advancement through organizations. What is your plan to work on the skill that does not come naturally to you?

Endnotes

1. *See Kathy Austin Quotes*, Goodreads, https://www.goodreads.com/quotes/622625-managers-light-a-fire-under-people-leaders-light-a-fire (last visited July 8, 2020). Kathy Austin is globally recognized for her work in theory of constraints (TOC) implementations, development, and facilitation. Her U.S. and international clients are both military and commercial, ranging from the shop floor to the boardroom. *About Us*, Focused Profit, https://focusedprofit.com/about-us/ (last visited July 8, 2020).

2. *See* John Kotter, *Management Is (Still) Not Leadership*, Harv. Bus. Rev. (Jan. 9, 2013), https://hbr.org/2013/01/management-is-still-not-leadership; Joseph Clarence Rost, Leadership for the 21st Century 129 (Greenwood 1991).

3. Steven Covey, The 7 Habits of Highly Effective People (Free Press 1989).

4. Roland B. Smith & Paul Bennett Marrow, *The Changing Nature of Leadership in Law Firms*, N.Y. St. B.J. 33 (2008).

5. N. Azad et al., *Leadership and Management Are One and the Same*, 81 Am. J. Pharmaceutical Ed. 102 (2017), *available at* https://doi.org/10.5688/ajpe816102.

6. *Id.*

7. Adapted, *see id.*; *see also* Steve Keating, *Management vs Leading*, Lead Today (Jan. 1, 2020), https://stevekeating.me/2020/01/30/managing-vs-leading-part-one/.

8. *Leadership*, WebFinance Inc. Business Dictionary (2020).

9. *What Is a Visionary Leader? 7 Traits of a Visionary Leader*, Status Net (2019), https://status.net/articles/visionary-leadership/.

10. J.P. Kotter, A Force for Change: How Leadership Differs from Management 3–8 (Simon & Schuster 2008) (1990).

11. *Id.*

12. *Id.*

13. *Management*, WebFinance Inc. Business Dictionary (2020).

14. Keating, *supra* note 7.

15. *Id.*

16. Ryan Fuller & Nina Shikaloff, *What Good Managers Do Daily*, Harv. Bus. Rev. (Dec. 14, 2016), https://hbr.org/2016/12/what-great-managers-do-daily.

17. *Id.*

18. *Id.*

19. *Id.*

20. *See* Forbes Quotes, *Thoughts on the Business of Life*, Forbes, https://www.forbes.com/quotes/theme/business/ (last visited July 8, 2015). *Dwight D. Eisenhower*, The White House, https://www.whitehouse.gov/about-the-white-house/presidents/dwight-d-eisenhower (last visited July 8, 2020).

21. *Management*, WebFinance Inc. Business Dictionary (2020).

22. *What Is a Visionary Leader? 7 Traits of a Visionary Leader, supra* note 9.

23. Shelley Frost, *How to Motivate Employees to Achieve Goal*, Hous. Chron., https://smallbusiness.chron.com/motivate-employees-achieve-goal-12303.html (last visited July 8, 2020).

24. Tara Mapes, *Walt Disney's Dream Culture*, Linked in (Jan. 30, 2017), https://www.linkedin.com/pulse/walt-disneys-dream-culture-tara-mapes/ (emphasis in original).

25. Fuller & Shikaloff, *supra* note 16.

26. Adapted, *see* Azad, *supra* note 5; *see also* Keating, *supra* note 7.

27. James Kerr, *Leader or Manager? These 10 Important Distinctions Can Help You Out*, Inc., https://www.inc.com/james-kerr/leading-v-managing-ten-important-distinctions-that-can-help-you-to-become-better.html (last visited July 21, 2020).

28. *See, e.g., Managing Partner — Law Firm Sample Job Description*, Monster, https://hiring.monster.com/employer-resources/job-description-templates/managing-partner-law-firm-job-description-sample/ (last visited July 21, 2020).

29. *Id.*

30. *See, e.g.,* Michael Short, *Signs That Origination Sharing Is NOT Working*, Law Vision (Sept. 7, 2018), https://lawvision.com/signs-that-origination-sharing-is-not-working/.

31. *Id.*

32. *See Managing Partner — Law Firm Sample Job Description, supra* note 28.

33. *See* Nicole Fallon, *35 Inspiring Quotes About Leaders*, Bus. News Daily (Nov. 29, 2015), https://www.businessnewsdaily.com/7481-leadership-quotes.html. Kenneth Thomas is an American author.

Part II

Leadership of Self: Growing into Leadership

Chapter 4

Understanding Leadership Theory

The most dangerous leadership myth is that leaders are born—that there is a genetic factor to leadership. That's nonsense; in fact, the opposite is true. Leaders are made rather than born.

Warren Bennis[1]

Purpose

Present different theories, strategies, and frameworks to help students consider approaches to leadership that may be effective in specific leadership circumstances.

Learning Objectives

At the end of this chapter, you should be able to:

- Discuss different approaches to the study of effective leaders and leadership.
- Critique strengths and weaknesses of particular strategies.
- Select one or more leadership approaches that might be a good fit with your personality and abilities.
- Identify leadership approaches that might work best within a specific scenario or environment.

Discussion

INTRODUCTION

"Leadership" defies simple explanation. In leadership stories, leaders create a vision, motivate a team, rally the troops when the going gets tough, and accept the accolades when the victory is won. While leadership may encompass that narrative, it can be "a complex process having multiple dimensions."[2] Some leaders make it look easy, which explains the notion that "great leaders are born, not made." In reality, leadership is hard work; it requires time and effort to study leadership and human nature. Leaders must consider various scenarios — and the potential responses to them — thoughtfully before they occur. Like war games where military leaders assess different options, leaders anticipate and assess what could go wrong and how best to respond given the goal or task, the people involved, and the resources available. While perhaps some leaders innately choose the correct action in a crisis, more make good decisions because they have studied, learned from mistakes, taken time to know their team, and have clarity of vision about the end goal. This process of leadership development differs for each of us, but learning the options for leading effectively applies to all. In this chapter, we present a number of leadership theories that have been widely researched. We encourage you to read this chapter with an intention to build a "toolbox" of leadership approaches that can be used in different situations.

WHY STUDY VARIOUS LEADERSHIP THEORIES AND APPROACHES?

Legal education and training typically did not include formal leadership development, although many aspects of the traditional law school curriculum provided knowledge, skills, competencies, and character formation needed for leadership. Beyond law school, law firms and bar associations provide some leadership training as part of their professional development programs. While lawyers, then, are not without any leadership training, the approach is indirect and informal, and lacks structure. We certainly would not apply this method of teaching to constitutional law or evidence. However, just as society expects lawyers to know evidence, society *expects* lawyers to be good leaders.

More directly of concern to young lawyers is the fact that law firms routinely evaluate their lawyers with an eye to their leadership potential. Beyond the need for a succession plan for the future of the firm's leadership, firms recognize that the same traits, characteristics, skills, and behaviors that make an effective leader translate to workplace success. Good leaders work well with others and have greater success in building new business for the firm. Whether the firm formally develops leadership talent or uses more indirect measures, leadership skills matter to your future employment potential. This means that law students who do not receive leadership training leave school without a needed competency to succeed in practice. Law students who recognize and integrate leadership theory and opportunities into their education come out of school better wired to meet firm expectations. Time spent in law school on leadership development can pay dividends as you enter the profession; you start with knowledge and experience to help you integrate more readily into a team, and you are ready to start developing beneficial relationships for yourself and your employer.

In this complicated and swiftly evolving world, uncertainty and change are givens. The curveballs thrown by this rapidly changing landscape can provide opportunity or they can devastate firms, clients, and communities. Leaders need to be prepared to assess situations and adapt as the circumstances dictate. No single approach to handling or leading a situation will work every time, and choosing wisely requires good judgment. Effective leaders select their approach for a given situation only after assessing the people involved (including themselves), the environment, and the goal to be accomplished. Different personalities, situations, relationships, and objectives need different techniques. The study of leadership theory teaches how to recognize, apply, mix, and transition between those approaches. With greater knowledge of the various approaches, including their strengths and weaknesses, you will be better prepared when you need to decide how to achieve the intended goal. And when the current approach is not working or becomes unfeasible, you will be prepared to implement another. The ability to adapt as a leader can be difficult, but with experience, you will be able to alter course more smoothly. The study of leadership, then, helps you prepare for situations before they arise and gives you the tools to lead effectively as challenges occur.

You will learn more about yourself as you study leadership, because leaders spend time on introspection. The more you know about your strengths, your weaknesses, your preferences, and your communication styles, the more successful you will be as a problem solver for your clients or a guide for teams you lead toward a goal. You will see throughout this study an emphasis on learning loops. In a learning loop, you assess, develop or change, evaluate, and reflect to master a skill or challenge. When you master the skill, you start the process over, allowing you to become more proficient. Learning is not static, and learning loops remind us that the pursuit of self-actualization requires learning again and again throughout life in pursuit of becoming the best person we can be. Consider the learning loop from tricycle to triathlete. At each step, you had to master a new and, at the time, challenging skill. Taking the training wheels off felt terrifying; 20 years later, clocking a hundred-mile ride presents the new horizon to reach. Had you simply stopped as a child, you would not have become the rider you are as an adult.

As you search for keys to success when guiding groups and leading projects, we encourage you consider these questions:

- *Who am I?* What are my natural inclinations, personality traits, and responses in difficult or stressful situations? Are there adjustments I need to pursue?
- *What do I have to offer?* What knowledge, skills, and professional competencies do I have? What knowledge, skill sets, and professional competencies do I still need to be prepared for situations in which I might find myself?

- *Where am I going?* Do I understand the environment or circumstances where I will be working? What is the vision, mission, or purpose of the organization or the goals or objectives of the project? Do I know whom I will be working for or with? What information do I need about the background or history of the organization or task that might impact the current work? What is the working relationship of those currently involved in the project?
- *Who will be my colleagues?* What type of relationship do I have with the people with whom I will be working? Do I know their strengths, weaknesses, and motivations? Do I know them well enough to understand their motivations and goals? Will I be sensitive to cultural or other influences?

The questions can be part of your learning loop. Addressing these questions when approaching a new position or project will enable you to create a plan, strategy, or framework to start the new project. Studying a variety of theories and approaches will enable you to implement the plan based upon your initial assessment and, if need be, adjust and modify as you gain information or circumstances change. This is the natural evolution of leadership learning.

THEORIES AND FRAMEWORK FOCUSED ON DEVELOPING THE LEADER

Thousands of books and articles describe leadership theories, and "as many as 65 different classifications systems have been developed to define the dimensions of leadership."[3] Fortunately, those theories can be sorted into three categories that group similar approaches. The first grouping looks at theories that focus the study on the *attributes* of the leader, including those that consider traits, characteristics, behaviors, actions, and styles of a particular leader. The second grouping includes studies that concentrate on the *situation*—the tasks or objectives to be completed and the needs of the followers to complete the task or meet the objective. The theories in the final grouping emphasize the *relationship* or interaction between the leader and the followers. Studying leadership from all three perspectives frames the issues and approaches from all the different perspectives that leaders will need as they try to develop a successful leadership style. The study of personal attributes looks inward as you examine your own traits and capabilities and assess their strengths and shortcomings in various situations. The other two perspectives involve external forces that must be assessed before determining a course of action. These three perspectives combine to create the complex process that is leadership and thus should be studied in all of their dimensions.

LEADERSHIP THEORIES BASED ON COMMON ATTRIBUTES AND BEHAVIORS OF LEADERS

The statement "Leaders are born, not made" reveals common biases about personal attributes the public expects to see in leaders. Leaders, for example, are tall men.

A large body of social science evidence demonstrates that the public perceives tall men as more persuasive and capable and "are more likely to attain leadership positions than women, or even shorter men."[4] If height is a foundational attribute, then leaders must be born — we cannot affect how tall we are. No wonder the first attempts to study "great" leadership in the early twentieth century[5] concentrated on the common "innate qualities and characteristics possessed by great social, political, and military leaders (e.g., Catherine the Great, Mahatma Gandhi, Indira Gandhi, Abraham Lincoln, Joan of Arc, and Napoleon Bonaparte)."[6] While effective leadership derives from more than a common set of personal attributes, taking inventory of your own traits, characteristics, and natural inclinations still provides a strong foundation for planning a course of action. Once you know more about yourself, you can better predict and change your reactions to situations.

Personal Traits and Characteristics of Leaders

In *Leadership: Theory and Practice*, Peter Northouse summarized common leadership traits identified in studies conducted over the last hundred years, focusing on twenty-five different terms from six major studies. Some traits like intelligence/cognitive ability, confidence, and initiative appeared on most lists; others like openness and problem solving appeared only in one study.[7] Northouse highlights five traits as central to leadership: *intelligence, self-confidence, determination, integrity,* and *sociability*.[8]

Studies of Leadership Traits and Characteristics

Stogdill (1948)	Mann (1959)	Stogdill (1974)	Lord, DeVader, and Alliger (1986)	Kirkpatrick and Locke (1991)	Zaccaro, Kemp, and Bader (2004)
Intelligence	Intelligence	Achievement	Intelligence	Drive	Cognitive abilities
Alertness	Masculinity	Persistence	Masculinity	Motivation	Extroversion
Insight	Adjustment	Insight	Dominance	Integrity	Conscientiousness
Responsibility	Dominance	Initiative		Confidence	Emotional stability
Initiative	Extroversion	Self-confidence		Cognitive ability	Openness
Persistence	Conservatism	Responsibility		Task knowledge	Agreeableness
Self-confidence		Cooperativeness			Motivation
Sociability		Tolerance			Social intelligence
		Influence			Self-monitoring
		Sociability			Emotional intelligence
					Problem solving

SOURCES: Adapted from "The Bases of Social Power," by J. R. P. French, Jr. and B. Raven, 1962, in D. Cartwright (Ed.), *Group Dynamics: Research and Theory* (pp. 259–269), New York: Harper and Row; Zaccoro, Kemp, & Bader (2004). https://www.sagepub.com/sites/default/files/upm-binaries/30933_Northouse_Chapter_2.pdf

In multiple studies, leaders were found to have higher *intelligence* than their followers.[9] Leaders with IQs that were higher than those of their followers were perceived positively as long as the deviation of the leader's intelligence was not so great as to cause difficulty in communication.[10] In other words, the leader needed to be smarter than the followers but not so smart that the team could not communicate with him. Higher intelligence also gives the leader an advantage in complex problem solving and social judgment skills.[11] Lawyers generally score higher on intelligence tests than the average citizen and are trained in complex problem solving in law school, which helps explain why lawyers are well suited for leadership positions.

Self-confidence and *determination* help the leader work proactively. Self-assured leaders trust their own ability to make a difference; they are convinced that their "attempts to influence others are appropriate and right."[12] They do not hesitate to assume command, and they also persevere in the face of obstacles or others' doubt. Some law students lack self-confidence when facing the pressures of law school, even experiencing imposter syndrome ("Did they make a mistake in letting me in?"). Good leaders remember that they earn opportunities, and you should remember that you *earned* the seat you occupy with your abilities and your willingness to do the hard work it takes to pursue a law degree. You also knew law school would challenge your intellect and test your fortitude. You still signed up a course of study designed to stretch your capacity for handling important and stressful matters with integrity and strength. Good leaders reflect on their willingness to embrace and master challenging situations; this process helps build self-confidence and determination.

Comment 2 for ABA Model Rule 8.4 Misconduct: Maintaining the Integrity of the Profession
"[A] lawyer should be professionally answerable . . . for offenses . . . involving violence, dishonesty, breach of trust, or serious interference with the administration of justice. . . ."

Integrity in Northouse's lexicon is "the quality of honesty and trustworthiness" in people who "adhere to a strong set of principles and take responsibility for their actions."[13] This "commitment to a set of values or principles" could be good or bad, admirable or not.[14] Northouse, however, believes leaders need *moral* integrity and implies that a leader must be honest and trustworthy before anyone will follow. "Leaders with integrity inspire confidence in others because they can be trusted to do what they say they are going to do."[15] Lawyers are required to adhere to a code of ethics and, to be trusted, must demonstrate good moral character. Their training and ethical foundations, then, help lawyers have the needed moral integrity to lead. Integrity should be foundational to your career as a lawyer and as a leader. Much of the practice of law and leading is based on solid relationships, which are in turn based on trust. When you conduct your affairs with integrity, others believe in you, want to follow you, and will stay loyal to you.[16]

The final positive leader trait is *sociability* or, as teachers phrased it in kindergarten, the ability to work and play well with others. Social leaders have good interpersonal skills, and they are "friendly, outgoing, courteous, tactful and diplomatic."[17] Their concern for others' well-being encourages sensitivity to others' needs and builds cooperative teams.[18] Sociability may seem discordant given the adversarial nature of much of the legal profession, but being more likable and relatable actually helps lawyers succeed, making them more effective in a courtroom, more likely to get new business from clients, or even more likely to receive more favorable assignments from colleagues. Sociability fosters better relationships — we like to work with people we like.

Over the past twenty-five years, other researchers found a common connection between effective leadership and four of the five basic factors that make up our personality. Effective leaders tend to be more *extrovert, conscientious, open*, and *low on the scale of neuroticism*.[19] While this approach looks at personality traits, the research aligns closely with Northouse's five traits discussed above. For example, extroversion correlates highest with successful leadership, and extroversion is really about sociability. Extroverts tend to be sociable, talkative, assertive, and positive.[20] The next strongest correlation was conscientiousness, a trait that includes elements of integrity. Conscientiousness was described as the "tendency to be thorough, organized, controlled, dependable, and decisive."[21] The trait of openness includes the "tendency to be informed, creative, insightful, and curious"[22] and correlates with both intelligence and confidence. Finally, effective leaders with low neuroticism are less likely "to be depressed, anxious, insecure, vulnerable, and hostile."[23] Low neuroticism sounds like self-confidence. The last of the five basic factors for personality, agreeableness ("tendency to be accepting, conforming, trusting, and nurturing"), has only a weak association with leadership.[24]

Skills Approach to Leadership Development

The Katz Model

A 1955 article in the *Harvard Business Review* marked a departure from leadership studies that focused on defining traits of effective leaders as the method to study leadership.[25] Robert Katz's article promoted the view of leadership as a set of skills that can be acquired and developed through effort. In other words, leaders *can* be made. Katz's work designated three skill sets necessary for effective leadership: *technical, human*, and *conceptual*. Technical skill refers to the knowledge, analytical ability, and other specialized tools or techniques needed to perform specific activities or tasks. *Technical skills* are not always necessary to serve as the team leader, but technical proficiency in an area is typically necessary to establish credibility in a particular organization. As lawyers, technical competency is a starting point, but it only gets you to the door. True expertise opens many more doors of opportunity.

Human skills are people skills, which include the ability to work cooperatively with others by taking into consideration others' needs and motivations to accomplish a task or goal. This equates to sociability. In law's professional setting, being social means being likable and taking time to get to know your clients and colleagues at a personal level. These people skills translate to stronger relationships and a robust network, both of which are effective when building a book of business or looking to create connections.

The last facet is the development of *conceptual skills*. "Whereas technical skills deal with *things* and human skills deal with *people*, conceptual skills involve the ability to work with *ideas*."[26] More than thinking big thoughts or dreaming up new directions for an organization, leaders must shape concepts into a form that can be communicated to those who will do the actual work needed to accomplish the goal. Lawyers are trained to take ideas, themes, and theories and shape them into manageable and workable concepts that can be communicated to clients, judges, or juries. This skill translates well to effective leadership.

The specific types of technical, human, and conceptual skills needed for a position will depend on the level of authority that the person has in the organization. The president of the firm spends most of his time on big picture concepts such as whether the firm should merge with another firm. Managing partners may not be familiar with the software system used to process an expense reimbursement form; instead, they hand the receipt to an administrative staff person who is very skilled in using the software system. The firm's office manager charged with supervising office staff will need to oversee and train the administrative staff responsible for expense reports. Middle management should have a good mix of technical, human, and conceptual skills to be able to assist those above and below in the organization. The middle manager must understand the day-to-day operations to support the work of the lower-level managers and also be capable of helping the president analyze the costs and benefits of a merger.

Skills Needed

Top Management	Technical	Human	Conceptual
Middle Management	Technical	Human	Conceptual
Supervisory Management	Technical	Human	Conceptual

The Mumford Model

Beginning in 1990, a different skills-based model emerged, known as the Mumford model. Also referred to as capabilities model, the Mumford model recognized that leadership is not limited to those born with common leadership personality traits. Mumford suggested that by gaining knowledge and developing beneficial skills (capabilities), people can improve their effectiveness as leaders. The Mumford model is "a more complex picture of how skills relate to the manifestation of effective leadership."[27] This model has five components:

- *individual attributes*: cognitive ability, motivation, and personality;
- *competencies*: problem-solving skills, social judgment skills, and knowledge;
- *leadership outcomes*: effective problem solving and performance;

- *career experiences*: previous experience; and
- *environmental influences*: available resources.

At the heart of this model are three general competencies: *problem-solving skills, social judgment skills,* and *knowledge*[28] that "can be developed over time through education and experience."[29] The first competency, *problem-solving skills,* includes skills such as analyzing the relevant causes and goals, identifying the constraints, formulating plans, anticipating consequences, and creatively considering alternatives, while articulating a vision that inspires followers.[30] The *social judgment skills* competency includes the "capacity to understand people and social systems and work with people to solve unique organizational problems."[31] *Knowledge* "directly influences a leader's capacity to define complex organizational problems and to attempt to solve them."[32]

The Mumford[33] model recognized that a leader needs more than competencies to be successful. Leaders must be well-rounded. For example, a lawyer may have a national reputation as the leading expert in an obscure regulatory procedure, but that advanced knowledge does not mean she would be trusted as the managing partner. The *individual attributes* component recognizes that the influence of the leader's traits, such as intelligence, drive, or lack of humor, will limit or enhance her ability to gain or advance the three types of competencies. A leader's effectiveness is also influenced by skills and lessons learned in the past, i.e., *career experiences,* as well as factors that may be outside the leader's control, i.e., *environmental influences,* such as available resources or an economic downturn. *Leadership outcomes* (effective problem solving and performance) are the result of the leader's competencies, which can be impacted by the leader's attributes and experience and other influences over which the leader has no control.

Skills Model of Leadership

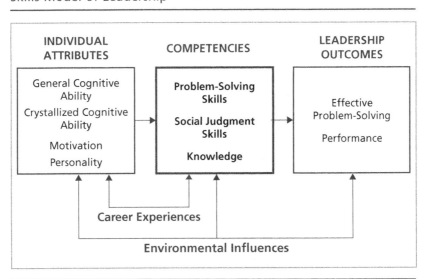

SOURCE: Adapted from "Leadership Skills for a Changing World: Solving Complex Social Problems," by M. D. Mumford, S. J. Zaccaro, F. D. Harding, T. O. Jacobs, and E. A. Fleishman, 2000, *Leadership Quarterly, 11*(1), 23. https://www.sagepub.com/sites/default/files/upm-binaries/45968_Chapter_3.pdf

Both models suggest leaders should spend time to acquire relevant knowledge and technical competency and to sharpen their analytical skills to assess the issues, anticipate obstacles, and develop a plan to address the issues as they arise. The ability to work with people in a cooperative manner is also recognized as essential to success.

Much of legal education prepares lawyers to excel at acquiring knowledge, developing technical skills, solving problems, and conceptualizing possible solutions. Little time is spent in law school to emphasize the importance of developing people skills, but the ability to effectively work with others can mean success in the practice of law. Take, for example, a tax lawyer who is asked to work on a merger of a client's corporation into another corporation. Knowledge of the relevant tax rules is necessary to achieve the client's goal of a tax-free merger. Proficiency with Excel worksheets lets the lawyer quickly tell the client if the proposed combination of cash and stock will meet the tax-free requirements. Those technical skills are essential to do the job. However, to get the client to hire her and to work as part of the larger team of lawyers and other professionals working on the deal or to successfully negotiate the best terms for the client, the lawyer's "people skills" become important.

Changing Behaviors to Improve Results

In the 1940s, researchers from Ohio State and University of Michigan studied the impact of leaders' behaviors rather their traits and skills.[34] They focused on what leaders do and how they act.[35] Leaders acted in one of two ways. In the first group, leaders focused on the technical aspects of production and created systems to organize the work. In other words, they built an efficient flow of work. The second group of leaders focused on employees, taking time to nurture them and recognize their value and contributions. This built camaraderie, mutual respect, and trust.[36] This research turned into the Leadership Grid®, which graphed a leader's concern for people (relationships) and results (production).

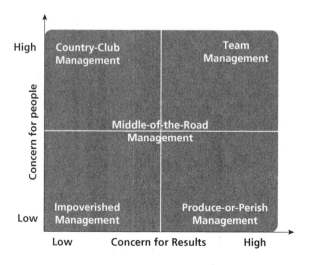

The grid presented five behavioral styles of leadership.[37] A leader with high concern for people and little emphasis on production was labeled a "country-club" manager. An individual who emphasized neither production nor people practiced "impoverished management." Emphasis on efficiency of production rather than the concerns of employees was a taskmaster exercising "authority-compliance management" (also known as "produce-or-perish.") Balancing concern for production and people was termed "middle-of-the-road" management. Finally, an individual who simultaneously exhibited a high concern for getting the job done while also valuing employees practiced "team management," which, according to the prescriptions of the grid, was the best leadership approach.

In addition to these five behavioral styles of leadership, scholars later identified two more styles that incorporate multiple aspects of the grid. Paternalism/maternalism is a combination of "country-club" and "produce-or-perish," which involves a " 'benevolent dictator' who acts graciously but does so for the purpose of goal accomplishment."[38] These leaders make the key decisions as the head of the organization (which is viewed as a family unit); loyalty and obedience are richly rewarded. Opportunism refers to leaders who may have a dominant style but can change at will. Their switch to another style, or any combination, is fueled by their self-interested pursuit of personal advancement.[39]

LEADERSHIP APPROACHES BASED ON THE SITUATION

Situational Leadership

As the name suggests, in this approach the leader acts based on the situation, evaluating whether the team is right for the task at hand, from both the competence and commitment perspectives. The task may be one that will require more supervision, or the team members may need a lot of hand holding. In a different situation, the team might be self-directed and enthusiastic either because of the task or because of the team's composition. This relationship behavior can be described as directive or supportive. This model tasks leaders with recognizing what needs to be done under the circumstances and adapting their style and strategy as the situation evolves.

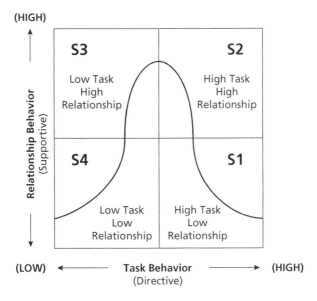

The Situational Leadership®II Model provides four distinct categories of directive and supportive behaviors that depend on the amount of time and energy the leader spends in directing the actions of the members in relation to the effort spent to support a member. *High directive–high support* style, similar to a coaching style, involves both high contact and direction with a high degree of emotional support. In the *high support–low directive* approach, the team member needs little direction — he has the expertise for the job — but needs significant supportive encouragement to succeed. In a *low directive–low support* situation, the leader sees little need for specific instruction or support as the team member is fully knowledgeable and self-sufficient. In this setting, the leader has more ability to *delegate* freely. *High directive–low supportive* behavior requires specific instructions about expectations that, once given, need little additional support.

In situational leadership, the leader continuously reassesses both the progress of the work and the development of the individual team members, adapting to meet the needs of both. Its flexible nature makes this approach appealing, especially as organizations aspire to become more inclusive environments. Cultural intelligence requires leaders to be more adaptable as they gain a better awareness of the different cultural influences within a group of individuals. Situational leaders approach each member individually to help members gain new skills as the work progresses while encouraging them to become more confident and capable.

Transactional Leadership

The price of success is hard work, dedication to the job at hand, and the determination that whether we win or lose, we have applied the best of ourselves to the task at hand.

Vince Lombardi

Transactional leaders tell group members what to do and when,[40] using a system of rewards and punishments to motivate followers. In this *quid pro quo* environment, behavior is bartered. Businesses reward successful employees with bonuses and "employee of the month" accolades. Motivation involves rewards and is outcome-driven, and the ends justify the means. Failure results in reprimands or other punishment. Athletic teams rely heavily on transactional leadership in which players are expected to conform to the team's rules and performance expectations. If they play well, they keep their starting position. Players who fail to meet expectations are benched or cut. Players are motivated to perform, even if it means playing with pain and injury, and a "win-at-all-costs" attitude pervades. Not surprisingly, military operations frequently rely on transactional leadership to achieve a given objective.

Transactional leaders set expectations and standards to maximize the efficiency and productivity of an organization. Constructive feedback, when given, keeps the employee on task to improve output; it is not given to better develop the team member as an individual. The relationship between leaders and subordinates is an exchange — you give me something for something in return. Maintaining the status quo is often the goal, rather than moving the organization forward, and that can discourage creativity.[41] Research shows transactional leadership is most effective in situations where problems are simple and clearly defined or when the goal is to keep the ship afloat in times of crisis.[42]

WHEN RELATIONSHIP INFLUENCES THE LEADERSHIP APPROACH

Transformational Leadership

Transformational leadership has developed as a popular approach in recent decades. Transformational leaders are influencers who engage with others to create a connection through intellectual stimulation. These leaders encourage their team members to think about problems and issues in new ways.[43] They may stimulate creativity and innovation to change an outdated or dysfunctional process or system. Research indicates that this high-energy and creative environment can have a positive impact on the psychological well-being of both the followers and the leaders.[44] "Mohandas Gandhi raised the hopes and demands of millions of his people and, in the process, was changed himself."[45]

Transformational leaders inspire by providing meaning and challenge to the work, and they involve team members emotionally with the shared vision.[46] Bass argued that transformational leaders motivate team members to do more than expected in three discrete ways: "(a) raising followers' levels of consciousness about the importance and value of specified and idealized goals, (b) getting followers to transcend their own self-interest for the sake of the team or organization, and (c) moving followers to address higher-level needs."[47] In other words, transformational leaders inspire followers to do more than was believed possible. Our country was established by the transformational leadership of our Founding Founders, who convinced the colonists to reject British rule and imagine a new form of government. Charismatic individuals' ability to convince others of their vision makes them effective as transformational leaders.

In business, transformational leaders encourage and motivate employees to innovate and create change that will help grow and shape the future success of the company. They often set "an example at the executive level through a strong sense of corporate culture, employee ownership and independence in the workplace."[48] Transformational leaders inspire and motivate their workforce without micromanaging. Experienced employees are trusted to make decisions in their areas and are given room to look for creative new solutions to old problems. They are encouraged to think about the future. "Employees on the leadership track will also be prepared to become transformational leaders themselves through mentorship and training."[49]

Bennis and Nanus highlighted "common strategies used by leaders in transforming organizations."[50] The four common strategies are:

1. Have a clear *vision* for the future direction of the organization that is simple enough to be understood, realistic enough to be believed and attractive enough to inspire followers to want to achieve it.[51]
2. Be the *social architects* for their organizations by creating new group identity or philosophy that can have a shared meaning for the people in the organization.[52]
3. Create *trust* by clearly articulating a position, being transparent, and then having the integrity to stand firm and follow through.[53]
4. Present themselves with a positive self-regard. By emphasizing their strengths, even though they are aware of their weaknesses, they create a sense of confidence and high expectations in the followers as well.[54]

Kouzes and Posner's leadership model for "how to get extraordinary things done in organizations"[55] takes transformative leadership a step further. Five fundamental practices enable leaders to accomplish extraordinary and transformative feats:

1. *Model the way.* Leaders have clarity about their own values and philosophy and they live out those values so that others are able to behave in a similar manner. Those values are reinforced through their conversations and interactions with others.
2. *Inspire a shared vision.* Leaders create compelling, uplifting visions of the future that inspire followers to join in the effort by appealing to their values, interests, hopes, and dreams.
3. *Challenge the process.* Leaders search for challenging opportunities to change, grow, and improve. A willingness to experiment and innovate means they are willing to take risks and learn from any mistakes.
4. *Enabling others to act.* Leaders foster collaboration by promoting teamwork and collaboration. Trust is built by engaging followers and developing their strengths and by treating others with dignity and respect. Followers are allowed to make choices and feel supported and valued.
5. *Encourage the heart.* Leaders recognize and reward individual contributions to the success of the project and celebrate the accomplishments of the team.[56]

Authentic Leadership

To thy own self be true.

Polonius, *Hamlet*[57]

"Authenticity has been explored throughout history, from Greek philosophers to the work of Shakespeare," but authentic leadership as a modern management science gained acceptance with the book *Authentic Leadership*.[58] The book described five basic qualities found in authentic leaders, and each is associated with an observable characteristic: *purpose* and *passion*, *values* and *behavior*, *relationships* and *connectedness*, *self-discipline* and *consistency*, and *heart* and *compassion*. When leaders demonstrate these qualities or characteristics, their followers respond positively, and the organization benefits.

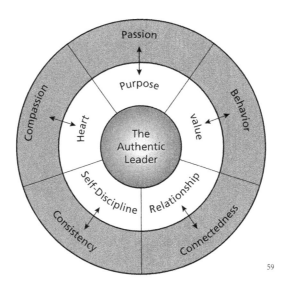

Nelson Mandela is an example of an authentic leader. A deeply moral man, Mandela had a strong conscience and set of values. "While fighting to abolish apartheid in South Africa, he was unyielding in his pursuit of justice and equality for all."[60] Even when imprisoned for 27 years, he never wavered, even when offered an early release if he compromised. With his leadership, apartheid ended. He also understood the need to connect with a variety of people, even those whom he once opposed, saying, "[Y]ou can't make peace with your enemy if you aren't willing to work with them and treat them with dignity."[61]

A study of authentic leadership emphasized four attributes of authentic leadership:

1. **Authentic leaders are self-aware and genuine.**

   Authentic leaders are self-actualized individuals who are aware of their strengths, their limitations, and their emotions. They also show their real selves to their followers. They do not act one way in private and another in public; they don't hide their mistakes or weaknesses out of fear of looking weak. They also realize that being self-actualized is an endless journey, never complete.

2. **Authentic leaders are mission driven and focused on results.**

   They are able to put the mission and the goals of the organization ahead of their own self-interest. They do the job in pursuit of results, not for their own power, money, or ego.

3. **Authentic leaders lead with their hearts, not just their minds.**

   They are not afraid to show their emotions and their vulnerability and to connect with their employees. This does not mean authentic leaders are "soft." In fact, communicating in a direct manner is critical to successful outcomes, but it's done with empathy; directness without empathy is cruel.

4. **Authentic leaders focus on the long term.**

   A key tenet in Bill George's model is that company leaders are focused on long-term shareholder value, not on just beating quarterly estimates. Just as George did as CEO of Medtronic, . . . leaders realize that to nurture individuals and to nurture a company requires hard work and patience, but the approach pays large dividends over time.[62]

Being authentic as a leader is hard work and takes years of experience in leadership roles. Krause shared, "Once a CEO reminded me, 'Leadership is acting.' And it surprises me when these same leaders seem shocked or confused when their employees don't trust them, don't like them, and can't really wait to work elsewhere."[63]

The definition of authenticity is not perfect, but "real or genuine; not copied or false; true and accurate."[64] It comes from the Greek word for author, which led author Warren Bennis to say, "You are the author of your life."[65] No one can be authentic without fail; everyone behaves inauthentically at times, saying and doing things that are regrettable. The essence of authentic leadership is emotional intelligence, or EQ, as articulated by Daniel Goleman.[66] The key to finding one's authentic self in the midst of life's imperfections is to have the self-awareness to recognize these times and listen to close colleagues who point them out.

Servant Leadership

The great leader is seen as servant first. . . .

Robert K. Greenleaf[67]

The term "servant leadership" originated in the writings of Robert K. Greenleaf in 1970 as a "theoretical framework that advocates a leader's primary motivation and role as service to others."[68] Greenleaf's writings were more prescriptive than descriptive and focused on the ideal servant leader to help create a better society. "I believe that caring for persons, the more able and the less able serving each other, is what makes a good society."[69] His theory for creating a better society encouraged leaders of institutions to reconsider their relationship with followers. He believed that if leaders put their followers' needs first and served their followers, "their influence may form a leaven that makes possible a reasonably civilized society."[70] In other words, he hoped that employees who are led and cared for by servant leaders would then lead and care for others out in the community. With his purposeful combining of "two seemingly contradictory terms, Greenleaf asks us to reconsider the very nature of leadership."[71]

Servant leadership is "a model which puts serving others as the number one priority. Servant leadership emphasizes increased service to others; a holistic approach to work; promoting a sense of community; and the sharing of power in decision-making."[72] Followers come first. Leaders must be attentive to the concerns of their followers, empower them, and help them develop to their fullest potential. "Furthermore, servant leaders are ethical and lead in ways that serve the greater good of the organization, community, and society at large."[73] According to Greenleaf:

> [T]he best test . . . is: do those served grow as persons; do they, *while being served*, become healthier, wiser, freer, more autonomous, more likely themselves to become servants? *And*, what is the effect on the least privileged in society; will they benefit, or, at least, will they not be further deprived?[74]

At the core of servant leadership is a "selfless, 'others-directed' motivation that resides within the leader."[75] Beginning with an analysis of the leader's motivation makes Greenleaf's model of leadership unique.[76] Accordingly, aspiring servant leaders must first scrutinize their personal principles and values and consider their motivation to lead. Strong ethics and commitment to those principles and values provide the foundation for all decisions and are "key to the long-term interests of the organization being served."[77] Servant leaders shift institutional power to followers and provide opportunities for them to "experience interdependence, respect, trust, and individual growth."[78] In addition to serving, servant leaders have "a social responsibility to be concerned about the 'have-nots' and those less privileged. If inequities and social injustices exist, a servant leader tries to remove them."[79]

Greenleaf's servant leadership emphasized ten core personal attributes: *listening, empathy, healing, awareness, persuasion, conceptualization, foresight, stewardship, commitment to the growth of people,* and *building community.*[80] Once purely Greenleaf's aspirational vision, servant leadership has been studied and confirmed by behavioral scientists. Greenleaf's list has been expanded to include more leadership attributes.

Functional Attributes	Attributes Accompanying
1. Vision	10. Communication
2. Honesty	11. Credibility
3. Integrity	12. Competency
4. Trust	13. Stewardship
5. Service	14. Visibility
6. Modeling	15. Influence
7. Pioneering	16. Persuasion
8. Appreciation	17. Listening
9. Empowerment	18. Encouragement
	19. Teaching
	20. Delegation

"When many leaders in an organization adopt a servant leadership orientation, a culture of serving others within and outside the organizations is created."[81]

Adaptive Leadership

Why do I always have to be the problem solver? Group problem-solving is a skill you will use your whole life. Figure it out.

Coach Robert "Lad" Ladouceur[82]

Ronald Heifetz's book *Leadership Without Easy Answers* introduced the concept of adaptive leadership. This leadership model is *follower-centered* and both situational and relational. It is a *process* of "mobilizing a group of individuals to handle tough challenges and emerge triumphant in the end." Adaptive leaders encourage people to face and deal with changes that need to be made to improve their lives.[83] Adaptive leaders do not want their followers to assume the leader will swoop in "as a savior who solves problems for people." Instead, adaptive leaders believe their role is to challenge and assist others to face difficult issues, such as drug abuse or microaggressions in the workplace.

The adaptive leader helps an individual or a group explore their values, change priorities and behaviors to address a challenge, or to improve and grow.[84] The goal is not for the leader to solve another's problem but to help the person address and resolve the issues on his own. This is the leadership equivalent of teaching a man to fish rather than giving him a fish. The leader must establish "an atmosphere in which people feel safe tackling difficult problems, but not so safe that they can avoid the problem."[85] Since the leader serves as a catalyst for addressing the issue, nurturing a relationship with the follower based on trust helps create that atmosphere.

Adaptive work may require leading in a situation where both the problem and the solution are unclear. In an environment of uncertainty, the role of an adaptive leader is to embrace the uncertainty and encourage followers to look for new approaches. Creating an inclusive environment where different perspectives are valued can result in a wider range of options. Employees who are encouraged to stretch beyond traditional thinking and approaches may find creative solutions. They should focus on thinking of possibilities rather than limitations.

Relationships matter in adaptive leadership, and in this approach, every member of the team is equally important. The leader must be able to inspire team members and encourage them to apply their best skills. Team members must be able to hold open dialogue with each other, which can lead to new insights and creative solutions. Solving tough institutional or societal issues is hard work. Everyone's voice is needed, and the leaders should be looking for any cultural barriers that might inhibit participation by all.

Adaptive leaders might consider the following six behaviors to enhance their leadership style. These are not steps that must be taken in a particular order but are guides to adaptive behavior.

1. *Get off the dance floor, get on the balcony.* The bigger picture can be seen only from the balcony above the dance floor, giving you broader perspective on the

situation. The leader may have to go through the exercise (step back to consider the overall picture) while still participating in the action. You may need to get on and off the balcony several times as you assess, take action, and reassess.

2. *Identify adaptive challenges.* "Failures in leadership often occur because leaders fail to diagnose challenges correctly."[86] If the problem is technical in nature, there is no need to invoke a process when it can be delegated and fixed. For example, when an assistant resigns, creating a backlog of work and hurting productivity, no process is necessary before hiring a replacement. On the other hand, if the adaptive challenge is a more complex challenge, such as a merger of your law firm with another, you will need to develop a process to work through issues such as different and incompatible policies or different compensation systems.

3. *Regulate distress.* People like consistency and predictability. Change creates uncertainty and can cause distress, which is normal and to be expected. "Too much distress is counterproductive and can be debilitating."[87] The leader should monitor the stress level of followers and be prepared to provide guidance or take action to help.

4. *Maintain disciplined attention.* The leader should find ways to keep followers focused on the work of addressing the tough problems or uncertainty. Avoidance techniques are common and can include ignoring the problem, blaming others, attacking others (even those who are trying to solve the issue), pretending it does not exist, or focusing efforts on unrelated areas.[88]

5. *Give the work back to the people.* Provide direction and structure but let them solve the problem.

6. *Protect leadership voices from below.* Listen carefully. "Be open to ideas from those who may be at the fringe, marginalized, or even deviant within the group."[89]

Adaptive leaders focus on processes that allow a team to work through problems and uncertainty in an ever-changing environment. They read the terrain, are well prepared, and expect plans to change. Although its origin is murky, many military leaders have adopted the adage, "No plan survives first contact with the enemy."[90] Adaptive leaders embrace change and create an environment in which their team members can respond to change, even when they are outside their comfort zones. Adaptive leaders build dynamic teams that can channel discomfort or fear into positive outcomes.

Leader-Member Exchange Theory

Leader-member exchange theory views leadership as the interaction between leaders and followers.[91] The leader's relationship with a follower depends on whether the follower is a member of the leader's inner circle, or "in-group." In-group members have a good and often close working relationship with the leader and they may have similar or complementary personalities. In-group members characteristically will take on extra tasks or responsibilities. By contrast, the leader's relationship with out-group members is more formal and conforms closely to formal job descriptions and hierarchical lines of communication. These employees may be less compatible with the leader, either because their personalities clash with the leader's or they hold dissenting opinions. Out-group members are less willing to take on additional assignments or responsibilities. You need only think back to social groups in junior high to understand these relationships. Not surprisingly, in-group members are more likely to get the best assignments, receive bigger bonuses, advance through the partnership track faster, and be invited to the join the partner at the client's house in Vail. The leader must avoid the appearance and reality of favoritism.

Leader-member exchange theory has important implications for diversity and inclusion efforts, both positive and negative. This type of in-crowd approach has been used to keep a "good ol' boys' club" leadership structure in law firms for years, giving an inside track to those most like the leader. Minorities, women, and LGBTQ+ persons likely comprise the majority of the out-group members. Both leaders and those in the out-group can alter this dynamic, however. Cultural awareness will help the leader identify and hopefully alter this dynamic. A leader's cultural intelligence will enable the leader to identify and dismantle barriers and find ways to connect with all members so that each individual feels valued. For followers, the lesson is easy: align yourself with the leader, volunteer to take on extra tasks, and assume additional responsibilities. The leader's greatest challenge is to find ways to turn out-group members into in-group members.

ADDING TO YOUR SKILL SET

Understanding these varied theories of leadership offers you a toolkit of options when problem solving. When you approach the study of leadership as the process of developing the skills in your skill set, you can be better equipped for a leadership situation when the time comes. Failing to prepare, as the adage goes, is preparing to fail. You are taught to practice preparedness from an early age — it is why we have fire drills. Knowing how to react before a crisis increases the likelihood that you will react well.

The leadership theories and approaches presented here are not an exhaustive collection. Through study and the passage of time, you doubtless will learn new and different approaches to leadership. Some will fit you better than others. Some will be more appropriate for certain situations than others. As you progress in your leadership journey and gain experience, you will become skilled in choosing, adapting, and modifying your approach as the circumstances dictate. You may discover that some leadership approaches overlap or are complementary and can be used in conjunction with one another. For example, transformational and transactional leadership complement each other as both are conducive to organizational effectiveness.[92] Transformational leadership may inspire employees with a new vision or an innovative way to improve upon an old way of operating. But a vision is a dream on a concept board — the professional version of a vision board—until someone can actualize a plan and implement the transactional steps to get there.

To get you started we offer these steps:

1. *Identify leaders who fit these styles.* As you read about these theories, did you recognize either someone you know or a famous leader who fit one of these styles? Think about the strengths and weaknesses of these leaders and what they did well versus what they did poorly. You can learn as much from the mistakes of others as you can from your own.

2. *Identify strengths and abilities.* Which approaches come most naturally for you? Some people are confident that their winning personality and sociability will allow them to influence the group. Others feel more comfortable allowing their expertise, skills, and experience to lead the way. Emphasizing your strengths will better your chances of success; knowing your weaknesses will help you build a team to compensate or identify an area for growth.

3. *Assess your tendencies.* Are you more likely to be focused on the people in a situation or on the situation as it affects people? Neither answer is wrong, but your answer may help guide you regarding the approach you need to take.

4. *Identify specific situations you are concerned about navigating.* Do you anticipate needing to have hard conversations with a boss or subordinate? How do you want that conversation to go? Which approach might be best suited based on the other person's personality type? Going through the mental exercise of creating situations and considering how you would resolve them ahead of time can help you when you are in the situation. Frequently, there is not time to pause and carefully think through each step, so having gone through the mental exercise in advance of the situation is tremendously helpful in getting to the right result.

CONCLUSION

The leadership theories in this chapter are neither an exhaustive list of approaches nor an in-depth study of the ones presented. We hope that they encourage you to consider which ones you want to investigate further and to explore multiple options. Leadership development can be a metaphorical toolkit filled with various different approaches. You can choose the tool that fits the situation and allows you to get the job done, but the same tool will not fix every problem. A study of all approaches will give you a broader understanding of the knowledge, skills, and competencies needed to suit your style and allow you to be effective in a variety of leadership situations.

The process of leadership is complex, layered, and constantly evolving as the people and the circumstances change and develop. Experience will help you determine which approach to try, and even with great study, experience may be your most valuable teacher. You may see the opportunity to grow through failure. The study of leadership helps develop the art of preparing for situations before they arise. Devoting time now to try out different approaches will better equip you for the challenges to come.

Exercise

Name That Leadership Theory

Choose one past or current famous leader with whom you are familiar enough to answer these questions:

- Which personal characteristics contributed to their position of influence as a leader?
- What skill sets did they possess that were essential to obtain their leadership position, and what additional skill sets did they possess that you think assisted with their obtaining or retaining that position?
- What behaviors contributed to their reputation, and how?
- What other factors may have played a role in their obtaining the role?
- What other factors may have played a role in their success or failure as a leader in that leadership role?
- What leadership theory do you think best describes their approach to leadership?
- Find a quote from or video clip of that person that best represents the public's perception of the individual as a person. Then find a second quote or video clip that best represents the public's perception of the individual as a leader. Social media posts from the leader count as quotes. Be prepared to share the quote or clip and discuss your answers to the above questions.

Journal Prompts

1. Choose someone, past or current, with influence over you and who held or holds some type of position of authority over you (parent, boss, coach, professor, etc.).

   a. Describe the personal characteristics and traits you believe contributed to their positive influence on you.

   b. Are there any negative characteristics or traits that diminished or damaged your relationship at any point? How was the relationship repaired?

   c. What skill sets do they possess that allowed them to have a positive influence on you?

   d. What behaviors of that person contribute to your relationship, and how?

   e. Which of your behaviors toward the other person contribute to your current relationship, and how? Were there other behaviors not directed to the other person but that were nevertheless observed by the other person that impacted your relationship?

    f. What other factors may have affected your relationship with that person?

    g. What leadership theory do you think best describes their approach to the influence they have had over you?

2. Consider the leadership theories presented in this chapter or elsewhere.

    a. Which leadership theory do you think fits most naturally with your personality and abilities? Describe what factors lead you to that conclusion.

    b. Which leadership theory do you think fits least naturally with your personality and abilities? What can you do to incorporate the best of that theory into your personality?

Endnotes

1. *Remembering Warren Bennis*, Harv. Bus. Rev. (Oct. 2014), https://hbr.org/2014/10/remembering-warren-bennis. Warren Bennis was an American scholar who is widely regarded as the pioneer of the field of leadership studies.
2. Peter G. Northouse, Leadership: Theory and Practice 1 (8th ed. 2019).
3. *Id.* at 5.
4. Erik Lindqvist, *Height and Leadership*, 94 Rev. Econ. & Statistics 1191 (Nov. 2012).
5. *See* Bert Spector, *Carlyle, Freud, and the Great Man Theory More Fully Considered*, 12 Leadership (2015), *available at* https://doi.org/10.1177/1742715015571392.
6. Northouse, *supra* note 2, at 19.
7. *Id.* at 22.
8. *Id.* at 23.
9. *Id.*
10. *Id.*
11. *Id.* at 24.
12. *Id.*
13. *Id.* at 25.
14. Nancy Schauber, *Integrity, Commitment and the Concept of a Person*, 33 Am. Phil. Q. 119, 120 (1996).
15. Northouse, *supra* note 2, at 25.
16. *Id.*
17. *Id.*
18. *See, e.g., Great Leaders Are Sensitive*, Sigma, https://www.sigmaassessmentsystems.com/sensitive-leaders/ (last visited July 22, 2020).
19. Northouse, *supra* note 2, at 26.
20. Kendra Cherry, *How Extraversion in Personality Influences Behavior*, Very Well Mind (May 9, 2020), https://www.verywellmind.com/what-is-extroversion-2795994.
21. Northouse, *supra* note 2, at 26.
22. *Id.*
23. *Id.*
24. *Id.*
25. Robert L. Katz, *Skills of an Effective Administrator*, Harv. Bus. Rev. 33 (1974), https://hbr.org/1974/09/skills-of-an-effective-administrator.
26. Northouse, *supra* note 2, at 45.
27. *Id.* at 57.
28. *Id.* at 46–47.

29. *Id.* at 47.

30. *Id.* at 48.

31. *Id.* at 50.

32. *Id.* at 51.

33. *Id.* Ch. 3, *available at* https://www.sagepub.com/sites/default/files/upm-binaries/45968_Chapter_3.pdf.

34. Behavioral Approaches to Leadership (Openstax 2012), *available at* https://opentextbc.ca/principlesofmanagementopenstax/chapter/behavioral-approaches-to-leadership/.

35. Northouse, *supra* note 2, at 73.

36. *Id.*

37. The initial name was "Managerial Grid," which has been renamed the "Leadership Grid." *Id.* at 76.

38. *Id.* at 78–79.

39. *Id.*

40. Bernard Bass, Leadership and Performance, Beyond Expectations (N.Y. Free Press 1985).

41. Athena Xenikou, *Transformational Leadership, Transactional Contingent Reward, and Organizational Identification: The Mediating Effect of Perceived Innovation and Goal Culture Orientations*, Front Psychol. 8 (2017), *available at* https//:doi:10.3389/fpsyg.2017.01754.

42. S. Wongyanon et al., *Analysis of the Influence of Leadership Styles of Chief Executives to Organizational Performance of Local Organization in Thailand*, 5 Int'l J. Applied Soc. 76–83 (2015).

43. Xenikou, *supra* note 41.

44. Northouse, *supra* note 2.

45. *Id.*

46. Xenikou, *supra* note 41.

47. Northouse, *supra* note 2 (citing Bass, *supra* note 40).

48. Sarah White, *What Is Transformational Leadership? A Model for Motivating Innovation*, CIO (Feb. 21, 2018), https://www.cio.com/article/3257184/what-is-transformational-leadership-a-model-for-motivating-innovation.html.

49. *Id.*

50. Northouse, *supra* note 2, at 175.

51. *Id.*

52. *Id.*

53. *Id.*

54. *Id.* at 176.

55. James Kouzes & Barry Posner, The Leadership Challenge: How to Get extraordinary Things Done in Organizations (6th ed. 2017).

56. *Id.*

57. William Shakespeare, *Hamlet*, Act I, Scene III (1603).

58. Kevin Kruse, *What Is Authentic Leadership?*, Forbes (May 12, 2013), https://www.forbes.com/sites/kevinkruse/2013/05/12/what-is-authentic-leadership/#65c60373def7.

59. Bill George, Authentic Leadership: Rediscovering the Secrets to Creating Lasting Value (John Wiley & Sons 2003).

60. Northouse, *supra* note 2.

61. Kevin Freiberg & Jackie Freiberg, *Madiba Leadership: 5 Lessons Nelson Mandela Taught the World About Change*, Forbes (July 19, 2018), https://www.forbes.com/sites/kevinandjackiefreiberg/2018/07/19/madiba-leadership-5-lessons-nelson-mandela-taught-the-world-about-change/#64238b5641ba.

62. Kruse, *supra* note 57.

63. *Id.*

64. *Authentic*, Merriam Webster Online Dictionary, https://www.merriam-webster.com/dictionary/authentic (last visited July 19, 2020).

65. Bill George, *The Truth About Authentic Leaders*, Harv. Bus. Sch. (July 6, 2016), https://hbswk.hbs.edu/item/the-truth-about-authentic-leaders.

66. *Id.*

67. Carol Smith, *The Leadership Theory of Robert K. Greenleaf* 3, Carol Smith (2005), https://www.carolsmith.us/downloads/640greenleaf.pdf.

68. *Id.*

69. Robert K. Greenleaf, The Power of Servant-leadership: Essays 17 (Berrett-Koehler 1998).

70. *Id.* at 18.

71. Smith, *supra* note 66.

72. Larry Spears, *Reflections on Robert K. Greenleaf and Servant-Leadership*, 17 LEADERSHIP & ORG. DEV. J. 33 (1996).

73. NORTHOUSE, *supra* note 2.

74. ROBERT K. GREENLEAF, THE SERVANT AS LEADER 15 (1970).

75. *Id.*

76. Smith, *supra* note 66 (citing Smith et al., 10 J. LEADERSHIP & ORG. STUD. 82 (2004)).

77. *Id.*

78. NORTHOUSE, *supra* note 2, at 229.

79. *Id.*

80. *Id.*

81. *Id.* at 240, *citing* R.C. Liden, S.J. Wayne, H. Zhao & D. Henderson, *Servant Leadership: Development of a Multidimensional Measure and Multi-Level Assessment*, LEADERSHIP Q. 19(2), 161–77 (2008), https://doi.org/10.1016/j.leaqua.2008.01.006.

82. Carmine Gallo, *The Coach Behind the Longest Winning Streak in Sports History Shows How to Build a Champion Business Team*, FORBES (Aug. 19, 2014), https://www.forbes.com/sites/carminegallo/2014/08/19/the-coach-behind-the-longest-winning-streak-in-sports-history-shows-how-to-build-a-champion-business-team/#6eca544d33a4. This occurred during a half-time when the players on Coach Lad's team were playing poorly. The team did "figure it out" and went on to win the game. *Id.*

83. NORTHOUSE, *supra* note 2, at 273.

84. *Id.* at 279.

85. *Id.* at 265.

86. *Id.* at 263.

87. *Id.* at 265.

88. *Id.* at 268.

89. *Id.* at 270.

90. Quote attributed to Helmuth Karl Bernhard Graf von Moltke. *See, e.g.*, SUSAN RATCLIFFE, OXFORD ESSENTIAL QUOTATIONS (Oxford Univ. Press 4th ed. 2016).

91. NORTHOUSE, *supra* note 2, at 139.

92. Xenikou, *supra* note 41.

Chapter 5

Character, Traits, and Characteristics of Leaders

A leader in sports, business, or any other field of endeavor should possess and provide the same qualities inherent in a good parent: character, consistency, dependability, accountability, knowledge, good judgment, selflessness, respect, courage, discipline, fairness, and structure.

John Wooden[1]

Purpose

Discuss traits and characteristics commonly observed in leaders and their impact on effective leadership.

Learning Objectives

At the end of this chapter, you should be able to:

- Identify character.
- Describe common traits and characteristics of leaders, both positive and negative.
- Identify leadership traits and characteristics in yourself and others.
- Describe the influence of those traits and characteristics on behaviors and decision making.

Discussion

INTRODUCTION

In *The Captain Class*, author Sam Walker set out to discover the common elements in the greatest sports teams of all time. He studied decades of successful teams across the globe and in all kinds of sports to discover the "secret sauce" that created these great teams. The results surprised Walker, who had assumed the key would be an inspiring coach, a team with the top talent, or the team with the most resources. He found instead that "the most crucial ingredient in a team that achieves and sustains historic greatness is the character of the player who leads it."[2] When using the phrase "the player who leads it," Walker meant the one whom the other players considered the captain, whether the player held the title or not. He wrote about one of the captains:

> Buried inside an obscure 1997 clinical psychology textbook called Aversive Interpersonal Behaviors, there is a chapter titled "Blowhards, Snobs, and Narcissists: Interpersonal Reactions to Excessive Egotism." The authors were a Wake Forest University professor and a handful of his undergraduate students. The paper concluded that self-centered people who project arrogance through their speech and body language tend to be viewed less favorably by others and can weaken a group's cohesion.[3]

Timothy Duncan was one of those student co-authors. At Wake Forest, Duncan was more than just another psychology major. He was the star of the basketball team and, later that year, the number one NBA draft pick for the San Antonio Spurs. "From the moment he arrived in San Antonio, Duncan seemed determined to abide by the conclusions of his undergraduate thesis. He never asked for special privileges, never skipped practices, never bristled at being dressed down after poor performances." On the court, he was known for his selfless approach. Off the court, Duncan did something shocking in a league known for players prone to jump ship for more money. Duncan took a pay cut for the good of the team. "The best way to look at one's teammates," Duncan said, is that "you're helping them as much as they're helping you."[4] Walker added, "It's as if Duncan had used his Wake Forest thesis as a blueprint for how to be an effective teammate in a league where 'narcissists' and 'blowhards' were the lords of the realm."[5] Tim Duncan was the unofficial team captain responsible for "leading" his teams to five NBA championships.

The study of human nature is fascinating and can benefit your efforts to develop as a leader. Study a handful of exemplary leaders, and you can create a list of desirable traits that likely played a role in their success. You will not find a single defined set of traits that applies to all great leaders. You will find that certain traits overlap or may be more prominent depending on the circumstances. The same is true for failed or destructive leaders.

A leader may naturally favor certain traits because they feel comfortable. Just as leaders have positive traits, they also have traits that could be best described as negative or a weakness. Interestingly, a trait that is a weakness in one situation (like stubbornness) can be a strength when the situation demands it. Some traits are innate and unlikely to change (like height), but most can be changed or developed. Not only will a study of traits help you to know yourself better, but you will find benefit in being able to identify and analyze tendencies of your clients, colleagues, and employees. Being aware of your characteristics and personality traits also helps predict how you and others may react in a given situation. Even noticing negative traits can help you become a better leader. Once identified, you can refine and polish your positive characteristics, and smooth the rough edges off the traits that may hold you back.

Identifying, developing, and honing your leadership characteristics is similar to developing the legal skills you will need to practice law. The more insight you have about your leadership traits and the traits of those on your team, the more effectively you can lead. The focus of this chapter is to explore character and to examine traits and characteristics that suit you and that equip you for success as a lawyer and leader. We will also discover techniques for transforming your character through intention and effort.

CHARACTER, TRAITS, AND CHARACTERISTICS: WHAT IS THE DIFFERENCE?

A person's character is the set of attributes unique to a person—strengths, weaknesses, virtues, vices, knowledge, and experience. The American Psychological Association defines character as "the totality of an individual's attributes and personality traits, particularly his or her characteristic moral, social, and religious attitudes."[6] Character development begins at birth with hereditary traits, continues to evolve until death, is shaped by experiential learning, and is influenced by culture.

Disagreement exists about the distinction between a trait and a characteristic. The two terms are often used interchangeably, and to most the distinction is irrelevant. However, to a biologist, it matters. In the field of biology, a characteristic is "a distinguishing quality, trait or feature of an individual, thing, disorder, etc." used "to designate [or] characterize" an organism.[7] The National Human Genome Research Institution explains a trait as "a specific characteristic of an organism. Traits can be determined by genes or the environment, or more commonly by interactions between them."[8] Traits are those inherent qualities that are present in an individual from birth, such as whether a person has red hair, is 5′8″, or is AB+ blood type. Certain genetic diseases, like sickle cell anemia, are also referred to as a "trait." Personality, such as shyness, is a trait. An example of a leadership trait is introversion versus extroversion (which is explored below). Unlike inherited traits, leadership traits can be developed, meaning that you can work on improving them. For example, if you want to develop the ability to clearly share your innovative ideas with others, you can practice and improve on message and delivery.

The term "characteristic" is a nod to the attributes that make up a person's character—that set of attributes and behaviors that create the distinctive qualities observable about a person and which form the basis of our assessment of a person. Such qualities can either be inherited or acquired over a period of time. Some gifts may come more naturally to some than others. Some are easier to adapt, shape, or mold over time.

TRAITS AND CHARACTERISTICS IN COMBINATION EQUAL CHARACTER

A combination of traits and characteristics form a person's character. When assessing someone else's character, we make a judgment based on observed behavior. Ashley is considered "good" because we observe her qualities of honesty, kindness, integrity, helpfulness, and cooperation. Helen is labeled as "bad" if we view her as dishonest, deceptive, manipulative, or a cheater.

Some traits and characteristics may be more visible. We judge people as creative, outgoing, energetic, optimistic, or confident as well as overly serious, lazy, negative, or shy. We may judge instantly — our first impression — if not upon first meeting them, then shortly thereafter. Hereditary traits like one's personality are easier to spot. They are largely static and slow to evolve. Though we may need more than one interaction to confirm the presence of these sorts of traits, by the time we decide they are present, we have usually amassed enough data to justify our conclusions.

"Character, on the other hand, takes far longer to puzzle out. It includes traits that reveal themselves only in specific — and often uncommon — circumstances, traits like honesty, virtue, and kindliness."[9] The evolving nature of character means that discerning a person's character takes longer. Our assessment of a person's character may be even more problematic because we may observe inconsistent behaviors in different circumstances. Because character is shaped by beliefs and life experiences, we need to apply cultural intelligence before assessing anyone else's character.[10]

With effort and motivation, we can change our perspective and view of the world, which can lead to a shift in character. Character development evolves over time, is transformed by experiential learning and influenced by culture. For example, good schools and strong parental support can help a child to generally exhibit good moral character. Growing up in economic poverty or raised by parents who are involved in criminal activity will influence the starting point of a child's character and put that child at a disadvantage in terms of character development. The influences, positive or negative, are not determinative, however, and their character can be changed.

Since character can change or evolve over time as we learn new behaviors or learn from mistakes or guidance, who you are today does not define who you will be in the future. Those past events, however, are not the only shaper of character; current circumstances or environments also impact character. Just as you can change a bad habit like smoking, you can also change your character. Your actions can become habit, and that which you do habitually will become part of your character.

INTENTION AND HABIT MOLD CHARACTER

Watch your thoughts, they become your words; watch your words, they become your actions; watch your actions, they become your habits; watch your habits, they become your character; watch your character, it becomes your destiny.

Lao Tzu[11]

Character is not the result of happenstance but of repeated action and influence. Being a lawyer and leader of good moral character requires constant attention to *right thinking* and consistent effort toward *right acting*. If we are not intentional in moving our thoughts and actions toward the *good*, we run the risk of inertia in our minds and behaviors, and we forgo growth. Even worse, we may be influenced by thoughts and actions that are expedient, convenient, and lucrative, but not good.

"Happiness is virtuous activity." That is Aristotle's way of saying that if we strive to live a virtuous life — to be the ultimate good that defines us — and are guided by practical wisdom, then we will succeed in achieving a virtuous character and we will find harmony:[12]

> What we need, in order to live well, is a proper appreciation of the way in which such goods as friendship, pleasure, virtue, honor and wealth fit together as a whole. In order to apply that general understanding to particular cases, we must acquire, through proper upbringing and habits, the ability to see, on each occasion, which course of action is best supported by reasons. Therefore practical wisdom, as he conceives it, cannot be acquired solely by learning general rules. We must also acquire, through practice, those deliberative, emotional, and social skills that enable us to put our general understanding of well-being into practice in ways that are suitable to each occasion.[13]

Developing virtue is no different than acquiring technical skills, according to Aristotle.[14] With practice and rational decision making, a person will determine action that is appropriate under the circumstances. The nineteenth-century psychologist William James observed, "All our life . . . is but a mass of habits."[15] "[H]abits are defined as actions that are triggered automatically in response to contextual cues that have been associated with their performance."[16] "Our habits will either make us or break us. We become what we repeatedly do."[17]

In *The Power of Habit*, author Charles Druhigg shared a discovery by a group of MIT researchers.[18] At the core of every habit is a simple neurological loop. "A habit is a formula our brain automatically follows: When I see CUE, I will do ROUTINE in order to get a REWARD."[19] Understanding these components helps in understanding how to create best practices and change bad habits. The habit loop is always started with a cue, a trigger that transfers the brain into a mode that automatically determines which habit (behavior or action) to use. The heart of the habit is a mental, emotional, or physical routine.[20] Finally, there is a reward, which helps the brain determine if this particular loop is worth remembering for the future.

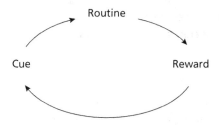

"Habits aren't destiny . . . Habits can be ignored, changed or replaced."[21] But because habits are automatic responses and can be deeply entrenched in our brains, changing habits can be challenging and take time.[22] To stop addictive habits or create desired practices, Duhigg's Golden Rule of Habit Change simply states: change your behaviors — replace the routine with another one. For example, "[i]f you remove drinking from your life, but replace it with nothing else, you'll likely be unhappy. The trick is to keep the cue (e.g. tired after a long day) and the rewards (e.g. social time, relaxation) while changing the routine (e.g. drinking)."[23]

Once you diagnose the habit loop of a particular behavior, you can look for ways to change the routine to replace old ways and old vices with new routines. Duhigg offers this framework to change a routine or an attitude that is a habit:

- *Identify the routine.* What is the habitual behavior you want to change?[24]
- *Experiment with rewards.* "Rewards are powerful because they satisfy cravings. But we're often not conscious of the cravings that drive our behaviors."[25]
- *Isolate the cue.* In your busy life, you may not be conscious of what is the habit cue. To identify the cue, consider the five categories of behaviors that trigger a habitual response: *location, time, emotional state, other people,* and *immediately preceding action.*[26]
- *Have a plan.* To re-engineer that formula, you need to identify what action you will take to replace the old behavior that will satisfy the desire or craving at the root of the old behavior. The easiest way to do this, according to study after study, is to have a plan for new action. "Within psychology, these plans are known as 'implementation intentions.'"[27]

Some behaviors can be more difficult to change than others. Some habits take a long time to conquer. According to a 2009 study published in the *European Journal of Social Psychology*, it takes 18 to 254 days for a person to form a new habit, with an average of 66 days.[28] Repeated experiments may be necessary and temporary failures should be anticipated. "But once you understand how a habit operates — once you diagnose the cue, the routine and the reward — you gain power over it."[29] Belief is a critical element of such a change.[30] Often people who join support or accountability groups are more successful in changing a behavior.[31]

These principles apply to lawyers.[32] Clients expect lawyers to be virtuous. As a lawyer, you can be a better warrior for justice, advocate for the powerless, and problem-solver for your community if you strive to spend your energy and talents to be good so you can do good. By the same token, if you disregard your ethical obligation as a lawyer, you can cause genuine harm to clients and the system of justice.

A multitude of good actions can confirm the good character of a person, but what does one bad action mean? Is this now a person whose character is less good than originally thought, or was this a specific and isolated moment of weakness? Either way, one bad act *can* call good character into question. As Pope John Paul cautioned, "[O]ne bad act can change one's orientation to the good. Each action must orient one towards the good."[33] Aquinas, in *Summa Theologica*, devotes an extensive portion of his book to habits: the momentousness of habits, how good habits lead to virtuous conduct, and how bad habits induce vice.[34] One bad behavior might signal an area in need of work — a character flaw in an otherwise good person. Many famous leaders celebrated for their great leadership had known character flaws, President John F. Kennedy being a well-known example.

Benjamin Franklin offers perhaps the best advice: "It is easier to prevent bad habits than to break them."[35] This may be true, but unfortunately none of us is perfect, and we all have bad habits. Thankfully, we are reminded that our character is formed and reformed over time with intention and habit.[36]

ARE LAWYERS DIFFERENT FROM NON-LAWYERS?

Empirical research spanning more than 50 years suggests that yes, lawyers are different from non-lawyers.[37] Studies find that lawyers tend "to be more competitive, dominant, achievement-oriented, focused on the economic bottom line, and analytical than the general population."[38] Lawyers are more likely "to respond to stress by becoming more aggressive and ambitious (not affiliative)."[39] Perhaps because of their traditional training in law school, attorneys "may prefer to make decisions on the basis of rights, rules, logical analysis, rationality, and justice, as opposed to contextual factors such as interpersonal relationships, emotions, harm to others, or mercy."[40]

With their more logical, analytical orientation, attorneys "may not be interpersonally sensitive or skilled, albeit they prefer to be perceived as socially ascendant, confident, and dominant."[41] Lawyers may be more motivated by external rewards and achievements. Lawyers also "suffer from higher rates of psychological distress and alcoholism."[42]

Certainly, some law students arrive at law school with these traits in full bloom, but some researchers who study legal education believe our traditional approaches to legal education reinforce those traits. While several of these traits mesh with the skills needed for effective lawyering, "such as practical judgment, motivation, diligence, self-confidence, managing one's own work, and influencing others, other typical lawyer traits work against lawyers' proficiency in skills, such as understanding and dealing with others, listening, collaborating in teams, stress management, and general mood."[43]

Other studies found that certain logical, analytical personality traits and decision-making preferences were more prevalent among lawyers and law students than among non-lawyers. Some suggested that these "lawyer traits" contributed to an uneven development of skills among lawyers—an imbalance, or a tendency to overemphasize logic, rationality, and the economic bottom line. Consequently, lawyers at times may overlook interpersonal and emotional concerns.[44]

STUDYING TRAITS OF LEADERS

The challenge is to be strong, but not rude; kind, but not weak; bold, but not a bully; thoughtful, but not lazy; humble, but not timid; proud, but not arrogant; have humor, but, without folly.

Jim Rohn[45]

The study of leadership is the study of leaders. We can study leaders, examine their actions, and learn lessons to apply to our own leadership approaches. By examining a wide variety of leaders, we can identify traits of leaders. Without study, people still can describe traits of the ideal leader: visionary, trustworthy, confident, humble, committed, creative, as well as has integrity, a positive attitude, and communicates well. If you asked the same people to describe a bad leader, they might identify these traits: aggressive, micromanages, demanding, insecure, immature, reacts negatively to criticism, unwilling to change, and bad listener.

Many people relate leadership traits (both positive and negative) to leaders whom they have known,[46] making it hard to separate the trait from the person. By studying traits through the people who exhibit them, we can learn more about how to incorporate positive traits into our personalities and avoid negative traits. We begin with an in-depth discussion of introverts and extroverts to provide a roadmap for how to examine traits of leadership.

Introverts versus Extroverts: Can Both Be Leaders?

There is no such thing as a pure extrovert or a pure introvert. Such a man would be in the lunatic asylum.

Carl Jung[47]

There is a common misperception that all leaders are naturally outgoing and are charismatic extroverts. After all, who would follow a quiet, bookish person into battle? Yet history and social science teach us that both introverts and extroverts can lead effectively. Extroverts make fine leaders, but introverts also bring a valuable skill set to leadership.

Notable extroverted leaders include Benjamin Franklin, Catherine the Great, Marie Antoinette, Winston Churchill, Ronald Reagan, Bill Clinton, and Margaret Thatcher.[48] Leonardo da Vinci, a purported extrovert, touted the trait when he said, "People of accomplishment rarely sit back and let things happen to them. They go out in the world and happen to things."[49] These charismatic, witty and outgoing leaders rallied support, sometimes in extremely difficult situations. In other circumstances, those same extroverts found that their charisma led to their downfall. Marie Antoinette certainly had a charming personality but could not be said to have effectively led her people; her extravagant personality and ways led her to the guillotine.[50]

Extroverts, however, are not the only ones who lead effectively. Some 30 to 50 percent of corporate leaders describe themselves as introverts rather than extroverts. Extrovert Steve Jobs may have sold a billion iPhones, but Bill Gates, Marissa Mayer, and Steve Wozniak[51] are famously introverted leaders who have also accomplished great things. Both introverts and extroverts can be exemplary leaders; different attributes of each contribute to effective leadership.

Extroverts versus Introverts

What are common characteristics of extroverts? They tend to be energized by socializing. They solve problems through discussion and love to talk to people. They are open and willing to share, and they are often described as friendly and approachable. Extroverts enjoy being the center of attention and tend to act before thinking. Their energy and enthusiasm are contagious, although sometimes exhausting.

Introverts feel comfortable spending time alone. Audrey Hepburn purportedly once commented, "I have to be alone very often. I'd be quite happy if I spent from Saturday night until Monday morning alone in my apartment. That's how I refuel." While introverts enjoy people, they tend to do so in limited doses. "After an hour or two of being socially on, we introverts need to turn off and recharge."[52] Introverts also are more willing to listen to team members, accept input, and think creatively in a leadership position than are extroverts.

We paint these stereotypes with a broad brush, but even describing yourself as an introvert or extrovert presupposes that it is an all or nothing situation. As emphasized in the quote above, Jung points out that being purely one or the other is unlikely. A better approach places these personality types on a spectrum from extreme introversion to extreme extroversion. Most people fall somewhere in the middle range of the introvert/extrovert (I/E) spectrum. There are outliers, or people at the extreme ends of the bell curve, but most of us lean moderately toward one side or the other.[53] Where you land on this spectrum may depend on how you recharge your energy source. Extroverted leaders tend get energy from being with others. Introverted leaders tend to need to recharge alone after spending time with people. This is but one of several hallmarks of the introverted versus the extroverted leader.

Introverted Leaders

Introverts have natural abilities that work well in leading teams and solving problems:

1. *They look before they leap.* A hallmark of an introverted leader is thinking before speaking, in order to give a considered answer to a question or a thoughtful opinion about an issue. This practice leads to teams in which the participants are comfortable sharing their ideas and feel that they will be given due consideration rather than dismissed. Introverted leaders listen when others speak.
2. *They work well alone.* Introverted leaders can think deeply about issues and spend time in solitude, which allows them to focus on problems and solve those problems creatively. Deep thinking combined with a willingness to listen to others and innate humility makes introverted leaders effective. "As an introvert, you can be your own best friend or your worst enemy. The good news is we [introverts] generally like our own company, a quality that extroverts often envy."[54]
3. *They solve problems well.* Introverts solve problems well because they approach problem solving creatively and stick with a problem until it is solved. Albert Einstein spoke eloquently about these aspects of an introvert's leadership life: "It's not that I'm so smart, it's just that I stay with problems longer. . . . I believe in intuitions and inspirations. I sometimes feel that I am right. I do not know that I am."[55]

Extroverted Leaders

Extroverts enjoy advantages as leaders in distinct areas: emotional, interpersonal, and motivational/performance[56]:

1. *They are emotionally positive and happy.* Extroverts are generally happy leaders who more regularly experience positive emotions with a glass-half-full approach. This naturally rosy outlook leads to greater satisfaction at work and in their leadership roles. The positive demeanor also helps buffer them from stress or setbacks. It also motivates those around them and provides encouragement.
2. *They have good interpersonal relationships.* Since extroverts enjoy others and get positive energy from interactions, they may adapt better to social situations and be more persuasive and likeable. We often describe this as charisma. They also like to solve problems in a group setting and through discussion, which can lead to greater input and broader buy-in.
3. *They are highly motived and perform at a high level.* Extroverts are goal-oriented and derive great satisfaction from setting and achieving a goal. Their ability to persuade others translates to better success on projects. Being part of an extrovert's team, then, feels like being part of a winning endeavor.

Does Being an Introvert or Extrovert Affect Your Skills as a Lawyer?

Both introverts and extroverts can be successful as attorneys. Each brings strengths and potential weaknesses to leadership in the legal field. Mixing both introverts and extroverts on the same team may bring unique energy and talents in a better combination.

In a law firm, the extroverts bring energy and enthusiasm to the team. Their natural resilience does well in the legal profession, where positive feedback may not be the norm. They engage well with others and shine in developing good relationships with clients, court staff, and juries. They are confident in expressing opinions quickly, which may be valuable when under the gun from a senior partner or a judge.

Extrovert attorneys, however, may also be impulsive and offer opinions that are not fully considered or researched. Given their love of the spotlight and natural independence, they may not share the stage or listen well to other team members' ideas. This can cause the others to feel as if they are not a valued member of the team.

By comparison, introverts do well working long hours, even in solitary conditions. They are good problem solvers. While perhaps not as glib as their extroverted counterparts, they seek creative solutions for challenging legal issues. They are thoughtful and willing to work collaboratively, which translates to being willing to take others' ideas into account. This openness to others often serves the client's interests well. As such, introverts can lead a team effectively through a difficult problem or challenging legal issue.

Their solitary approach, however, can keep introverts from networking effectively. The desire to think deeply may not work well on a tight deadline. Their natural reticence may keep the introvert from speaking up effectively, particularly in acrimonious settings or in a crowd. Introverts can seem aloof, shy, or not "leadership material" in a culture that prizes extroversion.

As you look at the various skill sets of introverts and extroverts, you can see how each could lead effectively in given circumstances. Developing positive attributes from each personality style can make leaders even more effective. A more naturally extroverted person could work on listening to others and sharing more credit with team members. Introverts might work on streamlining decision making so that they can meet deadlines. When it comes to introverts and extroverts, neither corners the market on effective leadership.

COMMON LEADERSHIP TRAITS

Understanding the common traits of introverts and extroverts can help you self-assess your own tendencies as a lawyer and leader, to better understand how your skill set comes into play, and how to utilize and optimize those natural traits in different situations and settings.

Many traits can be beneficial in one scenario but detrimental in another. There may be more than one path to accomplishing a goal, with one action being better or easier than another.

Leadership Traits Commonly Viewed as Positive Characteristics

The following positive traits are some of those most commonly cited as necessary for good leadership.

Vision

Visionary leaders are those who dream big, ignite passion, and are resolved to realize their vision.[57] They set the direction for an organization based on a belief of where the organization needs to be. The ability to see things as they should be or could be — not as they are — is a hallmark of visionary leadership, especially when combined with the ability to inspire the team to see it as a shared vision. Creating a vision for an organization calls for creativity; sustaining one requires discipline.[58]

Vision can address short-term goals, or it can look to a more distant future. Long-term goals tend to be the ones that have the most impact but require planning and perseverance. Achieving long-term visions requires a strategic plan with interim steps and regular assessment and reevaluation. Time spent looking at the big picture — working *on* the business — is just as important as working *in* the business.

In 1980, according to Inc., Apple's then-president Mike Scott sent out an office memo:

> EFFECTIVE IMMEDIATELY!! NO MORE TYPEWRITERS ARE TO BE PURCHASED, LEASED, etc., etc. Apple is an innovative company. We must believe and lead in all areas. If word processing is so neat, then let's all use it!
>
> Goal: by 1-1-81, NO typewriters at Apple. . . . We believe the typewriter is obsolete. Let's prove it inside before we try and convince our customers.[59]

Steve Jobs capitalized on this vision. In 1985, Jobs predicted the eventual rise of home computer usage and the use of computers for entertainment rather than just work projects. The tech icon also predicted that people would one day buy computers for the primary purpose of being connected to a "nationwide communications network" — the modern Internet.[60] Given the limited use of computers at the time, and the cumbersome size and expense of the technology, his pronouncement was astonishing. Jobs became a crusader and driving force behind the technological wave that has impacted every aspect of the way we live now and work.

Optimism

Effective leaders inspire and motivate others. Not all leaders have a charismatic personality but anyone can encourage their team team using an upbeat attitude. Many teams find the energy of an optimistic "can-do" leader to be contagious. Teams watch how their leader approaches everything from colossal challenges to tedious daily tasks. Those leaders who exhibit optimism set a powerful example for employees, encouraging a positive, productive attitude among team members. Optimism is not an idealistic naivete that disregards challenges; optimism combined with reality instead acknowledges the difficulties but perseveres in the knowledge that any challenge can be faced and overcome. "Realistic optimists . . . believe they will succeed, but also believe they have to *make success happen*—through things like effort, careful planning, persistence, and choosing the right strategies," Heidi Grant, Ph.D., explains in the *Harvard Business Review*. "They recognize the need for giving serious thought to how they will deal with obstacles. This preparation only increases their confidence in their own ability to get things done."[61]

Optimists with a growth mindset focus on the positive and look for solutions. They understand that an individual who overcomes a challenge grows stronger. Modeling this attitude is a strong leadership skill. Coupling this with conduct that inspires your team is important as well. Remember: It is not what you do; it is why and how you do it that gets people behind you[62] and leads to loyalty. Showing a willingness to shoulder the load with your team can be inspiring:

> More than 200 years ago, a man in civilian clothes rode past a small group of battle-weary soldiers digging what appeared to be an important defensive position. The leader of the group made no effort to help; instead he shouted orders and threatened punishment if the work was not completed within the hour.
>
> "Why aren't you helping?" asked the stranger on horseback.
>
> "I'm in charge. The men do as I tell them," said the leader. "Help them yourself if you feel so strongly about it."
>
> To the leader's surprise, the stranger dismounted and helped the men finish the job. The stranger congratulated the men for their work, and before he left, approached the leader.
>
> "You should notify top command next time your rank prevents you from supporting your men—and I will provide a more permanent solution," said the stranger, now recognizable as General George Washington.[63]

The ability to lead comes not from a title but from being able to capture the hearts and imagination of the team. Leaders can inspire others to share in and realize the vision, whether by providing the right words to show the vision or, as Washington did, by leading by example. The leader's infectious enthusiasm for the goal spreads through the team. Inspiring leaders are effective by organically motivating their followers, rather than motivating by force or rewards.

Integrity

The supreme quality for leadership is unquestionably integrity. Without it, no real success is possible, no matter whether it is on a section gang, a football field, in an army, or in an office.

Dwight D. Eisenhower[64]

A person of integrity commits to a set of ideals or principles — whether good or bad — no matter the cost. "At a minimum, the person of integrity manifests the trait of consistency or steadfastness."[65] She is true to her commitments, even in the face of personal disadvantage or social pressure to do otherwise.[66]

People generally expect that a professional who has integrity will exhibit morality, ethics, honesty, trustworthiness, justice, and compassion.[67] Such an assumption and expectation is appropriate for lawyers, who are required to prove their good moral character to gain and maintain a license to represent members of the public with their legal matters.

Leader and lawyer integrity is not situational; it is a state of mind.[68] "Integrity means doing the right thing because it's the right thing to do"[69] and doing the right thing when no one else is looking.[70] Leaders with integrity build trust because those with whom they deal can rely on them to be treated fairly. Leaders with integrity make hard choices, even if those choices come at a personal cost, because to do so is consistent with their principles no matter the cost.

In the 1920s, the Ku Klux Klan ("the Klan") was at the height of its power, with membership numbers in the millions.[71] In Texas, its members were in every community and included a U.S. Senator, the mayors of Dallas, Fort Worth, and Wichita Falls, and countless lower-level politicians and law enforcement officers.[72] White opponents of the Klan were assaulted or threatened in bids to take over political institutions.[73]

In Waco, Texas, Judge James Patterson Alexander of McLennan County was the last public official who refused to join the Klan.[74] Some Klansmen came to the courthouse and brought Judge Alexander into the hall to force him to take the oath of the Klan.[75] The judge refused, saying that doing so would conflict with his oath of office, and he walked away. At the time, the Klan controlled local elections, winning by two-to-one majorities.[76] Judge Alexander knew that his position, although the right one to take, would cost him his job when he sought reelection. It did, but he kept his integrity.[77]

Morality

The term "morality" refers to "certain codes of conduct put forward by a society or a group (such as a religion), or accepted by an individual for her own behavior."[78] Leadership is a moral undertaking.[79] Lawyering is also a moral undertaking because only persons of good moral character may earn and maintain a law license.

Morality cannot be taken for granted, and for leaders and lawyers it is critical because of the far-reaching effects of their actions or inaction on other people. The absence of morality can turn the influence of a powerful leader into a disastrous out-come. Hitler was a powerful leader but devoid of a morality that valued all human life. Lawyer leaders must work to preserve the direction of their inclinations to do good and to be good, and to fight the temptation to acquiesce to that which is not in accordance with the standards of the profession and society.

The term "morality" often intertwines with "integrity," the implication being that the person is also morally trustworthy. "Integrity requires more than good intentions, sincerity and conviction about holding fast to principles one believes in. It requires judgement that, while not infallible, is epistemically trustworthy and is grounded in the moral know-how of the agent."[80]

Adaptability

You have to be fast on your feet and adaptive or else a strategy is useless.

Charles de Gaulle[81]

The only constant is change, so leaders need to be able to adapt and adjust as the circumstances change — sometimes by the minute. Different times, different proj-ects, different teams all call for customized approaches tailored to the event. Take, for example, the recent Covid-19 pandemic, altering the economy, law, and businesses in ways never seen before; leaders with carefully crafted visions for their teams had to adapt to these new scenarios. Adaptive leaders know how to read the terrain and pre-pare for it, and they expect the plan to change.[82] To be effective, leaders must respond to circumstances as they unfold. They must not be afraid to try something new if the current approach is not working. A rigid, fearful, or inflexible leader rarely is effec-tive; leaders must be open to creative solutions.[83] Adaptive leaders get better results because they build dynamic teams that embrace change and channel fear into positive outcomes.[84]

Adaptive leaders must also be willing to reevaluate team goals as the landscape changes to see if those goals are still relevant. The leader may decide that the vision is still on point, but the methods for achieving it — the materials, the team, the timeline — need to change. By contrast, the leader may decide the goal itself is meaningless under the current circumstances. For example, the goal of having more in-person client con-tact during a worldwide pandemic with stay-at-home orders is completely unrealistic; however, that vision can be adapted to increase client contact virtually, demonstrating a nimble vision and willingness to change with the times.

Adaptability can also evolve over time. President Abraham Lincoln's decisions leading up to the Emancipation Proclamation and the Gettysburg Address showed his ability to be adaptable as a leader. While people remember President Lincoln as a staunch advocate for freedom, he did not always hold the opinion that all people should be free. In the 1858 debates with Stephen Douglas, Lincoln did not advocate for the emancipation of slaves or their equal rights; he favored allowing the Southern states to continue the practice of owning slaves but abolishing slavery in the Northern states. Lincoln lost that Senate race, but it gave him a platform for the Presidency.[85]

Three years later, during his inaugural address in 1861, Lincoln appealed for the preservation of the Union. He tried to retain his support in the North without further alienating the South. He hoped the Southern states would willingly give up slavery. This strategy failed when the Southern states seceded and the Civil War began. Lincoln tried other approaches. One idea was the relocating of freed slaves to the Panama Canal, but this did not go over well with Black leaders. The Emancipation Proclamation only freed slaves in the Northern states, but not in the Northern territories or the Southern states. Not until the Gettysburg Address did Lincoln espouse the principle of racial equality as necessary for the entirety of the United States. Over time, Lincoln's actions and words changed. Whether it was pragmatism or changing beliefs, he eventually got to the right answer. He adapted to the circumstances and the situation to achieve the goals he sought.[86]

Confidence

As a leader one of the things that's most important is to know your team needs to see you as confident.

Steve Kerr[87]

A leader must be someone in whom people can believe and trust. To inspire others to believe in the leader and in the goal, the leader must have plenty of self-confidence. Confidence doesn't mean arrogance, braggadocio, or the need to denigrate others, although a little swagger can go a long way. A truly confident person is simply aware of his abilities, knows his competencies and strengths, and is willing to accept responsibility and pressure in times of crisis and stress. Confident leadership imparts strength and assurance to others; part of a leader's responsibility is to maintain team morale and keep moving forward.[88] Confidence inspires trust.[89]

Before he became a Justice on the United States Supreme Court, Thurgood Marshall was the architect of the National Association for the Advancement of Colored People's (NAACP) plan to desegregate the public school system through civil lawsuits. Marshall planned to file a series of cases around the country that pushed the issue until the goal of desegregation was achieved. Marshall was confident that his plan would work, but he needed to recruit plaintiffs to make it work. Without the right plaintiffs, the right cases could not move forward, and the right opinions would not be written.

The NAACP actively pursued integration of higher education through several coordinated cases.[90] In 1946, Heman Sweatt attended an NAACP meeting held to solicit "students to serve as a plaintiff in a law school desegregation case."[91] The NAACP lawyers' confidence in the plan inspired Sweatt to answer the call.[92] He fit the admissions criteria for the University of Texas Law School but, as the NAACP suspected, had been denied entrance because of his race.[93] That denial gave Sweatt, and indirectly the NAACP, standing to challenge the unequal treatment of black people in higher education.

The issue in the landmark case of *Sweatt v. Painter* was whether the Equal Protection Clause of the Fourteenth Amendment prevented states from distinguishing between "students of different races in professional and graduate education in a state university."[94] In 1946, Heman Sweatt applied to the University of Texas Law School but was denied admission solely because of his race.[95] The Supreme Court held that Sweatt must be admitted and given equal protection under the law.[96] In the end, *Sweatt* was an important case on the road to desegregation — one that would not have happened had Marshall not had vision and the confidence to see it through.

Decisiveness

Decision making is at the heart of what it means to lead. A leader must make the final call and determine what course the team will take. Leaders do not always have the luxury of time; but once the choice is made, the leader needs to stand behind it. Strong leaders choose a plan and then throw their whole weight behind it. Pursuing weak half-measures or wasting time waffling back and forth between two options is bad leadership. Decisiveness is important in that it

- saves time;
- fosters respect;
- serves as motivation;
- prevents conflict; and
- increases productivity.[97]

Decisiveness saves time by encouraging clear direction and purpose, delegation, effective use of time, and enhanced productivity. This clarity of vision and purpose also develops respect and motivates the team. Following a self-assured, well-informed leader helps the team feel confident, knowing they can trust that leader to steer them in the right direction.[98] They, in turn, learn the skill of decisiveness and can become more independent.[99]

The notion of judicial review — and judicial supremacy — is based on the decisive actions of one of our Founding Fathers, Justice John Marshall.[100] Early in our nation's constitutional experiment, it was unclear whether the President or Congress was to interpret the Constitution. In *Marbury v. Madison*, Justice Marshall announced that the courts had the authority to strike down statutes. This fact is not surprising to any lawyer or law student, but it should be — the Constitution does not give the courts the authority to do so. Justice Marshall laid the groundwork to vest authority to interpret the Constitution in the courts.

Marshall wove together a series of clever decisions related to constitutional interpretation. In late 1800, the lame-duck Federalist Congress created several judgeships by the Judiciary Act of 1801. President John Adams, who would vacate the Presidency for Thomas Jefferson, appointed Federalist judges to fill the new seats and retain control of the judiciary. These "midnight appointments" were not valid until James Madison, the new Secretary of State, sent commissions to the new Federalist judges. Upon taking office, Jefferson ordered Madison not to issue the commissions, and William Marbury, one of the newly appointed judges, sued Madison to force issuance of the commission.[101] In 1803, the Supreme Court agreed to hear the case, and most anticipated Marshall would order Madison to issue the commissions. Similarly, most expected Madison would ignore such an order from the Court. Marshall, however, had a different plan. After chastising Jefferson for his actions and expounding upon the Court's ability to interpret the constitutionality of statutes, the Court dismissed the case for lack of jurisdiction. Procedurally, a dismissal for want of jurisdiction does not require or warrant discussing the merits. By writing the opinion this way, however, Marshall planted the seeds for judicial review and supremacy in a way Jefferson was unlikely to challenge. Jefferson got what he wanted, and the Court retained the power to interpret the Constitution.[102] This decision has shaped the role of the Court and the Constitution ever since.

Trustworthiness

The public, generally speaking, does not trust lawyers.[103] That is a major problem because trust is the foundation of any relationship, whether with a loved one, a colleague, or a client. Clients must be able to trust their lawyer, but that trust must be earned. Here are suggestions for earning that trust:

- *Embrace your professional obligations.* Pledge to conduct your personal life and your professional life as a person of good moral integrity.
- *Be honest in all your dealings.* Tell the truth, even when it would be easier to avoid doing so. People deserve the truth, even if they might not want to hear it.
- *Be available.* A lawyer who does not respond to a client in a timely manner is not one the client will call the next time there is a need. Make sure you have a system to respond in a manner to meet or exceed your client's expectations.
- *Be personable.* You will be busy and feeling the pressures of meeting deadlines and billing expectations, but spending time with your clients is important. Learn more about them beyond their legal issues. You cannot bill the client for this time, but it is an investment in the relationship. People do business with people they know, like, and trust. Be likeable.
- *Be respectful.* This legal matter is a significant issue in your client's life. Treat your clients and their legal matters with the respect they deserve. Be culturally aware and serve them with humility.
- *Be competent, be efficient, and be effective.* When you conclude the matter, you should be satisfied that you gave it your all. Be organized and prepared, and pay attention to details.

Courage

Courage is not the absence of fear, but rather the assessment that something else is more important than fear.

Franklin D. Roosevelt[104]

Courage is something you hope you have when you need it, but you will not know until you do. Only when you face an uncertain situation will you know if you have the fortitude to take action. Courage is "the ability to face adversity without being overcome by fear."[105] Courage, like grit, requires the determination to persist in spite of the risks. The courageous are willing to risk failure rather than settle for the comfort of the status quo. Do you have the courage to leave the security of a steady paycheck to follow your dream or to follow someone else's dream? Remember from the movie *Jerry Maguire* when secretary Dorothy Boyd is the only one who followed Maguire out the door to start his new sports agency? Neither could be confident the new venture would work, but both were willing to follow the dream.

Ethical dilemmas test whether you have the courage to do what is right over what is expedient. To give an example: You know that your client failed to disclose money hidden in secret accounts and that you should end your representation; to let him go as a client, however, means saying goodbye to enough money to pay for college for your children. That takes courage but also integrity. The two are often coupled.

In Georgetown, Texas, a young, aspiring district attorney named Dan Moody decided to take on the Klan.[106] On April 1, 1923, members of the Klan came upon Ralph Waldo Burleson and Fannie Campbell returning from a picnic with their friends.[107] Suspecting they were having an affair, the Klan members pulled Burleson out of his car.

> Burleson was pistol whipped and had a sack put over his head. He was threatened with castration if he did not cooperate. A padlocked horse trace chain was placed around his neck. He was dragged to a nearby thorn tree where the chain was thrown over a limb and Burleson was dragged from the ground, his body scraping into the thorns. His arms were tied behind him with a rope. His trousers and underwear were pulled off and the men took turns whipping him with a leather strap. All the time, a gun was being held to his head and he was instructed not to holler. He admitted, under pressure, to the affair. When the whipping stopped, they drove him to City Hall in the center of Taylor, [Texas,] and tied him to a nearby blackberry tree. A bucket of creosote was dumped over his head.[108]

Although most Klan victims refused to press charges, District Attorney Moody convinced Campbell and Burleson to do so.[109] Moody secured the convictions of five Klansmen and sent them to jail.[110] Moody is not without his flaws, but he was the first prosecutor in the United States who had the courage to take on the Klan.[111] He did so despite the "very real danger to himself and to those that helped him. When others waffled, quailed and backed down, he was relentless."[112] His victories in Williamson County were the "first big steps to break the Klan's hold on Texas."[113]

In times of fear and uncertainty, people need strong leaders to show true courage. Lawyers have that kind of courage when they stand up to a consortium of wealthy investors trying to bully a holdout homeowner into selling that last linchpin property for their $50 million commercial project. Courage is acknowledging that a long-standing practice is not equitable and inspires people to stand up for change. A young lawyer shows that kind of courage when she does not give in to self-doubt or threats of vicious social media attacks in deciding to run for office against a representative who vilifies those who disagree with him.

Be brave. Be bold. That is easier for some than others. Courageous leaders also are unafraid of fresh ideas, ingenuity, and out-of-the-box thinking, such as those offered by a group of millennial associates advocating for change. Brave leaders surround themselves with the best talent and know-how, even as they worry they cannot compete. Courageous leaders are prepared to fail, and if they do, they do so gracefully.

Negative Characteristics

Although the study of leadership often focuses on what to do, as much can be learned by studying what *not* to do. The following negative characteristics, though not an exhaustive list, exemplify ways leaders fail to lead:

Lack energy and enthusiasm. They see new initiatives as a burden, rarely volunteer, and fear being overwhelmed. One such leader was described as having the ability to "suck all the energy out of any room."

Accept their own mediocre performance. They overstate the difficulty of reaching targets so that they look good when they achieve them. They live by the mantra "Underpromise and overdeliver."

Lack clear vision and direction. They believe their only job is to execute. Like a hiker who sticks close to the trail, they're fi ne until they come to a fork.

Have poor judgment. They make decisions that colleagues and subordinates consider to be not in the organization's best interests.

Don't collaborate. They avoid peers, act independently, and view other leaders as competitors. As a result, they are set adrift by the very people whose insights and support they need.

Resist new ideas. They reject suggestions from subordinates and peers. Good ideas aren't implemented, and the organization gets stuck.

Don't learn from mistakes. They may make no more mistakes than their peers, but they fail to use setbacks as opportunities for improvement, hiding their errors and brooding about them instead.

Don't learn from mistakes. They may make no more mistakes than their peers, but they fail to use setbacks as opportunities for improvement, hiding their errors and brooding about them instead.

Lack interpersonal skills. They make sins of both commission (they're abrasive and bullying) and omission (they're aloof, unavailable, and reluctant to praise).

Fail to develop others. They focus on themselves to the exclusion of developing subordinates, causing individuals and teams to disengage.[114]

We add an important note here: Every one of us is flawed and we all make mistakes. Falling prey to one of these negative attributes is not fatal to your leadership. Being aware of these negatives and trying to improve where and when you can, will set you on the road to becoming an even better leader.

CONCLUSION

Few people are born strong leaders with all their attributes fully developed. More often leaders emerge through sustained effort to improve their abilities and gain wisdom through experience. Leadership requires commitment to making the best possible decisions under the circumstances and taking actions that are consistent with the character of a leader who is trusted and revered. Everyone has natural inclinations in their thoughts and deeds, but you can develop attributes — traits, competencies, and skills — that will allow you to succeed and thrive in your professional and personal lives. Included in many motivational speeches is a helpful reminder: "You are the author of your life."

Exercise

MBTI/16 Personalities Tests

The MBTI test identifies four different preferences in people's behavior.[115] The MBTI test, developed by Katharine Cook Briggs and her daughter Isabel Briggs Myers in the 1940s, categorizes people into 16 different types based on the combination of the individual's preferences. The four preference dichotomies are

- extraversion and introversion
- sensing and intuition
- thinking and feeling
- judging and perceiving[116]

A variety of websites offer this test for free and explain what each of the four preferences represents and what each different type means. The MBTI test has become a staple among personality tests.[117] It has relevance in many diverse areas — education, career development, organizational behavior, and team development.[118] Anyone studying leadership should take the MBTI (or a similar test) as a baseline. The 16 Personalities variant is a useful, free tool.

Take a personality test such as the Myers-Briggs Type Indicator (MBTI) test or the 16 Personalities test. Review your results and see whether you agree with what the test results show. Bring your results to the group discussion.

Discussion Questions:

1. What were your results?
2. Do you agree with them? Why or why not?
3. What can you do to improve the strengths of your type?
4. What can you do to improve the weaknesses of your type?

Journal Prompts

1. Choose one leader you admire. Describe attributes of his or her character that you admire and identify any attributes that are less than admirable. Do you believe that person is an introverted or an extroverted leader, and why?

2. Where do you fall on the introvert/extrovert spectrum? What experiences in leadership make you believe that?

3. Do you wish you were more introverted or extroverted? What would that add to your leadership style? How do you think you could move along the introvert/extrovert spectrum?

4. Write down five positive traits you believe you possess, and explain how they can be a strength.

5. Write down five negative traits you believe you possess, and explain how they might be a weakness. Describe how you might improve.

Endnotes

1. John Wooden, Wooden on Leadership: How to Create a Winning Organization (McGraw-Hill 2005). John Wooden was an American basketball player and coach of the UCLA men's basketball team.
2. Sam Walker, The Captain Class 17 (Random House 2017). His study revealed seven traits common to the captains who were responsible for sparking successful dynasties, including aggressive and intense focus on the work, "willingness to do thankless jobs in the shadows," "democratic communication style," "motivates others with passionate nonverbal displays," conviction and courage, and "ironclad emotional control." *Id.* at 91.
3. *Id.* at 138.

4. *Id.* at 141.

5. *Id.*

6. The American Psychological Association defines character as "the totality of an individual's attributes and personality traits, particularly his or her characteristic moral, social, and religious attitudes." *Character*, American Psychological Association, https://dictionary.apa.org/character (last visited July 22, 2020).

7. *Characteristic*, Biology Online, https://www.biologyonline.com/dictionary/characteristic (last visited July 19, 2020).

8. *Trait*, National Human Genome Research Institute, https://www.genome.gov/genetics-glossary/Trait (last visited July 19, 2020).

9. Alexi Lickerman, *Personality vs. Character*, Positive Psychology (Apr. 3, 2011), https://www.psychologytoday.com/us/blog/happiness-in-world/201104/personality-vs-character.

10. *See* Chapter 17 for a discussion of cultural intelligence.

11. Quote attributed to Lao Tzu. *See, e.g.*, Lucy King, *Who Said Your Character Is Your Destiny?*, Mindset Matters (Nov. 15, 2019), https://medium.com/mindset-matters/who-said-watch-your-thoughts-they-become-your-words-d645dff454b8. Lao Tzu was an ancient Chinese philosopher. Joshua Mark, *Lao-Tzu*, Ancient History Encyclopedia (July 9, 2020), https://www.ancient.eu/Lao-Tzu/.

12. *Aristotle's Ethics*, Stanford Encyclopedia of Philosophy, https://plato.stanford.edu/entries/aristotle-ethics/ (last visited July 19, 2020).

13. *Id.*

14. *Id.*

15. Charles Duhigg, The Power of Habit: Why We Do What We Do in Life and Business xv (Random House 2014).

16. Benjamin Gardner, Phillippa Lally and Jane Wardle, *Making health habitual: the psychology of 'habit-formation' and general practice*, 62 Br J Gen Pract. 664–666 (2012), doi: 10.3399/bjgp12X659466.

17. *William James on Habit*, FS Blog, https://fs.blog/2013/05/william-james-on-habit/ (last visited July 19, 2020).

18. Duhigg, *supra* note 15 at 13-17.

19. *Id.* at 18.

20. *Id.*

21. *Id.* at 19.

22. *Id.* at 25-27.

23. Jocelyn K. Glei, *Hacking Habits: How To Make New Behaviors Last For Good,* https://99u.adobe.com/articles/7230/hacking-habits-how-to-make-new-behaviors-last-for-good (last visited September 25, 2020).

24. *How Habits Work*, Charles Duhigg, https://charlesduhigg.com/how-habits-work/ (last visited July 19, 2020).

25. *Id.*

26. *Id.*

27. *Id.*

28. Phillippa Lally, Cornelia H. M. van Jaarsveld, Henry W. W. Potts, & Jane Wardle, *How are habits formed: Modelling habit formation in the real world,* 40 Eur. J. Soc. Psychol. 998–1009 (2010).

29. *Id.*

30. Duhigg, *supra* note 15 at 78.

31. *Id.* at 89.

32. Robert F. Blomquist, *The Pragmatically Virtuous Lawyer?*, 15 Widener L. Rev. 93 (2009).

33. Louise A. Mitchell, *Integrity and virtue: The forming of good character*, 82(2) Linacre Q. 149, 153 n. 14 (2015) (citing John Paul II, *Veritatis Splendor*, Vatican (1993), http://www.vatican.va/content/john-paul-ii/en/encyclicals/documents/hf_jp-ii_enc_06081993_veritatis-splendor.pdf).

34. Blomquist, *supra* note 32 (citing Thomas Aquinas, The Summa Theologica (1273), *reprinted in* Robert Maynard, 20 Great Books of the Western World 1, 60 (Robert Maynard Hutchins ed., 1952).

35. *Ben Franklin Quotes*, Brainy Quote, https://www.brainyquote.com/quotes/benjamin_franklin_163842 (last visited July 22, 2020).

36. Duhigg, *supra* note 15, Ch. 4.

37. Susan Swaim Daicoff, *Expanding the Lawyer's Toolkit of Skills and Competencies: Synthesizing Leadership, Professionalism, Emotional Intelligence, Conflict Resolution, and Comprehensive Law*, 52 Santa Clara L. Rev. 795, 829–30 (2012), *available at* http://digitalcommons.law.scu.edu/lawreview/vol52/iss3/4.

38. *Id.*

39. *Id.*

40. *Id.*

41. *Id.*

42. *Id.*

43. *Id.*

44. Susan Daicoff, Comprehensive Law Practice: Law as a Healing Profession 9–15 (2011).

45. Rachel Wolfson, *Uncovering the Two Keys to Leadership Legacy,* HuffPost (Oct. 31, 2017), https://www.huffpost.com/entry/uncovering-the-two-keys-to-leadership-legacy_b_59f89e89e4b0de896d3f2b7e?ncid=engmodushpmg00000006.

46. Peter G. Northouse, Leadership: Theory and Practice 19 (Sage 2019).

47. *See* The Editors of Encyclopedia Britannica, *Introvert and Extrovert Psychology,* Britannica (July 20, 1998) (hereinafter *Introvert and Extrovert Psychology*). Carl Jung was a Swiss psychologist who founded analytical psychology. *Carl Jung,* Britannica, https://www.britannica.com/biography/Carl-Jung (last visited July 11, 2020).

48. *See, e.g.,* Jack Flesch, *Why You're You: The Science Behind Introverts, Extroverts,* The Northerner (Feb. 25, 2019), https://www.thenortherner.com/news/2019/02/25/why-youre-you-the-science-behind-introverts-extroverts/ ("Ben Franklin was a greatly known extrovert. . . ."); Gene Landrum, Profiles of Female Genius 163 (Prometheus 1994) ("Catherine the Great [was] a classic extroverted, intuitive, thinker judger or Promethean temperament."); *Marie Antoinette Biography: The Face of Royal Excess During the French Revolution,* Biographics (Dec. 18, 2017), https://biographics.org/marie-antoinette-biography-face-royal-excess-french-revolution/; Bryan Walsh, *The Great Introverts and Extroverts of Our Time, Winston Churchill,* TIME (Jan. 26, 2012), https://healthland.time.com/2012/01/27/the-great-introverts-and-extroverts-of-our-time/slide/winston-churchill-politician/; *Presidential Personality Types,* L.A. Times (Aug. 18, 2000), https://www.latimes.com/archives/la-xpm-2000-aug-18-ss-6680-story.html.

49. Quote Attributed to Leonardo da Vinci, Goodreads, https://www.goodreads.com/quotes/8056089-people-of-accomplishment-rarely-sat-back-and-let-things-happen.

50. Richard Covington, *Marie Antoinette,* Smithsonian Magazine (Nov. 2006), https://www.smithsonianmag.com/history/marie-antoinette-134629573/.

51. "I don't believe anything really revolutionary has ever been invented by committee. . . . I'm going to give you some advice that might be hard to take. That advice is: Work alone. . . . Not on a committee. Not on a team." Steve Wozniak with Gina Smith, iWoz Computer Geek to Cult Icon: How I Invented the Personal Computer, Co-Founded Apple, and Had Fun Doing It (W.W. Norton & Company Inc. 2016).

52. Johnathan Rauch, *Caring for Your Introvert,* The Atlantic (March 2003), https://www.theatlantic.com/magazine/archive/2003/03/caring-for-your-introvert/302696/.

53. *Introvert and Extrovert Psychology, supra* note 47.

54. Laurie Helgoe, Introvert Power: Why Your Inner Life Is Your Hidden Strength (Sourcebooks 2008).

55. Quote by Albert Einstein. *See* James P. Grey, *It's a Grey Area: Einstein's Brilliant Thoughts to Today's Woes,* L.A. Times (May 31, 2013), https://www.latimes.com/socal/daily-pilot/opinion/tn-dpt-me-0602-gray-20130531-story.html.

56. Don Campbell, *Extroverts Enjoy Four Key Advantages According to a New UTSC Study,* U. Toronto Scarborough (May 29, 2019), https://utsc.utoronto.ca/news-events/breaking-research/extroverts-enjoy-four-key-advantages-according-new-utsc-study-here-they-are.

57. Scott Jeffrey, *Visionary Leadership,* CEOSage (2020), https://scottjeffrey.com/visionary-leadership/.

58. Dave Lavinsky, *Are You a Visionary Business Leader?,* Forbes (Apr. 26, 2013), https://www.forbes.com/sites/davelavinsky/2013/04/26/are-you-a-visionary-business-leader/#1e950c957bbf.

59. Tom Huddleston, *In 1981, This Was Steve Jobs' Vision for the Office of the Future,* CNBC (Oct. 17, 2019), https://www.cnbc.com/2019/10/17/steve-jobs-vision-for-the-office-of-the-future-in-the-1980s.html.

60. *Id.*

61. Heidi Grant, *Be an Optimist Without Being a Fool,* Harv. Bus. Rev. (May 2, 2011), https://hbr.org/2011/05/be-an-optimist-without-being-a.

62. Elite Daily Staff, *Why Charismatic People Are More Powerful,* Elite Daily (Mar. 27, 2013), https://www.elitedaily.com/money/entrepreneurship/charismatic-people-successful.

63. *Adapted from* Michael Rodgers, *A Great Leader by Example — Powerful Leadership Story,* Teamwork Leadership (July 2012), https://www.teamworkandleadership.com/2012/07/a-great-leader-by-example-powerful-leadership-story.html.

64. Terri Williams, *Why Integrity Remains One of the Top Leadership Attributes*, THE ECONOMIST (2020), https://execed.economist.com/blog/industry-trends/why-integrity-remains-one-top-leadership-attributes. Dwight D. Eisenhower was an American army general who served as the 34th President of the United States from 1953 to 1961. During World War II, he became a five-star general in the Army and served as Supreme Commander of the Allied Expeditionary Force in Europe. *Dwight D. Eisenhower*, THE WHITE HOUSE, https://www.whitehouse.gov/about-the-white-house/presidents/dwight-d-eisenhower (last visited July 8, 2020).

65. Nancy Schauber, *Integrity, Commitment and the Concept of a Person*, 33 AM. PHIL. Q. 119, 120 (1996).

66. Jody L. Graham, *Does Integrity Require Moral Goodness?*, 14 RATIO 234, 234 (2001).

67. Michael E. Palanski & Francis J. Yammarino, *Integrity and Leadership: A Multi-level Conceptual Framework*, 20 LEADERSHIP Q. 405, 406 (2009).

68. Brian Tracy, *The Importance of Honesty and Integrity in Business*, THE ENTREPRENEUR (Dec. 7, 2016), https://www.entrepreneur.com/article/282957.

69. *Id.*

70. Col. Eric Kail, *Leadership Character: The Role of Integrity*, WASH. POST (July 8, 2011), https://www.washingtonpost.com/blogs/guest-insights/post/leadership-character-the-role-of-integrity/2011/04/04/gIQArZL03H_blog.html.

71. PATRICIA BERNSTEIN, TEN DOLLARS TO HATE: THE TEXAS MAN WHO FOUGHT THE KLAN (Texas A&M University Press 2017).

72. *Id.*

73. *Id.*

74. Interview by Thomas Charlton and W. Frank Newton with Judge Leon Jaworski in Waco, Texas (Mar. 4, 1976).

75. *Id.*

76. *Id.*

77. *Id.* Luckily, it did not end his career. Judge Alexander taught Practice Court at Baylor Law School for over 20 years. *See History*, BAYLOR LAW, https://www.baylor.edu/law/index.php?id=930137 (last visited July 21, 2020). Leon Jaworski, "who at 19 was the youngest law graduate in the history of Texas," was one of his students. Judge Alexander later became the Chief Justice of the Supreme Court of Texas. *Id.*

78. Bernard Gert & Joshua Gert, *The Definition of Morality*, THE STANFORD ENCYCLOPEDIA OF PHILOSOPHY (Fall 2017 ed.), https://plato.stanford.edu/archives/fall2017/entries/morality-definition/.

79. JAMES MACGREGOR BURNS, TRANSFORMING LEADERSHIP: THE PURSUIT OF HAPPINESS (Atlantic 2003).

80. Graham, *supra* note 66 at 235.

81. *See* Vennli, *10 More of the Best Growth Strategy Quotes*, VENNLI CONTENT INTELLIGENCE BLOG (Oct. 9, 2015), https://www.vennli.com/blog/10-more-of-the-best-growth-strategy-quotes-part-3. Charles de Gaulle was a French President and former Army officer who lead the Free French Forces against the Nazis in World War II.

82. Brent Gleeson, *Why Adaptive Leadership Is the Only Way to Get Results*, INC.COM (2016), https://www.inc.com/brent-gleeson/why-adaptive-leadership-is-the-only-way-to-get-results.html.

83. Lauren Clarke, *Qualities That Define a Good Leader*, 6Q BLOG (2020), https://inside.6q.io/qualities-that-define-a-good-leader/.

84. *Id.*

85. Sarah Pruitt, *5 Things You May Not Know About Abraham Lincoln, Slavery, and Emancipation*, HISTORY.COM (June 23, 2020), https://www.history.com/news/5-things-you-may-not-know-about-lincoln-slavery-and-emancipation.

86. *Id.*

87. *See* Adam Mendler, *What Leaders Can Learn from Steve Kerr*, FORBES (July 10, 2018), https://www.forbes.com/sites/forbesbusinessdevelopmentcouncil/2018/07/10/what-leaders-can-learn-from-steve-kerr/#70842071604e. Stephen Douglas Kerr is an American professional basketball coach and former player who is the head coach of the Golden State Warriors of the National Basketball Association. He is an eight-time NBA champion, having won five titles as a player as well as three with the Warriors as a head coach.

88. *8 Leadership Qualities to Motivate and Inspire Your Team*, DEAKINCO., https://www.deakinco.com/media-centre/article/8-leadership-qualities-to-motivate-and-inspire-your-team (last visited July 19, 2020).

89. *Id.*

90. *A Dignified Response: Heman Marion Sweatt*, U. TEX. DIVISION OF DIVERSITY AND COMMUNITY ENGAGEMENT (June 1, 2014), http://diversity.utexas.edu/integration/2014/06/a-dignified-response-heman-marion-sweatt/.

91. *Id.*

92. *Id.*

93. *Id.*

94. 339 U.S. 629, 631 (1950).

95. *Id.* at 632.

96. *Id.* at 636.

97. Mark Williams, *5 Reasons Why Decision Making Skills Are So Important in Management*, MTD (2018).

98. *Id.*

99. *Id.*

100. *See Marbury v. Madison*, 5 U.S. 137 (1803).

101. *Id.*

102. *Id.*

103. Stacey Zaretsky, *Scientific Study Concludes No One Trust Lawyers*, Above the Law (Sept. 24, 2014), https://abovethelaw.com/2014/09/scientific-study-concludes-no-one-trusts-lawyers/.

104. *Franklin D. Roosevelt,* The White House, https://www.whitehouse.gov/about-the-white-house/presidents/franklin-d-roosevelt/ (last visited July 8, 2020). Franklin Delano Roosevelt, often referred to by his initials FDR, was an American politician who served as the 32nd President of the United States from 1933 until his death in 1945.

105. James M. Kouzes & Barry Z. Posner, Learning Leadership 129 (2016).

106. Patricia Bernstein, *Commentary: Dan Moody Was Not Simply a Racist*, Austin-American Statesman (Oct. 3, 2017), https://www.statesman.com/news/20171003/commentary-dan-moody-was-not-simply-a-racist.

107. *Id.*

108. *Id.*

109. *Id.*

110. *Id.*

111. *Id.*

112. *Id.*

113. *Id.*

114. Jack Zenger & Joseph Folkman, *Ten Fatal Flaws that Derail Leaders,* Harv. Bus. Rev. (June 2009), https://hbr.org/2009/06/ten-fatal-flaws-that-derail-leaders.

115. Naomi L. Quenk, Essentials of Myers-Briggs Type Indicator Assessment 5 (John Wiley & Sons 2009).

116. *Id.* at 5–9.

117. *Id.* at 4.

118. *Id.*

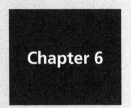

Chapter 6

Skills, Competencies, and Leadership Style

Debate is common about which leadership style is most effective. The answer, of course, . . . it all depends.

Thomas Kohntopp[1]

Purpose

Discuss the influence of lawyering skills and competencies on a leader's style and the need to develop over time a variety of leadership approaches.

Learning Objectives

At the end of this chapter, you should be able to:

- Define leadership style.
- Discuss leadership skills and professional competencies expected of lawyers.
- Discuss leadership skills and professional competencies developed in law school that are beneficial in leadership.
- Assess effective leadership styles in different scenarios.

Discussion

INTRODUCTION

Leaders bring their own distinctive style to an organization, for better or for worse, and there can be a sharp learning curve while you discover what style is effective and what style simply does not work for you. *Entrepreneur Magazine* shared a confession from one CEO:

> When he first became a business leader, admits Krister Ungerboeck, CEO of Courageous Growth, in St. Louis, Mo., he was a bit of a jerk. "I assumed that the CEO should be the smartest person in the room" . . . . That was a mistake Ungerboeck now acknowledges. Thanks to that mentality, he says, he tended to lead through criticism, he says. And that in turn led him to doubt the abilities of his team and created an unproductive work environment.

> But after receiving less-than-stellar feedback on an employee survey, Ungerboeck says he realized his leadership style wasn't working. "When I finally realized that my leadership style left my employees struggling to feel inspired, I made a major transformation," he wrote. "I learned that criticism is lazy leadership that is intended to pump up the ego of the boss by making the employee feel smaller."

> Since that epiphany, Ungerboeck has tried to do better by leading through encouragement. He now refers to himself as a "recovering a-hole."[2]

Leadership style requires more than just a certain personality type; it incorporates the competencies and skills that underpin a leader's effectiveness. Competencies such as judgment, vision, listening, emotional intelligence, and relationship building are vital to being a good leader, but not all leaders have developed these competencies well, especially early on in the role. Talented, successful people may find themselves in leadership positions without having been trained or given expectations for what the role entails. To make things more complicated, in more than a thousand studies, researchers could not reach consensus on a "clear profile of the ideal leader."[3] Instead, effective leadership hinges on the characteristics, skills, and competencies of individuals in different contexts. When considering what would make for an effective leadership style, then, it helps to know the competencies and skills needed in the leadership toolkit.

In this chapter, we discuss the core elements of leadership style. Each person develops a leadership style — the manner in which you approach a situation. In exploring leadership style, we focus on lawyering skills and professional competencies that help lawyers succeed in the legal profession and as leaders.

MATCHING YOUR LEADERSHIP STYLE TO YOUR CHARACTER, SKILLS, AND COMPETENCIES

In matters of style, swim with the current; in matters of principle, stand like a rock.

Thomas Jefferson[4]

Technical competencies and skills, including those taught in law school, uniquely drive our leadership style. Competencies and skill are the technical aspects of leadership that, when melded together, produce a leadership style. Developing an effective style requires that you candidly assess where your strengths and weaknesses lie. Research bears out that the leaders who most significantly impact their organizations critically evaluate themselves and the organization.[5] Most self-aware leaders have better insight and ability to assess not only themselves and their followers but also the situation. Decisions can be made with better clarity about all the components and influences.

Leadership style is the manner in which you lead, using the technical expertise you have amassed. Merriam-Webster defines style as "a distinctive manner of expression; a distinctive manner or custom of behaving or conducting oneself; a particular manner or technique by which something is done, created, or performed."[6] Your leadership style will be determined by

1. your distinctive manner of expression through your character;
2. your distinctive manner of behaving or conducting yourself through your abilities (knowledge, skills, and competencies); and
3. a particular manner or technique to approach situations through a leadership theory.

Leaders learn to combine their behavior and approach to problem solving and goal setting with their moral center. In other words, leaders have the technical knowledge to lead and the moral certainty that they are leading in the right direction.

CHARACTERISTICS, SKILLS, AND COMPETENCIES DESIRED BY LEGAL EMPLOYERS

A leader's style is influenced by character, skills, and competencies, but which of those aspects of leadership will be learned in law school? We know that lawyers need certain core skills and competencies to represent clients effectively. Surprisingly, many of those same competencies translate well to leadership. Professor Susan Daicoff synthesized six studies of lawyering skills, finding that the "competencies or traits named consistently in three of the six studies" were "drive, honesty, integrity, understanding others, obtaining and keeping clients, counseling clients, negotiation, problem solving, and strategic planning."[7]

In 2008, Marjorie Shultz and Sheldon Zedeck conducted hundreds of interviews with lawyers, law faculty, law students, judges, and clients to define successful or effective lawyering.[8] They wanted answers to two fundamental questions: "What does it mean to be a lawyer?" and "What are lawyering's constituent competencies?" Some of the 26 competencies (also referred to as effectiveness factors) included the very skills at the core of legal education: analysis and reasoning, influencing and advocating, and writing. Others, while clearly useful to lawyering, were not explicitly a core part of the law school curriculum, such as problem solving, practical judgment, listening, organizing and managing work, building and developing professional relationships, and the ability to see the world through the eyes of others. These 26 effectiveness factors correlated with the skills and competencies in the other studies reviewed by Professor Daicoff. Daicoff then divided those skills and competencies not clearly taught in the traditional law school curriculum into four categories, loosely based on Daniel Goleman's emotional intelligence theory,[9] listing the skills in each category not by order of importance but rather from the most general to the most specific:[10]

Intrapersonal (Self) Awareness, Values, and Abilities

- intrapersonal skills
- practical judgment
- maturity
- passion and engagement
- motivation
- diligence
- drive for achievement and success and a need to compete and win
- intense detailed focus and concentration
- self-confidence
- strong sense of self and self-knowledge
- integrity, honesty, and ethics
- reliability
- independence
- adaptability
- creativity/innovation (in a practical sense)

Intrapersonal Management Competencies

- organizing and managing one's own work
- self-development
- continued professional development
- stress management
- general mood

Interpersonal (Other) Awareness, Values, and Abilities

- understanding human behavior
- an intuitive sense of others by which one can "read" what is implicit or understand subtle body language and gestures
- ability to see the world through the eyes of others
- tolerance and patience
- ability to read others and their emotions

Interpersonal Management Competencies

- dealing effectively with others
- questioning and interviewing
- influencing and advocating
- instilling others' confidence in you
- speaking
- listening
- providing advice and counsel to clients
- obtaining, building relationships with, and keeping clients
- developing business
- working cooperatively with others as part of a team
- organizing and managing others (staff/colleagues)
- evaluation, development, and mentoring
- negotiation skills
- mediation
- developing relationships within the legal profession (networking)
- community involvement and service
- problem solving
- strategic planning

These four bundles of skills were "identified by lawyers and social scientists as important to success in the legal workplace and in the practice of law."[11] More importantly for young lawyers, these competencies aligned with those employers look for when they are hiring.

IAALS—Whole Lawyer Quotient

Reinforcing the earlier work on skills and competencies noted above was a 2016 report published by the Institute for the Advancement of the American Legal System (IAALS). The IAALS report focused on skills and competences law firms expect of new lawyers straight out of law school. The survey of more than 24,000 lawyers across the nation revealed that new lawyers need character as much as or more than knowledge and skills.[12] "[W]e have been, by far, most struck by what our study says about the importance and urgency of characteristics and, to a lesser extent, professional competencies—particularly when compared with legal skills."[13] Again, the skills and competencies bridged both the explicit and implicit curriculum of law school. Eighty-four percent of respondents indicated that intelligence was necessary, but intelligence and knowledge of the law was not viewed as enough; new lawyers needed to "come to the job with a much broader blend of legal skills, professional competencies, and characteristics that comprise the whole lawyer."[14]

The IAALS survey delved into a much longer list of skills and competencies (the study used the term "attributes") and asked respondents to rank the 147 attributes based on their contribution to the short-term or long-term success of lawyers. When ranking the attributes, study participants were asked to emphasize those needed for short-term success in the first year of law-related work. Surprisingly, only 27 percent of the desirable attributes were legal skills, such as legal drafting, research, and trial skills. Almost half (45 percent) of the desired attributes addressed professional competencies. These competencies addressed interpersonal skills such as working on a team and working well collaboratively. Desired characteristics, such as integrity, trustworthiness, resilience, and respect for others, comprised the other 28 percent of the top results.

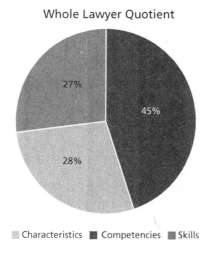

Whole Lawyer Quotient

■ Characteristics ■ Competencies ■ Skills

The message was clear: Law firms expected new lawyers to have the following attributes by the time they graduated:

- *Characteristics*: integrity, work ethic, common sense, trustworthiness, conscientiousness, emotional intelligence, empathy, self-control, self-awareness, being a self-starter, courtesy and respect for others, adaptability, resilience, and possessing a strong moral compass;
- *Professional competencies*: listening attentively and respectfully, tact and diplomacy, working well with a team, arriving on time; and
- *Legal skills:* use of dispute resolution techniques to prevent or handle conflicts, drafting policies, preparing a case for trial, and conducting and defending depositions.[15]

As the IAALS report concluded:

> When we talk about what makes people — not just lawyers — successful we have come to accept that they require some threshold intelligence quotient (IQ) and, in more recent years, that they also require a favorable emotional intelligence (EQ). Our findings suggest that lawyers also require some level of character quotient (CQ).[16]

LEADERSHIP SKILLS AND PROFESSIONAL COMPETENCIES DEVELOPED IN LAW SCHOOL

Law students expect to develop technical competencies in law school, in terms of both substantive knowledge and practical skills. Fewer students expect to receive formal leadership development in law school, and generally leadership skills are not widely taught in a formal sense. The research shows, however, that lawyering skills actually foster leadership skills. The substantive knowledge learned, the skills acquired and honed, and the professional attitude developed make lawyers well suited to leadership. Benjamin Heineman, Jr., former general counsel to General Electric, in addressing the topic of leadership and the law at Yale Law School, noted that the complexities of modern-day society requires leaders with

> vision, wisdom, and energy to lead. Such leadership will require many skills and multiple perspectives. No one is totally suited for such tasks, but no one is better suited than a lawyer with broad training and experience. Properly defined, the lawyer's core skills of understanding how values, rules, and institutions interrelate with social, economic and political conditions is central to the demands of contemporary leadership.[17]

Much of the training in law school lays the foundation for future leadership positions. Developing characteristics, skills, and competencies is a lifelong process, but many of them can be refined during law school. Some of the skills and competencies stressed in law school as essential for effective lawyering also prepare you for leadership.

Identifying, Researching, and Analyzing Issues

The explicit law school curriculum emphasizes issue identification, research, and analysis to offer good legal solutions. By the end of their law school coursework, students are proficient in analyzing facts, applying the relevant law, and reaching conclusions or recommending a course of action. Those skills, recognized as fundamental to good lawyers, are likewise effective for leadership. Leaders must listen to the client, understand the issues, determine the available options, and then find a way forward. Whether solving an organization's current problem or developing a vision for the future, leaders must comprehend and analyze the current data and circumstances (whether involving facts or people). Research requires leaders to look for patterns in the available information that others did not notice. Just as you gain technical expertise in these areas in your second and third year of law school, so will you develop the technical competency and analytical skills in leadership settings.

Ethics and Professionalism

Law students spend time, again as part of the formal curriculum, learning about their ethical and professional duties in the practice of law. Their understanding of these ethical requirements is tested in the Multistate Professional Responsibility Exam, a prerequisite to becoming licensed. Thanks to the efforts of Deborah Rhode and others, the standards governing all ABA-accredited law schools now require students to complete a course in ethics and professional responsibility. Ethical issues are commonly part of a student's clinical or other experiential training opportunity.[18] This same underpinning of ethical responsibility helps leaders choose the morally or ethically right course of action, and lawyer leaders are well equipped to understand the ethical guardrails when leading.

Good Judgment

The essence of providing legal services is the rendition of good judgment. In law school, you are asked about and tested on your ability to make good judgment calls based on the available information. The more you repeat this process in your classes, the more practiced and experienced you become in making judgment calls. The same skill set holds true for leading. Noel Tichy and Warren Bennis, authors of *Judgment: How Winning Leaders Make Great Calls*, describe judgment as "the ability to combine personal qualities with relevant knowledge and experience to form opinions and make decisions" and proclaim it to be "the core of exemplary leadership."[19] What they really mean, of course, is *good* judgment. Implicit in the term "judgment" as a leadership competency is the ability to make good decisions and reasonable choices when a solution is not clear. We want leaders who are able to form opinions, interpret evidence, and make sound choices. Judgment requires active learning and experience:

> Good judgment requires that you turn knowledge into understanding. This sounds obvious, but as ever, the devil is in the details—in this case your approach to learning. Many leaders rush to bad judgments because they unconsciously filter the information they receive or are not sufficiently critical of what they hear or read. The truth, unfortunately, is that few of us really absorb the information we receive. We filter out what we don't expect or want to hear, and this tendency doesn't necessarily improve with age. (Research shows, for example, that children notice things that adults don't.) As a result, leaders simply miss a great deal of the information that's available—a weakness to which top performers are especially vulnerable because overconfidence so often comes with success.[20]

Deciding on a plan of action does not end leadership responsibilities; good judgment extends to execution of the plan. How, and by whom, will the course of action be implemented? Is the decision feasible? Judgment involves considering the implications of the decision as well as the decision itself.

Strong Communication Skills: Effective Written and Oral Advocacy

Not surprisingly, lawyers and leaders need effective communication skills. While those skills can be developed elsewhere, law school curriculum integrates both written and oral advocacy effectively for those who practice law and those who lead. Law students take legal writing courses as part of their first-year curriculum and learn to convey ideas clearly and concisely in memorandum form. They progress to writing fluidly and persuasively in appellate briefs for their moot court arguments and then learn to present the essence of their position during oral argument. Often, judges or opposing counsel attack your weaknesses, question your authority, and force you to hone the skill of defending your stance — a valuable skill for leaders as well.

Sharing a vision and communicating achievable goals both require persuasion. Leaders need to inspire, course correct, and, to be effective, be good communicators who can translate thoughts and ideas into words the team can understand. Clear communication minimizes the risk that employees will not understand the mission and goals of the organization. When we think of effective leaders throughout history, we often remember them through their powerful words.

> [W]e shall fight in the fields and in the streets, we shall fight in the hills; we shall never surrender . . . .

> We choose to go to the moon in this decade and do the other things, not because they are easy, but because they are hard . . . .

> I have a dream that one day this nation will rise up and live out the true meaning of its creed: *We hold these truths to be self-evident, that all men are created equal.* . . .

Even without attribution, you likely know the names of the speakers who uttered these words. Churchill, Kennedy, and King all communicated their passion when they spoke and wrote. They crafted phrases that captured the hearts and minds of their listeners — phrases that became a touchstone for their vision. Communication by a leader may differ depending on the audience and the circumstances. Inviting and receiving feedback can enhance buy-in and bring the vision to life.[21]

Conflict Resolution and Negotiation

To study law is to study conflict. When parties cannot resolve their own conflicts, judges and juries do so for them. Law school teaches a variety of technical ways through which conflict can be resolved, as well as some of the art of doing so. Whether in a business law class discussing corporate issues or an employment course addressing disagreements between employers and employees, law school instills the technical and substantive knowledge for resolving conflicts and bringing parties together. These same skills work for leaders.

Former U.S. Secretary of State James A. Baker III was known for his ability to bring parties together and get a deal done. He had a skill set for resolving conflicts:

> When satisfied the person on the other side of the table was trustworthy and sensitive to the pertinent circumstances in play on a deal, Baker knew when to depart from a formal arm's-length attitude, shift his internal gear, and open up with candid disclosure calculated to get his counterpart to do the same. When operating in his candor mode, Baker often saw obstacles to compromise disappear in a flash, allowing progress to proceed on a faster track toward making a final agreement.[22]

Although Abraham Lincoln successfully resolved many conflicts by going to court, he had this advice for lawyers: "Discourage litigation. Persuade your neighbors to compromise whenever you can. Point out to them how the nominal winner is often a real loser — in fees, expenses, and waste of time. As a peacemaker the lawyer has a superior opportunity of being a good man. There will still be business enough."[23]

Conflict resolution is also a common task for leaders. Effective leaders do not shy away from facing conflict, whether it involves the leader personally or requires the leader to mediate a solution for others. When managed poorly, conflict can mean failure to meet an objective or harm the organization as a whole. But disagreement can be healthy if managed appropriately. The circumstances will dictate the leader's approach.

Innovation and Creativity

Lawyers solve problems through creative arguments and innovative approaches to advance client interests. While there are many definitions of innovation,[24] it best can be understood as "the transformation of knowledge into new products, processes, and services[,] involv[ing] more than just science and technology." Lawyers learn to apply existing precedent in new ways as circumstances change. Arguing for a good faith extension of the law is part of the formal curriculum. Taking this skill and applying it to problem solving is a hallmark of both good lawyering and good leading.

Professional Development or Formation

In more recent years, law schools have created professional development or professional formation programs.[25] These programs are designed to help law students recognize, understand, and develop their professional identities as lawyers. They commonly incorporate leadership as part of the professional development training. These programs guide students' understanding of, and reflection upon, both ethical and personal considerations in law and leadership.

Technical Competency

Being competent is a prerequisite for both leading and lawyering. A lawyer is ethically required to develop and maintain technical competence. As a leader, "one cannot succeed . . . and one will seldom get the opportunity to lead, without first demonstrating technical competence."[26] As a lawyer, your professional obligation is to be competent in a matter in order to represent a client. Comment 2 to Rule 1.1 clarifies that you do not have to be an expert in all matters: "Competent representation can also be provided through the association of a lawyer of established competence in the field in question."[27] If you do not have the needed expertise, you can assemble a team to assist.

> **ABA Model Rule 1.1: Competence**
> A lawyer shall provide competent representation to a client. Competent representation requires the legal knowledge, skill, thoroughness and preparation reasonably necessary for the representation.

Leadership requires not only general competencies, but job-specific, technical competencies. Specific tasks require the application of knowledge and skills for effective performance in a given job. Demonstrating competence or expertise in your areas of responsibility will build trust and respect within the team. Showing an interest in, and at least a basic understanding of, your team member's work can enhance the relationship and enable you to maintain control, which is important because you are ultimately responsible for the work.

DEVELOPING YOUR STYLE OVER TIME

Self-awareness gives you the capacity to learn from your mistakes as well as your successes. It enables you to keep growing.

Lawrence Bossidy[28]

Knowledge, skills, and competencies gained in law school will influence your approach to leadership. Through experience you become more comfortable with trying new approaches. You will learn which approaches work best in different circumstances. Virtually no leader follows a single leadership style all the time; most either blend aspects of different styles or adapt their style for different people or situations. In a law firm, the partner known as a dictator to his young associates may be far more collaborative and affiliative when meeting with a client. Effective leaders choose their style for a given situation by asking, "What do I need to do to accomplish my objectives in this situation?" For example, when President Lyndon Baines Johnson (LBJ) coerced a member of Congress to vote for a civil rights bill, he likely chose his approach before even picking up the phone. He might have contemplated what argument would motivate this member to care about the bill. How might he persuade him that a "yes" vote on the civil rights bill was the right thing to do? What would motivate the member to vote with him? These thoughts, to the extent that they occurred, represent a mix of visionary, affiliative, democratic, and commanding styles. LBJ understood he could not dominate or bully everyone all the time, because he would likely need to work with them in the future. He used his formidable talents to accomplish goals, but that does not mean that he was willing to destroy his long-term relationships.

When observing leadership styles of others, think about what made that leader's style successful. Was it the personality and abilities of the leader? Were they the right person at the right confluence of circumstances? By studying leaders' actions in specific scenarios and considering their character and capabilities in relationship to their followers and the circumstances, we can better analyze the factors that most likely led to their success or failure. In doing so, we can learn more about ourselves and better prepare for our time to be the person others look to for direction and motivation.

Daniel Goleman described six leadership styles: visionary/authoritative, coaching, affiliative, democratic, pacesetting, and commanding/coercive.[29] Goleman's styles framework is one of many vehicles for discussing how different styles might be best used in different scenarios and for considering both positive and negative ramifications in particular situations. Goleman's descriptions should be taken as *categories* of leadership style rather than rigid descriptions. Leaders rarely fit neatly into a single category and all have to adapt to changing circumstances. Good leaders are adept at transitioning from one style to another as the situation changes. For example, a naturally self-confident and aggressive leader might be inclined to bark orders and disregard input from the team. When the circumstances call for buy-in to a strategic initiative, however, the leader understands the benefit of active listening and bringing everyone together through a more collaborative style. Similarly, when crisis strikes, a collaborative leader may need to jettison consensus in favor of decisive action. Consider these styles and examples as you develop your own leadership style.

Goleman's Six Leadership Styles

Visionary	Motivates people toward a vision	"Come with me"	Self-confidence, empathy, change catalyst
Coaching	Developing people for the future	"Try this"	Developing others, self awareness, empathy
Affiliative	Creates harmony and builds emotional bonds	"People come first"	Empathy, building relationships, communication
Democratic	Forges consensus through participation	"What do *you* think?"	Collaboration, team leadership, communication
Pacesetting	Sets high standards for performance	"Do as I do, now!"	Conscientiousness, drive to achieve, initiative
Commanding	Demands immediate compliance	"Do what I tell you!"	Drive to achieve, initiative, self-control

Based on **primal Leadership** by Daniel Goleman, Richard Boyatzis, and Annie McKee

Visionary—"Come with Me"[30]

This style has also been described as "self-confident, and likely to be respected and obeyed." Visionary leaders earn respect by mobilizing people with enthusiasm and a clear vision.[31] Visionary leaders give people leeway to innovate and take calculated risks, provided they move in the direction of the stated vision.[32]

Steve Jobs was a visionary leader. He narrated the iconic "Think Different" Apple commercial featuring images of Albert Einstein, Martin Luther King, Jr., Mahatma Gandhi, Amelia Earhart, Pablo Picasso, and other visionaries. He said:

> Here's to the crazy ones. The misfits. The rebels. The troublemakers. The round pegs in the square holes. The ones who see things differently. They're not fond of rules. And they have no respect for the status quo. You can quote them, disagree with them, glorify or vilify them. About the only thing you can't do is ignore them. Because they change things. They push the human race forward. And while some may see them as the crazy ones, we see genius. Because the people who are crazy enough to think they can change the world, are the ones who do.[33]

Coaching—"Try This"[34]

Coaching leaders delegate well and are willing to tolerate short-term failures provided they lead to long-term development. Leaders who practice the coaching leadership style recognize a potential weakness in an employee and turn it into a strength.[35]

Not surprisingly, a great example of the coaching style of leadership comes from the world of sports. In 12 seasons, the De La Salle Spartans put together a legendary winning streak: 151 consecutive games. Their coach, Bob Ladouceur, exemplified leading by coaching and viewed the sport of football as a training ground for life. "Coach Lad" emphasized the development of his players by instilling values like commitment, character, love, respect, and discipline. He did not push his players to win. In his focus on players over victories, Coach Lad actually threw trophies and other mementos into a dumpster at the end of the season. The things that motivated this coach were not the same things that motived others in sports.

During one team meeting, Coach Lad told the players, "I'm focused one hundred percent on you guys as a team. I want you to become what you're capable of becoming. It has nothing to do with wins." Every word, every action supported Coach Lad's bigger mission to develop the players' discipline, character, and dedication to the team's success. But the coach also knew that at times the team had to be its own leader. During half-time of a game, his team naturally looked to him to coach them. When his team played poorly, rather than using a pep talk, he said, "Why do I always have to be the problem solver? Group problem-solving is a skill you will use your whole life. Figure it out." And with that the most successful high school football coach in history walked out, leaving the players to come up with their own solution.[36]

Affiliative— *"People Come First"*[37]

An affiliative leader wants to create harmony in the workplace and build emotional bonds with employees.[38] For this type of leader, the way that an employee feels at work is paramount.[39] To accomplish this, the affiliative leader spends time on relationship building and provides positive reinforcement for team members about their performance.

In *Shoe Dog*, Phil Knight, the founder of Nike, intertwines his life story with the success of his company. Knight credits his leadership team as the driving force behind the success of the brand. The group all knew each other extremely well and got along. The team affectionately nicknamed Knight, an accountant, "Bucky the Bean Counter" for his focus on the bottom line.[40] Knight attributes their effectiveness to annual retreats to develop new ideas and strategies. These meetings became known as the "Buttface Retreats":

> [Jeff] Johnson coined the phrase, we think. At one of our earliest retreats he muttered: "How many multi-million-dollar companies can you yell out, 'Hey Buttface,' and the entire management team turns around?" It got a laugh. And then it stuck. And then it became a key part of our vernacular. Buttface referred to both the retreat and the retreaters, and it not only captured the informal mood of these retreats, where no idea was too sacred to be mocked, and no person was too important to be ridiculed, it also summed up the company spirit, mission and ethos.

> I can see myself so clearly at the head of a conference table, shouting, being shouted at — laughing until my voice was gone. The problems confronting us were grave, complex, seemingly insurmountable . . . . Yet we were always laughing. Sometimes after a really cathartic guffaw, I'd look around the table and feel overcome by emotion. Camaraderie, loyalty, gratitude. Even love. Surely love.[41]

Democratic— *"What Do You Think?"*[42]

With a democratic leader, everyone has a seat at the table and everyone's voice is heard.[43] Consensus is achieved through participation. All ideas are considered. Only after examination and critique of those ideas is a decision made.[44]

George Washington reportedly used this style to build trust, respect, and commitment among people at many points in his life, mostly notably when he abstained from participating in the 1787 Constitutional Convention. He served instead as the president of the Convention.[45] At the end, like a good democratic leader, he supported the proposed Constitution without providing formal input on the mechanics of this new government. Washington's approach created solidarity. The delegates emerged united behind a single document. This unity was critical for the future of the young nation.[46]

Pacesetting—"Do as I Do, Now!"[47]

The attributes of a pacesetting leadership style sound admirable. Pacesetting leaders who set extremely high standards for performance—and achieve those standards themselves—surely motivate their team to accomplish tasks at an effective rate.[48] The high energy of these leaders theoretically trickles down to their followers. Pacesetters often achieve the goals that have been set out and willingly throw themselves into projects. Working with a pacesetter can be an adrenaline rush, full of positive interaction, for those who can keep up.

When Steve Jobs came back to a distressed Apple in the late 1990s, he held a conference to ask high-level employees what was wrong with the company. "After some murmurings and bland responses, Jobs cut everyone off. 'It's the products! So what's wrong with the products?' Again, more murmurs. Jobs shouted, 'The products suck!'"[49]

> Jobs set out to right the company, starting with the products. He wanted to make the best products possible and worked tirelessly to achieve it—working from 7:00 a.m. to 9:00 p.m. every day. Jobs modeled this behavior for his Apple employees because he was trying to get them to join him in his vision. [Jobs] wanted Apple to be a company of "A players," which meant regularly cutting B and C players, or pushing them with great fervor—bullying them, to some extent—to become A players.
>
> Before Apple launched the Macintosh, one of the engineers charged with building a mouse that could easily move the cursor in every direction—not just up/down and left/right—told Bill Atkinson, one of the early Apple employees who developed graphics for the Mac, that there was "no way to build such a mouse commercially." After Jobs heard about the complaint over dinner, Atkinson arrived at work the next day only to discover Jobs had fired the engineer. The first words said by the engineer's replacement were, "I can build the mouse."[50]

Commanding—"Do What I Tell You!"[51]

Commanding leaders demand immediate compliance with directions or orders. Commanding leaders use their position in the hierarchy to enforce or persuade people to get things done.[52] When the team is undergoing drastic changes in operation or experiencing a stressful time or crisis, someone needs to take charge to provide clarity and give direction. When commanding leaders push too aggressively, they can become coercive leaders. Lawyer personalities can tend toward a commanding style even though most firms do not work well in the long run with coercive leaders at the helm.

U.S. Congresswoman Barbara Jordan was revered as a powerful force in the House of Representatives:

> As a member of the House Judiciary Committee, she was thrust into the national spotlight during the Watergate scandal. Jordan stood as a moral compass during this time

of crisis, calling for the impeachment of President Richard M. Nixon for his involvement in this illegal political enterprise. "I am not going to sit here and be an idle spectator to the diminution, the subversion, the destruction of the Constitution," she said in a nationally televised speech during the proceedings.[53]

Perhaps the most widely cited example of a commanding leader who could drift to the coercive side is President Johnson.[54] Throughout his career, LBJ was famous for using his intimidating size and demeanor to coerce his colleagues. He was said to possess "an animal sense of weakness in other men" and

> studied, analyzed, catalogued, and remembered the strengths and weaknesses, the likes and dislikes, of fellow politicians as some men do stock prices, batting averages, and musical compositions. He knew who drank Scotch and who bourbon, whose wife was sick . . . who was in trouble . . . and who owed him.[55]

His reputation as an arm-twister was forged when he was the Senate Majority Whip, a position he earned just one year into his service in the Senate. In the House and Senate, where LBJ had no actual authority to command other members of Congress to do as he said, he had to find ways to persuade others to join his causes.[56] He started with vision and a purpose—a compelling reason that a goal needed to be accomplished. Once he had the end in mind, he would master the details. Like a good trial lawyer (he attended Georgetown Law for a semester[57]), he would learn all the details and be ready to debate them.[58] He also knew how to identify the right people and motivate them to join his cause. When necessary, however, people got the "Johnson treatment":

> For better or worse, he would harangue, threaten, flatter and bully. This was evident in Johnson's dealings with his mentor, longtime Georgia Senator Dick Russell. In establishing the Warren Commission—which was responsible for investigating the Kennedy assassination—Johnson knew Russell didn't want to serve, but announced Russell's involvement before asking him then bullied him into it in a phone call. As recorded in *Indomitable Will*, he then pushed past Russell—a dedicated segregationist—to get Civil Rights Act passed, telling him, "Dick, I love you and I owe you. But . . . I'm going to run over you if you challenge me on this civil-rights bill." He did just that—leading to Russell boycotting the Democratic convention in 1964. Similarly, after Bloody Sunday in Selma, Johnson summoned George Wallace to a meeting at the White House . . . in which he physically loomed over the man and badgered him for hours on subjects from voting rights to protecting demonstrators. He made people uneasy. He invaded their space. And he kept after them. This kind of persistence is uncomfortable for most of us but essential for LBJ.[59]

Many people found LBJ high-handed and abusive. He was famous for the amount of time he spent on the phone to achieve his goals.[60] Willing to make the fight personal, LBJ made many enemies during his political career. By whatever means, his efforts paid off. During his tenure as President, LBJ orchestrated the passing of momentous civil rights bills—the Civil Rights Act of 1964 and the Voting Rights Act of 1965—at a time in America when deep racial tensions divided the nation.

Although willing to be a coercive leader, LBJ mixed this style with others. He also had notable compassion and the ability to put himself in the shoes of others to figure out how he could help them — if he did not run them over.[61] Even this classically coercive leader realized it was a tool to be used sparingly.

Building Your Leadership Toolkit

As leaders face new responsibility, they may find themselves in a variety of different situations where an approach or style that was effective in the past just will not work now. When the circumstances call for a different approach, you need to step out of your comfort zone and find a way to lead effectively in that moment. We encourage you to think of leadership development as building a toolkit that is filled with characteristics, skills, and competencies developed over time for use as you need them. Daniel Goleman uses the analogy of clubs in a golf bag.[62] The leader may have a favorite approach, or golf club, but she must know how to use all of them.[63] The study of leadership broadens your capabilities and helps develop the art of preparing for situations before they arise. Devoting time now to try out different approaches will help you be better prepared for the challenges to come. As you gain experience and expand your toolkit, you will be a more effective lawyer and leader.

LEADERSHIP STYLES IN LAW FIRMS

Law firm leadership is unique. Most law firms are fairly "flat" structures of authority, with equal tiers of membership such that, typically, no one member of any tier has more formal authority than other members of the same tier. A typical firm hierarchy moves from equity partners and non-equity partners to senior associates, mid-level associates, and associates.[64] Even managing partners, while they have the title and influence, usually do not have more votes than anyone else.[65] Lawyers, generally, are autonomous and resistant to authority.[66] At most law firms, a majority of equity partners also operate in silos — managing the work for their clients alone or with a small team of other lawyers.[67] As such, law firm structure does not naturally create a designated leader, and the different styles of the members may influence who actually leads.

Lawyer personalities can tend toward a commanding style, which may work well, or even be expected, when working on a client's legal matter. Commanding and pacesetting are common and may work within a *team* in a law firm and may be necessary when time is short and deadlines loom, but trying those styles with colleagues in the same tier or above will likely not go over well.[68] Instead, law firm leaders are more likely to be affiliative or democratic when dealing with other members of the same tier or above.[69] Coaching would be beneficial but the economic pressures in most firms discourage investing in others the time suggested by coaching approaches. As always, lawyers-leaders should be mindful of the organizational structure, the team dynamics, the situation, and the people involved when considering actions and approaches to achieve goals.

CONCLUSION

Gaining knowledge and acquiring skills are unquestionably the primary mission of law school, but successful lawyers are much more than technical experts in the law. Character and professional competencies are equally important. The same is true for leadership. Your clients and colleagues will judge you not only based on the job you do but also the behaviors they observe. Same with your loved ones and friends. Developing character, skills, and competency is a lifelong process that began before law school and will continue long after law school.

Exercise

Leadership Styles

Divide into four groups to discuss the different leadership styles (as described by Daniel Goleman). Be prepared to discuss the following prompts for each style:

- How would you describe the leadership style?
- What are the pros and cons of the leadership style?
- When is it effective? When is it not effective?
- Give two examples of a leader that you believe exhibits the style, and explain why you believe each leader exhibits the style.

Journal Prompts

1. Think back to the six styles listed above ((1) visionary, (2) pacesetting, (3) coaching, (4) democratic, (5) affiliative, and (6) commanding).

   a. Which one or two leadership styles do you believe is a more natural fit for you?

   b. What about your characteristics and traits influences your preference for that style?

   c. List two positive features of that style.

   d. List two negative features of that style.

   e. In what circumstances do you think that style might work best?

   f. In what circumstances do you think that style might be problematic and what alternative style do you think would work better?

2. Recall a time when you worked in a group on a specific project in a previous school or work environment.

   a. Create a table for each person and list some defining traits, skills, competencies, and behaviors you observed. (Ex., Tom interrupted people, was overconfident and loud, was a persuasive speaker, was a clear and concise writer.)

   b. What formal or informal role did each person play? (Ex., Tom became the presenter for our group project.)

   c. How did the group make the decision about what role each would play? (Ex., We all discussed and then Tom volunteered to present.)

   d. What made that person effective or ineffective in that role? (Ex., Tom was a good presenter but did not include some important information provided to him by one of the other team members.)

   e. How did the individuals in the group relate to one another? (Ex., The group did not get along.)

   f. If you had been the leader of the group, knowing what you know now, what approach would you have taken?

Endnotes

1. *See* Salford Professional Development, *What Makes a Successful Leader?*, U. SALFORD (2015), https://blogs .salford.ac.uk/onecpd/2015/12/24/973/. Dr. Thomas Kohntopp is an industrial-organizational psychologist with more than 30 years' experience serving a variety of public and private-sector organizations in North America and Europe. He earned his Ph.D. from the College of Business at the University of Tennessee.
2. Heather Huhman, *5 Stories That Will Make You Rethink Your Leadership Style*, ENTREPRENEUR (May 11, 2017) https://www.entrepreneur.com/article/293842.
3. BILL GEORGE ET AL., DISCOVERING YOUR AUTHENTIC LEADER 163 (Harv. Bus. Rev. Pub. 2007).
4. Quote attributed to Thomas Jefferson, THE JEFFERSON MONTICELLO, https://www.monticello.org/site/ research-and-collections/matters-style-swim-currentspurious-quotation (last visited July 22, 2020).
5. JIM COLLINS, GOOD TO GREAT 88 (Harper Collins Publishers, Inc. 2001).
6. *Style*, MERRIAM-WEBSTER ONLINE DICTIONARY, https://www.merriam-webster.com/dictionary/style (last visited July 19, 2020).
7. Susan Swaim Daicoff, *Expanding the Lawyer's Toolkit of Skills and Competencies: Synthesizing Leadership, Professionalism, Emotional Intelligence, Conflict Resolution, and Comprehensive Law*, 52 SANTA CLARA L. REV. 795, 828 (2012), *available at* http://digitalcommons.law.scu.edu/lawreview/vol52/iss3/4.
8. Marjorie M. Shultz & Sheldon Zedeck, *Predicting Lawyer Effectiveness: Broadening the Basis for Law School Admission Decisions*, 36 LAW & SOC. INQUIRY 620 (2002).
9. *See* Chapter 14.
10. Daicoff, *supra* note 7.
11. *Id.* at 828.
12. Alli Gerkman, *Foundations for Practice*, U. DENVER, *available at* https://iaals.du.edu/sites/default/files/ documents/publications/foundations_for_practice_whole_lawyer_character_quotient.pdf (last visited July 22, 2020).
13. *Id.* at 3.
14. *Id.* at 5.

15. *Id.* at 3.

16. *Id.*

17. Benjamin W. Heineman, *Law and Leadership*, Lecture as part of the Robert H. Prieskel and Leon Silverman Program on the Practicing Lawyer and the Public Interest 11 (Nov. 27, 2006).

18. *See, e.g.*, Deborah L. Rhode, *Ethics by the Pervasive Method*, 42 J. Legal Educ. 31, 31–56 (1992).

19. Sir Andrew Likierman, *The Elements of Good Judgment*, Harv. Bus. Rev. (January–February 2020), https://hbr.org/2020/01/the-elements-of-good-judgment.

20. *Id.*

21. *See* Chapter 10 for more on giving and receiving feedback.

22. Talmage Boston, Raising the Bar: The Crucial Role of the Lawyer in Society, Ch. 1 (State Bar of Texas 2012).

23. *Abraham Lincoln's Notes for a Law Lecture*, Abraham Lincoln Online, http://www.abrahamlincolnonline.org/lincoln/speeches/lawlect.htm (last visited July 21, 2020).

24. Eric Shaver, *The Many Definitions of Innovation*, Ericshaver.com (June 6, 2014), https://www.ericshaver.com/the-many-definitions-of-innovation/#:~:text=%E2%80%9CInnovation%20is%20the%20process%20of,5).

25. *See* Louis D. Bilionis, *Professional Formation and the Political Economy of the American Law School*, 83 Tenn. L. Rev. (2016), *available at* https://papers.ssrn.com/sol3/papers.cfm?abstract_id=2783790.

26. Leary Davis, *Why Law Schools Should Emphasize Leadership Theory and Practice*, Law and Leadership: Integrating Leadership Studies into the Law School Curriculum (2013).

27. Model Rules of Prof'l Conduct R. 1.1, *available at* https://www.americanbar.org/groups/professional_responsibility/publications/model_rules_of_professional_conduct/rule_1_1_competence/comment_on_rule_1_1/ (last visited July 19, 2020).

28. *Lawrence Bossidy Quotes*, A-Z Quotes, https://www.azquotes.com/quote/830299 (last visited July 8, 2020). Lawrence Arthur "Larry" Bossidy is an American author and retired businessman. He served as CEO of AlliedSignal in the 1990s, prior to which he spent more than 30 years rising through executive positions at General Electric.

29. Daniel Goleman, *Leadership That Gets Results*, Harv. Bus. Rev. (2000), https://hbr.org/2000/03/leadership-that-gets-results. There are many, many other guides to leadership styles.

30. *Matthew* 4:19.

31. *Id.*

32. *Id.*

33. *The Iconic Think Different Apple Commercial Narrated by Steve Jobs*, FS Blog, https://fs.blog/2016/03/steve-jobs-crazy-ones/#:~:text=Here's%20to%20the%20crazy%20ones,re%20not%20fond%20of%20rules%E2%80%A6&text=These%20are%20people%20who%20think,into%20the%20square%20corporate%20box.

34. Goleman, *supra* note 29.

35. *Id.*

36. Adapted from Carmine Gallo, *The Coach Behind the Longest Winning Streak in Sports History Shows How to Build a Champion Business Team*, Forbes (Aug. 19, 2014), https://www.forbes.com/sites/carminegallo/2014/08/19/the-coach-behind-the-longest-winning-streak-in-sports-history-shows-how-to-build-a-champion-business-team/#40b579ce33a4.

37. *Id.*

38. *Id.*

39. Joanne Trotta, *Understanding and Leveraging the Affiliative Leadership Style*, Leaders Edge Inc. (Dec. 3, 2018), https://www.leadersedgeinc.com/blog/understanding-and-leveraging-the-affiliative-leadership-style.

40. Goleman, *supra* note 29.

41. Phil Knight, Shoe Dog: A Memoir by the Creator of Nike (Simon & Schuster 2016).

42. Goleman, *supra* note 29.

43. *Id.*

44. *Id.*

45. Richard Ketchum, *6 Key Players at the Constitutional Convention*, George Washington's Mount Vernon (2020), https://www.mountvernon.org/george-washington/constitutional-convention/6-key-players-at-the-constitutional-convention/.

46. Ron Chernow, Washington: A Life (Penguin Group 2010).

47. Goleman, *supra* note 29.

48. Daniel Goleman, *Use the Pacesetting Leadership Style Sparingly*, Daniel Goleman (2014), http://www.danielgoleman.info/daniel-goleman-use-the-pacesetting-leadership-style-sparingly-2/.

49. Dave Smith, *The Steve Jobs Guide to Manipulating People and Getting What You Want*, Bus. Insider (2019), https://www.businessinsider.com/steve-jobs-guide-to-getting-what-you-want-2016-10.

50. *Id.*

51. *Id.*

52. Ajay Ramamoorthy, *A New Way to Think About Leadership*, Upshotly (July 16, 2019), https://www.upshotly.com/blog/coercive-leadership.

53. *Barbara Jordan*, Biography.com, https://www.biography.com/law-figure/barbara-jordan (last visited July 22, 2020).

54. Goleman, *supra* note 29.

55. Roderick Kramer, *The Great Intimidators*, Harv. Bus. Rev. (2006), https://hbr.org/2006/02/the-great-intimidators.

56. John Coleman, *The Johnson Treatment: Pushing and Persuading Like LBJ*, Forbes (July 30, 2018), https://www.forbes.com/sites/johncoleman/2018/07/30/the-johnson-treatment-pushing-and-persuading-like-lbj/.

57. Aleksi Tzatzev, *Six Law School Dropouts Who Went on to Become President*, Bus. Insider (Sept. 8, 2012), https://www.businessinsider.com/six-presidents-who-dropped-out-of-law-school-2012-9.

58. Goleman, *supra* note 29.

59. *Id.*

60. *Id.*

61. Diane Coutu, *Lessons in Power: Lyndon Johnson Revealed*, Harv. Bus. Rev. (2006), https://hbr.org/2006/04/lessons-in-power-lyndon-johnson-revealed.

62. Goleman, *supra* note 29.

63. *Id.*

64. Sally Kane, *Guide to Law Firm Titles and the Career Ladder*, The Balance Careers (Aug. 13, 2019), https://www.thebalancecareers.com/legal-jobs-part-i-lawyer-careers-2164537.

65. *Id.*

66. *Id.*

67. *Id.*

68. *Id.*

69. Cary Gray, Presentation at Baylor Law School (Jan. 6, 2020).

Chapter 7

Fixed versus Growth Mindset: "I Can't" Meets "I Can't Yet"

Love challenges, be intrigued by mistakes, enjoy effort, and keep on learning.

Carol S. Dweck[1]

Purpose

Encourage the development of a growth mindset in order to expand an individual's view of his or her potential and help overcome perceived limitations.

Learning Objectives

At the end of this chapter, you should be able to:

- Explain the differences between a growth mindset and a fixed mindset.
- Describe how a growth mindset can affect the decisions we make.
- Illustrate how a fixed mindset can create artificial limits on our ability to accomplish a task.
- Evaluate your mindset, identify areas where your mindset falls more on the fixed mindset spectrum, and develop a plan to establish a growth mindset in those areas.
- Explain the difference between internal and external loci of control and how these controls can direct our view of ourselves and our circumstances.

Discussion

INTRODUCTION

For generations, society has debated whether nature or nurture produces greatness in the form of a talented athlete, a genius scholar, or a virtuoso musician.[2] Many believe that we are born with a fixed set of gifts and abilities that predetermine what we can achieve.[3] Others view those innate talents as a jumping off point that allows fuller and richer development of abilities.[4] The same thinking applies to leadership. Are great leaders born leaders who fulfilled their destinies, or are they individuals who identify and develop leadership skills that enable them to attain positions of influence? How you answer these questions — and the belief structure behind your answers — says a great deal about whether you have a fixed or a growth mindset. Your mindset, in turn, impacts how you lead and how you live.

Many people struggle with whether they are cut out to succeed. This can happen in school, in their careers, or when they have an interesting idea they would like to bring to market. In the late 1990s, Larry Page struggled to sell his software product. Although he thought the product was innovative, no one wanted to buy it.[5] At what seemed like a dead end, Page finally set up his own company, Google.[6] His company revolutionized how we search for information, and it is so ubiquitous that we now use his noun as a verb: We google to find an answer. Page likely did not foresee that his product would be as successful as it is, but he was willing to take a risk.[7] Page is an advocate of moonshot thinking, which he defines as "having a healthy disregard for the impossible."[8] Page approached the challenge of failing to sell as an opportunity to innovate. Approaching challenges as learning opportunities is a skill you can develop once you understand the distinction between a fixed mindset and a growth mindset.

Our willingness to tackle challenges may be informed by the narrative we believe about ourselves. Sometimes we write this narrative; other times, it is a narrative that comes from friends, family, or teachers. "I came to law school because I'm bad at math." "She's the smart one in the family." "He's just not artistic." These blanket pronouncements, which impose arbitrary limits on people and their potential to achieve, reflect what is known as a fixed mindset. Fixed mindsets assume that we are each given a certain bucket of ability. If a skill is not in our pre-ordained bucket, we can never achieve that skill with any meaningful competence. We are good at math or we are not. We are athletic or we are not. Others can contribute to this fixed narrative as well by labeling us as: "good student," "does not work and play well with others," or "not law school material." Fixed mindset perspectives discount the ability to grow or learn beyond the core talent set.[9]

A growth mindset, by contrast, looks at the innate ability as a starting point rather than the end result. The more we invest in learning and developing our innate abilities, the better those abilities become. This is true even in areas where we have little natural ability. In a growth mindset, challenges become opportunities to get better and increase our skill set. Thomas Edison famously conducted thousands of experiments before creating a lightbulb, and his attempts to find the right material for a battery numbered over ten thousand. When his friend and associate Walter S. Mallory commented on the tremendous amount of effort without results, "Edison turned on me like a flash, and with a smile replied: 'Results! Why, man, I have gotten lots of results! I know several thousand things that won't work!' "[10] The distinction is crucial: Edison's approach accepts failure as part of the process of success. Michael Jordan, one of the greatest basketball players of all time, said:

> I've missed more than 9,000 shots in my career. I've lost almost 300 games. I've been trusted to take the game winning shot and missed. I've failed over and over and over again in my life. And that is why I succeed.[11]

Fixed mindset restrictions can become more pronounced in law school. For example, some students who were accustomed to being at the top of the academic standings find themselves earning average or below average grades. It can be daunting to examine why you are not doing well when others are and to question whether you have what it takes to be a lawyer. The educational process of law school teaches a new way of thinking and processing material that does not come easily to many students. Additionally, law professors may use teaching methods that force students to think on their feet and to make connections that are not readily apparent. At some level, we worry the professor will say, "You're not cut out for this and you will never be a lawyer." Law students may also suffer from imposter syndrome, worrying there was a mistake in the admissions process and the error soon will be discovered and rectified. This thinking falls into the fixed mindset trap, assuming that failing to achieve at the accustomed level means you will not succeed in law school. Combining the fear of failure with a high-stakes, highly competitive environment can reinforce a fixed mindset because the skills being learned are untested by prior academic or life experience. It feels safer to enhance natural talents rather than focus on improving skills that are more difficult. This choice, however, deprives students of the ability to become well rounded and to gain the satisfaction of becoming proficient after hard work. It is both normal and natural to struggle in law school. For these reasons, being open to the challenges of law school can be best addressed with a growth mindset.

Beyond academic success, a growth mindset affects our interactions with others. Growth mindset leaders absorb setbacks by seeing them as opportunities to change and adapt.[12] Growth and success as a leader require reflecting on how we perceive ourselves and what limits we self-impose.[13] Once we know how we (or others) try to limit our potential, we can explore how to break through those boundaries. Applying a growth mindset—not only to ourselves, but also to our team members—is important to developing as a leader. Implementing a growth mindset requires a solid understanding of the differences between a growth and a fixed mindset.

THE FIXED MINDSET

A fixed mindset imposes internal constraints on what you can and cannot do based on the belief that our talents and abilities are innate and immutable.[14] A fixed mindset assumes that intelligence, athletic ability, and even academic performance are determined largely by heredity or other factors over which we have little control. In other words, nature supersedes nurture.[15] The dangers in thinking and behaving this way are as varied as they are predictable. It means success is all about showing how smart or talented you are. It's all about validating yourself, not due to effort but thanks to good genetics. Those with a fixed mindset avoid challenges or trying something new as it may expose weakness. And the last thing a person with a fixed mindset wants to do is acknowledge and address a weakness; better to pretend it does not exist. On those rare occasions when forced to confront weakness, fixed mindsets resort to the key weapons of the fixed mindset: blame, excuses, and stifling critics and rivals.[16]

When confronted with a situation calling for abilities outside the natural skill set, those with fixed mindsets default to the idea that they will not succeed.[17] They struggle to view criticism as constructive and instead react defensively. They discount or ignore the criticism because any criticism of how they handled the situation feels like a personal attack rather than an assessment of how to improve. After all, if the talents were given and not achieved, the criticism strikes at who the person is, not how he performed. The natural consequence results in fear-based choices and an avoidance of risk and failure at all costs. While he wants to succeed, a fixed mindset leader dodges challenges and settings that pull him out of his comfort zone.[18] Fixed mindset leaders invest energy in trying to *seem* smart or talented instead of trying to *be* smart and talented.

This fixed mindset is common among lawyers for a variety of reasons.[19] First, lawyers are uncomfortable with ambiguity.[20] "Ambiguity represents the degree of lack of confidence, or lack of reliability, of the information one has concerning the relative likelihood of events."[21] "Ambiguity aversion is a person's rational attitude towards the indeterminacy of the probability that attaches to his future prospects, both favorable and unfavorable."[22] Law school teaches students to avoid ambiguities. Even though case study naturally involves ambiguity,[23] students are taught to be as "unambiguous as possible in their thinking, writing, and speaking."[24] Our legal system is based on precedent, the concept of using past decisions to guide future ones.[25] Precedent, as we learn in law school, promotes predictability in the law so that lawyers and clients can rely on prior cases to guide decision making and predict rulings in individual cases. Lawyers find comfort in the fixed mindset promoted by precedent.

Risk aversion and fear of failure are common traits of a fixed mindset that lawyers must battle to overcome. Few law students were admitted to law school on the strength of their failures; they were chosen because of their successful academic and social endeavors. Many law students have limited experience with failure. The success-oriented model is reinforced in law school with the pressure to do well in each class, make law review, and pass the bar exam on the first try. If students do not achieve these benchmarks, they fear they may struggle to find a job. Once in practice, there is even more pressure not to fail. Our clients depend upon us to win (and some want us to win at all costs). Further, failures such as lapses in judgment or unethical behavior can be sanctionable or lead to malpractice suits or even disbarment. With such harsh consequences, lawyers not only fear failure, but many try to avoid admitting to more senior lawyers or clients that a mistake has been made. This leads to a doubly-problematic situation. When a mistake is acknowledged early and in a forthright manner, the consequences can be mitigated more readily. Mistakes that are covered up, however, fester, have more serious effects, and can lead to irreparable breaches of trust. This fear of failure also fosters a reluctance to take risks. Our legal training reinforces this risk aversion by providing lawyers with the tools to examine all possibilities of failure and risk in order to mitigate it — it is what our clients pay us to do.

In addition to these biases that affect individual lawyers, law firm structure can foster a fixed mindset. From a business perspective, the practice of law has not meaningfully changed in over a hundred years.[26] This means that firms can be reluctant to grow and change their structure. Firms engage in the status quo bias, both because of the security of what they know and the fear that change will have negative consequences.[27] This fear fosters a fixed mindset approach. Lawyers perceive safety in following the system, even when the system is antiquated and less effective than it could be. Unfortunately, this approach stifles innovation both in the business model and in the provision of efficient and effective legal services.

All these factors contribute to developing and entrenching a fixed mindset in lawyers. However, like many biases, the proper way to inoculate against a fixed mindset is to learn more about it.[28] Even better, learning how to develop a growth mindset and overcome challenge and setbacks are the keys to success. Whether it be losing a trial or having a transactional deal fall apart, lawyers frequently encounter setbacks in practice. By looking for the learning opportunities in challenges and setbacks, lawyers can continually improve their skill set.

THE GROWTH MINDSET

A growth mindset endorses the idea that while we start with a base level of ability, we can always learn and do better.[29] A growth mindset pushes us to develop and cultivate the skills we have while striving to acquire more abilities and expertise. People with a growth mindset enjoy challenges and look forward to trying new things.[30] When those with a growth mindset fail at something, they do not view themselves as inferior or incapable; rather, the failure provides an opportunity to grow and improve.[31] The growth mindset pushes us to learn from our successes as well as our failures. As Carol S. Dweck noted, "In a growth mindset, challenges are exciting rather than threatening. So rather than thinking, oh, I'm going to reveal my weaknesses, you say, wow, here's a chance to grow."[32]

The biggest advantage to the growth mindset is that you do not fear failure. Growth mindsets help you to see your flaws not as negatives but as ways to improve and change.[33] Criticism from colleagues, friends, and family feel like an opportunity to find new ways to improve yourself.

Fixed Mindset[34]	Growth Mindset
Perceives intelligence and talents as static, leading those with this mindset to	Perceives intelligence and talents as traits that can be developed, leading those with this mindset to
■ avoid challenges ■ give up easily ■ view trying harder as pointless ■ ignore criticism or become defensive when criticized ■ feel threatened by the success of others	■ embrace challenges ■ persist even at times of failure ■ view effort as the way to grow ■ learn from and accept criticism ■ be inspired by the success of others and try to learn from it

While this sounds easy, the truth is that adopting a growth mindset can be daunting. Few law students or young lawyers want to acknowledge errors for fear they will be seen as less worthy than their colleagues or competitors. This ignores a fundamental truth: we are all human and will all make mistakes. Mistakes and failure are inevitable and inexorable. Admitting to a mistake takes a quiet courage that, while uncomfortable in the moment, actually builds trust. Many senior partners, while frustrated initially by a mistake, vastly prefer the young lawyer who has the integrity to admit a mistake over the one who attempts to cover up errors or refuses to acknowledge mistakes or failures.

This scenario occurs commonly in law firms. Imagine you have just joined a law firm as an associate and a senior partner asks you to draft a motion for an important case. He tells you there is a short timeline so he needs a draft by the end of the day. You spend all day working on this motion, skipping lunch, working past five, and finally, you send him the motion before heading home. You are confident the work is the best you could do given the short deadline. When you get to work the next morning, you see the draft on your desk with a sticky note that says, "This is a good start, but here are changes I need you to make." You peel the sticky note off, and that's when you see the damage. The motion is covered in so much red ink that it looks like a crime scene.

In a fixed mindset, you might think: "This isn't fair. One day wasn't enough time. I'll never be able to write well enough for this guy. What I did the first time was good, and this partner is just out to make my life hard." In a growth mindset, while you still might find the number of edits a little daunting, you can see the good work you did and how the edits make it even better. Instead of "one day wasn't enough time," you think, "I did what I could in one day and got him a solid working draft." Rather than "he is just trying to make my life hard," you think, "I am going to learn so much from these changes he made, and the work we do for the client will be better. I'm glad someone with so much experience is helping me develop these skills." By changing how you view your abilities, you reflect a more positive light on your successes, your failures, and your life in general.

It helps to have as a boss and mentor an attorney who likewise shares a growth mindset. A fixed mindset boss might make comments that suggest your work is never going to be good enough. Unfortunately, that is not an uncommon approach with attorneys. Determining whether your boss has a growth mindset and will provide feedback from the perspective of that mindset can be a challenge, but engaging your work and training with such an approach is the only real way to learn and grow as an attorney.

EXTERNAL VERSUS INTERNAL LOCUS OF CONTROL

Related to growth versus fixed mindset are the concepts of external and internal locus of control.[35] These concepts address what or who we believe controls the things that happen to us, the causes of our failures, and to what we attribute to our successes.[36] In an external locus approach, good things are believed to happen as a result of luck or fate and bad things are beyond your control.[37] Whether you call it fate or destiny, the external locus of control belief system holds that individuals are boats bobbing along in life at the mercy of the wind and waves. External locus of control thinking promotes a fixed mindset, that what is going to happen will happen no matter what and your circumstances cannot be changed by any amount of effort.

Internal locus of control thinkers understand that they do have control in their lives.[38] That control may not extend to the ultimate outcome (diagnosis of cancer, winning the Pulitzer) but rather recognizes we have control over the effort in working toward a goal and our reaction to life events.[39] We also have control over how we respond to events. Hard work, effort, and attitude all contribute to better outcomes.[40] Not surprisingly, internal locus of control thinking goes hand in hand with a growth mindset. When looking at a problem or task from the perspective that outcomes can be affected, you focus on what you can do and what you can learn regardless of the outcome. Whether couched as locus of control or mindset, approaching your work with an intention to take control and improve your circumstances will pay dividends in the practice of law.

The movie *Legally Blonde* highlights how two different young women perceive locus of control. Elle Wood routinely expresses her confidence that she is in control of her fate. When her ex-boyfriend gets admitted to Harvard Law, Elle studies for and takes the LSAT, films a very individual application video, and gets into Harvard — "like it's hard?"[41] Vivian Kensington, by contrast, meekly accepts the role of coffee-fetcher for a more senior lawyer and cannot seem to find her voice to change her own circumstances.[42] While the movie is a light-hearted fiction, these two characters still illustrate vividly the mindsets of internal versus external locus of control.

Whether lawyer or law student, if you feel powerless to alter the course of your life, you can easily become depressed and dissatisfied. When you combine a willingness to learn from mistakes with the idea that your doing so can alter the course of events, you marry growth mindset with internal locus of control. Both give you power to change your situation for the better.

HOW A GROWTH MINDSET AND INTERNAL LOCUS OF CONTROL BENEFIT LAWYERS

Just as law students can grow more effectively when they are willing to learn from mistakes and failures during their education, lawyers can become more effective advocates if they are willing to employ this same growth technique. There are many opportunities for lawyers to fail, especially in the courtroom setting. Losing a hearing can become an indictment that you are not a good trial lawyer, or it can be an opportunity to learn how to better advocate for your client. Experienced trial lawyers universally acknowledge that if you haven't lost a trial, you haven't tried very many cases. They will also acknowledge that they learned far more from the cases they lost than from the ones they won — these are painful but valuable lessons. Those who thrive within the profession are those who are willing to acknowledge their mistakes and learn the lessons they teach. Shifting your perspective toward a growth mindset can benefit you personally as well as professionally.

While we have described fixed and growth mindsets as separate concepts, it is rare that anyone has an exclusively fixed or growth mindset.[43] Fixed versus growth mindset tends to exist both on a scale and situationally. Rarely does a student make it to law school with an entirely fixed mindset or a fully developed growth mindset. Different situations, especially those that challenge our comfort zone, may bring out or provoke fixed mindset tendencies. Many people engage a fixed mindset at least occasionally and in areas where they tend to feel insecure.[44] Changing from a fixed to a growth mindset, or moving to a stronger growth mindset disposition, involves incremental change and can happen using small and easy alterations to help break free from fixed mindset tendencies.

As you approach a challenge, listen for the seeds of doubt a fixed mindset sows: "Am I sure I can do it? Maybe I don't have the talent. Let's stay in our comfort zone and protect our dignity."[45] As you hit an obstacle, the voice says, "This would be easy if I really had talent; it's not too late to back out and save face." As you face criticism, it quickly says, "It's not my fault."[46] Learning to hear what your fixed mindset voice sounds like is important. If you do not realize you are engaging in fixed mindset behavior, you are less likely to change the conduct.

The next step engages your internal locus of control by acknowledging that you have a choice in the situation. That choice may not include the ability to change the outcome. If the judge has ruled and you lost the hearing, you cannot simply choose to win. What you can choose is how you respond to the situation. You can decide that you lost the hearing because you are not a very good lawyer, or you can decide that you need to approach the next hearing differently. This may mean conducting more research, framing your arguments differently, learning more about the judge, or talking to a senior partner before the hearing.

Talking back to the fixed mindset voice may sound funny until you think honestly about how often we talk to ourselves. There is power in self-talk, with both positive and negative effects.[47] As you hear the fixed mindset "not enough" voice, you need to gently but firmly correct it. Remind your fixed self that if you do not try, you will never know if you can succeed. If you do not listen to and address what is being criticized, you are unlikely to grow and succeed within the organization. Sometimes, talking back to the fixed mindset simply involves asking, "What do I have to lose by trying?"

Finally, you need to put the growth mindset into action. While this can be difficult, take on the challenge. Change in response to feedback. Work on a new skill. Be willing to laugh a little along the way. If you can alter your response to setbacks, you are on the road to a happier and more productive life. This is easily said but not as easily done. What, then, are some concrete steps you can take in working toward a growth mindset? Here are some suggestions:

1. *Acknowledge and embrace imperfection.* You do not have to be perfect or get it right all the time, nor will you. It is acceptable to make mistakes.[48]
2. *Face your challenges bravely.* Fear is the fixed mindset's best friend. Find the courage to take the next step even if you're afraid to do so.[49]
3. *Stop seeking approval from others.* Fixed mindset individuals conform to what others expect of them, even when those expectations are limiting. You do not have to agree that you will never be good at math.[50]
4. *Cultivate a sense of purpose.* If you have a strong sense that you are working for something bigger than just yourself, you will want to grow and serve that purpose.[51]
5. *Turn criticism around until you find its gift.* While criticism can be hard to hear, you need to find the lesson for growth in that criticism.[52]
6. *Value the process, not just the end result.* Learning how to do better is as or more important than simply doing the task better. Understanding "why" and "how" can help you the next time you face a situation.[53]
7. *Learn from the mistakes of others.* You do not have to repeat someone else's error to learn from it. If you hear a partner giving feedback to a colleague, be willing to apply it to your own work.[54]
8. *"Not yet" is okay.* Change is a gradual process. Be willing to be patient in growing and changing.[55]
9. *Be realistic.* While you can improve with effort, be realistic about where you are headed. If you take up gymnastics at age 40, it is highly unlikely that you can become an Olympic gymnast even though you become proficient or even skilled.[56]
10. *Own your attitude.* Your attitude toward situations and people is yours to control. No one "makes" you mad; you choose your reaction.[57]

Becoming more growth-oriented is not as simple as flipping a light switch. As with most behavioral change, intentionally committing to change and taking small but concrete actions on a regular basis can help you transition to a growth mindset. The next time you receive negative feedback on a memo from a professor, or from a partner, take note of how you feel. Think objectively about the comments that were made. Ask what you can learn and see how you could improve your work product. You may not want to hear the criticism, but you can make it work for you.

Lawyers and leaders need to be willing to accept challenges, enhance their skills, and continue learning at a high level, long after they leave law school. The most successful lawyers and leaders are not stifled by a fixed mindset; they understand they do not know everything and that it will take effort to be the best lawyer they can be. Tackling the limits of a fixed mindset paves the way for a more vibrant career.

CONCLUSION

By making the conscious decision to have a growth mindset, you can alter the way you respond to adversity and create a new habit and mindset for every challenge. This skill can be cultivated by anyone. Lawyers in particular will benefit from becoming more accepting of new experiences and challenges.

Exercises

The Mindset Quiz[58]

Take this mindset quiz. Be prepared to discuss your results.

Part A: For each statement, check the column that identifies the extent to which you agree or disagree:

	Strongly Agree	Agree	Disagree	Strongly Disagree
1. Your intelligence is something very basic about you that you can't change very much.				
2. No matter how much intelligence you have, you can always change it quite a bit.				

	Strongly Agree	Agree	Disagree	Strongly Disagree
3. You can always substantially change how intelligent you are.				
4. You are a certain kind of person, and there is not much that can be done to really change that.				
5. You can always change basic things about the kind of person you are.				
6. Music talent can be learned by anyone.				
7. Only a few people will be truly good at sports—you have to be "born with it."				
8. Math is much easier to learn if you are male or maybe come from a culture that values math.				
9. The harder you work at something, the better you will be at it.				
10. No matter what kind of person you are, you can always change substantially.				
11. Trying new things is stressful for me and I avoid it.				
12. Some people are good and kind, and some are not—it's not often that people change.				
13. I appreciate when parents, coaches, and teachers give me feedback about my performance.				
14. I often get angry when I get feedback about my performance.				

	Strongly Agree	Agree	Disagree	Strongly Disagree
15. All human beings without a brain injury or birth defect are capable of the same amount of learning.				
16. You can learn new things, but you can't really change how intelligent you are.				
17. You can do things differently, but the important parts of who you are can't really be changed.				
18. Human beings are basically good, but sometimes make terrible decisions.				
19. An important reason why I do my school work is that I like to learn new things.				
20. Truly smart people do not need to try hard.				

Part B: Circle the number in the box that matches each answer from Part A. Calculate your total to see your results:

	Strongly Agree	Agree	Disagree	Strongly Disagree
1. ability mindset—fixed	0	1	2	3
2. ability mindset—growth	3	2	1	0
3. ability mindset—growth	3	2	1	0
4. personality/character mindset—fixed	0	1	2	3
5. personality/character mindset—growth	3	2	1	0
6. ability mindset—growth	3	2	1	0
7. ability mindset—fixed	0	1	2	3
8. ability mindset—fixed	0	1	2	3

	Strongly Agree	Agree	Disagree	Strongly Disagree
9. ability mindset—growth	3	2	1	0
10. personality/character mindset—growth	3	2	1	0
11. ability mindset—fixed	0	1	2	3
12. personality/character mindset—fixed	0	1	2	3
13. ability mindset—growth	3	2	1	0
14. ability mindset—fixed	0	1	2	3
15. ability mindset—growth	3	2	1	0
16. ability mindset—fixed	0	1	2	3
17. personality/character mindset—fixed	0	1	2	3
18. personality/character mindset—growth	3	2	1	0
19. ability mindset—growth	3	2	1	0
20. ability mindset—fixed	0	1	2	3
Total				
Grand Total				

RESULTS

Strong Growth Mindset:	45–60 points
Growth Mindset with Some Fixed Ideas:	34–44 points
Fixed Mindset with Some Growth Ideas:	21–33 points
Strong Fixed Mindset:	0–20 points

Discussion Questions:

1. Are you surprised by your results? Why or why not?
2. What steps can you take to develop a growth mindset?

Growth versus Fixed Mindset

Complete this chart. In the Fixed Mindset column, indicate how the fixed mindset person would react to each scenario. In the Growth Mindset column, indicate how the growth mindset person would react to each scenario. Be prepared to discuss your answers.

Situation	Fixed Mindset	Growth Mindset
Struggling with a new skill (striking out in your first baseball at-bat, losing your first debate, etc.)		
At a party/reception, you find yourself talking to a group that you believe is comprised of people much smarter than you		
Getting called on in class and the professor says "good job" after you answer		
Getting called on in class and you are unable to answer		
Getting an A in a class		

Locus of Control Quiz[59]

For each pair of statements, circle A or B for the statement you believe is the most accurate. Remember, there are no right or wrong answers. Be prepared to discuss your results.

A: Bad luck is what leads to many of the disappointments in life.
B: Disappointments are usually the result of mistakes you make.

A: Political unrest and war normally occur in countries where people don't get involved or assert their political rights.
B: No matter how much people get involved, war and political unrest will occur.

A: You "reap what you sow." In the end, your rewards will be directly related to what you accomplish.
B: Despite your effort and hard work, what you accomplish will probably go unnoticed.

A: Teachers treat students fairly and evaluate their performances as objectively as possible.
B: The grades you earn in school have more to do with factors such as how much the teacher likes you or your mood on the day of a test.

A: To become a leader, you must be in the right place at the right time.
B: Those who are capable of leadership but don't lead have failed to capitalize on the opportunities afforded to them.

A: There are some people in this world who will not like you, no matter what you do.

B: If you have good interpersonal skills and know how to get along with others, then getting people to like you is not difficult at all.

A: If something is meant to happen, it will; there is little you can do to change it.

B: You decide what will happen to you. You don't believe in fate.

A: If you are prepared for an interview, you increase your likelihood of doing well.

B: There is no point preparing for an interview because the questions they ask are completely random and determined by whim.

A: To be successful in your career takes a lot of hard work and dedication, because effort is what makes the difference.

B: It's who you know, not what you know, that determines how good a job you get.

A: One person can have an impact on government policy and decisions.

B: Normal people can't do much to change the world; the elite and powerful make all the decisions.

A: If you set a reasonable goal, you can achieve it with hard work and commitment.

B: There's no point in planning ahead or setting goals because too much can happen that you can't control.

A: Luck doesn't play a large role in getting what you want out of life.

B: Life is like a game of chance. What you get or what happens to you is mostly a matter of fate.

A: Managers and supervisors got those positions by being in the right place and knowing the right people.

B: To be a manager or supervisor you have to demonstrate that you know how to get things done through, and with, people.

A: Accidents or twists of fate are what really determine the course of a person's life.

B: The notion that luck largely determines your life is a fallacy.

A: People have so many ulterior motives; it's impossible to determine who actually likes you and who doesn't.

B: How you treat people largely determines whether they like you.

A: After all is said and done, the positives and negatives of life are basically half and half.

B: When something negative happens, it is usually a result of apathy, lack of knowledge, inability, or a combination of these.

A: Corruption in politics can be eliminated if we all put in enough effort.

B: Once a politician is elected, there is little anyone can do to control him or her.

A: The assessments I get at work are completely at the whim of my supervisor; I don't understand them at all half the time.

B: How hard I work and how much pride I take in my job largely determines the results of my performance assessment.

A: I often feel that I have little control over my life and what happens to me.
B: I don't believe that luck or chance play a large role in determining what happens in my life.

A: If you're lonely, it's because you don't try hard enough to get along and be friendly.
B: Despite being friendly and pleasant, if someone doesn't like you, there's not much you can do to change his or her opinion.

A: The things that happen in your life are of your own doing.
B: You don't have much control over what happens in life or the direction in which your life is headed.

A: Why politicians make the decisions they do is anybody's guess!
B: The people are as much responsible for government decisions as the politicians themselves.

RESULTS: Calculate your total score to see your results. Each A = 1 point; each B = 2 points.

Score	Interpretation
22-25	Internal Locus of Control (strong)
	If you have a strong internal locus of control, you will likely feel that you're in full control of the events in your life. You are self-motivated and focused on achieving the goals you have set for yourself. For these reasons, people with a strong internal locus of control often make good leaders.
	However, there is a potential downside to having a very strong internal locus of control. Your powerful self-belief may mean that you find it difficult to take direction, so be careful to avoid seeming arrogant or "walking over" other people in pursuit of your objectives. And be sure to manage risks properly—random events do occur for all sorts of reasons.
	A very strong internal drive may lead you to believe that you can control everything, and if your plans don't work out you may feel responsible for their failure—even when events were genuinely beyond your control. This can lead to frustration, anxiety, and, in extreme cases, stress or depression.
26-33	Internal Locus of Control (moderate)
	You likely see your future as being in your own hands. As a result, you engage in activities that will improve your situation: You work hard to develop your knowledge, skills, and abilities, and you take note of information that you can use to create positive outcomes.
	However, few people have a wholly internal or external locus of control: Most of us fall somewhere between the two ends of the spectrum. Your locus of control may vary in different situations—at work and at home, for example—and it may change over time. People often tend toward a more internal locus of control as they grow older and their ability to influence the events in their lives increases.

Score	Interpretation
	Having a moderate, rather than strong, internal locus of control may make you more able to accept situations that you can't influence, and to manage them effectively when they arise.
34-44	External Locus of Control
	If you have an external locus of control, you likely believe that what happens to you is the result of luck or fate, or is determined by people in authority. You may tend to give up when life doesn't "go your way," because you don't feel that you have the power to change it.
	To overcome this, pay attention to your self-talk. When you hear yourself saying things like "I have no choice," or "There's nothing I can do," step back and remind yourself that you can always make choices. Set goals for yourself and note how you are making positive changes in your life by working toward and achieving these goals. You'll find that your self-confidence quickly builds.
	You may find it useful to develop your decision-making and problem-solving skills. These tools can enable you to take greater ownership of situations, rather than blaming circumstances or forces "beyond your control" when things go wrong.

Discussion Questions:

1. Do you agree with your results?
2. How can you develop a stronger internal locus of control?

Journal Prompts

1. Think about a time when you were faced with a challenging situation and you chose to embrace the challenge.

   a. What was that situation?

   b. What skills did you think you did not have to complete the task?

   c. How did you have to reach outside your comfort zone to complete the task?

2. Think about a time when you were faced with a challenging situation and you chose *not* to embrace the challenge.

   a. What was that situation?

   b. Why did you decide not to complete the task or challenge?

   c. Looking at the situation now, could a growth mindset have changed your decision?

3. List three views you have that are fixed mindset views. List three views you have that are growth mindset views. Discuss how the attributes you listed that are growth mindset views will help you adopt a growth mindset. Discuss how to overcome the fixed mindset views you have to sustain a growth mindset.

4. Think about the last time you got a grade back on a test that you were not happy with.

   a. What was your first reaction?

   b. Was it the teacher, the course, or you that caused you not to get the grade you wanted?

   c. Based on the answers to these questions, do you classify yourself as having an external or internal locus of control perspective?

5. Think about a mistake you made in the last couple weeks, preferably one that is not too emotionally charged. It could be anything — a mistake you made while learning something new, where maybe you misunderstood the instructions for a task at work and did it incorrectly, or maybe a social faux pas where you said something you wish you hadn't, or you snapped at someone and regretted it later.

   a. What happened? What were the consequences? Did you have the opportunity to correct the mistake? If so, how did it go and how did it make you feel?

   b. Create and complete a reflection chart:

Recall: In this column, write what you remember saying to yourself about the mistake. Think about what you said both immediately afterwards and later on. Try to be as honest as possible and give as many phrases as you can recall or that you might say in a similar situation.	Reflect: Is there a way you would like to reframe any of your selftalk to be more tolerant of your mistake and to reflect a growth mindset? Use this column to reframe relevant statements.

Endnotes

1. Carol Dweck, Mindset: The New Psychology of Success (Random House 2006). Dweck is the Lewis and Virginia Eaton Professor of Psychology at Stanford University.
2. Saul McLeod, *Nature vs. Nurture in Psychology*, Simply Psychology (2018), https://www.simplypsychology .org/naturevsnurture.html.
3. *Id.*
4. *Id.*
5. Nicolas Carlson, *The Untold Story of Larry Page's Incredible Comeback*, Bus. Insider (Apr. 24, 2014), https:// www.businessinsider.com/larry-page-the-untold-story-2014-4.
6. *Id.*
7. *Id.*
8. Larry Page, University of Michigan Commencement Address (May 2, 2009).
9. Dweck, *supra* note 1.

10. Thomas A. Edison Papers Project, *Did Edison Really Have 10,000 Attempts to Develop the Light Bulb?*, 9 THE EDISONIAN (2012), https://edison.rutgers.edu/newsletter9.html.

11. Eric Zorn, *Without Failure, Jordan Would be False Idol*, CHI. TRIB. (May 19, 1997), https://www.chicagotribune.com/news/ct-xpm-1997-05-19-9705190096-story.html.

12. Carol Dweck, *What Having a "Growth Mindset" Actually Means*, HARV. BUS. REV. (Jan. 13, 2016), https://hbr.org/2016/01/what-having-a-growth-mindset-actually-means.

13. *Id.*

14. DWECK, *supra* note 1.

15. *Id.*

16. *Id.*

17. *Id.*

18. *Id.*

19. *Overcoming Lawyers' Resistance to Change*, THOMSON REUTERS, https://legal.thomsonreuters.com/en/insights/articles/overcoming-lawyers-resistance-to-change (last visited July 22, 2020).

20. Stephen Rispoli, *The Walking Dead: Psychological Biases That Keep the Billable Hour Alive*, U. ALA. SCH. OF LAW'S J. LEGAL PROF. (2019), *available at* SSRN: https://ssrn.com/abstract=3594532.

21. Alon Harel & Uzi Segal, *Criminal Law and Behavioral Law and Economics: Observations on the Neglected Role of Uncertainty in Deterring Crime*, 6 AM. L. & ECON. REV. 276, 302 (1999).

22. Uzi Segal & Alex Stein, *Ambiguity Aversion and the Criminal Process*, 81 NOTRE DAME L. REV. 1495 (2006).

23. Anthony J. Luppino, *Minding More Than Our Own Business, Educating Entrepreneurial Lawyers Through Law School-Business School Collaborations*, 30 W. NEW ENG. L. REV. 151, 157–58 (2007).

24. Rispoli, *supra* note 20 (citing Luppino, *supra* note 23).

25. *Id.*

26. Thompson Reuters, *supra* note 19.

27. *Id.*

28. *See generally Lawyers and Resistance to Change, supra* note 26.

29. DWECK, *supra* note 1.

30. *Id.*

31. *Id.*

32. *Id.*

33. *Id.*

34. Table adapted from DWECK, *supra* note 1.

35. DWECK, *supra* note 1.

36. *Id.*

37. *Id.*

38. *Id.*

39. *Id.*

40. *Id.*

41. *Legally Blonde* (2001).

42. *Id.*

43. DWECK, *supra* note 1.

44. *Id.*

45. *See* Terry Waghorn, *Are You Trapped in a Fixed Mindset? Fix It!*, FORBES (Apr. 20, 2009), https://www.forbes.com/2009/04/20/mindset-psychology-succcess-leadership-careers-dweck.html#1ff123b911ad.

46. DWECK, *supra* note 1.

47. *Id.*

48. *See* Tchiki Davis, *15 Ways to Build a Growth Mindset*, PSYCHOLOGY TODAY (Apr. 11, 2009), https://www.psychologytoday.com/us/blog/click-here-happiness/201904/15-ways-build-growth-mindset.

49. *Id.*

50. *Id.*

51. *Id.*

52. *Id.*

53. *Id.*

54. *Id.*

55. *Id.*

56. *Id.*

57. *Id.*

58. *Mindset Quiz*, U. Ill. Chi., http://homepages.math.uic.edu/~bshipley/MindsetQuiz.w.scores.pdf (last visited July 22, 2020) (adapted from Emily Diehl, *Motivating Students with Mindset Coaching and How Brains Work (Dweck)*, Classroom 2.0 (Oct. 7, 2018), https://classroom20.com/forum/topics/motivating-students-with).

59. Mind Tools Content Team, *Loss of Control: Are You in Charge of Your Destiny?*, Mind Tools, https://www.mindtools.com/pages/article/newCDV_90.htm (last visited July 8, 2020).

Chapter 8 | Grit and Resilience

To be gritty is to keep putting one foot in front of the other. To be gritty is to hold fast to an interesting and purposeful goal. To be gritty is to invest, day after week after year, in challenging practice. To be gritty is to fall down seven times, and rise eight.

Angela Lee Duckworth[1]

Purpose

Distinguish grit and resilience, discuss the importance of each, and provide techniques for developing these traits.

Learning Objectives

At the end of this chapter, you should be able to:

- Describe the concept of grit.
- Describe the concept of resilience.
- Discuss the relationship between grit and resilience.
- Explain the advantages of leaders who have strong grit and resilience capabilities.
- Identify techniques to help develop grit and resilience.

Discussion

INTRODUCTION

For many students, law school is the most challenging academic experience they have faced. The hours are long. The coursework is intense. When you graduate, you are not finished. The bar exam stands between you and a law license. Although billed as a test of minimum competence, the bar carries a huge downside: "What if I fail?" The process of studying for the bar, then, adds to the marathon that is law school. Adding to that pressure in the summer of 2020, many students who had planned for an in-person July bar exam were faced with cancellation and delay due to the Covid-19 pandemic. This left many of them uncertain about how to proceed with studying given the uncertainty of when and how the bar would be administered and what effect that would have on employment.

The ability to succeed in the face of adversity and uncertainty requires commitment to the long-term goal of becoming a lawyer as well as the ability to dig deep, do the work, and bounce back from disappointments and challenges. This involves two qualities known as grit and resilience. Grit is the strength of will to persevere when others might quit. It is dedication to working toward long-term goals in spite of difficulties. Resilience is the ability to overcome adversity or rebound after a setback. Resilience, when combined with grit, helps you power through short-term challenges that present roadblocks to your long-term goals. Gritty, resilient people are usually optimists with a strong sense that they are able, through their own actions, to impact their circumstances positively. They cope with adversity by being flexible and adaptable. They are able to transform a challenge into an opportunity to grow or improve. This perspective enables people to succeed in the face of adversity and challenges and can be invaluable to those in the legal profession as well as anyone in a leadership position.

Knowing that grit and resilience are important does not translate into becoming grittier or more resilient. Studying how grit and resilience have helped others facing difficult situations through history can provide insight into how gritty, resilient people tackle adversity.

GRIT AND RESILIENCE: WHAT THE HANOI HILTON TEACHES ABOUT GRIT AND RESILIENCE

While law students might jokingly refer to themselves as prisoners of war, studying law is a privilege and nothing like what real prisoners of war (POW) experience. Studying historical examples from real prisoners of war can teach us a great deal about grit and resilience. Admiral James Stockdale spent seven years as the senior ranking officer among American prisoners of war in the "Hanoi Hilton," a gruesome prisoner camp in Vietnam.[2] During that time, Stockdale and his fellow prisoners suffered torture repeatedly but managed to maintain both personal and group integrity.[3] How they not only survived, but thrived, had much to do with how Stockdale led his men through this unimaginable time.

To help his men maintain community and communicate, Stockdale created an elaborate communication system that consisted of tapping on the walls of their cells. The system was essentially a crude Morse Code[4] that the prisoners used despite the official prohibition on prisoner contact. Each new POW was brought into the support community and schooled in the tap code.[5] Stockdale understood that being able to share the difficulties with others lessened the sense of isolation and the sadness that came with being imprisoned away from home and family.

The POWs also learned quickly that the official military Code of Conduct[6] did not save them in the face of torture. Stockdale created a new set of rules for prisoner conduct that would allow them to survive their imprisonment while staying true to their country. His new system, using the acronym BACK-US, adapted to the reality of long-term imprisonment and torture by identifying what the keys points of conduct were:

> **B:** don't Bow in public (this denied the captors propaganda footage of Americans bowing in humiliation);
>
> **A:** stay off the Air (POWs must not make any statement that could be broadcast for propaganda value);
>
> **C:** admit no Crimes;
>
> **K:** never Kiss them goodbye (do not show goodwill, curry favor or garner special treatment); and
>
> **US:** Unity over Self.[7]

Stockdale's system worked both during the period of imprisonment and also after the POWs were freed. An Air Force psychiatrist tasked with evaluating the POWs after they returned home found that they not only survived their imprisonment but also reported significant life improvement, from stronger personal relationships to improved values.[8] A subsequent formal study measured against a control group of Vietnam veterans showed the POWs to be more mentally fit as a result of their experience. The men were more optimistic, had stronger religious values, and a greater perspective on their lives.[9] The experience required the men to develop both grit and resilience, maintaining their resolve through unthinkable difficulty (grit) and bouncing back from repeated adversity (resilience).

Stockdale attributed his resilience to Epictetus, a Greek philosopher of the Stoic school who believed that "men are disturbed not by things, but by the view they take of them."[10] The admiral urged his men not to be concerned with things that were beyond their power.[11] The men could not control when they would be released, who would be tortured, or whether there would be an execution. With Stockdale's guidance, the

Hanoi Hilton prisoners reframed their powerlessness into the ability to control how they reacted. As Stockdale succinctly put it, "No matter what the situation is, you can control your response to it."[12]

Stockdale's creation of community kept the prisoners from acting out of blatant self-interest whereby prisoners could be turned against each other to avoid punishment or get extra rations.[13] He instilled in them the idea that "you are your brother's keeper."[14] When asked what sustained him through his POW years, Stockdale replied simply, "The man next door."[15] Stockdale's recipe for resilience also included a dose of realistic optimism. He never lost faith that he would one day make it home and that he would emerge a stronger man.[16] This formula worked for many of the POWs, but when asked who did not survive the POW experience, he responded, "Oh, that's easy . . . the optimists."[17] This seeming contradiction came to be called the Stockdale paradox. The paradox noted the difference between those who could face reality, without losing hope, and those who simply could not accept the reality in which they lived. Stockdale noted, "You must never confuse faith that you will prevail in the end — which you can never afford to lose — with the discipline to confront the most brutal facts of your current reality, whatever they might be."[18]

Lawyers frequently face brutal facts. Sometimes those facts are their clients' atrocious realities. Sometimes the lawyer is facing crushing obstacles in her own career. The fortitude to face those facts with grit and resilience can mean the difference between making it through those difficult times successfully or not making it.

GRIT

Leaders are made, they are not born. They are made by hard effort, which is the price which all of us must pay to achieve any goal that is worthwhile.

Vince Lombardi[19]

How did grit become a topic of leadership? What intangible qualities beyond raw talent contributed to success? Psychologist Angela Duckworth studied why some people persist and succeed in goals while others fall short of that finish line. Duckworth settled on the concept of "grit" as the key quality that enables individuals to overcome challenges time and again.[20] Grit can be defined either as "perseverance and passion for long-term goals" or "the tendency to pursue long-term goals with sustained zeal and hard work."[21] Thus, grit suggests a combined ability to see the long game while consistently working on the short game.

In a sense, "perseverance and passion for long-term goals" comes closer to a tautology than a definition. To succeed in the long run, you must persevere, but grit requires both effort and interest. Sticking to something you hate is not grit; it's drudgery or punishment. Adding passion to effort changes the scenario. Law students selected for mock trial teams frequently attend class all day and then spend several hours each night in practice. For those only interested in earning a grade or résumés boost for their participation, these practices may feel like drudgery. For those who have dreamed of being a trial lawyer, the ability to hone their skills under the tutelage of an experienced trial lawyer is deeply fulfilling. The effort may not be fun, but there is never a sense that they wish they were not on the team. Effort, when expressed in statements such as "I am diligent" and "setbacks don't discourage me," reflects a person willing to put in the needed effort to accomplish the task.[22] Passion reflects a long-term interest for a project that remains even when a different opportunity comes along.

Mere interest alone, however, does not translate to grit; the interest must run deep. Gritty people develop interests and pursue them, but deepen the commitment to those interests over time.[23] Those interests go beyond mere pleasure or amusement, moving to that which is meaningful and fulfilling—what are known as motivational orientations. Motivational orientations push people to seek happiness through meaningful activities, through engagement with their activities, or through the pleasure they derive from their activities. Grittier people are more likely to be motivated by meaning and engagement and less likely to be motivated by the pursuit of immediate pleasure.[24] In other words, gritty people are willing to invest in long-term benefits, even if the cost is delayed gratification.

In addition to interest and effort, gritty people tend to think of their challenges and setbacks optimistically, believing that they can affect their futures and change outcomes.[25] They demonstrate practice, purpose, and hope.[26] Practice reflects a focus on improvement that includes being willing to acknowledge weaknesses and to work to eliminate them.[27] Rather than being defensive, gritty people are open to receiving constructive criticism as a means to self-improvement.[28] They also tend to exhibit a growth mindset, believing that their skills and abilities can be developed over time, and that the challenges of life present opportunities for just such development.[29] Purpose recognizes that the work matters both to the individual and to others.[30] There is a sense that the engagement serves a higher goal or purpose. Hope, as used in this context, might be better described as persistent optimism rather than idealistic wishing. Hope comes from the knowledge that things can improve and that the gritty person has an active hand in that improvement. The perseverance inherent in grit requires hope, for one must have hope to face seemingly insurmountable challenges.[31]

Milana Hogan, while a doctoral candidate at the University of Pennsylvania, undertook a study of whether grit predicted success of women lawyers employed at BigLaw firms.[32] Combining Duckworth's grit with Carol Dweck's concept of growth mindset,[33] Hogan found that grit strongly correlated to a higher number of hours billed per year and a more positive perception on the lawyer's part of the quality or importance of the work assigned.[34] In numerical terms, a partner classified as "very gritty" could be expected to bring in almost $300,000 more per year than one of average grit. A very gritty associate would be expected to bring in about $155,000 more per year than an average associate.[35] When interviewed, the successful women lawyers tended to give very grit-heavy explanations for how they succeeded in the practice of law despite ever-present adversity and challenge.[36] Hogan's work suggests that grit correlates strongly with success in the practice of law in a tangible, measurable way.

RESILIENCE

When you stumble, there your treasure lies.

Joseph Campbell[37]

Successful attorneys, those who could land the promotion, close a multi-billion-dollar, multi-year merger, or win the trial, achieved their long-term goals because they had the willpower to persevere through challenges and obstacles in their path. The inevitable setbacks they faced did not derail them from achieving success. As noted above, grit is more powerful when combined with resilience. Resilience, then, would seem to be an essential quality in a profession where setbacks are a common occurrence.

While grit and passion provide longevity, resilience is needed for the inevitable bumps in the road. Resilience is defined by the American Psychological Association as "the process of adapting well in the face of adversity, trauma, tragedy, threats, or significant sources of stress. . . ."[38] Resilience is bouncing back from difficult experiences.[39] Psychologist George Vaillant characterized resilient people as being like "a twig with a fresh, green, living core. When such a twig bends, it does not break; instead it springs back and continues to grow."[40] In its most essential form, human resilience means bending and not breaking no matter the stress applied. Resilience is characterized by optimism, flexible coping with challenges, and a belief that one's efforts to overcome those challenges can create positive results.

Ten "Resilience Factors"

Psychiatrist Steven Southwick conducted resilience studies interviewing three groups of people who had demonstrated great resilience:

1. prisoners of war during the conflict in Vietnam;
2. Army Special Forces instructors in the Survival, Evasion, Resistance and Escape program; and
3. civilians exposed to severe psychological trauma, such as violent crime or child sex abuse.[41]

Even though the three groups had been exposed to very different types of pressure and adversity, all demonstrated consistent and reproducible traits that helped them overcome traumatic experiences. The three groups overlapped in the types of coping mechanisms they used to deal with traumatic events and their later effects.[42] Southwick identified ten "resilience factors" that seemed to help the individuals deal effectively with stress or trauma:[43]

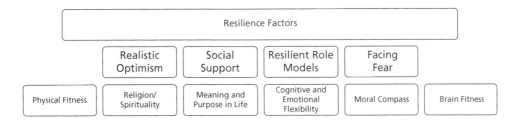

Of the ten factors identified, every person surveyed demonstrated four of the traits: realistic optimism, facing fear, giving and receiving social support, and making use of resilient role models.[44] These four traits can be considered the core of resiliency. Understanding these four universally helpful traits can help develop resilience in a variety of settings.

Resilience Trait 1: Realistic Optimism

Realistic optimism is "a future-oriented attitude involving hope and confidence," coupled with a belief that one's efforts can improve one's situation.[45] Realistic optimists manage stress with active problem-solving steps rather than passive avoidance strategies like self-pity, denial, or resentment.[46] The connection between realistic optimism and resilience is clear: Taking active steps to solve one's problems rather than shrinking from them is necessary to bounce back from adversity. Because dealing with adversity requires very active coping, Southwick calls optimism "the fuel that ignites resilience."[47] This ability to face problems without shrinking from them directly ties into the second intrinsic and universal characteristic of resilience — the ability to face fear. In a fear-based approach, the consequences of action and inaction weigh heavily on the individual.

Southwick found his resilient people were flexible in their thinking while managing adversity, both in the way they perceived events and the way they crafted responses.[48] They could accept circumstances they could not change, but showed agility in conceiving and employing coping strategies.[49] This approach mirrored the strategies the survivors of the Hanoi Hilton used in dealing with their captivity. Southwick noted the interviewees engaged in "cognitive reappraisal," by which they "reframe the negative, search for opportunity in the midst of adversity, and extract positive meaning from trauma and tragedy."[50] Humor was an effective tool of cognitive flexibility, often involving the reframing of negative events as something positive.[51]

For lawyers who have spent a year or longer preparing for trial, pretrial rulings by the judge can unexpectedly derail the best-laid litigation strategy. The unexpected exclusion of a witness's testimony or key piece of evidence can alter a carefully planned trial strategy. Walking away from the trial simply because of an adverse ruling, however, is not an option. A resiliently optimistic lawyer will recognize the impact that the court's ruling will have, but quickly comes up with a work-around strategy. Realistic optimism may include counseling the client about the impact of the ruling, including whether this now presents an appellate issue post trial.

Resilience Trait 2: Facing Fear

While trauma survivors may have faced fears involving an actual life or death situation, anyone can develop resilience skills by facing whatever it is that they fear. Resilience can be just as effectively applied to a young lawyer who fears killing a business deal or being fired. Often, however, the fear we face becomes more manageable when held up to the light of honest assessment. Resilience tells us that "you can't win them all" and that we probably will find another job even if we are fired. It also reminds us that we are not likely to be fired for turning in one bad memo, while grit reminds us to dig deep, listen to constructive feedback, and work to improve.

Resilience Trait 3: Giving and Receiving Social Support

Acts of kindness, no matter how small and no matter to whom directed, actually have a significant effect on the giver and the receiver. Performing an act of kindness does make you feel better, and it connects you to the other person in a way that encourages hope and faith in humanity. Not surprisingly, this connection makes both of you feel more positive. There is also a ripple effect that you may not fully appreciate, in which your supportive words are later passed on to another. Having enough love and generosity of spirit to give or receive support reminds you that things cannot be that bad if you can still help another.

While lawyers must frequently be opponents, there are many opportunities for small kindnesses that build relationships and professionalism, and ultimately can help the client. A lawyer who desperately needs a discovery extension will remember with genuine appreciation that you were gracious about agreeing to that extension. Many lawyers have found the shoe on the other foot when they needed a discovery extension and were glad to have set the collegial tone of civility with opposing counsel early in the litigation process.

Resilience Trait 4: Resilient Role Models

Many of us have people we admire about whom phrases like "indomitable spirit" or "ceaselessly optimistic" are used. We marvel at the friend from the gym battling cancer who, despite her bald head, always seems to be a well of hopeful energy. We watch videos about the survivors of the Boston Marathon bombing who not only survived the experience but emerged determined to run the race again, even on a prosthetic limb.

In a law firm setting, watch closely how other lawyers react to bad news, for example, the partner who lost an important trial. Resilient role models are those who kept calm during a difficult trial, accepted the adverse verdict with grace, thanked the team, and called the client with the bad news and presented the next steps. You know that lawyer is tired from weeks in trial, and saddened by a setback for the client, but he continues to advocate for the client through seeking a new trial, settlement, or appeal. Modeling the behavior of other resilient lawyers makes us more resilient as well.

RESILIENCE PROMOTES WELL-BEING

Dr. Larry Richards, a researcher who runs the consulting firm LawyerBrain, revealed that 90 percent of lawyers score in the bottom half of the resilience scale.[52] "Low resilience people tend to be relatively thin-skinned, defensive, and easily wounded by criticism, rejection, or other setbacks. They do not bounce back well from adversity."[53] Lawyers who lack resilience struggle in the profession. Practicing attorneys face criticism and even failure on a regular basis, but many seem to handle it poorly, which perhaps explains, at least in part, the rising dissatisfaction of those in the legal field. Richards's research suggests that lawyers who are able to thrive are those who work to develop grit and resilience, both for professional success and for personal happiness.

In 2006, the *Wall Street Journal* reported that 37 percent of new associates at large law firms quit within three years.[54] In a survey of 12,825 employed attorneys published in 2016, 20.6 percent screened positive for "hazardous, harmful, and potentially alcohol-dependent drinking,"[55] nearly double the 11.8 percent rate for a broader sample of highly-educated workers.[56] In addition, 28 percent reported mild or higher levels of depression, while 23 percent reported mild or higher levels of stress.[57] Both those who sought treatment and those who did not reported "not wanting others to find out they needed help" and "concerns regarding privacy or confidentiality" as major impediments to seeking treatment.[58] The concerns are not limited to mental health; they extend to physical health problems as well. Lawyers have a higher incidence of heart disease than the general population.[59] These statistics paint a picture of a proud but secretive group, suffering from significant pathology, unwilling to seek help and with poor resilience.

Nor is this a recent change in the profession. Benjamin N. Cardozo wrote on the topic in 1933:

> As to being happy, I fear that happiness isn't in my line. Perhaps the happy days that Roosevelt promises will come to me along with others, but I fear that all troubles in the disposition that was given to me at birth, and so far as I know, there is no necromancy in an act of Congress that can work a resolution there.

Cardozo, of course, had a stellar legal career, not only in private practice but as a respected jurist who served as an Associate Justice on the United States Supreme Court. The quote above was uttered by Justice Cardozo shortly before his death.

Could lawyer unhappiness be related to the fact that lawyers consistently score poorly on measures of resilience?[60] The problem appears to start in law school. In a study of the effect of optimistic and pessimistic explanatory styles on law school performance, an unexpected result emerged: While optimism typically predicted higher school performance in other environments, optimism predicted lower GPAs in law school.[61] In other words, "the poor 'C' law students tend to be optimists while the higher achievers are non-optimistic."[62] A profession whose top graduates are pessimists is unlikely to attract or create robustly resilient lawyers.

This natural pessimism is compounded by another problem for lawyer resilience: low decision latitude reflecting the number of choices you have or, actually, the number of choices you believe you have. Low decision latitude is seen in occupations that combine high pressure with low decision-making authority, such as nursing, secretarial work, and being a lawyer. These careers present a special risk of low morale, depression, and poor physical health.[63] Low decision latitude is likely a special problem for young lawyers. They are under significant pressure and feel they have little ability to refuse an assignment, work less than the "mandatory minimum," or leave early for a family engagement. Low decision latitude is compounded by the zero-sum game nature of much of the practice of law, in which one party's gain is another's loss. Zero-sum game participants tend to end up "anxious, angry, and sad."[64]

Happiness and resilience are related, so increased resilience can lead to a more satisfying professional and personal life for lawyers. In a 2011 study, leaders who rated themselves high on a happiness scale scored in the "incredibly resilient" range twice as often as did leaders who rated themselves low on the happiness scale.[65] If we can help lawyers learn to be more resilient, the data suggests we will also help lawyers be happier.

While the need to improve lawyer resilience is clear, solutions specific to the practice of law are sparse. Lawyers burdened by the zero-sum game might boost their happiness and resilience by moving toward a positive-sum area of practice, such as facilitating business transactions.[66] Another possibility is to reshape your practice area. For example, the traditionally hostile area of family law has become more positive through collaborative family law practices. In a collaborative approach, the structure of the divorce or custody dispute requires cooperation and includes counselors, financial advisors, and other consultants whose goal is to preserve the family and its assets. When changing your practice area is neither desirable or feasible, changing how you react to the adversity becomes your best strategy. Reminding yourself of your long-term commitment to this area of practice and employing strategies to bounce back when you stumble can help with long-term satisfaction.

METHODS OF BUILDING GRIT AND RESILIENCE

Deliberate Practice

Perhaps because grit is a relatively new field of study, or perhaps because it is defined by properties rather than methods, the recommendations on how to develop grit are sparse. Angela Duckworth, the pioneer researcher of grit, maintains that grit can be intentionally cultivated.[67] Her recommendations for how to become grittier echo the steps for becoming more resilient: Find someone you think has grit and start practicing those traits. What might those gritty traits look like?

Emulating a gritty role model means finding things about which you are passionate and working consistently to get better at those skills. This may require that you engage in deliberate practice, focused on improving specific weaknesses and achieving specific goals. For example, if you want to be a better writer at work, practice writing; study the work of people in your firm who write well; and listen to the feedback you receive from partners and then incorporate it into your next draft or project. Once you have achieved the goal or addressed the weakness, start again, finding yet another way to improve your legal writing.[68] This cycle allows for continued growth and development, and the practice becomes a habit. Seek and find a purpose or interest and observe the behavior of another person who demonstrates purposefulness. Get their insight on effort and how that made a difference for them. Try to work with gritty people in the firm. People often conform to the behaviors of other people with whom they associate.[69] Take steps to build an optimistic explanatory style and a growth mindset. With practice, these strategies can become a way of life, reframing and reshaping an individual's course in life. For lawyers, these techniques can prevent stagnation and despondency and ultimately contribute to a successful career.

Likewise, while we know much about how resilient people behave, how can you develop the skill? Observing that resilient people tend to be optimistic, spiritual, in touch with reality, or high in self-esteem does not provide much of a recipe for resilience. No one would list butter, sugar, flour, and eggs and expect a child to know how to bake a cake, especially if the child does not have the ingredients or know how to get them. Children do learn, however, from watching others. Emulate the resilient behaviors of someone in your office. Listen to the way they respond to adversity in different situations, perhaps with a client, a judge, or opposing counsel. Choose one or two identified resilience factors and habitually practice them.[70]

Mindfulness

Mindfulness techniques can improve resilience as well. Being thoughtful and intentional about resilience can lead to positive changes. The act of intentionally surrounding yourself with resilient people can help you emulate their resilient habits and behaviors. Noticing optimistic thinking and consciously choosing to apply it can help create a more resilient attorney. In addition to observing positive behaviors in others, mindfulness can help you notice negative behavior and redirect it. For example, mindfulness helps the pessimistic thinker stop the freight train of negative thoughts and consciously replace it with a different method of thinking. For this reason, yoga, meditation, and other mindfulness techniques prove useful in building resilience, because they focus on a clear mind, acknowledging a negative thought without dwelling on it, and choosing either to remove it from the mental space or to replace it with a positive thought.

Transformational Coping

For Salvatore Maddi, founder of the Hardiness Institute, the key to resilience training lies in the development of transformational coping skills in which you embrace adversity as a problem to solve and then actively plan and execute solutions.[71] The three key behaviors in Maddi's model of transformational coping are:

1. broadening perspective;
2. deepening understanding; and
3. creating and acting on a plan.[72]

Broadening perspective reframes a problem into a challenge or an opportunity for growth. A lawyer who loses a court hearing might reframe the loss by thinking "I may have lost that battle, but not the war." *Deepening understanding* explores features of the problem that may not be immediately apparent. For example, you might need to ask yourself, "What information did I glean as a result of that loss?" Did you need to do more thorough research or organize the argument differently? Could you have developed better rapport and communication with the judge? A deeper understanding helps delve into why the result came about and, importantly, provides insight into how you can have a different outcome should that issue arise again. Finally, Maddi suggests *creating and acting on a plan* to deal with the problem. Once you can identify the lessons learned, you can find the tools to change the outcome. Identify specific changes you can make to have a better outcome next time. Have a partner look over your hearing outline or listen to a practice version of your argument. Talk to other lawyers about their experiences in front of this judge. Coming up with a plan to deal with the problem adds a volitional, internal locus of control for dealing with the adverse outcome.

To put this into context, imagine that you just sent the client an email reminding her of the upcoming trial setting that is just a month away and asking for time to meet and prepare. The client responds in a tone that can best be described as furious. The client indicates she was unaware of the trial setting and will not be in town. If the case is going to trial, she will need to cancel a family vacation. She is also upset that you have not sent a pretrial report, including your assessment of the likelihood of winning, the possible range of exposure, and the trial budget. This client is important to the firm and the consequences of her taking her business elsewhere will be damaging to the firm (both reputationally and financially). What's worse, the client has copied the senior partner on the email. You did not realize the client was not sent a copy of the Notice of Trial Setting when the court sent it initially, and you have never done a pretrial report on your own.

Using Maddi's strategy, first broaden your perspective. Do some fact checking to be sure that no one sent the client the notice. It is understandable if the client misplaced the notice or failed to calendar the trial date, but she may have been told about the trial. If not, look at the bigger picture. While the mistake is an important one, it did not happen on the eve of trial; there is still a month to prepare. You also do not know if yours is the only case on the court's docket, and you have time to find out the likelihood the case will be reached. You also have time, if needed, to file a motion for continuance. You need to apologize for the error, but you at least have some options for the client to mitigate the harm. Next, deepen your understanding. There were several important communication steps that were skipped, and it will be important to learn not only about these but about other routine communications and notifications that you may not be aware of. You need to sit down with the partner on the case and have a conversation about client communications, why they are important, and the best format for them. To have good client relationships, you will want to build good patterns of communicating with the client. A well-informed client is better prepared when the unexpected twists of litigation occur. Finally, develop a plan. Engaging the partner and your assistant in identifying the kinds of documents and reports that should routinely be sent to the client and what processes are in place to send them can protect against a repeat of the error. You also may need to offer the firm's assistance in getting a refund for the travel costs or providing some other relief for the canceled trip. Mistakes will happen, but many clients gain comfort from your candidly acknowledging the error and having a plan for mitigating its impact.

You also can practice transformational coping by listing life stressors, rating each one on a scale of one to ten in magnitude. Next, classify each as either acute (a transient condition) or chronic (an ongoing problem). Reflect on the stressful circumstance to gain perspective on the nature of the problem. The first part of this step involves a technique called "situational reconstruction," in which you describe the problem fully, imagine alternative scenarios with both better and worse outcomes, and then place the problem in its proper perspective.[73] This may help you realize that the problem is not as bad as it could be, that the problem won't last forever, or that others have faced the same situation and managed it. Having done that, you can evaluate your own role in the problem — whether altering your behavior can change the situation or if it is a problem outside of your control and must be accepted.[74] Finally, create and execute a plan of action to resolve or improve the situation, by setting a goal, identifying the actions that can lead to that goal, and adjusting the plan as the steps are carried out and real-world feedback is received.[75]

CONCLUSION

Considering the important role that lawyers play in society as problem solvers, guardians of our democracy, and protectors of our rights and freedoms, grit and resilience are vital to our profession. Lawyers carry the burden of significant responsibility and face overwhelming challenges in dealing with the increasing complexities of our ever-changing world.

A leader who models grit and resilience for the team creates an atmosphere in which tenacity is expected and mistakes and challenges create opportunities to learn and improve. Knowing that you have the ability to develop grit and resilience can make you a better leader and a happier lawyer. Thankfully, both grit and resilience are learnable skills.

Exercise

Angela Duckworth's "Grit Scale" Test

Developed by Professor Angela Duckworth, the grit scale measures how "passionate and persevering" the test taker views herself as being.[76] The test consists of ten multiple-choice questions that ask the test taker to evaluate her response to situations and how she manages her productivity. The test provides the user with a grit score between zero and five and a comparative/percentile ranking. Professor Duckworth's website, the only website that administers this test, also provides information about her studies on self-control and grittiness, as well as links to her scholarly research on the subject and to her nonprofit organization, Character Lab, Inc.

Take the test in advance and bring your results. Be prepared to discuss the following questions:

- Were you surprised by your results? Why or why not?
- What habits can you form to be grittier?
- When faced with a challenge or setback:
  - Are your first thoughts positive or negative?
  - How might your natural inclination toward positivity or negativity influence your response?
  - What plan of action might help you respond more positively in order to achieve your goal?

Journal Prompts

1. The demands of law school require a great deal of grit and resilience.

   a. What is an example of a time in law school where you exhibited grit?

   b. What is a different example of a time in law school where you exhibited resilience?

   c. What is different about these two examples?

   d. How did your grittiness and resilience help you?

2. List a specific goal you want to accomplish. It does not have to be a professional goal. Be specific about your plan and the goal you want to achieve — the more specific, the better.

   a. Using grit building techniques, how will you ensure that you accomplish your goal?

   b. What are a series of "next right steps" you can take in achieving that goal or overcoming that challenge?

3. Think about a feedback session you experienced in the past that you remember as a negative experience. After today's discussion about your ability to control how you receive the information, re-analyze that session.

   a. What, if anything, did you constructively take from the experience at the time?

   b. Looking back at that experience, what, if anything, can you constructively take from the experience now?

   c. What, if anything, would you change about how you handled the experience?

4. Analyze a recent failure. Using Maddi's model of transformational coping, go through the steps: (1) broadening perspective, (2) deepening understanding, and (3) creating and acting on a plan to re-analyze it.

Endnotes

1. Angela Lee Duckworth is an American academic, psychologist, and popular science author. She is the Christopher H. Browne Distinguished Professor of Psychology at the University of Pennsylvania, where she studies grit and self-control. About Angela, ANGELA DUCKWORTH (last visited July 8, 2020), https://angeladuckworth.com/about-angela/.
2. PETER FRETWELL & TAYLOR BALDWIN KILAND, LESSONS FROM THE HANOI HILTON: SIX CHARACTERISTICS OF HIGH-PERFORMING TEAMS (U.S. Naval Institute Press 2013).
3. *Id.*
4. *Id.* at Ch. 1.
5. *Id.*
6. The Code of Conduct was supposed to cover what a prisoner did or did not disclose to his captors. This code, however, presupposed that the captors were not torturing the prisoners.
7. *Id.* at Ch. 5.
8. *Id.* at Introduction.
9. *Id.*
10. *Id.*
11. *Id.* at Preface.
12. *Id.* at Foreword.
13. James B. Stockdale, *The Melting Experience*, NATIONAL REVIEW 1534 (Dec. 25, 1981).
14. *Id.* at 1535.
15. *Id.* at 1536.
16. JIM COLLINS, GOOD TO GREAT: WHY SOME COMPANIES MAKE THE LEAP . . . AND OTHERS DON'T 85 (HarperBusiness 2001).
17. *Id.*

18. *Id.* at 85.

19. Mattson Newel, What You Can Learn from Vince Lombardi's Timeless Leadership Wisdom, Inc., https://www.inc.com/partners-in-leadership/what-you-can-learn-from-vince-lombardis-timeless-leadership-wisdom.html (last visited Oct. 15, 2020)." (See endnote 52 for style.) Vince Lombardi had many coaching positions throughout his life, but was most famous for being the head coach of the Green Bay Packers in the 1960s. Under his leadership, the team won five NFL championships, including Super Bowls I and II. *About Vince Lombardi,* http://vincelombardi.com/about.html (last accessed July 8, 2020).

20. Angela L. Duckworth & Christopher Peterson, *Grit: Perseverance and Passion for Long-Term Goals,* 92 J, PERSONALITY & SOC. PSYCHOL. 1087, 1087 (2007).

21. Katherine Von Culin et al., *Unpacking Grit: Motivational Correlates of Perseverance and Passion for Long-Term Goals,* 9 J. POSITIVE PSYCHOL. 306, 306 (2014).

22. *Id.*

23. *Id.* at Ch. 6.

24. Von Culin, *supra* note 21.

25. *Id.*

26. ANGELA DUCKWORTH, GRIT: THE POWER OF PASSION AND PERSEVERANCE (Scribner 2018) (2016).

27. *Id.*

28. *Id.* at Ch. 7.

29. *Id.*

30. *Id.* at Ch. 5.

31. *Id.*

32. Milana L. Hogan, *Non-Cognitive Traits That Impact Female Success in BigLaw* (unpublished EdD dissertation, University of Pennsylvania) (2013).

33. *See* Ch. 7 for more information about fixed and growth mindsets.

34. DUCKWORTH, *supra* note 26, at 117–19.

35. *Id.* at 118.

36. *Id.* at 101–16.

37. JOSEPH JAWORSKI, SYNCHRONICITY: THE INNER PATH OF LEADERSHIP 118 (Betty Sue Flowers ed., Berrett-Koehler Publisher, Inc. 1996). Joseph John Campbell was an American professor of literature at Sarah Lawrence College who worked in comparative mythology and comparative religion.

38. David Palmiter et al., *The Road to Resilience,* AMERICAN PSYCHOLOGICAL ASSOCIATION (Feb. 1, 2020), http://www.apa.org/helpcenter/road-resilience.aspx.

39. *Id.*

40. GEORGE E. VAILLANT, AGING WELL: SURPRISING GUIDEPOSTS TO A HAPPIER LIFE (2002), *as quoted in* STEVEN M. SOUTHWICK, RESILIENCE: THE SCIENCE OF MASTERING LIFE'S GREATEST CHALLENGES 6 (Cambridge University Press 2012).

41. STEVEN M. SOUTHWICK, RESILIENCE: THE SCIENCE OF MASTERING LIFE'S GREATEST CHALLENGES 8–11 (Cambridge University Press 2012).

42. *Id.* at 11.

43. *Id.*

44. *Id.*

45. *Id.* at 21.

46. *Id.* at 28.

47. *Id.* at 21.

48. *Id.* at 141.

49. *Id.*

50. *Id.* at 147.

51. *Id.* at 150–52.

52. Dr. Larry Richards, *Building Lawyer Resilience,* LAWYER BRAIN, http://www.lawyerbrain.com/our-services/building-lawyer-resilience (last visited July 22, 2020).

53. *Id.*

54. Ashby Jones, *The Third-Year Dilemma: Why Firms Lose Associates,* WALL ST. J. (Jan. 4, 2006), https://www.wsj.com/articles/SB113571843977932357.

55. Patrick R. Krill et al., *The Prevalence of Substance Use and Other Mental Health Concerns Among American Attorneys,* 10 J. ADDICTION MED. 46, 46 (2016).

56. *Id.* at 50.

57. *Id.* at 51.

58. *Id.* at 50.

59. Todd D. Peterson & Elizabeth W. Peterson, *Stemming the Tide of Law Student Depression: What Law Students Need to Learn from the Science of Positive Psychology,* 9 Yale J. Health Pol'y & Ethics 357, 358 (2009).

60. Dr. Larry Richard, *Resilience and Lawyer Negativity,* Lawyer Brain Blog (Sept. 19, 2012), http://www .lawyerbrainblog.com/2012/09/resilience-and-lawyer-negativity/.

61. Jason M. Satterfield et al., *Law School Performance Predicted by Explanatory Style,* 15 Behavioral Sci. and the Law 95, 100 (1997).

62. *Id.*

63. Martin E. P. Seligman et al., *Why Lawyers Are Unhappy,* 23 Cardozo L. Rev. 33, 41–42 (2001).

64. *Id.* at 47.

65. Elle Allison, Renewal Coaching Fieldbook: How Effective Leaders Sustain Meaningful Change (Jossey-Bass 2011).

66. *Id.* at 49.

67. Duckworth, *supra* note 26.

68. *Id.* at Ch. 7.

69. *Id.* at Ch. 12.

70. *Id.* at 170.

71. Salvadore Maddi, *The Personality Construct of Hardiness,* 51 Consulting Psychol. J. 83 (1999).

72. *Id.* at 87–89.

73. *Id.* at 110–16.

74. *Id.* at 116–19.

75. *Id.* at 124–28.

76. Angela Duckworth, *Grit Scale,* Angela Duckworth (2020), http://angeladuckworth.com/grit-scale/.

Chapter 9 — Setting Goals

You need a plan to build a house. To build a life, it is even more important to have a plan or goal.

Zig Ziglar[1]

Purpose

Encourage the use of goal-setting techniques to create meaningful and achievable personal, professional, and organizational goals.

Learning Objectives

At the end of this chapter, you should be able to:

- Explain the importance of setting goals.
- Describe some best practices for setting goals.
- Use the SMART method for goal setting.
- Describe the potential impact of goal setting on unethical behavior.

Discussion

INTRODUCTION

If you are in law school, you probably know something about setting goals. After all, you graduated from high school and then chose, attended, and graduated from college with the stellar academic record necessary to be admitted to law school. These are terrific accomplishments. In looking at the path you took educationally, you may have set some of the academic goals for yourself; other goals may have come through family expectations, insight from mentors, or even peer pressure. It is interesting to consider whether you intentionally set the goal of law school or attended by default. Some of you came to law school with career-oriented goals such as getting a job in an AmLaw 100 firm. This is a worthy goal, but you may discover such a path is not the best fit for you, and may not address all that you need or want in life. Whether your experience with setting goals is robust or minimal, the ability to set goals is an important skill. Effective leaders set goals for both personal and professional achievements. Learning how to set meaningful goals has tremendous power and can change your life. Setting goals is not difficult, but it does take time, thought, and, sometimes, a team.

In 1969, while a complete unknown in Hollywood, Bruce Lee wrote a letter to himself in which he set out personal and professional goals:

My Definite Chief Aim

I, Bruce Lee, will be the first highest paid Oriental super star in the United States. In return, I will give the most exciting performances and render the best of quality in the capacity of an actor. Starting in 1970 I will achieve world fame and from then onward till the end of 1980 I will have in my possession $10,000,000. I will live the way I please and achieve inner harmony and happiness.

Bruce Lee
Jan. 1969

These were bold and confident aspirations, but they were also specific and vivid. In just four sentences, he laid out his objectives, made a deal with himself, and kept his word. In just four years, he achieved every one of these goals. In just four years, he tragically died.

WHY SET GOALS?

Life without goals is like a road trip with no destination. You may be enjoying the trip, but you have no idea where you are going. Without some sense of where your intended destination lies, you likely will spend a lot of time and money meandering. By contrast, knowing where you want to go helps you create an intentional, purpose-driven life. You may still have detours or ultimately change destinations, but you have some sense of what you really want.

How much time do you spend thinking about what you want in life? When you do think about what you want in life, can you describe your dreams in ways that are real and specific or are your plans vague? Goals can cover a wide range of topics, from the weighty — "I want to start a foundation to provide clean water in my community" — to those purely for fun — "I want to run a marathon dressed like a banana." Unless you identify goals, however, you are unlikely to achieve them. It can help to think of goals that cover different aspects of your life, including financial goals, fitness or health goals, and relationship goals. Do you want to climb a mountain? Do you want to stand on all seven continents or read every word written by Jane Austen? Do you want to speak multiple languages? Goals focus your attention on what you want and ways in which you want to live your life. Individual goals are important because they help you with your own contributions and aims. A key part of living the life you want is spending time thinking about and identifying your goals.

Setting goals at work is important for professional development and success. An important step in professional goal setting is understanding how your employer measures success in her employees. If hours billed is the metric by which young associates are measured, developing business will not help you at this year's annual review. Developing business may be a desirable long-term or personal goal, but it will not help you advance in this particular firm if it takes time away from billable work. As you set work goals, you should ask the partner(s) evaluating you what benchmarks they will use to evaluate your work as an associate. It is hard to succeed if you do not know the rules.

Not all work goals, however, are designed for the job you have now; some are designed to lead you to the job you want. Your first job may be a wonderful entrance into the legal profession, but as you learn more your objectives may change. Some professional goals help you move to the next phase of your career. Identifying skills or connections necessary to move in-house or to a different firm can help you when you are ready for the next step.

Goal setting is just as important to organizations. Without clear objectives and desires, the firm, or a team within the firm, does not function as effectively. Some law firms actually have goal-setting or strategic vision retreats; others are less intentional about spending time to set goals. You may have already been involved in a goal-setting session within a student organization to plan for activities in the upcoming term or year. You also may have experienced frustration with student organizations that did not set goals or create steps to accomplish their plans. Even worse, you may have been the one who stepped in to save the day when others failed to set goals and plans as promised. Setting organizational goals and then establishing interim steps or team goals is critical to efficient operations of organizations.

Team goals help the group understand where the work is going, what the objectives are, how each person can participate, and how success will be measured on a given project or within a certain department. Some firms have goal-setting or vision-casting workshops to help delineate goals for the coming year. This time away from the daily grind allows everyone to participate in setting the vision for what will be achieved. Doing this exercise as a retreat also provides focus and time to work *on* the business rather than just *in* the business. In other words, it can be difficult to identify big picture objectives when you are at your desk trying to bill time. Stepping away, physically and mentally, provides space for big dreams. Moreover, the process of goal setting together helps every team member feel more invested in the team's goals. Discussing where you want the team to go provides opportunities to be heard and validation of different perspectives, which can also boost morale.

Basketball player Michael Jordan wrote the following about goal setting in his book, *I Can't Accept Not Trying: Michael Jordan on the Pursuit of Excellence*:

> I approach everything step by step. . . . I had always set short-term goals. As I look back, each one of the steps or successes led to the next one. When I got cut from the varsity team as a sophomore in high school, I learned something. I knew I never wanted to feel that bad again. . . . So I set a goal of becoming a starter on the varsity. That's what I focused on all summer. When I worked on my game, that's what I thought about. When it happened, I set another goal, a reasonable, manageable goal that I could realistically achieve if I worked hard enough. . . . I guess I approached it with the end in mind. I knew exactly where I wanted to go, and I focused on getting there. As I reached those goals, they built on one another. I gained a little confidence every time I came through.
>
> . . . . If [your goal is to become a doctor] . . . and you're getting Cs in biology then the first thing you have to do is get Bs in biology and then As. You have to perfect the first step and then move on to chemistry or physics.
>
> Take those small steps. Otherwise you're opening yourself up to all kinds of frustration. Where would your confidence come from if the only measure of success was becoming a doctor? If you tried as hard as you could and didn't become a doctor, would that mean your whole life was a failure? Of course not.
>
> All those steps are like pieces of a puzzle. They all come together to form a picture. . . . Not everyone is going to be the greatest. . . . But you can still be considered a success. . . . Step by step, I can't see any other way of accomplishing anything.[2]

THE IMPORTANCE OF A WRITTEN GOAL

While identifying goals is good, writing them down is even better. Several neuropsychological reasons explain why written goals are more likely to be achieved. As Mark Murphey wrote in *Forbes*:

Writing things down happens on two levels: external storage and encoding. External storage is easy to explain: you're storing the information contained in your goal in a location (e.g. a piece of paper) that is very easy to access and review at any time. You could post that paper in your office, on your refrigerator, etc. It doesn't take a neuroscientist to know you will remember something much better if you're staring at a visual cue (aka reminder) every single day.

But there's another deeper phenomenon happening: encoding. Encoding is the biological process by which the things we perceive travel to our brain's hippocampus where they're analyzed. From there, decisions are made about what gets stored in our long-term memory and, in turn, what gets discarded. Writing improves that encoding process. In other words, when you write it down it has a much greater chance of being remembered.[3]

The process of writing things down correlates with improved retention of information. Neuropsychologists attribute this to what they call the "generation effect."[4] The generation effect suggests that we remember things we create better than things we read. In other words, when we generate the idea or content, our brains hold onto that information longer and more effectively. This explains why taking notes in class helps you remember the concepts better; you decided what was important as you listened and then created a written version of the important things being said. Writing goals down capitalizes on the generation effect. With goal setting, you can access the generation effect twice — first, when you generate or visualize the goal and second, when you write it down.[5]

Writing your goals is good; revisiting and sharing them is better. Professor Gail Matthews, a psychology professor at Dominican University in California, conducted a study on setting and writing goals.[6] Her sample group included 267 participants from all walks of life and different geographic areas. Dr. Matthews found that people with written goals were 42 percent more likely to achieve them. The study also compared whether actively engaging with goals increased the likelihood of success. To test this, Dr. Matthews divided the participants into five groups, each assigned a different method for handling their goals.[7]

Group 1 was asked to think about their goals and rate the importance of that goal using various criteria.

Groups 2-5 were asked to write their goals before rating their importance.

Group 3 wrote and rated goals but also formulated action commitments.

Group 4 formulated action commitments but also sent their written goals and action commitments to a supportive friend.

Group 5 did the Group 4 steps but also were sent weekly reminders to email quick progress reports to their friend.

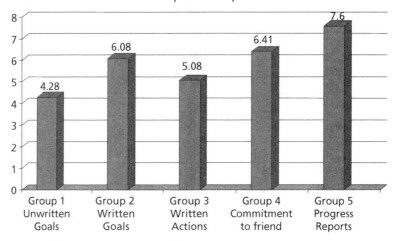

Mean Goal Achievement
Group 5 > Groups 4,3,2,1
Group 4 > Groups 3,1
Group 2 > Group 1

All participants had notable success with achieving goals. Even those who merely identified goals boasted a 42 percent achievement rate. The Group 5 participants, however, had a stunning 76 percent achievement rate for their goals, suggesting that active engagement and an accountability partner played vital roles in success. While 42 percent of the goal identifiers achieved at higher rates than those who did not set goals, Dr. Matthews's study suggests that the more active the goal setter is in thinking and acting on goals, the more likely the goal is to be achieved.[8]

BETTER GOAL SETTING

Many of us have set goals that we did not achieve.[9] While the amount of effort we put into the goal could be why we failed, it may be the goal itself that was the problem. To achieve what you want, you need to create more attainable goals. It turns out that the way you create and identify your goal matters. Goals should be specific, measurable, and vivid. Compare, for example, a goal to look better by losing weight with a goal of losing ten pounds in two months. The first goal is ill-defined and subjective. How much weight? When? Who will decide whether you look better? By contrast, a ten-pound weight loss is measurable within a time increment of two months. You can verify whether the second goal is achieved or not. In a professional setting, "have more client contact" is vague; "call and/or meet in person with four clients each quarter" is specific and measurable.

Goals that are so vivid that you can visualize them are also more likely to be achieved. Some financial advisors suggest that you save money by putting funds into a named account, such as "Hawaii fund" or "house down payment fund." Putting funds toward a specific and desirable goal encourages saving because you want to go to Hawaii and can imagine your trip there. Vision boards can help with vivid goals, as they use images as part of the depiction of the goal. Cutting out a magazine photo of a beautiful Hawaiian beach makes your vacation goal more real every time you look at the image. Whether the goal picture is clear in your head or you use physical images to make it real, if you can "see" it, you are more likely to achieve it. To test whether your goal is specific enough, consider sharing that goal with a supportive friend, and ask if the friend will be able to tell when you achieved the goal.

While vision boards and goal-setting sessions can help develop achievable goals, another way is to use the SMART goal-setting method.[10] SMART goals are

SPECIFIC

MEASURABLE

ACHIEVABLE

REALISTIC

TIMELY

Each attribute contributes to setting attainable goals.[11] Specificity means a goal that is concrete, detailed, focused, and well defined. Bruce Lee set a specific financial goal of having $10 million in the bank by a date certain. To see if your goal is specific enough, consider asking these questions about your goal:

What am I going to do?
Why is this important for me to do?
Who is going to do what?

To see if a goal is measurable, look at how you will compare where you are now to where you will be when the goal is accomplished — it is the standard used for comparison. For example, a goal to increase revenue by $5,000 per month is measurable compared to a goal to "improve our cash flow." In deciding how you will measure your achievement, you might ask:

How will I know that the change has occurred?
Can the measurements be obtained?

Achievable goals can be accomplished in a given time frame with available resources. Running the Disney Princess Marathon involves knowing the date of the race, owning a good pair of running shoes, and having a set amount of time to train. It may mean paying the entry fee, registering, and being able to get to Florida. To know if a goal is achievable, you need to ask:

> Do I understand the limitations and constraints?
> Can we do this with the resources we have?
> Has anyone ever done this successfully?
> Is this possible?

While we encourage you to dream big, goals need to be realistic so that you can get the job done with resources that you have. If you do not have running shoes, you either need to have the resources to get them or be willing to run the race barefoot. You need to know:

> Do I have the resources available to achieve this objective?
> Do I need to revisit priorities to make this happen?
> Is it possible to achieve this objective?

The "timely" attribute combines multiple different concepts. You need to know whether this is the right time for you to work on this goal, and that may involve deciding if it is a "now" goal or a "later" goal. Similarly, you need to decide whether you have the time or are willing to make the time for this goal. If you just started a new job, your goal of climbing Mount Everest may need to wait until you have more vacation time. The goal also needs to be timely for the environment, requiring you to ask questions such as "Are market conditions right?" for the goal. If the housing inventory in your price range is limited, it may not be the best time to buy your first house. When each new listing hits the market with numerous offers over the list price, an inexperienced home buyer might get caught in the excitement of a bidding war and over-commit.

These filters are not meant to dissuade you from setting and achieving goals, even if they feel big or improbable. What they do provide is a structure for identifying and achieving goals that enhances your likelihood of success. Using the SMART goal framework provides a toolkit for creating goals that you are likely to achieve because you have thought through what you need to make the goal a reality. There are other approaches to setting meaningful goals. Find one that works for you and put it to use.

TIME FRAME FOR GOALS

While some people discuss goal setting in terms of where they want to be in five or ten years, that may be too distant a time frame for meaningful goals.[12] Think about where you were ten years earlier. If you are in law school now, ten years ago you were likely a 13-year-old, dealing with middle school drama and hormones. The goals of that teenager probably would not apply to you at your current age. Even five years ago, you were either just starting college or had not even moved into the dorm. The truth is that our world changes quickly, so setting goals more than about three years in the future may not work. One way to think about goals, then, is to consider where you want to be in three years. To be there in three years, where do you need to be in two years? In one year? In six months? In three months? Breaking down goals into these chunks can help you identify what steps need to happen to get you to the ultimate goal. As the old joke goes, "How do you eat an elephant? One bite at a time!" Similarly, if you want to be out of debt in three years, you need to identify what that would look like two-thirds of the way there. Have you paid off high interest credit cards? Were you able to take a part-time job or work more hours at the firm? By contrast, the three-month goal may be to have made a spreadsheet of each debt and to have called each creditor, asking for a more favorable interest rate. Ironically, many of the three-year goals can be accomplished earlier because of the methodical identification of steps needed to reach the goal.

Not all goals are long-term goals; some are short-term or mid-term goals. If you want to run a half-marathon (assuming a basic level of fitness), there are training programs that take only 12 weeks from decision to starting line. If you want to cook meals at home three days a week, you can accomplish that goal in week one. It can be helpful to set goals that you accomplish in different time frames. Having a consistent sense of motivation and accomplishment lends to your sense of contentment and development. Checking a goal off your list as "done" increases a sense of mastery; you don't always want to wait a year or more to experience that satisfaction.

Whatever time frame you choose, set a time to revisit your goals.[13] For those who find comfort in planning, having a document that categorizes your goals from short term to long term can be part of your "to do" list, reviewed daily or weekly.[14] Perhaps it is a quarterly reminder on your calendar to have coffee with your mentor to review your goals. For some, setting New Year's resolutions is part of a periodic review of your life and your goals. Whatever the method, make reflection on your life and goals, as well as a review of your progress and status on each, a part of your routine.

THE ETHICAL COST OF GOAL SETTING

Goal setting works to motivate employees and improve performance, but negative consequences are possible as well. "Unethical behavior may often be the result of breakdowns in individuals' moral reasoning, which can be impacted by supervisory practices such as goal-setting."[15] One of the most infamous displays of unethical behavior in business led to the collapse of Enron Corporation. Leading up to filing for bankruptcy, $320 million in bonus payments and other special cash distributions were paid to Enron executives in accordance with performance-based programs. Prosecutors argued that the executives' unethical decisions and behavior (setting up shell entities to hide financial losses, etc.) could be traced to large bonuses paid based on the financial performance of the organization.[16] The corruption that ruined lives and toppled a global powerhouse organization ensued from incentivized, performance-based goal setting in an environment devoid of ethical leadership at the top.

Goal setting that is too aggressive can lead to unethical behavior in the workplace, which might occur without conscious awareness (or at least until it is too late). Research supports the "notion that goal-setting impacts ethical decisions by influencing individuals' perceptual weighing of costs and benefits of engaging in unethical behavior."[17] In an effort to achieve a stated goal, it is easier to justify bad behavior or to rationalize moral disengagement, especially if the personal stakes are high, such as when a million-dollar fee is on the line or when you are concerned about losing your job.

Research also indicates that ethical behavior requires more energy and uses more cognitive resources, which can be a concern when a person is already operating at capacity.[18] Goals are designed to increase effort and performance, which occupies a person's attention and diverts those cognitive resources away from evaluating the morality of work. The propensity to neglect ethical issues is especially acute when an individual's cognitive resources are already taxed. Exhausted or stressed individuals are more susceptible to behaving unethically *not* because they are immoral but because they tend to be distracted and neglect to think about ethical considerations. This can be especially acute when individuals are consumed with chasing challenging goals with individualized consequences.

"[T]hose committing corrupt acts in organizations are often no more ill-intentioned than those who lead saintly organizational lives."[19] Recognizing the potential for unethical behavior in all individuals is an important first step. As part of goal-setting protocols, organizations should create and implement policies, practices, and procedures to set ethical boundaries and to hold people accountable.[20] Setting reasonable goals, emphasizing the importance of ethical conduct, and monitoring *how* goals are achieved will reduce the likelihood that an organization experiences unintended consequences of goal setting.[21]

CONCLUSION

Whatever your intention for today or tomorrow and whatever your phase of life, the process of setting goals helps you focus on what is important to you. Goal setting helps you identify where you want your life to go and to think meaningfully about how to get there. Leaders who set goals can inspire the team to perform better, achieve more for the organization, and have happier, more productive employees.

Exercise

Identify Your Goals

Be prepared to write down a specific goal you want to achieve in three years. Think about the specific steps it will take to achieve that goal and write down where in the process you want to be in two years, then in one year, then in six months, then in three months.

Journal Prompts

1. Write down a short-term goal, perhaps something that can be achieved in the next three to six months. Using the SMART analysis, how will you ensure that you meet this goal?

2. Is it difficult for you to set goals? Why or why not?

   a. If it is difficult for you to set goals, what might be holding you back? How might you create a better environment to identify goals and achieve them?

   b. Regardless of whether or not it is difficult to set goals, have you encountered difficulty in achieving them? Why or why not? How might incorporating the SMART analysis help you with achieving them?

3. Accountability in goal setting:

   a. Who would be a good accountability partner for goal setting?

   b. What would you ask that person to do to help hold you accountable?

   c. Is that person also in a position to point out any feasibility issues or ethical concerns? If yes, consider how to ask for that feedback.

Endnotes

1. Attributed to Zig Ziglar, *in* Unleash Your Hidden Potential (Bhavin J. Shah & Avinash Poddar) (Notion Press 2017). Ziglar was well known as a motivational speaker, specifically for assisting and training employees in sales-based companies.
2. Michael Jordan, I Can't Accept Not Trying: Michael Jordan on the Pursuit of Excellence (HarperCollins 1994).
3. Mark Murphy, *Neuroscience Explains Why You Need to Write Down Your Goals If You Actually Want to Achieve Them*, Forbes (2018), https://www.forbes.com/sites/markmurphy/2018/04/15/neuroscience-explains-why-you-need-to-write-down-your-goals-if-you-actually-want-to-achieve-them/#7aa2ed527905.
4. *Id.*
5. *Id.*
6. Gail Matthews, Goals Research, summary available at https://www.dominican.edu/sites/default/files/2020-02/gailmatthews-harvard-goals-researchsummary.pdf.
7. *Id.*
8. *Id.*
9. Ashira Prossack, *Struggling to Reach Your Goals? Here's Why*, Forbes (Dec. 29, 2018), https://www.forbes.com/sites/ashiraprossack1/2018/12/29/goal-setting-roadblocks/#45c08c021f19.
10. Paloma Cantero-Gomez, *The 5-Step Road to Achievement*, Forbes (June 20, 2019), https://www.forbes.com/sites/palomacanterogomez/2019/06/20/the-5-steps-road-to-achievement/#6ce59d4084f8.
11. *Id.*
12. Expert Panel, *11 Ways to Establish, And Then Reach, Your Long-Term Goals*, Forbes (Nov. 13, 2018), https://www.forbes.com/sites/forbescoachescouncil/2018/11/13/11-ways-to-establish-and-then-reach-your-long-term-goals/#57ecd1fc7273.

13. Pia Silva, *Why Your Goal Setting Process Is Broken and What to Do About It*, Forbes (Jan. 3, 2018), https://www.forbes.com/sites/piasilva/2018/01/03/why-your-goal-setting-process-is-broken-and-what-to-do-about-it/#77f8c5d97e09.

14. *Id.*

15. Adam Barsky, *Understanding the Ethical Cost of Organizational Goal-Setting: A Review and Theory Development*, 81 J. Bus. Ethics 63–81 (2008).

16. *Id.*

17. *Id.*

18. *Id.*

19. *Id.*

20. Lisa Ordóñez et al., *Goals Gone Wild: The Systematic Side Effects of Overprescribing Goal Setting*, 23 Acad. Mgmt. Persp. 6–16 (2009).

21. *Id.*

<table>
<tr><td>Chapter 10</td><td># Giving and Receiving Feedback</td></tr>
</table>

Chapter 10 — # Giving and Receiving Feedback

The fastest way to change the feedback culture in an organization is for the leaders to become better receivers.

Sheila Heen[1]

Purpose

Improve the giving and receiving of feedback in a constructive manner so that it can be heard, accepted, and integrated into performance and will enrich relationships.

Learning Objectives

At the end of this chapter, you should be able to:

- Give more constructive feedback.
- Describe potential strategies for providing feedback to others in various scenarios.
- Explain feedback triggers and their effect on receiving and incorporating feedback.
- Receive and learn from feedback more effectively.
- Discuss the different roles a coach, mentor, and sponsor can play in your development and advancement.

Discussion

INTRODUCTION

"Constructive criticism" seems like an oxymoron given that criticism suggests there is something wrong that needs improvement. How often does criticism build you up as opposed to inspiring doubt? Sheila Heen and Douglas Stone offered this perspective on feedback in the *Harvard Business Review*: "The [feedback] process strikes at the tension between two core human needs — the need to learn and grow, and the need to be accepted just the way you are."[2] None of us is immune to the need for feedback, and the art of both giving feedback and receiving it is a crucial aspect of leadership and professional development. Leaders need to be able to give feedback so that team members individually or as part of the whole know whether they are on track to meet the team goals. Leaders need to hear feedback from the team to stay in touch with how the project is going and to gauge team morale. Leaders also need feedback from clients and customers to meet client objectives and stay in touch with the market. Feedback plays a crucial role from a business perspective because "[i]t improves performance, develops talent, aligns expectations, solves problems, guides promotion and pay, and boosts the bottom line."[3]

The best leaders ask for more feedback, as research by Jack Zenger and Joseph Folkman demonstrates. In a study of over 50,000 executives, Zenger and Folkman found that "leaders who ranked at the top 10% in asking for feedback were rated, on average, at the 86th percentile in overall leadership effectiveness."[4] Feedback is also tied to employee engagement. In a separate study of over 22,000 leaders, Folkman found that when employees discovered their leaders did not give honest feedback, the employees reported the leaders showed a lack of interest in the employees' work.[5] Conversely, a leader rated in the top 10 percent at giving honest feedback was ranked by his team for his engagement in the top 23 percent.[6] A leader who wants feedback to take root in the culture needs to ask for it. As Ed Batista noted, "We can't just sit back and wait for feedback to be offered, particularly when we are in a leadership role. If we want feedback to take root in the culture, we need to explicitly ask for it."[7]

A leader who does not provide feedback is as problematic as one who gives only harsh or painful feedback. Team members need to understand what is expected of them and whether or not they are meeting those expectations. Good leaders, then, develop feedback skills that provide honest input, help motivate team members, and keep them on track.[8]

Just as leaders need to hone their skills in this area, team members need to hear and accept criticism or feedback in a positive way.[9] Hearing direct commentary on your performance can enhance your individual development and make you a more valuable part of the team.[10] Think about watching a professional sporting event. When a player returns to the bench, a coach will often walk over and talk to the player about what just happened on the field. You can see the coach reviewing a play or offering comments on how to adjust or course correct the situation. Players may occasionally demonstrate anger while being coached, but more often, you see them studying the images and listening intently as the coach, who has a different, broader perspective, helps the player improve. A player who will not listen is labeled "not coachable" and does not stay on the team for long. When a willing listener gets useful feedback, both the individual and the team benefit.

This same principle is true in law school. On moot court or mock trial teams, small groups of students work closely with an advocacy professor to hone their advocacy skills. To prepare for the competition, the team will meet frequently to try the case or practice the argument. The advocacy professor will frequently start and stop the exercise in order to coach the student regarding the best way to present or phrase an argument. The best teams do not necessarily have the students that are most naturally talented regarding advocacy. Instead, winning teams are frequently comprised of good students who are willing to listen, learn, and incorporate their advocacy professor's feedback into their next presentation. Like the "uncoachable" athlete, exceptionally talented students who do not listen are not often asked to be on another team.

We often think of feedback as criticism with its negative connotation, which may explain why people are reluctant to even hear feedback or to accept constructive criticism. The process of providing feedback, though, does not always mean corrective action. Highlighting past conduct that should be repeated will reinforce good behaviors, which is as important as addressing undesirable ones that need to be avoided or changed.[11] Just as a tennis player learns the sweet spot on the racquet by feel and sound, a team member will better understand expectations when the good is reinforced and the bad is pointed out in a constructive manner.

This chapter will discuss the art of giving feedback and the process of receiving it. Even though law students are more likely to receive than give feedback, we start with giving feedback because thinking through that delivery will help contextualize how it feels to be on the other side and be the one receiving the feedback. We will also discuss how feedback can feel hurtful — the "triggers" of feedback — and how to inoculate against it. Next, we examine how to build upon feedback to be continually learning through "feedback loops." Finally, we discuss the importance of finding a coach, mentor, and sponsor for you and your career.

GIVING FEEDBACK

Learning to give feedback takes effort, but it is an important endeavor for your team to perform effectively in achieving client and firm goals.[12] Not every first effort is successful, particularly when the lawyers or employees are young or the subject matter is new or challenging. As a leader, your responsibility is to ensure quality work is delivered in a timely manner. Given the thin skin of lawyers, however, providing feedback in an effective way can be challenging.[13] Good leaders learn to give feedback in a way that helps the hearer not only absorb the message but also want to do better.[14] Advice offered by Coach Bud Grant: "If you have something critical to say to a player, preface it by saying something positive. That way when you get to the criticism, at least you know he'll be listening."[15] There are several keys to giving feedback that people want to hear — some are systemic and some are personal, but all require thoughtful preparation.

Environment Matters

The best feedback comes from a leader who creates an environment of trust, where it is safe to make mistakes, speak up, and collaborate without concern that novel and untested ideas will be met with scorn or derision.[16] A leader who publicly denigrates the ideas of others on the team will find team members who are reluctant to speak up because they fear public ridicule.[17] If the leadership does not create an atmosphere of safety and relationships built on trust, the likely alternative is a climate of blame and shame.[18] In an atmosphere of trust, leaders also remove obstacles that would keep a team member from moving toward the goal.[19] When you build a solid relationship as a leader, the team is more likely to listen to and heed your comments.[20]

Consider this situation: The senior partner of a law firm gathered several junior partners and associates to brainstorm about how to land the real estate business of a local company. As different team members would offer suggestions about business development, the senior partner would dismiss the ideas as either too expensive or unworkable. By the time the partner shot down the fourth or fifth idea, the team members clammed up. It was clear that the partner was not actually interested in hearing their suggestions or having a meaningful exchange of ideas. The younger lawyers left the meeting feeling discouraged, and there was no apparent plan on the table to land the real estate business.

Contrast this with a different approach that the partner could have taken. Rather than dismissing ideas, the partner offered encouraging words and asked thoughtful follow-up questions about cost or feasibility. By asking a question such that the lawyer proposing the idea had to think of the answer and whether it was a possibility for the firm, the younger lawyers quickly grasped that the scope of work was complex and called for a creative solution. As the conversation developed, the lawyers worked collaboratively to address feasibility and execution concerns in the proposal. The senior partner concluded the meeting by assigning responsibilities in executing the plan. The team was engaged and energized by the process and felt that everyone had contributed to solving the problems identified in the feedback session, with everyone feeling that the plan was much better because of its collaborative nature. By offering criticism in a constructive environment — here through carefully worded questions — the senior partner guided the team through a constructive problem-solving exercise, and no one left feeling that they had been unfairly criticized.

Self-Control Matters

Choose the time and place to give your feedback so that your response is objective and not emotional.[21] It can be very frustrating to assign a project — especially an important one — and have inferior work turned in or the project derailed by a missed deadline. Giving feedback in that setting, for example, is unlikely to be effective because it can catch the recipient off guard. While we cannot always schedule an appointment for feedback when a project is on a tight deadline, setting aside time for meaningful feedback is a good investment. Both the giver and receiver of the feedback are more prepared for the conversation, and emotion is not the driver. This more likely affords a better opportunity for the recipient to take the advice to heart rather than respond defensively. By the same token, the leader who gives feedback in a productive setting is more likely to be heard by the team. When a leader cannot be trusted to give feedback calmly and factually but chooses instead to yell or act out, the team suffers. The inability to give input to team members and treat them like professionals damages the effectiveness of the team.[22] Team members are more likely to discount the feedback because the leader's conduct undermines its validity.[23]

We have all received reactionary feedback that, while needed, may have been unnecessarily harsh. Email and text messaging are notoriously prone to tone issues, and that is exacerbated in the feedback context. For example, the associates working on a business deal exchange emails with proposed changes to the contract. The associate for the seller seeks an indemnity clause highly favorable to her client. Without consulting the senior partner, the buyer's associate attorney agrees. Minutes after reading the email, the senior partner storms into the associate's office, furious that he was not consulted about a potentially significant change in the terms. He yells at the associate for making this concession without his or the client's approval. While the criticism is valid — the associate should have consulted the partner and potentially the client — the associate is unlikely to receive that criticism well because of the delivery. As such, the associate may discount what the partner said because of how the partner said it. Had the partner taken time to cool off and calmly explain why an indemnity provision was a significant deal term, the associate might have learned a valuable lesson and been less likely to make a similar mistake in the future.

Content Matters

Just as the "when" matters with feedback, so does the "what." There are several aspects to good feedback.[24] How you deliver the message and what you say matters.[25] Bill Walsh, head coach of the San Francisco 49ers, noted, "People thrive on positive reinforcement. They can take only a certain amount of criticism, and you may lose them altogether if you criticize them in a personal way. . . . [Y]ou can make a point without being personal. Don't insult or belittle your people. Instead of getting more out of them you will get less."[26]

There are several aspects to delivering the message well. Some leaders advocate mixing positive feedback with the negative, claiming that if you "sweeten the pot," the listener is more likely to pay attention.[27] You can often find something positive to add — even a stopped clock is right twice a day. Pointing out specific good behaviors that you want repeated serves as positive reinforcement and makes it more likely that they will be repeated.[28] For example, if the work was not of the quality you wanted but

was turned in by the deadline, reinforce that you appreciate the team member's attention to timeliness. This will not be the last deadline you face and having a team member
who understands the importance of a deadline may save another project. Others, however, caution that you should be direct in what you want to say and avoid the sandwich
of praise, criticism, praise.[29] Praise that is simply to salve feelings dilutes your message,
and neither party leaves satisfied. The leader often feels that she held back, and the
receiver does not understand the real issue.[30] You will need to evaluate which style
works best for you and your team.

When you need to correct a team member, do not only identify what went wrong,
but also offer concrete suggestions or comments on how to fix it. Telling a young lawyer
that her analysis was wrong does not help her understand why she was off track or what
she could do about it. Pointing out deficient conduct without a way forward can lead
team members to feel hopeless; if they knew how to do it right, they probably would
have done so in the first place. A young lawyer who routinely arrives late to the office
may not understand the firm's expectation for when the work day begins. In the legal
profession, it is often true that if you are not early, you are late. Help the young lawyer
explore strategies for planning ahead, setting alarms, creating time buffers — whatever
strategy will get her where she needs to be on time. It may also be important for the
young lawyer to understand the effect being late has on the team. If the associate is late,
the team cannot function as effectively.

Timing Matters

Effective leaders know when to speak and when to be quiet. Feedback — positive
or negative — that is targeted, well framed, and delivered at the right moment can make
or break your team.[31] Well-timed words of support and congratulations are terrific and
an important aspect of reinforcing positive behavior. By contrast, you need to gauge
when a team member will be able to hear and absorb criticism — even if it is justified.[32]
Leading means evaluating whether you need to correct conduct or provide moral support until you can have a more targeted discussion. Kicking someone when they are
down rarely works well, but ignoring a team member who is struggling is not effective
leadership either. The ability to discern the proper time and place to deliver feedback is
a skill that must be mastered in order to be a great leader.

Trials are stressful. The trial team has to juggle many different aspects all at the
same time — examining witnesses, watching for objectionable testimony, ensuring
that the necessary elements of the law are all being met, and preserving the record for
appeal, to name a few. In the midst of this, inexperienced trial lawyers may miss crucial
statements or objections during a witness's testimony. If the experienced trial lawyer
can correct the mistake to benefit the client, that should be done; but if the experienced
trial lawyer notes a mistake and decides to chastise the less experienced lawyer in the
middle of the trial when nothing can be done, all the feedback will do is discourage him
and distract him from the task at hand. Similarly, if the lawyers lose the trial, moments

after they walk out of the courtroom is probably not the best time to point out all the things that the less experienced lawyer could do better. Instead, waiting for a more appropriate time to review the things that went well and the things that did not in an effort to learn from them will be a more productive conversation.

Compassion Matters

As you give feedback to others, consider all aspects of the situation, which may include cultural issues. The emotional self-control of the person giving the feedback is important, but you should evaluate the emotional state of the person receiving the feedback. An associate who is exhausted from pulling an all-nighter probably is not in an emotional place for a constructive feedback session. Moreover, feedback does not exist in a vacuum, and requires an appreciation for the hearer's background, circumstances, and previous experiences, all of which can play a role in receiving feedback.

RECEIVING FEEDBACK

Let's face it, criticism hurts. While many of us say that we want feedback on our work, we really don't. What we actually want is to be liked and praised and told how wonderful we are. Criticism, by definition, reminds us that we have some work to do, perhaps personally as well as professionally.[33] This can dent our self-worth and ego, but getting better at anything takes feedback from others.[34] How, then, can you prepare yourself both to receive feedback and be able to put that feedback to use? Here are some steps to consider:

Adjust Your Attitude

For many people, it can be difficult to hear criticism without becoming defensive.[35] Many conversations with students (or even associates) about feedback turn into the student explaining why the feedback is wrong or the student is misunderstood, etc. This cuts off the opportunity to learn and may actually keep you from getting the feedback you need to hear. Students are in school to learn, and it would be unfair to expect students to navigate law school without any feedback. But the feedback loop can only succeed when the message can be conveyed without a defensive wall being built.[36] This process starts over when you get to your first law firm job. There is much to learn, and defensive or justifying behavior makes people hesitant to give feedback, which means you miss the chance to improve. If you seem approachable and receptive to feedback, you are more likely to receive valuable advice and learning opportunities. You also create the impression that you are coachable and willing to learn.

When you get your first written assignment feedback during your summer clerkship, ask the supervising attorney what you could have done differently or better. There may be clues written on the document or contained in the "comments" section, but seek additional feedback actively. Rather than giving the impression that you are not a very good writer, your genuine interest suggests a desire to become a better writer. If the feedback already suggests that your work did not meet expectations, try to understand why without defending the work. Even if you do not get the full-time job, you do get the benefit of understanding what a law firm partner is looking for in written work.

Recognize Your Triggers

When you find yourself becoming defensive, angry, flustered, or deflated, you may be experiencing a trigger from your past.[37] You may feel a surge of emotion — your heart pounds, your stomach tightens, your mind races in a million directions — which becomes a distraction and blocks the learning that can come from feedback.[38] In *Thanks for the Feedback*, Douglas Stone and Sheila Heen describe three "triggers" that can become obstacles to growth in the feedback process. If you experience a trigger, you need to address those emotions in order to effectively manage your reactions and engage in the feedback conversation.[39] There are three triggers to watch for:

1. *Truth trigger.* "You're wrong." Somewhere in the feedback something is not right, not helpful, or simply untrue. In response, we feel indignant, wronged, and exasperated.[40]
2. *Relationship trigger.* "Who are you to say that to me?" The feedback is overshadowed by the relationship between the giver and the receiver. We react based on what we believe about the giver or feel toward the giver based on past treatment. Our focus shifts from the feedback itself to the audacity of the person delivering it.[41]
3. *Identity triggers.* "That's not really me . . . is it?" Something about the feedback — right or wrong — causes us to question our identity and our value. We feel overwhelmed, threatened, ashamed, or off balance.[42]

Our reactions to these triggers are not unreasonable, but they keep us from engaging in what could and should be a helpful conversation.[43] If we do not recognize the influence of our triggers, we might discard potentially valuable feedback. We also run the risk of taking to heart feedback that is better left at the curb.[44]

Receiving feedback is a process of sorting and filtering information in a constructive and healthy manner.[45] Information received can help us see a situation from the other person's perspective.[46] The receiver might feel empowered to try new ideas or a different approach that is outside his comfort zone. The person giving feedback may gain understanding about the relationship and why the feedback is perceived as not being helpful. Both parties may see their relationship in a clearer light such that the relationship can be strengthened through an effective feedback process.

Disentangle the "what" from the "who." To combat the relationship trigger, try not to focus on the person giving the feedback.[47] In other words, dissociate that person from the words so that you can hear the feedback without attaching emotion or triggers to it. Even if you do not believe the person giving you feedback can do so appropriately, you may still learn a valuable lesson. Sometimes feedback hurts more because of the close relationship to the person giving you feedback. If this is the case, remember that in a close relationship, the person giving feedback may truly want what is best for you and is not giving feedback to hurt you.

Be a reflective listener. One way to demonstrate you are receptive to feedback (and thus get the right feedback) is to reflect the comments back to the provider. This helps ensure that you heard the message accurately, and often the provider will appreciate that you truly are hearing what he is saying.[48] Rather than using defensive responses, try phrases such as "what I hear you saying is that my analysis needs to be deeper or more robust. I stopped at too shallow a level."[49] This approach gives the provider a chance to agree or to provide more clarity or detail, while at the same time you can quiet the little voice in your brain that wants to argue or deny. Reflecting the comments back is the equivalent of taking a deep breath or counting to ten.[50] It also validates the person giving the feedback.[51] Even if you ultimately do not agree with him, you demonstrate respect for the comments, which can be especially important if the provider is a professor or a boss. Finally, reframing or reflecting the comments helps you understand the other point of view.

Ask clarifying questions. As with reflective listening, asking questions can help make sure that you understand the feedback.[52] This practice keeps the focus on the feedback, not your feelings. You may also want to ask for examples or stories that illustrate the feedback. Hearing specific times or ways that the issue came up can help you process what might need to change. The concrete is usually easier to understand than the abstract.

Check for accuracy. Feedback from one source does not mean the comments are right or uniformly shared by other team members, the client, or your boss. If the comments feel like outliers or are not something you have heard before, you may want to check their reliability with others. In some areas, feedback is based on stylistic preference; the comments may reflect that person's opinion rather than a more universal issue.[53]

Evaluate feedback slowly. Similarly, decide what *you* think about the feedback, and take your time in doing so. Get in the practice of evaluating the feedback slowly.[54] Chew on it for a day or more. Does the criticism ring true; is it something you already knew was a limitation? Does the giver have expertise or credibility to support her observation? Have other people said similar things to you? These are valid considerations to mull over as you evaluate feedback.

Never argue; just say thanks. Your natural tendency may be to turn your "clarifying questions" into an explanation of why you are right.[55] The problem is that even if you are right and the feedback is wrong or off-base, defending yourself signals to the giver that you are unreceptive. You do not want to shut down future feedback or get labeled as "uncoachable" within your organization. The most appropriate response to constructive criticism: "Thank you."

Evolve. When you get feedback that is legitimate and designed to make you a better lawyer or leader, take it to heart.[56]

SEEKING FEEDBACK—THE FEEDBACK LOOP

Part of being a successful leader involves lifelong learning, the process by which you meaningfully continue to improve throughout your life and career. Whether you receive feedback spontaneously or actively seek it, good leaders work feedback into their personal and professional routines. Try asking a close friend or mentor the probing question posed by Sheila Heen: "What's one thing you see me doing (or failing to do) where I am getting in my own way?"[57] This look at your own conduct can lead to a growth phase or *feedback loop*:

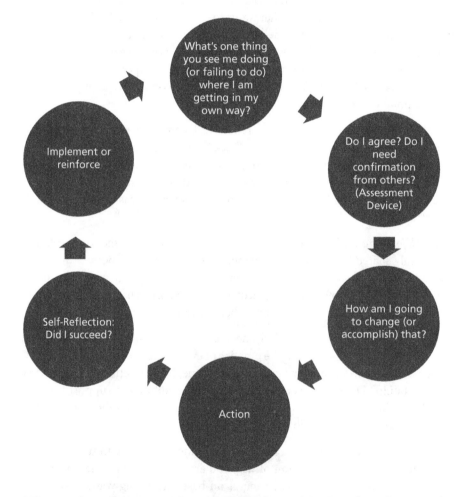

When you hear the answer, ask yourself, "Do I agree? Do I need confirmation from others?" If you do agree with the criticism, ask yourself, "How am I going to change (or accomplish) that?" Next, act on your self-assessment of how to fix the problem. Once you feel you've made progress, ask, "Did I succeed?" You may have made progress but not as much as you want. At this point, you may need to implement again or reinforce behavior. You can continue to grow with the feedback loop by asking the question again or to a different colleague: "What's one thing you see me doing (or failing to do) where I am getting in my own way?" By repeating the process of the feedback loop, you learn more from successive analysis.[58]

This process, while painful or uncomfortable at first, allows you to work actively through issues and create actionable steps to solve problems. Over time, this method of seeking feedback becomes part of your personality as you work constantly on improving.

In law school, each grade you receive provides a reflection point for your academic studies, highlighting where you did and did not do well in a course. Treating these as a one-off reflection after each course, however, keeps you from seeing patterns and maximizing your effectiveness. For example, making your own outline in first-year Property led to a higher grade than when you borrowed someone else's outline for Contracts. You learned that making your own outline helped you learn the material better. The next semester, you made your own outline for each class but also joined a study group for Criminal Law. Discussing hypotheticals and learning with a group deepened your understanding of the issues and also made studying more fun. You did better in Criminal Law than in Constitutional Law, where you studied alone. With each successive semester, you learned what worked best for you, not only in terms of comprehension but also enjoyment. For many law students, this reflective learning continues when they are in practice, holding team meetings where the ideas for a case or a deal are round tabled by a group.

As an associate in a law firm, you can look for more experienced lawyers to mentor you to become a better lawyer. They become ideal candidates to whom you can pose the question, "What's the one thing you see me doing (or failing to do) where I am getting in my own way *at this firm*?" For example, a more senior lawyer might point out that you should arrive each morning before the partners do. These lawyers may see it from the perspective that the early bird gets the worm, and equate early arrival with being an industrious, hard worker. You decide to try it and arrive early every day for a month. You start getting more interesting and challenging assignments as you are the only associate at the firm in the early morning hours. You have more time to meet with senior lawyers when the phones are not ringing and the staff has not arrived. In other words, the suggestion that you arrive early is paying off noticeably. Once your early morning starts become a habit, ask the question again, "What's the one thing you see me doing (or failing to do) where I am getting in my own way *at this firm*?" By turning this feedback loop into a habit, you create a system for career improvement, one useful step at a time. These incremental changes cumulatively provide a greater impact than the individual steps alone.

FIND A COACH, MENTOR, OR SPONSOR

Seeking help from someone with more experience can jumpstart your performance. As in the sports world, a good coach can provide specific constructive suggestions for achieving better results.[59] A good coach bridges the gap between the theory you learned in law school and the practical challenges of the workplace.[60] An experienced coach can guide you as you learn specific skills related to your area of law, can suggest networking opportunities, can offer suggestions on marketing and social media, and can guide you on how to manage the stresses of the profession.[61] By comparison, a mentor is more likely to take a holistic approach, offering guidance on career choices and decisions over an extended period of time.[62] Both coaches and mentors help you help yourself, promoting personal growth and professional development.[63] A sponsor plays a different role and champions you to others. Sponsors use their influence, power, and networks to promote you and connect you with good jobs and lucrative opportunities.[64] All three can serve as role models for you and play critical roles in your life.[65]

When looking for a coach, a mentor, or a sponsor, consider whether one person can realistically fill all three roles. Many young lawyers look first for a coach because of the need for practical help early on. In professional sports, while the team has a head coach, it also utilizes other coaches with special expertise to develop talent. You may find that you want or need to work with different coaches on different areas in your life. You may find a coach in your firm or you may feel more comfortable working with someone outside your office.[66] Your firm may have a formal leadership development program.[67] Even firms without a formal mentoring program or leadership development program may have informal programs or lawyers who are willing to coach or mentor if asked. Identify potential candidates and approach them about working with you.[68] You can also look for opportunities to be coached, mentored, or sponsored by more than one person. To get the relationship started, pick up the phone, write an email, or invite them to lunch.[69] Finding a good match starts by putting yourself out there and respectfully offering to take someone out to lunch and ask some questions. Young lawyers tend to overthink this and worry about being turned down. Even if the person is not in a position to help you, it is still flattering to be asked.

Before entering a coaching or mentoring relationship, set appropriate expectations. A coach or mentor is not meant to do your job for you. A sponsor cannot be expected to deliver the job of your dreams or create a professional reputation for you. Good coaches, mentors, and sponsors will provide you with information, resources, and perspective.[70] They will ask good questions that help you understand yourself and your situation better. Treat them as an investment. They are a trusted source of guidance. The endorsement of established, respected lawyers, and the networking opportunities that go along with these relationships, can be invaluable to your career.[71] Accordingly, nurturing these relationships should be a priority. Be respectful of their time and demands.[72] Be prepared with questions for your coach or mentor — do not expect them to lead the conversation.[73]

Look for ways to make these relationships a two-way street[74] and add value to the relationship. You may be more technologically savvy than an older attorney. If so, offer some help or training on a novel software product. You may be involved in organizations where your coach, mentor, or sponsor would value a speaking invitation. You can and should be a cheerleader for your coach, mentor, or sponsor.[75] Send notes and emails with items of interest or copies of news items where they are featured. Active participation is the essence of any relationship.[76]

You can find coaches, mentors, and sponsors outside the legal profession. Most communities have organizations that host formal leadership development programs. Check with your local chamber of commerce or young professional programs in your area. A number of state bar associations and young lawyers' associations have leadership development programs for lawyers involved in those associations. Joining professional organizations in your community can provide leadership development training as well as provide a network for potential coaches, mentors, and sponsors. When looking for growth, think creatively and resourcefully.

CONCLUSION

The art of giving and receiving feedback can be difficult to master.[77] Like any other skill, becoming proficient in receiving feedback takes time and practice but is well worth the investment in your personal development. Similarly, learning to give feedback effectively can move the task from one you dread to one that, with the right attitude and strategies, can strengthen relationships and improve interactions with others.[78] Effective feedback strategies extend beyond law school and the practice, and can be useful in interactions at home, in the community, or at a social gathering.

Learning to receive feedback in a constructive and positive manner will help you grow as a person and a leader.[79] Hearing feedback can be emotionally charged, especially if unexpected or if the nature of the criticism is personal.[80] By understanding the feedback triggers and learning techniques to allow you to receive feedback in a constructive manner, even hurtful feedback can be helpful. Learning to filter feedback to find the positives or to discard that which is not helpful is an important aspect of the process.[81] Using these techniques to rationally assess the feedback can help you grow and even embrace a regular practice of seeking feedback improvement.[82]

Finally, finding mentors, coaches, and sponsors to provide assistance at various times throughout your career can make all the difference in your success. No matter your current position or season of life, having someone you trust to help you think through situations and give you advice and support is an invaluable asset.

Exercise

How to Say It

Divide into small groups. Each group should come up with phrases that reinforce positive behavior, point out negative behavior, and suggest how to change. Have a scribe in each group write down some of the phrases, and then have each group share its top two or three in each category. Have everyone altogether discuss what they think is or is not effective in terms of feedback.

Journal Prompts

1. Watch Sheila Heen's video, "How to Use Others' Feedback to Learn and Grow." Try out the tip mentioned in Sheila Heen's TEDx Talk — ask a mentor/coach/relative/close friend, "What is one thing you see me doing (or failing to do) where I am getting in my own way?" In your journal, note the following:

   a. their feedback;

   b. how you responded to it in the moment;

   c. whether you agree or need to consult with another; and

   d. if you agree, what is your plan to act on the feedback?

2. Think about a feedback session that you experienced in the past that you remember as a negative experience. After today's discussion about your ability to control how you receive the information, re-analyze that session:

   a. What, if anything, did you constructively take from the experience at the time?

   b. What triggers did you experience and how did they hinder your ability to receive the feedback?

   c. Looking back at that experience, what, if anything, can you constructively take from the experience now?

   d. What, if anything, would you change about how you handled the experience?

3. What are the biggest challenges you face when receiving feedback?

4. When have you been given hurtful but helpful feedback? What did it help you accomplish?

5. How can you learn to give feedback in a more constructive way?

6. Do you have a coach, mentor, and sponsor?

   a. If not, how will you cultivate each?

   b. If yes, how effective have you been at utilizing the skills and advice of each? Why?

Endnotes

1. Interview with Sheila Heen, Lecturer on Law at Harvard Law School (Oct. 4, 2016), *available at* https://www.bcwinstitute.org/blog/use-feedback-strengthen-leadership/. Heen is also the founder of Triad Consulting Group.
2. Shelia Heen & Douglas Stone, *Finding the Coaching in Criticism*, Harv. Bus. Rev. (2014), https://hbr.org/2014/01/find-the-coaching-in-criticism.
3. *Id.*
4. Zack Zenger & Joseph Folkman, *Overcoming Feedback Phobia: Take the First Step*, Harv. Bus. Rev. (Dec. 16, 2013), https://hbr.org/2013/12/overcoming-feedback-phobia-take-the-first-step.
5. Joseph Folkman, *The Best Gift Leaders Can Give: Honest Feedback*, Forbes (Dec. 19, 2013), https://www.forbes.com/sites/joefolkman/2013/12/19/the-best-gift-leaders-can-give-honest-feedback/#54827a8e4c2b.
6. Jack Craven, *Being a Great Leader Means Giving and Receiving Feedback*, Forbes (2018), https://www.forbes.com/sites/forbescoachescouncil/2018/01/16/being-a-great-leader-means-giving-and-receiving-feedback/#26938ebbebc9.
7. Ed Batista, *Building a Feedback-Rich Culture*, Ed Batista Executive Coaching (Dec. 24, 2013), https://www.edbatista.com/2013/12/new-post-at-hbr-building-a-feedback-rich-culture.html.
8. Skye Schooley, *10 Ways to Become a Better Leader*, Business News Daily (Aug. 26, 2019), https://www.businessnewsdaily.com/4991-effective-leadership-skills.html.
9. *See* Nicole Lindsay, *Taking Constructive Criticism Like a Champ*, The Muse (2020), https://www.themuse.com/advice/taking-constructive-criticism-like-a-champ.
10. *Id.*
11. *See Encouraging Expected Behavior, in* MO SW-PBS Team Workbook 149 (2019), *available at* https://pbismissouri.org/wp-content/uploads/2018/08/Tier-1-2018_Ch.-5.pdf.
12. Karen Naumann, *5 Reasons Why Feedback Is Important*, Huff. Post (Dec. 8, 2016), https://www.huffpost.com/entry/5-reasons-why-feedback-is_b_8728332.
13. Larry Teply et al., *Giving Feedback on Practical Legal Skills*, Legal Business World Publications (Feb. 3, 2020), https://www.legalbusinessworld.com/single-post/2020/02/03/Giving-Feedback-on-Practical-Legal-Skills.
14. Georgia Hardavella et al., *How to Give and Receive Feedback Effectively*, Breathe (Dec. 2017), *available at* https://www.ncbi.nlm.nih.gov/pmc/articles/PMC5709796/.
15. Quote attributed to Coach Bud Grant, *in* Creating a Season to Remember (Jack Perconte) (Second Base Pub. 2017).
16. *See* Amy Jen Su, *Do You Really Trust Your Team? (And Do They Trust You?)*, Harv. Bus. Rev. (Dec. 16, 2019), https://hbr.org/2019/12/do-you-really-trust-your-team-and-do-they-trust-you.
17. *Id.*
18. Liz Ryan, *Ten Ways to Build Trust on Your Team*, Forbes (Mar. 17, 2018), https://www.forbes.com/sites/lizryan/2018/03/17/ten-ways-to-build-trust-on-your-team/#a8d6ea424454.
19. Marie Gervais, *Removing Obstacles to Team Success*, Shift Management (2020), https://shiftworkplace.com/removing-obstacles-team-success/.
20. Brian Gallagher, *Making Time for Your Employee*, Milestones (Nov. 18, 2019), https://www.milestonescompany.com/making-time-for-your-employee/.
21. *Giving and Receiving Feedback*, Skills You Need (2020), https://www.skillsyouneed.com/ips/feedback.html.

22. Leah Fessler, *Good Managers Give Constructive Criticism––But Truly Masterful Leaders Offer Constructive Praise*, Quartz at Work (July 22, 2017), https://qz.com/work/1010784/good-managers-give-constructive-criticism-but-truly-masterful-leaders-give-constructive-praise/ (citing Jim Harter & Amy Adkins, *Employees Want a Lot More from Their Managers*, Gallup (Apr. 8, 2015), https://www.gallup.com/workplace/236570/employees-lot-managers.aspx).

23. Roger Schwarz, *The "Sandwich Approach" Undermines Your Feedback*, Harv. Bus. Rev. (Apr. 19, 2013), https://hbr.org/2013/04/the-sandwich-approach-undermin.

24. Jory MacKay, *The 7 Essential Qualities of Effective Feedback*, Zapier (Sept. 5, 2017), https://zapier.com/blog/how-to-give-effective-feedback/.

25. *Id.*

26. Attributed to Bill Walsh, head football coach of the San Francisco 49ers, *available at* https://www.azquotes.com/quote/695992.

27. Jack Zenger & Joseph Folkman, *The Ideal Praise-to-Criticism Ratio*, Harv. Bus. Rev. (Mar. 15, 2013), https://hbr.org/2013/03/the-ideal-praise-to-criticism.

28. *Id.*

29. Schwarz, *supra* note 23.

30. *Id.*

31. Bruce Jones, *How Positive Reinforcement Keeps Employees Engaged*, Harv. Bus. Rev. (Feb. 28, 2017), https://hbr.org/sponsored/2017/02/how-positive-reinforcement-keeps-employees-engaged.

32. *Id.*

33. *Id.*

34. *Id.*

35. Douglas Stone & Sheila Heen, Thanks for the Feedback: The Science and Art of Receiving Feedback Well (2014).

36. *Id.*

37. *Id.*

38. *Id.*

39. *Id.*

40. *Id.*

41. *Id.*

42. *Id.*

43. *Id.*

44. *Id.*

45. *Id.*

46. *Id.*

47. *Id.*

48. *Id.*

49. *Id.*

50. *Id.*

51. *Id.*

52. *Id.*

53. *Id.*

54. *Id.*

55. *Id.*

56. *Id.*

57. *Id.*

58. David Sturt & Todd Nordstrom, *3 Ways You Can Provide a Feedback Loop Employees Will Value*, Forbes (Feb. 19, 2018), https://www.forbes.com/sites/davidsturt/2018/02/09/3-ways-you-can-provide-a-feedback-loop-employees-will-value/#2cd8867567d3.

59. Geertje Tutschka, *Legal Coaching: The New Fish in the Pond*, Legal Business World (Apr. 25, 2019), https://www.legalbusinessworld.com/single-post/2019/04/25/Legal-Coaching-The-New-Fish-in-The-Pond.

60. *Id*

61. *Id.*

62. Allison R. Day, *The Importance of Having a Mentor in the Legal Profession*, Daily Business Rev. (May 29, 2019), https://www.law.com/dailybusinessreview/2019/05/29/the-importance-of-having-a-mentor-in-the-legal-profession/.

63. Kelli Richards, *The Difference Between a Coach and a Mentor,* FORBES (Oct. 15, 2015), https://www.forbes .com/sites/ellevate/2015/10/15/the-difference-between-a-coach-and-a-mentor/#7ccd56467556.

64. Julie Koepsell, *Want to Advance Your Career Faster? Get a Sponsor,* FORBES (Nov. 25, 2018), https:// www.forbes.com/sites/juliekoepsell1/2018/11/25/want-to-advance-your-career-faster-get-a-sponsor/ #6830a92a65ed.

65. "A coach talks to you, a mentor talks with you, and a sponsor talks about you." Catalyst, *Coaches, Mentors, and Sponsors: Understanding the Differences,* NEW YORK: CATALYST (Dec. 11, 2014), https://www.catalyst .org/research/infographic-coaches-mentors-and-sponsors-understanding-the-differences/.

66. Dorie Clark, *Find the Career Coach Who's Right for You,* HARV. BUS. REV. (Mar. 31, 2015), https://hbr.org/ 2015/03/find-the-career-coach-whos-right-for-you.

67. *See, e.g.,* Kathleen Bradley, *Leadership Development That Works,* AMERICAN BAR ASSOCIATION (2018), https://www.americanbar.org/groups/law_practice/publications/law_practice_magazine/2018/ND2018/ ND2018Bradley/.

68. Kate Harrison, *4 Tips for Finding a Career Mentor,* FORBES (Jan. 3, 2018), https://www.forbes.com/sites/ kateharrison/2018/01/03/4-tips-for-finding-a-career-mentor/#300eeec852cf.

69. *Id.*

70. *Id.*

71. Ashira Prossack, *How to Be a Great Mentee,* FORBES (Apr. 27, 2018), https://www.forbes.com/sites/ ashiraprossack1/2018/04/27/how-to-be-a-great-mentee/#5c17bfcf512b.

72. Vineet Chopra & Sanjay Saint, *What Mentors Wish Their Mentees Knew,* HARV. BUS. REV. (Nov. 7, 2017), https://hbr.org/2017/11/what-mentors-wish-their-mentees-knew.

73. *Id.*

74. *Id.*

75. *Id.*

76. *Id.*

77. *See, e.g., Mastering the Art of Giving Feedback,* ADVANCEMENT FORM, https://www.advancementform .com/resources/master-giving-feedback/ (last visited July 22, 2020); Johana Tommervik, *The Art of Giving and Receiving Feedback,* PRINDIT, https://blog.prindit.com/2016/09/20/the-art-of-giving-and-receiving-feedback/ (last visited July 22, 2020).

78. Mind Tools Creative Team, *Giving Feedback: Boosting Your People's Confidence and Ability,* MIND TOOLS (2016), https://www.mindtools.com/pages/article/newTMM_98.htm.

79. Mike Jenner et al., *How to Master the Art of Receiving Feedback,* HAYS (Feb. 4, 2019), https://social.hays .com/2019/02/04/receiving-feedback-work/.

80. *See id.*

81. Courtney Seiter, *How to Give and Receive Feedback at Work: The Psychology of Criticism,* BUFFER BLOG (May 9, 2018), https://buffer.com/resources/how-to-give-receive-feedback-work/.

82. *Id.*

The Importance of Well-Being: Thriving in the Legal Profession

Chapter 11

Forget balance, find harmony. Lady Justice has a set of scales, and we advocate every day to ensure those scales remain fair and balanced for our clients. It makes perfect sense that we might also seek balance in our personal and professional lives. But, in that regard, balance is misleading. It implies that we should have a formula for allocating equal time to work, family, friends, and other personal activities. That thought alone creates a heightened sense of anxiety. Instead, find ways to integrate different parts of your life to reduce the stress of juggling all the activities simultaneously. In music, harmony is described as the art of combining different pitches into chords. Still, a harmony doesn't have to be "harmonious." Harmonization occurs when there is a blending of "tense" and "relaxed" moments.

Victor Flores[1]

Purpose

Introduce the concept of wellness and encourage the development of healthy practices and habits for long-term well-being.

Learning Objectives

At the end of this chapter, you should be able to:

- Describe common factors that make lawyers susceptible to physical and mental illness.
- Find resources for lawyers in need of assistance.

- Discuss the benefits of incorporating physical exercise and wellness practices into your life.
- Develop a plan to balance work and wellness practices in your personal and professional life.

Discussion

INTRODUCTION

Attorneys push themselves mentally and physically in practice, whether dealing with a demanding client, an imminent trial, or an aggressive negotiation, and it is stressful. Some of the pressures are external, stemming from workplace cultures that thrive on high-intensity situations. Other pressures are internal, stemming from the same drive and competitiveness that draw people to the profession. Regardless of its source, stress can have a profound impact on physical and mental well-being. To compound the effect, the same drive that pushes us to succeed makes us reluctant to admit weakness. What lawyer looks across counsel table to the opposing attorney and says, "I am not really ready for trial. I've had a million other things going on." Even within your firm, if you are trying to make partner, you are unlikely to admit that you drink heavily at night to deal with the possibility you might not make the cut.

Studies show that after basic needs such as food and shelter are met, "wellness emerges from nourishing six dimensions of your health: physical, emotional, cognitive, social, spiritual, and environmental."[2] It may seem daunting to balance all these dimensions of health, but they are closely intertwined.[3] Research shows that cumulatively developing each dimension is better than focusing on an individual part. This chapter will divide wellness into two general types: mental health and physical health. The discussion will start with the challenges that lawyers face generally and then discuss steps that you can take to improve each in your daily life.

WHY WELLNESS MATTERS FOR LAWYERS

Study after study demonstrates the toll stress takes on attorneys physically and mentally.[4] Lawyers suffer mental health issues, drug and alcohol addiction, and heart disease at a higher rate than the average population.[5] Stress drives or worsens many of these health conditions.[6] Lawyers not only worry about their own career advancement, but they also carry the weight of worry for others. Lawyers feel the burden that comes with the professional responsibility for protecting their clients' interests. Lawyers also recognize the profession's obligation to uphold the integrity of our justice system, increase access to justice, maintain public confidence in the judiciary, and more.[7] As such, lawyer wellness impacts not only individual attorneys but their clients, the judicial system, and the broader integrity of the system — all reasons for lawyers to protect their health and wellness.

While practicing law can take a toll, lawyers also get tremendous satisfaction from seeing the difference they can make in the lives of their clients and in their communities. Anecdotally, lawyers tell meaningful stories about people they have helped, but more formalized studies demonstrate high lawyer satisfaction as well. A study of the first women who enrolled in Harvard Law School found that, despite the challenges, *all* of them were satisfied with the decision to become lawyers.[8] This suggests that despite the heightened pressures, lawyers who manage the stress levels can thrive in the practice. While some lawyers suggest finding a work-life balance, this suggests a ledger that can be equalized on a daily, weekly, or monthly basis. For most busy attorneys, that is not feasible; each day does not offer the same allocation of hours. So consider instead finding a harmonious mix of work and wellness as a key to thriving. A holistic approach to your mental and physical well-being will help you find that balance over time.

HEALTH CHALLENGES FOR LAWYERS

Undoubtedly, the demands of this profession can take a toll on the mental and physical health of its members. Lawyers must be cognizant of the risks and take steps to avoid falling victim to unhealthy habits and harmful behaviors. Lawyers have an obligation to tend to their own mental and physical health. While mental health challenges once carried a stigma, the profession now recognizes that mental health issues could and should be addressed in a supportive fashion.

Mental Health

Depression, Anxiety, and Stress

A survey conducted by the *Journal of Addiction Medicine* looked at depression, anxiety, and stress levels of attorneys in America.[9] The results were troubling. Roughly 28 percent of attorneys surveyed showed symptoms of depression. Male attorneys showed slightly higher levels of depression than their female counterparts. Lawyers who had practiced for less than 10 years were almost twice as likely to suffer from depression than lawyers who had been working in the field for more than 40 years.

Nineteen percent of the lawyers surveyed showed serious symptoms of anxiety, with female attorneys showing slightly higher levels of anxiety than their male counterparts. Attorneys aged 30 or younger were nearly 1.5 times more likely to experience symptoms of anxiety than lawyers between the ages of 61 and 70. Comparable numbers reflected the stress levels in the profession. Not only did 23 percent of those surveyed experience stress, but the levels were constant irrespective of the legal environment in which the person worked. Private firms, sole practitioners, in-house government, in-house corporations, and law professors reported stress at similar levels. When broken down by position within a firm, stress levels were equivalent for clerks and paralegals, junior associates, senior associates, junior partners, senior partners, and managing partners. No matter where you work or what position you hold in a law firm, the stress is there.

Alcohol Use

Lawyers drink to decompress after an exhausting day and the liquor flows to celebrate big wins in the courtroom or boardroom. Whatever the occasion, lawyers turn to alcohol as a coping mechanism to deal with the stress, anxiety, and depression that often accompanies being a lawyer.[10] Whether a lawyer's drinking habits come from choice, a genetic tendency toward dependence, or some combination of the two, the legal profession has gained a reputation for drinking in ways that are often not healthy.[11]

Alcoholism is a disease in which the human brain depends on alcohol to function, and without which the person experiences symptoms of withdrawal.[12] In surveying members to evaluate alcoholism rates among practicing lawyers, many state bar associations found common symptoms of alcoholism:

- drinking alone and/or attempting to hide it from others;
- inability to place a limit on consumption;
- missing family-related and/or business events;
- feeling irritable when unable to drink;
- relationship issues stemming from alcohol use;
- legal troubles stemming from alcohol use (for example, driving under the influence);
- sweating and nausea when alcohol is withheld.[13]

In 2016, a national survey of lawyers from 19 states indicated that between 21 and 36 percent of lawyers exhibit drinking habits that are consistent with "problematic use."[14] Lawyers under age 30 showed particularly high rates of alcohol issues, with 31 percent demonstrating problematic use.[15] These high rates are alarming and indicative of mounting stress and pressure on lawyers.

Drug Use

Misuse of drugs is also a problem for some in the legal profession. Drug addiction to prescription (e.g., Adderall or Xanax) or street drugs (e.g., marijuana or cocaine) can change the way your brain functions.[16] Those changes can have devastating effects on your family, career, clients, and firm. Knowing the warning signs can help identify whether a friend or colleague may be struggling with drug use disorders:

- bloodshot eyes or pupils that are abnormally larger or smaller than usual;
- changes in sleep schedule;

- sudden weight loss or weight gain;
- tremors, slurred speech, or impaired coordination;
- decrease in attendance or performance at work;
- secretive or suspicious behaviors;
- unexplained financial problems;
- unexplained changes in personality or attitude;
- sudden mood swings, irritability, or angry outbursts;
- unexplained lack of motivation or lethargic appearance;
- appearing anxious, paranoid, or fearful for no reason.[17]

Drug and alcohol use can affect not only the individual user but those around him. Knowing that chemical dependency can happen in the profession should prompt not only self-awareness of the risk but also help for those who may be struggling.

Physical Health

Attorneys who bill by the hour laugh at the cushy concept of a 40-hour work week. Many firms expect their attorneys to work long hours, whether to get the work done for a client, maximize firm revenue, or both. Even when not required by the firm's culture, the nature of many litigation and transactional practices involves work days that start very early in the morning and end late each night for days or weeks or months at a time. Fast food is hurriedly consumed at the desk while wading through documents, and a workout is simply out of the question. As the months go by, suits that used to fit no longer do, you are not sleeping well, and you lack the energy you once had. Your physical wellness is taking a hit, not only in terms of physical appearance, but also in how you feel and how well you can perform.

In 2014, the National Center for Biotechnology Information conducted a study on the prevalence of obesity by occupation among U.S. workers.[18] The survey found that 26 percent of workers in the legal field were obese, up 8.3 percent since 2004. Another study published by the *American Journal of Preventative Medicine* found a positive correlation between unhealthy eating habits (burgers at your desk or handfuls of candy) and the stress that accompanies long work weeks.[19] The same study found that factors such as work weeks of more than 40 hours, hostile work environments, and job insecurity were leading factors linked to obesity.[20] Obesity, in turn, is linked to diabetes, hypertension, high cholesterol, strokes, and heart disease.[21] Age is not the protective factor it used to be; more and more people in their 30s and 40s are having heart attacks and strokes.[22]

Stress can mean different things to different people but generally reflects the harmful physical and emotional responses that occur when job requirements do not match the capabilities, resources, or needs of the worker. Stress increases when there is too much work and too little time, and most lawyers understandably feel that pressure.

Billable hour quotas drive lawyers to spend far more than 40 hours working each week, and the pressure is higher on younger attorneys who do not control their own workflow. Using a conservative estimate, an associate attorney required to bill 2,000 hours a year must bill an average of 40 hours every week. To capture 40 billed hours, however, requires that the associate work more than that. The most efficient associate can only bill about 80 percent of the hours she actually works.[23] The younger and less experienced the lawyer, the less that 80 percent efficiency rating applies. This calculus does not take into account any sick leave or holiday time.

Add to that pressure a hostile work environment. Some attorneys thrive on cracking the whip or have a naturally angry and hostile management style, both of which contribute to the stress on subordinates. Economic changes and industry-specific recessions means tenuous job security that is not guaranteed. Clients leave, partners change firms, and it can be difficult to predict where the axe will fall. Even in a good economy, harsh standards used at some firms create an "up or out" mentality, naturally causing attorneys to worry about job security.

LAWYERS' WELL-BEING: HAPPINESS, PRODUCTIVITY, ETHICS, AND PROFESSIONALISM

If life in a law firm is so stressful, can there be such a thing as a happy lawyer? A 2015 *George Washington Law Review* article by Professors Lawrence Krieger and Sheldon Kennon published the results of their study of lawyers and happiness[24] and concluded that lawyers are no different from other people when it comes to what makes them happy. "Simply stated, there is nothing in these data to suggest that attorneys differ from other people with regard to their prerequisites for feeling good and feeling satisfied with life."[25] Their conclusion was that "[i]n order to thrive, we need the same authenticity, autonomy, close relationships, supportive teaching and supervision, altruistic values, and focus on self-understanding and growth that promotes thriving in others."[26] Citing earlier research, the article suggested that happier employees showed "improved accomplishment of complex mental tasks, generally improved work performance, greater culturally valued success" as well as "health, energy, optimism, creativity, and altruism."[27] The benefits extended to law firms as well, since "happier employees also tend to remain with employers longer and raise the morale (and hence performance and retention) of others in the organization" while "less happy employees impose high costs on employers in terms of increased absence and turnover and poor work performance."[28] Since they found no distinction between lawyers and the general public in terms of happiness, it is reasonable to assume these benefits will apply to lawyers in law firms and other organizations.

Professors Krieger and Sheldon's study included law students, those results indicating a strong correlation between "increased well-being and internal motivation (resulting from enhanced autonomy[,] support[,] and need satisfaction)" and "better grades and bar exam performance."[29] While their study did not seek to measure professionalism or ethics,

[i]t did measure psychological factors that are virtually certain to be important sources of ethical and professional behavior for lawyers — authenticity (which is essentially

identical to integrity), competence, relating well to others, helping and community values, and valuing self-understanding and growth. These factors also include the strongest predictors of well-being in our subjects, suggesting that one powerful approach to raising the level of professional behavior among lawyers is to teach law students and lawyers to maximize their own happiness.[30]

Lawyers who intentionally commit time and effort to wellness tended to be healthier and happier. While the steps are simpler than you might think, as with any habit, they require you to stick with it to see the full benefit.

TIPS FOR IMPROVING AND MAINTAINING PHYSICAL WELLNESS

Physical activity can make you feel, function, and sleep better, as well as reduce the risk of a large number of chronic diseases.[31] The Centers for Disease Control and Prevention (CDC) recommend adults ages 18 to 64 spend 150 to 300 minutes (2-1/2 to 5 hours) each week doing moderate-intensity aerobic activity.[32] Moderate-intensity aerobic activities are those that noticeably increase your heart rate and breathing rate, but during which you are still able to carry on a conversation, for example, activities such as brisk walking, bicycle riding, jumping rope, and swimming.

The benefits of physical exercise reach beyond bodily health. Studies by the CDC found a strong correlation between physical activity and mental and emotional wellness.[33] Habitual physical activity improves attention, memory, crystalized intelligence (the ability to retrieve and use information acquired over time), and processing speed in adults over the age of 50.[34] Habitual physical activity also improves sleep efficiency and sleep quality, which reduces daytime sleepiness.[35]

Calendar It

The trick, of course, is making time for that physical activity and sticking with it. Spending 300 minutes a week exercising sounds like a huge time commitment until you realize that each week contains 10,080 minutes. Finding 300 minutes to invest in your physical and mental health sounds more feasible when compared to that number. The first step is to treat your exercise time as you would any other appointment: Put it on your calendar. Once you have already committed to spending that time exercising, you are less likely to schedule other things in that space. The ill-defined "after work" workout almost never happens. A potential solution is joining a yoga or spin class on Tuesday and Thursday at 6:30 p.m., especially with friends, turns workouts into social events with built-in accountability. For many people, the easiest time to commit to a workout is early in the morning. There are no hearings or client meetings at 5:30 or 6:00 a.m. For parents, the children are usually still asleep, giving you uninterrupted time for exercise. And online exercise programs offer community even at that hour.

Some firms make a commitment to fitness, going on group runs or heading to noon exercise classes. Having a friend or colleague who will work out with you also makes it more likely you won't skip a class. Many successful attorneys turn their competitive instincts toward workouts and are very committed to their physical fitness. You may be able to build better relationships with attorneys in the firm as you spend consistent time walking, running, or cycling together. Find one of those attorneys and either join in or take a page from their fitness goals.

Stay on Track

If you still do not believe that you can exercise 300 minutes a week, remember that you can break this up into smaller increments. Get up once an hour from your desk, walk the halls or climb the stairs for 5 minutes; you will get 30-40 minutes of exercise a day. Fitness trackers prompt you to get up and move; some even remind you to breathe. Take the stairs instead of the elevator. Park an extra block or row away (safety permitting). No matter how you decide to exercise, commit to at least six weeks of consistent effort to initiate your exercise routine. Behavioral psychology suggests that it takes about that long for something to become a habit.[36] By the time you've made exercise a habit, you will likely feel more motivated to keep going. Exercise is an investment in your health, and you are worth it.

TIPS FOR IMPROVING AND MAINTAINING MENTAL WELLNESS

Physical health is important, but it only addresses part of true wellness. Leaders need to be mentally healthy both for their own goals and to lead their team effectively. This is true in law school and in practice. What seems like a hectic pace in law school is unlikely to slow down when you enter practice, and just as it can be hard to take care of yourself physically, it may be difficult to maintain mental and emotional wellness. Here are some tips that require minimal time but can make all the difference in lowering the stress and anxiety levels that you frequently face:

Challenge the Unhelpful Thinking

Some topics or people seem to trigger anxiety. Whenever you notice that a particular topic makes you feel anxious, take a moment to write it down and acknowledge the effect it has on you. Then ask yourself, "What *evidence* is there that this thought is *factual*?" As a first-year associate, for example, you might feel anxious asking your supervisor a question, thinking to yourself, "If I ask this question, my supervisor will think I'm an idiot who isn't up to par with the other associates." Compare that thought to this one: "I'm not the only first-year associate at this firm. There is a strong chance that the other associates have similar questions even if they haven't asked. At the end of the day, my supervisor would prefer that I get the job done properly, even if that requires asking a few questions." The first thought may be a fear, but it is not a fact. The second thought is much more likely to be grounded in factual reasoning.

This process helps you separate anxiety from fear. A counselor once asked a nervous client if he knew the difference between anxiety and fear. "Anxiety," the counselor said, "is being concerned there is a tiger on the other side of the door. Fear is when there really *is* a tiger on the other side of the door." They are far more imagined tigers in the world than actual tigers. Reminding yourself of the difference can help you manage those overblown concerns.

Gratitude Practice

Many studies show that "people who consciously count their blessings tend to be happier and less depressed."[37] Research suggests many benefits from a practice of expressing gratitude. In various studies, grateful people were found to be healthier.[38] Gratitude was found to "improve people's health and encourage them to adopt healthier habits."[39] Other studies found that "more grateful people are happier, more satisfied with their lives, less materialistic, and less likely to suffer from burnout."[40] Specific gratitude practices, such as writing in a "gratitude journal" or writing a letter of gratitude, can increase your level of happiness and lift your overall mood. In one study, "grateful cardiac patients reported better sleep, less fatigue, and lower levels of cellular inflammation."[41] Grateful people "experience less depression and are more resilient following traumatic events."[42] In other studies, gratitude was found to encourage "the development of other virtues such as patience, humility, and wisdom."

Harness Meditation Techniques

Take a moment to practice mindfulness techniques.[43] When we feel stress and pressure, our body naturally responds. In evolution, the stress response — sometimes referred to as the "fight or flight response" — was designed to be activated in dangerous situations.[44] Now that we rarely face true physical danger, that same response can be activated from psychological or mental stress. When activated, your body releases a flood of hormones, which can create a physical reaction that includes

- increased heart rate and blood pressure;
- pale or flushed skin with cold and clammy hands;
- dilated pupils;
- edginess — looking and listening for things that are dangerous;
- alteration of memory;
- tense or trembling hands;
- gastrointestinal and bladder reactions.[45]

All of these triggered responses physiologically limit your ability to deal with the stressful circumstance.[46] However, you can harness your parasympathetic nervous system to calm things down. The same techniques used in yoga and meditation can help you manage a stress reaction:

- slow controlled breathing;
- mindfulness, calmly acknowledging the current situation;[47] and
- noticing the stressful thoughts and detaching from them.[48]

Being physically and mentally calmer shows professionalism and self-control. Some law students are trained during mock trial exercises to take a few slow, deep breaths while still sitting at counsel table. They are told to envision the "walk up" to the well of the courtroom, much as a baseball batter has a walk up to the plate. By controlling their fight or flight reactions and envisioning success, they are better able to stay calm and cool as they start the opening statement.

GETTING THE HELP YOU NEED — MENTAL HEALTH AND LAWYER ASSISTANCE PROGRAMS

Sometimes healthy habits alone are not enough to handle the stress levels and mental health challenges faced by those in the legal profession. Counselors and assistance programs can provide tremendous relief. Law students, however, have shown reluctance in seeking help for substance abuse and mental health issues.[49] Among the reasons cited for not seeking help:

Factors Discouraging Law Students from Seeking Help	Percentage Regarding Substance Use	Percentage Regarding Mental Health
Potential threat to bar admission	63%	45%
Potential threat to job or academic status	62%	48%
Social stigma	43%	47%
Concerns about privacy	43%	30%
Financial reasons	41%	47%
The belief that they could handle the problem themselves	39%	36%
Not having the time	36%	34%

[50]

Many law students fear that treatment or diagnosis of a mental health condition will keep them from being licensed to practice or being offered a job. This is an unfortunate perception with long-term consequences. Hiding issues rather than addressing them directly can be disastrous in a lawyer's personal and professional life. Bar boards and law firms want to know that those with mental health issues are addressing the problem and following treatment plans.[51]

Every state has at least one lawyer assistance program (LAP) to help judges, lawyers, and law students suffering from substance abuse and mental health challenges.

Their services are completely confidential. If you recognize some of the symptoms or have concerns for yourself or someone you know, you are strongly encouraged to reach out to these services. Above all, keep in mind that it is possible to overcome these challenges and live a healthier and happier life.

HARMONY, NOT BALANCE

Looking at how to cope with physical and mental health challenges may leave you wondering how to balance your time at work with wellness. You probably have heard the term "work-life balance," but have you considered what that balance would look like in the midst of law school or a busy law practice? Firms interviewing law students raise the issue often, portraying a culture that encourages a life outside of work. Whether that is realistic is debatable. Even with a supportive firm, you often face challenges that include a mountain of work on your desk, more deadlines than you can meet, and distraught family members feeling neglected. You have tried to maintain a work-life balance as best you can, but it seems like there are not enough hours in the day. Why is it so hard to maintain work-life balance? Could it be that work-life balance does not really exist — at least in the traditional way we picture it? Perhaps a paradigm shift is in order.

One of the problems with trying to achieve work-life balance is that the term "balance" suggests things in equilibrium. Most lives, however, do not have a predictability that allows for balance. Your children do not get sick on a predictable and convenient schedule. The opposing counsel does not call to see if today is a convenient time to file her emergency order. Your client in crisis mode does not care if you have plans to go jogging during lunchtime. Work-life balance also suggests that work is not part of your life, that the two are in opposition to each other. This simply is not true, especially for those in the legal profession. Work is a huge and rewarding part of life. So how do you achieve that place where your work and non-work goals mesh? Instead of seeking work-life balance, perhaps you should seek work-life harmony.

Rather than focusing on a daily balance between work and life, work-life harmony focuses on making your office life and personal life work together in the bigger picture. If work-life balance focuses on the day-to-day, then work-life harmony focuses on the year-to-year. There will undoubtedly be times when you work more than 40 hours a week, meaning time for your personal life takes a hit. Work-life harmony says, "When your work needs more time, give it more time, and when your personal life needs more time, give it more time." If it seems like work and personal life "need more time" every day, consider reevaluating what it really means for work or family to "need more time."

For example, perhaps you are handling a case set for trial soon. You have spent months on discovery and the parties are nowhere near settling the case. You need to reach a stopping point on your other files so you can focus on this trial. You have experts to woodshed, exhibits to make, opening statements to prepare, witness examinations to map out, local rules to research, evidentiary motions to file, clients to keep informed — the list goes on and on. Understandably, you practically live in your office. For every evening you spend working, you miss dance recitals, baseball games, parent-teacher conferences, and the like. Work is ruling your life. Finding harmony, then, means taking time after trial is over to reconnect with others and recalibrate how you spend your time. Remind your friends and family that they are as important to you as your work.

Finally, think about your priorities. Just because you are working for a firm or company that pays you well does not necessarily mean that makes you happy. As noted earlier, the billable hour quota can be draining. If you are not fulfilled by the job you have, think about what you might like instead and make a positive change. It is not uncommon for lawyers to leave prestigious BigLaw firms to join a less prestigious and less lucrative one because it makes them happy. Sometimes, that new job requires working just as many hours or more, but the difference is the sense of satisfaction when you believe in the work and it "fits." Finding a position that makes you happy *can* help you find that sense of harmony and peace. If you are fortunate enough to receive multiple job offers, do not be short-sighted or induced by more money. You owe it to your long-term success and happiness to consider the work, the people, the environment, and the firm's reputation as well as the monetary offer.

In law school, students may face the same struggle to find purpose and meaning in the work. Students who work long hours, and do so happily, probably are able to do so because they enjoy the work and the people, and they see the purpose of the task. For example, practicing nights and weekends for a negotiation competition is exhilarating for one who cannot wait to be negotiating lucrative real estate deals in practice. But the long hours and difficulty can seem like drudgery when you are not enjoying the tasks and do not see the relevance. For the tasks you wish you could skip, you have to see those as necessary steps on your journey to graduation day. While keeping your priorities straight and maintaining your grades, you should also seek out interests that inspire you. Join a student organization. Volunteer in a clinic. Investigate opportunities to help in your community. Do something that brings you purpose and joy while in law school and beyond.

CONCLUSION

As part of the legal profession, you will play an indispensable role in society and for your clients. But if you are running on empty, neglecting your health and well-being, everyone will suffer. Taking care of your mental and physical wellness is the first step to happiness and fulfillment within the legal field. Make it a priority. Watch for warning signs both in your own life and with your colleagues. If you see the signs, do not hesitate to ask for help for yourself or offer help to others. Use the practice tips mentioned in this chapter to help alleviate some of the daily stresses. Strive for that optimal work-life harmony, and you will thrive, not just survive, in this profession.

Exercise

ABA Grit Project: Struggling with Your Workload

Watch the ABA Grit Project's video "Struggling with Your Workload," but disregard the prompted questions at the end of the video.

Assume that Jane will say yes to John and begin working on his intellectual property work, which is her passion. John has agreed to help Jane with shifting some responsibilities at the firm so that she can do so, but she is still going to be billing 2,500 hours per year. To do this, she must bill 50 hours every week (assuming two weeks of vacation). Billing 50 hours per week frequently means working at least 62.5 hours per week, assuming that 25 percent of her time is non-billable (which is common for relatively new lawyers). There are only so many ways to split up 62.5 hours over a seven-day period. As such, once you factor in a 30-minute commute (each way), eight hours of sleep each night, spending time with family and friends, and meals, there is not much time left for other activities.

However, Jane has also been approached to join the board of a local business incubator nonprofit organization. This nonprofit helps entrepreneurial members of the community start their small businesses. This organization is one that Jane has been interested in for years, and one that she identified right out of law school as an activity in which she would like to be invovled. She spent the last few years going to events and meeting people in the organization in order to be considered for a board position when one became available. In addition to being something about which Jane is passionate this position may be beneficial to her career because those incubator businesses may need intellectual property help and turn to her for that work.

This board position will require, at a minimum, that she dedicate two hours per month to board meetings. However, to gain the maximum benefit from being part of this organization, it will require that she attend weekly organization events where she can engage with other board members and the business owners they help. These weekly events can include business openings, advising sessions, and informal social events. Each of these events is likely to last only a couple of hours, not including travel time.

As Jane considers each hour individually, it does not seem like much time and she is inclined to say yes; however, as she thinks about the demands of her overall schedule, she is worried about the cumulative effect.

- Without compromising her sleep schedule, how might Jane make this work? To run this analysis, create a weekly schedule that outlines work, commute, sleep, and this volunteer position.
- How will Jane ensure that she maintains her relationships with her family and friends?

- Should she seek John's input or approval before agreeing to serve on the nonprofit board? Create the talking points for her conversation with John.

Journal Prompts

1. How are you doing in law school with self-care? Self-assess your habits.

2. What would a healthier lifestyle look like for you?

3. Have you seen anyone in law school struggling with mental or physical health issues?

   a. Have you done anything to help them? Why or why not?

   b. What might be the barriers to their acknowledgment of the problem?

   c. Are there any barriers to your offering help and how might you overcome them?

4. Find a mindfulness exercise on the Internet and complete it.

   a. What did you like (or not like) about the experience?

   b. Now think back to a previous challenge or setback. How could a mindfulness exercise have reframed the situation and helped you determine the next best course of action?

5. One aspect of finding harmony, not balance, is identifying the people and activities that are important to you and making time for them. Over the next five years, what is your plan or process to ensure that you make time for the people and activities that are important to you? Will you develop weekly or monthly goals? What would these goals look like?

Endnotes

1. Victor A. Flores, *Officer, I Wasn't Going That Fast*, 82 TEX. B.J. 638 (2019). Victor Flores served in the Marine Corps, is an Iraq War veteran, practices government law in McAllen, Texas, and served as the 2019-2020 Texas Young Lawyers Association President.

2. *See* Diana Roth Port, *Lawyers Weigh In: Why Is There a Depression Epidemic in the Profession?*, A.B.A. J. (May 11, 2018), https://www.abajournal.com/voice/article/lawyers_weigh_in_why_is_there_a_depression_epidemic_in_the_profession.

3. Troy Adams et al., *The Conceptualization and Measurement of Perceived Wellness: Integrating Balance Across and Within Dimensions*, 11 AM. J. HEALTH PROMOTION 208–18 (1997), https://doi.org/10.4278/0890-1171-11.3.208.

4. Katherine Keyes et al., *Stress and Alcohol*, 34(4) ALCOHOL RES. 391–400 (2012); *see also* Rajita Sinha, *How Does Stress Increase Risk of Drug Abuse and Relapse?*, 158 PSYCHOPHARMACOLOGY 343–59 (2001).

5. Priscilla Henson, *Addiction & Substance Abuse in Lawyers: Stats You Should Know*, AM. ADDICTION CENTERS (Feb. 19, 2020), https://americanaddictioncenters.org/rehab-guide/workforce/white-collar/lawyers.

6. Keyes et al., *supra* note 4; *see also* Sinha, *supra* note 4.

7. Bree Buchanan & James Coyle, *Report from the National Task Force on Lawyer Well-Being*, AMERICAN BAR ASSOCIATION (Mar. 20, 2020), https://www.americanbar.org/groups/lawyer_assistance/task_force_report/.

8. *Women as Lawyers and Leaders*, 1(4) THE PRACTICE 1 (2015), https://thepractice.law.harvard.edu/article/women-as-lawyers-and-as-leaders/. One hundred percent of the women respondents in the class of 1953 felt this way. Ninety-three percent of the men in the class, for comparison, felt the same way.

9. Patrick R. Krill et al., *Prevalence of Substance Use and Other Mental Health Concerns Among American Attorneys*, U.S. NATIONAL LIB. OF MED. (Mar. 20, 2020), https://www.ncbi.nlm.nih.gov/pmc/articles/PMC4736291/.

10. Joseph L. Wielebisnki, *Culture Shock*, 79 TEX. B.J. 229 (Mar. 20, 2020).

11. Patrick Krill, *The Legal Profession's Drinking Problem*, CNN (Feb. 6, 2016), https://www.cnn.com/2016/02/06/opinions/lawyers-problem-drinkers-krill/index.html.

12. Juan Harris, *What Is an Alcoholic? Am I an Alcoholic?*, QUITALCOHOL.COM (Mar. 20, 2020), https://www.quitalcohol.com/what-is-an-alcoholic.html.

13. Krill, *supra* note 9.

14. *Id.*

15. *Id.*

16. *Id.*

17. Commission on Lawyer Assistance Programs, *Drug Use Disorders*, AMERICAN BAR ASSOCIATION (Mar. 31, 2020), https://www.americanbar.org/groups/lawyer_assistance/resources/drug_abuse_dependence/.

18. Ja K. Gu et al., *Prevalence of Obesity by Occupation Among U.S. Workers*, 56 J. OCCUPATIONAL ENVTL. MED. 516 (Mar. 20, 2020).

19. Sara E. Luckhaupt et al., *Prevalence of Obesity Among U.S. Workers and Associations with Occupational Forces*, 46 AM. J. PREVENTATIVE MED. 237 (Mar. 1, 2014), https://www.ajpmonline.org/article/S0749-3797(13)00617-X/fulltext.

20. Within the context of the study conducted by the *American Journal of Preventative Medicine*, "hostile work environments" means being threatened, bullied, or harassed while on the job, and "job insecurity" means concern about becoming unemployed. *Id.*

21. *Id.*

22. Penn Heart & Vascular Blog, *Think You're Too Young for a Heart Attack? Think Again*, PENN MEDICINE (Jan. 24, 2019), https://www.pennmedicine.org/updates/blogs/heart-and-vascular-blog/2019/january/not-too-young-for-heart-attack.

23. Katy Lewis, *Law Firm Hours — The Real Story*, ABOVE THE LAW (July 20, 2012), https://abovethelaw.com/career-files/law-firm-hours-the-real-story/.

24. Lawrence S. Krieger & Kennon M. Sheldon, *What Makes Lawyers Happy? A Data-Driven Prescription to Redefine Professional Success*, 83 GEO. WASH. L. REV. 554 (2015), *available at* https://ir.law.fsu.edu/cgi/viewcontent.cgi?article=1093&context=articles.

25. *Id.* at 621.

26. *Id.*

27. *Id.* at 662.

28. *Id.*

29. *Id.*

30. *Id.* at 623.

31. *Physical Activity Guidelines for Americans*, U.S. DEP'T HEALTH AND HUMAN SERVICES (2d ed. 2018), https://health.gov/sites/default/files/2019-10/PAG_ExecutiveSummary.pdf.

32. *Id.*

33. *Id.*; *see also Physical Activity*, CDC, https://www.cdc.gov/healthyplaces/healthtopics/physactivity.htm (last accessed July 8, 2020).

34. *Physical Activity Guidelines for Americans*, *supra* note 31.

35. *Id.*

36. *See, e.g.*, Phillippa Lally et al., *How Habits Are Formed: Modelling Habit Formation in the Real World*, 40 EUR. J. SOC. PSYCHOL. 998 (2010), *available at* http://citeseerx.ist.psu.edu/viewdoc/download?doi=10.1.1.695.830&rep=rep1&type=pdf.

37. Joel Wong & Joshua Brown, *How Gratitude Changes You and Your Brain*, GREATER GOOD MAGAZINE (June 6, 2017), https://greatergood.berkeley.edu/article/item/how_gratitude_changes_you_and_your_brain.

38. Summer Allen, *The Science of Gratitude*, GREATER GOOD SCIENCE CENTER AT UC BERKELEY (May 2018), https://ggsc.berkeley.edu/images/uploads/GGSC-JTF_White_Paper-Gratitude-FINAL.pdf?_ga=2.66445038 .1376612137.1594160711-2093851938.1594160711.

39. *Id.*

40. *Id.*

41. *Id.*

42. *Id.*

43. *See* Rasmus Hougaard, *The Dalai Lama on Why Leaders Should Be Mindful, Selfless, and Compassionate*, HARV. BUS. REV. (Feb. 20, 2019), https://hbr.org/2019/02/the-dalai-lama-on-why-leaders-should-be-mindful-selfless-and-compassionate?utm_medium=social&utm_campaign=hbr&utm_source=linkedin.

44. *Understanding the Stress Response*, HARV. MED. SCH., HARV. HEALTH PUB. (2018), https://www.health .harvard.edu/staying-healthy/understanding-the-stress-response.

45. *Id.*

46. *Id.*

47. "Mindfulness is the basic human ability to be fully present, aware of where we are and what we're doing, and not overly reactive or overwhelmed by what's going on around us." *Getting Started with Mindfulness*, MINDFUL.ORG, https://www.mindful.org/meditation/mindfulness-getting-started/ (last visited July 22, 2020).

48. *Id.*

49. Jerome M. Organ, David B. Jaffe, Katherine M. Bender, *Suffering in Silence: The Survey of Law Student Well-Being and the Reluctance of Law Students to Seek Help for Substance Use and Mental Health Concerns*, 66 J. Legal Educ. 116, 144 (2016).

50. *Id.* at 141.

51. *See, e.g., Supplemental Investigation Form from the Texas Board of Law Examiners, available at* https://ble. texas.gov/supplemental-investigation-form (last visited July 22, 2020); *Health and Wellness Resources for Baylor Law's Current Students, available at* https://www.baylor.edu/law/currentstudents/index .php?id=934058 (last visited July 22, 2020).

Chapter 12 — Integrity and Character

Leadership is a combination of strategy and character. If you must be without one, be without the strategy.

H. Norman Schwarzkopf[1]

Purpose

To understand the challenges and practical importance of ethics in leadership roles.

Learning Objectives

At the end of this chapter, you should be able to:

- Explain the meaning of integrity and discuss the importance of a leader's integrity.
- Describe how a person's character is formed and influenced.
- Explain what it means to be a person of good moral character.
- Cite examples of valuable lessons about ethics learned from studying past leadership failures.
- Describe important elements of an environment that promotes ethical behavior and leadership.

Discussion

INTRODUCTION

In the 1925 U.S. Open, golfer Robert "Bobby" Tyre Jones was in contention for the lead when he called a two-stroke penalty on himself. He told tournament officials that he caused the ball to move as he addressed his ball. No one saw the ball move, and no one would have known of the infraction otherwise. Jones lost the tournament by a single stroke. One year later, Jones again approached the rules official to self-report a two-stroke penalty that, again, only Jones saw. This time, however, Jones won the 1926 U.S. Open and went on to win 12 other majors as an amateur golfer. Jones never turned pro; he maintained his amateur status because his chosen profession was the law. Jones became an accomplished lawyer in Georgia. He led the organization that built the famous Augusta National Golf Course, home of the annual Masters golf championship. His reputation as a lawyer and leader mirrored his reputation as a golfer — that of a person with good moral character and the highest integrity.[2]

ABA Model Rules of Professional Conduct, Preamble & Scope [9] In the nature of law practice . . . conflicting responsibilities are encountered. Virtually all difficult ethical problems arise from conflict between a lawyer's responsibilities to clients, to the legal system and to the lawyer's own interest in remaining an ethical person while earning a satisfactory living. The Rules of Professional Conduct often prescribe terms for resolving such conflicts. Within the framework of these Rules, however, many difficult issues of professional discretion can arise. Such issues must be resolved through the exercise of sensitive professional and moral judgment guided by the basic principles underlying the Rules. These principles include the lawyer's obligation zealously to protect and pursue a client's legitimate interests, within the bounds of the law, while maintaining a professional, courteous and civil attitude toward all persons involved in the legal system.

How easy it would have been for Jones to ignore the little motion of that ball. He was already doing well in the tournament, and the slight motion as he addressed the ball was unlikely to affect the tournament outcome. Yet Jones knew that the rules required him to report such an event, so he did. He did the the right thing even when no one was looking.

Ethical leadership requires a commitment to acting with integrity and striving to live as a person of good moral character. While the two are intertwined, they actually describe different attributes and behaviors. A person of integrity commits to a set of ideals or principles — for better or worse — no matter the cost. Character defines who we are and how we behave, which again can be virtuous or not. Character is formed by both innate hereditary traits (height) as well as characteristics that are not fixed and are behavioral in nature (introvert). Experience, beliefs, and learned behaviors can alter and shape those characteristics as can the situational influence of our current circumstances. Our character affects our outlook on the world and our actions in the world. Morals then connect us to our fundamental beliefs about right and wrong.

Lawyers face a complex mix of obligations ranging from the practical (productivity and profitability) to the professional (meeting their clients' demands and legal needs) to the ethical (valuing the clients' best interest over the attorney's self-interest, supporting the system of justice, and serving society).[3] Balancing these commitments with your desire to be a person of integrity and good moral character is challenging. In this chapter, we examine the impact of integrity and character on the success and reputation of the lawyer-leader and suggest steps for ethical leadership.

LAWYERS' ETHICAL AND PROFESSIONAL OBLIGATIONS

Ethics guidance comes from a variety of sources. Law students study the ABA Model Rules of Professional Conduct in order to pass the Multistate Professional Responsibility Exam and obtain a license. Once licensed, lawyers must abide by the applicable codes of professional responsibility for the state(s) in which they are licensed. They may also need to adhere to additional codes of conduct when admitted to practice in a specific court or as members of specialty boards or organizations. These rules generally set *minimum* standards of conduct for lawyers. A code of professional responsibility will not determine who you are as a lawyer, what type of cases or clients you will represent, how you will practice law, or how you will be remembered. Your commitment to integrity and ethical behavior will determine the answer to those issues.

> **ABA Model Rules of Professional Conduct, Preamble & Scope [1]**
> A lawyer is . . . a representative of clients, an officer of the legal system and a public citizen having special responsibility for the quality of justice.

True professionals look beyond that which they *must* do to ways of behaving that enhance their reputation and the profession. Civility, candor, and respectful communication exceed the mandatory minimums. These concepts are aspirational in the truest sense of the word and reflect what we hope or aspire to be and apply not only generally but in specific situations. Choosing to respond civilly to a hostile opposing counsel or admitting to the court that your position is the minority approach requires courage but also says much about the kind of person you are.

This tradition of integrity and character is deeply interrelated with the historical obligation lawyers have to serve their clients and society. As Alexis de Tocqueville recognized in the 1830s, lawyers are keepers of the rule of law as well as trained problem solvers and advocates with "a separate station in society."[4] He labeled lawyers the "American Aristocracy," using that title in the European tradition in which lords were responsible for their charges.[5] The charge for American lawyers is our democracy. The special status of lawyers requires more than mere provision of legal services; lawyers must protect the rule of law.

To keep this tradition alive will require a more robust discussion about what it means to be a member of a profession whose rich history of status and privilege came from rigorous intellectual pursuit and legal training. Here are some of the questions you should consider as you establish your professional identity:

- *What does it mean to be a member of the legal profession?* While this may sound like a broad question, the emphasis should be, "What does it mean for *you* to be a member of the profession?" Why do you want to be a lawyer? What draws you to holding a law license? Is it helping people in their time of need by using your specialized skills and knowledge? Is it financial security? A combination of the two?
- *What is the lawyer's role in society?* Put another way, what do you want *your role* in society to be? The legal profession has a long history, and lawyers were involved in all aspects of the founding of our country and many significant events in our history. But what does it mean to you to be a part of the profession? What, or who, do you want to use your skills and knowledge to benefit?
- *What does a client expect of a lawyer?* What is the lawyer role and relationship with clients? Sometimes clients want "bulldog" lawyers who will intimidate others, utilize hardball tactics, and do anything to win. Is that the type of lawyer you want to be? Or do you want to be the lawyer who acts with conviction and compassion; someone who is able to treat others with respect and civility, but hold them accountable?
- *What kind of lawyer do you want to be?* How do you want to be remembered? What do you want the highlights of your career to be? Will they be the *pro bono* cases you took? Will they be the clients who became lifelong friends after you built a meaningful relationship with them? Many successful lawyers with spectacular records (large deals negotiated or big verdicts) regard some of their smaller cases as more meaningful because of the stories and the people at the center of them.

International Bar Association Professional Integrity
A lawyer shall at all times maintain the highest standards of honesty, integrity and fairness towards their clients, the court, colleagues and all those with whom the lawyer comes into professional contact.[6]

These questions should promote deep discussion both as you look inside yourself and as you progress in your career. The answers may be difficult and require periodic re-evaluation. The standards may provide a framework of minimally ethical conduct, but how will you both avoid ethical traps and reach above the minimum? Knowing how you want to be regarded and what you want your reputation to be will help guide you. The guide to earning the reputation you desire is integrity and good moral character.

INTEGRITY

Integrity is doing the right thing, even when no one is watching.

C.S. Lewis[7]

Integrity is often associated with good moral character when, in reality, integrity and good moral character are separate concepts. Integrity derives from the Latin adjective *integer*, meaning "whole or complete."[8] *Merriam-Webster's Dictionary* defines integrity as a "firm adherence to a code."[9] Moral philosophers describe integrity using four primary character traits:

1. Steadfast commitment to one's values and principles, maintained even in the face of negative consequences;

2. Deliberative flexibility;

3. Clear sense of those values and principles; and

4. Consistency, both in the application of those principles and between word and deed.[10]

People with integrity act with conviction consistent with a set of principles — their moral values. The term "morality" refers to "certain codes of conduct put forward by a society or a group (such as a religion), or accepted by an individual for her own behavior."[11] The group's morality is not always virtuous, even though its integrity cannot be attacked. In the movie *Pirates of the Caribbean: The Curse of the Black Pearl*, the pirates demonstrated impeccable integrity as they followed the Pirates' Code.[12] The pirates adhered to a common set of values and acceptable conduct even though their victims (and the rest of society) might not ascribe to the code. The fidelity to that code is what bound the group, such that each member adhered to the shared set of values or principles. As Dwight Eisenhower put it, "The supreme quality for leadership is unquestionably integrity. Without it, no real success is possible, no matter whether it is on a section gang, a football field, in an army or in an office."[13]

Integrity calls for people to act with consistent commitment to a set of principles to which they pledge allegiance regardless of the circumstances, regardless who will benefit, and regardless if the action works to their detriment. This view of integrity does not include a reference to concepts of good versus evil or right or wrong.[14] Integrity looks at the degree of adherence to the code, not at whether the code should be adhered to. In the legal profession, integrity requires commitment to representing a client in the face of adversity, including public scorn, loss of income, or damage to personal relationships. This is true even if a client is guilty of the conduct with which he is charged. Lawyers endure these sacrifices because their clients deserve representation; lawyers serve a system of justice that guarantees due process irrespective of guilt or innocence.

Integrity, in the setting of legal representation, can be difficult. Lawyers do not decide if their client is guilty or innocent, culpable or not, and then determine how much due process or zealous representation the client gets. The core of being a lawyer of integrity requires that you adhere strictly to the lawyers' code to ensure the full measure of due process and zealous advocacy is given as equally to a client in the wrong as to a client who is wrongly accused. Why is this so difficult? Because it is unpopular in many settings. Representing the persons accused of setting bombs at the finish line of the Boston Marathon is not popular, especially when they have already been tried in the court of public opinion. Defending a man accused of raping a four-year-old child is not popular. We hear often, "How can you represent that monster?" The integrity-based answer is because the lawyers' code protects the guilty and innocent alike.

In *To Kill a Mockingbird*, Atticus Finch agrees to represent Tom Robinson, even though he knows that doing so will jeopardize his practice and earn the scorn of his neighbors.[15] Finch does so because he firmly believes that every person deserves representation. But there's another consideration: while representing Tom Robinson was the right thing to do, is vigorously defending someone you believe to be guilty the morally right thing to do?[16] Put another way, even when you know that duty requires this type of integrity, you can still struggle on moral grounds with representing a client whom you believe is guilty of the crime. How do you square morality with your duty of integrity?

MORAL CHARACTER

Character is like a tree and reputation like a shadow. The shadow is what we think of it; the tree is the real thing.

Abraham Lincoln[17]

A person's character is the set of attributes unique to a person — their strengths, weaknesses, virtues, vices, knowledge, and experience. The American Psychological Association defines character as "the totality of an individual's attributes and personality traits, particularly his or her characteristic moral, social, and religious attitudes."[18] As individuals make decisions and take action, they are guided by, and simultaneously forming, their character. Character is shaped by one's background and the influences of previous actions and beliefs. This means character can change or evolve over time as we learn new behaviors or learn from mistakes or guidance. Who you are today does not define who you will be in the future. In addition, while past events shape character, current circumstances or situations also impact character. Even when we know or believe something is the right thing to do, we do not always translate that belief into action. "[I]ndividuals can be exemplary with respect to some key traits but not others, and their character-related qualities can vary across situations and evolve over time."[19]

In our desire to be people of good moral character, knowing what is "right" is essential. Aristotle described a virtuous person as one who has the knowledge of what is "right" (defined by a set of acceptable standards within the group of community) and who desires to do it.[20] Aristotle recognized that in societies, most people know what is *good* and are more or less able to do it most of the time. Consider these four ways in which we can train ourselves to be morally good:

1. Simply doing good and avoiding evil;

2. Deliberately placing ourselves in situations of moral significance (e.g., volunteering at a soup kitchen);

3. Imagining ourselves in such situations and acting rightly; and

4. Reflective thinking about moral matters.[21]

This advice sounds like something we might have heard from our mothers ("Idle hands are the devil's helpers." "Nothing good happens after midnight — you get home before then." "You knew you were doing something wrong and did it anyway."). Taking that sage advice and applying it consistently can build a moral structure to your life, reflexively skewing toward right over wrong.

REVIEW OF ETHICAL ISSUES IN THE LEGAL PROFESSION

How does morality combine with ethics? While morality contemplates how you view right and wrong, ethical guidelines inform what the profession sets as mandatory minimums for right and wrong behavior. You want to make decisions in practice looking through the prism of integrity and good moral character, irrespective of your practice area. Ethical decision making can be difficult. Lawyers face situations that are often complicated and messy. Both within law firms and in various state bars, dedicated committees review and decide ethical issues that arise. A law firm committee may have to decide whether accepting representation creates a conflict of interest with an existing client or whether suing a client to collect an unpaid fee would be improper or simply ill-advised. Similarly, state bar ethics committees review ethics rules, evaluate grievances made against attorneys, and take disciplinary action when lawyers step outside the ethical boundaries. Self-regulating lawyers' conduct helps maintain both integrity within the profession and the outside perception of lawyers as ethical champions of integrity.

While law firms review the ethical ramifications of a proposed action, not all take the next step to consider the moral aspects of the conduct. Simply determining that the action does not violate the minimum standards of the relevant code of professional conduct or ethics guidelines does not mean that morally, the firm *should* take the case or pursue the action. The ethical issues may be gray; the moral judgments even more so. In the business world, entities may be jointly owned by multiple family members. When the lawyer meets with them, it may not be clear to these co-owners that the entity is the actual client. The individual owners may seek the firm's advice on other business issues, investments, and opportunities. While accepting that ancillary business may be ethically permissible, the firm should consider whether morally, giving that type of advice would likely cause confusion about whose interests were being

ABA Model Rule 1.6(b)

A lawyer may reveal information relating to the representation of a client to the extent the lawyer reasonably believes necessary:

   (1) to prevent reasonably certain death or substantial bodily harm;

   (2) to prevent the client from committing a crime or fraud that is reasonably certain to result in substantial injury to the financial interests or property of another and in furtherance of which the client has used or is using the lawyer's services;

   (3) to prevent, mitigate or rectify substantial injury to the financial interests or property of another that is reasonably certain to result or has resulted from the client's commission of a crime or fraud in furtherance of which the client has used the lawyer's services; . . . .

18 U.S.C. § 1957

Whoever . . . knowingly engages or attempts to engage in a monetary transaction in criminally derived property of a value greater than $10,000 and is derived from specified unlawful activity, shall be punished . . . .

   [However,] monetary transaction. . . does not include any transaction necessary to preserve a person's right to representation as guaranteed by the sixth amendment to the Constitution.

served at any given time. These considerations of ethical versus moral decision making can be complicated, especially when balancing the attorney's interest in retaining the business (and its financial benefits), the fiduciary obligation to put the client's interests above the attorney's, and the professional obligations to protect the rule of law. Independent of the lawyer's duty not to advance self-interest, the larger obligations are not divorced from each other; one cannot ethically serve a client's interest at the expense of the integrity of the system.

For example, while lawyers strictly protect client confidences, they do not do so at risk to a potential victim of crime or our system of justice. The ethical rules permit lawyers to divulge what would otherwise be kept confidential, if necessary to protect a potential victim of a serious crime or to protect society from a crime related to fraud or injury to financial interest or property. We will visit this issue later as we examine the Enron financial scandal and the conduct of the lawyers involved in it.

Failure to adhere to ethical obligations also can result in moral and potentially criminal concerns for the lawyer. Lawyers who know that they are accepting "dirty" money — money that was used in a crime or otherwise obtained illegally — may violate federal law.[22] The rule, however, does not bar the lawyer from accepting dirty money in order to represent a criminal defendant. The lawyer must consider the potential criminal exposure for accepting dirty money; even if he legally can accept it, does the lawyer morally feel that accepting money from human trafficking, for example, is acceptable?

Ethical dilemmas arise even before you enter the practice of law. Law students face issues that challenge their integrity, some of which require consideration of the school's honor code. Time pressure and the importance of grades and class rank may tempt students to cheat. Research shows cheating is a common, and often unpunished, habit of students from middle school all the way up to graduate school. Donald McCabe, a leading expert in the academic integrity field,[23] conducted regular anonymous surveys of students at all academic levels. His published work focused upon cheating at the college level.[24]

According to McCabe's surveys, published in *U.S. News & World Report* in 1999:

- 80 percent of "high-achieving" high school students admit to cheating.
- 51 percent of high school students did not believe cheating was wrong.
- 95 percent of cheating high school students said that they had not been detected.
- 75 percent of college students admitted cheating, and 90 percent of college students didn't believe cheaters would be caught.
- Almost 85 percent of college students said cheating was necessary to get ahead.[25]

McCabe's surveys of over 70,000 high school students at more than 24 high schools in the United States demonstrated that 64 percent of students admitted to cheating on a test, 58 percent admitted to plagiarism, and 95 percent said they participated in some form of cheating. These statistics reflect the overall trends uncovered over the past 12 years.

	Graduate Students	Undergraduates [26]
Number responding:[27]	~17,000	~71,300
% who admit cheating on tests:	17%	39%
% who admit cheating on written assignments:	40%	62%
% total who admit to written or test cheating:	43%	68%

In graduate programs, a majority (56%) of the graduate students in business acknowledged they cheated at least once, compared with 47 percent in other fields.[28] "Some business students have developed a bottom-line mentality," explains McCabe. "Getting the job done is what matters; how you do it is less important."[29] Law school students clocked in at 45 percent. "The stakes are much higher for law students," McCabe said.[30] "There's a fear you may not be able to take the bar exam after having spent these three years in law school."[31] When questioned about why the cheating trend has seen no decrease over time, McCabe responded that "[s]tudents today are much more willing to make their own decisions about what's okay and what's not okay."[32]

Preparing for challenging scenarios is easier if you study the ethical rules, and think through issues before you encounter them. Variations between different states and different courts complicate the task, but that challenge illustrates the potential for missteps and highlights the need to do your homework and be prepared. Set clear expectations with your team for interaction with your clients, opposing counsel, and the court. If you are the new lawyer on the team, understand the team's expectations for that conduct. When the time comes and an issue arises, as it inevitably will, you will have a good foundation with the rules and expectations for an ethical solution.

> **ABA Model Rules of Professional Conduct: Preamble & Scope [7]**
> Many of a lawyer's professional responsibilities are prescribed in the Rules of Professional Conduct, as well as substantive and procedural law. However, a lawyer is also guided by personal conscience and the approbation of professional peers. A lawyer should strive to attain the highest level of skill, to improve the law and the legal profession and to exemplify the legal profession's ideals of public service.

Beyond the ethical solution, consider the moral solution. When facing a tough decision, look at it from a future perspective. Will your decision withstand retrospective analysis, such that no matter how hard the decision or how difficult the consequences, you still are proud of what you did? The ability to stand by difficult choices is important to long-term success in both life and the practice of law. Taking time to conduct a meaningful review of tough choices also helps guide you in future decision making; you will have more confidence in your ability to choose wisely.

LEARNING FROM ETHICAL FAILURES OF THE PAST

In law a man is guilty when he violates the rights of others. In ethics he is guilty if he only thinks of doing so.

Immanuel Kant[33]

While many of us believe we have sufficiently good moral character that we would naturally make the ethical choice, history teaches us a different lesson. A classic example of where lawyers let situational constraints pull them from the ethical and moral path was General Motor's ("GM") handling of faulty ignition switches in several of its cars.[34] Over roughly a decade, GM built more than 2.6 million cars with faulty ignition switches.[35] The defect in the ignition switch caused the car's engine to turn off and kept the airbags from deploying, all while the car was still moving.[36] This faulty ignition switch caused at least 54 accidents and 13 deaths.[37] At issue was how lawyers for GM could let the switch continue to be used without telling their client to do the right thing and replace the faulty ignition switch. In hindsight, it seems obvious that someone should have spoken up about the right thing to do. Instead, highly qualified in-house counsel did nothing while faulty switches continued to injure customers. Why was it so hard for these lawyers to do the right thing? Did they not have the needed information? Were they afraid for their jobs? Did a groupthink mindset[38] take over? Irrespective of the motivation, the retrospective analysis shows an ethical breach.

Once the matter was investigated, six lawyers were fired — not because there was an intentional cover-up of the faulty ignition switch, but because of a "pattern of incompetence and neglect."[39] We may never fully know what led to the decision to turn a blind eye, but this decision may cast doubt on the integrity and character of the lawyers involved for quite some time.

It is impossible to discuss ethical leadership without mentioning the Enron scandal. Enron was once the epitome of the successful American business and one of the largest companies in the nation.[40] Enron went from powerhouse success story to one of the largest bankruptcies in the nation and a story of a $10 billion fraud. "Most of the public's attention was focused on Enron's political connections and the failure of Wall Street's so-called gatekeepers — the analysts, banks, credit agencies and analysts — to sound a warning bell."[41] But the inside story of Enron was a corporate culture of "greed, betrayal and deception — and its human costs, in broken friendships, ruined careers, and worse."[42]

> **ABA Model Rule 5.4 Professional Independence of a Lawyer**
>
> . . .
>
> (c) A lawyer shall not permit a person who recommends, employs, or pays the lawyer to render legal services for another to direct or regulate the lawyer's professional judgment in rendering such legal services.
>
> (d) A lawyer shall not practice with or in the form of a professional corporation or association authorized to practice law for a profit, if:
>
> . . .
>
> (3) a nonlawyer has the right to direct or control the professional judgment of a lawyer.

Enron produced fraudulent financial statements year after year using complex and unethical accounting practices designed to hide its financial misdeeds from the public. Where were the lawyers at Enron? Shamefully, they were in the middle of the transactions. Prominent law firms served as outside counsel to Enron, structuring transactions, negotiating deals, giving advice about the transactions, drafting documents, and preparing SEC disclosure filings. "Yet, the lawyers did nothing to stop these transactions or even insist on proper disclosure."[43] The bankruptcy examiners' report alleged the lawyers failed to discharge their professional responsibilities.[44] The lawyers defended their actions by saying that "they had no reason and no obligation to challenge their client."[45] Can this be right? ABA Model Rule 5.4 protects the exercise of a lawyer's professional judgment "free of compromising influences and loyalties."[46] At some point, did the lawyers not have a responsibility to point out that filing misleading documents with the SEC was wrong? That structuring deals to misappropriate assets was wrong? Where were the lawyers?

Enron's collapse provides a dramatic example of failed leadership and economic catastrophe that, according to Ronald E. Berenbeim, happened due to a failure of ethics.[47] Enron *had* a code of ethics, but that code was not part of Enron's culture and not reflected in the actions of Enron's leadership. If integrity is adherence to a code, ignoring the internal code of ethics was, by definition, a breach of integrity.

The Enron scandal teaches that merely having an ethics code on paper does not translate to ethical leadership.[48] Enron executives fundamentally did not believe they needed to be truthful — in the accounting documents, in disclosures to the government, or in disclosures to their employees. Top-level executives actually dumped Enron stock in anticipation that the truth would come out and they appeared to have no moral or ethical qualms about doing so. All of these actions violated Enron's own code of ethics. Why did Enron executives feel comfortable ignoring the code of ethics? Because the leaders made lack of integrity part of Enron's culture: executives were not required to adhere to the code. In testimony before the Special Investigations Committee, William C. Powers, the chief investigator of the Enron scandal, noted that "[l]eadership and management begin at the top with the CEO," and the CEO lacked integrity.[49]

When leadership commits to ethical practices in the organization, that tone will trickle down to the rest of the organization. If the leadership shows it is acceptable to cut corners, fudge figures, and be less than honest, that conduct will trickle down through the organization as well. Enron's lawyers willingly certified the legality of documents showing dubious accounting or investment practices. More damning, when the client was at risk of being investigated for those practices, these lawyers subtly advised executives to destroy incriminating documents rather than retain and turn them over to the investigating authorities when lawfully requested.[50]

Outside counsel may have claimed they had "no reason" to question the Enron dealings; but ample red flags existed that the in-house attorneys ignored. For example, Kristina Mordaunt, an in-house lawyer in Enron's financial group, invested $6,000 in a subsidiary company at the invitation of a senior financial officer of Enron. She received $1 million in return shortly thereafter.[51] Should she have questioned whether ethically, a return that large was possible in such a short time period, particularly in light of the other financial irregularities? In light of Enron's collapse, Mordaunt's conduct looks naive at best and legally troublesome at worst. How could she not have suspected illegal conduct? Yet her behavior highlights the situational difficulties lawyers face. One million dollars is an almost impossible return on such a small investment, which should have signaled a significant financial irregularity. Assuming she had concern, should she have held the money in trust and contacted the management of the company? Knowing now the outcome of a full investigation into Enron, this disclosure was unlikely to trigger action by management. If management did not act, what should have been Mordaunt's next step? Should she have contacted the board or the SEC or other legal authorities to report on her own client and employer, Enron? Mordaunt faced a difficult dual responsibility: her duty to her client and our system of justice. Had she been willing to speak up about actions she knew to be wrong, the shareholders and employees of Enron, who were devastated financially by the fraud, might have been shielded from the full impact of the company's actions.

Both inside and outside counsel hired to guide and advise Enron failed in their fiduciary duties to ask pointed questions and to delve into suspicious or incomplete answers to questions that were asked. Well-regarded lawyers from highly respected law firms were among those failed professionals. Lawyers whose practices are organized around the priority of profit-maximization seem likely to engage in an ongoing strategy of deference to clients (or influential individuals who work for the clients) in a way that compromises, rather than enhances, the exercise of independent counsel to clients.[52] Enron is yet another warning to lawyers not to let the client or others sway their independent judgment. Lawyers have a duty of candor to their clients as well as a duty to protect society. Integrity requires lawyers to meet those ethical obligations even if it means losing a lucrative client.

ETHICAL LAWYERING

They're certainly entitled to think that, and they're entitled to full respect for their opinions . . . but before I can live with other folks I've got to live with myself. The one thing that doesn't abide by majority rule is a person's conscience.

Harper Lee, *To Kill a Mockingbird*[53]

Many adages try to capture the fleeting essence of character and reputation: "character is like glass; it can shatter in an instant and will never be the same again" or "character takes a lifetime to build and an instant to destroy." This is particularly true for lawyers. No matter how large a city in which you practice law, the legal community is comparatively small and tight-knit. Word will spread about your character and integrity as you practice law. Do you want to be known as a lawyer who can be trusted ("my word is my bond") or as the lawyer with whom every single agreement — no matter how small — must be documented?

Advocating effectively for your clients does not require that you push ethical boundaries or damage your credibility. In fact, your integrity and credibility will benefit your clients. Many jurisdictions have a procedural rule by which attorneys can make written agreements during litigation; these typically must be signed by all parties to the agreement and filed with the court to become enforceable. A lawyer who tells you she does not need a signed agreement because your word is good enough clearly respects your integrity. When the opposing counsel respects you as a trustworthy lawyer, both parties can have more open conversations about the case and work toward a resolution more efficiently. By doing so, you can save your clients a great deal of money and achieve the same result. As one trial lawyer related:

> As a young lawyer, I thought I was supposed to battle the other lawyer on everything. I made things difficult that should have been done by agreement — scheduling depositions, working out discovery issues — and was costing my client money that he didn't need to spend. One day, the lawyer on the other side called me. He introduced himself and said he wanted to apologize. He had been difficult too and told me that was not what was in his client's best interest. He asked if we could start over and work collaboratively on getting the case ready for trial. I remember feeling ashamed of my petty behavior; it had not helped my client at all. We not only worked out all future depositions and discovery disputes civilly, we became friends. I always respected his willingness, as a more senior lawyer, to be humble, civil, authentic, and to do what was right for both our clients.[54]

ABA Model Rule 3.3(a): Candor Toward the Tribunal

A lawyer shall not knowingly:

(1) make a false statement of fact or law to a tribunal or fail to correct a false statement of material fact or law previously made to the tribunal by the lawyer;

(2) fail to disclose to the tribunal legal authority in the controlling jurisdiction known to the lawyer to be directly adverse to the position of the client and not disclosed by opposing counsel; or

(3) offer evidence that the lawyer knows to be false. If a lawyer, the lawyer's client, or a witness called by the lawyer, has offered material evidence and the lawyer comes to know of its falsity, the lawyer shall take reasonable remedial measures, including, if necessary, disclosure to the tribunal. A lawyer may refuse to offer evidence, other than the testimony of a defendant in a criminal matter, that the lawyer reasonably believes is false.

Collegial and ethical conduct can lead to your developing deep relationships with other lawyers, even when they are frequently your opposing counsel. Lawyers Keith Langston and Scott Skelton were on opposite sides of more than four thousand cases in a five-year period. While they shared a common alma mater, they otherwise could not be more different — until the day Keith donated a kidney to Scott.[55] These relationships lead not only to a more satisfying personal life, they also create a community of like-minded lawyers who trust and respect each other. This models for the public the kind of legal community that can be trusted and respected. If lawyers do not trust and respect each other, we can hardly expect the public to do so.

This credibility extends to appearances before the court. Lawyers are supposed to be truthful both in their affirmative statements and when an omission would leave a false impression. Lawyers are supposed to correct false statements or misleading information on their own initiative when dealing with the courts.

Judge Ed Kinkeade, U.S. District Judge for the Northern District of Texas, has taught ethics at several Texas law schools for decades. He frequently tells students about the importance of maintaining credibility with the court. Once a judge discovers that a lawyer has lied (whether it be a lie of commission or omission), that lawyer will forever be on the list of lawyers that the judge does not trust. Even worse for the lawyer, as Judge Kinkeade often remarks, "judges have an invisible billboard in the sky with the list of lawyers who are not to be trusted. Once someone gets on that list, all the other judges know about it soon enough."[56] At the heart of ethical lawyering, then, is the duty and desire to be scrupulously honest, forthright in your dealings, and oppositional only when it is truly necessary.

SUGGESTIONS FOR ETHICAL LEADERSHIP

Always do right. It will gratify some people and astonish the rest.

Mark Twain[57]

The lessons of ethical lawyering translate into ethical leadership, both of which mean doing the right thing in the right way for the right reasons.[58] As we discussed above, ethical conduct sounds easier than it is when the situations are difficult. The pressure to be stronger, better, and faster can lead to the temptation to cut ethical corners in order to come out on top.[59] "No defensible theory of professional ethics can guarantee a correlation between ethical action and the financial interests of the actor, and most, if not all, lawyers face an inevitable 'tension between doing good and doing well.'"[60]

Ethical dilemmas arise not just in the practice part of the law but in the internal leadership issues in law firms. Firm leadership sets the ethical tone in a way that either promotes integrity or looks like Enron. For example, firms that charge based on a billable hour model face tremendous pressure to maximize revenue, a practice than can easily lead to overbilling. A "bill at all costs" approach actually puts pressure on lawyers to charge for work they have not done or to overstate the time spent on a given task. This practice became so widespread that many clients now use software to audit bills so as to spot systematic overbilling.

Why do some leaders cave to this pressure while others refuse to? Making decisions based upon moral and ethical duties (such as maintaining independent judgment, utmost candor with the client, and the fiduciary obligation not to profit inappropriately from a client) sends the message that profit does not come first. They stay true to behaviors expected of ethical leaders, including honesty, trustworthiness, integrity, and courage. These characteristics must both be internalized by the leader and woven into the fabric of an organization to be truly effective.

Honesty Creates Trust

Merriam-Webster's Dictionary defines honesty as "adherence to the facts" and "fairness and straightforwardness of conduct."[61] Leaders must choose to tell the truth, both to themselves and to their clients and teams. Fundamentally, the failed leaders behind the Enron debacle stopped telling the truth.[62] Telling difficult, hard truths can be challenging, and lawyers face many hard truths. The client may be facing jail time. The judge rules against request for custody of the children. The invention is not patentable. Even harder truths include admissions of personal errors, such as, "I missed a deadline." The client will be unhappy, the boss will be disappointed, and the shareholders will be angry. Even when truth-telling is initially difficult, it is universally easier than lying now and being discovered later. Telling hard truths, surprisingly, builds trust because it demonstrates a willingness to accept reality and deal with things as they are. Even when truth-telling gets a bad reaction, the reaction is not because you are telling the truth. Often, the reaction is to the situation, not to your candid disclosure of the situation. Clients will appreciate that you are honest and respect your willingness to be straight with them. Your candor leads them to making good decisions in difficult situations. Moreover, those above and below you in the organization will trust you more when they know you are scrupulously honest. That honesty creates an institutional atmosphere of trust.

In addition to telling the truth, an ethical leader is open and receptive to hearing the truth.[63] Listen to what others are saying and actively participate in the team discourse. Employees who trust you to listen will be more comfortable approaching you with the tough issues. If you are known as a leader who only wants to hear good news, your team will not trust you with the bad. As a leader, you can then get blindsided if people in your organization are not forthcoming in sharing bad facts, and this can undermine your effectiveness as a leader and as a team. Inviting input and actively listening creates an atmosphere where honesty, trust, and collaboration can flourish.

Integrity Builds Reputation

Warren Buffett once remarked, "[I]n looking for people to hire, look for three qualities: integrity, intelligence, and energy. And if they don't have the first, the other two will kill you."[64] Integrity takes honesty and marries it to consistency. Consistency means "doing what you say[;] it's following up and following through, and a pattern that when you say something, people believe it because historically when you've said it, you've followed through."[65] For an ethical leader, integrity, then, is about having the courage to do the right thing, being incorruptible, and being honest, whether anyone is looking or not.

In a survey of nearly 3,500 executives and employees, both groups placed a high premium on integrity.[66] This finding comes as no surprise. Leaders with integrity take responsibility, they do not shift blame, and they provide a consistent and reliable work environment. Not only do honorable leaders with integrity take the blame when warranted, they are secure enough to give credit where credit is due. If you are a young associate or team member who did the lion's share of the work on a project, it is a confidence and career booster to have your boss acknowledge the contribution; it undermines your trust in that leader, however, if they claim your work as their own.

In seeking to become an ethical leader who is known for integrity, consider several essential steps and practices. First, keep your word. If you make a promise, explicitly or implicitly, honor that promise, even if it is inconvenient to do so. Make fair decisions and give credit where credit is due. The perception that you are fundamentally a person of integrity who treats the team well will stand you in good stead when you need backing on a tough decision. Be aware of the bottom line, but be willing to make financial decisions for the right reasons even when it might hurt profitability.

Organizational Culture Reinforces Behavior

When working within an organization, you can create an environment that promotes integrity and good moral character in everyone within the organization. Roland E. Berenbeim, in his article *Why Ethical Leaders Are Different*, explains why ethical leaders are necessary to the success of any business or organization.[67] He suggests four steps to ethical leadership:

Step 1—Allow Institutional Limits on Power

Power corrupts, and absolute power corrupts absolutely.[68] By opening your conduct and actions to review, input, and scrutiny, you create a culture of openness. Ethical leaders know that criticism and public scrutiny of you or other members of leadership allow for accountability.[69] Institutional arrangements that allow for public scrutiny and criticism range from anonymous tip lines and HR processes for reporting misconduct (with anti-retaliation protections) to making decisions publicly and allowing input from those on the team below. In the law firm world, these actions must take place while safeguarding client confidences and maintaining the integrity of the work product and attorney-client privileges.

At a conference titled *Insight from the Ethics*, the conference organizers used input from 60 experts to identify "25 Truths of Measuring the Impact of Ethics in an Organization."[70] One of those truths was that merely having an ethics reporting procedure is not enough—the employees must trust the organization.[71] Trust in reporting procedures is earned by acting on reports—whether at the top or bottom tier of the organization.

Uncensored debates promote ethical leadership. Open discussion can foster common goals among your organization. Creating an atmosphere where all opinions are welcome is key to being a better leader and to getting the full picture from your people. To determine whether your system is helping to promote ethical leadership, ask yourself these four questions:

1. Do employees ask leadership for advice when they face an ethical problem?
2. Are employees willing to speak up?
3. Do they report ethical violations to management?
4. Do they feel comfortable pushing back when goals seem unachievable?[72]

Step 2—Actively Participate in the Procedures

Part of earning the trust of team members comes from actively participating in the process. If the rules apply to everyone, those within an organization will come to understand that the rules do, in fact, apply to everyone. Meaningfully engaging in debate, in transparency, and in ethical leadership helps build confidence in the ethical health of the organization.

Step 3—Using What You Learn

Once you hear the comments and criticism, learn from it. Taking advice from others and acting on tips foster trusts between you as a leader and the people who follow you. To measure trust in your organization, you look to see if those at the bottom of the decision-making chain trust the top and not the other way around.[73] As comments are put into action, team members will trust that they are valued and heard. Trusted leaders thrive.

Step 4—Planning for a Future Without You

No one stays at one organization forever. Someday you will retire or leave for a new opportunity. The procedures and practices you create need to outlast you, and it is your job to ensure that the ethical procedures you helped put into place survive you or any one person in your organization.[74] If your institutional safeguards are in place long term, you lessen the likelihood of ethical erosion over time.[75]

Ethical failings in leadership can happen as an organization's culture changes over time.[76] Companies that begin with ethics as a core value can succumb to industry pressures or be seduced by the call of the almighty dollar, as happened with Enron. Keeping an organization on track is on the shoulders of the leaders—whether you run a small business or a large Fortune 500 company. An ethical tone at the top is critical. No matter your position or title within an organization, look for opportunities to foster this environment within the organization. Modeling this behavior on a daily basis will likely create allies in other key leadership positions to ensure these steps are being followed by others.

Think About What the Headline Would Say

On your leadership journey, your company may never get media attention. Nonetheless, when making important decisions, sometimes it's helpful to step back and think about how the headline would read: "Greedy Business Steps on the Less Fortunate for Gain," or "Organization Takes Steps to Help the Poor." Would a feature story about you as an individual reflect well on the choices you make? "Prominent Lawyers Indicted in Murder for Hire Plot" will lose more than clients if convicted; they will lose their license and their freedom. Integrity does not waver from the right path. Remember, integrity and trustworthiness are integral to being not only an ethical leader but a good leader.

CONCLUSION

Ethical lawyering means being a person of good moral character who practices with integrity. The expectation that you will be a person of good moral character began before law school. Character examination is part of the admission process for both law school and the bar. Good moral character is the price for continuing in your privilege of holding a law license. Being a person of good moral character is a lifelong pursuit to *know* what is right and to *take actions* consistent with that understanding. The legal profession also requires lawyers to practice with integrity — an unwavering commitment to live up to the aims and ideals of the profession. When a lawyer has a firm grasp of what is right and what is not, and the integrity to do what is right, even at great cost, that lawyer has what it takes to be an ethical lawyer and a respected leader.

Take the time now to think about what you want your reputation to be. Having those principles solidly fixed in your mind will help you when you are faced with making a difficult decision. If you practice what you preach as a leader, you can influence others to join with you in your commitment to ethical leadership and you will be well on your way to being a successful leader.

Exercises

The Ethics of the Billable Hour

Assume that you have landed a job at a prestigious law firm after graduating from law school. Your colleagues treat you well and you are enjoying your practice area. The firm has a minimum billable hour requirement: 2,400 hours a year. Assuming that you will work 50 weeks per year, you will need to bill an average of 48 hours per week to hit that goal. You also know that, on average, for every three hours spent working, only two hours will be considered billable time. This means that you need to work approximately 72 hours per week to hit your minimum billable hour requirement. Read the following scenarios and think about how you hope you will approach the situation. The following scenarios are to be read independently of each other.

- The first few months are going fine — you hit your numbers and are on track to bill 2,400 hours in your first year. However, in the fifth month of working at the firm, the Covid-19 pandemic breaks out and the main partner loses the largest institutional client. Your workload is suddenly cut in half. You no longer have plenty of work. Once you get caught up on all your other cases, you ask other partners and associates for work but are only working about 40 hours per week and only billing about 26 hours per week. At this rate, you will fall well short of your billable hour requirement for the year. Your senior partner told you the firm does not plan on laying off any lawyers in response to losing the large client, but you heard through the rumor mill that associates who do not meet the billable hour requirement are often fired at the end of the year. To make matters worse, you fear that no other firms are hiring because of the pandemic.

  To help work out a solution, you approach a senior associate about what to do. The senior associate tells you to do what he and the others in the office are doing: Simply work less efficiently and spend more time on client files in order to pad your numbers. What should you do?

- As a second-year associate you are generally working 12 hours a day, 6 days a week in order to meet your billable hour expectation. You are thrilled that the managing partner assigned you a case. Unfortunately, it is a bit out of your wheelhouse. You normally handle the firm's insurance work defending car and 18-wheeler wrecks, but the partner wants you to analyze a medical malpractice case. You believe that you might need some help navigating the complexities of med-mal work.
  - To get up to speed on the case, you believe you need to spend at least three days of billable time researching the applicable law to ensure that you are competent for the case. Keep the 2,400 billable hour requirement in mind. Should you bill for your time catching up on med-mal litigation issues? If not, how will you make up those three days' worth of work, given the long hours you already work?
  - To shortcut the learning curve, you ask for a meeting with a partner who does med-mal work at the firm. The partner agrees, but says that you need to ensure the client will pay for the partner's time as well as your time while you discuss the case. After checking, the client says that he will not pay for the time discussing the case with the partner. What should you do?

Nonprofit Dilemma

You must be prepared for a board meeting of the nonprofit, playing the role of the CEO of the nonprofit. Read the facts in the list below. What do you recommend that the board do and why? Be prepared to explain to the board the potential ramifications of any action that may be taken.

- You are a licensed lawyer and the CEO for a nonprofit organization. The nonprofit helps build schools for underprivileged children in developing or war-torn regions of the world.
- In some regions, the only way to import needed building materials into these countries without prohibitive taxes is through bribes to corrupt customs officials.
- Many of the necessary materials are not available locally.
- You have an architect and design team that has already tried to use as many local products as possible, but many of them are cost-prohibitive or cannot be used for the purpose of building adequate facilities.
- Company policy and several United States laws, including the Foreign Corrupt Practices Act (FCPA), clearly prohibit bribes, but the amounts are small and violations are so common that prosecution is unlikely.

Below is a primer on the FCPA, 15 U.S.C. §§ 78dd-1 et seq. Assume that it would be difficult or expensive for the nonprofit, a U.S. prosecutor, or reporter to discover if such a written local law exists to allow the practice.

- Foreign Corrupt Practice Act: The FCPA's anti-bribery provisions contain two affirmative defenses: (1) that the payment was lawful under the written laws of the foreign country (the "local law" defense); and (2) that the money was spent as part of demonstrating a product or performing a contractual obligation (the "reasonable and bona fide business expenditure" defense). Because these are affirmative defenses, the defendant bears the burden of proving them.

- The local law defense: For the local law defense to apply, a defendant must establish that "the payment, gift, offer, or promise of anything of value that was made, was lawful under the written laws and regulations of the foreign official's, political party's, party official's, or candidate's country." The defendant must establish that the payment was lawful under the foreign country's written laws and regulations at the time of the offense. In creating the local law defense in 1988, Congress sought "to make clear that the absence of written laws in a foreign official's country would not by itself be sufficient to satisfy this defense." Thus, the fact that bribes may not be prosecuted under local law is insufficient to establish the defense. In practice, the local law defense arises infrequently, as the written laws and regulations of countries rarely, if ever, permit corrupt payments. Nevertheless, if a defendant can establish that conduct was lawful under written, local law, he or she would have a defense to prosecution.

Journal Prompts

1. Who do you know that embodies the attributes of an ethical leader? What is it about that person that makes you feel that way?

2. How would you describe a person of good moral character? For you personally, what is the foundation or origin of these moral values?

3. Describe a situation where your actions were not consistent with your desire to be viewed as a person of good moral character. Why did you take those actions? If you could have a "do-over," what would you do differently?

4. Describe a situation that challenged your integrity. Do you feel you handled it well? If not, what should you have done?

5. As you think about an ideal employment situation, what are the most important aspects of that arrangement? How many of those attributes relate to the culture of the organization?

6. When considering employment or other working relationships, what might be indicators that a person's or an organization's actions might not match their proclaimed commitment to ethics?

Endnotes

1. Kevin Kruse, *Norman Schwarzkopf: 10 Quotes on Leadership and War*, FORBES (Dec. 27, 2012), https://www .forbes.com/sites/kevinkruse/2012/12/27/norman-schwarzkopf-quotes/#58d380384eeb. Herbert Norman Schwarzkopf Jr. was a United States Army general. While serving as the commander of United States Central

Command, he led all coalition forces in the Gulf War. Norman Schwarzkopf Jr., Biography.com, https://www.biography.com/military-figure/norman-schwarzkopf (last visited July 11, 2020).

2. Herbert Warren Wind, Following Through 126 (Echo Point Books & Media 2016) (1985).

3. For a discussion of the lawyer's role to balance duty to client and duty to society, *see* Sharon Dolovich, *Ethical Lawyering and the Possibility of Integrity*, 70 Fordham L. Rev. 1629 (2002) (discussion of the standard conception of a lawyer's role as amoral technician of zealous advocacy and an alternative contextual account of the lawyer's role as pursuer of justice developed by Deborah Rhode (Deborah Rhode, In the Interests of Justice: Reforming the Legal Profession (Oxford Univ. Press 2003))). "If lawyers want to claim for themselves the status of 'officers of justice,' they must accept greater obligations to pursue justice." Dolovich, at 1639 (citing Deborah L. Rhode, *In the Interests of Justice: Reforming the Legal Profession* 17 (2000)). Justice is "the achievement of a morally defensible balance of the competing interests at stake in any legal struggle. If lawyers are to do justice, they must be ready to take account in any given case of all the interests at stake — including the interests of third parties and not merely the interests of the client and the lawyers themselves. As such, before acting on behalf of a client, they must consider all the consequences of the actions they contemplate for all of these interests, not just legally but morally as well." Dolovich, at 1639 (internal citations omitted).

4. Alexis de Tocqueville, *Democracy in America* 302-309 (Henry Reeve trans., Pa. State U. 2002) (1835), http://seas3.elte.hu/coursematerial/LojkoMiklos/Alexis-de-Tocqueville-Democracy-in-America.pdf.

5. *Id.*

6. International Bar Association, IBA International Principles on Conduct for the Legal Profession 5 (2019), available for download at https://www.ibanet.org/Article/NewDetail.aspx?ArticleUid=BC99FD2C-D253-4BFE-A3B9-C13F196D9E60#:~:text=The%2010%20core%20values%20constituting,parties%3B%209)%20Competence%3B%20and.

7. *15 C.S. Lewis Quotes That Will Stand the Test of Time*, Goalcast, https://www.goalcast.com/2018/03/26/15-c-s-lewis-quotes/c-s-lewis-quote1/ (last visited July 8, 2020). Clive Staples Lewis was a British writer and lay theologian. He held academic positions in English literature at both Oxford University and Cambridge University. *C.S. Lewis*, Biography.com, https://www.biography.com/writer/cs-lewis (last visited July 11, 2020).

8. *Integer*, Dictionary.com, https://www.dictionary.com/browse/integer (last visited July 9, 2020).

9. *Integrity*, Merriam-Webster's Dictionary, https://www.merriam-webster.com/dictionary/integrity (last visited July 7, 2020); *Character*, Merriam-Webster's Dictionary, https://www.merriam-webster.com/dictionary/character (last visited July 7, 2020).

10. *Integrity*, Stanford Encyclopedia of Philosophy, https://plato.stanford.edu/entries/integrity/ (last visited Sept. 25, 2020).

11. Bernard Gert & Joshua Gert, *The Definition of Morality*, The Stanford Encyclopedia of Philosophy (Fall 2017 ed.), https://plato.stanford.edu/archives/fall2017/entries/morality-definition/.

12. *Pirates of the Caribbean: The Curse of the Black Pearl* (2003).

13. *See* Ty Kiisel, *Without It, No Real Success Is Possible*, Forbes (Feb. 5, 2013), https://www.forbes.com/sites/tykiisel/2013/02/05/without-it-no-real-success-is-possible/#7f9a96e3e491.

14. Dolovich, *supra* note 3, at 1649.

15. Harper Lee, To Kill a Mockingbird (2006).

16. There are, of course, exceptions here. Lawyers are not forced to take cases in which they cannot represent a person in good conscience. The rules provide mechanisms to allow lawyers to withdraw. *See* ABA Rule 1.16. Specifically, a lawyer may withdraw if "the client insists upon taking action that the lawyer considers repugnant or with which the lawyer has a fundamental disagreement." ABA Rule 1.16(b)(4).

17. Abraham Lincoln Quote, Liberty Tree, http://libertytree.ca/quotes/Abraham.Lincoln.Quote.7140 (last visited July 11, 2020). Abraham Lincoln was an American statesman and lawyer who served as the 16th President of the United States. Abraham Lincoln, The White House, https://www.whitehouse.gov/about-the-white-house/presidents/abraham-lincoln/ (last visited July 11, 2020).

18. *Character*, American Psychological Association, https://dictionary.apa.org/character (last visited July 7, 2020). https://dictionary.apa.org/character (last visited July 7, 2020).

19. Deborah L. Rhode, *Virtue and the Law: The Good Moral Character Requirement in Occupational Licensing, Bar Regulation, and Immigration Proceedings*, 43 Law & Soc. Inquiry 1027, 1030 (2018), *citing* John M. Doris, Lack of Character: Personality & Moral Behavior 115 (Cambridge Univ. Press 2005) (2002).

20. *Aristotle's Ethics*, The Stanford Encyclopedia of Philosophy, https://plato.stanford.edu/entries/aristotle-ethics/ (last visited Sept. 25, 2020).

21. Paul W. Taylor, *Moral Virtue and Responsibility for Character*, 25 Analysis 17, 22 (1964).

22. *See* 18 U.S.C §§ 1956-1957. *See also* Kathleen F. Brickey, *Tainted Assets and the Right to Counsel — The Money Laundering Conundrum*, 66 Wash. U. L.Q. 47 (1988).

23. Donald McCabe retired from Rutgers in 2014 and continued his research on academic integrity until his passing in 2016. Susan Todd, *Three Decades Uncovering the Truth About Student Cheating*, Rutgers (May 16, 2014), https://www.rutgers.edu/news/three-decades-uncovering-truth-about-student-cheating.

24. *See generally* Donald McCabe, Cheating in College: Why Students Do It and What Educators Can Do About It (JHUP 2017).

25. Peter Ashworth et al., *Guilty in Whose Eyes? University Students' Perceptions of Cheating and Plagiarism in Academic Work and Assessment*, 22 Stud. in Higher Educ. 187–203 (1997), *available at* https://doi.org/10.1080/03075079712331381034.

26. The undergraduate data excludes first-year students, code schools, and two-year schools.

27. This basic dataset was compiled based upon surveys that were conducted between fall 2002 and spring 2015, by Dr. Donald McCabe of Rutgers University and the International Center for Academic Integrity. Daniel McCabe et al., *Academic Integrity: How Widespread Are Cheating and Plagiarism?*, ICAI (2004).

28. Lucia Graves, *Which Types of Students Cheat the Most*, US News, https://www.usnews.com/education/articles/2008/10/03/which-types-of-students-cheat-most (last visited July 11, 2020).

29. *Id.*

30. *Id.*

31. *Id.*

32. *Id.*

33. Immanuel Kant Quote, Brainy Quote, https://www.brainyquote.com/quotes/immanuel_kant_134876 (last visited July 11, 2020). Immanuel Kant was an influential German philosopher in the Age of Enlightenment. Immanuel Kant, Stanford Encyclopedia of Philosophy, https://plato.stanford.edu/entries/kant/ (last visited July 11, 2020).

34. Martha Neil, *As Leaders Blame GM Lawyers for Ignition Woes, Lawmaker Asks: Why Wasn't General Counsel Fired?*, A.B.A. J. (July 17, 2014), https://www.abajournal.com/news/article/senators_ask_gm_why_wasnt_general_counsel_fired.

35. Tanya Basu, *Timeline: A History of GM's Ignition Switch Defect*, NPR (Mar. 31, 2014), https://www.npr.org/2014/03/31/297158876/timeline-a-history-of-gms-ignition-switch-defect.

36. *Id.*

37. Neil, *supra* note 34.

38. *Groupthink*, Merriam-Webster's Dictionary, https://www.merriam-webster.com/dictionary/groupthink (last visited July 7, 2020).

39. *Id.*

40. Jake Tapper, *How to Become an Enron Millionaire*, Salon (Jan. 29, 2002), https://www.salon.com/2002/01/29/enrons_human_cost/.

41. *Id.*

42. *Id.*

43. Bernard S. Carrey, *Enron-Where Were the Lawyers?*, 27 Vt. L. Rev. 871, 871–72 (2003).

44. Court-appointed examiner Neal Batson of the Atlanta law firm Alston & Bird, who led the investigation, advises corporate lawyers who encounter wrongdoing to recognize who their client is. "In most instances you're representing the corporation, not the officers," he says. "Individuals hire and fire you and make decisions about how you will be compensated, but you're not representing those individuals." Richard Acello, *Enron Lawyers in the Hot Seat*, A.B.A. J. (June 1, 2004), https://www.abajournal.com/magazine/article/enron_lawyers_in_the_hot_seat.

45. *Id.*

46. Comment 4, Tex. Disciplinary R. Prof. Conduct 5.04: Professional Independence of a Lawyer, Tex. Disciplinary R. Prof. Conduct (1989), *reprinted in* Tex. Gov't Code Ann., tit. 2, subtit. G, app. (Vernon Supp. 1995) (State Bar Rules art X, section 9), https://www.legalethicstexas.com/Ethics-Resources/Rules/Texas-Disciplinary-Rules-of-Professional-Conduct/V--LAW-FIRMS-AND-ASSOCIATIONS/5-04-Professional-Independence-of-a-Lawyer (last visited July 11, 2020).

47. Ronald E. Berenbeim, *The Enron Ethics Breakdown*, The Conference Board (Feb. 2002), https://www.conference-board.org/publications/publicationdetail.cfm?publicationid=519.

48. *Id.*

49. *Collapse of Enron: Hearing Before the S. Comm. on Commerce, Science, and Transportation*, 107th Cong. 25 (2002) (statement of William Powers, Member of Enron Board of Directors). William C. Powers, Jr., was the

former President of the University of Texas, dean of the Texas Law School, career law professor, and former Enron board member. He authored the 2002 Powers Report, which detailed the entire Enron scandal in 217-page "blistering" detail. "In 2001 he joined Enron's board and agreed to lead a committee to investigate the company's financial dealings. Its findings led to one of the nation's largest corporate scandals and the collapse of Enron, a Houston-based energy company that had started to implode in 2000. His blistering 217-page report found a culture of deception, self-dealing and self-enrichment at Enron. Controls, it said, had failed at almost every level, and the losers were the company's shareholders, to the tune of more than $60 billion. Some critics had feared that Mr. Powers would be soft on Enron because the company had donated $3.5 million to the University of Texas, including $276,000 to the law school. But those concerns evaporated once the report came out and Mr. Powers testified before Congress, saying that what he had found was 'absolutely appalling.' The Powers Report said that Enron executives had intentionally manipulated the company's profits, inflating them by almost $1 billion. The report, which served as a road map for more than a dozen congressional and executive branch investigations, placed the blame squarely on Kenneth L. Lay, Enron's longtime chairman and chief executive, and his protégé, Jeffrey K. Skilling, who was president and the next chief executive. Mr. Skilling, who was convicted on fraud and conspiracy charges in 2006, was released from federal custody last month after serving 12 years of a 24-year sentence; Mr. Lay faced the possibility of the rest of his life in prison but died of coronary artery disease at 64 before he was sentenced. After issuing his report, Mr. Powers returned to the law school, where he was an expert on product-liability law." Katherine Q. Seelye, *Obituaries: William Powers Jr.*, N.Y. TIMES, https://www.nytimes.com/2019/03/13/obituaries/william-powers-dead.html (last visited July 11, 2020).

50. Dolovich, *supra* note 3, at 1681.
51. Tapper, *supra* note 40.
52. Dolovich, *supra* note 3, at 1682.
53. Lee, *supra* note 15. Nelle Harper Lee was an American novelist best known for her 1960 novel *To Kill a Mockingbird*. It won the 1961 Pulitzer Prize and has become a classic of modern American literature. Harper Lee, BIOGRAPHY.COM, https://www.biography.com/writer/harper-lee (last visited July 11, 2020).
54. This was an experience and lesson learned by one of the authors, Elizabeth M. Fraley, during her years in private practice as a trial lawyer.
55. *Law Grads Share Baylor Background — And Now, a Kidney*, BAYLOR PROUD, https://www2.baylor.edu/baylorproud/2009/03/law-grads-share-baylor-background-and-now-a-kidney/ (last visited July 11, 2020).
56. From a conversation with Judge Ed Kinkeade and two of the authors, Elizabeth M. Fraley and Stephen L. Rispoli. Baylor Academy of the Advocate in St Andrews (July 30, 2017).
57. *See* Gwen Glazer, *Librarians' Favorite Twain Quotations*, NEW YORK PUB. LIB. (Nov. 29, 2016), https://www.nypl.org/blog/2016/11/29/librarians-favorite-mark-twain-quotations. Samuel Langhorne Clemens, known by his pen name Mark Twain, was an American writer, humorist, entrepreneur, publisher, and lecturer. Mark Twain, BIOGRAPHY.COM, https://www.biography.com/writer/mark-twain (last visited July 11, 2020).
58. Linda Klebe Treviño et al., *A Qualitative Investigation of Perceived Executive Ethical Leadership: Perceptions from Inside and Outside the Executive Suite*, 56 HUM. REL. 18 (Jan. 1, 2003).
59. Lyrics by Daft Punk, *Harder, Better, Faster, Stronger*, VIRGIN RECORDS (2007).
60. Dolovich, *supra* note 3, at 1667.
61. *Honesty*, MERRIAM-WEBSTER'S DICTIONARY, https://www.merriam-webster.com/dictionary/honesty (last visited July 7, 2020).
62. Alexi Barrionuevo, *Enron Chiefs Guilty of Fraud and Conspiracy*, N.Y. TIMES (May 25, 2006), https://www.nytimes.com/2006/05/25/business/25cnd-enron.html.
63. Klebe Treviño, *supra* note 58.
64. Marcel Schwantes, *Warren Buffet Will Only Hire People with High Integrity — Here Are 5 Ways They Separate Themselves from the Pack*, Bus. INSIDER (Dec. 17, 2019), https://www.businessinsider.com/warren-buffett-hire-people-with-integrity-heres-how-to-find-them-9.
65. Klebe Treviño, *supra* note 58.
66. Robert Half, *Which Leadership Trait Rises to the Top? Integrity*, ROBERT HALF (Oct. 27, 2016), https://www.roberthalf.com/blog/salaries-and-skills/which-leadership-trait-rises-to-the-top-integrity.
67. Berenbeim, *supra* note 47.

68. Quote attributed to John Emerich Edward Dalberg, Lord Acton, a British 19th-century historian. Christopher Shea, *Why Power Corrupts*, Smithsonian Magazine, Oct. 2012, https://www.smithsonianmag .com/science-nature/why-power-corrupts-37165345/ (last visited Oct. 19, 2020)

69. *Id.* at 2.

70. Sheri Rothman, *Truths About Measuring the Impact of Ethics Programs in Your Organization*, THE CONFERENCE BOARD 1 (July 2017), https://www.conference-board.org/publications/publicationdetail .cfm?publicationid=7550.

71. *Id.* at 5.

72. *Id.*

73. *Id.*

74. Ronald E. Berenbeim, *Why Ethical Leaders Are So Different*, THE CONFERENCE BOARD (May 2005), https:// www.conference-board.org/publications/publicationdetail.cfm?publicationid=961.

75. Rothman, *supra* note 70.

76. *Id.*

Chapter 13

The Right Leader at the Right Time

At the very moment when we are struggling to attain a sense of personal autonomy, we are also caught up in vital forces that are larger than ourselves, so that while we may be protagonists of our own lives, we are important participants in a larger drama. . . . As I was to discover, acting in the belief that I was part of a greater whole while maintaining flexibility, patience, and acute awareness led to "all manner of unforeseen incidents and meetings and material assistance which no man could have dreamed would have come his way."

Joseph Jaworski[1]

Purpose

Encourage preparedness and patience in anticipation of capitalizing on future opportunities.

Learning Objectives

At the end of this chapter, you should be able to:

- Discuss the importance of preparing for your next leadership role.
- Describe techniques for increasing your opportunities.

Discussion

INTRODUCTION

The biography *Churchill: Walking with Destiny* suggests that Churchill spent his life actively preparing to serve as British Prime Minister during World War II. In 1891, at just 16 years of age, Churchill told a friend that he foresaw "great upheavals, terrible struggles; wars such as one cannot imagine."[2] Churchill believed that London, at some point in the future "will be in danger, and in the high position I shall occupy, it will fall to me to save the capital and save the Empire."[3] His life was shaped by this belief, such that his military service, speech and writing experience, and even his failures in public life, led to his being the right person to lead Great Britain during the country's "finest hour."[4]

Churchill never considered as coincidence the life events and experiences that led to his succeeding Neville Chamberlain as Prime Minister as the Nazi threat became real.[5] Rather, his life experience allowed him to perceive clearly the threat that Adolf Hitler and his plans posed.[6] Whether Churchill was prescient or opportunistic, he saw a chance and took it. The benefit of seizing your chance cannot be overstated when it comes to leadership.

Preparing for future leadership positions is central to leadership development. Planning for the leadership position you want prepares you when the opportunity arises. In this chapter, we encourage you to broaden your perspective to plan for opportunities you do not yet see and to keep your eyes open.

BEING PREPARED FOR LEADERSHIP

We learn from Churchill and other leaders the role opportunity plays. You cannot predict when an opportunity will present itself. You must be ready to act when given the chance. As such, your life experiences, training, and education should prepare you for your next role and the one after that. Leaders commit to learning new skills and strengthening their existing skill sets continuously. As you study leadership styles, traits, and capabilities, you can compare them to your own, receive critical feedback to grow, and take steps to push your comfort zone. Leaders committed to learning, stretching, and growing are more likely to see and be ready to seize a new opportunity. How will you recognize the next opportunity? This is where timing and "luck" come into the equation.

TIMING IS EVERYTHING

Synchronicity [is] a meaningful coincidence of two or more events, where something other than the probability of chance is involved.

Carl Jung[7]

A convergence of hard work, experience, luck, and timing led to Winston Churchill's rise to Prime Minister in 1940. While no one would claim that Hitler's rise to power was good for the vast majority of people, it provided an opportunity for Churchill. He foresaw the rise of Hitler and the Nazi party and spoke out early about the Nazi threat even though it was an unpopular opinion at the time. Neville Chamberlain took office as Prime Minister in 1937, and he preferred to deal with the crisis on mainland Europe by appeasing Hitler. To that end, he signed the misguided Munich Agreement in 1938. By 1939, Britain had declared war on Germany, and Chamberlain resigned in 1940. Throughout Chamberlain's attempts at appeasement, Churchill led the opposition push to stand up to Hitler. Having already led the push to fight Hitler, he became the natural choice for Prime Minister in Britain's hour of need.[8]

But timing and opportunity work both ways. Churchill is famous for his leadership during World War II, but he was ousted from office as the war was ending. Germany surrendered on May 7, 1945, and Churchill was defeated in the July 1945 general election. Even so, Churchill maintained influence through the rest of the 1940s. The tide then turned again, and he was elected Prime Minister for a second time in 1952.[9] His opportunities to lead ebbed and flowed; the one constant was Churchill's willingness to lead.

Mastering the art of timing can be a lesson in patience and readiness. You work diligently to study leadership, develop personal and professional goals, enhance your strengths and minimize your weaknesses, even though there may not be a leadership position available to you at the time. The art of timing, however, involves knowing what you want so you can act quickly when the opportunity arises. Opportunity can come in many forms, including a new job, a new client, a new partnership track, or a new opening for a political office. No matter the situation, be mindful of your long-term goals and look for opportunity to capitalize on the right moment to achieve them.

MAKE YOUR OWN LUCK

Luck has nothing to do with it, because I have spent many, many hours, countless hours, on the court working for my one moment in time, not knowing when it would come.
Serena Williams[10]

Have you ever heard the phrase, "the harder I work, the more luck I seem to have"? "Luck" is often the result of years of intentional planning and practice, and execution at just the right moment. Take, for example, the real estate developer who often gets "lucky" breaks—the government or an energy company needs some land, and she has just what they need. She capitalizes on the situation and reaps the benefits. While some degree of luck may be involved, really, she is seeing her effort come to fruition. She works every day to find out what is going on around town, makes the right purchases at the right time, and waits for the right opportunity to present itself. Being prepared and informed while watching for opportunities and having the courage to act comprises a great deal of what we may think of as luck.

We can learn from others who are "lucky." They often exhibit patterns of behavior that optimize their environment and present them with advantageous opportunities. Lucky people tend to use the following behaviors:

1. *They meet new people.* They find or make opportunities to meet new people and get to know them. They are constantly working on the list of people that they know. This is not a superficial knowledge, but a genuine care to get to know others. At the same time, it builds a network of relationships for future opportunities.
2. *They make small talk.* They take the time to visit with others. This small talk does include the mundane (like the weather), but also includes the personal. In doing so, the lucky will ask questions that build relationships: Who is your spouse and what does he/she do? Do you have any children? What do you do for fun?
3. *They make connections.* They take the time to introduce people and make connections. This is also known as the art of networking.
4. *They listen.* Rather than trying to dominate the conversation, the lucky listen to others and seek ways to engage them. By listening carefully, you can learn a great deal about others and their goals.
5. *They ask for or offer help.* They are not afraid to ask for help. By asking others for help, you are validating them by telling them that you value their contributions and need them. By the same token, the lucky offer to help others and follow through on promises. Both asking for and offering to help create meaningful connections.
6. *They get off the beaten path.* They are bold — they are willing to take risks (within reason) and to learn from failures.
7. *They say yes.* Even when they want to, or should, say no, they step forward to answer the call when others need help or ask for a favor. That doesn't mean being a rubber-stamp yes-person. That means seeing the value in learning new skills, gaining valuable experiences, and meeting new people because you are willing to help. You never know what new opportunities you will discover along the way.[11]

Those who make their own luck practice these habits daily. One successful lawyer and entrepreneur goes out of his way to meet new people, learn about them, and offer to help them. When speaking to young lawyers, he coaches them on how to connect: hold personal conversations; make people feel special; make a good first impression; create meaningful relationships; fearlessly ask for something; and treat everyone as a friend. His business boomed as he leaned into these ideals and practices. He frequently says yes when he's asked to do something for someone else. Because of these efforts, he has many opportunities presented to him. While some might categorize those opportunities as "luck," he gratefully recognizes that opportunities flow from his earlier investment of time and effort. As such, he is able to pursue the opportunities that interest him.[12]

To increase your own professional luck, work as many of these practices into your daily life as you can. Some will be easy to incorporate. Some will take time and effort to develop and sustain and to do so with joy and genuine enthusiasm. All will help you make your own luck.

DON'T TAKE IT PERSONALLY

It is easy to celebrate a well-timed success; it is more difficult to acknowledge that defeat or rejection might happen at the right time as well. We often want a new opportunity, whether a job, a promotion, or a new client, but do not always get what we want. Even though we might be disappointed by the loss, there are two important lessons to take away from disappointment. First, learn not to take disappointment personally. People within organizations must do what they believe is best for the organization. Second, the disappointment may be happening at the right time to open the path to something better.

Rejection or defeat is not the end of the world — it may mean this was not the right opportunity for you after all. In 1965, Julie Andrews accepted the Academy Award for best actress for her role in *Mary Poppins*, but here is the rest of the story. Ms. Andrews was free to take the role only because Jack Warner refused to cast her as Eliza Doolittle in the movie version of *My Fair Lady*. Andrews originated the role of Eliza on both the London and Broadway stages, but Warner thought she wasn't pretty enough to star in the movie version. During her speech accepting the Oscar, Andrews displayed her usual class and charm by thanking Mr. Warner for giving the role to another actress.[13] Had he not, Andrews would not have won her first Oscar.

You cannot foresee all the twists and turns that alter the path of your life, personally or professionally. The opportunity in front of you may seem ideal, but there may be pitfalls you do not yet recognize. By the same token, this "ideal" opportunity may be inferior to another of which you are not yet aware. Do try to capitalize on desirable opportunities, but when the timing doesn't work, consider whether a better one may be waiting for you. Accept the decision with grace and know that one of two things can happen: You can show them they made a mistake by doing your absolute best work elsewhere, or, like Julie Andrews, you can thank them for freeing you to accept a better opportunity.

As part of your journey to grow and develop, learn from the decision. Spend time understanding why you were not the right choice. If possible, inquire about your application or interview by asking the person you believe will be in the best position to give you honest feedback. What skills, characteristics, qualifications, and experiences were most important in making their decision? What might you have needed to be considered the ideal candidate? Thank them for their time and honesty. Next, decide if you should and could develop those missing skills in preparation for the next opportunity. In thinking about the next opportunity, you should consider what might be available and where.[14] Sometimes you have to move on to move up,[15] either to be perceived as the right person by a different audience or because you have reached the highest available position in the current organization.

SOMETIMES NO IS THE RIGHT ANSWER

The art of leadership is saying no, not saying yes. It is very easy to say yes.

Tony Blair[16]

An important corollary to being prepared for the right leadership opportunity at the right time is keeping yourself available for that opportunity. Lawyers are often asked to serve on committees and boards, run for public office, and take leadership roles at a company or firm. Saying yes to every opportunity, however, may not be the right path. While other people may block some of life's paths for you, you can be intentional about choosing not to follow a path. Just because you are asked to take a path does not mean it is right for you. If you know your long-term goals well enough, you can identify the potential pathways that lead you to them, even if those pathways are not open to you at the moment. Some pathways present wonderful opportunities but do not lead or contribute to achieving your long-term goal. The danger of taking these pathways is that you do not have the time — your most valuable commodity — when the right opportunity becomes available.

Take, for example, a young lawyer pursuing a career as a tax lawyer. She wants to make partner at her firm in the next five years and is passionate about helping animals. Her community engagement goal is to join the board of the local zoo. She believes the board position will fulfill her desire to be engaged in the community while doing something she is interested in. Given the composition of the board, she thinks she could also make business connections. While she has expressed interest in getting on the board and applied for open positions, she has not yet been accepted. Several board members have told her that they want her on the board but the timing is not right yet.

A few months after her latest contact with the zoo, she is offered a board position with a local charity focused on helping local underprivileged children get meals for weekends. She believes the organization does good work and benefits the community, but it does not line up with her long-term goals. To make partner in the next five years, she'll need to manage her time carefully, work long hours, and bring new business to the firm to meet the criteria for equity partner. Accepting the invitation to join this board limits her time to spend on becoming a partner and would keep her from being able to accept a position on the zoo board when offered. In this situation, she can thank the nonprofit for the opportunity, but decline the invitation, even if she does not know when the zoo board opportunity will arise. Sometimes protecting your time by saying no is the right decision. Learning when to say yes and when to say no is an important part of becoming an effective leader.

CONCLUSION

Being prepared for leadership requires planning and patience. Churchill knew his ultimate goal and worked for a lifetime to achieve it. His preparation through various roles, his readiness for opportunities that led him down the right path, and his diligence in working toward his goal allowed him to be in the right place at the right time. Mastering these concepts and incorporating them into your leadership skill set will have you ready as leadership opportunities arise. You rarely are handed leadership opportunities without attention and effort; you must look for the opportunity and make your own luck.

Exercise

The Right Leader at the Right Time with the Right Speech

Go online to find print copies and videos of the following speeches by these noteworthy leaders. Share and discuss your thoughts and major takeaways. Why do you think these individuals were the right leader at the right time with the right speech?

- Winston Churchill: "We Shall Fight on the Beaches"
- John F. Kennedy: "We Choose to Go to the Moon"
- Martin Luther King, Jr.: "I Have a Dream"
- Barbara Jordan: "Constitutional Faith"
- Ruth Bader Ginsburg: oral argument in *Weinberger v. Wiesenfeld*

Journal Prompts

1. Revisit your long-term goals. What can you be doing right now to prepare to succeed with those goals?

2. Do you believe that you can make your own luck? Why or why not?

3. Do you struggle with saying no to others when asked to help with something? Why or why not?

Endnotes

1. JOSEPH JAWORSKI, SYNCHRONICITY: THE INNER PATH OF LEADERSHIP 88 (Betty Sue Flowers ed., Berrett-Koehler Publisher, Inc. 1996) (internal quote attributed to Johann Wolfgang von Goethe, a late eighteenth- and early nineteenth-century German writer and statesman). Joseph Jaworski, the son of Leon Jaworski, was one of the founding lawyers of Bracewell, but he resigned in 1980 to found the American Leadership Forum.

From there, he moved to London to lead the scenario planning group for the Royal Dutch/Shell Group companies. Jaworski returned to the United States to continue teaching leadership, founding Generon International and the Global Leadership Initiative.

2. Tunku Varadarajan, *"Churchill: Walking with Destiny" Review: A Life at Full Pelt*, WALL ST. J. (Nov. 16, 2018) (quoting Winston Churchill), https://www.wsj.com/articles/churchill-walking-with-destiny-review-a-life-at-full-pelt-1542372879.

3. *Id.*

4. *Their Finest Hour*, WINSTONCHURCHILL.ORG, https://winstonchurchill.org/resources/speeches/1940-the-finest-hour/their-finest-hour/ (last visited July 8, 2020).

5. *Who Was Winston Churchill and Why Was He So Important?*, BBC (Feb. 14, 2019), https://www.bbc.co.uk/newsround/31043477.

6. *Id.*

7. JAWORSKI, *supra* note 1. Carl Gustav Jung was a Swiss psychiatrist and psychoanalyst who founded analytical psychology. Jung's work was influential in the fields of psychiatry, anthropology, archaeology, literature, philosophy, and religious studies.

8. Biography.com Editors, *Neville Chamberlain Biography*, BIOGRAPHY.COM (Mar. 12, 2020), https://www.biography.com/political-figure/neville-chamberlain.

9. Biography.com Editors, *Winston Churchill Biography*, BIOGRAPHY.COM (Apr. 27, 2020), https://www.biography.com/political-figure/winston-churchill.

10. Jolie A. Doggett, *13 Secrets to Serena Williams' Success*, ESSENCE (Mar. 23, 2015), https://www.essence.com/celebrity/13-secrets-to-serena-williams-success/#150282.

11. This list was inspired by the Susan Roane's list of luck patterns, and expanded with the inclusion of additional thoughts. *See* SUSAN ROANE, HOW TO CREATE YOUR OWN LUCK 2 (Wiley 2004).

12. Leah Teague conversation with Bill Shaddock, Baylor Law School (Jan. 22, 2020).

13. Julie Andrews, Academy Award Acceptance Speech (1965).

14. *Luke* 4:24.

15. John Brubaker, *Can You Ever Be a "Prophet in Your Own Land"?*, ENTREPRENEUR (May 4, 2016), https://www.entrepreneur.com/article/275066.

16. Quote attributed to Tony Blair, former Prime Minister of the United Kingdom. *See, e.g.*, Deanna Maio, *The Art of Leadership Is Saying No, Not Saying Yes*, DELEGATED TO DONE, https://delegatedtodone.com/the-art-of-leadership-is-saying-no-not-saying-yes/ (last visited July 23, 2020).

Part III

Leadership with Others: Effective Group Dynamics

Chapter 14 — Leadership and Emotional Intelligence

> I don't want to be at the mercy of my emotions. I want to use them, to enjoy them and to dominate them.
>
> **Oscar Wilde[1]**

Purpose

Explain emotional intelligence and its impact on relationships and leadership, and offer suggestions for developing your emotional intelligence.

Learning Objectives

At the end of this chapter, you should be able to:

- Describe the concept of emotional intelligence and its importance to leadership effectiveness.
- Assess your emotional intelligence.

Discussion

INTRODUCTION

Dan Jansen competed in his first Winter Olympic Games at age 19, finishing fourth in the 500m speed skating event.[2] The American skater arrived in Calgary four years later with a recent world sprint championship and with high expectations that he would medal. The day before his first race, he learned his sister Jane was dying of leukemia; she died just hours before he skated. He fell on the first corner of his first race. Jansen raced again in the 1000m race and was in the lead with just a lap to go. Disastrously, he fell again and did not medal.[3]

Jansen qualified for the Albertville Olympic Games and again seemed likely to medal. He missed the 500m bronze by 0.20 seconds and was a dismal 26th in the 1000m. Despite continued success elsewhere in the speed skating world, Jansen consistently underperformed at the Olympics.[4]

Jansen skated in the Lillehammer Olympic Games, and his streak of misfortune continued. A small error in the 500m race landed him in eighth place. He laced up his skates for his final Olympic race thinking, "In a minute and a half, you're done and your Olympics will be over."[5] He lost his footing for a split second after 200m, and his wife had to look away. She needn't have. Jansen recovered his footing and skated to a world record in the 1000m race. The Olympic jinx was finally broken.[6]

Jansen's story of heartbreaking underachievement is etched in the annals of Olympic history. The lesson is not of Jansen's talent being enough to medal. Jansen's real story highlights his ability to overcome adversity and ultimately succeed. Like many individuals, teams, and groups, Jansen had more than enough talent, ability, and training, yet he consistently underperformed. Jansen ultimately medaled not due to innate talent and training; he had already succeeded in every world skating area. He medaled because he ultimately overcame frustration and doubt — connecting with his emotions and managing them. Instead of being remembered as the biggest "choker" in the sport, he retired with a world record and a gold medal.

The smartest or most talented person or team is not always the most successful. Their emotional intelligence can be their shortcoming. In sports, athletes have to deal with many expectations and demands, and the difference in performance is not due solely to physical training or nutrition. The athlete's mental state matters. Increasingly, top performers in sports and other endeavors believe emotional intelligence plays a key role beyond innate ability and training.

The same emotional intelligence issues translate to lawyers and leaders. Many a lawyer can tell you of winning a trial where they did not have the better case. They won because they were better prepared and mentally tougher when trial came along. This chapter will introduce you to the four quadrants of emotional intelligence and describe the benefits of developing your own EQ.

MASTERING EMOTIONAL INTELLIGENCE IS TIED TO SUCCESS

"[A] person's emotional intelligence — often referred to as 'EQ' — may be even more important than their IQ when it comes to predicting success, quality of relationships and overall happiness."[7] Emotional intelligence was defined in 1990 as "the ability to monitor one's own and others' feelings and emotions, to discriminate among them and to use this information to guide one's thinking and actions."[8] In other words, emotional intelligence is the ability to interact effectively with others and to control yourself. It involves connecting with your emotions and managing them. It requires motivating yourself, controlling your impulses, and overcoming frustration and doubt.

EQ applies to teams as well, but it is more complex because of the number of personalities on the team. Winning teams have high EQ, not just talent. What motivates one team member and how each controls frustration may differ from what works for another player. Interactions will vary among team members. The interplay of personalities and EQ can tip the balance to a more winning scenario or into the biggest chokes in sports history. Every sport is replete with examples of teams that blew 30-point leads, made mindless emotion-driven errors, drew senseless penalties, or did not have the emotional toughness to win. While difficult to quantify, EQ in the team setting is vital to success.

As in sports, a winning law firm needs more than just good people, it needs high EQ. Lawyers are almost universally highly intelligent and competent people. A lawyer-leader in a legal setting has the rare challenge of managing other lawyers who, by definition, are trained in acrimony. Leading a group of high-achieving individuals requires a high level of emotional intelligence. Successful leaders know when to mix authority and forbearance and to exert control of their own emotions. Picking where and when to assert authority, and in what measure, is more art than science. But it is an art that a successful leader must master.

DANIEL GOLEMAN'S MODEL OF EMOTIONAL INTELLIGENCE

Daniel Goleman, the author and psychologist who popularized the term "emotional intelligence," found that professionals such as doctors, lawyers, and business executives need above-average intelligence to enter their field. Once they master the technical competencies necessary to enter that field, however, intelligence and technical skills are often equal among successful leaders.[9] Emotional intelligence (self-awareness, self-regulation, awareness of the feelings and reactions of others, and highly effective communication skills) "becomes an important differentiator."[10] "To oversimplify, emotional intelligence (coined EQ after the IQ abbreviation) roughly equates to one's personal and human relations skills, sometimes commonly referred to as 'people skills.'"[11] Goleman found that emotional intelligence accounts for 80 to 90 percent of a person's success in moving up the ladder when IQ and technical skills are roughly equivalent.[12] Data also shows that with training, EQ skills can improve over time.[13]

A leader's emotional intelligence can make a significant difference when delivering difficult news — as lawyers often must do. Consider how British media giant BBC handled the firing of nearly 200 journalists who were part of an experimental news division. Despite a valiant effort by that division, management decided to close it and sent an executive to announce the decision. That executive assembled the staff and announced the layoffs. Before delivering the bad news, he began with a glowing account of how well rival divisions were doing. He next mentioned having just returned from a holiday in Cannes. Once he turned to address the closure, his "brusque, even contentious manner . . . incited something beyond the expected frustration. People became enraged — not just at the management decision, but also at the bearer of the news himself."[14] Concerned for the safety of the executive, security was called to usher him safely from the room.

The next day, a different executive was sent to visit the same staff. He engaged the group in a very different manner:

> He spoke from his heart about the crucial importance of journalism to the vibrancy of a society, and of the calling that had drawn them all to the field in the first place. He reminded them that no one goes into journalism to get rich — as a profession its finances have always been marginal, with job security ebbing and flowing with larger economic tides. And he invoked the passion, even the dedication, the journalists had for the service they offered. Finally, he wished them all well in getting on with their careers.
>
> When this leader finished speaking, the staff cheered.[15]

The key difference was the emotional impact each delivery had on the group. "One drove the group toward antagonism and hostility, the other toward optimism, even inspiration, in the face of difficulty."[16] How could the first executive so badly miss the mark? He did not think about the emotional impact of his words.

FOUR QUADRANTS OF EMOTIONAL INTELLIGENCE

Goleman divides emotional intelligence into four quadrants or domains, all of which can be learned, developed, and improved: *self-awareness, self-management, social awareness,* and *relationship management*.[17] The first two (self-awareness and self-management) focus on regulation of our thoughts, behaviors, and actions.[18] The second two (social awareness and relationship management) impact how we relate to others and how others perceive us.[19]

SELF-AWARENESS	**SOCIAL AWARENESS**
Emotional Self-Awareness	Empathy
Accurate Self-Assessment	Organizational Awareness
Self-Confidence	Service Orientation
SELF-MANAGEMENT	**RELATIONSHIP MANAGEMENT**
Emotional Self-Control	Developing Others
Transparency	Inspirational Leadership
Adaptability	Change Catalyst
Achievement	Influence
Initiative	Conflict Management
Optimism	Teamwork and Collaboration

Self-Awareness

How well do you understand your own emotions? What values do you hold dear? What motivates you? Having strong self-awareness means being realistic and honest about strengths and limitations, even to the point of being able to laugh at your own foibles.[20] Self-aware individuals understand their values, goals, and dreams. They are attuned to what "feels right" to them. Goleman's self-awareness cluster contains three competencies:

- *Emotional self-awareness*: Recognizing and understanding your emotions as well as recognizing the impact of your emotional state on the work performance of others and their relationship with you and others.
- *Accurate self-assessment*: Knowing your own strengths and limitations, including how well you are able to evaluate them realistically.
- *Self-confidence*: Having a positive and strong sense of your self-worth and capabilities, sufficient enough that you can be critically self-reflective.[21]

You may be tempted by an offer that comes with a large salary, but self-awareness leads you to turn it down because it is not a good fit with long-term goals of balancing family and work, or because in your heart, you know you want to work for a nonprofit that is important to you.

Self-Management

Self-management looks at how you manage your internal emotional and behavioral status, your impulses, and resources — in other words, how well you self-regulate. The self-management cluster contains six competencies:

- *Emotional self-control*: The ability to control disruptive emotions and impulses.
- *Transparency*: The ability to maintain standards of honesty and integrity by acting congruently with those values.

- *Adaptability*: The ability to be flexible in order to handle changing situations and to be adaptable to overcoming obstacles.
- *Achievement*: Striving to improve or meet an internal standard of excellence.
- *Initiative*: Readiness to seize opportunities and act.
- *Optimism*: Persistence in pursuing goals despite obstacles and setbacks.[22]

In a law firm or leadership setting, this can include things like not throwing temper tantrums, expressing expectations honestly, and being flexible when the situation changes while remaining focused on the ultimate goal. Litigation presents a variety of frustrating scenarios to the attorneys involved. The judge may rule against you or the jury may return a verdict that is not favorable to your client. The ruling may seem unfair or so legally wrong that you know you will appeal. You may be tempted to blame others for the loss — the associate could have done a better job writing the brief, your trial partner's cross-examination of the key witness could have been better, and so forth. Lashing out never helps the situation. Calm self-management maintains your professionalism and allows you to figure out the next step forward. An emotional outburst will not help the negative experience, and it distracts from the work needed to fix the underlying issue. By keeping calm, you can make a note to address any issues to be corrected at a later date when you do not face the pressure of the immediate issue.

Social Awareness

Social awareness turns the focus to others — how we handle relationships and awareness of others' feelings, needs, and concerns. The social awareness cluster contains three competencies:

- *Empathy*: Sensing and understanding others' feelings and perspectives and taking an active interest in their concerns.
- *Organizational awareness*: The ability to read a group's emotional currents, and to build decision networks and power relationships in order to navigate organizational politics.
- *Service orientation*: Anticipating, recognizing, and meeting the needs of others (customers, clients, etc.) but still with a desire to succeed.[23]

For example, in a business meeting you notice the solution offered by a male colleague, Thomas, is the same idea that was offered by a female colleague, Eliza, 15 minutes before. The suggestion, when offered by Eliza, was ignored until Thomas suggested it as if it was his own. You announce to the group, "I think that is the perfect solution. I am so glad Eliza came up with it and that Thomas agrees." A gentle, humorous nudge may diffuse the situation, validate Eliza, and get Thomas's support for the idea at the same time.

Relationship Management

Relationships are important in both legal and leadership settings. In fact, effective leaders spend considerable time building strong relationships, so how well a leader engages with others to work collaboratively on common goals is vital. Relationship management is the skill or adeptness at influencing others to accomplish a desirable response. The relationship management cluster contains six competencies:

- *Developing others*: Sensing others' development needs and bolstering their abilities through feedback and guidance.
- *Inspirational leadership*: Inspiring and guiding individuals and groups, which might also be considered visionary leadership.
- *Change catalyst*: Proficiency in initiating new ideas, managing change, and leading people in a new direction.
- *Influence*: Exercising a wide range of persuasive strategies, such as listening and sending clear, convincing, and well-tuned messages with integrity, to build bonds and maintain relationships with others.
- *Conflict management*: Negotiating and resolving disagreements and collaboratively developing resolutions.
- *Teamwork and collaboration*: Creating group synergy, promoting cooperation, and working well with others toward collective goals.[24]

Consider this situation: A law firm is on the brink of a major disruption because of the loss of an important client. Fingers are pointing as the head of the mergers and acquisitions department blames the tax attorneys for failing to find a solution to satisfy the client's request. As managing partner, it is your job to keep the firm together and moving forward while smoothing over bruised egos and concerns about lost revenue. Convincing those lawyers to work together and to think strategically about the future of the firm could heal the hurt and save the firm. This is where your relationship management skills come into play.

While a leader may not have natural strength and ability in each of these competencies, these are competencies that can be learned, practiced, and strengthened.[25] Highly effective leaders exhibit strength in a number of these areas, and effective leaders demonstrate at least one competence for each area.[26]

STEPS TO DEVELOPING EMOTIONAL INTELLIGENCE

Developing skills as a leader is a lifelong endeavor, and working on emotional intelligence is a worthwhile process. Strengthening and growing Goleman's EQ competencies will make you more emotionally intelligent. An easy quadrant to start with is self-awareness. "[E]motions can help you and they can hurt you, but you have no say in the matter until you understand them."[27] The ability to recognize your own emotions and how they affect your thoughts and behavior is a vital first step in emotional intelligence and in gaining self-confidence. Spending time to discover your strengths and limitations in the areas listed above is well worth the investment.

Self-awareness alone may not provide a full picture of strengths, weaknesses, and leadership styles — we are not always self-aware enough to assess accurately our own strengths and limitations. Even if we engage in self-reflection, we do not always reflect accurately. We can be a distorted mirror. A personal coach or trusted mentor may give you a more accurate assessment of your strengths and weaknesses, as can taking some of the personality and strengths tests available on the Internet.

As you work through the domains of emotional intelligence, you move from controlling emotions and adapting to changing circumstances in healthy ways to interacting with others in meaningful and beneficial manners. Expressing concern for others and recognizing their emotional responses helps you feel comfortable in group settings. Identifying the power dynamics in a group or organization allows you to participate more effectively. Improving communication skills enables you to be more successful as you build relationships, work in teams, manage conflict, and ultimately assume roles of influence.

LAWYERS' EMOTIONAL INTELLIGENCE

Emotional intelligence is one of the most important, yet overlooked, areas of law practice. It is a gift for lawyers and legal educators alike.

Daniel S. Bowling III[28]

Rhonda Muir, author of *Beyond Smart: Lawyering with Emotional Intelligence*, says lawyers' above-average intelligence but below-average emotional intelligence "plays a part in the public's low opinion of them."[29] Individually, emotionally intelligent lawyers are more successful and are healthier, both physically and mentally. Having emotionally intelligent lawyers in firms and organizations who work to improve their communication skills and their relationships with others can lead to better performance in the workplace, more successful client services, and an enhanced professional reputation.[30] Muir uses different terms from Goleman to describe emotional intelligence: *emotional perception, emotional empathy, emotional understanding*, and *emotional regulation*. She writes that "the emotionally intelligent have an accurate awareness of emotions in themselves and others, can tap into how those emotions feel and are able to understand and manage emotions so as to produce the desired results."[31]

Unfortunately, anything requiring a law student or lawyer to admit to, much less express, emotions is highly discouraged in most legal settings. Skills traditionally taught in law school emphasize the use of logic, reason, and analysis to perform as a lawyer.[32] Rarely are law students encouraged to be creative, imaginative, and artistic;

to focus on big picture tasks; or to be empathetic and caring in their interactions with others.[33] This "right-brain" law school orientation leaves law students unprepared for professional situations that call for judgment, maturity, self-awareness, self-control, compassion, collaboration, and conflict resolution, but these are all qualities expected of lawyers. How a lawyer relates to a client facing trauma, discrimination, financial ruin, and other life-altering events will set the tone for the relationship. Managing the situation while relating sympathetically to others in an emotionally-charged moment requires emotional intelligence.

Some experiences in law school offer students the opportunity to develop their emotional intelligence. For example, law students representing clients in an immigration clinic may need ways to control their anger when immigration authorities threaten to deport their clients; likewise, law students assigned to work with volunteer lawyers may require conflict resolution techniques when disagreements erupt over strategy and approach. Law students eager to prove they can fulfill their duty to zealously represent their clients may resort to sarcasm, harsh criticism, threats, and other hostile behavior. The compassionate law student "can lapse into over-identification with the client's cause and become overly emotionally invested in the success or failure of the client's case, resulting in 'emotions on rampage.'"[34]

In *Beyond Smart*, Rhonda Muir points out that "emotional awareness is the EI skill that lawyers usually score the lowest in," and she offers this suggestion for improving that skill: "You can start noting on whatever regular basis you are comfortable with — every meal, every time you walk through a doorway, every hour — exactly what you are feeling emotionally. Either mentally or literally, note the emotional and physical attributes of what you are feeling."[35] Thinking or talking about emotions is hard to do if you cannot name them.[36]

Another exercise Muir suggests for lawyers is watching a movie without the sound. Watch body language and facial expressions. Can you follow the course of the plot by simply reading the emotional cues? She suggests that you turn on the sound occasionally to see if you are following accurately.[37] This technique also can be used at a reception or public gathering. The practice of observing social interactions in any setting improves your skill in reading the emotional cues in your own professional interactions and personal relationships.

CONCLUSION

The success of many leaders cannot be explained by their talent, education, or training. Leadership is "work done well through other people."[38] Emotional intelligence often becomes the factor that differentiates leaders who are otherwise relatively equivalent in terms of talent, qualifications, and experience. "Emotional Intelligence is an active ingredient in great leadership."[39] Thankfully, our emotional intelligence is not a fixed commodity. We have the ability to change and develop our self-awareness, self-management, and social awareness while being mindful of the benefits of building and nurturing our relationships. Efforts spent to assess and enhance these capabilities can be difficult, emotional, and time-consuming, but the benefits of such work can be a game changer in your career as well as your personal relationships.

Exercises

Record Your Observation

During the next 24 hours, pick two different scenarios where you have the opportunity to observe a group without participating in the group. You also should be far enough away that you cannot hear what the individuals are saying to one another. Write down what actions you observe and what you think they mean. For example, if someone frowns, do you think that person is angry, is sad, disagreed with another person, or something else? Was the emotion directed at another person in the group or someone who you do not think was present? Spend at least ten minutes observing each group.

ABA Grit Project: Billing Credit Dispute

Watch the ABA Grit Project's video, "Billing Credit Dispute." Instead of answering the questions at the end of the video, be prepared to discuss these questions:

- What emotions do you think Kate might be feeling after Jim told her that he was going to take credit for the cybersecurity audit for the XYZ Corp.?
- What emotional intelligence skills did Kate show during the meeting with Jim?
- What do you think Jim's thought process was regarding the cybersecurity work based on his history and relationship with XYZ Corp.?
- What emotional intelligence skills *could* Jim have shown during the meeting with Kate?
- What emotional intelligence skills should Kate use if she decides to have a follow-up conversation with Jim to pursue receiving relationship and billing credit for the work?

Journal Prompts

1. Imagine a job you might find yourself holding in ten years. Which of the above emotional intelligence competencies do you think will be particularly important for you to be successful in that position?

2. Which three competencies listed in Daniel Goleman's four quadrants are particular strengths for you at this point in life? Describe why you believe those to be strengths and what experiences in your life help to develop those competencies.

3. Which three competencies listed in Daniel Goleman's four quadrants do you believe most need your time and effort to develop and strengthen? What is your plan for developing and strengthening them?

4. Ask someone you trust and who knows you well which of the competencies above are particular strengths for you. If you are ready to receive helpful feedback in a constructive manner, also ask which they recommend you focus upon developing.

Endnotes

1. OSCAR WILDE, THE PICTURE OF DORIAN GRAY (Random House 2004) (1890). Oscar Fingal O'Flahertie Wills Wilde was an Irish poet and playwright. After writing in different forms throughout the 1880s, in the early 1890s he became one of the most popular playwrights in London of the late Victorian era. Oscar Wilde, BIOGRAPHY.COM, https://www.biography.com/writer/oscar-wilde (last visited Sept. 25, 2020).

2. *Olympic Speed Skater Dan Jansen Falls After Sister Dies*, HISTORY.COM (Feb. 13, 2020), https://www.history .com/this-day-in-history/olympic-speed-skater-jansen-falls-after-sister-dies.

3. *Id.*

4. *Id.*

5. *Jansen Ends a Long and Painful Quest for Gold*, OLYMPIC.ORG (Nov. 6, 2017), https://www.olympic.org/news/ jansen-ends-a-long-and-painful-quest-for-gold (last visited Oct. 20, 2020).

6. *Id.*

7. Arkadin Blog Team, *The Heart in Your Head: A Primer on Emotional Intelligence*, ARKADIN (Oct. 6, 2017), https://blog.arkadin.com/en/the-heart-in-your-head-a-primer-on-emotional-intelligence/.

8. Peter Salovey & John D. Mayer, *Emotional Intelligence*, IMAGINATION, COGNITION, AND PERSONALITY (Mar. 1, 1990), *available at* http://citeseerx.ist.psu.edu/viewdoc/download?doi=10.1.1.385.4383&rep=rep1&type=pdf.

9. DANIEL GOLEMAN, EMOTIONAL INTELLIGENCE: WHY IT CAN MEAN MORE THAN IQ (Bantam 2005).

10. Laura Wilcox, *Emotional Intelligence Is No Soft Skill*, HARVARD PROFESSIONAL DEVELOPMENT BLOG (June 6, 2015), https://www.extension.harvard.edu/professional-development/blog/emotional-intelligence-no-soft-skill.

11. Susan Swaim Daicoff, *Expanding the Lawyer's Toolkit of Skills and Competencies: Synthesizing Leadership, Professionalism, Emotional Intelligence, Conflict Resolution, and Comprehensive Law*, 52 SANTA CLARA L. REV. 795 (2012), *available at* http://digitalcommons.law.scu.edu/lawreview/vol52/iss3/4.

12. *Id.*; *see also* Daniel Goleman, *Strategies to Become More Emotionally Intelligent*, YOUTUBE (Nov. 20, 2017), https://www.youtube.com/watch?v=pt74vK9pgIA; Daniel Goleman, *What Makes a Leader*, HARV. BUS. REV. (Jan. 2004), https://hbr.org/2004/01/what-makes-a-leader.

13. DANIEL GOLEMAN, EMOTIONAL INTELLIGENCE 238–39 (1995). This book spent more than a year and a half on the New York Times Best Sellers list.

14. *Id.*

15. DANIEL GOLEMAN, RICHARD BOYATZIS & ANNIE MCKEE, PRIMAL LEADERSHIP 3–4 (Harv. Bus. Rev. Press 2013).

16. *Id.*

17. *Emotional Intelligence*, Daniel Goleman (Apr. 21, 2015), http://www.danielgoleman.info/daniel-goleman-how -emotionally-intelligent-are-you/. For further explanation, see Goleman, *supra* note 9, at 253– 56.

18. *Id.*

19. *Id.*

20. Goleman, *supra* note 15, at 40.

21. Goleman, *supra* note 17.

22. *Id.*

23. *Id.*

24. GOLEMAN, *supra* note 15, at 38–40.

25. *Id.* at 40.

26. *Id.*

27. Nathalie Martin, *Think Like a (Mindful) Lawyer: Incorporating Mindfulness, Professional Identity, and Emotional Intelligence into the First Year Law Curriculum*, 36 U. ARK. LITTLE ROCK L. REV. 413, 421 (2014), *available at* https://lawrepository.ualr.edu/lawreview/vol36/iss3/6.

28. Daniel S. Bowing is a Senior Lecturing Fellow at Duke Law School. Daniel S. Bowing, Duke Law, https://law.duke.edu/fac/bowling/ (last visited July 13, 2020); Rhonda Muir, Beyond Smart: Lawyering with Emotional Intelligence (ABA Book Publishing 2017).

29. Muir, *supra* note 28.

30. *Id.*

31. *Id.*

32. Daicoff, *supra* note 11.

33. *Id.*

34. *Id.*

35. Rhonda Muir, *How Emotional Intelligence Makes You a Better Lawyer*, A.B.A. J. (Oct. 2017), https://www.americanbar.org/news/abanews/publications/youraba/2017/october-2017/how-successful-lawyers-use-emotional-intelligence-to-their-advan/.

36. *Id.*

37. *Id.*

38. Goleman, *supra* note 9.

39. *Id.*

Chapter 15 | Relationships and Influence

The pessimist complains about the wind. The optimist expects it to change. The leader adjusts the sails.

John Maxwell[1]

Purpose

Explore opportunities for influence as you create and nurture relationships built on competence and trust, and suggest practices for working well with others.

Learning Objectives

At the end of this chapter, you should be able to:

- Discuss the intersection of relationship and influence.
- Describe the role of competence and trust in developing relationships.
- List actions that will build trust in a relationship.
- Define civil discourse.
- List steps for successful engagement in civil discourse.
- Discuss techniques for navigating the difficult aspects of relationships.

Discussion

INTRODUCTION

When we think of leaders, we think not of a rugged individual, forging on alone, but of a visionary, inspiring and gathering a team to achieve a goal. We first develop our individual competencies and abilities to be in a position to lead, but we then need to establish relationships with our team members. As leaders accept new assignments or step into a new position, they draw on their expertise and competencies as they build their team to complete the assigned tasks. Past relationships may inform who joins the team and what duties are assigned. When new members join the team, the leader needs to develop relationships with the new members so that the team functions well as a whole. Both as the team is formed and as goals are being set, the leader is considering how the team will work together and how the leader can convince the team to pull together toward the goal. Getting the job done requires the ability to influence both people and situations. This intersection of relationship and influence is important, not only within a firm or trial team but also in businesses, bar activities, politics, nonprofit organizations, and government. Most of us do not like to be told what to do, but we are influenced by those we trust and respect.

Relationships not only help the team work more effectively and cohesively, they also help build our sphere of influence. Sphere of influence refers to those sets of people on whom we have an impact or where we have power to affect events or developments. We may have a tight sphere of influence primarily affecting our friends and family. We can extend that sphere as we develop professionally as lawyers and trusted advisors to our clients and as active members of our state and local bar associations. That influence extends even more as we become more connected and lead in our communities. The relationships we develop inform the spheres of influence we affect.

Influence in a relationship derives from a series of leadership traits that inspire us to want to follow another or teach us to lead well. We have better relationships with people we like and trust; we agree with the decisions of those who demonstrate good judgment and decision-making skills. We are more influenced by those who are knowledgeable and who listen well both to data and to the voices of other stakeholders. Finally, we are influenced by those who communicate effectively with us and others to motivate us toward an outcome. In this chapter we explore the qualities and characteristics that facilitate building relationships that allow you to influence others.

HOW LEADERS DEVELOP TRUST AND INFLUENCE

Good Judgment

In 2015, Robert Half surveyed attorneys from several law firms and companies throughout North America to identify important qualities that leaders in a corporate legal department should have.[2] Among the nearly 350 lawyers interviewed, 45 percent responded that good judgment was the most important lawyer attribute beyond legal knowledge.[3] For lawyers to make the difficult decisions the practice demands daily—whether in the courtroom, the boardroom, or the community—they must be able to weigh risks and think creatively, both alone and in collaboration with others.

Good judgment generally requires exercising problem-solving abilities to make good, strategic decisions.[4] In the absence of an obvious or straightforward answer, good judgment encompasses the ability to interpret the facts available to you and make the best decision based on the information you have.[5] Leaders who exercise good judgment are often good listeners who consider others' opinions when making a decision. Leaders who listen carefully better understand *what* others are saying, *why* they might be saying it, and *how* to incorporate that information into the decision. Even if you disagree with their input, hearing it helps clarify the issues and anticipate problems or resistance to the decision.

Good judgment acts as a counterbalance to undue influence. It is a foundational skill of an effective leader; without it, even the most charismatic leaders can take their followers down the wrong path. In his article *The Elements of Good Judgment*, Sir Andrew Likierman—former dean of the London Business School—outlined six basic components of good judgment to cultivate:[6]

1. *Learning.* Good judgment is the vehicle that turns knowledge into understanding.[7] You may know all the facts, but that knowledge is meaningless if you cannot interpret and make a sound decision from it.[8] Being a good listener allows you to sift information, absorbing what you need with a healthy skepticism of the parts that do not make sense. Take Soviet Lt. Col. Stanislav Petrov, the duty officer for the USSR's missile tracking center. While on duty in 1983, Petrov was told that Soviet satellites detected a U.S. missile attack on the Soviet Union.[9] If a missile attack were underway, Soviet nuclear doctrine dictated a full nuclear retaliation, without double-checking facts or negotiating with the United States.[10] The Soviet Union had 35,804 nuclear warheads, and the United States had 23,305,[11] meaning a retaliatory launch would kill millions; an all-out nuclear war would kill billions.[12] But Petrov's judgment told him that the probability reading was suspiciously high.[13] Rather than send the attack information and his assessment up the chain of command, Petrov instead reported a system malfunction.[14] An investigation revealed that the Soviet satellites confused reflected sunlight for missile engines.[15] Petrov's careful filtering of unreliable data helped him make the right judgment call and, arguably, save the world from nuclear war.[16]

2. *Trust.* Trust and good judgment are intertwined, because effective leaders acknowledge they cannot go it alone.[17] Without followers, leaders are but ambitious people taking a lonely walk. More important, the most effective leaders choose to work with followers who engage rather than follow commands like blind sheep.[18] Abraham Lincoln's cabinet was made up of people whom he respected but who did not shy away from disagreeing with him.[19] Leaders should recruit people who will tell them what they need to hear, not simply what they want to hear. By the same token, followers who can trust their leader because of the leader's character, integrity, knowledge

base, and truthfulness, are better followers. When in place, this symbiotic relationship leads to better overall judgments because of the trust-rich environment.

3. *Experience.* Facts and evidence have richer meaning when combined with experience. Leaders' background and experience influence how they make decisions.[20] Experience applied to our decision-making process helps provide context and connect the dots toward possible solutions.[21] When we take time to analyze and reflect upon past judgment calls that went well and those that went poorly, we[22] better recognize patterns in judgment and can correct issues going forward.[23] In addition to mining the wisdom of past experience, good leaders also seek diverse new experiences and accept new opportunities. This combination of accumulated wisdom applied to new experiences expands their capabilities and also helps avoid the leadership rut in which leaders with narrow experience often find themselves.[24] Varied experience provides perspective and context to apply similar experiences for better decision making.

4. *Detachment.* A leader's personal values and experiences can inspire others, but they also create biases that can affect judgment.[25] If the leader gets emotionally involved in a case, perhaps because of a contentious relationship with the opposing counsel or a close relationship with the client, these strong emotions may cloud judgment. When judgment is based too heavily on emotion, emotion rather than facts, experience, and training can drive the decision. Detaching emotionally from the source of bias changes the way we process information.[26] Lawyers are uniquely trained to detach and exercise good judgment in times of crisis,[27] allowing us to understand and evaluate the different viewpoints that play a role in the decision-making process.[28] Once the biases are acknowledged and dealt with dispassionately, the attorney can make the best judgment call under the circumstances.[29] Acknowledging bias suggests not only good judgment but also cultural humility.

5. *Options.* Leaders, even when presented with two options, try not to box themselves into thinking those are the only choices available.[30] The process of debating the options presented, and exploring why other options were not presented, can strengthen the ultimate plan of action.[31] George Washington's cabinet included both Thomas Jefferson and Alexander Hamilton. The two lawyers frequently took opposing views on issues and, when faced with difficult decisions, Washington would ask Jefferson and Hamilton to brief issues and argue their positions in cabinet meetings.[32]

The two famously clashed over Hamilton's controversial National Bank bill, which sought to create a national bank to serve as the central hub for "taxes, transfers, banknotes, and currency to be held and regulated."[33] The bank and all of its programs would be under Secretary of the Treasury Hamilton's control.[34] Jefferson and Representative James Madison vehemently opposed the bill.[35] Washington was neutral but needed to decide whether to support the bill. Washington asked Hamilton to respond to Jefferson and Madison's arguments, which he apparently did persuasively, because Washington signed the bill into law.[36] Washington thoroughly considered the opposing views of his cabinet members and advisors. He asked for their thoughts, weighed the options, and made the best decision he could with the information he had, shaping for centuries the financial policy of the United States.

6. *Delivery.* Using good judgment to make a decision is the first half of the equation; delivery is the second half.[37] The feasibility of executing the decision is integral to the exercise of good judgment. No matter how sound the decision in theory, if it cannot be executed in a feasible manner (considering cost, time, and resources), the decision is not a good one. Ferdinand de Lesseps, developer of the Suez Canal, pitched construction of the Panama Canal. Many thought his experience and judgment would be sufficient, but building a canal through sand differs markedly from building one through jungle. He never understood this crucial distinction in the ability to execute, and his approach proved to be a disaster. The U.S. government was forced to step in and complete the canal through different measures. Exercising good judgment means anticipating the risks of a chosen plan of action and how to best manage them during the execution phase.[38]

Artful Listening

Leaders need to communicate effectively, which involves both purposeful speaking and artful listening. A self-aware leader, then, considers how words and language affect others. This goes beyond actively listening to the content of what is said. The words we use to communicate, along with tone of voice and non-verbal gestures, impact the team. Even a benign message, when part of a terse email or brusque exchange, can carry disproportionate weight with a team member seeking your approval. Those we communicate with may read into communications messages that we do not intend to convey. The more trust you build with your team members, the less likely they will be to misunderstand your communication content or style. A focus on expressive speech is important, but leaders also need to consider how the ability to listen, and really hear, also affects those with whom we work.

Hearing words is easier than *listening* to the message. Leaders get bombarded with information, making it difficult to listen attentively. Mere passive listening, however, can lead to serious misunderstanding. Consider the story told by leadership author John Maxwell:

> Two hunters were out in the woods when one suddenly fell to the ground. His eyes rolled back in his head, and he seemed to stop breathing. The other hunter frantically took out his cellphone and called 9-1-1. As soon as the call connected, he yelled out, "My friend Bubba is dead! What can I do?" The operator calmly replied, "Take it easy. I can help. Just listen to me and follow my instructions. First, let's make sure he's dead."

A short pause ensued, and the operator then heard a loud gun shot. The hunter came back on the line and said, "Okay . . . now what?"[39]

Law school trains us to listen to respond rather than listen to understand. The distinction is key, particularly when personal relationships and difficult subjects are involved. From conducting *voir dire* to negotiating a business deal, real communication requires effective listening just as much as (if not more than) effective speaking.[40] Listening actively to what someone says rather than focusing on the literal meaning of the words spoken can provide greater insight and improve productivity within your organization.[41] Colleagues who feel they have been heard are more likely to feel valued and remain loyal to the organization.[42] In addition, leaders who actively listen catch things that others would miss and are better informed when making decisions.[43]

Artful listening includes hearing not only what is said but also what is not said.[44] Non-verbal cues — body language, posturing, and tone, for example — can convey a great deal about what is really being said.[45] Maintaining eye contact and using reassuring facial expressions convey to the speaker that you are hearing them. When you also confirm what you heard and ask open-ended questions to follow up, you increase the likelihood you are truly communicating. Resist the temptation to interrupt or think only about what to say next; both diminish your ability to listen closely.[46] Your non-verbal cues, especially those that signal you are bored or impatient, can overpower anything that you say.

Practicing artful listening can be done on a daily basis with friends, loved ones, and strangers alike. Becoming a master helps you build and maintain relationships that can pay dividends years after the first conversation. For lawyers, active listeners are better at witness examinations and *voir dire* during trial, at connecting with clients, and at catching the nuances of office politics. And for leaders, artful listening contributes to team trust, good decision making, and fewer unpleasant surprises.

BUILDING AND NURTURING RELATIONSHIPS

The world runs on relationships. Many children are taught the concept of "stranger danger;" if you do not know someone, they pose a threat. While the power of that concept diminishes as we mature, we still prefer to work with people whom we know and trust. "Regular communication, clarity, and honesty are fundamental to building a trusting relationship."[47]

In our profession, trust can only be built on a foundation of competence. Clients will not trust a lawyer who cannot perform as expected, which raises another important point in building a lasting relationship with your clients or others. You must set appropriate expectations so you can live up to those expectations. Do not over promise or under deliver. "Relationships don't grow just because you want them to; they grow and evolve because you have exceeded expectations."[48]

Results are very important, but to retain the client you must have "a good bedside manner," and "the ability to network and connect."[49] Start with rapport building and devote time to nurture connections, friendships, and professional relationships. Be mindful of developing your relationships on a daily basis. You never know when you will need to rely on one of your friends or colleagues. This may mean blocking time to make calls, send cards or letters, or even to post a happy birthday message on social media to convey that the person is worth your time.

Leaders who involve their colleagues in important decision making benefit especially from building these relationships. Better relationships build trust and make disagreements or difficult conversations easier. It also feels good to spend time on relationships. Everyone loves the colleague who remembers their birthday or congratulates them on their wedding or new baby. Staying in tune with the events and circumstances shaping people's lives makes for a thoughtful leader and in turn, a more dedicated and satisfied worker.

Research done at Northwestern Medicine has linked maintaining relationships to less stress, healthier behaviors, a greater sense of purpose, and even a longer life.[50] In fact, studies show that those who actively listen with the goal of understanding maintain better and happier relationships with colleagues.[51] Relationships help provide support and value to overall well-being and happiness both personally and professionally. Not surprisingly, when an organization's employees are happy, its productivity increases.[52]

Leading effectively, then, requires the leader and the team to build solid working relationships both within the team and in the broader sphere of influence. The nature of these relationships can vary; not all leaders can or should be friends with their subordinates; in other settings, the leader can easily lead a group of friends. Leaders need to appreciate and maintain healthy relationships with health boundaries.

EFFECTIVELY DEALING WITH PEOPLE: LESSONS WE LEARNED IN KINDERGARTEN

A kindergarten rubric evaluated whether we "work and play well with others." Business schools advise their students that "people do business with people they know, like, and trust." Whether dealing with a client, others in the firm, or opposing counsel, nurturing these three aspects of relationship is a worthwhile investment. Getting to know someone is hard if you do not spend any time with them, so a basic component of relationship building is the investment of time. Taking a few minutes at the beginning of a call to get to know someone or follow up on shared interests fosters a closer personal connection. If you do not spend any time asking your clients questions about their families or interests, you may be missing not only the chance to connect and deepen the relationship, but also missing the opportunity to gain insight into how they might view your advice on legal matters. This is an ongoing process that is handled best on a consistent basis. Getting someone to like you comes from engaging in authentic behavior and showing a genuine interest in the other person. Finding common ground builds likeability. Finally, trust is key. Lawyers and leaders need to be trustworthy in their personal and professional dealings. Using effective communication, empowering others, and remaining adaptable and open to feedback builds relationships, and leaders who build strong relationships with colleagues enjoy a more cohesive practice.

To lead, you must *understand others*. The most effective way to understand others is by asking yourself how you would expect your colleagues to treat you in the work-place or, from a cultural humility perspective, how they want to be treated. People appreciate being treated with respect, and trust and effective collaboration flow from respect. An excellent way to understand others is to listen to them actively. Leaders are in a special position to provide feedback, so giving feedback in a respectful manner positively affects team morale and confidence.

Be approachable. Your colleagues (and your organization) need to feel they can take concerns and questions to you. Your team is less effective if you are unapproachable or intimidating to the point that they cannot challenge your ideas. Just as they need to accept your feedback gracefully, you must acknowledge the courage it takes for your colleagues to stand up to the boss. To ensure that your colleagues challenge in a respectful way, you can lead by example. Your interests are aligned, so do not become defensive when ideas clash or debate becomes lively.

Show appreciation. There is no substitute for feeling like you bring value to a team. Think of a time when your boss told you he or she appreciated your work and how that made you feel. If your colleagues do not feel valued, rest assured they will leave for a place that does makes them feel important. Even small tokens of appreciation can go a long way in making your colleagues feel valued throughout the year, increasing their loyalty and confidence to further the organization's objectives.

THE ART OF INFLUENCE

Even though using influence to achieve a goal is normal and even commonplace, it often has the negative connotation that you used improper leverage to achieve a goal. That is not always the case; it simply means that, through your relationship with another person, you persuaded that person to help you. Often, you have developed a relationship with a person such that you are able to reach out, ask for a favor, and he or she will agree to expend time and energy for you.

John Maxwell identified five levels of influence that leaders can attain not by their title but by their character, experience, and knowledge.[53] In your own journey, take time to reflect on the type of influencer you are and whether that is the type you want to be.

1. *Position-level influence*: People follow you because they need to follow you.
2. *Permission-level influence*: People follow you because they choose to follow you.

3. *Production-level influence*: People follow you because of what you achieve.
4. *People-development-level influence*: People follow you because you have helped their development.
5. *Personhood-level influence*: People follow you because you have helped so many leaders' development for so long that you become larger than life.[54]

Think of using influence as drawing energy from a battery. Every person has a "relationship battery" with each of their friends and colleagues. This relationship battery is charged and depleted through interactions. Spending time with a friend or colleague, building goodwill, and helping with their projects – charging the battery – makes it easier for them to expend energy to help you. Spending time, in this context, is not necessarily measured by quantity, but it is measured by quality. How you develop quality time with each person should be tailored to the person — it may be dinner with one, playing video games with another, or mountain biking with yet another. The key is to find the activities that both of you enjoy and will enjoy doing together, not because you want to store energy with that person for future purposes but because you enjoy that time. The key to the relationship and time is genuine care and concern for the other person. When we feel someone is spending time with us because they want something (a favor, money, influence with another person), we are less interested in the connection. We may help anyway, but it is not the sort of experience we want to repeat.

CIVIL DISCOURSE

Leaders not only influence their team, leaders also can influence those with whom they disagree. This may include hostile judges, opposing counsel, political opponents — people who may not share our ideas or even common goals. The ability to influence through civil discourse, by disagreeing respectfully, is a crucial aspect of influence.

We seem to live in a time where discussions about difficult topics — race, gender identity, immigration, health care, the wealth gap, climate change (to name just a few) — turn into ad hominem attacks. "We" are right and "they" are wrong. If you disagree with me, you must be a bad person whose moral compass skews off true north. It feels as if our country has never been more divided, but history tells us otherwise. Our nation has faced division like this throughout its history. It may feel more pronounced now thanks to a 24-hour news cycle and social media, but that is just the method of delivery. Our Founding Fathers disagreed so vehemently that it led to duels with pistols at dawn. Alexander Hamilton, who had served as Secretary of the Treasury, died in a Duels with Aaron Burr, who had served as Vice President of the United States.[55] Duels were affairs of honor that rarely led to the actual firing of the weapons. Instead, they afforded the participants an opportunity to discuss their differences, which often led to resolution of the dispute. In other words, the offended parties resorted to civil discourse to settle their differences. Because of our training, lawyers can be key leaders in encouraging civil discourse, but the skill is one that can take time to develop.

What is meant by the phrase "civil discourse"? The American University School of Public Affairs created a Civil Discourse project, designed to promote free speech "not only as a matter of rights, but of responsibilities, values, and opportunities."[56] Stated differently, just because we can say something does not mean that we should. The project defines some parameters about civil discourse, which notes both what it is and what it is not.

Civil discourse is

    Truthful

    Productive

    Audience-based

    About listening *and* talking

    Each Speaker's own responsibility[57]

Civil discourse is not

    Mere politeness

    An exercise in martyrdom

    About telling other people who they are

    Purely performative[58]

Discourse involves not only hearing the words being said but also really hearing the place from which the other person is speaking and hearing that truth. If one side of an issue were so clearly right, there would be no basis for discussion. Moreover, our experiences (influenced by our cultural environment) and implicit bias can color our ability to understand the other side in ways we do not consciously appreciate. Leaders who engage in civil discourse must both explain their views authentically in a productive way but also be willing to hear — really hear — an opposing point of view.

Why is civil discourse so difficult? Because the issues are emotional, painful, and divisive.[59] There are truths on both sides, some of which force us to face longstanding bias or prejudice. The issues can threaten our sense of normalcy and security and disrupt what we believe to be true.[60] Coupled with powerful emotions such as anger, fear, outrage, and sadness, the setting for discussion is anything but calm and rational.[61] Yet our ability to have these important discussions enables change in our society, and in our law firms and law schools.

One young lawyer wrote thoughtfully about the difficult topic of Confederate-themed mascots. Her high school, Pine Bluff High (PHS) in Pine Bluff, Arkansas, long had a Rebel mascot, but in response to the Black Lives Matter movement, petitions circulated to change the mascot. The issue highlighted the debate between those who believe changing the mascot undermines and erases history versus those who believe holding onto such images perpetuates racial discrimination. She wrote:

This is my high school. It's a great school in a wonderful town, and I'm a proud alum. During my four years there, I served on student council, was a cheerleader, and was even "Miss PHS" my senior year. I was proud to be a Rebel and sang "Are You from Dixie?" at football games with the best of them. I obviously knew the Rebel General was a confederate symbol, but at the time I felt we were so far removed from the Civil War it was just a fun relic, a symbol of the south in general and not meant to be racist. I know I was wrong, and last night I signed the petition to change it.

I know the knee-jerk reaction for many people is to roll your eyes, get defensive, and protect what feels like an important school tradition. "It's always been that way." "I loved being a Rebel!" I get it. 10-15 years ago, I probably wouldn't have wanted it changed. "No one thinks of it like that," or "It's not hurting anyone," I would think. But the truth is, I felt that way because it wasn't hurting ME. I wasn't bothering to learn the history or to really listen to the argument in favor of change.

We have to look at the facts. PHS was established in 1952 during segregation, and it was the white school. Crepe Myrtle High School was the black school, and our own beloved Mayor Fields went there. Does anyone really think it was a coincidence that they decided in 1952, almost a century after the Civil War ended, to make the Rebel General the mascot of the white school? Take a look at the graphic in my comment[62] below charting the rise and decline of the Confederate Rebel mascot at schools nation-wide. It's no coincidence. Rebel mascots are not "suddenly" under attack. . . . [I]t's not something that has "just now" come up in the wake of George Floyd's death. Schools have been changing their Rebel mascots for decades. (By the way, someone at the University of Southern Mississippi wrote an entire 250-page dissertation on the use of the Rebel mascot, which is where I found that graphic.)

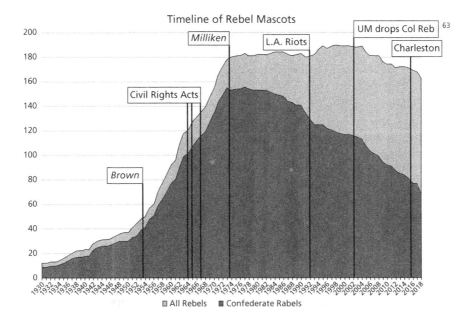

The south is full of wonderful traditions and some of the best people on the entire planet. It's a place where strangers treat you like friends and friends treat you like family. I loved growing up in the Deep South and wouldn't change it. But there is a painful past and, frankly, a painful and very real presence of overt racism still today. No one is trying to erase history. To the contrary, we have to acknowledge history and learn from it. We have to take what we have learned and grow and do better.

A school isn't a relic. It's a living, breathing body of people. Times change, hearts and minds change, and people change. PHS has not even been around for 70 years, and I hope it has a much longer future ahead of it and one we can all be proud of. Changing the mascot isn't going to take away my high school experience. It won't change any of the fond memories I have of friends and the fun times we had. If anything, it would just make me prouder to have been a part of it. I would rather be able to tell my kids and grandkids about how we were originally called the Rebels and why that was changed than to be the holdout school that refused to change and ended up on the wrong side of history. It's not about being liberal or conservative. It's not just the "popular" thing to do; it's the right thing to do.[64]

What makes this piece effective civil discourse? It acknowledges the truth of both positions. It does not attack the people who feel differently. It looks to facts to support the position. Whether or not you agree with her position, she prompts you to think about the issue from a different perspective.

Civil discourse may come up in a variety of settings. You may disagree with your employer, your professor, your spouse, or your client. In the heat of the moment, neither you or the other participant may adhere to the niceties of civil discourse. Learning to disagree well, however, pays benefits in your personal relationships, where you have a vested interest in the other person and the relationship.[65] It becomes an important skill in the employment setting, where you may need to stand up for a position without jeopardizing your place in the firm or the work of your team.[66] When disagreeing with a client, you want to protect the relationship but still need to give good counsel, even if it is not what the client wants to hear. And as for society, we will not be able to make progress on thorny social issues without the ability to vocalize and honor both sides of an issue. To wield true influence through social discourse, you should consider steps that make it more likely you can be heard.

Pick your battles. There may be times when you disagree with a position, but it may be a small enough point that you can just let it go.[67] A blowhard sitting across from you at a bar association luncheon spouting his opinion may be irritating, but it may not be important that you engage him on the topic. Having an important discussion with your law partners about how the firm will handle finances, though, may be critical to the long-term viability of the firm. Just as important as picking your battle is picking the time and place for the conversation. Trying to have a crucial conversation when there is an audience, or tempers are high, or there is a different important deadline looming, almost guarantees the conversation will fail. Talking about the firm finances on the eve of an important jury trial is not likely to be productive; those preparing for trial are likely tired and getting ready for a fight — but not with you.

Use data, not just emotion. Few children were persuaded by a parent whose rationale was "because I say so!" Similarly, just *feeling* that someone is wrong is not as persuasive as having data to back up your argument.[68] Scheduling your discussion will give you time to obtain the data you need to support your position. The data will help you frame the basis for your position, and can temper the emotions.

Aim to inform, not confront. Just as the duel between Burr and Hamilton did not change either's mind about the other, a confrontation designed to end up with a winner and a loser is unlikely to lead to common ground. When you enter into a disagreement with the idea that you have information both to share and to receive, you have a more open mind and may actually learn information you did not previously know.

Ask great questions. Gaining a better understanding of the issue will allow you to respond or defend your position.[69] The person on the other side of the issue may have information and experiences that you do not, but which inform his opinions. You may disagree with your brother-in-law about immigration policy. His position, though, might be based on having grown up in the Rio Grande Valley of Texas, where it was common to find the dead bodies of those crossing the border illegally in the fields of his family land. This traumatic and senseless loss of life understandably influenced his strong belief in strict immigration laws, and understandably so. Unless you ask the question "why," you will not fully understand the heart of the other person.

In many legal settings, asking great questions not only leads to better comprehension, it also may lead to greater respect. Lawyers who ask penetrating and insightful questions are perceived to be more skilled in the profession.[70] Leaders who are truly curious about another's perspective can lead to a better relationship, as you show genuine interest and enthusiasm for the person with whom you are disagreeing. Borrowing from the world of improv, you can also try the phrase "yes, and . . . ." This suggests that the other position is valid, but that perhaps there is another valid position as well.

Great listening is vital to civil discourse. Law students and lawyers are especially prone to be thinking about their next argument, question, or statement rather than listening to what another is actually saying. Rather than hearing the other person, they are in their own head, reinforcing their argument. There are several key components to listening well. First, don't take the disagreement personally.[71] If you believe that the disagreement is a measure of your worth as a person, you will not be able to disagree civilly.[72] Next, try to practice reflective listening, where you reflect back to the other person what you believe he has said.[73] Language such as "what I hear you saying is . . . . Is that right?" allows you to confirm that you are actually hearing the other person. It also can have a validating effect; we all like to feel that we are being heard when we feel strongly about a situation or issue. This may also allow you to find common ground. In your family disagreement about immigration policy, you may find that you can agree on many points that deal with the basic sanctity of human life and dignity. You may not discover the key to immigration reform, but you could agree the system is broken and that people are being hurt as a consequence. It is a start.

Finally, be willing and able to disagree with dignity, confidence, and humility.[74] Few minds are changed on social media; some minds are changed as a result of thoughtful discussion. At the end of the day, you may find you need to agree to disagree. You can make the conflict productive, however, by finding aspects on which you do agree and by agreeing on how to have difficult conversations in the future.[75] Recognize the possibility that you could be mistaken or that the situation could change. Be open to revisiting the conversation in the future. Canyons are not made by a single deluge; they are created through process of gradual erosion. While we may have a blinding "aha moment" about an issue, more frequently we change based on the accumulation of data and engaging in honest and meaningful discussion.

NAVIGATING THE DIFFICULT ASPECTS OF RELATIONSHIPS

With influence and solid relationships come responsibilities. As a leader, you must make tough decisions, manage conflicts (both in your team and outside of it), and have difficult conversations with others. None of these situations are easy. Rarely are the issues simple and often they arise out of a convergence of complex situations. Anticipating these situations before they occur will help you be prepared for them.

Difficult Decision Making

Whether for ourselves, our team, or our clients, we do not always make the wisest decisions. Decision making is a skill that is best acquired experientially through trial and error rather than a law school course or self-help book.[76] The keys to difficult decisions require different considerations based on context, but some common themes apply in a variety of situations:

1. Be clear in the decision you make.
2. Gather all the relevant facts.
3. Determine beforehand what a "successful" decision looks like.
4. Develop and evaluate your options.
5. Consider why other options are or aren't feasible.
6. Assess the risks of your options.
7. Execute your decision.[77]

This list does not differ much from Likierman's framework for exercising good judgment, which is not surprising: good decision making requires good judgment.[78] Both require you to weigh the available information and anticipate the risks for any plan of action you consider. As a leader, people look to you to make decisions, so develop a method that works for you and reassures you that the decisions you make are the best ones you can make at the time.

Integrity: Doing the Right Thing, Even When It Costs You

Every decision comes at a cost. Leaders may not fully understand the cost when they make decisions. At other times, leaders know the cost and choose the right thing anyway. These leaders value their integrity and believe in the mission of the organization, making difficult choices for the benefit of others.

History is littered with tough decisions with even tougher consequences. President George H.W. Bush famously promised, "Read my lips: no new taxes" at the 1988 Republican National Convention.[79] At the time, he was trailing Michael Dukakis in the race for President by several points in the polls. He made this promise to contrast himself with Dukakis, whom he painted as a "tax and spend liberal."[80] It worked; he won in a landslide.

Keeping his promise proved difficult. In 1990, the savings and loan crisis cleanup lingered and a recession threatened the country. Bush 41 needed to cut spending.[81] Democrats opposed pure spending cuts to measures that would affect government services and benefits created during the New Deal.[82] To avoid a recession and boost the economy, Bush 41 broke his promise.[83] In return for several tax increases, Democrats accepted spending cuts that were twice as large.[84]

This decision was the right one — the "1990s ended with the economy booming and the federal budget in surplus."[85] But it had cost Bush 41 dearly. Talk show host David Letterman reframed the phrase to, "Read my lips: I was lying."[86] Bush lost the presidential election to Bill Clinton.[87] When he made the decision, President Bush knew that it was likely to cost him the election.[88] While he may not have known at the time that the promise was one he could not keep, when he needed to break it he was willing to take the hit to his reputation and career because he believed it was the right thing to do.

Doing the right thing, however, can impact others in a way that is difficult for the leader as well. A young lawyer running a nonprofit legal aid office who faces a shortfall in funding may have to make the difficult decision to close one of the divisions. The division impacts a relatively small number of clients but has a full-time lawyer (and the associated salary). The division does important work, but the whole nonprofit will fail if she does not eliminate the cost associated with the division. Having to tell another lawyer he is being laid off and turning away clients who need help is very difficult and may feel in conflict with the goal of the nonprofit, but the move is life-saving for the organization.

Decisions like these test the mettle of a leader. Making the right decision, for the right reasons, is the courageous choice that leaders do not regret. These leaders must put their short-term gain aside for the long-term gain of the organization. They will face criticism — and often unduly harsh criticism — in doing so. Lawyers and leaders have to make painful and difficult decisions knowing that not everyone will agree. This means, however, that they need another skill — the ability to deliver bad news.

Difficult Conversations and Delivering Bad News

During the course of practicing law and leading in almost any setting, you will have to have difficult conversations, some of which involve your delivering bad news. The client is going to jail; the deal fell through; the grant application was denied; your associate did not make partner. When you have to deliver bad news, a natural instinct of the listener may be to shoot the messenger. You may never get to the point where you find it easy to deliver bad news, but there are definitely steps that can make the process better.

In other settings, leaders must have difficult conversations.[89] This may be with an underperforming team member, a client, the judge, the partners, the bar association — the list goes on. No matter the nature of the difficult conversation, most lawyers hate to have them but as lawyers and leaders we need to handle them well.

Even skilled lawyers who advocate fiercely for their clients can be surprisingly conflict-averse and avoid the potential confrontation that comes with difficult conversations.[90] Fear of criticism causes lawyers to become defensive when reaching an impasse. While these conversations may be difficult, the cost of staying silent is high. The need to hold them effectively outweighs the discomfort of confrontation and temporary conflict. If not resolved, the conflict can stymie productivity, create confusion, and negatively affect morale.[91]

Holding difficult conversations can be similar to delivering bad news, but they do have distinct differences. Not every difficult conversation requires delivery of bad news. The difficulty may involve personality styles, differences of opinion, disagreement, reprimand, and so forth. Some of the same skills that work when delivering bad news can be applied to difficult conversations, but the goal here is to work through the process and restore the relationship to a healthy place, which requires preparation. First identify the issue and then decide what to do about it. Once you've determined that the situation *must* be addressed (remember that some issues will be resolved with time or extenuating circumstances), you should develop a strategy for the conversation:

1. What do you want to accomplish by having the conversation? Consider any ulterior or inappropriate motives that would be unhelpful in the conversation. Try to ensure that the goal is a realistic one and that the conversation will be helpful and productive.[92]
2. What is the power dynamic between you and the others in the conversation? If the power roles are equal or those persons have a subordinate role, carefully think through the tone of the conversation. Avoid using a condescending tone — this can break down communication fairly quickly. If the other person

is your superior, work on remaining calm and respectful while making your needed points. Overall, going into the conversation, you should view the opponent as a partner in resolving the conflict.[93]

3. Be straightforward with the difficult points. Important points or messages should be made early so that the conversation can build around those points.[94]

4. Prepare for negative reactions and think about how you will deal with those reactions. Blaming, mirroring negativity, or reacting emotionally are common in difficult situations, but they are not conducive to moving the conversation forward.[95]

5. Decide if there is anything you can concede. If you have contributed to the problem, acknowledge your role. Be willing to listen to the other person without using the time to anticipate your next response. You may hear information you need to address fully. Even if you do not hear anything new, the conversation will go better if the other person feels she was heard by you.[96]

Once you've thought through the conversation, there are several other questions you should ask yourself about how to proceed before approaching the other person:

1. Are you the right person to confront him or her? Sometimes the person who has to have a difficult conversation is as important as the message. If you aren't the right person for the conversation, who is?[97]

2. What do you know about the other person? Is that person struggling with a personal issue, or are there other extenuating circumstances that are creating the problem? What is that person's personality like? What approach, based on the other person's personality, might work to successfully resolve the issue in a manner that's beneficial to everyone?[98]

3. Where do you plan to have the conversation? Will you have it in your office? What message does that convey? Be especially careful if the person is, or is perceived to be, senior (age, experience, or in the organizational structure) to you. Will you have it in the other person's office? Will that person feel like you are invading his or her space and get more defensive? Or should you pick a neutral location, such as a coffee shop or restaurant? This may be a good option, but be mindful of the time it may take to accomplish the goal, or, worse, to finish a meal if the conversation does not go well. You should also consider whether you will meet the person there or travel together.[99]

4. How will you set up the conversation? What will you tell the other person about the purpose of the meeting? You do not want this to be an ambush. How will you phrase the purpose so as not to put the person on the defensive and have him reject your message?[100]

5. Although you already thought about the messaging of the issue, during the meeting how do you plan to address the issue with the other person? How do you want the conversation to go? Where will you start the conversation? Will you start with small talk or get straight to it? How do you want to end

the conversation? Be sure to think through the entire conversation and the desired outcome before you start.[101]

6. After the meeting, is there likely to be any action needed? Is it something that you need to do or is something that someone else needs to do? What will you do to document the conversation in case there is a dispute about it later?[102]

7. If the situation is not resolved after a conversation, what will you do? Are there others that need to be involved? Can you avoid the situation going forward?[103]

The conversation is more likely to have a positive outcome if you consider these questions in advance. It is unlikely you can answer them all, but try to answer them using what you know about the person and your relationship. The approach will change with each situation and with each person. What works for a conversation with a close colleague may not work with someone you met recently working on a nonprofit board. This process is more art than science.

The goal in a difficult conversation is not necessarily to be right; it may be to find a solution that works.[104] Good trial skills are not necessarily the most effective for handling workplace conversations — this may not call for rigorous cross-examination. By framing the conversation in terms of what is most beneficial for the organization, you can more easily find common ground and separate the person from the conflict so you control the conversation in a productive way. Difficult conversations are never easy, but they come with the territory of being a leader. The sooner you embrace that reality, the easier it will be to keep your team on track to meet its objectives.

Conflict Management

Lawyers, no matter their role in an organization, deal with conflict every day, which is normal when working with many people who have different priorities and roles. When managed poorly, conflict can harm the organization as a whole and prevent it from achieving its objectives for clients or otherwise.[105] Effective conflict management draws from many of the different leadership capabilities discussed elsewhere in this chapter. For example, artful listening helps minimize miscommunication and identify common ground for agreement. Body language and non-verbal cues can set the tone for a professional, cordial discussion instead of a heated and destructive one.

In either case, effective leaders do not shy away from facing conflict, whether it involves the leader personally or requires the leader to mediate a solution for others.[106] Disagreement can be healthy, especially to prevent mindless followership, but leaders should be wary when disagreement is characterized by noncooperation or bullying.[107] In that setting, the leader may need to bring the conflict into the open and address the underlying differences that led to it.[108] The leader may need to guide the team members through the conversation or help them brainstorm solutions. As the leader, intervene appropriately. If the parties cannot reach an agreement on their own, use your judgment to step in and make a decision on how to get past it.

CONCLUSION

Effective leaders build effective teams one relationship at a time. Those relationships help leaders develop and expand their spheres of influence throughout their personal, professional, and community arenas. You begin to develop your lawyer leadership skills and competencies in law school but continue after law school as you develop relationships with other professionals, clients, and leaders. The time and effort spent on relationships is important to your growth and influence. When done well, healthy relationships provide you with a network of individuals who support you and your goals.

Exercises

Difficult Conversations

A student organization on campus is responsible for hosting an Adoption Day at the law school. The students in the organization are primarily responsible for picking a theme for the day (i.e., "Adoptions Are Incredible," with the theme being borrowed from Disney's *The Incredibles*) and then decorating the law school accordingly. This annual event brings significant attention to the law school each year. The local news stations send crews to film the decorations and the festivities. Alex, the president of the organization, asked for volunteers to lead several committees with discrete tasks. There are three major committees: decorating the law school, sponsorships from the community, and coordination with adoption agencies, lawyers, and the law school administration. One of the committees, the decorating committee, is responsible for building some of the sets/ props that will be placed around the law school. One student, Jordan, volunteered to lead the decorating committee and three other students volunteered to help. Since then, all the committees except Jordan's have made significant progress on their tasks. With only three weeks until the event, Jordan has not yet called a meeting or made any plans to accomplish the tasks of the committee. Alex knows how long it takes to build the sets/ props and believes that time is getting short for the committee to complete its task. The decoration around the school is one of the highlights for the children going through the adoption process, so Alex wants to make sure that these tasks get accomplished. Alex has set a meeting with Jordan to discuss the committee's progress.

Confidential instructions will be provided to the students playing Alex and Jordan.

Discussion Questions (for conversation after the meeting):

1. Questions for Alex:
   a. What was your approach to the conversation?

b. What did you hope to achieve? Was the outcome the resolution you wanted?

c. Where else could this conversation take place? Is there a better location than the law school for this type of conversation?

2. Any suggestions for either Alex or Jordan now that the role play is over?

Civil Discourse

Midway High School's male sports teams are called the Panthers. The female sports teams, however, are referred to as the Pantherettes. A student researched the issue and made a presentation to the school board suggesting that the use of the term "Pantherette" served to diminish women by suggesting that they were smaller versions of Panthers. She even noted that the female trustees on the school board would not want to be known as "trustee-ettes." The school board voted to change the name simply to Panthers for all teams.

Following the vote, the student and the board faced tremendous backlash. The student was attacked personally on social media by parents, students, and even her teachers. Her parents were subject to attacks for having done a poor job raising her. The school board trustees were accused of betraying the values of "Panther Nation" and caving to "liberal values." The board rescinded its vote, and the female teams were returned to being called the Pantherettes.

Discussion Questions:

1. Do you agree with the school board's actions in returning to the original terminology?

2. Do you agree that "Pantherette" is a diminutive term that implicitly discounts the female athletes? Why or why not?

3. Should the board have held public debate on the issues? If so, what rules should apply to promote civil discourse?

4. Should the teachers who posted their opinions on their private social media pages have been disciplined? Does an attack on a student, when made on a private social media account, constitute cyberbullying or is it freedom of speech and expression?

Journal Prompts

1. Describe your relationship with someone who had some type of influence on your life. It could be a recent influence, such as in making the decision to go to law school, or a person who helped you develop your moral compass. What about that person caused you to be influenced by him or her? Were you more influenced by the person's character or the relationship between the two of you? Do you have the same relationship today? If not, what happened?

2. Think about an important relationship. What could you be doing to better nurture that relationship?

3. Identify a person you admire and would like to get to know. What steps can you take to begin a relationship with that person?

4. Watch the ABA Grit Project's "Billing Credit Dispute" video. How would you approach Jim to discuss the issue? Assume that he is aware of the issue and intentionally trying to take credit, that you do not want to leave the firm but are willing to do so and believe the client would come with you, and you have asked for a meeting to discuss this issue. Be specific about the approach you would take:

   a. Where do you want the conversation to take place and why?

   b. How will you structure the conversation to address the issue?

   c. Liz is not the managing partner, but is a partner within the firm who cares about you and is willing to help you think this through. How will you talk about this issue with Liz in a constructive manner?

Endnotes

1. Dawn McCoy, *Adjust the Sails*, FLOURISH LEADERSHIP GROUP (Sept. 12, 2010), https://flourishleadership.com/2010/09/adjust-the-sails/#:~:text=John%20Maxwell%20once%20said%20that,be%20in%20a%20better%20space. John Maxwell is an American pastor, author, and an expert on the importance of leadership.
2. Robert Half, *Beyond Legal Expertise: What Makes a Lawyer a Great Leader*, ROBERT HALF BLOG (Feb. 16, 2015), https://www.roberthalf.com/blog/management-tips/beyond-legal-expertise-what-makes-a-lawyer-a-great-leader.
3. *Id.*
4. *See* Robert E. Shapiro, *Learning Good Judgment*, A.B.A. LITIG. J. (2015).
5. Sir Andrew Likierman, *The Elements of Good Judgment*, HARV. BUS. REV. (Jan. 2020), https://hbr.org/2020/01/the-elements-of-good-judgment.
6. *Id.*
7. *Id.*
8. *Id.*
9. *Id.*
10. Dylan Matthews, *36 Years Ago Today, One Man Saved Us from World-ending Nuclear War*, Vox (Sept. 26, 2019), https://www.vox.com/2018/9/26/17905796/nuclear-war-1983-stanislav-petrov-soviet-union.
11. *Id.*
12. Death tolls from a nuclear war between the USSR and the United States at the time would have ranged from 136 to 288 million people. *Id.*
13. Likierman, *supra* note 5.
14. *Id.*
15. *Id.*
16. Unfortunately, Petrov was never rewarded by the Soviet Union for his decision. *Id.* "Preventing the deaths of hundreds of millions, if not billions, of people was a costly decision for Petrov. If he had been wrong, and he somehow survived the [resulting, real] American nuclear strike, he likely would've been executed for treason." Matthews, *supra* note 10. For being right, he was "relentlessly interrogated afterward." *Id.* However, "[a]fter the Cold War, Petrov would receive a number of commendations for saving the world. He was honored at the United Nations, received the Dresden Peace Prize, and was profiled in the documentary *The Man Who Saved the World*. 'I was just at the right place at the right time,' he told the filmmakers." *Id.*

17. Likierman, *supra* note 5.

18. *Id.*

19. Doris Kearns Goodwin, Team of Rivals: The Political Genius of Abraham Lincoln (Simon & Schuster 2006) (2005).

20. Likierman, *supra* note 5.

21. *Id.*

22. *Id.*

23. *Id.*

24. *Id.*

25. *Id.*

26. *Id.*

27. *Id.*

28. *Id.*

29. *Id.*

30. *Id.*

31. *Id.*

32. Ron Chernow, Washington: A Life (Penguin Books 2011).

33. Jonathan Adams, *Department of the Treasury*, Mount Vernon (2020), https://www.mountvernon.org/library/digitalhistory/digital-encyclopedia/article/department-of-the-treasury/.

34. *Id.*

35. *Id.*

36. *Id.*

37. Likierman, *supra* note 5.

38. *Id.*

39. John C. Maxwell, Leadership Gold: Lessons I've Learned from a Lifetime of Leading 50 (Thomas Nelson 2008).

40. *See* Elle Kaplan, *"Active Listening": The Key to Strong Workplace Relationships, Productivity, and Personal Empowerment*, Medium (Aug. 22, 2018), https://medium.com/@ellekaplan/active-listening-the-key-to-strong-workplace-relationships-productivity-and-personal-72650f32da4c.

41. *Id.*

42. *Id.*

43. *Id.*

44. Likierman, *supra* note 5.

45. Kaplan, *supra* note 40.

46. *Id.*

47. Phoebe Bower & Pervin R. Taleyarkhan, *Building Effective Client Relationships: Practice Tips from In-House*, 11 Landslide, American Bar Association (Jan. 2019), https://www.americanbar.org/groups/intellectual_property_law/publications/landslide/2018-19/january-february/building-effective-client-relationships/.

48. Jennifer Smuts, *Relationship Development in Today's Law Firm*, Law Practice Today (Aug. 14, 2015), https://www.lawpracticetoday.org/article/relationship-development-in-todays-law-firm/.

49. *Building Better Client Relationships [Podcast]*, Nat'l L. Rev. (July 15, 2019), https://www.natlawreview.com/article/building-better-client-relationships-podcast.

50. *Why Healthy Relationships Are So Important*, Northwestern Medicine, https://www.nm.org/healthbeat/healthy-tips/5-benefits-of-healthy-relationships (last visited Apr. 21, 2020).

51. Kaplan, *supra* note 40.

52. Camille Preston, *Promoting Employee Happiness Benefits Everyone*, Forbes (Dec. 13, 2017), https://www.forbes.com/sites/forbescoachescouncil/2017/12/13/promoting-employee-happiness-benefits-everyone/#70cfe781581a.

53. John C. Maxwell, The 21 Irrefutable Laws of Leadership: Follow Them and People Will Follow You 11–22 (HarperCollins 2007) (1998).

54. *Id.*

55. *Aaron Burr Slays Alexander Hamilton in Duel*, History.com, https://www.history.com/this-day-in-history/burr-slays-hamilton-in-duel (last visited July 14, 2020).

56. *The Project on Civil Discourse*, American University, https://www.american.edu/spa/civildiscourse/ (last visited July 14, 2020).

57. *What Is Civil Discourse?*, American University, https://www.american.edu/spa/civildiscourse/what-is-civil-discourse.cfm (last visited July 14, 2020).

58. *Id.*

59. Lisa Lerer, *The New Culture War*, N.Y. Times (May 7, 2020), https://www.nytimes.com/2020/05/07/us/politics/liberal-conservative-coronavirus.html.

60. *Id.*

61. *Id.*

62. Patrick Smith, *The Rebel Made Me Do It: Mascots, Race, and the Lost Cause* (2019), *available at* https://aquila.usm.edu/dissertations/1654.

63. Patrick Smith, *The Rebel Made Me Do It: Mascots, Race, and the Lost Cause*, Dissertations, 1654, Univ. S. Miss. (2019), available at https://aquila.usm.edu/cgi/viewcontent.cgi?article=2725&context=dissertations.

64. Reprinted with permission of the author, Jennifer Hamlett Saucedo. It was first published on Facebook but has since been republished elsewhere.

65. *See Building Personal Relationships*, Medscape, https://www.medscape.com/courses/section/911175 (last visited July 14, 2020).

66. *See, e.g.*, Kate Ashford, *The Art of Disagreeing with Your Boss Without Losing Your Job*, Monster, https://www.monster.com/career-advice/article/how-to-disagree-with-your-bosswithout-losing-your-job-hot-jobs (last visited July 14, 2020).

67. Celestine Chua, *7 Tips to Choose Your Battles and Fight for What Matters*, Personal Excellence Blog, https://personalexcellence.co/blog/choose-your-battles/ (last visited July 14, 2020).

68. *See, e.g.*, *Making an Argument*, Lumen Learning, https://courses.lumenlearning.com/suny-geneseo-businesscommunication/chapter/making-an-argument-2/ (last visited July 14, 2020).

69. MindTools Content Team, *Conflict Resolution*, MindTools, https://www.mindtools.com/pages/article/newLDR_81.htm (last visited July 14, 2020).

70. Daniel Hemel, *A Good Lawyer Asks Good Questions*, The University of Chicago Law School (Sept. 25, 2018), https://www.law.uchicago.edu/news/good-lawyer-asks-good-questions.

71. Abigail Brenner, *How to Stop Taking Things Personally*, Psychology Today (Aug. 26, 2014), https://www.psychologytoday.com/us/blog/in-flux/201408/how-stop-taking-things-personally.

72. *Id.*

73. *Reflective Listening*, Syracuse University, https://www.maxwell.syr.edu/uploadedfiles/parcc/cmc/reflective%20listening%20nk.pdf (last visited July 14, 2020).

74. Brenner, *supra* note 71.

75. *Id.*

76. Daniel Roberts, *Wise Decisions for Lawyers*, Coaching for Lawyers, https://www.coachingforlawyers.com/wise-decisions-for-lawyers (last visited Apr. 22, 2020).

77. *See id.*

78. *See* Likierman, *supra* note 5.

79. Philip Klein, *How George H.W. Bush's Broken "No New Taxes" Pledge Changed American Politics and Policy Forever*, Wash. Examiner (Dec. 1, 2018), https://www.washingtonexaminer.com/opinion/how-george-h-w-bushs-broken-no-new-taxes-pledge-changed-american-politics-and-policy-forever.

80. *Id.*

81. John Harwood, *George HW Bush's Compromise on Raising Taxes Defied Conservatives — and Altered American Politics*, CNBC Politics (Dec. 4, 2018), https://www.cnbc.com/2018/12/04/george-hw-bush-defied-gop-by-raising-taxes-paid-steep-political-price.html.

82. *Id.*

83. *Id.*

84. *Id.*

85. *Id.*

86. Lily Rothman, *The Story Behind George H.W. Bush's Famous "Read My Lips, No New Taxes" Promise*, TIME (Dec. 1, 2018), https://time.com/3649511/george-hw-bush-quote-read-my-lips/.

87. Harwood, *supra* note 81.

88. Fred McClure, speech delivered to Baylor Law students (Jan. 15, 2020).

89. *See, e.g.*, *Effective Leadership: How to Manage Difficult Conversations*, IE University (Feb. 28, 2017), https://www.ie.edu/insights/articles/effective-leadership-how-to-manage-difficult-conversations/.

90. Rhonda Muir, *Lawyers in Conflict*, Law People Blog (Oct. 25, 2015), https://www.lawpeopleblog.com/2015/10/lawyers-in-conflict/.

91. Kimberlee Leonard, *The Importance of Interaction in Workplace Issues*, Hous. Chron. (Aug. 15, 2018), https://smallbusiness.chron.com/importance-interaction-workplace-issues-11429.html.

92. *See, e.g.*, *How to Improve Teamwork in the Workplace*, GALLUP, https://www.gallup.com/cliftonstrengths/en/278225/how-to-improve-teamwork.aspx#ite-282719 (last visited July 14, 2020).

93. Judy Ringer, *We Have to Talk: A Step-By-Step Checklist for Difficult Conversations*, MEDIATE.COM, https://www.mediate.com/articles/ringerJ1.cfm (last visited July 14, 2020).

94. *See id.*

95. *See, e.g.*, Christine Pearson, *The Smart Way to Respond to Negative Emotions at Work*, MIT SLOAN MGMT. REV. (Mar. 13, 2017), https://sloanreview.mit.edu/article/the-smart-way-to-respond-to-negative-emotions-at-work/.

96. *See* Belle Beth Cooper, *5 Habits of Highly Effective Communicators*, BUFFER (Aug. 8, 2013), https://buffer.com/resources/why-talking-about-ourselves-is-as-rewarding-as-sex-the-science-of-conversations/.

97. *Manager's Guide to Difficult Conversations in the Workplace*, AUSTRALIAN GOV., https://www.fairwork.gov.au/how-we-will-help/online-training/online-learning-centre/difficult-conversations-in-the-workplace-manager-course (last visited July 14, 2020).

98. *See, e.g.*, *The Benefits of Understanding Personality Types in the Workplace*, ALL THINGS ADMIN (May 7, 2019), https://www.allthingsadmin.com/benefits-understanding-personality-types-workplace/.

99. Rachel Manning, *5 Tips for Navigating Difficult Conversations with Your Employees*, STAFF LEASING (Oct. 8, 2019), https://staffleasing-peo.com/human-resources/difficult-conversations-with-your-employees/.

100. Ringer, *supra* note 93.

101. *See, e.g.*, Manning, *supra* note 99.

102. *See, e.g.*, Tia Benjamin, *Importance of Documenting Verbal Conversations*, HOUS. CHRON., https://smallbusiness.chron.com/importance-documenting-verbal-conversations-31306.html (last visited July 15, 2020).

103. *See, e.g.*, Ellevate, *Should You (Ever) Go Over Your Boss's Head?*, FORBES (Mar. 21, 2014), https://www.forbes.com/sites/85broads/2014/03/21/should-you-ever-go-over-your-bosss-head/#111a8aa04bc9.

104. *See Difficult Conversations*, CHARLES.IO (May 14, 2017), https://charles.io/difficult-conversations/ (reviewing DOUGLAS STONE ET AL., DIFFICULT CONVERSATIONS (Penguin Books 2010)).

105. David L. Masters, *Managing Conflict*, 40 COLO. LAW. 5 (2011).

106. *See* Rick Goodman, *Transformational Leaders Don't Shy Away from Conflict*, BUSINESS 2 COMMUNITY (Apr. 24, 2019), https://www.business2community.com/leadership/transformational-leaders-dont-shy-away-from-conflict-02193215.

107. *Id.*

108. *Id.*

Chapter 16 Followership

You cannot be a leader, and ask other people to follow you, unless you know how to follow, too.

Sam Rayburn[1]

Purpose

Consider the interplay between leading and following and the importance of followers to the leadership process.

Learning Objectives

At the end of this chapter, you should be able to:

- Describe the role of followers.
- Discuss behaviors and styles of followers that can contribute to the success or failure of an organization.
- Describe approaches to constructively challenging a leader.

Discussion

INTRODUCTION

No one really grows up dreaming of becoming a follower; we are taught to seek leadership positions, whether the line leader in kindergarten, the student council president, or the captain of our sports team. The view from the front is better, right? A quick Google search for the term "leadership" produces over 4.7 billion results, while "followership" ekes out just over a million responses.[2] While we may prefer to lead, the practical reality is that one leads only after learning to follow and function effectively as a team member — an art and practice known as followership. Followership, in many ways, is the first phase in the development of leadership. Especially as a young lawyer, you will more likely start off as a follower or, put another way, as part of the team. It may take courageous initiative to be the first follower of a leader. This calls to mind the movie *Jerry Maguire*, in which Maguire, inspired by his new vision for a sports agency, asks, "Who's coming with me?" A young secretary is his lone follower, and Maguire's disappointment is palpable. But that follower becomes instrumental in his success, and greater opportunities arise for her as well.

The ability to follow secures your position as a reliable team member and can open paths for additional responsibility and leadership. While we know this intuitively, we still do not like to be labeled a follower. One reason followership gets a bad name is the misconception that followers are like sheep, blindly following their leader. Being a good follower, however, does not mean you jettison independent thinking. Good followership involves active participation in pursuing an organizational goal. Each follower must work independently, be accountable for his actions, and take ownership of his role. While the leader may be responsible for vision, followers turn that vision into reality. In this chapter, we explore what it means to be a follower and discuss the opportunities to contribute as one who is not in charge.

DEFINING FOLLOWERSHIP

Many can identify the qualities of a great leader, but few take the time to consider the characteristics of a great follower. The *Cambridge Dictionary* does not even define the term "followership."[3] *Merriam-Webster's Collegiate Dictionary* defines "followership" as the "capacity or willingness to follow a leader."[4] Lawrence Suda suggests that followership is "the willingness to cooperate in working toward the accomplishment of the mission, to demonstrate a high degree of teamwork and to build cohesion among the organization members."[5] Followership may not have a universally accepted meaning, but all definitions implicitly recognize the interrelated nature of followership and leadership. In a way, good followership requires "leading" within the structure that the individual in the leader role provides. Orchestral musicians, for example, are superior "followers." They follow the conductor's lead, but in doing so, each brings the full measure of her skill, experience, and talent to create something beautiful. At its core then, followership involves the ability to work with others — leaders and peers — in an effective way. Followership is the manifestation of leadership's vision.

A hiking group includes both a guide at the front and a sweep at the back. The guide, acting as "leader" of the group, clears the path, sets the pace, and navigates the group to its destination. The sweep, although a "follower," plays a critical role in ensuring the group's success and may have a more demanding position than that of the guide. The sweep must ensure the pace is appropriate, watch the group for signs of developing injury, and keep an accurate count of the hikers. Sweeps observe the group from an entirely different perspective than the leader; in fact, they have a view the leader may never see. Without the unique view and responsibilities of the sweep, the group may not make needed adjustments or even finish the hike. Skilled sweeps predict what their guides need and get it done before the guides even ask for it.

This same dynamic plays out in leader/follower relationships in law, business, and government where there is a visionary leader and a team that executes that vision. Leaders need sweeps to ensure their teams make their destination. As Dr. Barbara Kellerman[6] of Harvard's Kennedy School noted, "Followers are more important to leaders than leaders are to followers." Like the guide and the sweep, followership recognizes that followers may be in a better position than leaders to recognize the everyday struggles of an organization. An effective sweep knows how best to address an organization's obstacles. The follower's role is not one-dimensional, and good followership requires the adaptability to address the ever-changing needs of the team.

THE DIMENSIONS OF FOLLOWERSHIP

The Four Roles of Followership

Cory Bouck, author and leading expert on corporate leadership, identifies four main followership roles, all of which focus on a single goal: facilitation.[7] Good followers facilitate the organization's pursuit of its goals, although the follower's responsibilities are not static.[8] Like the tango, good followers adapt to their environment and the fluctuating needs of their leader and organization at various points in time. The four suggested follower roles are as follows:

1. *Valet*: The valet knows what lies ahead and lays out the tools necessary for the team and its leaders to be successful. If there is a gap, the valet fills it without waiting to be told.[9] This is the role butler Alfred plays for Bruce Wayne in the *Batman* movie/comic series.
2. *Socratic mentor*: The mentor asks provocative, counterintuitive questions. The mentor not only knows his own job but also knows the leader's job.[10] For those

who have seen the *Star Wars* franchise movies, Yoda plays the Socratic mentor role for many a young Jedi.

3. *Chameleon*: The chameleon develops the professional maturity to know when to stand out and when to be subtle or even invisible. While followership is not about being the center of attention, it also does not mean allowing others to take advantage. An effective chameleon can be a standout even when blending in.[11] In *The Simpsons*, Smithers is a quintessential chameleon, adapting to Mr. Burns's changing and often capricious needs while still being his own person.

4. *Pastor-parent role*: The pastor-parent role is twofold. Pastors hear the sins and complaints of an organization without recrimination. Parents never think twice about putting us back on track when we have gone astray. Be both. By being reliable and genuine, you will soon become a trusted advisor within your organization.[12] In the movie *Good Will Hunting*, Robin Williams's character, Sean, serves as the pastor-parent to Will, the character played by Matt Damon.

These traits of good followership vary depending on the circumstances.[13] A follower may occupy one role on a given project and change to another for a different project. A follower may become the go-to person for that skill within a number of teams. Some follower roles come with time and familiarity with the organization or the work. Each follower role, however, facilitates the objectives of the organization and is important. While the leader may have the authority, followers lack neither power nor influence and can be agents of change by behaving proactively within the frameworks created by their leaders.[14]

Styles of Followership

Just as there can be styles of leadership, business expert Robert Kelley suggests there are styles of followership. He divides these styles into categories that depend on the level of engagement and the degree of independent thinking.[15] Though neither exclusive nor restrictive, these five styles identify common responses of those in the follower role:

1. *The sheep*: Sheep are passive in thinking and engagement, motivated by their leader rather than being self-motivated. They lack a strong sense of responsibility.

2. *The yes-people*: Yes-people readily act with positive energy when told what to do, but they often depend on their leader to do most of the thinking for them.

3. *The alienated*: The alienated are independent thinkers who can effectively carry out their individual roles, but they often bring skepticism and cynicism to the team, rarely contributing to the positive direction of the organization.

4. *The pragmatics*: Pragmatics are more reserved, exhibiting minimal levels of independent thinking and engagement. They are more willing to become involved when they understand the end goal; otherwise, they prefer the status quo.

5. *The star followers*: Star followers are independent thinkers, positive in energy, and actively engaged. They are adaptable and amiable, but they also challenge the leader if they disagree, offering constructive alternatives.[16]

The different follower styles impact the team dynamic. Imagine a team made up entirely of sheep — all too fearful or insecure to participate actively, unwilling to take any ownership in the project. This followership style is unlikely to result in successful outcomes. The leader's style, however, may play a role in creating sheep-like followers. If the leader has an authoritarian, coercive, or commanding approach that demeans team members and creates an atmosphere of insecurity or blame, the result may well be sheep. Yes-people can be helpful in that they have enthusiasm for the leader's ideas and are willing to execute specific tasks given to them. The downside, however, is an echo effect where no one challenges the leader's ideas or approach. This means the project is not tested or vetted during a time when changes could be made, and the result may not withstand challenge. Having an alienated team member can be exhausting in terms of the energy drain on the team. Pragmatic followers need to be engaged with the end product but are reluctant to change; this can keep the team from making needed progress. Sometimes, these various follower responses represent a developmental response, with members evolving to a higher level of followership when they see better conduct modeled, either by another team member or the leader. Evolution also happens when the team has a dynamic conducive to learning and where it is safe to make mistakes.

Followership: Serving a Common Purpose

At the heart of good followership is the ability to embrace one's role and assume responsibility for the common purpose of the organization. A follower can be a bystander or can choose to engage in the team's efforts by embracing a can-do attitude and taking a collaborative approach to the work. Good followers embrace five different follower attitudes and behaviors,[17] which call for the courage to:

1. support the leader;
2. assume responsibility for the common purpose;
3. constructively challenge the leader's behaviors;
4. participate in necessary transformations; and
5. take a moral stand when warranted to prevent ethical abuses.[18]

Followers who see themselves in service for something greater than themselves develop the courage and self-confidence to do whatever is necessary for the overall success of the organization or the greater cause.

DEVELOPING YOUR FOLLOWERSHIP SKILLS

The symbiotic nature of leaders and followers requires an effective relationship with your leader.[19] Just as leaders cannot succeed with disengaged followers, followers cannot succeed with a failing leader.[20] Learning to "manage your boss" and to become a better follower through practical steps can help build an effective relationship.[21]

Take Responsibility for Building an Effective Working Relationship with Your Leader

Your ability to thrive and contribute means you need to work well with your boss. This may be an easy relationship to develop or it may be challenging, depending on the personalities involved and the nature of the work. Not all personalities mesh immediately, but a good follower makes an effort to participate in, and set the tone for, a healthy working relationship. You are on this team for a reason — perhaps a job you need or a cause about which you feel strongly. This means you need to work within the confines set out by the leader, even if your leader fails to put any intentional effort into creating this relationship.[22]

How do you build an effective relationship? Start by being reliable, trustworthy, self-motivated, and an independent worker. Show your leader that, when she reaches out, she can depend on you to handle whatever task she throws your way. Demonstrate to your leader that you do not need constant direction or attention to get the job done, even if that requires working alone or being out of the spotlight. And above all, prove to your leader that you are someone that can be trusted not to leak information or speak disparagingly about her or your peers. Build the relationship by being the person the leader can trust.

Learn Your Leader's Goals and Support Achieving Them

Leaders and followers need to understand their respective roles to execute them effectively. Knowing the team's goals and the leader's vision helps. Seek a firm understanding of where you fit in a team and how your skills can further the team's objectives. This may come from other team members but should come from your leader. Ask about the leader's objectives. Seek input from her on what role she would like you to play. Once you have this information, it is easier not only to follow but to contribute in every way possible.[23]

Understand the Pressures on Your Leader

Followers sometime complain their leader lacks empathy for the pressures on the team. If only the leader took the time to understand the many duties you juggle at any given moment. Perhaps he does, but do you understand the pressures under which *he* operates on a regular basis? Many leaders shield their team members from financial pressure, client pressure, and deadline pressure, which protects the team but creates a gap between the reality the leader faces and the reality the team perceives. Take time to ask or at least imagine the pressures on your leader. That empathy can strengthen your relationship. Effective leaders voice their understanding of what the team is going through; effective followers show emotional support for the leader as well.

Evaluate Whether You Help or Hinder Your Leader's Effectiveness

What are you bringing to the team or project? While we all like to feel that we are invaluable contributors to any endeavor, there are times when we are more hindrance than help. Ask any senior partner in a law firm, and you will hear of work product from an associate that was so far off the mark that the leader simply did the work herself and never told the associate it was useless. To be an effective follower, then, listen to the direct feedback you received, and if you are not getting feedback from a busy leader, speak up. While many teams build in feedback or review sessions, you should not wait a full year to see if you are on track. If appropriate, take your boss to lunch and ask about the things you do well, those you do poorly, and what you could do to make her life easier.[24] Be prepared to hear and receive constructive criticism and feedback, which means leaving your ego at the door. Feedback is only helpful if you are prepared to listen honestly and be ready to act on it. The sooner you know where you can improve, the sooner you can become a more effective member of your organization.

Learn Your Leader's Preferred Work Habits

No two people work alike, but your leader's work habits set the tone for the team. A fundamental responsibility of an effective follower is understanding how and when your leader likes work to be done and how she reacts to various situations.[25] What are the things that make your leader tick? If she is an early bird and you get to the office at 9 a.m., hours after she arrives, this is not conducive to meshing your work styles. If your leader prefers to hear bad news in person, do not send a text or email. A follower's job is to facilitate the workings of the team and leader, which generally means aligning with the leader's preferred work style.

Case in point, a trial lawyer once worked for a partner who disliked it when his associates responded with "OK" or "Sure" when he assigned them work via email. He explained that a simple "I'll get right on it" or "Sure thing" was a minor tweak that made all the difference. This change in tone showed him that the associate appreciated the opportunity to do the work. While not substantive, taking this small step strengthened the relationship with this leader.

Know Your Leader's Strengths and Weaknesses

Teams are only as strong as their weakest link, and the leader-follower relationship is no exception. Leaders bring their own strengths and weaknesses to the team. A good follower identifies those weaknesses and helps pick up the slack.[26] For example, if your leader is known for losing original documents, file the original in a safe place and provide copies for the team to work with. You will know where the original is if needed.

Keep Your Leader Informed

The principle is simple: do not unfairly surprise your leader.[27] This obviously does not apply to birthday cards or celebrating bosses' day; those are great relationship builders. Withholding important information that the leader needs to know is unacceptable. Maybe you were afraid to share bad news. Maybe you got busy and forgot. Either way, this is bad followership. Always keep your leader informed. Use the type of communication your boss prefers, and in a timely manner. For matters that are urgent or time sensitive, dropping by her office may be needed. For others, sending an email or leaving a printed memo on her desk at the end of the week may be sufficient. If a response from her is needed, or the matter is time sensitive, request a "read receipt" or otherwise follow up. Some leaders get hundreds of emails a day, so do not assume yours will be read.

This extends to scheduling issues and personal requests. If you are running behind, need to leave early for an appointment, or have another issue, be transparent about it. Be courteous so that everyone can plan ahead and avoid any failures that may accompany last-minute surprises.

Manage the Flow of Information to Your Leader

Keeping the leader informed also means doing so in a manner that helps the work get done. Dumping a problem on your boss, or standing in the doorway with a "what do you want me to do about it" expression on your face, does not solve a problem.[28] Likewise, interrupting an important meeting, or dropping a news bomb at 5:00 p.m. on a Friday, is unlikely to help the situation. Strategize about the time and place to convey information to your leader, and when you do, be prepared to offer a solution. Even if you have not figured everything out yet, show your leader that you have thought about it and are ready to share the responsibility.[29] She may choose a different solution, but your willingness to take ownership will be remembered.

Make Decisions Easy

As a final step tying the others together, provide your leader with the information needed to make an informed decision.[30] Know the strengths and weaknesses of your work, and disclose those before she makes a decision. With the information you provide her, she should be able to make a quick and appropriate decision without doing any more of the legwork herself.

CONSTRUCTIVELY CHALLENGING YOUR LEADER

While good followers support their leader, occasionally the leader needs to be challenged if he is off track or missing an important aspect of the project. Good followers have the courage to express their concerns without undermining the leader's authority.

When challenging leaders, consider the following strategies that can pave the way for robust yet constructive dialogue:

Do Your Homework First

It is easy to criticize but much harder to find a solution. Before challenging your leader, invest time in looking for a better solution. Consider the alternatives from both the follower and the leader positions, since different perspectives may shed light on why certain decisions were made. Engage in productive discussions and endeavor to be open to different ideas. Finally, give your leader the benefit of the doubt — she may have good reasons for the proposed solution.

Consider the Time and Place

Disagreeing does not mean acting unprofessionally; it is important to find the right time and place to raise your concerns. Occasional disagreement during one-on-one meetings with your leader is one thing but voicing your disagreement at staff-wide conferences or client meetings is problematic for various reasons. Challenging your leader during staff meetings where the issue is not on the agenda is counterproductive unless there is time and space for that discussion. Similarly, disagreeing with the partner during a client meeting does little to facilitate discussion and may cause the client to lose faith in your organization; disagreements about a proposal should be discussed and settled before meeting with the client.

In addition to choosing the right time and place for raising questions, pick your battles. While you might have different ideas from your leader, the team will suffer if you expect the leader to defend every decision. It slows the work of the team and tells the leader you lack confidence in her judgment, which in turn weakens the team. Focus on the bigger issues, the more important points. Raise the issue in the right way at the right time.

Ask Result-Oriented Questions

Rather than telling a leader he is "wrong," try asking questions. Opening a dialogue through questions is an effective way to voice concern while also trying to understand the thought process. Looping the questions back to the results your team is striving to achieve will promote discussion that will either resolve the issue or help the team understand *why* the leader has chosen a particular approach.

Offer Solutions Based on Common Ground

Leaders and followers are on the same side — colleagues, not opponents. Rather than criticize the leader's ideas or judgment, ground your discussion in shared objectives. Explain your concerns about whether certain ideas will be effective in reaching the team's goals. Support your concerns with facts and data. Leaders are often open to reasoned arguments aimed at the common good of the organization.

Support the Leader's Ultimate Decision

Good followership means sharing your opinion under the proper circumstances. Ultimately, however, it is the leader's decision, and you need to respect and support that decision even if you disagree. Embracing your leader's decision is not the same thing as being a yes-person; if the issue has been vetted and discussed, then the team has been heard. A leader's decision may also be based on factors of which the follower may not be aware. The decision may have been made at a higher level by a superior. Once made, however, the team should be all in.

Challenging a leader often stems from mere strategic disagreement rather than a fundamental ethical issue. But if following your leader's decision would entail ethical abuse, you may need to step back or leave the team to prevent ethical violations.[31] Lawyers owe a fiduciary responsibility to the client and an ethical duty to the court and our system of justice. Though it may not be easy, part of becoming an effective follower includes recognizing when a leader's decisions overstep the boundary into ethical impropriety. You need to walk away — even when no one else does.

LAWYERS AND FOLLOWERSHIP

Even though lawyers tend to be autonomous, strong-minded, and risk-averse individuals,[32] they still are often called on to be followers. This role is not always comfortable for the Type A personalities (driven, hardworking, determined to succeed) drawn to the legal profession. Moreover, if collaborative work is not emphasized in your law school, you may not be adequately prepared to be a good follower. Today's lawyers need to be able to work in a team setting, whether as a leader or a follower. Many trial teams are comprised of different levels of lawyer help, with each assigned to an aspect of the case. Younger lawyers may be doing research and handling document production while more senior associates take more responsibility for hearings and depositions, leaving the partner-level attorneys to cover expert witnesses, client contact, and trial strategy. Each of these roles is important in the process of working up the case, and each level needs to work well with the others to coordinate representation and maximize the outcome for the client.

The same followership principles are true on the transactional side and even with mostly senior lawyers. Lawyers involved in a corporate deal may need expertise in widely varied practice areas from securities regulation to tax, antitrust, and intellectual property. It would be unlikely that a single lawyer or even section could address all of these legal specialty areas. Whether the specialists work for the same firm or not, they still need to work as a team. Each lawyer in this deal cannot be the leader; in fact, the majority will fill a supportive or follower role. This means they answer to and work under the lawyer in charge, either because that lawyer has the client relationship or because she has been designated the leader, either by the client or by the firm. If the lawyers in the follower roles fail to embrace their position or attempt to undermine the leader, the client and the work can suffer from unnecessary delay and cost, or a bad outcome may result for the client. Young associates must learn to work as part of the team, because they typically lack the needed expertise to take on legal matters without any supervision.

Being a good follower requires a good work ethic and the ability to work independently. Assigned tasks need to be done well and on time. A follower also needs to communicate to the team and/or leader about the status of the work and any issues that arise, and get questions answered promptly. In addition to handling the individual work assigned, good followers also offer to help other team members. The primary goal is to timely deliver quality work and results to the client.

Being a good follower, however, can cause work prioritization issues. In a firm with multiple partners or an overwhelming list of open client matters, young associates can be inundated with work assignments. One of the questions young associates are most afraid to ask is whether (and when) to say no to more work if they are overwhelmed. Rather than saying no, a better follower strategy might be to discuss with the assigning partners the pending deadlines and priorities for getting the work done. Your concerns about whether an unmanageable workload will have a negative or detrimental effect on the quality of your work are valid. The partners who assign work may not know about your other assignments or deadlines. Once they do know, they can either restructure the deadlines or bring in additional help. Again, communication is key. Being a good team player also means being a realistic team player. You may not understand the overall deadlines or sensitivity of a given project, so let the leaders lead on this. Manage your time efficiently so you can be as effective for your team as possible, while keeping your leaders in the loop. Over promising when you cannot realistically get the work done does not help the ultimate goal or enhance your standing as a team member.

CONCLUSION

Followership is underrated. Even though followership often takes the back seat to leadership, it is essential. Leaders need followers to accomplish together that which would be impossible alone. Become an active participant and take ownership of your role.

Spend time thinking about what type of follower you are currently and what type of follower you want to be. Decide what changes are necessary to move in that direction and become a more effective follower. Simple adjustments can shift a leader's reliance on you. Important assignments and responsibilities may come your way. Being a valued follower may accelerate your path to the leadership position you want. When you are the leader, you will be more successful if you understand the value of good followers and better utilize their skills and talents.

Exercises

Helping Your Professor with a Research Article

Good news! You have been selected to be a research assistant for one of your law school professors. This professor is the preeminent scholar in evidence law, specifically hearsay.

At your first meeting with the professor, you learn that she wants to write a new article about witnesses not being able to testify in court to their own out-of-court statements. She tells you that some practicing lawyers have approached her for such an article because local judges and attorneys believe that just because the witness-declarant is in the chair and subject to cross-examination that their out-of-court statements are not hearsay. As the cornerstone of her article, she wants you to find a "white horse" case that cannot be disputed, such as one from the U.S. Supreme Court or your state's supreme court that backs her thesis. Although your professor has not done the research, she is confident that such a case exists. After all, "it reflects what the rule says."

You are excited about the project and get started right away. However, after hours of extensive research, you cannot find a single case that supports her position.

Discussion Questions :

1. What should you do?
2. How will you tell the professor that no case supports her position?
3. When will you tell her this?
4. What more might you want to do before meeting with the professor?

Law Firm Setting—Assignment That Raises an Ethical Issue

You have recently been handed an assignment by your senior partner. The firm has been engaged by the founder of a local company to represent his company in a shareholder dispute. The company sells and installs trucking equipment for 18-wheelers, such as drive shafts, truck accessories, tires, etc. In this lawsuit, the son of the founder of the company has sued the company. The father owns 51 percent of the company and the son owns 49 percent. The son is claiming that the father has wrongfully shut him out of the operations of the company and is stripping the company of all assets to leave the son bankrupt. The father has expressed concerns about the son's ability to manage the company.

As part of your initial case investigation, you discover that your senior partner has represented the company before in a different matter. In that case, the firm represented the company in a tortious interference with a contract dispute. The plaintiff in that case had a similar business to the client, and alleged that the father and son were contacting the plaintiff's clients and spreading false statements in an effort to steal business from the plaintiff. Your firm took extensive notes about the operation of the business from the father and son to defend the previous suit, including the operation of the business, their roles in it, and the finances of the business. In the notes from the previous suit, the son mentioned that he was skimming some money out of the business to feed a drug and alcohol problem, but he did not believe that his father knew about it. After mentioning this to the partner, the partner said that she did not tell the father about the issue because she felt it was irrelevant to the then-pending lawsuit. That case settled on the eve of trial for $100,000.

You are concerned that the firm is conflicted out of the current matter because of the firm's involvement in the previous case. After consulting the ethical rules, you see that ABA Model Rule 1.9 states:

> (a) A lawyer who has formerly represented a client in a matter shall not thereafter represent another person in the same or a substantially related matter in which that person's interests are materially adverse to the interests of the former client unless the former client gives informed consent, confirmed in writing.

> (b) A lawyer shall not knowingly represent a person in the same or a substantially related matter in which a firm with which the lawyer formerly was associated had previously represented a client

> > (1) whose interests are materially adverse to that person; and

> > (2) about whom the lawyer had acquired information protected by Rules 1.6 and 1.9(c) that is material to the matter; unless the former client gives informed consent, confirmed in writing.

> (c) A lawyer who has formerly represented a client in a matter or whose present or former firm has formerly represented a client in a matter shall not thereafter:

> > (1) use information relating to the representation to the disadvantage of the former client except as these Rules would permit or require with respect to a client, or when the information has become generally known; or

> > (2) reveal information relating to the representation except as these Rules would permit or require with respect to a client.

After discovering the issue, you send the relevant information to the law firm's ethics committee, highlighting the issue, the ABA rule, and the relevant facts. The committee, after reviewing the information you sent, states that there is no conflict. The committee's response specifically referenced comment [1] to Rule 1.9:

> After termination of a client-lawyer relationship, a lawyer has certain continuing duties with respect to confidentiality and conflicts of interest and thus may not

represent another client except in conformity with this Rule. Under this Rule, for example, a lawyer could not properly seek to rescind on behalf of a new client a contract drafted on behalf of the former client. So also a lawyer who has prosecuted an accused person could not properly represent the accused in a subsequent civil action against the government concerning the same transaction. Nor could a lawyer who has represented multiple clients in a matter represent one of the clients against the others *in the same or a substantially related matter* after a dispute arose among the clients in that matter, unless all affected clients give informed consent [emphasis added].

The committee determined that, because this matter is not substantially related to the previous matter, no conflict of interest exists. You are concerned because the senior partner has given you her notes and consulted on the case, but you are signing all the court filings as well. You're concerned that this is a conflict of interest and that your bar license may be in jeopardy.

Discussion Questions:

1. What should you do now?
2. If you decide to talk to the senior partner on the case, how will you approach that conversation?

Journal Prompts

1. Describe a time when it was easy to play the role of a follower. What about that situation allowed you to be comfortable in the role of follower rather than wishing to be in charge?

2. Some people are naturally inclined to jump in and determine the direction for a project. Others are naturally inclined to look to the group for direction and be a good team player to make sure the job gets done.

   a. If your natural inclination is to look for direction from the group and perhaps need encouragement to seek leadership opportunities, describe a situation where you wish you had been more courageous and volunteered to determine the direction or next steps. What prevented you from taking that action?

   b. If your natural inclination is to take charge in a group, describe a situation where your directions were not well received and the group or project was not successful. What can you learn from that experience?

3. Looking back to Robert Kelley's descriptions of followers, think of people you have observed in the past that fit into one or more of those categories.

   a. Identify two types of followers you have observed in particular situations. How did their behavior affect the group?

b. Identify two scenarios where the followers negatively impacted a project. Thinking back, how could the followers have been more helpful to the project if they had adopted a different approach?

Endnotes

1. *See* Office of the Historian, *Samuel Taliaferro Rayburn Biography,* U.S. House of Representatives History, Art & Archives (2020). Sam Rayburn (1882-1961), was a Texan lawyer and congressman who served as Speaker of the U.S. House of Representatives for 17 years.
2. *Leadership,* Google.com (last visited Apr. 5, 2020).
3. *See* Cambridge Dictionary, https://dictionary.cambridge.org/us/ (last visited Sept. 25, 2020).
4. *Followership,* Merriam-Webster's Collegiate Dictionary (11th ed. 2003).
5. *See* Lawrence Suda, *In Praise of Followers,* Project Management Institute (Oct. 29, 2013), https://www.pmi.org/learning/library/importance-of-effective-followers-5887.
6. Dr. Kellerman is the James MacGregor Burns Lecturer in Public Leadership at the Harvard Kennedy School. She is the founding executive director of the school's Center for Public Leadership.
7. Cory Bouck, *The Four Roles of Followership,* Address at the Integrated Data Storage 2015 Kickoff Meeting (Mar. 23, 2015), *video available at* https://www.youtube.com/watch?v=D_lq0z0fino.
8. *Id.*
9. *Id.*
10. *Id.*
11. *Id.*
12. *Id.*
13. Barbara Kellerman, Followership: How Followers are Creating and Changing Leaders 236 (Harv. Bus. Rev. Press 2008).
14. *Id.*
15. Ronald E. Riggio, Ira Chaleff & Jean Lipman-Bluman, The Art of Followership: How Great Followers Create Great Leaders and Organizations 5–15 (Jossey-Bass 2008).
16. *Id.*
17. *Id.* at 67–87.
18. *Id.* at 87.
19. Janis L. Johnston, *Managing the Boss,* 89 Law. Libr. J. 21, 22–29 (1997).
20. *Id.*
21. *Id.* at 22–29.
22. *Id.* at 22–23.
23. *Id.* at 23.
24. *Id.* at 24–25.
25. *Id.* at 25.
26. *Id.* at 26–27.
27. *Id.* at 27.
28. *Id.* at 28.
29. *Id.*
30. *Id.* at 28–29.
31. *Id.*
32. *See generally* Dr. Larry Richards, *About Lawyer Brain Blog,* LawyerBrain LLC, https://www.lawyerbrainblog.com/about/ (last visited July 13, 2020).

Chapter 17

Diversity, Inclusion, and Cultural Intelligence

You never really understand a person until you consider things from his point of view—until you climb into his skin and walk around in it.

Atticus Finch[1]

Purpose

Explore the ongoing challenges to creating an inclusive environment, highlight the benefits of leading a diverse team, help lawyers become more inclusive leaders in a diverse workforce, and develop cultural intelligence.

Learning Objectives

At the end of this chapter, you should be able to:

- Explain the differences among diversity, equity, and inclusion.
- Discuss the importance of diversity in organizations.
- List benefits of an inclusive environment.
- Describe the current status of diversity in the legal profession.
- Develop a strategy for addressing diversity and inclusion issues.
- Describe the influence of a person's cultural background on viewpoints, decisions, actions, and behaviors.
- Describe the attributes and benefits of cultural intelligence.

Discussion

INTRODUCTION

I look to a day when people will not be judged by the color of their skin, but by the content of their character.

Dr. Martin Luther King, Jr.[2]

The traditional model of an American law firm, likely drawn from its British predecessors, contained distinguished white men going to private clubs, arguing points of law, and passing knowledge on to their junior partners. They knew the same people, golfed at the same clubs, and married pretty, passive wives who took care of the children and ran a gracious home. Depending on the era, they might have owned slaves. Law schools reflected this path to the legal profession, with white male professors teaching white male students. Many states had laws requiring that lawyers be males.

Notably and explicitly absent were women and people of color. Change came slowly. Laws that excluded women were eventually amended through the efforts of women such as Clara Shortridge Foltz, who, in 1878, found herself raising five children alone when her husband abandoned her. She decided to become a lawyer, but under California law, "any white male" could become an attorney; women and minorities could not. She ultimately drafted and saw passed the Woman Lawyer's Bill, paving the way for "any citizen or person" to become a licensed attorney.[3]

Women and people of color slowly gained admission to law school and the bar, but firms would not hire them. Supreme Court Justice Sandra Day O'Connor graduated from Stanford Law School third in her class, having excelled on the law review and in moot court, and having been named Order of the Coif. A friend's father, a partner in the Los Angeles office of Gibson, Dunn & Crutcher, agreed to meet her, so she traveled to LA one day in 1952. The partner told her, "You have a fine resume, Miss Day . . . but this firm has never hired a woman lawyer. I don't see that it will. Our clients won't stand for it." He then went on to suggest that if she typed well enough, they might find her a job as a legal secretary.[4] Justice O'Connor and her eventual colleague on the court, Justice Ruth Bader Ginsburg, often quipped that had the traditional law firm paths been available to them, they would never have made it to the Supreme Court.[5]

The late Judge A. Leon Higginbotham, Jr., who during his career served as Chief Judge of the U.S Court of Appeals for the Third Circuit, faced similar roadblocks. Judge Higginbotham, an African-American man, graduated Yale Law School in 1952, only to find that his Yale diploma and his various awards opened no doors for him. One of the premier law firms in Philadelphia granted Higginbotham an interview, wrongly assuming that his name meant that he was white. Although the interviewing attorney found Higginbotham's resume impressive, he informed Higginbotham, "Of course, you know there's nothing I can do for you."[6]

These stories seem like historically interesting footnotes about the travails of women and minorities as they tried to become lawyers in the past. Sadly, the impediments diverse lawyers face remain prevalent. Barriers, both overt and implicit, keep the power structure of the law and law firms largely white, straight, and male. Attorney Beth Wilkinson, who enjoyed a "formidable reputation" at a BigLaw firm, left to start her own firm because "she was never in the inner circle. BigLaw is a male-dominated place, and it is very hard for women to thrive in an institution built that way."[7]

The problem is not limited to BigLaw; it pervades the practice:

> What makes the issue especially vexing are the sources of the bias — judges, senior attorneys, juries, and even the clients themselves. Sexism infects every kind of courtroom encounter, from pretrial motions to closing arguments — a glum ubiquity that makes clear how difficult it will be to eradicate gender bias not just from the practice of law, but from society as a whole.[8]

Indeed, both people of color and women are often the subjects of the refrain, "You don't look like a lawyer," whether that refrain is express or implicit. In other words, people of color and women do not fit the predominate image that lawyers are white and male. Ask virtually any woman or person of color and they are likely to recount their own anecdote of being mistaken for a secretary, paralegal, or support staff. In her book, *You Don't Look Like a Lawyer*, Tsedale M. Melaku tells the story of Philomena, a young Black associate who succeeded in gaining entry to a reputable law firm only to be essentially invisible as an attorney there.[9] The head of the firm repeatedly mistook Philomena for a secretary. One can imagine how that might affect Philomena's chances for advancement at that firm.

The problem of overt bias, which includes such things as female lawyers being called "honey" and "sweetie," was so pervasive that the American Bar Association amended the Model Rules of Professional Conduct to make it unethical to

> (g) engage in conduct that the lawyer knows or reasonably should know is harassment or discrimination on the basis of race, sex, religion, national origin, ethnicity, disability, age, sexual orientation, gender identity, marital status or socioeconomic status in conduct related to the practice of law. This paragraph does not limit the ability of a lawyer to accept, decline or withdraw from a representation in accordance with Rule 1.16. This paragraph does not preclude legitimate advice or advocacy consistent with these Rules.[10]

For those who were uncertain about the intent of that amendment, the comments clarified that

> [s]uch discrimination includes harmful verbal or physical conduct that manifests bias or prejudice towards others. Harassment includes sexual harassment and derogatory or demeaning verbal or physical conduct. Sexual harassment includes unwelcome

sexual advances, requests for sexual favors, and other unwelcome verbal or physical conduct of a sexual nature. The substantive law of anti-discrimination and anti-harassment statutes and case law may guide application of paragraph (g).[11]

The fact that the ABA needed an explicit statement that harassment and discrimination were inconsistent with the ethical and professional obligations of lawyers underscores the lack of progress minorities and women have made. The fact that the rule was passed as late as 2016 is even more disturbing. This chapter looks first at diversity, inclusion, and equity within the practice. It then examines cultural intelligence as a needed skill set for lawyers and leaders working with those who come from a different culture, background, or tradition.

DISTINCTION AMONG DIVERSITY, EQUITY, AND INCLUSION

Diversity, equity, and inclusion often are bundled without much thought to how they differ. If they all meant the same thing, though, we would not need all three words. Diversity, on a broad scale, is a numerical representation of different types of people.[12] At an individual level, diversity looks at whether the team encompasses "the range of human differences, including but not limited to race, ethnicity, gender, gender identity, sexual orientation, age, social class, physical ability or attributes, religious or ethical values system, national origin, and political beliefs."[13] Diversity is that which makes us unique from one another and includes lifestyles and life experiences, perspectives, and opinions.[14]

An inclusive environment makes it possible for each of the constituents to participate. Inclusion is the "how"—the behaviors that welcome and embrace diversity.[15] Inclusion involves an authentic and empowered participation and a true sense of belonging,[16] where the inherent worth and dignity of all people are recognized.[17] Inclusivity is about creating a working environment where each member feels empowered to contribute.

The ultimate goal, however, should be to achieve equity. Without equity, efforts to promote diversity likely will fail. The numbers game of diversity does not promote meaningful involvement of all team members. It does not address the attitudes that marginalize or exclude diverse team members from contributing, owning, and leading. *Merriam-Webster's Dictionary* defines equity as "fairness or justice in the way people are treated." But what exactly is fairness and how do we define justice?[18] If our view of fairness and justice are "shaped by each individual's worldviews and experiences, then the definition may be a perpetually moving target."[19] Striving for inclusion is a "step toward equity . . . but even those who feel included may not experience equity."[20] Dafina-Lazarus Stewart contrasts diversity and equity: "Diversity asks, "Who's in the room?" Equity responds: "Who is trying to get in the room but can't? Whose presence in the room is under constant threat of erasure?"[21]

The equitable community supports and uplifts the well-being and potential of *all* of its members, not just some. Equity "describes something deeper and more complex. It is about each of us getting what we need to survive or succeed—access to opportunity, networks, resources, and supports—based on where we are and where we want to go."[22] The goal should be to establish an environment where diversity moves beyond mere policy. Such efforts require leadership that begins with the enactment of goals and policies but is then lived out in word and deeds, in effort and actions throughout the organization.

DIVERSITY AND LEADERSHIP IN LEGAL SETTINGS

Lawyers value collective intellect, ingenuity, analytical skills, and decision making. Although the legal profession attracts highly intelligent people, diversity in the workplace further increases collective intellect. Diverse teams are more likely to reexamine facts and remain objective, and they encourage greater scrutiny of each member's actions, keeping their joint cognitive resources sharp and vigilant.[23] Scientists think the diversity of the team leads to more careful processing of information and questioning of assumptions, resulting in more innovation.[24]

Creating an energized, engaged, and innovative environment is needed to help the legal profession meet the challenges it faces[25] and a number of disruptors, both anticipated and unanticipated.[26] Rigid pricing and fee structures create a bar to access, meaning fewer citizens seek the help of lawyers for their legal needs. As a profession, lawyers need to find better ways to deliver legal services in an affordable and accessible manner. Innovation and more inclusive environments are needed.[27] In addition, corporate clients now demand true inclusion and equity. Firms who do not demonstrate equity lose the legal work. The moral and economic reasons for diversity and inclusion continue to mount, but the profession continues to lag.

How Is the Legal Profession Doing?

Given that lawyers advise and represent clients on issues involving equal protection statutes, employment law, and anti-discrimination statutes, one might assume the legal profession excels in creating environments that encourage inclusion and produce greater diversity. It does not.

Consider, first, the number of women and minorities attending law school. Data showed that in 1960, 3.5 percent of law students were women. In 1970, only 5 percent of law students were non-white. In 1980, 33.6 percent of law students were women. In 2005, 48 percent of law students were women and 17 percent were non-white. Today the number of women in law school exceeds the number of men—a trend seen across the board in higher education[28]; but minority representation still lags.[29]

The number of minority and women lawyers who graduate and enter the profession does not reflect our society, particularly in partner and leadership positions. The 2019 survey by the National Association for Law Placement (NALP) found that people of color accounted for 9.55 percent of partners in U.S. law firms and women accounted for 24.17 percent of partners in major firms. Associates of color represent 25.44 percent. Women associates were 46.77 percent and women of color were 14.48 percent.[30] Even when women make partner in a firm, they earn substantially less than their male counterparts. Women law partners faced a whopping 53 percent gap in pay at top U.S. law firms. Female partners earned an average of $627,000 annually compared to $959,000 for male partners, according to the 2018 Partner Compensation Survey, published at the end of 2018 by legal consulting firm Major, Lindsey & Africa. The survey underscored the earnings difference, which was 32 percent in 2010, the first year the big-firm survey was done. Two years later, the gap rose to 48 percent and the next year passed the 50 percent mark. Women, according to this study, are losing economic ground every year.[31]

Persons of color fare even worse than white women, both in terms of representation and power. Only 5 percent of active attorneys identified as Black or African American or as Hispanic or Latino in 2009; a decade later, in 2019, those percentages remain the same.[32] During the same period of time, the U.S. Census Bureau reported that in 2016 Black/African Americans made up 13.3 percent of the total U.S. population and Hispanic/Latino individuals made up 17.8 percent.[33] As of the writing of this book, some national law firms still did not have a single Black partner.[34]

The 2019 NALP Report also describes changes in representation for LGBTQ+ lawyers, summer associates, and partners.[35] While the number of LGBTQ+ lawyers, partners, and associates has not increased by more than 2 percent since 2004, the amount of summer LGBTQ+ associates has increased from 0.61 percent in 2004 to almost 7 percent in 2019.[36] It is not clear from the data whether this increase is due to greater representation or a greater willingness to self-identify orientation status. If numerically accurate, this increase in summer associates is encouraging considering the role that summer associate positions play in providing full-time jobs after graduation. On June 15, 2020, the United States Supreme Court held that Title VII of the Civil Rights Act of 1964, which prohibits discrimination on the basis of sex, protects LGBTQ+ employees.[37] This pivotal decision establishes critical protections for LGBTQ+ workers, who are now protected by law from harmful discrimination in the workplace. In his majority opinion, Justice Gorsuch wrote, "An employer who fires an individual for being homosexual or transgender fires that person for traits or actions it would not have questioned in members of a different sex."[38] Sex therefore plays a "necessary and undisguisable role" in the employment decision, violating Title VII.[39] This Supreme Court decision provides necessary protection to LGBTQ+ workers, and should encourage LGBTQ+ representation in the workplace. Whether employers act on the Supreme Court's urgings or turn the issue into a numbers game will be the next diversity challenge.

A number of studies and reports attribute the slow growth in diversity within the legal profession to factors including bias in the workplace,[40] inability of minority and women lawyers to find adequate access to mentors in the firm or law profession,[41] and insufficient pregnancy-leave and family-support polices at many firms. More firms have tried to promote diversity and inclusion through firm culture, personnel policies, retention and attorney support polices (such as maternity leave and partnership policies recognizing maternity and paternity leaves), and the creation of chief diversity officer positions and/or a diversity committee of key lawyers in the firm. While these are important steps, they are not sufficient and firm leadership still does not reflect the demographics of our society as a whole. More must be done to maintain meaningful professional opportunities in an increasingly diverse society.

Groups within the American Bar Association support diversity work within bar associations and offer advice to bar leaders. "Diversity and inclusion . . . takes persistence, innovation, and a deep commitment."[42] Being an inclusive bar leader requires effort to reach out to people, to listen to their concerns and desires, and to actively engage diverse members.[43] Bar associations should strive to create a culture in which bar associations are a welcoming place for all members.[44]

Why Diversity and Inclusion Initiatives Are Not Working

The reasons why women and minorities are systematically excluded are myriad. Overt sexism and racism, while less prevalent, still take place. When Clara Foltz argued a case in the late 1800s, a male prosecutor told the jury to reject Foltz's arguments on these simple grounds: "She is a woman, she cannot be expected to reason. God Almighty declared her limitations." That attitude pervades today. In 2015, a male lawyer filed a motion "to preclude emotional displays" during trial. The motion did not address the personal injury plaintiff but instead, the lawyer representing him. "Counsel for the Plaintiff, Elizabeth Faiella, has a proclivity for displays of anguish in the presence of the jury, including crying," the attorney wrote in his motion.[45] Faiella insisted to the judge that she had never cried once in a trial. The motion was denied, but this raises the question: What man has ever had to defend himself against an unwarranted claim that he was going to cry in trial? Faiella said of the motion and others like it, "I cannot tell you how much it demeans me. Because I am a woman, I have to act like it doesn't bother me, but I tell you that it does. The arrow lands every time."[46]

In addition to overt racism and sexism, women face more subtle attitudinal pressure that does not apply to men. They are scrutinized for their clothing (too feminine or not feminine enough), hair and makeup (too feminine or not feminine enough), handshake (too firm or not firm enough) in ways that male attorneys simply are not. Influential women are asked in various settings about being "unapologetically female," a question that is so confounding it is hard to contemplate. Why should anyone be required to apologize for their gender and being authentically male or female?

Beyond appearance, women face a double bind from both men and women alike. In a landmark 2001 report on sexism in the courtroom, Deborah Rhode described what women face in the courtroom: a "double standard and a double bind." Women, she wrote, must avoid being seen as "too 'soft' or too 'strident,' too 'aggressive' or 'not aggressive enough.'"[47]

Women who advocate strongly for a better salary — a skill men are taught from an early age — are viewed as grasping and too aggressive. If women do not advocate for an equitable salary, they are paid less. This creates a setting where it can feel impossible for women to advocate effectively for themselves and their clients, and they may be forever disadvantaged economically. A salary gap at initial hiring is rarely corrected and often grows.[48] Assume a starting salary of $100,000 for a woman and $110,000 for a man. If both receive no more than an annual 3 percent cost of living raise, the woman's salary is $103,000 and the man's $113,300 the next year. In ten years, the woman's salary is only $134,392 compared to the man's salary of $147,830. With larger raises and bonus disparities, the gap worsens.

The challenges are certainly not limited to women; minorities face the same or greater barriers in attitude and access. Black men in the United States are often turned away from jobs because they are not "the right fit."[49] By the same token, Black men and Black women lose opportunities because they do not "look like a lawyer." The norms of success, ability, and competence are tied to looking a certain way — usually white and male.[50] Diverse lawyers face substantial pressure in terms of appearance to conform to white norms of professional attire, both of which are costly to women of color.[51] Professionals of color (and women) often are subject to what some authors call an *invisible labor clause*. "They are required to perform added, unacknowledged, and uncompensated labor and to pay additional 'taxes' for their inclusion in these social and professional spaces that would otherwise view these professionals' inherent differences as obstacles to their career advancement."[52] They also must spend resources of all kinds to gain entry to and acceptance from traditionally white and male institutional spaces.[53] In addition to needing to appear "white," they also need to work longer or harder to get noticed and to be flawless because of implicit bias about incompetence.

> The research of numerous scholars, including David B. Wilkins and G. Mitu Gulati, Catherine H. Tinsley and Robin J. Ely, and Heather Sarsons, reveals that women and people of color tend to be significantly penalized for marginal errors, as compared with white men. In Ashleigh Shelby Rosette and Robert Livingston's study, black women leaders in particular were punished more harshly than their white counterparts for making a mistake. . . . That adds up to some very real costs of the you-don't-look-like phenomenon: receiving less pay for equal hours; doing the work but not receiving the credit; encountering difficulty with breaking into social and professional networks; and dealing with the discomfort of white male colleagues.[54]

Beyond the perception issues faced by women and minorities, the economic disparity is one of the most significant barriers to equity. Most law firm structures look at work originated as a key component of power. The rainmakers get more credit than do the workers. Women and minorities lag in getting introduced to the clients and to mentorship in rainmaking. Diverse lawyers are not taken to client development functions. Men's golfing and hunting trips are routinely off limits to female attorneys. Events held at private clubs with unwritten restrictions on minority access limit networking opportunities. The vague "the client doesn't feel comfortable with a woman/Black/Asian lawyer" is used as an inviolate bar to access. When women and minorities do get business from an existing client of the firm, the accounting metrics often credit the origination fee to the original partner, not the diverse member who has the current relationship. This keeps the diverse partner at an economic disparity vis-à-vis the original members, but law firms have shown reluctance to change the financial structure to benefit women and minority shareholders.

Legal organizations have tried to address the issues of diversity, equity, and inclusion. Some do so because they believe it to be the morally and ethically right thing to do and also recognize that diversity and inclusion enhances the profession. Bonnie Mayfield, an African-American female Member at Dykema and a Board Member of the International Association of Defense Counsel (IADC), highlights the IADC as an example. According to Mayfield, the IADC has a genuine and tangible commitment to diversity and inclusion, and that the IADC's leadership includes women and diverse individuals. She also notes that in the wider world of society at large, hearts, minds, and the law must change and that one change cannot wait upon the other.[55]

THE IMPACT OF IMPLICIT BIAS ON DIVERSITY AND INCLUSION

We all contain a bundle of different biases, some of which we readily acknowledge and some of which we are wholly unaware. For example, confirmation bias affects how we see information, whether from memory or other resources, as we are often "biased in favor of information that is consistent with [our] desired conclusion."[56] Social media algorithms play to confirmation bias by directing more confirmatory information onto your feed.[57] Those same algorithms can create a filter bubble by sending news from the same source, which isolates people from diverse perspectives and strengthens confirmation bias.[58] Self-serving bias informs our judgments of fairness or right and wrong in the "direction of their own self-interest."[59] The status quo bias reflects a person's natural preference for the current state of affairs, even if a change would be advantageous to him.[60] These biases do not represent an exclusive list of all the ways we can be biased, but bias has been studied for decades.[61] These forms are so entrenched in our society that government policies have been written with behavioral economics in mind to encourage citizens to make better decisions.[62]

In more recent studies, researchers have studied implicit bias in "social categories, such as genders and races."[63] These implicit biases are driven by attitudes and stereotypes about social categories. While the two concepts overlap, the relationship and differences between attitudes and stereotypes is important.

> An attitude is an association between some concept (in this case a social group) and an evaluative valence, either positive or negative. A stereotype is an association between a concept (again, in this case a social group) and a trait. Although interconnected, attitudes and stereotypes should be distinguished because a positive attitude does not foreclose negative stereotypes and vice versa. For instance, one might have a positive overall attitude toward African Americans and yet still associate them with weapons. Or, one might have a positive stereotype of Asian Americans as mathematically able but still have an overall negative attitude towards them.

> The conventional wisdom has been that these social cognitions — attitudes and stereotypes about social groups — are explicit, in the sense that they are both consciously accessible through introspection and endorsed as appropriate by the person who possesses them. Indeed, this understanding has shaped much of current antidiscrimination law. The conventional wisdom is also that the social cognitions that individuals hold are relatively stable, in the sense that they operate in the same way over time and across different situations.[64]

The conventional wisdom, however, may be wrong.[65] These biases can be implicit, meaning that a person who holds them may not be able to sense them through introspection.[66] As such, the person acts on these biases in an unthinking manner, even in ways that the person, if aware of them, would not endorse.[67] Explained another way:

> [E]xplicit biases are attitudes and stereotypes that are consciously accessible through introspection and endorsed as appropriate. If no social norm against these biases exists within a given context, a person will freely broadcast them to others. But if such a norm exists, then explicit biases can be concealed to manage the impressions that others have of us. By contrast, implicit biases are attitudes and stereotypes that are not consciously accessible through introspection. If we find out that we have them, we may indeed reject them as inappropriate.[68]

Structural biases "lock in past inequalities, reproduce them, and indeed exacerbate them" even when the person affected by them is not being treated any differently than others.[69] To better understand the bias, it can be helpful to take the issue outside of an emotionally charged setting.

> Because thinking through biases with respect to human beings evokes so much potential emotional resistance, sometimes it is easier to apply them to something less fraught than gender, race, religion, and the like. So, consider a vegetarian's biases against meat. He has a negative attitude (that is, prejudice) toward meat. He also believes that eating meat is bad for his health (a stereotype). He is aware of this attitude and stereotype. He also endorses them as appropriate. That is, he feels that it is okay to have a negative reaction to meat. He also believes it accurate enough to believe that meat is generally

bad for human health and that there is no reason to avoid behaving in accordance with this belief. These are explicit biases.

Now, if this vegetarian is running for political office and campaigning in a region famous for barbecue, he will probably keep his views to himself. He could, for example, avoid showing disgust on his face or making critical comments when a plate of ribs is placed in front of him. Indeed, he might even take a bite and compliment the cook. This is an example of concealed bias (explicit bias that is hidden to manage impressions).

Consider, by contrast, another vegetarian who has recently converted for environmental reasons. She proclaims explicitly and sincerely a negative attitude toward meat. But it may well be that she has an implicit attitude that is still slightly positive. Suppose that she grew up enjoying weekend barbecues with family and friends, or still likes the taste of steak, or first learned to cook by making roasts. Whatever the sources and causes, she may still have an implicitly positive attitude toward meat. This is an implicit bias.

Finally, consider some eating decision that she has to make at a local strip mall. She can buy a salad for $10 or a cheeseburger for $3. Unfortunately, she has only $5 to spare and must eat. Neither explicit nor implicit biases much explain her decision to buy the cheeseburger. She simply lacks the funds to buy the salad, and her need to eat trumps her desire to avoid meat. The decision was not driven principally by an attitude or stereotype, explicit or implicit, but by the price. But what if a careful historical, economic, political, and cultural analysis revealed multifarious subsidies, political kickbacks, historical contingencies, and economies of scale that accumulated in mutually reinforcing ways to price the salad much higher than the cheeseburger? These various forces could make it more instrumentally rational for consumers to eat cheeseburgers. This would be an example of structural bias in favor of meat.[70]

The manifestation of these hidden biases becomes evidence in various settings. Some are innocuous, such as our American infatuation with a British accent, which we associate with intelligence and sophistication.[71] Children in Chicago considered Southern accents to be "nicer" than Northern accents.[72]

Implicit biases involve associations we make without necessarily being aware we are doing so and can arise in a variety of settings. More personal fouls are called against NBA players when they are officiated by an opposite-race officiating crew than by a crew of their own race. "The bias in foul-calling is large enough so that the probability of a team winning is noticeably affected by the racial composition of the refereeing crew assigned to the game."[73] As late as 2006 in Milwaukee, non-white families were 2.7 times more likely to be denied for a home loan than white families, even when they had similar incomes.[74]

These biases are also exhibited in the workplace. Tall white men disproportionately hold high-level leadership positions and earn more than other similarly situated individuals.[75] When resume content (such as work experience and education) are equal, resumes of individuals with "Black-sounding" names are 50 percent less likely to be selected for an interview.[76] Partners at a law firm rated a legal memo 3.2/5 when told the author of the memo was a Black man, yet rated the same memo 4/5 when the memo was attributed to a white man. In addition to the score disparity, memo comments for the Black man critiqued his average performance and cited a need for improvement, while the memo attributed to a white man was praised for its analysis.[77]

Unfortunately, our court systems have not fared better. A study in Los Angeles in 1985 found that prosecutors were more likely to charge Black defendants with crimes than white defendants.[78] Moreover, on average, non-white offenders owed more in court costs and fines than white offenders with similar offenses and criminal histories.[79] Most concerning are the statistics indicating that Black defendants get longer sentences and are more likely to get the death penalty than white defendants.[80] As recently as 2018, the U.S. Supreme Court dealt with a *Batson* challenge case where state prosecutors routinely and systematically used race to discriminate during jury selection.[81]

These social group biases are not limited to race; they apply to gender and socio-economic status (among others) as well. Gender bias by professors at Harvard Law School resulted in female students receiving lower grades than their male peers, until the introduction of blind grading mitigated the practice.[82] In a 1983 study, participants were asked to evaluate the intelligence of a young girl based on an oral interview.[83] When told the girl was from a poor family, the participants stated that she was not very smart.[84] When told that the girl came from a rich family, they believed her to be smart.[85]

These are learned biases. Children do not innately attribute characteristics — positive or negative — based on gender, religion, or race. We learn bias in our families, in school, and from the media. Our families teach us, directly or indirectly, their beliefs and stereotypes about people. At school, teachers try to make us "fill in the boxes" to conform to stereotypes. Apparently, only one gender can like computers or stomp rockets or play with Barbies.

The media likewise reinforces stereotypes to the detriment of the cultural groups involved. Movies and television shows routinely perpetuate the idea that smart and competent women still need to be saved by a man. Even politicians, supposedly on their best behavior as they seek elected office, can be culturally tone-deaf. President Donald Trump certainly has attacked women and other groups on a number of occasions,[86] but the practice is not limited to him. When an interviewer confused Sen. Cory Booker with former Attorney General Eric Holder, former Secretary of State Hillary Clinton "quipped" that she understood the confusion since "they all look alike."[87]

Implicit bias creates a strong barrier to cultural intelligence, a concept discussed below. As noted above, implicit bias reinforces stereotypes and beliefs of which we are not consciously aware. For example, consider the image below and decide which is the longer line:

You probably decided that B was the longer line when, in fact, the lines are of equal length. You were implicitly biased by the arrows.[88] A key contribution to modern research on implicit bias "is the realization that people can be biased implicitly not only by arrows but also by social elements in our environments, that is, by elements indicative of the social group to which others belong (e.g., skin color)."[89] Implicit bias is a normal feature for most of us, and it does not necessarily carry negative moral implications. You were not expressing a societal prejudice by thinking line B was longer than line A. The fact that we carry a wide range of implicit biases, however, is a bar to cultural competence and humility because we must first recognize our biases and then be willing to act to remove them as a barrier to effective cultural communication.

THE SYSTEMIC EFFECT OF IMPLICIT BIAS IN THE WORKPLACE

Implicit bias not only has a systemic impact on organizations and society but also impacts individuals, particularly women and people of color. In *You Can't Change What You Don't See*, the American Bar Association Commission on Women in the Profession and the Minority Corporate Counsel Association examined issues of racial and gender bias in the legal workplace.[90]

Regularly, women and men of color are required to go "above and beyond" to receive the same recognition and respect as their white male colleagues.[91] This "prove it again" bias is reported by women of color 35 percent more than by white men.[92] Women and men of color regularly experience bias for not meeting the expected appearance of a lawyer. In fact, this bias goes so far that women of color report being mistaken for administrative staff or janitorial staff at a level 50 percentage points higher than white men.[93] Even when women and men of color effectively achieve this heightened standard as a professional, bias also impacts their chances at promotion. Only 52 percent of women of color believed they were presented with fair opportunities for advancement, in contrast to approximately 75 percent of white men who believed the playing field was even.[94]

While career women have seen some advances, many continue to report difficulties navigating the "tightrope" that is being a hard worker and a woman.[95] "White women reported that their commitment or competence was questioned after they had kids at a level 36 percentage points higher than white men."[96] Often due to workplace bias, women report being assigned "office housework," including office party planning, ordering coffee and other supplies, and administrative tasks such as taking notes at a meeting.[97] White women report these responsibilities at a level 21 percentage points higher than white men, and women of color report at 18 points higher than white men.[98] While regularly taking on such additional tasks, 70 percent of women of color still report being paid less than their colleagues of similar experience and seniority.[99]

Such statistics should prompt us to consider how our unconscious bias may play a part in projecting certain experiences or roles onto others. Recognizing implicit bias should in turn bring to our attention systems and other circumstances where bias impedes the success, and even safety, of others. In *You Can't Change What You Don't See*, the authors highlight the extent to which training materials focus on "how individual lawyers could *overcome* barriers in the workplace . . . rather than *removing* those barriers."[100] Rather than placing a burden on the disadvantaged individual, changes to procedures and systems must be implemented if we hope to eradicate harmful bias and create a fair playing field for all employees.[101] In other words, rather than teaching women and minorities how to climb the wall, we should remove the wall.

EFFECTIVE LEADERSHIP IS ESSENTIAL TO THE SUCCESS OF DIVERSITY AND INCLUSION EFFORTS

The difference between a broken community and a thriving one is the presence of women who are valued.

Michelle Obama[102]

Those who make up the majority in the legal profession, those who make the decisions and have the power, need to understand how biases disproportionately affect those whose appearance or life experiences are not like theirs. Only with awareness and effort can we help rectify the disparate treatment. Despite decades of diversity and inclusion training and countless studies proving the benefits of a diverse workforce, employers still struggle to have meaningful diversity in the workplace. Documented benefits of a diverse and inclusive environment include more innovation, improved creativity, enhanced performance, better decision making, better problem solving with complex tasks, greater collective intelligence, lower turnover, greater job satisfaction, and increased profitability.[103]

Despite overwhelming evidence of the benefits of diversity, embarrassingly little progress has been made. This failure is multifactorial; companies and firms have thrown significant resources at hiring women and racial minorities thinking that simply building the numbers would solve diversity issues. Firms have done poorly in changing attitudes toward, and meaningful access for, women and minorities. Being an employee is not the same thing as being a partner with equity in the firm. Being a partner is not the same as being included in business opportunities and decision making. And neither is the same as getting financial credit for client origination or case development. The data shows the pervasive attitude that hiring women and minorities is enough; the fact that the number retained melts significantly in a short period of time has not translated to different action.[104] Irrespective of your race or gender, the profession you have entered will not progress until this problem is erased, and each of you must consider how to address inequity on a one-to-one as well as a structural and systemic basis.

For decades, diversity has been a factor in hiring and promoting without measurable success.[105] As Meir Shemla's assessment of diversity noted:

> Too many organizations make the fundamental error of failing to align their diversity practices with their organizational goals. And in such situations, no matter how much

good will there is towards the concept of diversity, the harsh realities of running the business on a day-to-day basis, of keeping customers satisfied, of selling and delivering the product or service will keep undermining it. There is often a mismatch between how organizations design diversity policies and how they implement them. To put it another way, what looks good on paper too often falls apart in practice.[106]

Diversity initiatives started by simply hiring more broadly to increase the number of people from diverse backgrounds. Diverse hiring does not ensure the new hires' potential is recognized, their efforts supported, or their contributions appreciated. Inclusion requires more than checking a series of demographic boxes. Companies need to achieve equity — the pinnacle of effective diversity — where individuals are valued as colleagues, not simply tolerated as an HR requirement.

Firms have tried to implement diversity initiatives, but efforts to create a more inclusive workplace environment and increase the diversity of the workforce face resistance. Companies perceive "that the policies and practices are too expensive or unnecessary[,] or [there exists] implicit bias on the part of some of the key individuals from whom 'buy-in' is most needed."[107] It is possible "institutional efforts to enhance diversity may 'simultaneously produce more conflict and employee turnover as well as more creativity and innovation.'"[108] Because there has been resistance to efforts to enhance diversity, strong and committed leadership is even more important to oversee diversity initiatives, as is sound management of diversity policies, practices, and measurements.[109]

If you consider the movement from diversity to inclusion to equity, leaders must address each aspect, both on an individual and a firm or systemic basis. Some education must be directed toward helping those in the firm understand and appreciate the challenges faced by women and minorities and how to engage them meaningfully. The educational efforts do not stop there, however. They should involve clients of the firm as well. Systemically, recruiting women and minorities to increase diversity should remain a focus, but retaining that talent should be an even higher priority. What are the barriers to keeping diverse attorneys at the firm? Are the metrics used by the firm to address promotion ones that promote opportunity for diverse lawyers, or do they create barriers to progress within the firm? For example, if business origination is one of the metrics, but women and minorities are not given the same access to clients, the firm is using a measuring stick that guarantees failure, albeit using objective data.

Lawyers also need to speak up to get more women and minorities into leadership positions. As of the writing of this book, President Trump had 200 federal judges confirmed in 40 months. Not one of the 53 court of appeals nominees is Black; only one is Latino.[110] The district court appointees also have been largely white and male; only 25 percent have been women and only 15 percent Black or Latino or Asian.[111] Of the 93 U.S. attorneys appointed by President Trump, only 7 are women and only 2 are Black.[112] The white male appointment pattern, particularly at the federal level, entrenches a lack of diversity for the lifetime of each judge.

To be more inclusive, the legal system needs to place women and minorities in all facets of leadership in the bar, in the judicial system, and in law firm hierarchy, and they must be given an opportunity to contribute. Ask almost any woman or minority lawyer, and they can relate a personal experience of being told explicitly that the reason they were being put on a team was because of their minority status. Not only does this diminish the respect they are afforded (these are sometimes referred to as "token" appointments), it also undermines the individual's confidence. It is very difficult to know whether you were appointed because you are the best choice or appointed because you are the best Black choice.

Leading by Example: How Leadership Priorities Impact Diversity Efforts

Leaders can play a significant role in advancing the efforts to increase diversity. A leader must not only embrace the concept of diversity, that leader must remove barriers, engage team members, and enforce meaningful integration. Here are some suggested initiatives to support diversity, address implicit bias, and provide the best opportunity for creating a richly diverse and inclusive environment:

- Policies
  - Diversity required in each applicant pool.
  - Objective performance measurements used in evaluations.
  - Performance-based promotion practices.
  - Family-friendly policies that are used by all.
- Protocols, practices, and procedures
  - Careful selection of hiring committees to include a champion for inclusion goals.
  - Intentionality for inclusion of diversity in important committee roles and work assignments.
  - Protection of women and persons of color from too many non-billable and low-valued assignments.
- Training
  - Specific training on implicit bias for all.
  - Diversity/inclusion training for hiring committees.
  - Diversity/inclusion training for all in supervisory roles.[113]
- Mentoring programs
  - Coaches, mentors, and sponsors.
- Economic restructuring
  - Creation of opportunities and incentives for minority and female partners to both attract and retain customers and for partnership benefits.

Women and minorities who have made progress need to help those who come after them. The old model of white men mentoring men can be adapted. As Michelle Obama noted in her address to the 2012 Democratic National Convention, "When you have worked hard and done well and walked through that doorway of opportunity, you do not slam it shut behind you." Women notably have underperformed at helping other women. "In some cases, women who have broken the glass ceiling do not sponsor, promote, or support the career advancement of mid-career women leaders," explains Sophia Zhao, a senior researcher at the Center for Creative Leadership (CCL).[114] Sometimes referred to as the "queen bee syndrome," the term suggests that more senior women do not support other women in advancing. A variety of explanations have been tendered, from jealousy to control. In her white paper *Queen Bee Syndrome: The Real Reason Women Do Not Promote Women?*, Zhao posed the question: "So why wouldn't women — especially senior women — strive to support the advancement of other women?" Zhao's research suggests that senior-level women are penalized for supporting other women leaders.[115]

In another variant of the double standard/double bind conundrum, researchers at CCL found that female leaders who showed they valued diversity in the workplace received much lower competency ratings. By contrast, men's performance ratings actually increase when they show that they value diversity in the workplace.[116] Women who actually promoted other women were also penalized.

The researchers divided working adults into two groups, each of which was asked to evaluate the competency of a hiring manager interviewing candidates for a vacant senior vice president position. One group was told that the hiring manager chose a white male candidate because he "had the highest scores." The other group was told that the hiring manager chose a woman because she "had the highest scores and increases the racial and gender balance of our leadership team." When told that the hiring manager was a male, the group of working adults gave him the same competency rating whether he advocated for diversity or not. When the hiring manager was a female and hired a woman, her competency rating dropped dramatically, indicating a perception that she was showing favoritism.

Despite the message to women from that survey, women and minorities who consciously keep doors open for those who come after serve a valuable role. As Madeleine Albright admonished, "There is a special place in hell for women who don't help other women."[117] Sharing experience, providing guidance, and supporting colleagues can increase inclusiveness. For example, female attorneys should plan to go into a meeting designated to be the other's back-up. When one offers an idea, the other speaks up to validate the idea and ensure that the correct person gets credit for the proposal.

Although multiple interests are served by firms achieving diversity and inclusion, a gap still exists between organizations' commitment to diversity and the experiences of employees. Where does this disconnect come from? Many leaders know the right things to say about committing to inclusion, but they stumble on how to advance inclusion through their everyday behavior.[118]

Creating an Inclusive Environment

In a Gallup study of the world's most productive workplaces, three essential characteristics emerge when identifying an inclusive culture. First, employees are treated with respect — they both treat others and are treated with civility and decency.[119] Second, employees are valued for their strengths.[120] Third, employees believe their leaders do what is right.[121] Inclusive leaders intentionally create an environment where employees feel they can safely express themselves and where specific concerns can be raised with transparency and confidence.[122]

A commitment to inclusion must begin at the top, but a pronouncement alone, even when accompanied by a demonstrated personal commitment by the leadership, is insufficient. To change a culture and create a new environment, all members must understand why it matters to the organization and how diversity benefits all. People need to know how to answer the question, "Why should I care?" Change occurs when there is broad recognition of the *why* and *how*, followed up with a system of account-ability and assessment, and lived out in daily behavior of the leadership. Research tells us actions speak louder than words.[123]

Undoubtedly, leaders play a significant role in creating an inclusive environment, so inclusion should be recognized, developed, and prioritized as a distinctive leadership skill set.[124] A number of studies suggest how leaders can be more inclusive. Inclusive leaders share the following traits: authentic commitment to creating culture of inclu-sion, curiosity about cultural intelligence, cognizance of bias, courage to take actions, deliberately seeking out collaboration, humility, and willingness to seek feedback.

Authentic commitment to creating a culture of inclusion. One of the most important aspects of the leadership function is a clear understanding — a vision, in leadership parlance — of the goals, objectives, or aspirations of the diversity initiative. They must be clear, unambiguous, and directly related to key institutional, and sometimes existen-tial, goals. People want their leaders and peers to display inclusive behaviors on a daily basis.[125] The behaviors of leaders (be they senior executives or managers) can drive up to 70 percentage points of difference between the proportion of employees who feel highly included and the proportion of those who do not. Employees want leaders with an authentic commitment to diversity, who will challenge the status quo, hold others accountable, and make diversity and inclusion a personal priority.[126] A leader mod-els authenticity by treating everyone with fairness and respect; fostering environments where team members are comfortable, valued, and empowered; and caring about the well-being of others.[127] Inclusive leaders should encourage authenticity.[128] People tend to gravitate toward leaders who embrace these traits.[129]

Curiosity about cultural intelligence. An inclusive leader is willing to ask the people in the organization about the environment, the culture, and workers' feelings about the leader.[130] Inclusive leaders demonstrate an open mindset and deep curiosity about others, listen without judgment, and seek with empathy to understand those around them.[131] They look for opportunities to be curious about the lived experiences of oth-ers,[132] to learn about different cultures, and to become aware of other cultural con-texts.[133] *Cultural intelligence* or *fluency* is more than understanding cultural sensitivies intellectually; it is the ability to adapt effectively and work well across cultures by behav-ing in ways that respect and value the cultural differences of individuals.[134]

Cognizance of bias. Inclusive leaders understand the unconscious biases we all have as a result of our learned behaviors and natural preferences.[135] They show awareness of personal blind spots as well as institutional flaws in systems, and they work hard to address personal and organizational biases and strive for meritocracy.[136] They set up systems for accountability to ensure decisions can be made in a transparent, consistent, and informed manner.[137] Leaders who are cognizant of bias gain the respect of their employees.

Courage to take action and be visible and vocal. Inclusive leaders are willing to put in the hard work[138] to engage in tough conversations when necessary. They identify opportunities to be more inclusive, take ownership, and engage others.[139] They also tell a compelling and explicit narrative about why being inclusive is important to each employee personally and the business more broadly.[140] Inclusive leaders should be willing to advocate on the behalf of the employees.[141]

Deliberately seek out difference for effective collaboration. Leaders strive to create teams that are diverse in thinking.[142] They empower others, pay attention to diversity of thinking and psychological safety, and focus on team cohesion.[143] Ensuring that team members "speak up and are heard; making it safe to propose novel ideas; empowering team members to make decisions; taking advice and implementing feedback; giving actionable feedback; and sharing credit for team success" make diverse team members feel valued and participate more fully.[144] Effective leaders seek opportunities to work with cross-functional or multi-disciplinary teams to leverage diverse strengths.[145]

Humility. These leaders are modest about capabilities, create the space for others to contribute,[146] and acknowledge mistakes, even if their intentions were good.[147] A humble leader is willing to make the changes needed to achieve a truly diverse and inclusive working environment.

Check impact by seeking input and feedback. Great leaders look for signs that people are following their lead, more diverse groups of people are sharing ideas, and people are working together more collaboratively.[148] Strong leaders may ask a trusted advisor to give candid feedback on the areas the leaders have been working on.[149] Scheduling regular check-ins with members of your team to ask how you can make them feel more included also sends the message.[150] They seek feedback on whether they are perceived as inclusive, especially from people who are different. This will help them see blind spots, strengths, and development areas. It will also signal that diversity and inclusion are important. Then implement feedback, give actionable feedback, and share credit for team success.[151]

External Influence on Equity Efforts

Those who may ultimately have the greatest impact on law firm equity advances are in-house counsel at major corporations. The business world acted more quickly to require diversity in hiring, and women and people of color were recruited for general counsel roles. Those same men and women have risen to leadership positions and now demand that if a firm is going to do the corporation's work, it will be done by a diverse and inclusive team of lawyers. Where firms used to put a Black or female face at counsel table purely for a diversity show, general counsels who hire outside counsel now demand that the firm demonstrate leadership opportunities and true equitable investment by diverse counsel. Where the firm cannot show true equity, the work goes elsewhere. Organizations like the National Association of Minority and Women Owned Law Firms ("NAMWOLF")[152] and National Association of Women Lawyers ("NAWL")[153] help promote equity and provide support for women and minorities to secure lucrative pieces of litigation.

With intentionality and effort, leaders can both alter their behaviors and try to garner a set of skills that will allow them to be more effective in creating a culture for inclusion. Among the most important behaviors/skills are developing effective relationships with members of the organization. People want to be heard, respected, and valued.

CULTURAL INTELLIGENCE

ABA Model Rule 8.4(g)

It is professional misconduct for a lawyer to: . . . engage in conduct that the lawyer knows or reasonably should know is harassment or discrimination on the basis of race, sex, religion, national origin, ethnicity, disability, age, sexual orientation, gender identity, marital status or socioeconomic status in conduct related to the practice of law. This paragraph does not limit the ability of a lawyer to accept, decline or withdraw from a representation in accordance with Rule 1.16. This paragraph does not preclude legitimate advice or advocacy consistent with these Rules.

[In explaining the evolution of Rule 8.4, the ABA noted that "Rule 8.4(g) calls for lawyers to educate themselves about reasonable standards of acceptable conduct; the rule prohibits conduct 'the lawyer knows or reasonably should know is harassment or discrimination.' *If nothing else, the rule is an invitation for lawyers to consider another person's viewpoint before speaking or acting.*"]

Atticus Finch, the just and ethical attorney in Harper Lee's novel *To Kill a Mockingbird*,[154] inspired many of us to become lawyers. The novel is set in the American South during the Great Depression and follows Atticus's appointment as defense counsel for a Black man wrongly accused of raping a white woman. While much of the action takes place in a courtroom setting, the story is less a legal drama than a reflection on human nature. The book explores many facets of prejudice and racial tension, not only in broad stereotype but in the actual relationships of the small community. Atticus suggests to his daughter, Scout, that until you walk a mile in another person's shoes and try to understand what it is like to be a different race or gender, you will not have the empathy you need to view him or her as a person.

We deal with cultural issues daily as they are broadcast on the news, posted on social media, raised in courtrooms, and encountered in our own life experience. As this book is being written, much of the rhetoric takes on an "us versus them" tone as "Black Lives Matter" competes with "All Lives Matter" and "Blue [Police] Lives Matter."[155] This phrasing, however, misses the point of cultural competency. It is true that the lives of all these groups are valuable and important. Cultural competency urges us to sincerely value the unique and precious nature of *each* cultural group. We do not value one at the expense of another. Cultural intelligence guides us to genuinely understand and recognize the humanity in each individual. To walk in the shoes of another requires true effort and understanding.

Racial tension, gender inequality, and misunderstanding of sexual orientation,[156] whether overt or as an implicit bias, create cultural rifts. Not only do we disagree on the solutions, we struggle to agree even on the language that should be used to address these issues. Representing persons from other backgrounds effectively and leading teams with different backgrounds and belief systems can be challenging. Cultural intelligence teaches us how to follow Atticus Finch's advice about walking a mile in someone else's shoes. Showing empathy and reaching out to understand another person's journey strengthens friendships and builds relationships. In looking to influence others, you must understand how that person makes decisions. An individual's life experience, including the cultural beliefs and values, can have a powerful impact on judgment.

WHAT IS CULTURAL INTELLIGENCE?

A cousin to emotional intelligence, cultural intelligence helps us not only walk a mile in another fellow's skin (to paraphrase Atticus Finch), but also to partner with and advocate for true equity for that fellow. Cultural intelligence, like artful listening, requires us to get beyond the words to hear and understand another person with different beliefs, values, and experiences. Only when we get beyond a superficial understanding of another person's cultural influences can we arrive at a deeper connection with that person.

To develop cultural intelligence requires that we understand its building blocks: *culture, cultural competence,* and *cultural humility*.[157] Culture has a number of characteristics and nuances beyond just race. *Culture* is multigenerational, as we hand down to our children and our children's children our shared "beliefs, values, customs, behaviors, and artifacts."[158] We create cultural groups using many different identifiers from the geographical (i.e., "I'm a Southerner"; "I'm a New Yorker"; "I'm a Texan") to those including "race, religion, age, sexual orientation, gender, immigration status, social status, language, and geography."[159] Rarely does a person define his culture by a single characteristic; in many ways we are all multicultural, and each culture generates its own norms.[160] The influence of culture, then, drives our behaviors and values, including the way in which society "treats members of different groups. Culture is closely bound up with identity; it may be understood as an expression of group identity."[161]

Beyond how we view our own cultural expression or identity, culture also affects how we view and experience the world and the people in it.[162] Using the same contextual issues raised by emotional intelligence,[163] cultures in which women are expected to be submissive do not encourage women to speak up in a firm meeting — even when the woman has abandoned that culture and its norms.

We may not fully appreciate the extent to which we have absorbed our culture and cultural beliefs. The osmotic process of assimilation through childhood, family encounters, education, travel, religion, and so forth have us absorbing cultural information without even being aware that we are. We hear our parents or grandparents talk about people, religions, and political ideas in a way that denotes them as "other," and we assimilate that belief to one degree or another. We also assimilate culture through lack of knowledge and then fill in beliefs about other groups based on fear, ignorance, curiosity, or envy. We learn our values in a similar way.[164] Despite our background, individual identity and cultural identity evolve over time, as can the culture itself.[165] "The norms associated with a particular culture may change and . . . people who associate with a given culture may diverge significantly in their practices and beliefs."[166]

With an understanding of culture, we must next understand *cultural competency*, which may be considered the skill set and principles needed to "acknowledge, respect, and work towards optimal interactions between the individual and the various cultural and ethnic groups that an individual might come in contact with."[167] Cultural competence involves a depth of understanding and response to cultural variables and to the diversity of opinion and experience that another brings to an interaction.[168] The concept of cultural competence, when "loosely defined as the ability to understand, appreciate, and interact with people from cultures or belief systems different from one's own, has been a key aspect of psychological thinking and practice for some 50 years."[169]

Cultural competence alone does not create cultural intelligence. Another step in the journey incorporates *cultural humility*. Where cultural competence encompasses being respectful and responsive to the beliefs and practices of diverse population groups, cultural humility requires you to step outside of yourself and be open to other people's identities, in a way that acknowledges their authority over their own experiences.[170] The final evolution then is *cultural intelligence*. A person with cultural intelligence has "a seemingly natural ability to interpret someone's unfamiliar and ambiguous gestures in just the way that person's compatriots and colleagues would, even to mirror them."[171]

> Cultural intelligence is related to emotional intelligence, but it picks up where emotional intelligence leaves off. A person with high emotional intelligence grasps what makes us human and at the same time what makes each of us different from one another. A person with high cultural intelligence can somehow tease out of a person's or group's behavior those features that would be true of all people and all groups, those peculiar to this person or this group, and those that are neither universal nor idiosyncratic. The vast realm that lies between those two poles is culture.[172]

Discussions of cultural intelligence try to define what Atticus asked Scout to do: Walk a mile in someone else's shoes. While the discussions above suggest what cultural intelligence might be, it does not explain cultural intelligence in the leadership context.

CULTURAL COMPETENCE AS A BASIS FOR RELATIONSHIP BUILDING

All interviewing and counseling is multicultural. Each client comes to the session embodying multiple voices from the past.

Dr. Paul B. Pedersen[173]

The goal of cultural competency is effective communication across different cultures to build better relationships. When you first arrive in an unfamiliar country, you may find it difficult to communicate. You do not speak the language or understand how the currency works. People drive on the "wrong" side of the road, and every time you go to cross a street, you do so risking life and limb. In those lost, strange days, you struggle to understand and to be understood. Cultural intelligence recognizes that some of that strangeness and lack of understanding takes place whenever we encounter someone from a different cultural background — even if that encounter takes place in the halls of a law school or law firm.

Respecting the impact of diversity on communication remains a key aspect of cultural competency. In an article aptly titled *A Historical Perspective of Cultural Competence*, Professor Kwame McKenzie noted that our understanding of cultural competence in the United States began to take shape in the early 1970s to assist with mental health and social service needs for East Asian refugees and inner-city African Americans who had different cultural models of understanding.[174] Early and influential research on the subject came from counseling psychologist and professor Paul B. Pedersen,[175] who pioneered the field, viewing all behavior and learning in a cultural context.[176]

That the initial focus on cultural competency originated in the field of counseling and psychology explains the emphasis on individual "awareness, knowledge, attitudes and skills."[177] A culturally competent practitioner could better "understand the individual in order to offer a service," unimpaired by ignorance of cultural factors and communication styles that the practitioner did not share.[178] Over time, however, those in the field increasingly recognized that the inequities often experienced by persons of diverse cultural backgrounds were systemic and needed to be addressed on a broader scale than individual counseling could manage.[179]

Cultural humility approaches the same issues but goes deeper to incorporate the idea that this is a process or continuum. As the American Psychological Association described it, there are three steps in developing cultural humility. The first is a *lifelong commitment to self-evaluation and self-critique*[180] and the knowledge that we are never finished learning. "Therefore, we must be humble and flexible, bold enough to look at ourselves critically and desire to learn more. . . . Willingness to act on the acknowledgement that we have not and will not arrive at a finish line is integral to this aspect of cultural humility as well."[181]

The second feature of cultural humility is a desire to *fix power imbalances* where they should not exist.[182] In the context of providing health care, the imbalance can be corrected by recognizing that each person brings different but valuable perspective to the conversation. The patient, for example, is the expert on his or her own life, symptoms, and strengths. The practitioner holds a body of knowledge and experience that the patient does not. Both people must collaborate and learn from each other for the best outcomes.[183] The same is true in a legal setting. The client is an expert on the facts, the problem, and the impact of the problem on the client's life; the lawyer is the expert on the legal and procedural remedies for the problem. Unless the two collaborate, however, and incorporate the other's expertise, the problem will not be solved to the client's satisfaction.

The third feature of cultural humility includes aspiring to develop partnerships with people and groups who advocate for others:

> Though individuals can create positive change, communities and groups can also have a profound impact on systems. We cannot individually commit to self-evaluation and fixing power imbalances without advocating within the larger organizations in which we participate. Cultural humility, by definition, is larger than our individual selves — we must advocate for it systemically.[184]

Cultural intelligence becomes a key leadership skill to build closer and more authentic relationships and to have greater influence with individuals and on a systemic basis. Lawyers, as leaders, have some of the skills and abilities to foster and contribute to these partnerships. With greater cultural intelligence, lawyers can advocate for true partnerships within multicultural groups and bridge communication and language gaps given their training in effective advocacy.

BARRIERS TO CULTURAL INTELLIGENCE

Time and time again, we are reminded that structural and systemic racism, intolerance, and hate—evidenced in behaviors and policies—show their ugly faces in as much an epidemic fashion as Covid-19. These infectious agents are not as visible as the signs above water fountains and restrooms in the Jim Crow era, but the inability or unwillingness of our nation to root out race-based violence and the marginalization of people of color doggedly persists.

Dean Brad Toben[185]

Cultural intelligence is a learned rather than innate skill for many of us regardless of our background. It is a crucial skill for leadership since overt bias, although not eradicated, is less of a leadership issue than are more subtle forms of bias. A leader who lacks cultural intelligence, however, may confuse the lack of explicit bias with an absence of bias. "While explicit sexism, racism, and other forms of bias persist, they have become less prominent and public over the past century."[186] As discussed above, while explicit statements of bias are still a problem,[187] implicit biases are the other part of the equation — the "attitudes or stereotypes that affect our understanding, decision-making, and behavior, without our even realizing it."[188] Cultural intelligence helps a leader recognize implicit biases, including those derived due to cultural ignorance or blindness, and course correct the team.

CULTURAL INTELLIGENCE AS A LEADERSHIP TOOL

Cultural intelligence for leaders is vital to success, both in terms of achieving goals for the team or organization and for each team member to feel invested and understood. In the health care field, the importance of cultural competence is fairly obvious. When a physician does not understand a Jehovah's Witness's religious aversion to blood transfusion, the therapeutic relationship breaks down. Cultural barriers may impact treatment if the provider does not understand who is the decision maker: the husband or wife. If the patient speaks a language other than English, is she receiving effective and accurate translation of the physician's words? Are there moral or religious prohibitions against, for example, birth control that the patient and provider need to navigate to protect the mother's health? An understanding of the patient's cultural background assists with communication and treatment, including prejudice against certain types of treatment, barriers to access, and lack of family support. Outside of health and linguistic issues, cultural competence grows in significance as our economy and our society become more global in scope. Young professionals, including lawyers, must consider the influence of culture both on themselves and the people whom will serve.

For Lawyers in Client Relationships

Clients look to their attorneys for advice and problem-solving skills. To provide those effectively, though, the attorney has to understand the cultural issues from the client's perspective. Providing sound advice requires an understanding of a client's goals and the ability to communicate the impact and consequences of that advice within the context of the client's cultural background, practices, and beliefs. While a lawyer must represent her client's rights and interests zealously, she cannot disregard her duty to act in accordance with the law as an officer of the court.[189] Clients whose sense of justice is discordant with the system they will face here may need additional counseling; you can only know this if you appreciate their cultural background. This dual role compounds the need for cultural competency so the lawyer can understand the client's needs and counsel the client about the options available in protecting the client's interests. Similar understandings and sensitivities are necessary in other practice areas, such as business, family law, and estate planning. A lawyer cannot fully understand the client's needs and goals without considering the impact of the client's cultural background and personal experience.

ABA Rule 1.1: Competence
A lawyer shall provide competent representation to a client. Competent representation requires the legal knowledge, skill, thoroughness and preparation reasonably necessary for the representation.

[Subsequent cases and interpretations of this Rule focus upon legal knowledge and adequate representation. However, we encourage you to adopt a broad definition of competence to include, among other competencies, cultural and linguistic competence.]

This means the lawyer must be able to set aside personal biases to thoughtfully consider the available options and not skew the client's decision due to personal preference or prejudice. The attorney's recommended course of action may be influenced not by the client's needs but by the attorney's own background. Evaluating the situation through a cultural competence lens reduces the likelihood of misguided advice.

The Model Rules of Professional Conduct require competent representation. While this does not require that an attorney know everything needed to represent a client before accepting that representation, there are necessary levels of skill and preparedness that must be used.[190] The Rule specifically notes that the intended definition of competence should be broad and should include cultural and linguistic competence. In other words, knowing the law is not enough; you must know your client and his background to know how the cultural influences affect representation. A lawyer may not know or appreciate initially the cultural and linguistic influences that may arise during the course of the representation, but for an attorney to lead the client to an effective resolution of the matter, cultural competence is a necessity.

Take, for example, the issue of the venue in which to file a lawsuit. Lawyers have long understood the strategic importance of venue. Each juror's life experience affects the lens through which the jury perceives the litigants, issues, and evidence. Rural jurors may be more suspicious of "foreigners," making a client with an accent less credible to them. You must understand the cultural influences of that region and how they might impact decision making during deliberations. These cultural influences can be benign, or they can manifest as outright prejudice. The attorney must be cognizant of the cultural issues when choosing which would be the better venue for the client.

Cultural intelligence impacts case development beyond simply venue considerations. In a personal injury case, you need to understand the various cultural perspectives on pain. Is complaining about pain regarded as a sign of weakness? Has the client minimized her complaints because of this? Is the jury full of stoics who don't tolerate "whiners"? These cultural effects shape what the lawyer must know both in interviewing a potential client and proving the extent of damages. The injured client may be reluctant to acknowledge the extent of pain, while a treating physician could objectively and scientifically explain the issue without minimizing. Language can be an additional barrier both in communicating with the client and in communicating to the jury. How you handle these sensitive but important issues will affect the attorney-client relationship and the competence with which you assist the client.

Culture issues are magnified in criminal law, since understanding what might influence a person's decision-making process is critical to prosecution or defense of a case. Sociological research shows that race, gender, and socioeconomic status affect how a crime is viewed and how the accused is viewed — to the extent that for many years, some district attorney offices provided handbooks to young prosecutors advising them not to seat Black jurors on panels because they would not convict other Blacks.[191] While such broad prejudice cannot be tolerated, understanding the cultural implications of the crime, the accused, and the victim is critical to effective representation on all sides of the issue. A related issue is the culture of the defendant and how that can affect the lawyer's representation. For example, culture may influence whether defendants feel that they have the autonomy to make decisions about plea negotiation.

> A criminal defense lawyer might assume she is operating in her client's best interests when negotiating a plea deal in exchange for a reduced sentence . . . and may not understand that her client's community will not allow her to admit guilt as it would bring shame on the community.[192]

Culture also plays a role in many family law situations. Family lawyers, then, must be aware of cultural differences that may influence their representation.

> One prominent expression of culture is the way in which people show love to, and the way in which they discipline, their children. In some cultures, keeping children physically close is an expression of love, while in others fostering independence is valued more highly. In some cultures, discipline is practiced by separating a child from her environment (a "time-out"), while in other cultures, spanking is the norm. These parenting approaches are central to child custody cases, which examine the behavior of parents in light of the "best interests of the child." A family lawyer will face the task of understanding her client's parenting approaches and explaining them to the trier of fact to make the case that the parent is acting in the best interests of her child.[193]

A family lawyer who does not understand these cultural issues and barriers cannot meet a client's needs or give competent advice. If the case is going to be tried, though, the lawyer will need cultural intelligence not only in dealing with the client but also in dealing with those involved in the trial.

For Lawyers in the Courtroom

Cultural intelligence plays a role during hearings and trials. Judges are not always culturally aware, and the legion of stories where judge called lawyers of color "boy" or female attorneys "little lady" are not a thing of the past. Bar associations should demand that judges have, as part of their training, better cultural intelligence. The litigants who appear in their courtrooms want to feel justice is being dispensed in a way that acknowledges their culture. The lawyer must also consider the biases and cultures of the jurors. Just as jurors might wonder what motivates a person to commit a crime, they also question the victim in what is known as victim blaming. These jurors might wonder: "Why didn't the victim fight back?" "Why didn't she leave the abusive relationship?" "Why didn't she call for help?" "Why did she dress in a provocative manner?"[194] While not the focus of the case, the prosecutor must now deal with this reality to ensure that justice is done for the victim. Thus, the lawyer best serves the public and the victim by addressing the bias openly, discussing implicit bias, and debiasing the jurors in order to focus on the defendant and his conduct.

A criminal defense lawyer begins her *voir dire* with a demonstration on why and how we are *all* biased for natural and reasonable purposes. She defines bias and its purpose in helping us make beneficial associations instantaneously. As a child, we learned that we get burned if we touch a hot skillet with our bare hands. As an adult, we waste no mental energy but automatically reach for a potholder. She continues with questions such as "What sport do you follow? What team do you follow? And why do you have those preferences? Why is a Cheesehead from Green Bay so loyal to the Packers but someone from Los Angeles is a die-hard Lakers fan?" Different sports, different teams. Often the answer comes from preferences established as a child. There is no malintent here, just learned biases resting in our unconsciousness until we are called to think about them and defend them. These techniques underscore the importance of knowing and understanding implicit bias enough to explain it to others — your case and your client may depend on it.

For Lawyers in Their Own Firms

As discussed in the section above, applying cultural intelligence in the law firm itself will be crucial to making progress with diversity, equity, and inclusion efforts. Truly understanding a colleague's background, culture, and viewpoint takes time and effort; recognizing the power of that alternate viewpoint and background can make the field more just. In addition to being the right thing to do, there is a pragmatic reason to embrace cultural intelligence and diversity: The firm will likely profit from doing so.[195] Those who are reluctant to embrace other cultural perspectives might consider their own perspective and that of the clients. Increasing pressure from clients and published "accountability" reports cannot be ignored. Failure to support diversity initiatives that actually work could mean the loss of lucrative business and damage to the firm's reputation.

For Leaders in All Fields

The reason cultural competence is important for leaders in all fields is simple. Leaders cannot guide others well without an understanding of what influences another's decision-making process. Today's increasingly global business world has more companies considering the impact of different cultures on how they conduct business. Replicating the U.S. business model in another country may be unsuccessful in that country's culture. Whether religious, ethnic, or gender-based, American norms do not apply equally and globally. Businesses that move toward a more global approach necessarily must assess and adjust their company culture to fit the cultural differences of societies where they enter the market. Companies have to take cultural preferences into consideration when they advertise, seek new business connections, or work to find creative solutions to everyday problems. Cultural intelligence is a must for leaders in a global organization or any international market.

DEVELOPING PRACTICAL SKILLS FOR CULTURAL INTELLIGENCE

Conceptually understanding the importance of cultural intelligence is one thing—achieving it is another. Below are five basic steps that can help you move toward cultural intelligence.

Awareness of Differences

Developing cultural competency requires understanding your own cultural worldview. Without realistically assessing how your own background and belief system shape your view of the world, you cannot hope to put those influences aside or fully understand the influence another person's culture has on decision making. As noted above, these unconscious or implicit biases are often harder to recognize because they are not conscious decisions or judgments. Even if confronted with an implicit bias, a person might deny its impact on his decision making.

Addressing Implicit Bias

To combat implicit bias, we must acknowledge that it exists to some degree in all of us; these unconscious attitudes impact perception and behavior toward members of a group. Raising awareness of implicit bias is an important step, but it will not lead to equity. Active steps must be taken to *unlearn* these behaviors and replace them with awareness of difference, compassion for another's journey, and appreciation for that person's contributions.

Attitude of Openness

You must be aware of your cultural worldview before you can change it. Knowing your predisposition to view cultural difference, however, is a starting point that next requires you to take conscious steps to improve your attitude toward cultural difference. Truly understanding how your worldview impacts your attitude toward other cultures and working on that attitude can develop a greater appreciation of the value brought by diversity.

Developing an understanding of these different approaches helps us fight an attitude that "our way is the best way" or "this is the way we've always done things." Keeping an attitude of openness that looks for opportunity in collaboration is essential to moving toward cultural competency.

Knowledge Creates Understanding

While understanding your own worldview and developing an attitude of openness and receptivity to other cultures is important, the diverse nature of human experience means you need to learn more. Even persons from the same families—and, arguably, the same cultural background—can develop an entirely different worldview based on their individual perspective and factors unique to their experience. Experience is a good teacher, but where experience is not an option, you can gain knowledge and understanding of different cultural practices and worldviews through books, blog posts, and studies - anything containing human stories. Lifelong learning is a hallmark of good leaders, and includes learning about others and their culture.

Cross-Cultural Skills Lead to Advancement

Developing cross-cultural skills assists in effective communication and interaction with people from different backgrounds and cultures. Like any skill, developing cultural intelligence goes beyond an academic understanding to the application of one's knowledge of cultural differences. Here are some tools for developing cross-cultural skills:

- journaling and self-reflection;
- active listening with peers and clients;
- mirroring what people say in conversations to be certain you are understanding correctly; and
- practicing effective communication through discussion with a mentor with a different cultural background from your own.

UTILIZING CULTURAL INTELLIGENCE SKILLS WITH CLIENTS

Cross-cultural lawyers[196] use their cultural intelligence to reach across cultural barriers to provide more effective representation. The concept is based upon five "facets" of representation: "degrees of separation and connection, rings in motion, parallel universes, red flags and remedies, and the camel's back."[197] The first facet, *degrees of separation and connection*, focuses on identifying "similarities and differences between the lawyer and the client" to help the lawyer better understand the common ground they share and how to identify differences and compensate for them.[198] For example, by thinking about your background and your path to becoming a lawyer, can you ask questions in the initial client meeting that help you understand your client's background and the path to his or her current position? The second facet, *rings in motion*, encourages the lawyer to apply the similarities and differences analysis to all other parties in the case: lawyer, client, opposing counsel, and, if it is a litigation case, the judge and jury.[199]

In the third facet, *parallel universes*, the lawyer considers alternative explanations for client behavior rather than making assumptions about the behavior.[200] For example, if a client misses a meeting, rather than assuming that the client does not care, you should think of all the other reasons missing the meeting, such as missing the bus, a sick child, or work obligations that ran over.[201] The fourth facet, *red flags and remedies*, helps the lawyer look for "red flags" that signify the client is losing interest or not understanding. Here are some of the red flags to look for:

- The client appears bored, disengaged, or even actively uncomfortable;
- The client has not spoken for many minutes, and the lawyer is dominating the conversation;
- The client has not taken any notes for many minutes;
- The client is using the lawyer's terminology instead of using the client's words;
- The lawyer is judging the client negatively;
- The client appears angry; or
- The lawyer is distracted and bored.[202]

If you notice any red flags in a client conversation, subtly pause the conversation. Try using artful listening techniques by asking questions to ensure that the client is engaged in the conversation. If necessary, try rephrasing questions or offering examples to explain a complex concept.[203] If the conversation involves difficult or uncomfortable subjects, try asking indirect questions. For example, rather than asking, "Did you yell at her?," try asking "Was anyone yelling?"[204] Similarly, to get the full picture, ask open-ended questions (as you would during direct examination in a trial) such as "What happened next?" rather than specific questions.[205] You can tailor the questions later if need be, but more open-ended questions help with conversation flow and can make it easier for the client to be open because she is using her own words. If none of these techniques work, you can try these approaches:

- Turning the conversation back to the client's stated priority;
- Seeking greater detail about the client's priority;
- Giving the client a chance to explain her concerns in greater depth;
- Asking for examples of critical encounters in the client's life that illustrate the problem area;
- Exploring one example in some depth;
- Asking the client to describe in some detail what a solution would look like; and
- Using the clients' words.[206]

The final facet, *the camel's back*, relates to minimizing negative influences that might disrupt the attorney-client relationship.[207] The legal profession is stressful, and in high-pressure situations, people tend to fall back on their implicit and explicit biases.[208] By ensuring that you are taking care of yourself and giving yourself enough time and emotional bandwidth to handle a client's case, you can avoid situations that might cause you to fall back on biases and bad habits.[209]

Cultural intelligence works toward true understanding of what it means to have grown up in a different culture. Applying these principles, though, requires a further understanding of what it may mean to have grown up in a different gender or sexual orientation. That deeper understanding then needs to be applied so that teams (and law firms, companies, and so forth) contain a diverse group of people from different backgrounds and life experiences whose contributions can be valued by the team. In a sense, until you understand what it is like for another person, you may struggle to understand why that person needs a seat at the table. Giving different voices a seat and power at the decision-making table is what we refer to as diversity, inclusion, and ultimately equity.

CONCLUSION

I am cognizant of the interrelatedness of all communities and states. I cannot sit idly by in Atlanta and not be concerned about what happens in Birmingham. Injustice anywhere is a threat to justice everywhere. We are caught in an inescapable network of mutuality, tied in a single garment of destiny. Whatever affects one directly, affects all indirectly. Never again can we afford to live with the narrow, provincial "outside agitator" idea. Anyone who lives inside the United States can never be considered an outsider anywhere within its bounds.

Dr. Martin Luther King, Jr., *Letter from a Birmingham Jail*[210]

The world continues to get smaller as we can connect and transact with individuals all over the globe. Recognizing the influence a person's life experiences and cultural background have on decision making and behavior is essential when interacting with people. Effectively communicating with clients, customers, and employees in business or in law is essential to building meaningful relationships. It is also our obligation to understand another person's worldview and cultural experiences to appreciate our differences and find value in learning from one another. Societies will succeed when we are successful in relating to one another.

The movement toward greater diversity in law has been slow. The progress made came because lawyers, judges, and policy makers fought for more inclusive workplaces and articulated sound reasons for enhancing diversity. Early diversity began as "the right thing to do"; now business, ethical, and moral reasons for diversity are clear and well-documented. More diverse law firms are more productive and responsive to clients' expectations and requirements, all of which can impact the bottom line. Much more needs to be done to achieve true diversity and equity. That will require leadership from a new generation of law firm and law organization leaders with a deeper understanding of cultural intelligence and the true value of inclusion.

Exercises

Discovering Our Implicit Biases

As an exercise in discovering bias, do the following:

- Watch SmarterEveryDay's "Backwards Brain Bicycle" video.
- Take one of the "Harvard Implicit Associations Tests."
- Watch Valerie Alexander's "How to Outsmart Your Own Unconscious Bias" TEDxPasadena presentation.

Discussion Questions :

1. What non-social biases do you have?
   a. What is your favorite breakfast food?
   b. Who is your favorite singer, artist, or band?
   c. What is your favorite fast food restaurant?
   d. What is your favorite vacation destination?
2. Given the recent issues related to race, gender, or sexual orientation injustice, do you believe that inequities still exist? Why or why not?
3. Regarding Valerie Alexander's TEDx presentation:
   a. Do you examine your behavior? Why or why not?
   b. Visualize situations before they happen.
      i. What mental pictures do you see?
      ii. Can you change them and open your eyes to different pictures?
   c. In your daily life, how will you ensure that you're using this technique when preparing for new experiences and meeting new people?
   d. Exposure to the unexpected.
      i. Do you expose yourself to the unexpected?
      ii. Think back to a time when you did expose yourself to the unexpected. What did you learn?

Toy Shopping[211]

Shop online for a child who is celebrating her or his fifth birthday. Half the group should shop for a girl and half should shop for a boy. Search for toys you think would be desired by the child. Do not use a search term such as "toys for boys" or "toys for girls." In 3-5 minutes, choose a toy in the $10-20 range. Then reconvene as a group to compare your choices. What conclusions can you draw from the results? Do you think your answer would have been different before reading this chapter?

Journal Prompts

1. Which of the specific statistics or studies discussed in this chapter surprised you, and why?

2. If you have not already done so, watch SmarterEveryDay's "Backwards Brain Bicycle" video. How do you think the backward bicycle video relates to your attitude about diversity and inclusion? How will you use this information?

3. Write about a time that you heard someone in a leadership role say something that seemed utterly tone-deaf. Explain why it struck you as insensitive. Also discuss any aspect of your own life experience that may contribute to your reaction to the statement.

4. Write about a time you said something to a friend or a peer that you later realized was insensitive.

   a. Why did you later determine it was insensitive?

   b. How could you have communicated differently to avoid this?

   c. Did you discuss it with the person then or later?

   d. Were you hesitant or uncomfortable about having the conversation?

   e. How did you feel after?

   f. How did the conversation affect your relationship?

5. Think about a big decision you have made in your life.

   a. What made it difficult?

   b. What factors of your unique background played into your decision making to make it easier or harder to choose?

   c. Did you consult anyone in making that decision? Who? Why?

6. Take one of the "Harvard Implicit Associations Tests" (if you took one for the exercise noted above, choose a different one).

   a. Were you surprised by the results? Why or why not?

   b. What do you think you can do to address any implicit bias you may have?

7. After reading the material in this chapter, describe how diversity on your team helps you.

8. In your ideal law firm, what will diversity, inclusion, and equity look like?

9. As discussed by Sheryl Sandberg in *Lean In*, your own personal empowerment is necessary to achieve your full potential. This applies to all of us regardless of

our background or circumstances. Identify for yourself one aspect that could potentially keep you from seeking opportunities outside your comfort zone. What is your plan to overcome this inhibition?

Endnotes

1. Harper Lee, To Kill A Mockingbird (Philadelphia: Chelsea House Publishers 1999) (1960). Atticus Finch is a lawyer and resident in small town Alabama in the book.
2. Martin Luther King, Jr., *I Have a Dream*, speech delivered at the March on Washington, Washington, D.C. (1963). Martin Luther King, Jr. was an African-American minister and activist who became the most visible spokesperson and leader in the civil rights movement from 1955 until his assassination in 1968.
3. Rebecca Hooley, *California's Women Lawyers: 134 Years and Counting*, Cal. B.J., https://www.calbarjournal.com/March2012/TopHeadlines/TH4.aspx (last visited July 20, 2020).
4. Evan Thomas, First — Sandra Day O'Connor 43 (Random House 2019).
5. Nina Totenberg, *Does Justice Ruth Bader Ginsburg Have Any Regrets? Hardly*, NPR (July 28, 2019), https://www.npr.org/2019/07/28/745304221/does-justice-ruth-bader-ginsburg-have-any-regrets-hardly.
6. William Glaberson, *Leon Higginbotham Jr., Federal Judge, Is Dead at 70*, N.Y. Times (Dec. 15, 1998).
7. Lara Bazelon, *What It Takes to Be a Trial Lawyer If You're Not a Man*, The Atlantic (Sept. 2018), https://amp.theatlantic.com/amp/article/565778/.
8. *Id.*
9. Tsedale M. Melaku, *Why Women and People of Color in Law Still Hear "You Don't Look Like a Lawyer,"* Harv. Bus. Rev. (Aug. 7, 2019), https://hbr.org/amp/2019/08/why-women-and-people-of-color-in-law-still-hear-you-dont-look-like-a-lawyer.
10. Model Rules of Prof'l Conduct R. 8.4(g) (2020).
11. Model Rules of Prof'l Conduct R. 8.4 cmt. 3 (2020).
12. *Id.*
13. *Diversity and Inclusion Definitions*, Ferris State University (2020), https://www.ferris.edu/HTMLS/administration/president/DiversityOffice/Definitions.htm.
14. Ella Washington & Camille Patrick, *3 Requirements for a Diverse and Inclusive Culture*, Gallup (Sept. 17, 2018), https://www.gallup.com/workplace/242138/requirements-diverse-inclusive-culture.aspx; Janet Foutty et al., *Shift/Forward: Redefining Leadership: The Inclusion Imperative*, Deloitte (June 2018), https://www2.deloitte.com/content/dam/Deloitte/us/Documents/about-deloitte/us-shift-forward-redefining-leadership.pdf.
15. William Arruda, *The Difference Between Diversity and Inclusion and Why It Is Important to Your Success*, Forbes (Nov. 22, 2016), https://www.forbes.com/sites/williamarruda/2016/11/22/the-difference-between-diversity-and-inclusion-and-why-it-is-important-to-your-success/#4be41445f8f5.
16. Kris Putnam-Walkerly & Elizabeth Russell, *What the Heck Does "Equity" Mean?*, Stan. Soc. Innovation Rev. (Sept. 15, 2016), https://ssir.org/articles/entry/what_the_heck_does_equity_mean.
17. *Diversity and Inclusion Definitions*, supra note 13.
18. *Id.*
19. *Id.*
20. *Id.*
21. Dafina-Lazarus Stewart, *Language of Appeasement*, Inside Higher Ed (Mar. 30, 2017), https://www.insidehighered.com/views/2017/03/30/colleges-need-language-shift-not-one-you-think-essay.
22. *Id.*
23. *Id.*
24. Foutty et al., *supra* note 14.
25. Paula Davis-Laack, *6 New Leadership Literacies Lawyers Must Build*, Forbes (Feb. 28, 2018), https://www.forbes.com/sites/pauladavislaack/2018/02/22/6-new-leadership-literacies-lawyers-must-build/#73d7b9ff2334.
26. Michelle R. Pistrone & Michael B. Horn, *Disrupting Law School: How Disruptive Innovation Will Revolutionize the Legal World*, Clayton Christensen Institute for Disruptive Innovation (March 2016), *available at* https://eric.ed.gov/?id=ED568678.
27. *Id.*

28. "Fifty years ago, 58 percent of U.S. college students were men." In 2019 "for the first time, the share of college-educated women in the U.S. workforce passed the share of college-educated men, according to the Pew Research Center. It's not just that more women opt for college. It's that fewer men do, affecting their opportunities and lifetime earnings. *The students disappearing fastest from U.S. campuses? Middle-class ones.*"

"It's a crazy cycle," said Adrian Huerta, an assistant professor of education at the University of Southern California who focuses on college access and gender. "We know that when you have a college education, there are good outcomes with health. You're more likely to live longer. It matters for employment stability and civic engagement. You're less likely to rely on social services." Jon Marcus, *The Degrees of Separation Between the Genders in College Keeps Growing*, Wash. Post (Oct. 27, 2019), https://www.washingtonpost.com/local/education/the-degrees-of-separation-between-the-genders-in-college-keeps-growing/2019/10/25/8b2e5094-f2ab-11e9-89eb-ec56cd414732_story.html.

29. Melissa Heelan Stanzione, *Law School Enrollment Up Overall, But Not for Minorities*, Bloomberg Law (Dec. 12, 2019), https://news.bloomberglaw.com/us-law-week/law-school-enrollment-up-overall-but-not-for-minorities.

30. The American Bar Association's National Lawyer Population Survey shows a growth in women in the profession from 31 percent in 2009 to 36 percent in 2019. Allison E. Laffey & Allison Ng, *Diversity and Inclusion in the Law: Challenges and Initiatives*, American Bar Association (May 2, 2018), https://www.americanbar.org/groups/litigation/committees/jiop/articles/2018/diversity-and-inclusion-in-the-law-challenges-and-initiatives/.

31. *Female Law Partners Face 53 Percent Pay Gap, Survey Finds*, Bloomberg Law (Dec. 6, 2018), https://news.bloomberglaw.com/business-and-practice/female-law-partners-face-53-percent-pay-gap-survey-finds.

32. *Id.*

33. *Id.*

34. Vivia Chen, *Yes, Cravath Still Has Zero Black Partners*, The American Lawyer (July 7, 2020), https://www.law.com/americanlawyer/2020/07/07/yes-cravath-still-has-zero-black-partners/.

35. *Report on Diversity in U.S. Law Firms*, National Association for Law Placement (December 2019), https://www.nalp.org/reportondiversity.

36. *Id.* at 31.

37. Robert Barnes, *Supreme Court Says Gay, Transgender Workers Protected by Federal Law Forbidding Discrimination*, Wash. Post (June 15, 2020), https://www.washingtonpost.com/politics/courts_law/supreme-court-says-gay-transgender-workers-are-protected-by-federal-law-forbidding-discrimination-on-the-basis-of-sex/2020/06/15/2211d5a4-655b-11ea-acca-80c22bbee96f_story.html?arc404=true.

38. *Id.*

39. *Id.*

40. Karen Sloan, *43% of Young Women Lawyers Experience Bias, Fla. Survey Finds*, Nat'l L.J. (Mar. 1, 2016), https://www.law.com/nationallawjournal/almID/1202751069129/.

41. Laffey & Ng, *supra* note 30.

42. Marilyn Cavicchia, *Energy, Commitment, and Connection: Doing the Work of Diversity and Inclusion*, 43 A.B.A. Leader (May-June 2019), https://www.americanbar.org/groups/bar_services/publications/bar_leader/2018_19/may-june/energy-commitment-and-connection-doing-the-work-of-diversity-and-inclusion/.

43. *Id.*

44. *Id.*

45. Bazelon, *supra* note 7.

46. *Id.*

47. Brock Pronko, *Backward and in High Heels*, Central Penn Bus. J. (June 28, 2019), *available at* https://law.stanford.edu/press/backwards-and-in-high-heels/.

48. Average salary increase in law firms was 2.6 to 4.7 percent. *What Is the Average Pay Raise?*, JDSUPRA (Jan. 4, 2019), https://www.jdsupra.com/legalnews/what-is-the-average-pay-raise-15382/#:~:text=Recent%20studies%20show%20that%20the,pay%20raises%20larger%20than%20that%3F.

49. Leigh Donaldson, *When the Media Misrepresents Black Men, the Effects Are Felt in the Real World*, The Guardian (Aug. 12, 2015), https://www.theguardian.com/commentisfree/2015/aug/12/media-misrepresents-black-men-effects-felt-real-world.

50. Melaku, *supra* note 9.

51. *Id.*

52. *Id.*

53. *Id.*

54. *Id.*

55. Author Elizabeth M. Fraley conversation with Bonnie Mayfield (July 22, 2020).

56. Linda Babcock & George Loewenstein, *Explaining Bargaining Impasse: The Role of Self-Serving Biases*, 11 J. Econ. Persp. 109, 114 (1997) (quoting Rasyid Sanitioso et al., *Motivated Recruitment of Autobiographical Memories*, 59 J. Personality & Soc. Psychol. 229, 229 (1990)).

57. Giovanni Luca Ciampaglia, *Biases Make People Vulnerable to Misinformation Spread by Social Media*, Scientific American (June 21, 2018), https://www.scientificamerican.com/article/biases-make-people-vulnerable-to-misinformation-spread-by-social-media/.

58. *Id.*

59. *Id.*

60. Status quo is defined as "the existing state of affairs." *Status quo*, Merriam-Webster Online Dictionary, https://www.merriam-webster.com/dictionary/status%20quo?utm_campaign=sd&utm_medum=serp&utm–source=jsonld (last visited July 13, 2020). In this discussion, the billable hour method of charging for legal services is the "status quo"; *see also* Daniel Kahneman et al., *Anomalies: The Endowment Effect, Loss Aversion, and Status Quo Bias*, 5 J. Econ. Persp. 193, 194 (1991).

61. Jerry Kang, Judge Mark Bennett, Devon Carbado, Pam Casey, Nilanjana Dasgupta et al., *Implicit Bias in the Courtroom,* 59 UCLA L. Rev. 1124, 1126 (2012).

62. Shlomo Benartzi et al., *Governments Are Trying to Nudge Us into Better Behavior. Is It Working?*, Wash. Post (Aug. 11, 2017), https://www.washingtonpost.com/news/wonk/wp/2017/08/11/governments-are-trying-to-nudge-us-into-better-behavior-is-it-working/.

63. Kang et al., *supra* note 61, at 1128.

64. *Id.* at 1128–29.

65. *Id.* at 1129.

66. *Id.*

67. *Id.*

68. *Id.* at 1132.

69. *Id.* at 1133.

70. *Id.* at 1133–34.

71. Kevin Bennett, *Why Do British Accents Sound Intelligent to Americans?*, Psychology Today (Sept. 9, 2016), https://www.psychologytoday.com/us/blog/modern-minds/201609/why-do-british-accents-sound-intelligent-americans.

72. Individuals make social judgments based on accents, reflecting unconscious bias. *Id.*

73. Joseph Price & Justin Wolfers, *Racial Discrimination Among NBA Referees*, 124 Q. J. Econ. 1859, 1884–85 (2010).

74. John Eligon & Robert Gebeloff, *Affluent and Black, and Still Trapped by Segregation*, N.Y. Times (Aug. 20, 2016), https://www.nytimes.com/2016/08/21/us/milwaukee-segregation-wealthy-black-families.html.

75. Francesca Gino, *Another Reason Top Managers Are Disproportionally White Men*, Scientific American (Sept. 12, 2017), https://www.scientificamerican.com/article/another-reason-top-managers-are-disproportionally-white-men/.

76. "This paper suggests that African-Americans face differential treatment when searching for jobs and this may still be a factor in why they do poorly in the labor market. Job applicants with African-American names get far fewer callbacks for each resume they send out. Equally importantly, applicants with African-American names find it hard to overcome this hurdle in callbacks by improving their observable skills or credentials." Miriam Bertrand & Sendhil Mullainathan, *Are Emily and Greg More Employable Than Lakisha and Jamal? A Field Experiment on Labor Market Discrimination*, 94 Am. Econ. Rev. 991–1013 (2004).

77. "Half [of the partners] were told the memo was written by an African-American man named Thomas Meyer, and half were told the writer was a Caucasian man named Thomas Meyer. Fifty-three partners completed the task. Of those, 29 received the memo supposedly by a white man and 24 received the memo supposedly by a black man." Debra Cassens Weiss, *Partners in Study Gave Legal Memo a Lower Rating When Told the Author Wasn't White*, American Bar Association (Apr. 21, 2014), https://www.abajournal.com/news/article/hypothetical_legal_memo_demonstrates_unconscious_biases.

78. Kang et al., *supra* note 61, at 1140.

79. Erik Eckholm, *Court Costs Entrap Nonwhite, Poor Juvenile Offenders*, N.Y. Times (Aug. 31, 2016), nytimes.com/2016/09/01/us/court-costs-entrap-nonwhite-poor-juvenile-offenders.html.

80. Kang et al., *supra* note 61, at 1148.

81. *Foster v. Chatman*, 136 S. Ct. 1737 (2016).

82. Dev A. Patel, *In HLS Classes, Women Fall Behind*, Harv. Crimson (May 8, 2013), https://www.thecrimson.com/article/2013/5/8/law-school-gender-classroom/.

83. *Id.* at 1161 (citing John M. Darley & Paget H. Gross, *A Hypothesis-Confirming Bias in Labeling Effects*, 44 J. Personality & Soc. Psychol. 20, 22–23 (1983)).

84. *Id.*

85. *Id.*

86. *See, e.g.*, *30 of Donald Trump's Wildest Quotes*, CBS News, https://www.cbsnews.com/pictures/wild-donald-trump-quotes/8/ (last visited July 14, 2020). "You know, it really doesn't matter what they write as long as you've got a young and beautiful piece of ass."

87. Emily Bernbaum, *Clinton Teases Interviewer Who Confused Holder and Booker: "They All Look Alike,"* The Hill (Oct. 29, 2018), https://thehill.com/homenews/administration/413754-clinton-teases-interviewer-who-confused-holder-and-booker-they-all.

88. *What Is Implicit Bias?*, Psychology Today (Oct. 13, 2019), https://www.psychologytoday.com/us/blog/spontaneous-thoughts/201910/what-is-implicit-bias.

89. *Id.*

90. Joan C. Williams et al., You Can't Change What You Can't See, Executive Summary (ABA 2018).

91. *Id.*

92. *Id.*

93. *Id.*

94. *Id.*

95. *Id.*

96. *Id.*

97. *Id.*

98. *Id.*

99. *Id.*

100. *Id.* (emphasis added).

101. *Id.*

102. Former First Lady Michelle Obama at the 2009 State Department Women of Courage Awards.

103. Washington & Patrick, *supra* note 14.

104. *See, e.g.*, Kellianne Payne, *Diversity Needs to Extend to Leadership in the Legal Profession*, Law.com (Feb. 28, 2020), https://www.law.com/thelegalintelligencer/2020/02/28/diversity-needs-to-extend-to-leadership-in-the-legal-profession/.

105. In a survey of human resource executives, 55 percent of respondents reported "that their employers' policies promote diversity and inclusion, and both issues are rated as an important issue by 69% of execs, according to a Deloitte study." Washington & Patrick, *supra* note 14.

106. Meir Shemla, *Why Workplace Diversity Is So Important, and Why It's So Hard to Achieve*, Forbes (Aug. 22, 2018), https://www.forbes.com/sites/rsmdiscovery/2018/08/22/why-workplace-diversity-is-so-important-and-why-its-so-hard-to-achieve/#1704e3e13096.

107. Leah Witcher Jackson Teague, *Training Lawyers for Leadership: Vitally Important Mission for the Future Success (and Maybe Survival) of the Legal Profession and Our Democracy*, 58 Santa Clara L. Rev. 633, 635–37 (2018); Donald J. Polden, *Leadership Matters: Lawyers' Leadership Skills and Competencies*, 52 Santa Clara L. Rev. 899, 901–04 (2012).

108. Thomas Kochan et al., *The Effects of Diversity on Business Performance: Report of the Diversity Research Network*, 42 Hum. Resource Mgmt. 3, 3–21 (2003).

109. *Id.*

110. Russell Wheeler, *How Close Is President Trump to His Goal of Record Setting Judicial Appointments?*, Brookings (May 5, 2020), https://www.brookings.edu/blog/fixgov/2020/05/05/how-close-is-president-trump-to-his-goal-of-record-setting-judicial-appointments/amp/.

111. Sophia Nelson, *White, Male and Conservative: Trump's Damaging Legal Legacy*, USA Today (July 3, 2020), https://www.usatoday.com/story/opinion/2020/07/03/trump-and-judiciary-lack-diversity-column/5357852002/. At the time of writing this book, Judge Amy Coney Barrett had just been appointed to the United States Supreme Court to replace the late Justice Ruth Bader Ginsburg. Although we are pleased that President Trump nominated a woman, it did not add diversity to the Court because she was replacing an iconic female Supreme Court Justice.

112. *Id.*

113. Pooja Jain-Link et al., *5 Strategies for Creating an Inclusive Workplace*, Harv. Bus. Rev. (Jan. 13, 2020), https://hbr.org/2020/01/5-strategies-for-creating-an-inclusive-workplace.

114. *Women Pay a Price for Promoting Other Women*, Center for Creative Leadership, https://www.ccl.org/articles/leading-effectively-articles/queen-bee-women-pay-a-price-for-not-promoting-other-women/ (last visited July 17, 2020).

115. *Id.*

116. *Id.*

117. Keynote speech at *Celebrating Inspiration* luncheon with the WNBA's All-Decade Team (2006), https://www.goodreads.com/quotes/14328-there-is-a-special-place-in-hell-for-women-who.

118. Foutty et al., *supra* note 14.

119. Washington & Patrick, *supra* note 14.

120. *Id.*

121. *Id.*

122. *Id.*

123. Foutty et al., *supra* note 14.

124. *Id.*

125. *Id.*

126. Laura Sherbin & Ripa Rashid, *Diversity Doesn't Stick Without Inclusion*, Harv. Bus. Rev. (Feb. 1, 2017), https://hbr.org/2017/02/diversity-doesnt-stick-without-inclusion.

127. Foutty et al., *supra* note 14.

128. *Id.*

129. *Id.*

130. Washington & Patrick, *supra* note 14.

131. Foutty et al., *supra* note 14.

132. Samantha McLaren, *4 Important (and Sometimes Difficult) Steps Leaders Must Take to Create a More Diverse and Inclusive Team*, LinkedIn Talent Blog (Nov. 5, 2019), https://business.linkedin.com/talent-solutions/blog/talent-on-tap/2019/steps-leaders-must-take-to-create-diverse-inclusive-teams.

133. *Id.*

134. Kori S. Carew, *You Say Tomaydo, I Say Tohmahtoh: Why You Can't Improve Diversity Without Culturally Fluent Leaders*, 59 DRI For Def. 100 (2017).

135. Foutty et al., *supra* note 14.

136. Sherbin & Rashid, *supra* note 126.

137. *Id.*

138. McLaren, *supra* note 132.

139. Sherbin & Rashid, *supra* note 126.

140. *Id.*

141. *Id.*

142. *Id.*

143. *Id.*

144. *Id.*

145. McLaren, *supra* note 132.

146. *Id.*

147. *Id.*

148. Sherbin & Rashid, *supra* note 126.

149. *Id.*

150. McLaren, *supra* note 132.

151. Sherbin & Rashid, *supra* note 126.

152. National Association of Minority and Women Owned Law Firms, https://namwolf.org/, (last visited Sept. 25, 2020).

153. National Association of Women Lawyers, https://www.nawl.org/ (last visited Sept. 25, 2020).

154. *Id.*

155. Josiah Bates, *Pro-Police Agitators and Black Lives Matter Protesters Clash in Brooklyn*, TIME (July 13, 2020), https://time.com/5866336/police-supporters-black-lives-matter-protesters-brooklyn/.

156. This is not intended to be a complete list of all the groups and issues affected by a lack of cultural competency, but a full list would subsume the message of this chapter.

157. Debra Chopp, *Addressing Cultural Bias in the Legal Profession*, 41 N.Y.U. Rev. L. & Soc. Change 367, 371 (2017).

158. *Id.* (citing Daniel G. Bates & Fred Plog, Human Adaptive Strategies 3 (1991)).

159. *Id.* (citing Sue Bryant & Jean Koh Peters, *Five Habits for Cross-Cultural Lawyering, in* RACE, CULTURE, PSYCHOLOGY & LAW 48 (Kimberly Barrett & William George eds., 2004); *see* Paul R. Tremblay, *Interviewing and Counseling Across Cultures*, 9 CLINICAL L. REV. 373, 379 (2002); *see generally* Joseph R. Betancourt, *Cross-Cultural Medical Education: Conceptual Approaches and Frameworks for Evaluation*, 78 ACAD. MED. 560 (2003)).

160. *Id.* (citing Tremblay, *supra* note 159, at 379; Kimberle Crenshaw, *Mapping the Margins: Intersectionality, Identity Politics, and Violence Against Women of Color*, 43 STAN. L. REV. 1241, 1242 (1991).

161. *Id.*

162. *Id.* (citing Betancourt, *supra* note 159, at 561).

163. For a discussion of emotional intelligence, see chapter 14.

164. *Id.* at 372 (citing Charles R. Lawrence III, *The Id, the Ego, and Equal Protection: Reckoning with Unconscious Racism*, 39 STAN. L. REV. 317, 337–38 (1987); *see also* Robert M. Ortega & Kathleen Coulborn Faller, *Training Child Welfare Workers from an Intersectional Cultural Humility Perspective: A Paradigm Shift*, 90 CHILD WELFARE 27, 29 (2011)).

165. *Id.* (citing Ortega & Faller, *supra* note 164, at 29. *See also* Robert C. Post, *Law and Cultural Conflict*, 78 CHI.-KENT L. REV. 486, 492–93 (2003) (explaining that culture is as much about difference as it is about unity and noting the challenge for law to respect and reflect culture in a multicultural state).

166. *Id.*

167. *Understanding Cultural Competency*, HUMAN SERVICES EDUCATION GUIDE (2018), https://www .humanservicesedu.org/cultural-competency.html.

168. *Cultural Competence*, AMERICAN SPEECH-LANGUAGE-HEARING ASSOCIATION (2017), https://www.asha .org/Practice-Portal/Professional-Issues/Cultural-Competence/.

169. Tori DeAngelis, *In Search of Cultural Competence*, 46 MONITOR ON PSYCHOL. 64 (2015), https://www.apa .org/monitor/2015/03/cultural-competence.

170. Robert Wood Johnson Foundation, www.rwjf.org (last visited July 13, 2020).

171. P. Christopher Earley & Elaine Mosakowski, *Cultural Intelligence*, HARV. BUS. REV. (Oct. 2004), https://hbr .org/2004/10/cultural-intelligence.

172. *Id.*

173. Allen Ivey, *In Memoriam*, AMERICAN COUNSELING ASSOCIATION (Feb. 7, 2017), https://www.counseling .org/aca-community/in-memoriam/in-memoriam/2017/02/07/dr.-paul-b.-pedersen. Dr. Paul B. Pedersen was a counselor and leader in cultural competency awareness.

174. Kwame McKenzie, *A Historical Perspective of Cultural Competence*, 1 ETHNICITY & INEQUALITIES HEALTH & SOC. CARE 1, 5–8 (June 1, 2008).

175. *Id.*

176. Ivey, *supra* note 173.

177. McKenzie, *supra* note 174.

178. *Id.*

179. *Id.* This broader development of cultural competence began through work at the University of Georgetown. "The now National Centre for Cultural Competence at Georgetown, University Centre [sic] for Child and Human Development developed out of child psychiatry and social services centre [sic]."

180. Melanie Tervalon & Jann Murray-Garcia, *Cultural Humility Versus Cultural Competence: A Critical Distinction in Defining Physician Training Outcomes in Multicultural Education*, 9 J. HEALTH CARE FOR THE POOR AND UNDERSERVED 9, 117–25 (1998); *see also* Dustin Rynders, *Battling Implicit Bias in the Idea to Advocate for African American Students with Disabilities*, 35 TOURO L. REV. 461, 475 (2019).

181. Amanda Waters & Lisa Asbill, *Reflections on Cultural Humility*, AMERICAN PSYCHOLOGICAL ASSOCIATION, https://www.apa.org/pi/families/resources/newsletter/2013/08/cultural-humility (last visited July 13, 2020).

182. Tervalon & Murray-Garcia, *supra* note 180.

183. Waters & Asbill, *supra* note 181.

184. Tervalon & Murray-Garcia, *supra* note 180.

185. Bradley J.B. Toben, *Statement on George Floyd Tragedy/A Message from Dean Brad Toben*, Baylor Law School (June 5, 2020). Dean Toben graduated from Baylor Law with the J.D. degree, with honors, in 1977, after completing his B.A., with honors, in political science at the University of Missouri-St. Louis. He received the LL.M. from Harvard Law School in 1981 and then taught at Indiana University School of Law-Indianapolis.
He joined the Baylor Law faculty in 1983 and was named as Dean of the Law School in 1991.
Dean Toben is the longest serving dean of any U.S. law school. Dean Brad Toben, Law School Faculty, BAYLOR UNIVERSITY, https://www.baylor.edu/law/facultystaff/index.php?id=933507 (last visited July 14, 2020).

186. Kang et al., *supra* note 61.

187. *Id.*

188. *Id.*

189. *See, e.g.,* Texas Lawyer's Creed — A Mandate for Professionalism (1989).

190. 1.1 Competence, Ann. Mod. Rules Prof. Cond. § 1.1.

191. *See* Associated Press, *Report: Dallas Prosecutors Bar Black Jurors,* NBC News (Oct. 22, 2005), http://www
.nbcnews.com/id/9033376/ns/us_news-life/t/report-dallas-prosecutors-bar-black-jurors/#.XvDwrGpKjGI.

192. Chopp, *supra* note 157, at 373.

193. *Id.* at 372–73 (internal citations omitted).

194. To understand this phenomenon better, watch the following TEDx talk by Prosecutor Ryan Calvert.
Ryan Calvert, *A Mile in Her Shoes: Changing Perspective on Domestic Violence,* TED (Feb. 10, 2020), *video
available at* https://www.youtube.com/watch?v=wLNa6qwVpbA.

195. Evan Parker, *Forum Magazine: Racial & Ethnic Diversity — A Multiplier for Law Firm Probability,* THOMSON
REUTERS (May 17, 2019), https://www.legalexecutiveinstitute.com/forum-magazine-diversity-law-firm-
profitability/.

196. Rynders, *supra* note 180 (citing Susan Bryant & Jean Koh Peters, *Five Habits for Cross-Cultural Lawyering,
in* RACE, CULTURE, PSYCHOLOGY & LAW 47–63 (Kimberly Holt Barret & William H. George eds., 2005)).

197. Rynders, *supra* note 180.

198. *Id.*

199. *Id.*

200. *Id.*

201. *Id.*

202. *Id.* at 477.

203. *Id.*

204. *Id.*

205. *Id.*

206. *Id.* at 478.

207. *Id.*

208. *Id.*

209. *See id.*

210. Martin Luther King, Jr., *Letter from Birmingham Jail* (1963), *available at* https://liberalarts.utexas.edu/
coretexts/_files/resources/texts/1963_MLK_Letter_Abridged.pdf.

211. Mary Kite, Marli Diane Simpson & Bridget Ryan, *Gender Stereotypes Activity,* BREAKING THE PREJUDICE
HABIT, http://breakingprejudice.org/teaching/group-activities/childrens-gender-stereotypes-activity/ (last
visited July 20, 2020).

Chapter 18

Communication Styles, Public Relations, and Crisis Management

Losing your head in a crisis is a good way to become the crisis.

C.J. Redwine[1]

Purpose

Examine different communication styles that may be more or less effective for different audiences and prepare students for the important role lawyers often serve in assisting clients with public relations during a crisis.

Learning Objectives

At the end of this chapter, you should be able to:

- Describe different styles of verbal and non-verbal communication.
- Discuss why a leader might use a particular style for a specific audience.
- Identify situations that require special cultural attention.
- Describe the importance of crisis preparation and management efforts for organizations.
- Describe the role a lawyer might assume when an organization experiences a crisis.

Discussion

INTRODUCTION

Everyone has an individual communication style. While there are commonalities, how we process, internalize, and communicate information is unique to each individual, both in expressive speech and in receptive speech. A leader must be able to communicate well with each member of the team, meaning the leader must know his own communication style as well as the communication style of the people on the team.

Communication styles and their effective uses gain particular importance when representing a client in the public arena and during a crisis. Clients frequently rely upon their lawyers to be the spokespersons during a crisis. The lawyer's skill in these instances can be invaluable in a company's "make it or break it" moments. A lawyer whose comments exacerbate the crisis can worsen the damage to the client. By contrast, a lawyer who gives the right message at the right time can mitigate the damage in a bad situation.

This chapter explores the different styles of communications — the ways in which people communicate with each other in different situations. Effective communication styles can ensure your words are not going to get lost in translation as you lead others. Non-verbal communication, including the signals that can be sent without uttering a word, is as important as explicit verbal speech. Meshing verbal and non-verbal messages is highly important. Finally, we discuss the importance of effective communication in situations that require public relations and/or crisis management.

COMMUNICATION STYLES

Do you lead with emotions or do you lead with facts? Would you say something like "we are off to a good start this quarter" or "sales are up by 7.2 percent"?[2] Some communication styles work better in different contexts. Learning about each communication style can help leaders get their message across effectively in any given situation, especially given that the leader and the follower may use different styles. Theories of communication styles can be broken down into four fundamental categories: (1) analytical, (2) intuitive, (3) functional, and (4) personal.[3]

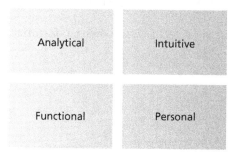

Analytical

Analytical communicators like hard data and real numbers, and tend to be suspicious of people who are not in command of the facts.[4] Those with an analytical communication style may have little patience for emotional words in communication.[5] An advantage of this style is the ability to look at issues logically and dispassionately. This style also creates the perception that you are competent in handling high levels of information and that people can trust your expertise.[6] By the same token, a very analytical, data-driven style may seem cold or insensitive. For example, when an analytical communicator interacts with a personal communicator, the warm and chatty personal style may be irritating to an analytical communicator.[7] Analytical communicators are not necessarily unemotional, but they prefer to focus on the facts.[8] When analytical communicators deal with sensitive subjects or try to get group consensus, they may need to be cognizant of the audience's perspective, perhaps by softening or warming the tone of the data-driven message. Leaders who adhere too rigidly to a communication style at the expense of their listeners may have trouble effectively getting the team on board, especially the personal communicators.

Speaking an Analytical Communicator's Language

- Focus on facts and data.
- Be clear, concise, and logical.
- Prepare facts to back up any proposal, argument, or idea you share.
- Don't push for immediate decisions.
- When possible, present ideas with options for possible outcomes.
- Be prepared to answer questions—and anticipate them—so you can have well-thought-out responses. [9]

Intuitive

An intuitive communicator focuses on the big picture but can get bogged down by details.[10] This leader tends to skip right to the main point and present it in a broad overview style, which causes tension with functional communicators who prefer step-by-step analysis.[11] An intuitive communicator delivers messaging that is quick and to the point in a manner that focuses attention well.[12] This communicator's message does not get stalled by unnecessary details, keeping the focus on the end goal.[13] The tendency toward a broad message, however, can leave out important and necessary details, which may lead to questions about the feasibility of the idea. Leaders who cannot identify and organize the details may have trouble accomplishing the overall goal.

Speaking an Intuitive Communicator's Language

- Share big-picture vision.
- Focus on the end product; only zoom in on critical details.
- Remember that getting in the weeds will only frustrate this leader.
- When discussing ideas, provide a variety to consider.
- Use existing visuals or sketch out ideas to ensure your points are sticking. [14]

Functional

The polar opposite of an intuitive communicator is a functional communicator, for whom the devil is always in the details.[15] This communication style thrives on process, detail, timelines, and well-thought-out plans.[16] Step-by-step communication ensures that nothing gets missed.[17] On a team, the functional communicators may be chosen to implement plans because others have confidence in their process and attention to details.[18] For some, the minutiae can become an irritation if dwelt on before implementation is imminent.[19] Functional communicators need to adapt to managing the details while keeping sight of the bigger picture.

Speaking a Functional Communicator's Language

- Connect conversations and points to a plan.
- Provide clear context and structure with your communication—have an outline.
- Specifically discuss how a certain action (or inaction) could impact current or future tasks.
- Emphasize the importance of each step of the process. [20]

Personal

Personal communicators value emotional language and connection. These communicators tend to be good listeners, skilled at smoothing over conflicts and focusing on the relational health of the organization.[21] Personal communicators are emotionally intelligent and can pick up on "vibes" that others might miss.[22] Personal communicators may clash with analytical communicators and their focus on facts over feelings. Personal communicators may need to augment their touchy-feely style with fact-driven analysis to communicate better with analytical communicators.

Speaking a Personal Communicator's Language

- Use emotive language with details to help connect your point to this leader's emotional way of thinking.
- Be authentic in establishing a personal relationship.
- Listen and show genuine interest in the leader's thoughts and ideas.
- Talk through situations and outcomes through the lens of how they will affect others. [23]

These styles describe types of communicators, but rarely will an individual fall solely into one style. As with introversion and extroversion, most people utilize a mix of communication styles depending on the situation and their natural comfort level. Studying the different styles of communication to understand the strengths and weaknesses of each one can help you tailor your messages to better connect with different audiences. In a meeting with the company's auditors, you may want to stick to facts and figures. In a closing argument, you may adopt a far more emotional tone, tuning into the pathos of the case. Use these different communication styles strategically to keep your organization on the right track, both personally and professionally.

Finally, as with other aspects of leadership, finding your own personal style of communication is essential to authenticity. Before the Battle of Midway in WWII, Admiral "Bull" Halsey became ill. His replacement, Ray Spruance, came to the hospital to ask for guidance on the attack. Halsey responded, "When you're out there, don't play it the way you think I'd play it; play it the way you think it should be played."[24] Understanding your own communication style, and understanding that of others can foster growth within your team. As long as you use styles to communicate in a way that is authentic for you and your team, the message will be heard.

VERBAL AND NON-VERBAL COMMUNICATION

Richard Nixon—Founding Father of "Strategery"[25]

In an adversarial or emotionally charged environment, an effective communication strategy becomes a necessity. In 1952, Richard Nixon, the Republican candidate for Vice President, was accused of maintaining a secret slush fund for his personal benefit. The resulting media frenzy caused a rift with some in the Republican National Convention wanting Nixon off the ticket to avoid damage to the Republicans in the upcoming election. An attorney and politician, Nixon believed he could save his bid for the vice presidency if he were able to appeal directly to the public. Using the new medium of television, Nixon gave a live 30-minute address now widely referred to as the Checkers Speech.[26]

In the speech's two parts, Nixon used distinct verbal and non-verbal styles to convey the two different messages. At the beginning of the speech, he explained the fund to the American people using a conversational tone and seated behind a desk. He referred to the viewers as "folks" and "you," with informal word choices and fillers such as "well" and "now." He denied any illegal conduct, appealed to his daughters' emotional attachment to Checkers, the family dog, and portrayed his family in a relatable, middle-class light. His colloquial language and direct eye contact with the camera made viewers feel they were part of a personal conversation.

In the second half of the speech, Nixon attacked notable Democrats for their conduct. His tone shifted to a more political one. He stood up from the desk and moved toward the camera with fists clenched, conveying the outrage he wanted viewers to share. Such non-verbal cues served to remind the public that he was a powerful political leader motivated to end corruption.

The reactions of commentators now and at the time were mixed, with many believing the speech was calculated and insincere. Nixon's strategy, however, resonated with the intended audience — the American people in the 1950s. Over two million telegrams and three million letters supporting Nixon's remaining on the ticket flooded the RNC offices. Later that year, the Republicans won the presidential election in a landslide. Through the remainder of his political career, Nixon viewed the speech as one of his greatest successes.

While Nixon faced criticism for rehearsing the speech down to his gestures and pauses, the Checkers Speech is a prime example of how strategy in communications can enrich the message. Nixon also provides a chilling example of how communication skills can be used to twist and deceive rather than rally and persuade. Nixon declared in the wake of the Watergate scandal, "I am not a crook." Nixon, and others, provide a cautionary reminder that the tools of advocacy can be abused.

Good leaders understand the need to hone and polish their message without using the stage to be disingenuous or dishonest. We now look at some of those advocacy techniques and communication tools that make argument more persuasive. Whether as lawyers or leaders, understanding the power of verbal and non-verbal tools enhances communication to best serve a given situation.

Verbal Communication—Better Content for Your Speech

Effective advocacy does not distract from or disguise the true content of the argument but must start with a firm factual and substantive base. As discussed above, communication style is the ability to weave data, facts, and emotion into the verbal message. That basic content, though, can be enhanced or diminished by verbal tools referred to as paralinguistics. Paralinguistics focuses on the sound and delivery of the communication rather than the actual words used.[27] The comment "I could just sit and listen to her read a phone book" refers to a speaker whose delivery is so appealing that the words matter less than the sound the speaker makes. There are actors whose vocal tone is so appealing they make a good living doing voiceover work. Proper use of tone, modulation, and volume will make lawyers and leaders appear both knowledgeable and trustworthy.

Your most important objective is to achieve clarity with verbal communications. Matching the tone and volume to the setting can help you sound more natural. If the delivery is jarring, distracting, or irritating, the listener cannot focus on the message. For some speakers a smooth delivery is more natural, but it is a skill that can be learned and enhanced.

Effective verbal communication requires the speaker to adjust to the space and the audience. The venue can alter communication significantly due to size and acoustics. To command the attention in a smaller space, you can replicate a conversation by using a lower, friendly tone of voice. The listener feels more engaged and, as appropriate, able to participate in the conversation. Conversely, commanding the attention of jurors in a large courtroom requires the attorney to project and fill the space, whether making a powerful point or a more subtle one. The amount and type of emotion in the argument affects the tone. When reaching for crescendo emotions like outrage, excitement, or fear, the attorney's tone needs to match the emotion. This can involve taking the volume up or down, but the tone should depart from the baseline to convey the weight of these emotions. Pace, likewise, conveys meaning. Speed (including pauses), staccato delivery, and slow and deliberate comments all add impact to the words spoken. Master verbal communicators know that both substance and delivery matter.

Finally, the content of the message should be conveyed in digestible, yet appealing language. When Johnnie Cochran notably declared, "If [the glove] doesn't fit, you must acquit,"[28] he seared into jurors' minds the weight they should give to a single piece of evidence when returning their verdict. Appealing and memorable verbiage does not mean using cutesy or kitschy phrases. Verbalizing key points in a marketable manner, however, does enhance the content of your communications. Vivid imagery, alliterative statements, and rhetorically structured arguments all make the point in a memorable way.

When you are to speak in an important setting, spend time preparing — not memorizing — what you are going to say. Great actors and conductors do not take the stage without rehearsing. They have not only spent time on what they will say or play, they have marked up the script or score with directions: when to go fast, when to slow down; when to be louder, when to be softer; when to pause, when to continue. If you approach important communications as if you were performing a great play or symphony, you may feel more comfortable thinking through how to enhance the verbal and non-verbal parts of your performance.

Some people think that good oratorical skills flow naturally such that you should not spend time on the details of presentation. This could not be further from the truth. Consider the movie *The King's Speech*, which detailed the importance of preparation for both the individual speaker and the audience. King George VI took the throne after his brother, Edward VIII, abdicated to marry divorced commoner Wallis Simpson. The nation was reeling from the abdication and headed into what would become World War II. His subjects needed to feel confidence in the monarchy. Not only was George not a naturally good speaker, he also had a profound stammer that was exacerbated by nerves. King George worked extensively with his wife and a speech therapist before making one of the most important speeches of his life: the declaration that Britain would be joining the war after Hitler violated the Munich Pact. The long hours of preparation paid off: King George VI gave a brilliant speech and inspired the nation.

Lawyers will face situations that feel as significant for their clients: a presentation to the board of directors regarding the sale of the company; an opening statement in a heated custody case; the closing argument in a capital murder trial. The idea that you would go into any of those settings without preparing the most persuasive performance you can is foolish. Be willing to work at the craft of presentation, down to the details, and see just how compelling a presentation you can give. Each time you do so successfully, you become a better advocate, lawyer, and leader.

Non-Verbal Communication — Supplementing the Content of Your Speech

More than 90 percent of what a person "says" comes through non-verbal communication.[29] Even physical appearance and clothing are non-verbal behavior that may affect the way that listeners interpret our messaging. We get non-verbal messages when a colleague regularly speaks up at meetings — she communicates an interest and eagerness for work. By contrast, the colleague who is checking a cell phone or social media account conveys strongly he is not interested in what is being said at the meeting. Actions really do speak louder than words.

People can sense your attitude not only by the way you speak but by your demeanor. A positive attitude, while it may not turn you into a more knowledgeable lawyer, is unquestionably contagious.[30] Think of how different it feels to walk into a meeting with a groggy and hostile colleague as opposed to an energetic and good-humored one. You can almost feel the mood in the room shift. Setting the tone with a positive attitude signals to your colleagues that you trust them and creates a more collegial environment entirely.[31] You can show a positive attitude not only through the energy you bring into the room, but also the words you use and how you treat your colleagues.[32]

Body Language — Being Consistent with the Content of Your Speech

Non-verbal communication refers to a full range of conduct, whereas body language is specific to the gestures and movements that we make, consciously or subconsciously, through our body and facial expressions.[33] We constantly communicate signals through body language.[34] Since first impressions are formed in a matter of seconds, those impressions may be shaped in part from our body language. In a criminal case, for example, the body language of the lawyers trying the case can impact a guilty verdict or an acquittal.[35] When negotiating a business transaction, your posture at the conference table can signal confidence or desperation. Verbal speech does not overcome poor body language.

1. *Eye contact.* How and when to make eye contact depends entirely on the customs of where you are, who you are with, and the social setting. In some cultures, making

direct eye contact can be a sign of aggression, rudeness, or disrespect.[36] Other cultures and some religious groups consider eye contact between men and women inappropriate and either threatening or flirtatious. In many Asian cultures, avoiding eye contact with a member of the opposite sex or a superior is seen as a show of respect.[37]

In the United States and most of Europe, making and maintaining eye contact evokes presence and projects confidence to your listeners. In countries where eye contact is not only seen as appropriate but is necessary for establishing yourself as a powerful professional or confident leader, you should practice eye contact. When you are out in public, make eye contact with those whose paths you cross. Try to notice their eye color or, if that is uncomfortable, simply acknowledge them with a simple head nod or verbal gesture as you pass them. See what it feels like to make the connection.

2. *Firm handshake.* As with eye contact, the firmness of a handshake, or whether to shake hands at all, depends on the culture (and sometimes circumstance, such as the recent Covid-19 pandemic). A bone-crushing grip and fist-pumping handshake is considered rude in Middle Eastern countries. In Brazil, the custom is a longer handshake than in the United States. In the United States, a strong handshake exudes confidence and sets the tone not only for your abilities but also your personality and leadership style. Do not overthink it. Make palm-to-palm contact but do not crush the other person's hand. Make eye contact during the handshake; it can feel awkward to shake someone's hand who does not look at you.[38]

3. *Hand gestures.* When people speak passionately about a particular topic, they engage their body. Many of us talk with our hands. Some cultures are more animated with their gestures. The use of hand gestures should be tailored to the situation.[39] The hand gestures that are appropriate for oral arguments at the Supreme Court are not the same gestures you should use in a meeting with your colleagues, a consultation with a new business client, or a closing argument before a jury. Depending on your message and your audience, use your hands and arms to emphasize certain points and convey enthusiasm. Be deliberate in your movements for more effective communication, rather than letting them become a point of distraction or sign of nervous fidgeting.

4. *Posture.* Research from Northwestern University's Kellogg School of Management indicates that powerful posture can have a greater influence than formal titles or ranks.[40] Displaying "posture expansiveness," opening up the body and/or taking up greater space, triggers a sense of inner confidence.[41] Irrespective of the hierarchical role a person might hold in an organization, good posture produces a behavioral change that will lead that person to think and act more confidently.[42] In other words, be confident when owning your space.[43]

Non-Verbal Communication—The Reinforcer or Betrayer

Studies show that only 7 percent of an advocate's credibility comes from word choice, and only 38 percent depends on tone of voice. The remaining 55 percent depends on body language.[44] Non-verbal communications either complement or contradict the speaker's message, making it all the more necessary for attorneys to understand and command their non-verbal cues.

When leading or advocating, you should carry yourself in a manner that is appropriate for the message you are trying to convey. Are you asking for something from the listener? Are you making a declaration? Recall the Nixon example. When he was asking for understanding from the American people in the first part of his speech, he sat behind a desk with his shoulders hunched over in a manner that appeared more vulnerable. When the topic shifted to politics and corruption, he reinforced his role as a leader by rising and standing tall for the remainder of the speech. When determining how to present yourself, consider whether your posture aligns with your message.

Gestures reinforce or dilute a message. Our brains want the verbal and non-verbal messages to be in synch. If you say there are three reasons your audience should invest in a company, you would not hold up four fingers. By the same token, if an attorney tells the jury, "We have faith in your judgment and believe that you will reach the correct decision," the message conveys trust and openness. You would expect the attorney to lean forward toward the jury, with open and even expectant body language. If, instead, the attorney closes off his body language by tightly crossing his arms, turning his body away, and refusing to make eye contact, he is conveying non-verbally that he does not actually trust the jury. Other potential message-betrayers are gestures that indicate concealment or deception. Movements that appear involuntary, such as finger- and foot-tapping or fidgeting with clothes, convey uneasiness to the listener. Even gestures that may ordinarily strengthen a message, such as finger-pointing or fist-pounding, can do more harm than good if they appear overly angry or aggressive for the situation.

Finally, facial expressions are a key aspect of non-verbal communication that can be difficult to control, especially if the speaker is unaware of the expression he is making. Humans are naturally expressive and reactive through their facial expressions, but an advocate or leader may not want to show every emotion being felt. Learning to keep a neutral expression or one that looks engaged and anticipatory can be useful. Because there is often the potential for the unexpected to arise and surprise to come across your face, a useful advocacy skill is controlling your reaction to the opposition. Practice maintaining a neutral face that appears relaxed so you know what that expression feels like on you.

When you are trying to persuade, however, remember that interested and engaged facial expressions can help you. Showing interest and active listening makes clients and juries feel valued. You can convey surprise or anger without ever speaking a word. As with your body language and posture, become a student of how your facial expression speaks for you.

CULTURAL INTELLIGENCE IN EFFECTIVE COMMUNICATION

Communicating well means connecting with people effectively. That connection requires a certain level of understanding others. Connecting with those who have different life experiences and come from different communities can be challenging. "Most of us filter our communication skills and strategies through a limited lens that often does not translate across cultures and differences."[45] As leaders communicate with their followers and as lawyers build a relationship with their clients, they must be attentive to those differences.

The way in which people communicate (verbally and non-verbally) is framed by their worldviews and attitudes acquired through their culture. Culture is "a system of shared beliefs, values, customs, behaviors, and artifacts" that identify members of a society and are passed down through learning from one generation to the next.[46] It is "the lens through which we see and understand the world."[47] "Cultural groups can be based on a range of different identities including race, religion, age, sexual orientation, gender, immigration status, social status, language, and geography."[48]

Cultural intelligence or fluency is important to communications. The more pronounced the differences in backgrounds and worldview the more essential it is to recognize and value cultural differences and then adapt behavior in ways that convey understanding and respect. Kori S. Carew offers the following descriptions of some areas where cultural experiences will influence expectations.[49]

Direct versus indirect communication.[50] In direct communication cultures, priority is placed on precision, exactness, and efficiency. They rely on using words with explicit meanings that are simple and clear. In indirect communication cultures, common understandings or implicit meanings are sprinkled into messages. Communication relies on nuanced messages that are both stated and implied. Americans tend to be more direct.

High hierarchy versus low hierarchy.[51] People in high-hierarchy cultures are deferential to individuals with some type of authority. Low-hierarchy cultures are less class-conscious and emphasize individualism. A young lawyer from a high-hierarchy culture may be reluctant to speak in meetings and may be uncomfortable and underutilized in an environment that rewards *assertiveness*, as many law firms do.

Collectivism versus individualism.[52] Individualistic cultures emphasize a person's autonomy and believe that an individual should rely on personal power to succeed. In collectivist cultures, community comes first, family comes second, and the needs of individuals come last. The group's culture and obligation determine the decisions of each individual. Organizations that emphasize personal responsibility and self-determination can seem selfish to collectivist cultures, where duty to the group, cooperation, and collaboration are paramount. Competition thrives in individualistic cultures. Self-promotion and personal achievement are highly valued, and cooperation may not be necessary. An employee from a collectivist culture may appear unambitious if she waits for consensus in making decisions and relies on the collaboration of others. A gender difference is often observed here. Women's unwillingness to self-advocate may come from a cultural understanding that women should be more nurturing and less self-promoting than men. Some women experience repercussions for violating these cultural norms.

High context versus low context.[53] High-context cultures have a strong sense of tradition and rely on nuance and common understandings that are passed down and consistent throughout generations. Low-context cultures rely on stated words and rules to help newcomers understand expectations. High-context cultures tend to be more homogenous in race. Their traditions create unspoken understandings and loyalty. They have fewer rules and structures. They prioritize relationships and face-to-face communications. Conversely, low-context cultures rely on specific learning. "A low-context speaker may offend a high-context listener by being explicit about what the listener already understands and risks being interpreted as condescending. We see this in gender differences and cross-gender communication and leadership."[54]

Expressive versus nonexpressive.[55] The expression of emotion and the use of body language differ among cultures. Communication in expressive cultures is infused with drama, gestures, and vivid imagery. Other cultures frown on public displays of emotion. Leaders are expected to be contained, and body language is minimal. "American culture is typically more emotionally expressive than some cultures (e.g., Japanese culture) but less expressive than others (e.g., some Latin American and most African cultures). Imagine a female litigator described as hysterical because she was expressive, and imagine the effect on her career."[56]

Cultural humility. Failing to understand and interpret cultural and gender differences often results in miscommunications and failed leadership. Cultural humility requires you to open yourself to other people's identities in a way that acknowledges their authority over their own experiences.[57]

CULTURAL COMPETENCY IS INTEGRAL TO EFFECTIVE COMMUNICATION

ABA Rule 1.2(a): Scope of Representation and Allocation of Authority Between Client and Lawyer
[A] lawyer shall abide by a client's decisions concerning the objectives of representation and, as required by Rule 1.4, shall consult with the client as to the means by which they are to be pursued . . . .

ABA Rule 1.4(b): Communications
A lawyer shall explain a matter to the extent reasonably necessary to permit the client to make informed decisions regarding the representation.

Cultural competency is a critical skill for effective communication on any level. The ABA Model Rules expect lawyers to communicate effectively with their clients. However, they do not contemplate cultural or linguistic barriers. Lawyers should seek to understand the client's perspective in all communications and work to ensure the client has the full picture in order to "make informed decisions."[58] Consider the significance of a communication barrier, for example, at the negotiating table. Negotiations, including the participants' expectations and their outcomes, vary widely across cultures,[59] and the nuances of high stakes negotiation provide a clear illustration of cultural competency's role in effective communication. The consequences of negotiating while unaware of the traditions, expectations, or practices of the other party can range from missed opportunities all the way to unintentionally insulting behavior.

For those who negotiate in an international setting or with those from other countries, there are basic differences in approach that require awareness and adaptability. These include personal space, view of time, and conversation style.[60] As simple a task as standing or sitting at a mediation can trigger cultural issues, because individuals from different cultures have a greater or lesser need for personal space.[61] Sitting too close or seeming remote can influence the negotiation. How time is used or viewed is another issue; some cultures see time as very linear and structured, while others move at a more fluid pace.[62] Negotiators with an awareness of potential differences in cultural norms likely will be more effective. Their cultural competency better prepares them to meet these differences with an adaptable and patient mindset to help the parties come to terms.

British linguist Richard D. Lewis studies cultural communication patterns around the world, and in his book *When Cultures Collide: Leading Across Cultures*, he explores how cultural characteristics such as eye contact, pleasantries, and pragmatism impact a culture's norms.[63] Even countries with common heritage or geographic proximity, such as the United States and Canada, can take different approaches to negotiation.[64] Often, the subtle differences in body language and conversation structure can cause cross-cultural communication to fail.[65]

Determining cultural and national characteristics is inherently reductive, and there will always be individual exceptions. Lewis, however, insists on the importance of recognizing national norms in approaching cross-cultural conversation.[66] Illustrating the difference in flow, intensity, and duration of negotiation, Lewis's communication chart below provides insight into the wide variety of communication styles among cultures.[67]

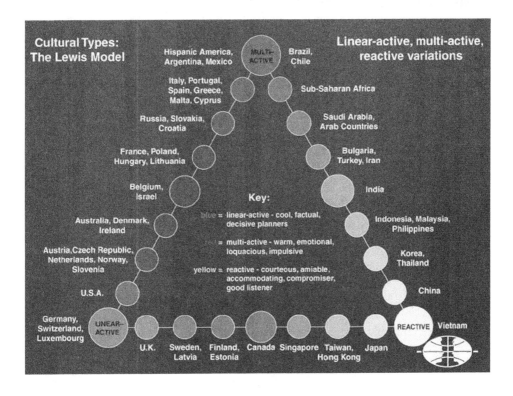

Lewis plots countries in relation to three categories:

> *Linear-actives* — those who plan, schedule, organize, pursue action chains, and do one thing at a time. Germans and Swiss are in this group.
>
> *Multi-actives* — those lively, loquacious peoples who do many things at once, planning their priorities not according to a time schedule, but according to the relative thrill or importance that each appointment brings with it. Italians, Latin Americans and Arabs are members of this group.
>
> *Reactives* — those cultures that prioritize courtesy and respect, listening quietly and calmly to their interlocutors and reacting carefully to the other side's proposals. Chinese, Japanese and Finns are in this group.[68]

Many of these nuances in style are subtle, rooted in a country's language and societal norms. The differences that make up a person's culture are learned by the person but also unconscious to the person. It is simply who he is and what he knows. Without an awareness of the influence of a person's culture and your culture's potential differences, communication can break down. For example, "frankness and directness in communication are a substantial value to the Americans and to a lesser extent to the French, but not to Mexicans in formal encounters, nor to Japanese at any time."[69] For example, Hungarians value eloquence over logic and are not afraid to speak over one another.[70] The Italians and Spanish also "regard their language as instruments of eloquence," taking a verbose, emotional approach to negotiations.[71] Negotiations in Singapore emphasize harmony, taking extended amounts of time to build trust before abruptly shifting to an aggressive discussion.[72] In Sweden, negotiations often embark on wide-ranging discussions before reaching a conclusion.[73] Each of these styles is in stark contrast to American communication, where expediency, logic, and succinct explanations are the norm. Someone from an Asian culture might be offended by the direct adversarial arguments presented by a colleague from the United States.[74] What Americans view as efficient and expedient may be perceived as rude by a person from China.

Where parties need to come to a common understanding of the issues and the resolution, such as a negotiation or client counseling session, an effective dialogue is required. Reaching a common understanding may be especially difficult when the parties have different native languages and relationship customs. A lawyer from the United States might make the mistake of assuming the silence of his Vietnamese client is an indication of consent to the proposal. The French expect to begin with the facts and principles on which a decision will be made. "Once this reasoning process is underway, it becomes relatively difficult to introduce new evidence or facts, most especially during a negotiation. Hence the appearance of French inflexibility."[75] As American lawyers, you are trained to adapt as new information is introduced and encouraged to be creative and malleable as a negotiation continues. When negotiating with the French, new information, ideas, and alternatives should be introduced early in the game.

Even when speaking the same language, cultural differences can impact negotiations. For example, British and Americans take very different approaches to negotiation because both nations have their own distinct communication style and strategy.

Americans approach the negotiating table with urgency and high stakes, unafraid of confrontation and eager to place all cards on the table.[76] The British, in contrast, value maintaining a light tone when negotiating, relying on subtlety and understatements to convey opinions.[77] Without attention to cultural differences, a conversation between citizens of these two nations, even those with much in common, could quickly lead to misunderstandings or offense. Approaching the discussion without cultural competency, an American could mischaracterize a calm British demeanor for apathy, and a British person could mistake an American's directness for aggression. Both sides enter the conversation with appropriate negotiation styles for their own cultures, but the negotiation may fail without recognizing the impact of the other's culture on communication.

Communicating in the day-to-day roles we play is important for relationships, courtroom success, and effective negotiations. The ability to communicate effectively, however, takes on heightened importance during a crisis. How, then, do lawyering skills get utilized when there is a genuine crisis or emergency?

LAWYERS SERVE IN IMPORTANT ROLES DURING A CRISIS

I'm sorry. We're sorry for the massive disruption [the oil spill]'s caused their lives. There's no one who wants this over more than I do. *I'd like my life back*.

Tony Hayward[78]

"I'd like *my* life back," was how British Petroleum (BP) CEO Tony Hayward ended several of his statements to the media following the *Deepwater Horizon* oil spill in the Gulf of Mexico.[79] The spill resulted from the explosion and sinking of the oil rig *Deepwater Horizon* on April 20, 2010, and released 4 million barrels of oil into the Gulf of Mexico over 87 days.[80] The disaster resulted in loss of life and severe personal injuries to rig personnel, and had a devastating environmental effect on the Gulf. BP reacted to the oil spill with a media campaign designed to minimize the public relations effect of the explosion, but Hayward's comment, made on June 1, 2010, was a disaster.[81] Not only did Hayward fail to acknowledge responsibility or express remorse, he equated his business inconvenience with the actual loss of life and limb for his employees and for the devastation to the Louisiana coastline. Hayward resigned as a result of the oil spill and the comments he made in dealing with the crisis.[82]

The BP oil spill saga is an example of what not to do in managing a crisis, and it is likely that at some point you will be involved in a crisis. Consider this adage: "There are only two kinds of organizations—those that have been through a crisis of some sort and those that are going to go through one."[83] While no organization wants to be involved in a crisis, all organizations need to prepare for one. Choosing the appropriate messaging and spokesperson is vital to crisis management. Surely if lawyers had been consulted, they could have explained to Hayward that saying "I'd like my life back" would be viewed unfavorably by other constituencies.[84]

Upping the stakes, crises often go hand in hand with litigation and media attention. In addition to the damage to the company's reputation, BP paid $14.3 billion to settle the litigation that resulted from the spill.[85] Lawyers play critical roles in planning for and managing a crisis, as they are equipped to advise their clients, advocate for them, and serve as spokespersons. "Business lawyers are familiar with the ground rules for managing legal crises in a court of law, but the stakes can be just as high when dealing with a crisis in the court of public opinion."[86] Lawyers are trained to stay rock steady in the storm experienced by their clients. Their dispassionate, analytical thinking, ability to assess and manage risk, and good communication skills serve well in time of chaos. Not surprisingly, lawyers who serve in leadership roles within organizations are called upon to be part of the team to manage the crisis and the related communications.

Crisis management is a critical organizational function. Failure can result in serious harm to the organization and its stakeholders. In the context of an organization, a crisis is any situation that threatens to harm people or property, interrupt operations, or damage reputation.[87] In crisis management, the threat is the potential damage a crisis can inflict on an organization, its stakeholders, and an industry. A crisis can create three related threats: (1) public safety, (2) financial loss, and (3) reputation loss.[88] Some operational crises, such as industrial leaks of hazardous chemicals, transportation accidents, and harmful products, can result in injuries and even loss of lives. Crises can create financial loss by disrupting operations, creating a loss of market share/purchase intentions or spawning lawsuits related to the crisis.

Lawyers have many roles to play in a crisis. They often need to coordinate the efforts and resources of the organization. If insurance potentially applies, the attorney may need to gather the different insurance resources and report the loss. Some insurance policies provide immediate funds to cover shortfalls; others have timeliness requirements about reporting. Ideally, an assessment of available coverage was done at the time the insurance was purchased, but if not, the attorney may need to dig into the fine print. In the wake of the MGM hotel shootings, the carriers provided funds for covering the immediate needs of victims and their families.[89] Not only was this the right thing to do, it also reflected compassion for the circumstances.

Attorneys are well suited to interview witnesses, gather documents, lock down extraneous commentary to the media, and otherwise preserve evidence.[90] Whether the organization anticipated litigation and acted accordingly can affect the attorney work-product privilege, and documenting the concerns can help later when the privilege is asserted in a lawsuit.[91]

Attorneys also can identify the steps that need to be taken immediately as opposed to those than can be delayed.[92] Time and resources need to be prioritized, and good counsel can help deploy those resources in the most effective manner.[93] Providing counsel may actually be the most important thing the attorney can do.[94] In times of crisis, people need to feel that there is a plan, that things will work out, and that the organization will weather the storm. Many New Yorkers looked to the daily briefings of Governor Andrew Cuomo during the Covid-19 pandemic for the factual content of those briefings, his no-nonsense assessment of the situation, and his calm messages of hope.[95] Blending fact, action, and hope helps organizations and people during a crisis.[96]

A crisis can reflect poorly on an organization and threaten to tarnish its reputation.[97] Managing the media becomes vital to the long-term health of the company.[98] Whoever speaks for the company sets the tone of the corporate response, and this also has ramifications for potential litigation.[99] Information provided to the media becomes an admission by the defendant and so, if shared prematurely, may cause problems at a deposition.[100] Allowing the CEO to be the spokesperson may create problems for a future deposition.[101] Having the attorney act as spokesperson has several benefits. The attorney tends to be a good communicator who can stay on message. The attorney has a sense of what might be used against the company in subsequent litigation and, if the attorney makes a damaging statement, the company can plausibly put distance between the attorney's actions and the company's conduct.

Careful thought must be given to messaging to ensure you take a reasoned approach. The legal department should be part of the crisis management team crafting strategy and language, especially when litigation is a possible concern.[102] As lawyers craft the message, they should keep the communication styles of different listeners in mind. If the message does not speak to all the communication types, the message may not be effective.

ABA Rule 3.6: Trial Publicity

(a) A lawyer who is participating or has participated in the investigation or litigation of a matter shall not make an extrajudicial statement that the lawyer knows or reasonably should know will be disseminated by means of public communication and will have a substantial likelihood of materially prejudicing an adjudicative proceeding in the matter.

(b) Notwithstanding paragraph (a), a lawyer may state:

   (1) the claim, offense or defense involved and, except when prohibited by law, the identity of the persons involved;

   (2) information contained in a public record;

   (3) that an investigation of a matter is in progress;

   (4) the scheduling or result of any step in litigation;

   (5) a request for assistance in obtaining evidence and information necessary thereto;

   (6) a warning of danger concerning the behavior of a person involved, when there is reason to believe that there exists the likelihood of substantial harm to an individual or to the public interest; and

   (7) in a criminal case, in addition to subparagraphs (1) through (6):

      (i) the identity, residence, occupation and family status of the accused;

      (ii) if the accused has not been apprehended, information necessary to aid in apprehension of that person;

(iii) the fact, time and place of arrest; and
(iv) the identity of investigating and arresting officers or agencies and the length of the investigation.
(c) Notwithstanding paragraph (a), a lawyer may make a statement that a reasonable lawyer would believe is required to protect a client from the substantial undue prejudicial effect of recent publicity not initiated by the lawyer or the lawyer's client. A statement made pursuant to this paragraph shall be limited to such information as is necessary to mitigate the recent adverse publicity.

Preparing the message is only half of the process. The top executives and designated spokespersons should receive media training to prepare them for "handling media inquiries and publicly communicating information under pressure — a little bit of professional training will go a long way when the time comes for those skills to be put to the test."[103] As these key people receive training on responding to questions, they should also be receiving training on speaking to each of the communication styles to ensure that their answers resonate with the audience no matter its makeup.

Here are some suggestions for those serving as spokespersons:

1. Avoid the phrase "no comment." People think it means the organization is guilty or trying to hide something.
2. Present information clearly and avoid jargon or technical terms. If you are not clear, people may believe the organization is being intentionally confusing to hide facts.
3. Appear pleasant on camera. Avoiding nervous habits that people interpret as deception. Be able to look at the camera; a spokesperson needs to have strong eye contact. Limit disfluencies such as "um" or "uh." Do not fidget or pace.
4. Brief all potential spokespersons on the latest crisis information and the key message points the organization is trying to convey to stakeholders.[104]

As the organization deals with a crisis, getting an outside perspective is always helpful.[105] Whether it be a trusted advisor, such as outside counsel, or a public relations professional, hearing from others about the other possible viewpoints regarding a crisis will help the team craft the right message and deliver it in the right way. Getting the message out clearly and effectively is difficult and often time pressured.[106] Organizations should always have a plan of action to implement if the situation ever arises.[107]

WORKING WITH PUBLIC RELATIONS PROFESSIONALS

When there is a significant risk of harm to the company's image and goodwill, the company may need to involve public relations (PR) professionals to manage the flow of communications related to the crisis.[108] The Public Relations Society of America (PRSA) defines public relations as "a strategic communication process that builds mutually beneficial relationships between organizations and their publics,"[109] by "influencing, engaging and building a relationship with key stakeholders across numerous platforms in order to shape and frame the public perception of an organization."[110] An important tactical and strategic function of public relations is media relations. "[M]edia relations is the systematic, planned, purposeful and mutually beneficial relationship between a public relations practitioner and a mass media journalist."[111] Lawyers often play an important role in media relations for a client during the management of a crisis. While the client may have hired a public relations professional, having a lawyer involved in the process will help protect the client from making ill-worded statements that affect the client later, such as in litigation or employment matters. As you interact with the different players in a crisis, having an understanding of their role will help you navigate the crisis in an effective and efficient manner.

Working with the Media

Never pick a fight with a man who buys ink by the barrel and paper by the ton.

Greener's Law[112]

It may appear that journalists and public relations professionals have an adversarial relationship, but if they know each other and have a good prior working relationship, the company can benefit from that trust.[113] Credibility and professionalism are at the heart of media relations, which means that the messaging from the company has to be trustworthy and the journalist reporting on it must be trustworthy as well.[114] Studies indicate the difficulties between the two professions can be overcome on an individual level, but widespread distrust continues.[115] Before hiring a PR company, then, the lawyer and the company need to vet the message managers to be sure that they help rather than hurt. Media coverage is an important part of managing the message, but social media allows public relations professionals to communicate directly with multiple stakeholder groups.[116] Having both an effective social media presence and strong relationships with journalists can help with credibility during a crisis.[117]

Messaging Advice from Public Relations Professionals

Great leaders are almost always great simplifiers, who can cut through argument, debate and doubt to offer a solution everybody can understand.

Colin Powell[118]

Public relations can play a critical role in preparing spokespersons for handling questions from the news media. The media relations element of public relations is a highly valued skill in crisis management. The public relations personnel can provide training and support because in most cases they are not the spokesperson during the crisis.[119]

Advice from PR professionals often includes the recommendation that organizations immediately take responsibility. This may not apply in all situations, and the company should seek legal advice about any such action and communications. If future litigation is possible, the company needs legal advice to avoid making a statement that admits liability. Here are excerpts of advice on handling statements to the media:

> [A] message of concern, sympathy, and compassion for those harmed or affected must be carefully reviewed to ensure it does not raise legal issues in matters of potential litigation. PR professionals recommend messages that are proactive with a sense of transparency to convene that they take responsibility, acknowledge people's concerns and questions, and respond appropriately and strategically. When put into action it looks like this: acknowledge the incident, accept responsibility, and apologize.[120]

> [S]tart communicating, apologizing, refunding, or whatever-ing now![121] Responses like "you'll look into it" do not satisfy anyone. Saying you're deeply saddened by what went down and will work on making things better is important. Then, immediately share how policies will be put in place so it doesn't happen again.[122]

> Extending a heartfelt apology is key to moving forward. Not doing so adds fuel to the fire and delays changing the narrative. Following a public apology, the company must offer a call to action. They must do something substantial to show that they are changing their ways moving forward.[123]

> Communicate all relevant details to key stakeholders. When asked to comment, never reply with "no comment." Even if you're still assessing a situation, simply say that. If you don't have a voice in the matter, people immediately assume guilt or make their own suppositions. Also, recognize when operational improvements are necessary and be transparent about how you're solving the situation.[124]

> Step back, put yourself in the consumers' shoes and ask, "How would I feel if this happened to me?" Looking in the mirror is the best PR advice there is when dealing with crisis situations. It ensures we do the right thing. And right beats spin every time.[125]

> Companies, brand representatives, or influencers often provide emotional, frenzied responses. Going silent on social media is not a bad thing when you are monitoring a crisis. Freeze all external communication until you can assess what's going on. Be sure that the first external communication following the crisis is a well-thought-out response that resonates with your consumers.[126]

Having a PR professional on the team in a crisis situation is tremendously helpful. As the lawyer for the client, you must remember that the client is ultimately responsible for the message. Your responsibility to the client is to provide advice about the advantages and disadvantages of any statement. Being available to help your client wordsmith any statement may save you and your client a lot of heartache in the future.

PROCESS FOR MANAGING CRISIS COMMUNICATIONS

The most fortunate of us all in our journey through life frequently meet with calamities and misfortunes which greatly afflict us. To fortify our minds against the attacks of these calamities and misfortunes should be one of the principal studies and endeavors of our lives.

Thomas Jefferson[127]

Crisis management is a process designed to prevent or lessen the damage from the crisis.[128] Crisis management can be divided into three phases: (1) pre-crisis, (2) crisis response, and (3) post-crisis.[129] The pre-crisis phase is concerned with prevention and preparation.[130] During the crisis response phase, management is actually responding to a crisis.[131] The post-crisis phase looks for ways to better prepare for the next crisis and fulfills commitments made during the crisis phase, including follow-up information.[132]

Pre-Crisis Phase

No one wants to be at the center of a scandal, but you may find yourself there. Scrambling around at the onset because you are unprepared to handle the scandal takes things from bad to worse. Whether fault is reality or perception, organizations must be prepared for such an event.[133] As the Forbes Agency Council puts it:

> The way you respond can either give you a much-needed image boost or significantly damage your brand, ultimately alienating your customer base and business partners. Especially in this day and age, when news goes viral almost instantly, organizations need to be ready to respond to any PR crisis quickly and efficiently, using all available platforms.[134]

The company needs to act quickly to protect the company's reputation.[135] Because of the organic nature of social media, companies can lose control of the message and the fallout, so there must be a plan already in place that anticipates the need for response and provides that response.[136] Preparing for any crisis requires that an organization spend time anticipating different potential types of crisis scenarios and establishing internal protocols for handling them.[137] The protocols should "outline who needs to be notified, your internal review process and the individuals who are authorized to speak publicly on your behalf."[138] The planning and preparation process allows crisis teams to react faster and to make more effective decisions. "Without a good plan ready to be deployed when the circumstances demand, you'll be playing catch-up from the outset of a crisis and will lose valuable time in the crucial early stages of a crisis while you hustle up a plan."[139]

Make sure you have an open line of communication with the employees and a channel in place for getting urgent news and information out to them immediately.[140] Make sure employees know whom to call and what to say when confronted by journalists or other third parties in the event of a crisis.[141]

As part of the crisis management plan, someone must be charged with monitoring news and posts about the organization and its product and people, using a Google Alert or something similar.[142] Organizations should be ready to message something immediately that is in line with the basic tenets of crisis communication, even before a specific strategy is developed.[143] Having some generic positive messaging statements available that can be rolled out in the early public hours of a crisis will help maintain control over the event and the brand.[144]

Initial Crisis Response

Effective crisis management handles the threats sequentially.[145] The primary concern in a crisis has to be public safety.[146] A failure to address public safety intensifies the damage from a crisis.[147] Reputation and financial concerns are considered after public safety has been secured.[148] Ultimately, crisis management is designed to protect an organization and its stakeholders from threats and/or reduce the impact felt by threats.[149]

Issuing a press release and social media posts can better control the situation and the message.[150] Here are some recommendations:

1. Be quick and try to have initial response within the first hour.
2. Be accurate by carefully checking all facts.
3. Be consistent by keeping spokespeople informed of crisis events and key message points.
4. Make public safety the number one priority.
5. Use all of the available communication channels including the Internet, Intranet, and mass notification systems.
6. Provide some expression of concern/sympathy for victims.
7. Remember to include employees in the initial response.
8. Be ready to provide stress and trauma counseling to victims of the crisis and their families, including employees.[151]

In 1996, the *New York Times* released tapes of some Texaco oil company executives making racist remarks and contemplating destroying evidence in a class action lawsuit alleging racial discrimination.[152] The relatively new CEO, Peter Bijur, released several public apologies the same day that the story broke in the *Times*.[153] Bijur also announced that an immediate investigation was being conducted by outside counsel into the employees alleged to have made the statements.[154] In addition to quick statements condemning the statements made by the executives, Texaco settled the lawsuit for a record-setting $176 million within two weeks of the story breaking.[155] Texaco's handling of the matter is cited by experts as a case study in how to respond to a crisis.[156]

Some crises call for reputation repair efforts.[157] Frequently, the published information and expressions of concern are enough to protect the reputation.[158] When a strong reputation repair effort is required, that effort will carry over into the post-crisis phase.[159]

Post-Crisis Phase

Damage control and reputation repair may be necessary for some short or long period after the crisis.[160] Keeping stakeholders informed will help restore trust.[161] Promoting positive results and reviews will be important to continued operations. Effective use of relevant Search Engine Optimization (SEO) keywords will help with

Internet searching. If you find information that is defamatory, incorrect, or slanderous, seek to have the negative webpages taken down unless the information has gone viral.

With any challenging situation and effort, time should be spent analyzing the response efforts.[162] Look for lessons that can be integrated into the organization's crisis management system.[163] The best defense is sometimes an effective offense.[164] In the world of crisis management, the effort to prevent a future crisis is a worthy investment of resources.[165] Pay attention to an organization's brand culture. A company that "treats customers badly likely treats its employees poorly too. Dig deep into organizational culture and service delivery and you'll find that new lows in brand experience always start at the top."[166]

In 1982, seven people in the Chicago area died from ingesting "cyanide-laced capsules of Extra-Strength Tylenol."[167] The Food and Drug Administration officials speculated that a killer had taken the bottles, injected the cyanide, and then replaced them in stores, while the Illinois Attorney General suspected a disgruntled employee in the Tylenol factory.[168] No matter the cause, the initial estimate of the disaster was that Tylenol would never recover from the scandal.[169] When the story broke, Johnson & Johnson, the parent company of Tylenol, immediately recalled 31 million bottles of Extra-Strength Tylenol and offered replacements of tablet-based forms of Tylenol to any consumers.[170] While this is a common method of dealing with consumer product defects now, it was unheard of at the time.[171] Tylenol also introduced tamper-proof packaging in an extensive media campaign as it relaunched Tylenol Extra-Strength.[172] These moves cost $100 million[173] (over $265 million in today's dollars[174]). As a result of the initial and post-crisis management and response, Tylenol recovered completely within a few years and serves as a case study for other crises today.[175]

Lawyers who are leaders in organizations are likely to be involved at each step of this process. While you are engaged in managing the crisis, be sure to keep your eye on the end goal as well. Create a plan with the end goal in mind and start executing it. Of course, "no plan survives first contact with the enemy,"[176] but it is important to have a plan with your crisis management strategy. Utilizing the communication styles and public relations strategy described above will help you navigate a crisis for a client.

CONCLUSION

Communication can inspire a group of persons to join a risky but promising venture. It also can destroy a family. A leader must be able to communicate well with others, which requires an effort to understand a person's experiences, desires, and worldviews. Words matter but so do tone, gestures, and posture. The more important the issue, the more preparation is necessary to convey the right message in the right way. Lawyers are trained to be strong communicators and advocates, but one must prepare for the specific audience and circumstances for those skills to be effective.

Preparation is also important to ensure an organization is ready to manage any crisis that threatens to harm people or property, interrupt operations, or damage reputation. Failure to plan can result in even more damage to the organization. Since lawyers play a number of critical roles in planning for and managing a crisis, lawyers should be prepared as well, and equipped to advise their clients, advocate for them, and serve as spokespersons.

Exercises

Media Exercise—Press Conference

Prepare and conduct a mock press conference about a current event of your choosing. Apply information you have learned from this chapter regarding communication styles (verbal and non-verbal), public relations, and crisis management.

Active Listening

This exercise demonstrates how difficult listening can be, and the importance of asking questions to help clarify understanding.

1. Have the participants get into pairs.
2. Ask each pair to arrange their chairs so they are sitting back to back.
3. Give one participant in each pair a piece of paper with a couple of shapes on it. The second participant should not be able to see his or her partner's paper (or anyone else's paper).
4. Give the second participant a blank piece of paper and a pencil.
5. Using only methods of communications as instructed, the second participant should try to draw his or her partner's shapes.
6. Have pairs compare their shapes and discuss ways they could improve communications for better results.

Journal Prompts

1. Describe what circumstances allow you to best speak with ease and confidence.

2. Describe what circumstances make it more difficult to speak with ease and confidence.

3. How has your communication style changed over time?

4. Do you change your speaking style when faced with different audiences? How so? Do you believe the change effectuates better communication?

5. How confident are you in your public speaking skills? What opportunities do you have during law school to strengthen or practice those skills? How might these opportunities be different from the role of spokesperson for an organization going through a crisis?

6. What did you find particularly interesting from the discussion about cultural communication patterns? Why?

7. The following questions ask you to reflect on the relationship you desire to establish with your clients. In many legal practice areas, lawyers want to be the first person their clients call when they have a crisis.

   a. What strategies will you adopt to establish that kind of relationship with your clients?

   b. How will you ensure that your clients know they are your priority in a crisis situation (such as the one in the media exercise)?

   c. How will you ensure that your clients know they are your priority during times of normal operation?

8. During a crisis situation, as the person responsible for reacting to the situation and being the spokesperson, what team would you want to assemble?

Endnotes

1. C.J. Redwine, Defiance (HarperCollins 2012). C.J. Redwine is an American young adult fantasy writer. Her notable works include the Defiance Trilogy and the Ravenspire series.
2. Mark Murphy, *Which of These 4 Communication Styles Are You?*, Forbes (Aug. 6, 2015), https://www.forbes.com/sites/markmurphy/2015/08/06/which-of-these-4-communication-styles-are-you/#533081363adb.
3. *Id.*
4. *Id.*
5. *Id.*
6. Brett Harned, *4 Communication Styles You May Find on Your Team (and How to Speak their Language)*, Team Gantt (Sept. 17, 2019), https://www.teamgantt.com/blog/4-communication-styles-and-how-to-speak-their-language.
7. Murphy, *supra* note 2.
8. Harned, *supra* note 6.
9. Adapted from Harned, *supra* note 6.
10. Murphy, *supra* note 2.
11. Harned, *supra* note 6.
12. Yaniv Masjedi, *4 Business Communication Styles and How to Work with Them*, Nextevia (Mar. 4, 2019), https://www.nextiva.com/blog/business-communication-styles.html.
13. Murphy, *supra* note 2.
14. Adapted from Harned, *supra* note 6.
15. Masjedi, *supra* note 11.
16. *Id.*
17. Harned, *supra* note 6.
18. *Id.*
19. Murphy, *supra* note 2.
20. Adapted from Harned, *supra* note 6.
21. Murphy, *supra* note 2.

22. Harned, *supra* note 6.

23. Adapted from Harned, *supra* note 6.

24. *The Seven Habits of Highly Ineffective Communicators*, 64 Tex. B.J. 378, 381 (2001).

25. *Saturday Night Live* coined this term in its humorous portrayal of the Bush-Gore debates. *Saturday Night Live, Presidential Bash* (Oct. 7, 2000).

26. The speech gets its name from Nixon's admission that the only gift his family received was a cocker spaniel named Checkers for his young daughters. Richard Nixon, California Senator and Vice-Presidential Candidate, Checkers Speech delivered in Los Angeles, California (Sept. 23, 1952).

27. John Townsend, *Paralinguistics: How the Non-Verbal Aspects of Speech Affect Our Ability to Communicate*, 9 J. Eur. Indus. Training 27, 27–31 (1985).

28. *See* David Margolicklos Angeles, *Simpson's Lawyer Tells Jury That Evidence "Doesn't Fit,"* N.Y. Times (Sept. 28, 1995).

29. Stewart Levine, *The Power of Leading an Engagement Effectively*, 21 No. 5 Law Prac. 42, 44 (2015).

30. Jennifer Post, *How to Develop a Positive Attitude in the Workplace*, Bus. News Daily (Oct. 1, 2019), https://www.businessnewsdaily.com/6912-develop-positive-mindset.html.

31. *Id.*

32. *Id.*

33. Celia W. Childress, *Body Language for Trial Lawyers: Persuasive Gestures, Postures, and Foot Movement in the Courtroom*, 84 Am. Jur. Trials 1 (2002).

34. Regina G. Carter, *Ready for the Next Century, Enhancing Professional and Personal Development*, 60 Tex. B.J. 347, 349 (1997).

35. *See* Charles F. Miller et al., *Body Language*, State Bar of Tex. Advanced Fam. L. 60 XXXI (2017).

36. *See* Pervez N. Ghauri, International Business Negotiations 124 (Emerald Publishing Limited, 2d ed. 2003).

37. *See id.* at 212.

38. *See id.*

39. *See id.*

40. Li Huang et al., *Powerful Postures Versus Powerful Roles: Which Is the Proximate Correlate of Thought and Behavior*, 22 Psychol. Sci. 95–102 (2011).

41. *Id.*

42. *Id.*

43. Amy Cuddy, *Your Body Language May Shape Who You Are*, TED (June 2012) *video available at* https://www.ted.com/talks/amy_cuddy_your_body_language_may_shape_who_you_are.

44. Sonya Hamlin, Now What Makes Juries Listen 121 (Thompson West 2008).

45. Kori S. Carew, *You Say Tomaydo, I Say Tohmahtoh: Why You Can't Improve Diversity Without Culturally Fluent Leaders*, 59 DRI for Def. 100 (2017).

46. Daniel G. Bates & Fred Plog, Human Adaptive Strategies 3 (McGraw-Hill College 1991).

47. Carew, *supra* note 45.

48. Sue Bryant & Jean Koh Peters, *Five Habits for Cross-Cultural Lawyering, in* Race, Culture, Psychology and Law 48 (Kimberly Barrett & William George eds., 2004).

49. Carew, *supra* note 45.

50. *Id.*

51. *Id.*

52. *Id.*

53. *Id.*

54. *Id.*

55. *Id.*

56. *Id.*

57. *Id.*

58. Model Rules of Prof'l Conduct r. 1.4(b) (Am. Bar Ass'n 2020).

59. Richard D. Lewis, When Cultures Collide: Leading Across Cultures (Nicholas Brealey Publishing 2005) (1996).

60. Lidi Albuquerque, *Different Cultures & Negotiation Styles Across the World*, BRIC Language Learning (June 2, 2014), https://briclanguage.com/guest-post-different-cultures-negotiation-styles-across-the-world/.

61. *Id.*

62. *Id.*

63. *Id.*

64. *Id.*

65. *Id.*

66. *Id.*

67. Jenna Goudreau & Gus Lubin, *23 Fascinating Diagrams Reveal How to Negotiate with People Around the World*, Bus. Insider (Aug. 14, 2015), https://www.businessinsider.com/how-to-negotiate-around-the-world-2015-8#australians-tend-to-have-a-loose-and-frank-conversational-style-19.

68. Gus Lubin, *The Lewis Model Explains Every Culture in The World*, Bus. Insider (Sept. 6, 2013), https://www.businessinsider.com/the-lewis-model-2013-9?IR=T.

69. Pervez N. Ghauri, International Business Negotiations 125 (Emerald Publishing Limited, 2d ed. 2003).

70. *Id.*

71. Victoria Guillén Nieto, *The invisible face of culture: why do Spanish toy manufacturers believe the British are most peculiar in business?* (2005), https://nemvat.com/the_invisible_face_of_culture_why_do_spanish_toy_manufacturers.pdf (last visited Sept. 25, 2020).

72. Ghauri, *supra* note 69.

73. *Id.*

74. *Id.*

75. *Id.* at 121.

76. *Id.*

77. *Id.*

78. Gus Lubin, *BP CEO Tony Hayward Apologizes for His Idiotic Statement: "I'd Like My Life Back,"* Bus. Insider (June 2, 2010), https://www.businessinsider.com/bp-ceo-tony-hayward-apologizes-for-saying-id-like-my-life-back-2010-6 (emphasis added). Tony Hayward was the former CEO of BP.

79. *Deepwater Horizon — BP Gulf of Mexico Oil Spill*, U.S. Environmental Protection Agency, https://www.epa.gov/enforcement/deepwater-horizon-bp-gulf-mexico-oil-spill (last visited July 14, 2020).

80. *Id.*

81. Lubin, *supra* note 78.

82. Tony Hayward, *BP's Tony Hayward: Resignation Statement*, The Guardian (July 27, 2010), https://www.theguardian.com/business/2010/jul/27/bp-tony-hayward-statement.

83. Author Leah Teague conversation with Bruce Gietzen, former KWTX news anchor and the director of student publications for Baylor University. Jan. 13, 2020.

84. Lubin, *supra* note 78.

85. EPA, *supra* note 79.

86. *Training for Tomorrow: The Court of Public Opinion: Best Practices for Attorneys in High-Profile or Crisis Situations,* A.B.A. Bus. L. Today (July 22, 2014), *available at* https://www.americanbar.org/groups/business_law/publications/blt/2014/07/training_tomorrow/.

87. Jonathan L. Bernstein, *The 10 Steps of Crisis Communications*, Management Help (July 22, 2020), https://managementhelp.org/crisismanagement/index.htm#ten.

88. Institute for PR, *Crisis Management and Communications*, Institute for Public Relations (Oct. 30, 2007), https://instituteforpr.org/crisis-management-and-communications/.

89. Autumn Heisler, *MGM's 800 Million Dollar Las Vegas Settlement Drives Home Mass Shooting Liability*, Risk & Ins. (Oct. 9, 2019), https://riskandinsurance.com/mass-shooting-liability-for-businesses/. In the experience of the authors, two years for such a complex case is a fast settlement.

90. Brandon Huffman, *Advising Clients in Crisis About the Media*, Lawyer Mutual (Oct. 26, 2018), https://www.lawyersmutualnc.com/risk-management-resources/articles/advising-clients-in-crisis-about-the-media.

91. Fed. R. Evid. 502.

92. John Allison, *Developing a Litigation Strategy for Your Case*, Nat'l Jurist (Sept. 14, 2018), http://www.nationaljurist.com/smartlawyer/developing-litigation-strategy-your-case.

93. *Id.*

94. *Id.*

95. Kevin Tampone, *Cuomo Offers Inspiration, Hope in Address to End Daily Coronavirus Briefings*, Syracuse.com (June 19, 2020), https://www.syracuse.com/coronavirus/2020/06/cuomo-offers-inspiration-hope-in-address-to-end-daily-coronavirus-briefings.html.

96. *Id.*

97. *See* Robert Dilenschneider, The Corporate Communications Bible (New Millennium 2000).

98. Huffman, *supra* note 90.

99. *Id.*

100. Fed. R. Evid. 801.

101. *See* Scott Mager, *CEOs Need to Understand How to Minimize Exposure to Depositions*, Mager Parúas, https://magerparuas.com/ceos-need-understand-minimize-exposure-depositions/ (last visited July 14, 2020).

102. Institute for PR, *supra* note 88.

103. *Id.*

104. *Id.*

105. Larry Clark, *Innovation in Time of Crisis*, Harv. Bus. Pub. (Mar. 26, 2020), https://www.harvardbusiness.org/innovation-in-a-time-of-crisis/.

106. Institute for PR, *supra* note 88.

107. *Id.*

108. *See id.*

109. *About Public Relations*, Public Relations Society of America (2020), https://www.prsa.org/all-about-pr.

110. *Id.*

111. Dustin W. Supa, *The Academic Inquiry of Media Relations as Both a Tactical and Strategic Function of Public Relations*, Institute for PR (Sept. 17, 2014), https://instituteforpr.org/academic-inquiry-media-relations-tactical-strategic-function-public-relations/.

112. William Greener, a press aide to President Gerald Ford and other political and corporate figures in the 1970s and 1980s called the admonition "Greener's Law." Ralph Keyes, Quote Verifier: Who Said What, Where, When (St. Martin's Press 2006).

113. Christian Fisher, *The Relationship Between Public Relations Practitioners and the Media*, Hous. Chron., https://smallbusiness.chron.com/relationship-between-public-relations-practitioners-media-67778.html (last visited July 14, 2020).

114. *Public Relations: Getting Attention to Polish Your Image*, Lumen Learning, https://courses.lumenlearning.com/clinton-marketing/chapter/reading-public-relations/ (last visited July 14, 2020).

115. *See, e.g.*, Jon White & Julia Hobsbawm, *Public Relations and Journalism*, 1 Journalism Practice 283 (Apr. 2017), *available at* https://doi.org/10.1080/17512780701275606.

116. *Public Relations: Getting Attention to Polish Your Image, supra* note 114.

117. *See* Paige Cooper, *How to Use Social Media for Crisis Communications and Emergency Management*, Hootsuite Blog (Mar. 27, 2020), https://blog.hootsuite.com/social-media-crisis-communication/.

118. Quotations from Chairman Powell, Government Leaders, GovLeaders.Com, https://govleaders.org/powell.htm (last visited July 9, 2020). Colin Luther Powell is an American politician and retired four-star general in the United States Army. During his military career, Powell also served as National Security Advisor, as Commander of the U.S. Army Forces Command, and as Chairman of the Joint Chiefs of Staff.

119. Institute for PR, *supra* note 88.

120. Quote by Lisa Allocca, Red Javelin Communications. Forbes Agency Council, *13 Golden Rules of PR Crisis Management*, Forbes (June 20, 2017) [hereinafter *13 Golden Rules*], https://www.forbes.com/sites/forbesagencycouncil/2017/06/20/13-golden-rules-of-pr-crisis-management/#3724918d1bcf.

121. Quote by Michael Levin, BusinessGhost, Inc., *13 Golden Rules*.

122. Quote by Nicole Rodrigues, NRPR Group, LLC, *13 Golden Rules*.

123. Quote by Leila Lewis, Be Inspired PR, *13 Golden Rules*.

124. Quote by Ashley Walters, Empower MediaMarketing, *13 Golden Rules*.

125. Quote by Kim Miller, Ink Link Marketing LLC, *13 Golden Rules*.

126. Quote by Coltrane Curtis, Team Epiphany, *13 Golden Rules*.

127. Letter from Thomas Jefferson to John Page (July 15, 1763) *available at* https://founders.archives.gov/documents/Jefferson/01-01-02-0004. Thomas Jefferson was an American statesman, diplomat, lawyer, architect, philosopher, and Founding Father who served as the third President of the United States from 1801 to 1809. He had previously served as the second Vice President of the United States between 1797 and 1801.

128. Institute for PR, *supra* note 88.

129. *Id.*

130. *Id.*

131. *Id.*

132. *Id.*

133. *Id.*

134. *Id.*

135. *Id.*

136. *Id.*

137. *Id.*

138. *Id.*

139. ABA, *Training for Tomorrow, supra* note 86.

140. Novid Parsi, *Communicating with Employees During a Crisis*, SHRM (Oct. 25, 2016), https://www.shrm.org/hr-today/news/hr-magazine/1116/pages/communicating-with-employees-during-a-crisis.aspx.

141. *See id.*

142. Meg, *11 Steps for PR Crisis Management*, Talkwalker (Jan. 15, 2019), https://www.talkwalker.com/blog/pr-crisis-management.

143. *Crisis Communication Strategy: One Size Does Not Fit All*, Institute for Crisis Management, https://crisisconsultant.com/crisis-specific-communication-strategy/ (last visited July 14, 2020).

144. *Id.*

145. Institute for PR, *supra* note 88.

146. *Id.*

147. *Id.*

148. *Id.*

149. *Id.*

150. *See id.*

151. *Id.*

152. Elizabeth Hoger & Lisa Swem, *Public Relations and the Law in Crisis Mode: Texaco's Initial Reaction to Incriminating Tapes*, 26 Pub. Rel. Rev. 425 (2000), *available at* https://www.sciencedirect.com/science/article/piiS0363811100000576.

153. *Id.*

154. *Id.*

155. *Id.*

156. *Id.*

157. Institute for PR, *supra* note 88.

158. *Id.*

159. *Id.*

160. *Id.*

161. *Id.*

162. *Id.*

163. *Id.*

164. *Id.*

165. *Id.*

166. Quote by Stephen Rosa, (add)ventures. Jade Minh, *The Golden Rules of PR Crisis Management*, Everything PR (Sept. 3, 2019), https://everything-pr.com/the-golden-rules-of-pr-crisis-management/.

167. Judith Rehak, *Tylenol Made a Hero of Johnson and Johnson: The Recall That Started Them All*, N.Y. Times (Mar. 23, 2002), https://www.nytimes.com/2002/03/23/your-money/IHT-tylenol-made-a-hero-of-johnson-johnson-the-recall-that-started.html.

168. *Id.*

169. *Id.*

170. *Id.*

171. *Id.*

172. *Id.*

173. *Id.*

174. *See, e.g.*, CPI Inflation Calculator, https://www.in2013dollars.com/us/inflation/1982?amount=100000000.

175. Rehak, *supra* note 167.

176. Quote by Helmuth von Moltke, a Prussian military commander, Oxford Essential Quotations (Oxford Univ. Press 4th ed. 2016), https://www.oxfordreference.com/view/10.1093/acref/9780191826719.001.0001/q-oro-ed4-00007547.

Chapter 19

How Organizational Structures Affect Leadership Roles

It is common understanding that communication is at the heart of any organization. So, why have organizational models not evolved accordingly? To truly leverage the potential of this information age, we need to rethink and redesign organizations.

Miguel Reynolds Brandao[1]

Purpose

Present the basic types of organizational structures and consider how different structures affect leadership styles and strategies.

Learning Objectives

At the end of this chapter, you should be able to:

- Describe the basic types of organizational structures and their decision-making processes.
- Discuss the effectiveness of different leadership styles in different organizational structures.
- Discuss which organizational structures work best for law firms.

Discussion

INTRODUCTION

Traditionally, law firms were staid organizations reluctant to change or break from tradition.[2] On the one hand, this suggested stability for clients.[3] On the other hand, clinging to tradition stifled innovation.[4] Recent cultural, financial, and social changes have created enormous pressure on the legal profession to alter its traditional approach.[5] This pressure originates from both inside and out. The number of law school graduates continues to climb.[6] The 2008-2009 recession resulted in economic pressure that left an extraordinary number of lawyers unemployed.[7] The more recent Covid-19 pandemic has created levels of unemployment not seen since the Great Depression, and the ripple effects through the legal industry on firms, courts, and clients are still unknown. Even before the latest round of unemployment, client expectations and demands, workforce diversifications, technology, information accessibility, attorney dissatisfaction and attrition, and globalization pushed for a new world of legal services.[8] To survive in today's legal profession, lawyers must "develop new and creative business models and ways of working seamlessly, collaboratively, and resourcefully."[9] "Long standing practices and policies . . . are being re-evaluated and modified to meet this new reality. Adapting to this *new normal* requires an examination of firms' people, systems, and processes."[10] Law firms may need to change fundamental aspects of practice, including the structure of their organizations.

Firms looking for greater efficiency must scrutinize their organizational structure because of its profound impact on the bottom line.[11] "Cold as it sounds, structure is more important for . . . performance than the people who fill its roles, because a bad structure will defeat competent individuals and a good one will generate overachievement."[12] Historically, law firms have lagged behind other organizations in realizing the importance of organizational structure.[13] This chapter looks at the basics of organizational structure both generally and in law firms, its influence on leadership styles, and the factors that influence which structure a firm chooses to utilize.

TYPES OF ORGANIZATIONAL STRUCTURES

Organizational structure describes both the manner in which a firm or business organizes its employees and how those employees interact with one another. Although we see increasing variety in organizational structures, the two primary forms are (1) vertical structures (also commonly referred to as tall or hierarchical); and (2) horizontal structures (also commonly referred to as flat).[14] A third, matrix structures, combines vertical and horizontal structures.[15]

Vertical Structures

In vertical structures, decisions filter down through the company from the top level, and are implemented via a narrow chain of command. While narrow, the chain can be long, with many layers of management between the top managers and ground-level employees. The manager oversees a small number of subordinates, and managers usually have little discretion to exercise independent decision making. This structure is useful for environments that prioritize detail and accuracy over speed. Employees are organized into departments and perform specialized roles on smaller teams, leaving little ambiguity concerning their role or the chain of command. Departments can be organized by function, geography, client, or another topic. Employees in vertical organizations are generally closer to their specific manager and find it easier to query them directly. Employees and managers become subject-matter experts, frequently performing the same tasks daily.

Vertical structures benefit from expert coordination, economies of scale, and long-term working relationships, which reduce transactional costs.[16] Communication in vertical structures can be slow, however, due to the number of layers of management. Directions passed down through many layers of management may also be subjected to multiple interpretations. Vertical organizations are more formal, traditional, bureaucratic, and less fluid or capable of evolving quickly to take advantage of industry changes. Vertical structures are common in larger, older, or more established organizations. Below is an example of what the organizational chart of an organization using a vertical structure may look like:

Vertical Organizational Structure

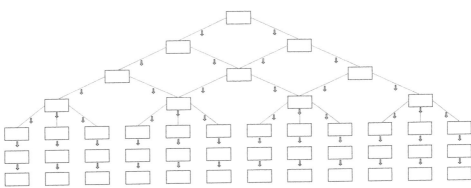

Horizontal Structures

In horizontal structures, decisions filter from the top, but the chain of command is wider, with fewer middlemen between top managers and employees. Individual managers in horizontal organizations oversee a higher number of employees than in a vertical structure. They are given more freedom to exercise independent decision making. Horizontal managers need greater latitude in decision-making power because the employees work on larger teams and handle a wider variety of tasks than their counterparts in vertical organizations. As a result of their greater range of responsibilities, managers and employees in horizontal organizations often have a deeper awareness of what the organization needs to function than do managers in vertical organizations. Horizontal managers gain a broader range of skills but also may lack the depth of expertise in a specific field that vertical structure managers acquire through repetition and specialization. Horizontal structures promote a culture of collaboration because employees at every level are more aware, involved, and responsible.

Horizontal structures place increased responsibility on a smaller number of managers. Some leaders may find this empowering as they can delegate and complete tasks much faster. Other leadership types may struggle, feeling less comfortable with delegating tasks or ceding control, and thus overwhelmed.[17] Horizontal structures are less formal, more modern, and better able to adapt to industry changes. Horizontal structures are common in smaller, newer, or less established firms.[18] Below is an example of what the organizational chart of an organization using a horizontal structure may look like:

Horizontal Organizational Structure

Matrix Structures

Growing in popularity, the matrix structure combines vertical and horizontal structures. A matrix uses two chains of command, and employees often report to two superiors. The chains of command are divided between functional activities and more traditional administrative activities but can be arranged in any number of ways. The leadership roles in matrix organizations are often fluid and work most efficiently when the leaders effectively share information for organizational success. Matrix structures attempt to employ the best of both vertical and horizontal structures to enhance their respective strengths and mitigate their weaknesses.[19] Below is an example of what the organizational chart of an organization using a matrix structure may look like:

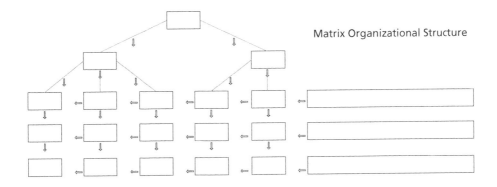

Matrix Organizational Structure

TYPES OF DECISION MAKING

The type of decision making an organization uses and its application influence how an organization develops both financially and culturally.[20] There are two primary types of decision making: centralized decision making and decentralized decision making.

Centralized Decision Making

An organization using centralized decision making consolidates power in a small group of individuals. Centralized decision making is more often found in a vertical structure. Since decision making is confined to one individual or a head office, decisions can be very detailed and finely tuned. The corporate values and decisions concerning finance and corporate image can be rendered as the owners or top-level managers prefer. Unfortunately, as businesses that utilize centralized decision making grow and enter diverse markets, their ability to adapt to local environments, and attend to those unique demands, diminishes. This type of decision making is less likely to succeed in new, emerging, or culturally diverse markets. Central decision making also significantly reduces the speed of decisions and slows the pace at which changes are implemented.

Decentralized Decision Making

The decentralized model distributes decision-making authority down or out to several groups to provide input or make the decisions. For organizations that need to adapt to changing environments to survive and succeed, decentralization allows more people to bring their ideas and suggestions to the table, with broader growth and engagement possibilities for the organization.[21] In business, this approach allows subsidiaries in different parts of the world or in different industries facing different issues, to apply specific solutions, unique to their situation. It enables businesses to keep their finger on the pulse of their market factors and adapt quickly to changes, which can be vital to success. The downside of decentralization, however, is that too many cooks can spoil the decision-making broth, making the process slower and more cumbersome than it needs to be. Conflict may occur when various divisions appear to have favor or enjoy more success than others.

Many organizations apply a complex mixture of centralized and decentralized decision making, applying the better strategy to specific tasks, such as using centralized decision making for designing products and services, and decentralized decision making for seasonal or local advertising purposes.[22] For example, McDonald's utilizes centralized decision making for purposes of controlling its brand, but recognizes that regional decision makers are better equipped to decide which products will appeal to local demographics. In China, McDonald's sells rice, sweet potato cakes, and Big Macs — only one of which is a traditional fare in the United States. McDonald's in France sells wine and Big Macs. In Israel, the restaurant provides separate kosher counters for meat and dairy menu items, but you can still create that Big Mac.[23] Similarly, Starbucks brews signature coffee drinks at their locations in Asia, but they also offer a more diverse selection of teas than is offered at their stores in Western countries, reflecting tea as a preferred choice of consumers in Asia.[24]

These brands benefit from strong global recognition because everything related to that brand from signage to the decor of their stores remains under centralized decision making. This combination of both centralized and decentralized decision making, sometimes referred to as "glocalization" or "selective decentralization," allows organizations to appeal to local markets while still benefitting from global brand recognition.[25] This combined decision-making process applies well to law firms. The firm as a whole controls the core identity while allowing different offices to specialize in what their region, city, or even country needs in terms of legal services.

LEADERSHIP STYLES

There is a variety of leadership styles and a number of labels for them. Not surprisingly, some leadership styles work better within one organizational structure than another. The six different leadership styles identified by Daniel Goleman, and how those styles interplay within the different types of organizational structures, are discussed below.[26]

Coercive Leaders

Coercive or commanding leaders, with their preference for extreme top-down decision making, are a natural fit for organizations with vertical structures.[27] Their reluctance to share information and work toward compromise is ill-suited to horizontal organizations, which rely on their leaders to share information freely to inform group decision making.[28] Coercive leaders may also perform better within vertical organizations due to the emphasis on standardization of processes. A vertical organization is better equipped to handle the high rate of employee dissatisfaction and turnover often associated with coercive leadership.[29] Coercive leadership is often blamed for suppressing the development of critical thinking among employees,[30] but this weakness can be mitigated by vertical organizations' reliance on standardization and specialized knowledge.

Authoritative Leaders

Authoritative or visionary leaders tend to be goal-setters and mobilize people through encouragement and enthusiasm.[31] Authoritative leaders are most effective when they do not micromanage their colleagues to get the work done after the vision has been explained. This style can work well within vertical structures unless the authoritative leaders are "working with a team of experts or peers" that have more experience or specialized knowledge.[32] In horizontal organizations, authoritative leaders can achieve impressive results and keep employee morale high by providing opportunities for employees to feel valued. Authoritative leaders in horizontal organizations, however, may struggle to communicate with their peers on the leadership team.[33]

Affiliative Leaders

Affiliative leaders develop rapport with their employees, cultivate comfortable professional relationships in which feedback is welcomed, and praise employees for their positive contributions.[34] This leader puts the employees first and believes that when the employees feel valued and encouraged the quality of their work will improve, resulting in benefits for the business as a whole.[35] Affiliative leadership encourages communication between employees and the free sharing of information.[36] Affiliative leaders are a good fit for horizontal organizations because of their skill at building relationships and consensus. Affiliative leaders' desire to maintain relationships and share feedback, however, can become problematic in vertical organizations, which tend toward large bureaucracies demanding strict compliance with top-down decisions. The "my way or the highway" approach is ill-suited to affiliative leadership.

Democratic Leaders

Horizontal organizations require leaders with well-developed democratic leadership skills who can build a strong sense of community in the leadership team and across the organization as a whole. Horizontal organizations are vulnerable, though, to the many downsides of this leadership style. Horizontal organizations with weak democratic leaders can find themselves in an endless cycle of meetings that resolve nothing. Employees can often be left feeling "confused and leaderless."[37] Democratic leaders, then, need to ensure that decisions still get made in a timely manner after input and collaboration from the team.

Leaders who prefer a democratic style may find themselves ill-suited to vertical organizations given the insistence on strict compliance with top-down decision making. This is not to say vertical organizations cannot benefit from democratic leaders. Vertical organizations often suppress feedback and criticism, but democratic leaders who encourage feedback and knowledge sharing can help improve standards and provide a clearer view of where the organization needs help and where it is excelling.

Pacesetting Leaders

Pacesetting leaders lead by example. They have high standards for themselves and their work and expect their employees to meet those same standards once shown how to implement the pacesetter's practices.[38] Pacesetters may find horizontal organizations a challenge because, although "[g]uidelines for working may be clear in the leader's head[,] . . . she does not state them clearly."[39] The pacesetter's tendency to leave employees in the dark can leave employees feeling overwhelmed and unsupported. This same negativity can also lead to good results if the horizontal organization has a talented and highly motivated team. The pacesetter's failure to provide clear direction enables employees to take ownership of a project and discover innovative ways of accomplishing tasks.[40]

Pacesetting leaders can work well within vertical organizations because those employees are often highly specialized, have fewer responsibilities, and follow more standardized procedures in completing their work. The fairly rigid hierarchy makes it easier for employees to meet the leader's exacting standards even in the absence of clear direction from that leader.

Coaching Leaders

Coaching leaders do not lead by example; they prefer to delegate, provide instructions and the opportunity to help others figure out the task, and follow up with detailed feedback.[41] The coaching style of leadership can work well within either vertical or horizontal organizations as long as the structure is one in which the coaching leader can develop personal relationships with employees or subordinates over longer periods. This relationship-driven style may work better in vertical structures made up of smaller and more intimate teams. However, this style takes a great deal of time to be effective. Coaching leaders may have trouble when situations demand decisive or quick action, which can be particularly problematic in vertical structures.

ORGANIZATIONAL STRUCTURES IN LAW FIRMS

Most law firms adhere to a basic structure with a top hierarchy of the firm's equity partners who share power on a one person/one vote basis. This may not reflect the true power dynamic within the firm nor the extent of ownership interest. Some firms have management committees and/or a managing partner to handle financial issues and resolve disputes or concerns. Depending on the partner and the firm, partner time is spent on legal work, developing client relationships, and supervising younger attorneys.

The next tier in the hierarchy is either the non-equity partners or the firm's associates. Both typically are salaried attorneys with less experience or who do not have a sufficient book of business to warrant an equity stake in the firm. These lawyers perform legal work under the supervision of the firm's partners and senior associates. They may be on the partnership track, being groomed to join the partnership, or they may be contract employees.

The firm's legal support staff including paralegals, legal secretaries, IT staff, as well as law clerks, runners, and so forth, form the remainder of the organizational structure. While some would argue they are the bottom tier, any lawyer worth her salt recognizes the vital role these employees fill. How much input the lower tiers have depends on the partner personalities and culture of the firm.

Equity partners who control their own book of business may be able to choose which associates and other partners they work with. Associates often work on multiple projects at once and can be assigned work by any of the firm's partners, although in a model where the firm has sections or teams, work generally stays in that unit. Associates are expected to manage their own workload while also engaging in client and business development as possible. Firms who place associates within specialized "practice groups"[42] have those associates under the supervision of a limited number of partners and work exclusively within one area of the law or industry. Legal support staff members usually work with and report to a set group of attorneys. In some firms, partners are expected to interview and hire their own support staff. In others, an office manager or human resource manager hires support staff and assigns them to an attorney or practice group.

Traditional Flat Structure

The traditional law firm is a decentralized, organic, flat structure that relies on the partners working together to reach consensus and share resources. However, economic forces through the years have required many firms to reconsider whether the traditional model is the best model in modern times.[43] Many law firms have turned to non-lawyers to help them organize and run their practices for now,[44] but with firms constantly looking to become more efficient, there is a growing need for lawyers who are business savvy.[45]

The traditional flat structure has many benefits. It permits firms to react quickly to changing economic and social environments. It encourages attorneys to be "self-starters."[46] It can also help build interpersonal relationships among the attorneys because partners have to constantly communicate and learn to work together to grow the firm.[47] Perhaps most importantly, the traditional flat structure can promote an environment of fairness because the firm's leaders (the partners) all share equal power.

There are also many downsides to using the traditional structure in a law firm. The lack of clear channels of authority common in the traditional structure can leave some associates feeling overwhelmed if partners do not communicate well with each other. Associates often feel enormous pressure to agree to help on every project they are asked to do and may be unsure which partner's projects to prioritize. Labor and processes can often require duplication if the firm's partners do not communicate among themselves concerning which projects have been assigned to which associates or which associates have already acquired specialized knowledge from previous projects.

Firms that adhere to the traditional model also commonly lack formal mentorship programs and rely on partners to voluntarily take on the responsibility of recruiting and hiring new associates. However, the emphasis on billing that is prevalent in most firms makes it difficult to incentivize partners to take on mentorship roles; instead they often opt to spend their hours at work racking up billable hours. The lack of formal mentorships can leave associates feeling unsupported and unappreciated, leading to increased job dissatisfaction and higher attrition.

Many traditional-model firms also lack formal compensation structures. Instead, employee compensation is decided by partner vote, which can lead to discrepancies in employee compensation that can breed employee dissatisfaction and tension in the ranks. On the other hand, firms with strong cultures that focus on transparency, fair employee compensation, and a shared sense of community can benefit greatly from the flexibility offered by this model. Finally, in the theoretical framework of the traditional model, power is divided equally among partners; the reality, however, is that many partners simply are not interested in participating in making the mundane decisions that occupy significant blocks of time. When the firm's other partners cease participating, the managing partners can be left feeling unsupported and too busy addressing administrative matters to manage their own billing and client relationships.

Firms that adhere to the traditional structure benefit from a strong focus on finding fluid personalities that "fit" and strong leaders who are skilled in democratic leadership, adept at managing meetings, and successful in building consensus.[48] In traditional firms with weak leaders, contentious factions can form within the firm and meetings can devolve into petty arguments.

Formalized Vertical Structures

As firms continue to restructure, many larger firms have begun to resemble large corporations more than traditional law firms, complete with separate legal practice departments and formal firm management structures organized into strict vertical hierarchies. These firms benefit from increased organization and better communication by being better positioned to take advantage of economies of scale. These firms often have centralized purchasing departments that can leverage the firm's size to obtain better prices for necessary services and products. Firms organized into more formal hierarchies can also survive poorer interpersonal relationships among employees because employees are separated into distinct departments and have fewer interactions with employees from other departments. Associates at firms with more formalized structures also commonly benefit from transparent criteria for advancement or compensation increases. Firms with more formal organizations are also better equipped to survive poor leadership because they rely more on processes than fit between personalities to keep business running smoothly.

Determining the Right Structure

There is no single organizational structure that works best for all law firms. It is not always apparent which structure would work best for a specific firm. The structure of a law firm must be flexible enough to permit it to evolve and meet the needs of its clients, many of whom are in industries that experience constant change (such as tech), yet rigid enough to forestall complete chaos.[49] When determining what structure is best for a particular law firm there are a few factors to consider, including the firm's size, age, use of technology, and its environment.

Size

The size of a law firm has an enormous impact on its organizational structure.[50] Most law firms start off as a small group of lawyers banding together to form a partnership. So long as the firm remains relatively small it can usually maintain a flat organization structure with the partners at the top all sharing power. However, as the size of the firm increases, the partners usually began finding it more difficult to reach a consensus (sometimes even on relatively trivial matters); the flat structure becomes increasingly inefficient. If a firm grows large enough, it will usually begin moving away from a flat structure and developing a more elaborate hierarchy.[51]

Age

The structure of a law firm is also significantly impacted by its age. As a firm grows older, it usually encounters a variety of issues that help it naturally develop better problem-solving techniques, which often take the form of formalized rules and operating procedures and a more hierarchical structure.[52] Partners also become more comfortable ceding control over certain aspects of the firm's management as the firm grows, and committees and departments slowly form to handle much of the day-to-day operations as the firm ages. And as partners grow their business and specialize, they can become more amendable to the creation of distinct practice groups that allow them to focus on the work that is most profitable or enjoyable for them.

Technology

Historically, the tools that lawyers used (a pen and notepad or typewriter) were not very advanced,[53] and lawyers primarily engaged in "unit production" (the production of small bespoke pieces designed to meet individual client needs).[54] This combination of low-tech tools and the need to produce specialized batches of work encouraged organic growth, informal working relationships, and resistance to rigid bureaucratic standardization.[55] However, in recent years technology has been transforming every segment of the legal ecosystem. Along the way, technology has "ended lawyer hegemony of legal delivery and, in the process, has helped debunk industry myths including: all work performed by lawyers is 'bespoke', only lawyers are competent to perform 'legal' tasks — as defined by lawyers, legal practice is synonymous with legal delivery, and 'every case is unique.'"[56] Technology has also impacted law firm's organizational structures. Many tasks once performed solely by lawyers are now being performed by legal support staff or service providers. The increasing need to utilize advanced technology and a variety of outside legal services has driven firms to develop more formal hierarchical structures to better take advantage of economies of scale and manage ongoing relationships with legal service providers.

Environment

A firm's environment can be measured by its stability, diversity of services, complexity, and hostility.[57]

Stability

Stability is the measure of how predictable a firm's work is.[58] Dynamic environments are those which require novel solutions and complex decision making by employees.[59] As a general rule of thumb, law firms are dynamic structures that tend to measure low on stability.[60] Moreover, customer demand is often unpredictable as the needs of a firm's clients are constantly evolving, which also encourages firms to remain flexible and informal.[61] However, the trend toward legal specialization has led to increased stability in some firms.

Diversity of Services

Diversity is the measure of a firm's range of customers, products, services, and geography.[62] A firm that serves distinct industries, or which specializes in many distinct areas of the law, is more likely to divide itself into units and develop formal hierarchical structures than firms with a more generalized practice.[63] Similarly, firms that serve a broader geographical area are more likely to have multiple offices and develop a hierarchical structure organized around different markets.[64]

Complexity

Complexity is the measure of the level of sophisticated knowledge a firm requires to serve its clients.[65] Complexity appears to be on the rise.[66] Businesses have increasingly grown their in-house legal departments, and their in-house counsel now commonly handle routine legal matters, so a business may require an outside law firm's services only for litigation and complex matters that require detailed technical knowledge.[67] The more complex the environment, the greater the need for flat, decentralized structures that permit lawyers greater freedom to meet the demands of the client.[68]

Hostility

Hostility measures the competition for clients and resources.[69] In hostile environments, there is more need for hierarchy and centralized decision making.[70] The legal industry is notoriously competitive and characterized by a high level of hostility.[71] However, the exact level of hostility a firm experiences fluctuates depending on practice area and geographic location. A firm with a "revolving door" practice in a small town will have less need for centralized decision making than a large firm in New York City that specializes in corporate mergers.

As firms grow and evolve they will usually move from being a flat, decentralized organization into a vertical hierarchical structure with equity partners at the very top who elect a governing committee or managing partner that is in charge of running the firm. However, these factors should be constantly evaluated to make an informed decision regarding the best structure for any particular firm.

CONCLUSION

Understanding organizational structures is important for leaders in any industry, including the legal profession. As firms face increasing economic and social pressure to become more efficient, the organizational structures they use will continue to be evaluated and tweaked. To thrive in this new legal environment, young lawyers need to understand how their firm is organized and what role they are expected to play within that organization. Law firm leaders also need to understand how the structure of their firm increases and diminishes the effectiveness of the different types of leadership styles in their toolbox.

Exercise

How Do Legal Organizations Function?

For those who worked or interned for a law firm or other legal organization, share with the group what you know about that organizational structure. How were departments organized (by practice, client, geography, etc.)? How did they organize their work? How did they structure the supervision of associate lawyers? Lead a discussion on the pros and cons of the structures and processes observed.

Journal Prompts

1. What kind of law firm structure do you believe would be a good (or better) fit for you? How do you think your view of the ideal structure might change as you gain experience?

2. Draw an organizational chart that represents the structure of an ideal firm.

3. What type of leader do you think would best lead in your ideal firm?

Endnotes

1. MIGUEL REYNOLDS BRANDAO, THE SUSTAINABLE ORGANIZATION (Createspace Independent Publishing Platform 2015). Miguel Reynolds Brandao has authored books and articles on strategic management systems, entrepreneurship, business brokering, and teleworking and has participated in several international events as a guest speaker.

2. Stephen Rispoli, *The Walking Dead: Psychological Biases That Keep the Billable Hour Alive*, U. ALA. SCH. OF LAW, J. LEGAL PROFESSION (Feb. 1, 2019).

3. *Id.*

4. *Id.*

5. Jane Harrington, *Organization Development in Law Firms: An Exploration of Opportunity, Challenge and Method* 4 (2013) (unpublished M.A. thesis, Sonoma State University); *see also* RICHARD SUSSKIND, THE END OF LAWYERS: RETHINKING THE NATURE OF LEGAL SERVICES (Oxford Univ. Press 2009); STEVEN HARPER, THE LAWYER BUBBLE: A PROFESSION IN CRISIS (Basic Books 2016) (2013); MITCHELL KOWALSKI, AVOIDING EXTINCTION: REIMAGINING LEGAL SERVICES FOR THE 21ST CENTURY (ABA 2012); MICHAEL TROTTER, DECLINING PROSPECTS: HOW EXTRAORDINARY COMPETITION AND COMPENSATION ARE CHANGING AMERICA'S MAJOR LAW FIRMS (Createspace Independent Publishing Platform 2012); JAMES MOLITERNO, THE AMERICAN LEGAL PROFESSION IN CRISIS: RESISTANCE AND RESPONSES TO CHANGE (Oxford Univ. Press 2013).

6. Karen Sloan, *Demand for Law Degree Continues to Climb Albeit Modestly*, LAW.COM (Aug. 5, 2019), https://www.law.com/2019/08/05/demand-for-a-law-degree-continues-to-climb-albeit-modestly/.

7. *See, generally, supra* note 5.

8. *Id.*

9. Harrington, *supra* note 5, at 4 (citing Deborah Epstein Henry, LAW & REORDER: LEGAL INDUSTRY SOLUTIONS FOR RESTRUCTURE, RETENTION, PROMOTION & WORK/LIFE BALANCE, Foreword, ABA (2010)).

10. Harrington, *supra* note 5, at 5 (internal citations omitted) (emphasis in original).

11. *See id.*

12. *Id.* at 12 (internal citations omitted).

13. *Id.*

14. Fred C. Lunenburg, *Organizational Structure: Mintzberg's Framework*, 14 INT'L J. SCHOLARLY, ACAD., INTELL. DIVERSITY 1, 1–8 (2012); Masahiko Aoki, *Horizontal vs. Vertical Information Structure of the Firm*, AM. ECON. REV. 971, 971–83 (1986).

15. *Id.*

16. Brian Bass, *Advantages and Disadvantages of Vertical Organization Design*, HOUS. CHRON., https://smallbusiness.chron.com/advantages-disadvantages-vertical-organizational-design-19024.html (last visited July 14, 2020); Bart Leahy, *Vertical, Horizontal, and Matrixed Organizations (And Why You Should Care)*, HEROIC TECH WRITING (Sept. 21, 2014), https://heroictechwriting.com/2014/09/21/vertical-horizontal-and-matrixed-organizations-and-why-you-should-care/.

17. *Id.*

18. WENDY WONG, INTERNAL AFFAIRS: HOW THE STRUCTURE OF NGOS TRANSFORMS HUMAN RIGHTS 53–83 (Cornell Univ. Press 2012).

19. Jason Westland, *Matrix Organizational Structure — A Quick Guide*, Project Manager (May 3, 2018), https://www.projectmanager.com/blog/matrix-organizational-structure-quick-guide.

20. Patty Graybeal et al., Principles of Accounting, Volume 2: Managerial Accounting (OpenStax Pressbooks 2019); *see also* M.C. Jensen & W.H. Heckling, *Specific and General Knowledge, and Organizational Structure*, 8 J. Applied Corp. Fin. 4–18 (1995).

21. Marshall W. Meyer, *Leadership and Organizational Structure*, 81 Am. J. Soc. 514, 514–42 (1975).

22. Lunenberg, *supra* note 14.

23. Hyo Jin Jeon et al., *Cultural Convergence in Emerging Markets: The Case of McDonald's in China and India*, 54 J. Small Bus. Mgmt. 732, 732–49 (2016); Uri Ram, *Glocommodification: How the Global Consumes the Local — McDonald's in Israel*, 52 Current Soc. 11, 11–13 (2004).

24. *Id.*

25. Hung-Che Wu, *What Drives Experiential Loyalty? A Case Study of Starbucks Coffee Chain in Taiwan*, 119 Brit. Food J. 468, 468–96 (2017).

26. Mary Uhl-Bien & Michael Arena, *Leadership for Organizational Adaptability: A Theoretical Synthesis and Integrative Framework*, 29 Leadership Q. 89, 89–104 (2018).

27. Deborah L. Rhode, Lawyers as Leaders 12–21 (2013).

28. *Id.*

29. *Id.*

30. Rosa R. Krausz, *Power and Leadership in Organizations*, 16 Transactional Analysis J. 85, 85–94 (1986); Dimitri Landa & Scott Tyson, *Coercive Leadership*, 61 Am. J. Pol. Sci. 559, 559–74 (2017).

31. Rhode, *supra* note 27, at 12–29.

32. *Id.*

33. Stephen Dinham, *Authoritative Leadership, Action Learning and Student Accomplishment*, Austl. Council Educ. Res. 33, 33–39 (2007); N. Iqbal et al., *Effect of Leadership Style on Employee Performance*, 5 Arabian J. Bus. Mgmt. Rev. 146 (2015).

34. Rhode, *supra* note 27, at 12–29.

35. *Id.*

36. *Id.*

37. *Id.*

38. *Id.*

39. *Id.*

40. *Id.*

41. *Id.*

42. LexisNexis Legal Business Community Staff, *Practice Groups as Part of Organizational Structure*, LexisNexis (Jan. 27, 2010), https://www.lexisnexis.com/legalnewsroom/legal-business/b/strategy/posts/section-2-11-of-how-to-manage-your-law-office-practice-groups-as-part-of-organizational-structure.

43. Susan S. Samuelson, *The Organizational Structure of Law Firms: Lessons from Management Theory*, 51 Ohio St. L.J. 645, 563 (1990).

44. Susan Balzer Spoerk, *Organizational Culture in Wisconsin Large Law Firms*, 36 Coll. Prof. Studies Prof. Projects 29 (2011).

45. *Id.*

46. Interview with Michael Miller, Former Managing Partner, Lowther Johnson Attorneys at Law (2020).

47. *Id.*

48. *Id.*

49. Spoerk, *supra* note 44, at 647.

50. *Id.* at 657.

51. *Id.*

52. *Id.* at 658.

53. *Id.*

54. *Id.*

55. *Id.*

56. Mark A. Cohen, *Lawyers and Technology: Frenemies or Collaborators?*, Forbes (Jan. 15, 2018), https://www.forbes.com/sites/markcohen1/2018/01/15/lawyers-and-technology-frenemies-or-collaborators/#1db4f2ed22f1.

57. Spoerk, *supra* note 44, at 659.

58. *Id.*

59. *Id.*
60. *Id.*
61. *Id.*
62. *Id.* at 659.
63. *Id.*
64. *Id.* at 660.
65. *Id.*
66. *Id.*
67. *Id.*
68. *Id.*
69. *Id.*
70. *Id.*
71. *Id.*

Chapter 20

How Leaders Manage Effectively

Make sure you're not just waiting for someone else to fix things, or hoping that things will improve . . . . Figure out what's going on and make a plan to improve things.

Kenneth Thomas[1]

Purpose

Promote efficient operations by dedicating time to building relationships with people in the organization, encouraging a commitment to the mission of the organization, appropriately delegating tasks and employing processes for smooth operation of meetings.

Learning Objectives

At the end of this chapter, you should be able to:

- Describe the relationship between an employee's loyalty to the mission of the organization and advancement within the organization.
- List specific processes to improve the efficiency of a meeting.
- Utilize the SMART technique for delegating work.
- Identify strategies to build relationships.
- Identify key aspects of giving evaluations.

Discussion

INTRODUCTION

No matter how good the team or worthy the goal, at some point, someone must take responsibility that the details are handled. Attributed to Benjamin Franklin (among others) is this proverb:

> For the want of a nail, the shoe was lost,
> For the want of a shoe, the horse was lost,
> For the want of a horse, the rider was lost,
> For the want of a rider, the battle was lost,
> For the want of a battle, the kingdom was lost,
> And all for the want of a horseshoe-nail.[2]

Like the proverbial missing nail, details matter. Every leader should be proficient in running the day-to-day operations of an organization. Good leaders must take ownership of execution. They often delegate to managers or team members so that the tasks are handled efficiently, but at the end of the day, the leader is responsible for ensuring the work is done. Attending to the details of operation is not always a glorious or prestigious job, but it is vital to organizational success. While we describe leaders as visionaries, that vision sputters if no one sees it to fruition. This chapter addresses some of the mechanical aspects of everyday leadership, which include being responsive and responsible, being clear in your expectations of others, running efficient, productive meetings, and building relationships based on trust and integrity.

KEEPING THE INTERESTS OF THE ORGANIZATION FRONT AND CENTER

Fans of *Hamilton* and history know that Alexander Hamilton desperately wanted to earn fame and glory on the battlefield. Early in the Revolutionary War, Hamilton left King's College (now Columbia) to organize and lead a raid to steal British heavy guns from Manhattan in 1775.[3] As Hercules Mulligan, one of Hamilton's close friends, recalled, "I was engaged in hauling off one of the cannons, when Mister Hamilton came up and gave me his musket to hold, and he took hold of the rope. . . . Hamilton [got] away with the cannon."[4] At the end of the raid, a group of volunteer militiamen had stolen 21 of 24 of the heavy guns.[5]

Hamilton's intellect, courage, and determination drew the attention of General George Washington, who recruited Hamilton to be one of his aides-de-camp. In this role, Hamilton assisted the general with battle strategy, organizing and administering the revolutionary forces, and correspondence with Congress.[6] General Washington needed Hamilton's brilliant strategic mind and prolific writing skills to win the war.

Hamilton's leadership in the Revolutionary War continued throughout his life. Hamilton poured himself into each role, whether it be militiaman, staff for General Washington, field commander, Secretary of the Treasury, or lawyer. Hamilton was determined to get the tasks done. He held firm beliefs about the right things to do and set about to do them. Hamilton was a master of seeing the big picture and being able to explain the vision, but also of seeing all the details that needed to be accomplished to achieve the goal.

In the book *Extreme Ownership: How Navy SEALs Lead and Win*, authors Jocko Willink and Leif Babin take their military experience and translate it to the workplace environment.[7] Both are former Navy SEALs who discuss the lessons learned on the battlefield, and distill them into principles that apply in their personal and professional lives. At the core of their approach is the belief that each person on the team should have "extreme ownership" of the mission, that every person is integral to the mission and should have a "do what it takes to achieve" mindset.

Adopting that type of mindset at the workplace requires commitment to the mission of your organization (whether it's a company, law firm, nonprofit, governmental agency, etc.), the specific project you are working on (a case at the firm, a new contract for the company, etc.), and the welfare and productivity of the entire team as you carry out your duties. This requires that you constantly reevaluate the situation to ensure that the goals of the organization, your team, and your project are being met.

Another way to approach this is by acting as if you had a fiduciary responsibility to the organization. Fiduciaries must act with the beneficiary's best interest in mind, applying a standard of the highest care.[8] Regarding yourself as a fiduciary of your organization — even when it is not required — adds a layer of responsibility. Staying true to the mission and guided by your North Star, you will be prepared for whatever situation comes your way.

Consider this example. A law firm faced a difficult situation. The night before trial started, the team discovered that instead of sending five copies of the trial exhibits (as required by the court's pretrial order), the document company sent only one copy. It was 9:00 p.m. The team — along with four more copies of the 231 exhibits — had to be at the courthouse at 8:00 a.m. the next morning. The natural response from the lead lawyer would have been to ask how this could have happened, why no one had checked the order, and generally berate everyone involved in the error. Instead, she picked up one of the boxes of exhibits and said, "Then I guess we'd better start making some copies." Every lawyer on the team, every paralegal, and every administrative assistant, pitched in and got the job done.[9]

Several important management lessons come from this story. First, yelling at your team for a mistake when there is a tight deadline accomplishes nothing. If your team is any good, the members *know* there has been a mistake and already feel bad about it.

Second, when the mission is at a critical state (the exhibits had to be copied and ready to go), that means "all hands on deck." Third, a leader pitching in to do the "grunt" work sends a strong message that you really are a team. And fourth, your mindset should be on keeping the client's interest protected and the firm's credibility with the client, opposing counsel, and the court, firmly intact. The better time to discuss where the process broke down — where the mistake happened — is after the trial is over.

THE MOVE FROM STRATEGY TO EXECUTION: HOW TO RUN A TEAM

Strategies most often fail because they aren't well executed.

Larry Bossidy[10]

Leaders envision goals for the organization, but not all leaders know how to move from a wish to a plan. Turning that vision into a strategic plan of action, with specific objectives, goals, and action steps requires management skills to translate that vision into organizational behavior and action.[11] Managers, especially those close to the front lines, are critical in turning a compelling vision into objectives, objectives into goals, goals into action. Without effective management, the execution will not follow and the vision will die.[12] As Jamie Dimon, CEO of JPMorgan Chase, stated, "I'd rather have a first-rate execution and second-rate strategy any time than a brilliant idea and mediocre management."[13]

What follows are some practical tips for the everyday but vitally important tasks of operating a vibrant and productive organization: running meetings, learning to delegate, accountability, evaluation, and building relationships.

Running Meetings

The best meetings get real work done. When your people learn that your meetings actually accomplish something, they will stop making excuses to be elsewhere.

Larry Constantine[14]

In every organization and human culture of record, people come together regularly in small groups at frequent intervals and in larger "tribal" gatherings from time to time. Without work meetings, people do not connect well to the organization; they will not be engaged members of the team.[15] A meeting defines the team in that those present belong to it; those absent do not.[16] Meetings provide an opportunity to share individual knowledge so that it becomes collective knowledge. This school of thought helps members do their jobs more intelligently, but also greatly increases the speed and efficiency of all communications.[17] When the combined experience, knowledge, judgment, authority, and imagination of a half dozen people are brought to bear on issues, ideas are born, plans are improved, tasks are accomplished, and sometimes organizations are transformed.[18]

Given that meetings are an avenue for ideas to be transformed, they should be structured to encourage participation.[19] Good leadership makes the meeting's objective clear. Before the meeting begins, an effective leader knows what the meeting is intended to accomplish, and by the time the meeting is over, whether that objective was met. With a set agenda, the team members know why they gathered and what they are supposed to accomplish.[20]

The objectives for just about any meeting fall into one of the following three categories: informative-digestive, constructive-originative, and executive responsibilities.[21] For an informative-digestive meeting, purely factual information may be better shared in a document; a meeting is unnecessary. Some information is communicated better in person, particularly if it is likely to generate questions or require clarification such as when the information is dense or has broader implications. Introducing a new employee health plan might require a meeting if the plan is changing significantly; otherwise, circulating a summary of new plan features should be enough. The constructive-originative function taps into the creative process. In this type of meeting, team members can contribute to the discussion.[22] As the ideas are fleshed out, the executive in charge decides who is responsible for the next steps and what are the deadlines.[23] The execution of executive responsbilities could be done outside the meeting, but discussing delegation in the meeting allows for collective input and gives each member a better understanding of how his or her piece fits into the bigger puzzle.

In contrast to some of the meetings described above, everyone has been part of unproductive meetings. Nothing is getting accomplished, and team members are counting the minutes until it ends so they can return to the matters they deem a more valuable use of their time. A similar time waster is the endless meeting. Even if necessary to move the project forward, the meeting takes far more time than is needed to accomplish the goal. Both of these problems can happen if the person leading the meeting does not control the time, process, and agenda. Lawyers, especially, are deadline-driven, which makes efficient meetings crucial. Well-run meetings serve an accountability function. Regular meetings ensure forward movement of a project in a timely manner.

The good news is that running effective meetings is a learnable skill that can be developed. Robert's Rules of Order provides a comprehensive set of rules regarding running meetings for an organization.[24] The following simple steps ensure everyone is prepared for the meeting and the meeting time is as productive as possible.[25]

1. *Setting the meeting.* Set the meeting at a time when others can attend. There are several ways to do this. If a small group is involved, check with the others ahead of time. If a larger group is involved, check with the key players — those whose presence is essential. Set the meeting with enough advance notice that is reasonable and courteous to ensure that at least most of the others can attend. Of course, if it is an emergency, the team leader will likely have to call the members of the team to get everyone on the same page (or in the same space — physical

or virtual) as quickly as possible. By the same token, if the team meets on a regular basis, set aside a dedicated day and time for the meeting so that it remains calendared for the team.

2. *Send the agenda and any supporting materials.* Send an agenda in advance of the meeting. The purpose of the agenda is to let others know what will be discussed and provide an order to the meeting. Be realistic with the agenda items, keeping in mind the time that you have for the meeting. No one appreciates meetings scheduled for an hour that drag on for two hours.

   At this point, follow up with those who are being asked to report on agenda items to ensure they are prepared for the conversation. You also should provide an expectation for how much of the meeting time is allocated to their agenda items. An agenda also allows the leader to seek input about items that need to be added, removed, or tabled in advance of the meeting. The agenda organizes the meeting so that the most important matters will be covered in the time allowed.

   Send a reminder of the meeting along with any materials for review sufficiently in advance of the meeting so that both can be reviewed. Whether that is a day or a week will depend on the nature of the materials, the agenda items, and the urgency of the issues. Sending an agenda 20 or 30 minutes before the meeting rarely gives attendees time to be adequately prepared. For those attending virtually, include the link or phone number for their convenience.

3. *Running the meeting.* How the meeting is conducted largely depends on the leader's particular style. The leader's primary job is to keep the conversation progressing through the agenda while managing the time allocated to the different contributions. Be sure to bring the agenda to the meeting and follow the items. Think about the following before and during the meeting:

   a. Is this meeting subject to the "open meetings act" in your state? Meetings connected to governmental entities are usually subject to such an act, which generally requires that certain aspects of the meeting must be made accessible to the public. If so, make sure you are in compliance.

   b. Are you prepared for the meeting? (This applies whether you are leading the meeting or not.)

   c. Be aware of the time—are you getting through the agenda?

   d. Are you running out of time? Are there any items you won't get to?

      i. What will you do when you realize this? Try to notify the others as soon as you recognize the issue and rearrange the agenda to deal with the most urgent and time-sensitive items.

      ii. If the meeting is a public one, has anyone come to the meeting who will not be heard? If so, how can you address the situation to be mindful of that person's time?

   e. When wrapping up an item on the agenda, do a quick recap of what was decided, agreed upon, left for another day, or remains in dispute.

   f. Ensure that good notes (or "minutes") are being taken by someone in the group.

4. *Managing the conversation.* In many meetings, it is important to ensure that the conversation is moving forward and that others are being heard. There are two categories of people that may need special attention: those who are being quiet and those who are being difficult.

   For the quiet ones who are not engaged, ask yourself why that person is being quiet. What is she thinking but not saying? Is she intimidated by the environment? Is there an issue outside the meeting that is distracting her? Attend to any cultural influences or barriers to ensure all persons feel included and valued. You want to hear from all interested parties to get the best decisions possible.

   For the difficult people at the meeting, you typically know who might need more attention to maintain order and to keep the conversation moving in a positive manner. If someone does try to hijack the meeting, stifle the discussion, or bully another participant, ask yourself why that person is acting that way. Is that person unaware of the way that he affects others? Does he think this is acceptable behavior? Is he having trouble being understood or getting his point(s) across? Or is that person just an unhappy soul? Is there something about his life experience or cultural background that explains the behavior and requires consideration and understanding by the rest? In your first encounter with such a person, it may be difficult to deal with the situation in an effective manner. Always remember to criticize in private and praise in public!

5. *Follow-up to the meeting.* After the meeting, it is critical that everyone who attends understands items discussed and the next steps planned. Quickly completing and distributing the minutes is a good practice. Follow up with any member with assigned tasks to see if she needs anything as she moves forward. If more work is required, set up the next meeting.

Learning to Delegate

Never tell people how to do things. Tell them what to do, and they will surprise you with their ingenuity.

General George S. Patton[26]

One of the more difficult transitions is the shift from doing to leading.[27] Leading a team through the execution of goal-oriented plans is the real job of running a workplace. Formulating a "vision" but assuming others will execute it without further structure is a surefire way to fail. Similarly, refusing to delegate and trying to do all the work alone leads to burnout if not outright failure. The skill of delegating — pushing power downward and across the organization — empowers people at all levels to make decisions and accomplish the team's goals. Through effective delegation and feedback, you will develop your team's self-sufficiency, which allows you to focus on those items that cannot or should not be delegated. Delegation is not a management technique that lets the boss work less; on the contrary, the leader generally carries the heaviest burdens.

Delegation is an effective tool to move the work to the best and most efficient personnel on the team, which allows all the team to participate.

In law school, you probably have already experienced team members who did not do their part, leaving others to pick up the slack. You also may have seen a person take on the entire group project to be sure the project was done "right." You may have been that person. Both situations demonstrate failures in appropriate management and delegation. The work that was delegated in the first situation did not get done, either because the team members were not held accountable or because they lacked the skills to do the work. The second broke down because of a refusal to delegate. When the team is not accomplishing goals, the breakdown can occur with the delegation of responsibility or in the accountability of the person or group for the work. As a team leader, you must be ready with strategies to prevent either scenario and protect the work flow.

The SMART acronym has been applied across a broad range of business strategies, because it seeks to focus the given inquiry into a usable, practical format.[28] You may have seen this used in goal setting as a way to test whether a goal has a likelihood of success. In the delegation setting, team leaders can use the SMART process to ensure that the work is being delegated appropriately to the right team members in a way that helps them understand what is being expected of them.

Specific ⇒ Measurable ⇒ Achievable ⇒ Relevant ⇒ Timebound

When you delegate tasks that are specific, measurable, achievable, relevant, and timebound, you provide well-defined expectations for the work.[29] A *specific* task has a clearly defined rubric of what the task is and how and why it needs to be accomplished. For example, a specific task assigned to a young associate might be to draft a traditional motion for summary judgment on the statute of limitations in a given case. A *measurable* task has a method for evaluation of progress. The partner might say, "Send me your draft of the motion in a format you believe is ready to be filed with the court." An *achievable* task defines likely obstacles but has realistic solutions. The motion is achievable but may require the associate to do some legal research; obtain documents, including an affidavit from the client; and check the court's local rules to be sure the draft motion meets the requirements for this court. The task also must be *relevant*, including a connection to core values, along with a clear *timeline* of the steps needed to complete the task.[30] In the example of the summary judgment motion, the firm's core values include representing a client's interests zealously and economically. Filing a well-conceived and legally appropriate motion for summary judgment can save the client time and money in defending litigation. Giving a realistic timetable for the delegated project includes both a deadline for when the work is due to the partner and the court's deadline for when such motions need to be filed, responded to, and set for hearing. This type of assignment should allow a young associate to succeed in this project.

Using the SMART process helps the delegation work better. The leader, however, needs to spend some time considering the following issues before she delegates:

1. *Start with "why delegate?"* Why should the task be delegated? Can it be done more inexpensively by someone else? Could the leader's time be used more effectively elsewhere? Asking whether it would be easier to do it yourself is not really the right question. While the leader may be able to do tasks more easily, research shows that lawyers who delegate earn more and get more done.[31] Effective delegation demonstrates that you know your strengths and weaknesses, and the value of your time.[32] It also acknowledges that others have different strengths and weaknesses, which make them better fits for certain tasks. Delegating allows others to advance their skills and shine.[33]

2. *Identify what to delegate.* Not everything needs your personal time and attention.[34] Identify the parts of the task someone else can do and prioritize. Assign the more crucial or challenging tasks to those in whom you have faith that the work will be done, and done well. Give others opportunities to start with small, low-risk tasks until they have proven ready for more.[35]

3. *Define expectations.* Take time to determine and clearly communicate your expectations in terms of process, work product, and timeline. Provide opportunities for questions about the project and a process for further questions. Share enough direction to explain what you need but leave space for them to take ownership. As General Patton noted in the quote above, "Tell them what to do, and they will surprise you with their ingenuity."

4. *Empower them to work.* Those to whom you delegate responsibility must also have the authority to carry out the task. You do not want to frustrate team members or inhibit their work by delegating a task to them but withholding decision-making power on all items that are needed to actually accomplish the task. Micromanaging their work is not effective delegation. At that point, you might as well have done the job yourself.

5. *Prepare for measured risk.* Perfection is not only an unrealistic expectation but sets up everyone involved for failure. Start by providing a SMART task. Ask the recipients to reflect back to you what they understand the task to be, just to make sure they start with a clear understanding. Patiently restate your expectations if needed. Check their progress periodically, and again, ensure they understand the expectations.[36] Determine the acceptable level of risk for the task assigned. Prepare for mistakes to be made and to have a plan if it does. Thomas J. Watson once stated, "I was asked if I was going to fire an employee who made a mistake that cost the company $600,000. No, I replied, I just spent $600,000 training him. Why would I want somebody to hire his experience?"[37]

Finally, delegation benefits others. Through delegation you are teaching, coaching, and mentoring.[38] Use your evaluation and feedback skills (see the evaluation section) to help the person improve.[39] Delegation increases communication between the managers and employees. Working closely together can strengthen relationships, and employees will be more invested in the work. These personal relationships are the backbone of a good team.

Accountability

Accountability breeds response-ability.

Stephen Covey[40]

Accountability in the workplace sets and holds people to a common expectation by clearly defining the company's mission, values, and goals.[41] Entrusting employees with responsibility for their piece of the puzzle allows the team to function more like a machine — all parts working together efficiently to produce the product.

Employees need clearly-defined expectations to achieve goals. Some may have ongoing responsibilities while others may be seasonal or temporary. With clearly defined expectations, employees can know what is expected of them. Only then can employees be held accountable for meeting those goals.[42] This is true at each level of the organization and creates a culture of accountability throughout the company. Here are five steps to promote accountability:

1. Define what people are accountable for.
2. Set and cascade goals throughout the organization.
3. Provide updates on progress.
4. Align development, learning, and growth.
5. Recognize and celebrate progress.[43]

Evaluation

One of the most tried and true forms of management is feedback.

Dr. Christopher Lee[44]

An employee evaluation is the assessment and review of a worker's job performance.[45] Regular employee evaluation helps remind workers of their manager's expectations for them in the workplace. Some employers have moved away from the traditional yearly employee evaluation to a more fluid line of communication to evaluate their employees.[46] Ideally, evaluation is another way to give feedback to your employees one on one. Employees want to know they are on the right track.

Evaluations serve as another way to manage performance. Whether the process is formal or informal, feedback helps align employees, resources, and systems to meet strategic objectives.[47] Time invested by both parties to learn how to better give and receive feedback will make evaluation conversations more productive and less emotional.

Performance management does not work without frequent, honest, open, and effective communication.[48] Productive daily shift huddles, toolbox talks, and after-action reviews can all work to manage performance of your employees.[49] Rewarding good performance is more effective than penalizing bad performance — which goes hand in hand with the employee evaluation. Managers should be quick to celebrate even the smallest progress within the team. Employees are a manager's best data source. To improve the success of the organization, the manager should have laser focus on the success of each individual.

Building Relationships

Building a professional relationship with each employee, or as many as possible, will pay dividends in terms of dedication to the mission and loyalty to the organization. Employee satisfaction is influenced by more than salary.[50] Small acts of appreciation, like small acts of kindness, can make all the difference. Share the praise and accept the blame. Praise in public and correct in private. Be intentional about using "we" and not "I" when talking about team accomplishments.

Make the rounds of the office (physically or virtually) regularly. Long conversations are not necessary. Simply greet people and acknowledge that they are important to the organization. Remembering someone's birthday or anniversary or sending emails to recognize good work is appreciated. Handwritten notes are treasured. Asking employees about family and taking interest in the answers as they share their proud moments lets them know that you care about them beyond your work expectation.

CONCLUSION

Setting vision and representing the organization to external constituents are important aspects of a leader's role in an organization, but effective leaders are so much more. They are insightful managers who understand the day-to-day operations of an organization, at least at a higher level, and they manage their direct reports well. Management responsibilities are aspects of everyday leadership. Expectations set at the top and carried through management duties will set the tone of the behaviors and attitudes of all.

Exercise

Delegation and Accountability Exercise

You are on a moot court team with two of your fellow law students, Blake and Drew. Your faculty member coach has designated Drew to be the brief writer for the competition. The case file has two main issues. You will be an advocate responsible for one of the issues and Blake will be the advocate for the other issue. After discussing the work with the team and your coach, you and the other team members will all help with researching the issues and drafting the brief.

Discussion Questions:

1. What is your plan of action to make sure that the brief gets done on time?
2. How can you use the SMART process to set tasks?
3. How can you use the five steps to accountability model noted above to help ensure the team members complete their tasks?

Journal Prompts

1. Taking "extreme ownership" of tasks requires initiative and determination that can be difficult to maintain on a daily or regular basis. What steps can you take to incorporate concepts of extreme ownership of tasks into your daily life?

2. Running meetings:

   a. Think about a meeting in which you were involved (for example, getting together to work on a group school project or working with a team in your previous employment to discuss an action item). What could have been done differently to make it more productive?

   b. What new tips did you learn from this chapter for running or participating in meetings?

3. Most of us struggle with delegation and accountability. We have all found ourselves working in a group and thinking, "Oh, I'll just do it myself." However, to achieve all of your goals, it is necessary to get everyone pulling in the same direction. How will you delegate tasks and keep others accountable?

   a. How could the SMART process help?

   b. How could you use the five steps to accountability model noted above to help?

   c. How could you apply these strategies in law student organizations?

4. It takes time and intention to build positive, productive relationships with members of your team or organization. From the reading above and thinking about your own inclinations, what specific actions can you take or what approaches can you try to assist with developing relationships?

5. Evaluations of others and giving feedback is difficult.

a. What will be your strategy to effectively do this without alienating the other person? Remember that the goal is to make the other person more effective and helpful for the task at hand.

b. How can you use what you know about the person's background and personality to ensure that your message is received well?

Endnotes

1. Kenneth Thomas, PhD, is an American author and academic. Nicole Fallon, *35 Inspiring Leadership Quotes*, Bus. News Daily (Nov. 29, 2019), https://www.businessnewsdaily.com/7481-leadership-quotes.html.

2. Quote by Benjamin Franklin, Goodreads, https://www.goodreads.com/quotes/626466-for-the-want-of-a-nail-the-shoe-was-lost (last visited July 14, 2020).

3. Willard Randell, *Hamilton Takes Command*, Smithsonian Magazine (January 2003), https://www.smithsonianmag.com/history/hamilton-takes-command-74722445/.

4. *Id.*

5. *Id.*

6. *Alexander Hamilton*, The American Revolution, http://www.ouramericanrevolution.org/index.cfm/people/view/pp0050 (last visited July 14, 2020).

7. Jocko Willink & Leif Babin, Extreme Ownership: How Navy SEALs Lead and Win (St. Martin's Publishing Group 2015).

8. Jean Murray, *What Are the Duties and Responsibilities of a Fiduciary?*, The Balance Small Business (Oct. 22, 2019), https://www.thebalancesmb.com/what-are-the-duties-and-responsibilities-of-a-fiduciary-4583851.

9. An experience of one of the authors, Elizabeth M. Fraley, from her time in practice.

10. Larry Bossidy, Execution: The Discipline of Getting Things Done (Penguin Random House 2002). Larry Bossidy is the former AlliedSignal CEO.

11. Ken Favaro, *Defining Strategy, Implementation, and Execution*, Harv. Bus. Rev. (Mar. 31, 2015), https://hbr.org/2015/03/defining-strategy-implementation-and-execution.

12. Chris Sowers, *The Real Difference Between Managing and Leading*, Management Matters (Apr. 26, 2018), https://medium.com/management-matters/the-real-difference-between-managing-and-leading-9a8bfae0238.

13. *Id.*

14. Larry Constantine Quotes, A-Z Quotes, https://www.azquotes.com/author/40418-Larry_Constantine (last visited July 9, 2020). Larry LeRoy Constantine is an American software engineer, professor in the Center for Exact Sciences and Engineering at the University of Madeira Portugal, and considered one of the pioneers of computing.

15. Anthony Jay, *How to Run a Meeting*, Harv. Bus. Rev. (1976).

16. *Id.*

17. *Id.*

18. *Id.*

19. *Id.*

20. Adam Bryant, *How to Run a More Effective Meeting*, N.Y. Times (2020), https://www.nytimes.com/guides/business/how-to-run-an-effective-meeting.

21. Jay, *supra* note 15.

22. *Id.*

23. Bryant, *supra* note 20.

24. Robert's Rules of Order, *available at* https://www.robertsrules.com/. The authors highly recommend that everyone have a copy of Robert's Rules of Order and learn the lessons contained therein for running meetings.

25. Mike Morrison, Running Effective Meetings presentation, Baylor Law School (Dec. 11, 2019).

26. *Thoughts on the Business of Life*, Forbes, https://www.forbes.com/quotes/theme/business/ (last visited July 9, 2020). George Smith Patton, Jr. was a general of the United States Army who commanded the U.S. Seventh Army in the Mediterranean theater of World War II, and the U.S. Third Army in France and Germany after the Allied invasion of Normandy in June 1944.

27. Jessie Sostrin, *To Be a Great Leader, You Have to Learn to Delegate Well*, Harv. Bus. Rev. (Oct. 10, 2017), https://hbr.org/2017/10/to-be-a-great-leader-you-have-to-learn-how-to-delegate-well.

28. Tony Freed, *Smart Product Management*, Medium.com (May 29, 2017), https://medium.com/@tony_freed/smart-product-management-47351d765717 (last visited Oct. 20, 2020).

29. Holloran Center, *Assessment of Student's Ownership of Continuous Professional Development Rubric*, U. St. Thomas (2019), https://www.stthomas.edu/media/hollorancenter/pdf/FINALSelf-DirectednessRubricMarch2019.pdf.

30. *Id.*

31. *Id.*

32. *Id.*

33. *Id.*

34. *Id.*

35. *Id.*

36. *Id.*

37. Gareth Garbutt, *What Would You Do If an Employee Made a $600,000 Mistake?*, People HR (June 26, 2015), https://www.peoplehr.com/blog/2015/06/26/what-would-you-do-if-an-employee-made-a-600000-mistake/.

38. *Id.*

39. *Id.*

40. Stephen R. Covey, *Discipline 4: Create a Cadence of Accountability*, FranklinCovey, https://www.franklincovey.com/the-4-disciplines/discipline-4-accountability.html (last visited July 9, 2020). Stephen Richards Covey was an American educator, author, businessman, and keynote speaker. His most popular book is *The 7 Habits of Highly Effective People.*

41. Matt Gasior, *Why Is Accountability Important in the Workplace?*, Power DMS (Mar. 14, 2019), https://www.powerdms.com/blog/accountability-workplace-important/.

42. *Id.*

43. Andrew Robertson & Nate Dvorak, *5 Ways to Promote Accountability*, Gallup (June 3, 2019), https://www.gallup.com/workplace/257945/ways-create-company-culture-accountability.aspx.

44. Dr. Christopher Lee is a human resources practitioner, lecturer, researcher, and author. Office of Human Resources, *About Performance Management*, Texas State University (2020), https://www.hr.txstate.edu/performance-management/background.html.

45. Susan Heathfield, *Employee Evaluation*, The Balance Careers (Sept. 24, 2019), https://www.thebalancecareers.com/employee-evaluation-1918117.

46. Liz Ryan, *Ten Reasons Your Performance Review Doesn't Matter*, Forbes (May 7, 2016), https://www.forbes.com/sites/lizryan/2016/05/07/ten-reasons-your-performance-review-doesnt-matter/#5d349b3563f6.

47. Raffaele Carpi et al., *Performance Management: Why Keeping Score Is So Important, and So Hard*, McKinsey & Company (Oct. 4, 2017), https://www.mckinsey.com/business-functions/operations/our-insights/performance-management-why-keeping-score-is-so-important-and-so-hard.

48. *Id.*

49. *Id.*

50. *Id.*

Part IV

Leadership Within Community:
Service and Impact

Chapter 21 Lifelong Learning

The only certainty about the future is change.

Joseph Aoun[1]

Purpose

Encourage a lifelong commitment to studying leadership development and pursuing leadership development opportunities.

Learning Objectives

At the end of this chapter, you should be able to:

- Describe what lifelong learning is and why it is important.
- Consider how you can start the process of lifelong learning now.
- Discuss the role lifelong learning plays in leadership development.

Discussion

INTRODUCTION

Law professors caution students that the study of law does not end at graduation and that law school begins a lifelong pursuit of knowledge and wisdom. While law school provides a solid base, you will need additional knowledge as you take on more complex matters and as the law and society continue to evolve. Many lawyers can attest (somewhat painfully) that growth comes from failure far more than from success. The process of acquiring new knowledge, advancing your understanding of people, and assessing circumstances helps you gain wisdom. Wisdom acquired over years of education, training, and life experience provides value as you advise clients, complete tasks for your employer, and lead in your communities.

Lawyers need technical competence to gain trust of their clients and to successfully perform the work. Acquiring technical competence requires ongoing learning and training well beyond that which a lawyer can acquire in law school.

In litigation, you need a thorough understanding of the subject matter. Before preparing your case theory, cross-examining the other side's expert, and explaining to the jury how the "thing" works, you need to have an understanding of the material that is so deep that you and the expert can have a technical conversation. You may have to learn exactly what brain surgery entails for a medical malpractice case, or how Apple iPhone technology works for an intellectual property case. On the transactional side, to advise your client you need to understand your client's business. Failing to understand critical issues at the heart of the deal could mean a failed negotiation. Other issues might not be detrimental to a particular deal, but harmful to the long-term goals of the business. A real estate client who wants you to negotiate the terms for a land deal may not understand the ramifications of needed groundwater contamination remediation work. If you do not understand the issue either, the client may be responsible for a significant expense that outweighs the purchase price. From mastering the details to protecting the client's future, developing technical skills is a crucial part of the lawyer's journey. Learning new information is at the core of being a good lawyer.

Your leadership skills need to develop as well. You may graduate with some concept of leading, but those skills need to grow, evolve, and mature as you face more challenging leadership positions with bigger teams and more complex environments. Continue the process of self-exploration and sharpening your skills. Spend time learning more about your personality style, work on developing leadership competencies, reflect on your strengths and weaknesses, and you will continue to improve as a leader. A leader's commitment to seeking new knowledge, new skills, and new perspectives through self-actualization tops Maslow's hierarchy of needs.[2] According to Maslow, as basic human needs are met, growth-motivated individuals are freed to focus on personal and professional development to reach their full potential and to fulfill a mission, calling, or destiny.[3]

Your journey as a lawyer and leader is just beginning. The energy and effort you devoted to completing law school gives you a good template for continuing to learn as you enter the profession. Invest in a life of striving to *know* yourself, to *be* your best self, and to *do* your best in every situation. Lifelong learning guides this process. This process occurs naturally in your community. As you get involved in your community, new leadership development opportunities will arise, and you will enhance your professional competencies, gain experience, and build relationships.

BENEFITS OF LIFELONG LEARNING

Your brain — like with your muscles — needs ongoing challenges to keep it strong and healthy. When you are familiar with information or tasks, your brain runs efficiently but it is not being exercised. New activities help avoid atrophy.[4] Learning a new skill, trying a new sport, or tackling new technology can create, strengthen, and reorganize neural pathways.[5] Tasks as simple as brushing your teeth with your nondominant hand provide mental stimulation. The more you discover about new topics or current events, the more you want to learn. Learning to think differently also stimulates your brain.[6] Exchanging viewpoints and ideas with other learners helps you see the other side of an issue and gain perspective.

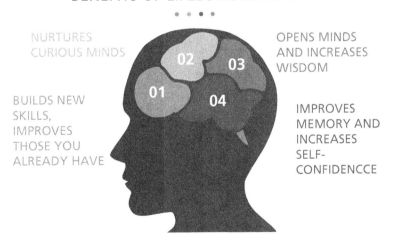

BENEFITS OF LIFELONG LEARNING[7]

NURTURES CURIOUS MINDS

OPENS MINDS AND INCREASES WISDOM

BUILDS NEW SKILLS, IMPROVES THOSE YOU ALREADY HAVE

IMPROVES MEMORY AND INCREASES SELF-CONFIDENCCE

Learning throughout your life can improve self-esteem while increasing optimism and life satisfaction.[8] Gaining a new skill can boost your confidence in your own abilities just as it did when you were a child. Think back to the first time you went off the high dive into the pool or rode a bicycle without training wheels. You *knew* that you had accomplished something. In our personal lives, this confidence lends a sense of accomplishment and satisfaction. In our professional lives, this self-confidence can produce a feeling of trust in our knowledge and the ability to apply what we have learned.

A willingness to learn makes life more interesting and can open future opportunities. You never know where your interests will lead you. For example, learning to sew requires problem solving. Learning to draw involves developing creativity. Not only can your new skill help develop interpersonal skills, creativity, and problem solving, you may meet like-minded aficionados who could use your skills in their organization. Whether pursuing personal interests and passions or chasing professional ambitions, lifelong learning can help you achieve personal fulfillment and satisfaction.

Managing Change Requires Lifelong Learning

Ongoing education keeps workers and their employers competitive.[9] While the legal profession mandates a certain amount of continuing legal education for licensure, the minimum may not be enough to keep you abreast of current developments in your area of practice. Technology is changing the practice in significant ways. New technologies can make practice more efficient but only if you learn to use them. The job you have now may not be your forever job. You may need — or want — a career change. One benefit of a law degree is the ability to reinvent yourself professionally as the world changes. Rapidly evolving and challenging times call for a new kind of education beyond that which is required to maintain your law license. Self-initiated education includes both personal and professional development.

Universities are not the exclusive venue for lifelong learning. Learning occurs in all realms of our existence when approached "with the aim of improving knowledge, skills, and competences within a personal, civic, social and/or employment-related perspective."[10] The *Oxford Handbook of Lifelong Learning* provides several other definitions of lifelong learning. "A simple definition of lifelong learning is that it is 'development after formal education: the continuing development of knowledge and skills that people experience after formal education and throughout their lives.'"[11] Here is a more detailed definition:

> The combination of processes throughout a lifetime whereby the whole person — body (genetic, physical, and biological) and mind (knowledge, skills, attitudes, values, emotions, beliefs, and senses) — experiences social situations, the perceived content of which is then transformed cognitively, emotively or practically (or through any combination) and integrated into the individual person's biography resulting in a continually changing (or more experienced) person.[12]

Many believe that a commitment to lifelong learning is the only way to succeed in the dynamic environment in which we live. Joseph E. Aoun, president of Northeastern University in Boston, Massachusetts, wrote of lifelong learning that "it is a necessity rather than a possibility or a luxury to be considered,"[13] because "[c]reation will be at the base of economic activity and much of what human beings do in the future."[14] His call for colleges and universities to "shape students into professionals but also creators"[15] should resonate powerfully with you as you prepare to advise, advocate, and lead.

FOCUS ON NEW LITERACIES

Knowledge acquisition should include what Dr. Aoun calls the new literacies: technological literacy, human literacy, and data literacy. The need for technological literacy comes as no surprise — technology is making our world smaller and more connected, but also more complicated, requiring new forms of education. The need for technical know-how to navigate the modern digital world is a given in today's environment. Similarly, data literacy — the ability to understand the enormous amounts of information generated by machines — is a vital component of the practice of law. Computers create not only the data we see as we use software but also a trail of data not immediately visible to the user. An entirely new industry in data retrieval and protection now exists to help lawyers manage big data in litigation, regulatory, and other legal areas.

Human literacy — "the ability to engage others, think creatively, and be entrepreneurial"[16] — resonates particularly in the study of leadership. No matter the extent that machines permeate society, what really matters is human contact and interaction. Machines and artificial intelligence could soon rival humans for cognition, precision, and power, but the human traits of sociability and creativity make the difference. As Aoun explains, "Other animals apply intelligence to solving problems: crows fashion tools to pluck bugs out of wood, and sea otters yield rocks to crack clamshells. But only human beings are able to create imaginary stories, invent works of art, and even construct carefully reasoned theories explaining perceived reality."[17] Interestingly, the skills that will continue to be valued and in demand are those prioritized in a liberal arts education. "These skills include judgment, collaboration, curiosity, communication, empathy, team work, leadership, and many others. These creative, social, and leadership qualities represent tasks that can't be automated."[18]

In addition to new literacies, we also need to develop our cognitive capacities, including entrepreneurship, systems thinking, and cultural intelligence.[19] "Entrepreneurship will be increasingly valuable as a means for humans to distinguish themselves in the digital workplace," Aoun writes, "as machines invade the labor market."[20] Entrepreneurship does not necessarily mean launching a new company; it may describe looking at things in a different way and changing the structure or processes of an existing company.

The skills of issue spotting and making innovative arguments that connect disjointed concepts will have value in the digital age. Machines may be able to understand complex systems and how the variables interact, but they are not very good at knowing how to apply this information to different contexts.[21] The human ability of systems thinking "sees the details and the entire tableau, exercising our mental strength to weigh complexity while also testing our grasp on multiple strands of thought."[22] Lawyers learn to look for the "less obvious . . . relationships between different ideas and processes," which gives them the comparative advantage.[23] These are skills taught in law schools and should be honed after graduation.

Another competitive advantage for those trained in the law is *cultural agility*, or the ability to perform in multiple different settings and with a variety of people.[24] Machines cannot interact and respond based on body language, tone of voice, or non-verbal conduct. Lawyers are trained to gauge these reactions and adjust accordingly whether the setting is a jury trial, a mediation room, or a tense boardroom.[25]

Ironically, Aoun notes a paradox in learning these skills. "Technical proficiency appears lower on employers' agendas than things such as initiative, work ethic and, notably, leadership. In fact, the last of these is frequently cited as the most desirable of employment skills." He also found that "employers increasingly want to see recruits with deep listening skills, the ability to rapidly summarise and share their knowledge, alongside the capacity to conceptualise, synthesise and communicate effectively."[26] Aoun concluded:

> These are complex questions requiring intellectual discipline and nuanced thought — and the professional workplace of tomorrow is only getting more complex. Soon enough professionals will function in tandem with intelligent machines. Whatever the industry — finance, law, manufacturing, media or any other — it will require cognitive capacities that equip it for tasks we might not even be able to imagine yet. These capacities are mindsets rather than bodies of knowledge — mental architecture rather than mental furniture. Going forward, people will still need to know specific bodies of knowledge to be effective in the workplace, but that alone will not be enough when intelligent machines are doing much of the heavy lifting of information. To succeed, tomorrow's employees will have to demonstrate a higher order of thought . . . . Because critical thinking and systems thinking are crucial for the human employees of the future, it is imperative we instill them through the education of the present.[27]

Learning for life and mastering human literacy will give lawyers an advantage in their professional roles as well as in other spheres of influence. Even as the world continues to become more automated, certain qualities cannot be duplicated by artificial intelligence. Capabilities developed in law school, such as judgment, teamwork, creativity, communication, and leadership, will be increasingly in demand and valued.

ADOPTING LEARNING AS A WAY OF LIFE

Humans have a natural drive to explore, learn, and grow, but a commitment to lifelong learning must be self-initiated and motivated by a desire for personal development. By paying attention to the ideas and goals that inspire us, we are encouraged to improve our own quality of life.[28] There is a downside, however, to being a jack of all trades but master of none. Here are some suggestions to consider as you engage in lifelong learning:

Make a List of What You Want to Learn

Professionally

- What knowledge or skill sets do you need to succeed in your current position?
- What knowledge or skill sets do you need to be qualified and prepared for the position you want next?
- What resources are available to help?
- How much time is involved and when will you have time?

Personally

- What are you most interested in learning?
- What would help you be more well rounded?
- Is there a group or organization involved with that interest?
- How do you get started and how do you schedule time to pursue?

Make a Commitment

Once you thoughtfully identify an area of interest in which to learn, commit to pursuing your learning goal. You should use the SMART (Specific, Measurable, Achievable, Realistic, and Timebound) method for goal setting to set realistic goals. After setting a goal, commit to learning, keep your focus and motivation, and hold yourself accountable.[29]

For example, if learning history is your passion, explore what specific areas of history might better hold your interest, such as the Tudors versus the American Civil War. Is there a more specific area within the broad topic that is more intriguing to you, such as the Battle of Gettysburg? You could look for books, blogs, articles, and podcasts dedicated to the subject, or visit museums or historical collections. Perhaps your interest is so strong that you want to pursue an advanced degree. Executive and online programs are available even when you are in the full-time practice of law.

Think about what format fits with your schedule. If you have limited time, you may do better learning from a computer-based program or an app. If you have more time, you can investigate community college classes or other classroom offerings. Understanding the time and space you can devote to the learning goal can help you to stick with the goal in the long run.

CONCLUSION

Life moves fast. The world is in a state of constant change, and some changes we can see more readily than others. A commitment to lifelong learning will help you stay relevant and better serve your family, your clients, and your communities. As advancements in technology and artificial intelligence change the way business will be conducted and organizations will operate in your communities, the need for lawyering skills will only increase. Opportunities to lead in your communities will allow you to continue to hone your skills and competencies.

Exercises

The Bucket List

Create a bucket list with at least five entries of achievements you want to accomplish — experiences you want to have or skills you want to learn. What is your plan to achieve these goals? What resources (skill, knowledge, money, time, etc.) do you need to achieve these goals?

Applying Lifelong Learning to Your Organization

Discussion Questions :

1. What opinion that you held in the past have you changed your mind about? (For example, "As a restaurant patron, the customer is always right.")
2. What is your revised opinion? (Revised opinion from previous example, "In a restaurant, the customer is not always right.")
3. What caused you to change your opinion? What knowledge or skills did you learn that caused you to change your perspective and examine the issue from another angle? (Returning to the previous example, "After working at a restaurant as a server, I learned that sometimes customers can be unreasonable in their requests, but you still try to be as accommodating as possible.")

Your answers can range from simple ideas (such as the one noted above) to complex ones (such as important societal issues commanding attention in our nation today).

Journal Prompts

1. What does lifelong learning mean to you?

2. What do you see as the benefits of lifelong learning?

3. For the literacies identified by Dr. Aoun:

   a. Which one are you most comfortable with?

   b. Which one are you least comfortable with?

   c. Which one do you believe law school is most helping you develop?

   d. Which one do you believe law school is least helping you develop?

4. How will you incorporate lifelong learning into your routines?

Endnotes

1. Joseph Aoun, *Higher Education in the Age of Artificial Intelligence*, ROBOT-PROOF, http://robot-proof.com/#about (last visited July 9, 2020). Joseph Elie Aoun is the seventh president of Northeastern University in Boston, Massachusetts, where he took office on August 15, 2006. Previously, Aoun was dean of the College of Letters, Arts, and Sciences at the University of Southern California.

2. In his influential paper of 1943, A Theory of Human Motivation, American psychologist Abraham Maslow proposed that healthy human beings have a certain number of needs, and that these needs are arranged in a hierarchy, with some needs (such as physiological and safety needs) being more primitive or basic than others (such as social and ego needs). Maslow's so-called hierarchy of needs is often presented as a five-level pyramid, with higher needs coming into focus only once lower, more basic needs are met. When their basic needs are unmet, people feel incomplete. Without food security and a roof over our heads, for example, our need for security dominates our attention. Once these needs are fulfilled and we feel secure, we can shift away from these exigent external needs and focus more attention on our internal need for growth. Neel Burton, *Our Hierarchy of Needs: True Freedom Is a Luxury of the Mind. Find Out Why*, PSYCHOLOGY TODAY (May 23, 2012), https://www.psychologytoday.com/us/blog/hide-and-seek/201205/our-hierarchy-needs.

3. Scott Jeffrey, *A Complete Guide to Self-Actualization: 5 Key Steps to Accelerate Growth*, CEOSAGE (2014), https://scottjeffrey.com/self-actualization/.

4. BrainMD Life, *12 Ways to Strengthen Your Brain*, BRAINMD (Mar. 19, 2015), https://brainmd.com/blog/use-it-or-lose-it-your-mind-is-like-a-muscle-12-ways-to-strengthen-your-brain/.

5. *Id.*

6. Amy Morin, *How to Train Your Brain to Think Differently*, PSYCHOLOGY TODAY (Oct. 10, 2017), https://www.psychologytoday.com/us/blog/what-mentally-strong-people-dont-do/201710/how-train-your-brain-think-differently.

7. *See Benefits of Lifelong Learning*, CENTER FOR INTERACTIVE LEARNING AND COLLABORATION (2020), https://www.cilc.org/Lifelong-Learners/Lifelong-Learners.aspx.

8. Thomas Oppong, *Want to Boost Your Confidence? Consider Learning a New Skill*, MEDIUM (Oct. 22, 2019), https://medium.com/@alltopstartups/want-to-improve-your-confidence-consider-learning-a-new-skill-71ca8439fa51.

9. Lynne Doughtie, *The Changing Nature of Work: Why Lifelong Learning Matters More Than Ever*, FORBES (Apr. 23, 2018), https://www.forbes.com/sites/kpmg/2018/04/23/the-changing-nature-of-work-why-lifelong-learning-matters-more-than-ever/#11fb92731e95.

10. Manuel London, The Oxford Handbook of Lifelong Learning (The Oxford Library of Psychology 2011).

11. *Id.*

12. *Id.* (citing Peter Jarvis, The Routledge International Handbook of Lifelong Learning 9–18 (Routledge 2009)).

13. *Id.*; *see also* G. Fischer, *Lifelong Learning: More Than Training,* 11 J. Interactive Learning Res. 265, 265 (2000).

14. Joseph E. Aoun, Robot-Proof: Higher Education in the Age of Artificial Intelligence (MIT Press 2017).

15. *Id.*

16. *Id.*

17. *Id.*

18. Joshua Kim, *If You Read One Higher Ed Book This Year, Make It "Robot-Proof,"* Inside Higher Ed (Apr. 18, 2018), https://www.insidehighered.com/digital-learning/blogs/technology-and-learning/read-robot-proof-if-you-only-read-one-higher-ed-book.

19. *See* Chapter 17.

20. Russell Flannery, *How to Make Yourself Robot-Proof,* Forbes (May 13, 2019), https://www.forbes.com/sites/russellflannery/2019/05/13/how-to-make-yourself-robot-proof/#6a84ce4524b1

21. *Id.*

22. *Id.*

23. *Id.*

24. *Id.*

25. Aoun, *supra* note 14.

26. *Id.*

27. *Id.*

28. *Lifelong Learning,* Valamis (2020), https://www.valamis.com/hub/lifelong-learning#what-is-lifelong-learning.

29. *See* Chapter 9.

Chapter 22

The Complete Lawyer: Service and Significance

Dedicated lawyers, devoted to the profession of law, of high moral and ethical standards always will occupy an important and admired place in our society. This is inescapably true because this type of lawyer in the practice of his profession will be serving the public interest. He will be playing a prominent part in fashioning the rules of conduct for the welfare of our society. What other profession is privileged to make a greater contribution?

Leon Jaworski[1]

Purpose

Present the four components that comprise the complete lawyer, discuss the benefits of adopting service as a value and a priority, and provide practical steps to identify service opportunities that can help you find meaning and purpose.

Learning Objectives

At the end of this chapter, you should be able to:

- Describe the four components of a "complete" lawyer.
- Discuss the personal and societal benefits of community involvement.
- List steps for identifying opportunities for involvement in your community.
- Articulate the reasons why you want to join a particular organization.
- Discuss the benefits of community service.
- Identify common ethical issues when volunteering.

Discussion

INTRODUCTION

I WENT ON A SEARCH,

 to become a leader. I searched high and low; I spoke with authority and people listened. But at last there was someone who was wiser than I and they followed him.

I sought to inspire confidence but the crowd responded, "Why should we trust you?" I postured and assumed the look of leadership with a countenance that glowed with confidence and pride. But the crowd passed by and never noticed my air of elegance.

I ran ahead of the others pointing new ways to new heights. I demonstrated that I knew the route to greatness. And then I looked back and I was alone. "What shall I do?" I queried. "I've tried hard and used all that I know."

And then I listened to the voices around me, and I heard what the group was trying to accomplish. I asked, "Are we all together in what we want to do, and how will we get the job done?" And we thought together and struggled toward our goal. I found myself encouraging the faint-hearted; I sought the ideas of those too shy to speak out.

I taught those who knew little at all. I praised those who worked hard. When our task was completed, one of the group members turned to me and said, "This would not have been done but for your leadership." At first I said, "I did not lead — I just worked with the rest."

And then I understood: leadership isn't a goal or a laurel. I lead best when I forget about myself as a leader and focus on my group: their needs and their goals. To lead is to serve; to give; to achieve together. — *Anonymous*[2]

The study of leadership helps develop lawyers who are *complete* in the traditional sense. They are technically competent in the practice of law, wise counselors in helping clients navigate challenging situations and decisions, and effective leaders of organizations and institutions.[3] From law school through practice, complete lawyers hone the skills needed for each of these roles. Moreover, each role — technical expert, wise counselor, and effective leader — builds on the previous one and incorporates the lawyers' ethical duties and professional obligations to society. "Complete" is something of a misnomer in suggesting that the work of development is finished; effective lawyers never stop learning. Complete as used here, however, denotes wholeness — the full attributes of an accomplished attorney.

A lawyer who lacks technical competence will not be trusted as a wise counselor. A lawyer who is not viewed as a competent lawyer or a trusted advisor will not be effective as a leader.[4] Lawyers who combine expertise, good counsel, and integrity are more likely to be respected as leaders. They know that without weaving their ethical obligations into every aspect of being a complete lawyer, they fall short, not only in service to their clients but also society.[5] Complete lawyers derive their ethical base from several sources, which include:

> the spirit and letter of the Model Rules of Professional Conduct; an implied social contract between state-licensed professionals and the rest of society; the enlightened self-interest of the institutions in which lawyers serve; the role of law, regulation, and norms as the foundation and expression of public policy and private ordering; and lessons about lawyers' roles in the history of our constitutional democracy and political economy.[6]

Armed with a sense of duty and an important moral commitment to society, the complete lawyer incorporates aspects of servant leadership, authentic leadership, adaptive leadership, and transformational leadership. This includes a servant's heart, a commitment to being your authentic self, the ability to adapt as circumstances dictate, and a desire to inspire transformation in an organization or a community. Many of you came to law school to make a difference; through these roles, lawyers can both make a positive difference and live a meaningful life. We remind you of Margaret Mead's advice: "Never doubt that a small group of thoughtful, committed citizens can change the world; indeed, it's the only thing that ever has."[7]

In this chapter, we discuss what it looks like when lawyers *see* themselves within the context of the four components of a complete lawyer and what lawyers *do* with their lives in response. The benefits to a lawyer's professional satisfaction and personal well-being are well established. The potential positive impact on society and in communities is exponential.

USING YOUR RESOURCES TO SERVE OTHERS

The meaning of life is to find your gift. The purpose of life is to give it away.
William Shakespeare[8]

Frequently, lawyers who have experienced financial success and professional accolades hit a point in their career when they reflect on their path and recount the story of helping a *pro bono* client. The feelings of pride and joy, humility, and grace can be overwhelming when the client expresses heart-felt gratitude for gaining custody of a child, recovering his life savings, or providing financial security when catastrophically injured. The sense of meaning and purpose in those moments lasts far longer than the celebration after closing a multi-million-dollar deal for a client. You enjoy the accolades and financial success, but somehow service brings greater meaning to your practice. As Sam Levenson puts it, "As you grow older, you will discover that you have two hands—one for helping yourself, the other for helping others."[9] As complete lawyers search for meaning, they encounter the challenge posed by Martin Luther King, Jr.: "Life's most persistent and urgent question is, What are you doing for others?"[10]

Jim Sandman is a lawyer who reflected on the meaning and purpose of life earlier in his career than most. Sandman began his career at Arnold and Porter, spending 30 years with the firm and eventually becoming managing partner of the nationwide firm. He left at the peak of his career, though, to take a much less lucrative job. Jim Sandman served as president of the Legal Services Corporation (LSC) from 2011 to 2020. The LSC uses congressional funding to support 132 legal aid programs and over 850 offices throughout the United States.[11] As he describes his career path:

> I went to Arnold and Porter because they had a *pro bono* program that was unlike any other firm I had ever heard of then. Arnold and Porter's most famous and important client is not a global corporation. It was a poor drifter by the name of Clarence Earl Gideon. Arnold and Porter did *Gideon v. Wainwright pro bono*. When I came to the firm, and for my 30 years there, the firm's policy was to encourage lawyers to spend up to 15% of their time on *pro bono* work. I've never heard of another firm that had a quota that high.
>
> The partners did *pro bono* work. There was a time in the early days of the firm in the 1950s when more than half the firm's work was *pro bono*, representing government employees and academics whose livelihoods were at risk because their loyalty to the United States was being questioned. They were thought to be Pinkos, communist sympathizers, and every lawyer on the firm spent some time every day helping clients answer questionnaires that they had received in the mail. These were terrified people. And these were cases that no other law firm would touch. They were toxic because anti-communism was a non-partisan American value.
>
> So that culture, that value, had everything to do with why I chose that firm. I did *pro bono* work at Arnold and Porter from the day I joined until the day I left the firm 30 years later, including throughout the 10 years I served as the firm's managing partner.[12]

Sandman learned the importance of service during his years at the firm and left the firm to become general counsel for the D.C. public schools.[13] When the opportunity to serve on a larger stage arose, he became president of LSC. With Sandman at the helm, LSC's funding grew to $440 million, the largest ever[14]—despite efforts by the Trump administration to zero out the LSC funding. Each time, Sandman got the money restored plus more.[15] Sandman recently became president emeritus of LSC, allowing him to teach at the University of Pennsylvania Carey School of Law.[16] Sandman epitomizes servant leadership—looking for opportunities where he can pour himself into making a difference in other people's lives.

Jim Sandman is more likely an exception to the rule than typical of lawyers in the practice of law today. We encourage you to be more intentional about your path.

Choosing to prioritize service will not be easy. In fact, you are guaranteed to face challenges and barriers. Economic pressures, peer pressures, and even family obligations may dissuade you from prioritizing service. No one promised a life of a lawyer would be easy, but it can be gratifying and fulfilling.

COMMITMENT TO SERVICE

No attorney can be faulted for meeting the minimum expectations of clients, employer's obligations, and the lawyers' code of professional responsibility. For all lawyers, the parameters of your life at any given moment, or during a specific phase of life, may dictate a goal of doing what you must just to survive. Struggling to learn a new area of the law requires dedicated time and concentrated effort — much like law school. Juggling work and young children consumes so much time that you fight for precious little sleep. Meeting or exceeding the expectation of a certain number of billable hours may often occupy your nights and weekends. Client demands will vary and a case or a transaction may need your attention for 16-hour days. But somewhere along the way we encourage you to reflect, set priorities, and assess your life. A life of bare minimums or just surviving is not likely to lead to finding purpose and meaning — it may keep you from thriving. Tremendous satisfaction occurs when lawyers recognize their potential for making a difference in the lives of their clients and communities.

The servant leadership model has a lot to offer lawyers aspiring to become a complete lawyer.[17] By seeking to place others' interests before yours, you benefit not only them, but also the organization, yourself, and society as a whole. Lawyers with a servant's heart inspire people to also serve others, which can change the culture within an organization, a profession, or a community.[18] Servant leaders put people first, but not at the expense of the goal and objective of the organization.[19] The purpose is to inspire all persons in the organization and all other related parties, so that they also want to serve one another as everyone works toward a goal.[20] The product is produced and the bottom-line expectations are met *because of* the work ethic and attitude of the individual people on the team.[21] In other words, by serving others you raise the consciousness of all, you care about and inspire all, and in the process, you change the culture. The goals of the organization will be achieved through the joint ownership and effort of all.

Some have criticized the servant leader model as aspirational only.[22] But maybe that is what is missing in the legal profession today. Setting aspirational standards can help lawyers become the best professional they can be. These aspirational standards begin with studying yourself and society, striving to maintain integrity and character, and committing to support the rule of law and democracy through your work and service. We offer aspirational standards or duties in four distinct categories:

1. Responsibilities to the people and organizations that their own institution serves (such as corporate stakeholders, law firm clients, and law students and faculty).

2. Responsibilities to the legal system and rule of law that are the foundation of our political economy and constitutional democracy, including contributing to access to justice, strengthening the rule of law and legal institutions in the United States and around the world, and supporting efforts by other lawyers to uphold their own professional responsibilities.

3. Responsibilities to the institution in which lawyers work — e.g., corporations, law firms, and law schools — and to the people employed by such institutions, such as a corporation's global workforce or a law firm's or law school's diverse employees.

4. Responsibilities to secure other broad public goods and enhance sound private ordering complementary to the rule of law — in order to create a safe, fair, and just society in which individuals and institutions (including major corporations, major law firms, and major law schools) can thrive over the long term.[23]

Contributing more broadly to bettering others can be daunting, particularly when leaders of law firms or companies focus primarily on the outcome or the bottom line. Servant leaders flip this model by putting people first in order to meet the aspirational responsibilities noted above.[24] Robert Greenleaf's servant leadership model is perhaps the most appropriate for lawyers because it focuses on others, which is consistent with a lawyer's fiduciary obligation to put the needs and goals of a client first. Greenleaf views servant leadership as "a model which puts serving others as the number one priority. Servant leadership emphasizes increased service to others; a holistic approach to work; promoting a sense of community; and the sharing of power in decision-making."[25] Valuable aspects of servant leadership include listening, empathy, healing, awareness, persuasion to achieve group consensus, conceptualization of solutions, the foresight to predict the next steps needed, acting as a trustee for the group, a commitment to the growth of people, and building community. These are useful tools in the lawyer's toolkit.[26]

True servant leaders have the vision to see goals, the ability to share that vision, an ethical overlay that creates right action, the ability to adapt to challenges and setbacks along the path, and a genuine concern for others. This combination translates to a team that is highly motivated to achieve those goals.

Coach Bob "Lad" Ladouceur used this model during the 12 seasons he led the De La Salle Spartans.[27] During that time, the team set one of the longest winning streaks in sports history — 151 games.[28] Coach Lad viewed winning as the result of the bigger mission, not the mission itself.[29] He believed his role as a high school football coach was to focus on "commitment, character, love, respect, and discipline" for his players, rather than wins, trophies, and accolades.[30] He told his players during a team meeting, "I'm focused one hundred percent on you guys as a team. I want you to become what you're capable of becoming. It has nothing to do with wins."[31] He fulfilled this promise every day and his players remember it still.

There doubtless are coaches across America who also are invested in their players but whose teams do not set record winning streaks. What made Ladouceur different? His actions were consistent with his values, and his team saw that happen. At the end of a season, Ladouceur would actually throw away the trophies and awards the team had won. For Coach Lad, they did not represent the actual victories won that season. The impact on each player as a young man was the only mark of achievement that mattered.

THE OBLIGATION AND BENEFIT OF SERVICE

The special responsibility described in the Model Rules Preamble drives lawyers to use their distinctive passion, talents, and skills to serve communities in a variety of ways. You can spend time and energy persuading law firms and companies to fight for a more just world. You can help those without meaningful access to our judicial system by volunteering in a

> **ABA Model Rules: Preamble and Scope**
> A lawyer is a representative of clients, an officer of the legal system and a public citizen having special responsibility for the quality of justice.

legal clinic to advise veterans, battered spouses, or small business owners in disadvantaged neighborhoods. "Every lawyer has a professional responsibility to provide legal services to those who are unable to pay."[32] Although many equate *pro bono* with representing an indigent client free of charge, other service can fulfill your obligations.[33] The Rules contemplate fulfilling this obligation by serving on a nonprofit board or volunteering with an organization that lobbies for changes in law to help those in the community.[34] Aligning your service with your passion benefits those you serve as well as your own career and values. As one young lawyer related:

> At first, I got involved with the local young lawyers' organization because one of the senior partners told me I should. I started going to meetings and realized that it was a great way to meet other lawyers in my community. The more meetings I went to, the more I volunteered to help. I didn't have much money, so I couldn't contribute much financially to some of the projects, but I was able to volunteer my time. By following through on the promises I made, I was given more and more responsibility. I ended up being President of the local young lawyers, and then active in the state young lawyers' association. I was building meaningful relationships with other lawyers, both in my community and beyond. I enjoyed helping with projects, but I also realized that I was building a great referral network. When a client came to one of my friends needing a lawyer, if it was something that they didn't do but knew that I did, they would send those clients my way. Not only was I getting to help my fellow lawyers, but I was getting additional business from it, too.[35]

The ability to serve can arise from need, stepping in when a crisis arises. In 2008, authorities arrested Warren Jeffs, the polygamist leader of the Fundamentalist Church of Jesus Christ of Latter-Day Saints (FLDS) in Eldorado, Texas, for the sexual assault of several children.[36] As a result, the Texas Department of Child Protective Services brought more than 400 children from the FLDS compound to San Angelo, Texas, in what would be the largest child custody case in U.S. history.[37] San Angelo is a small town with far too few lawyers to represent all the children.[38] The local judge asked lawyers across

Texas to take the children's cases *pro bono,* and 263 lawyers from Houston, Dallas, San Antonio, and elsewhere undertook the representation.[39] For context, San Antonio to San Angelo is a more than six-hour drive, and flights are not an option. These were not glamorous cases to take and the issues involved were difficult (emotionally and legally), but lawyers took them anyway because it was the right thing to do.

CHOOSING YOUR PATH FOR SERVICE

While we are encouraged to serve outside our full-time job, very real issues create barriers to doing so. The demands of your job, especially as a new associate, can be overwhelming. Every project you are assigned involves a new skill, and young lawyers often feel that they are barely managing all the new learning they have to do. Law firms frequently require that associates bill a certain number of hours, and may frown on activities that interfere with associates' meeting that minimum. Some view community involvement as hindering career advancement because it takes time away from climbing the firm's internal ladder of success. Even firms that claim they value *pro bono* work may subtly discourage you from taking time away from billing. Fortunately, not all firms take this approach, and you may find your firm not only supportive of your *pro bono* endeavors but also cognizant that community involvement can actually bolster your career. They recognize that community involvement, as well as meeting community leaders or others with whom you share a passion, adds to your base of influence and referral sources.

Telling you to "find your passion," though, can be like trying to follow the punch recipe from a small-town cookbook that begins with the directive "First, fashion a swan of ice." With no instructions about how to do it, the task seems impossible. There are many worthy causes out there that deserve your time, talent, and energy. Finding service activities that engage you and that can help you professionally takes time and attention. It may involve talking to mentors and understanding how outside interests could also work with your commitments to your law firm. So, how can you determine where your passions align with your interests and your career? Each person's answer will be different, but here are three fundamental questions to ask yourself:

1. What interests me and what do I want to do?
2. What strengths, skills, or talents do I have that can benefit the community through service?
3. Where do I want to be in five or ten years? What steps must I take to make myself known and build my professional reputation?

To answer the first question, think back to what drew you to the law and what captivated you during your studies. Did you love working in a clinic? Did you really thrive writing a law review article? Did you enjoy your school's clothing drive for the homeless? Thinking back to both what you enjoyed and why helps focus your interests and the needs of your community. This approach is used by philanthropists when deciding how to contribute. Cecilia Boone, who with her husband founded The Container Store, shared their approach to giving at a philanthropy luncheon in Dallas, Texas. As you can imagine, the Boones amassed significant wealth and were often asked for contributions to hundreds — if not thousands — of causes. They found that they were not making an impact with that approach. They began starting each year by identifying the specific causes they would support that year and then making a significant commitment of time and resources to those charities.[40] Bill and Melinda Gates take a similar view through their Gates Foundation.[41] Not only does directing their charitable gifts through their own foundation ensure responsible use of the funds, it also lets the Gates family make meaningful change. The Gates have a clear mission statement and identity for their goals:

> We work with partners worldwide to tackle critical problems in five program areas. Our Global Health Division aims to reduce inequities in health by developing new tools and strategies to reduce the burden of infectious disease and the leading causes of child mortality in developing countries. Our Global Development Division focuses on improving the delivery of high-impact health products and services to the world's poorest communities and helps countries expand access to health coverage. Our Global Growth & Opportunity division focuses on creating and scaling market-based innovations to stimulate inclusive and sustainable economic growth. Our United States Division works to improve U.S. high school and postsecondary education, and support vulnerable children and families in Washington State. And our Global Policy & Advocacy Division seeks to build strategic relationships and promote policies that will help advance our work. Our approach to grantmaking in all five areas emphasizes collaboration, innovation, risk-taking, and, most importantly, results.[42]

These are examples of impact philanthropy, a common approach to grant funding by foundations because they see the results. Funding decisions are made by focusing efforts to support a strategic impact.[43]

You can learn from these givers in terms of focusing your efforts. You have three different kinds of gifts you can share: time, talent, and treasure. Each one can be an important way to contribute. If you are paying off student loans and trying to buy a house, you may have more talent and time than you do treasure. As you get older and have a more stable financial situation, you may choose to make monetary contributions in a significant way. At each point in your professional life, you have much to give. What issue is your community facing that strikes a chord within you? Does the idea of finding solutions to that issue get you excited and thinking about the next meeting? The key is to find those challenges that animate you, then join organizations in which you have a genuine interest and where you believe in the mission. You want to be able to actively dedicate yourself to accomplishing the organization's goals. Otherwise, if you lose interest, you will find it difficult to commit the time necessary to the organization, and you risk being seen as an opportunist. You must commit to actively and fully focus upon the mission at hand.

For the second question, take the time to identify your strengths and how they can benefit an organization.[44] Research the organization or talk to a member to better understand what the organization needs. Pay attention to how you can combine your abilities with the organization's needs to add value to a community organization. You can enhance the experience by using your skills to communicate well with others, being responsive to people's needs, and having a genuine understanding of, and concern for, people's problems. Finally, you want to be present and appropriately engaged with everyone you encounter.

The ability to be present while working a demanding job in the legal profession is a challenge, and you may need to assess candidly the extent to which your work schedule affects your ability to volunteer. You may be best suited to a group where you can volunteer on nights and weekends rather than one whose board meetings take place in the middle of a work day. If a group needs a well-written newsletter or press release, you could draft that without coordinating with someone else's schedule. If your firm is supportive, look for opportunities to reflect your service back on the firm. Can you add your volunteer efforts to the firm's website? Could you wear a firm logo shirt in pictures for the charity? Can you connect other board members or volunteers who might need, for example, a will drafted with a partner in your firm who specializes in wills? Even if the firm is reluctant initially, it may be persuaded by the results of your volunteer efforts. The best results come when you are the one who acts to make the situation beneficial for all involved.

Next, analyze your personal goals and objectives so you can reasonably articulate and plan your ideal career path. You may not realistically know what the future holds, but as you begin to envision it, you play a more active role in making that future a reality. If you aspire to public office, having experience with grassroots political organizations or the local League of Women Voters can provide both practical insight into how campaigns run as well as connect you with people who observe your skill and efforts at work. The key is to be intentional in deciding how serving in this particular manner can benefit your career. Will it help you develop a skill you need? Will it give you the experience in resolving a complex issue that prepares you for future leadership roles? Will it expose you to key movers within the community? Finding a public service opportunity where you can incorporate your own interests increases the potential for your success and impact.

Once you have identified an organization that fits these criteria, the next step is getting involved. The simplest way to do this is simply show up, volunteer, and follow through. When you are reliable in a volunteer post, you build confidence and a reputation for being reliable within the community — people know you can be counted on.

BUILDING TRUST

You must honor commitments you make whether you are paid or not. While you may think volunteer work is less important than your paid job, you must treat it respectfully and give it the attention you said you would. Otherwise, those in the organization may overlay your lack of follow-through on your professional competence, believing you are not able to commit to and achieve goals. You will not feel good about leaving the charity in the lurch, and you may undermine future opportunities.

If you donate your time and consistently follow through with your commitments, you will build trust within the community. People who trust you are more likely to call you for legal representation or to refer a friend or family member. Even if the case is outside your area of practice, people still trust you to know the right person to handle the matter. Trust goes not only to your competence but also to your counsel.

Core values like loyalty, excellence, and integrity are crucial for attorneys, both in their professions and in their volunteer endeavors. Committing to and completing the obligations you make is an inherent component of these values. Be willing to put in the hard work needed to achieve the goals of your organization. You also build trust when you show an ability to communicate with others and are responsive to people's needs. If you demonstrate these skills in a volunteer setting, prospective clients assume you would be as competent when you are being paid. Likewise, showing genuine understanding for people's problems suggests an empathy that would be reassuring in a professional setting. As you work in the volunteer world, you model the kind of lawyer you are and the kind of person you are.

Finally, be present and engaged with everyone you encounter. If you seem too busy to engage, future clients will assume you are too busy for their case. One of the best ways to build your practice is through word of mouth. As a lawyer, you will routinely hear stories of trials and tribulations from your clients. After a while, it is not hard to get compassion fatigue, because you have heard different versions of your clients' stories before. While their stories may not seem unique to you, to your clients, the reason that they are coming to see you may be the most troubling time in their lives. As one experienced lawyer relayed:

> As a young lawyer I was meeting with a client for the initial consult on a divorce case. As I listening to my client's tale about the struggles of her marriage, my mind began to drift and I started thinking about lunch. The client, a woman nearly twice my age, reached across the table and put her hands on each side of my face to get my attention. And she had it. She paused for a moment and said, "I know that you've probably heard something like this before, but to me, deciding to leave my husband of many years has been one of the most difficult decisions of my life. If you don't care enough to listen, I am just fine finding another lawyer who will." I was floored. I apologized profusely, and took the time to really hear what she had to say. It was important to her case, but more fundamental, it was important to her.[45]

Take the time to connect with those around you, whether they be clients, friends, family, or neighbors. People will know you in return, and respect you because of it.

ENGAGE YOUR PASSION

Once you identify a potential group with whom you feel a connection, get involved and see how it goes. You may choose wisely the first time, or it may take several attempts to find your true connection with a group or cause. Do not be concerned if the first group you work with does not turn out to be the right one. Just as not every first date works out, so too you may need to "date around" to find the right opportunity for you. Every experience, whether successful or not, teaches you valuable lessons. You will find the right combination of people, mission, and responsibility. You may also find that your passions and commitments change as you move through your life. Groups that serve and involve young children may have more meaning when your own children are young. Later in life, you may find more passion for ensuring the arts are a vibrant part of your community. Just as you grow and evolve, so may your interests. This is part of being a lifelong learner and can keep your passion for helping others alive and growing.

Ways to Get Involved and Related Ethical Considerations

Getting involved in your local community depends in part on where you live. A lawyer's community involvement may differ depending on whether the practice is in a big city, small town, or a rural area. Ask your friends and colleagues, do an Internet search, read the local newspaper, and get a feel for opportunities and needs in the community. Joining then is a matter of showing up and offering your time.

Access to Justice

The access to justice gap encompasses the inability and perceived inability of low- and middle-income Americans to afford lawyers in the United States and should give all lawyers and legal scholars cause for concern. The ABA's 2016 "Report on the Future of Legal Services in the United States" highlights the reality that much of the American population does not have access to civil legal services.[46] The inability of many Americans to access such services means that "many Americans cannot afford to hire a lawyer" and thus "are forced to either represent themselves or avoid accessing the legal system altogether."[47] Further difficulties for these would-be users of the system include encounters with underfunded programs meant to assist them.[48] This finding is particularly surprising considering that the legal system of the United States is considered the standard on which other systems are modeled and by which they are judged.

The report found that 100 million low- and middle-income Americans cannot afford legal representation for "basic human needs,"[49] which includes cases related to shelter, sustenance, safety, employment, health care, and custody of children and dependent adults.[50] These needs "emerge 'at the intersection of civil law [in the justice system] and everyday adversity.'"[51] Although different people face these problems at different times in their lives, "they are defined by a central important quality: they are justiciable."[52] All of these issues "have civil legal aspects, raise civil legal issues, have consequences shaped by civil law, and may become objects of formal legal action."[53]

Of that 100 million Americans, "an estimated thirty to forty million litigants" do access the civil justice system,[54] and are involved in over 19 million civil cases every year in state trial courts.[55] In Texas alone, nearly 5.8 million people qualify for legal aid.[56] Out of all those that qualify, however, only 100,000 Texas families are assisted by a legal aid organization.[57] It is thus unsurprising that at least one party is not represented by a lawyer in up to 90 percent of cases in America's civil courts.[58] In a recent study by Rebecca L. Sandefur, just over a fifth (22%) of people facing a civil justice issue sought help outside of their immediate social network.[59] Even fewer actually sought the help of the legal system, with 8 percent contacting a lawyer and 8 percent getting involved with a court.[60] Instead of turning to lawyers or the legal system, the vast majority chose to "do nothing" or try to handle it on their own.[61] These statistics and issues are not new — they are merely the latest in a long line of concerning reports from the ABA.[62] Of course, opportunity exists within every problem, and these unmet needs represent pent-up demand waiting to be served by an innovative approach.

Even more remarkable is the reality that the gap in legal services does not just affect low- and moderate-income individuals. High-income individuals and businesses are hurting too — lawyers in large law firms joke that they could not afford to hire themselves. People making $250,000 per year may not have the disposable income to afford a $10,000 legal bill.[63] To a law student that may seem unimaginable, but to a parent of three college-aged kids with car payments and a mortgage, an unexpected $10,000 bill will wreak havoc on a budget. "More than 13 million, or nearly 60%, of all small businesses have experienced significant legal events in the past two years."[64] "Despite the fact that nearly all respondents listed at least one legal issue as one of the 'greatest threats to their business,'" "nearly 60% . . . reported not hiring [a lawyer] to help them."[65] The primary reason was the cost associated with hiring a lawyer.[66]

To address the significant access to justice issue in the United States, lawyers should creatively address the provision of services and payment for those services. Firms can close the gap by charging lower fees for legal services, especially by dealing more efficiently with cases to make the same amount while charging less. Given the unmet legal need in the United States, if lawyers can meet that need by more efficiently dealing with a higher volume of cases, they can still profit. Scalability and process efficiency of legal services are critical to solving the gap in access to justice.

There are over 1.3 million lawyers in the United States.[67] If every lawyer had a *pro bono* case on his or her docket at all times, the number of people helped would expand exponentially. While the need is great, each individual client helped is important, as illustrated by *The Star Thrower* story:

> A man walking along the beach noticed a boy picking up a starfish and gently throwing it into the ocean. Approaching the boy, he asked, "What are you doing?" The youth replied, "Throwing starfish back into the ocean. The surf is up and the tide is going out. If I don't throw them back, they'll die." "Son," the man said, "don't you realize there are miles and miles of beach and hundreds of starfish? You can't make a difference!"
>
> After listening politely, the boy bent down, picked up another starfish, and threw it back into the surf. Then, smiling at the man, he said . . . "I made a difference for that one."[68]

Look for opportunities to close the access to justice gap. You will find that these cases provide meaning. Often, these are the cases that are remembered at the end of a long and distinguished career, rather than the big verdicts or big business deals closed. One young lawyer recalls helping a *pro bono* client with a simple will. The client could not afford to pay him, but she did deliver a cake to his office. "I'll remember that cake more than any check I ever got from any client."[69]

Bar Service

Getting involved with your state or local bar association is a great way to meet other lawyers, build relationships, and work toward the 50-hour aspirational goal for *pro bono* service.[70] The bar tailors opportunities to areas of practice, gender, age, and skill sets.

> **ABA Model Rule 6.1: Voluntary Pro Bono Publico Service**
> Every lawyer has a professional responsibility to provide legal services to those unable to pay. A lawyer should aspire to render at least (50) hours of pro bono publico legal services per year.

No matter what kind of law you intend to practice, service in the bar can be good for the community and your career; you meet your future colleagues, judges, and opponents at bar functions and get to know them outside the framework of a case. As you build a reputation as someone who is trustworthy and gets things done, you will grow your network and create more referral and collaborative opportunities.

Criminal Appointments

Of course, the lawyers as a whole can never be popular. They represent minority groups and stand for individual rights. They must place themselves athwart the current of public opinion when waves of prejudice roll. There always have been and doubtless will be gibes and disparaging remarks hurled at our profession. We should not be overly concerned about that, but should be concerned about rekindling a resolve to overcome and smother them by lives of rectitude and public service.

Chief Justice John E. Hickman, Supreme Court of Texas[71]

Accepting criminal appointments can help sharpen your trial skills and serve the vital role of representing an accused citizen. The classic *pro bono* case brings to mind images of actors Gregory Peck as Atticus Finch[72] and Matthew McConaughey as Jake Brigance.[73] While criminal appointments are vital to the administration of justice, not all are popular.[74]

The need for *pro bono* criminal representation predates the founding of our country. One of the Founding Fathers played an instrumental role in the unpopular defense of British soldiers. In early March 1770, tensions were high between the colonists and British soldiers in Boston. On March 5, a mob of colonists gathered at the Boston Customs House and taunted the British sentries on duty. They hurled not only insults but "snowballs, ice, oyster shells, and even lumps of coal." After one soldier was knocked down, he fired at the crowd and the other soldiers followed suit. The incident became known as the Boston Massacre.[75]

On March 13, 1770, 13 indictments for murder were issued. Captain Thomas Preston, as the officer of the guard at the Customs House the night of the Boston Massacre, would be tried first. No one wanted to represent Captain Preston until John Adams, a Patriot leader and future President, agreed to defend Preston and the other soldiers. Adams's position as a staunch Patriot made the decision an unpopular one, but he believed the men should receive fair trials.[76] Adams's representation was successful; Captain Preston was acquitted because he never gave an order to his men to fire on the colonists.[77]

ABA Model Rule 6.2 reminds that lawyers are not to avoid appointment except for good cause, in settings when:

(a) representing the client is likely to result in violation of the Rules of Professional Conduct or other law;

(b) representing the client is likely to result in an unreasonable financial burden on the lawyer; or

(c) the client or the cause is so repugnant to the lawyer as to be likely to impair the client-lawyer relationship or the lawyer's ability to represent the client.

Six soldiers were acquitted and only two were found guilty of manslaughter, rather than murder, which would have been punishable by death. Because the two British soldiers, threatened by the angry crowd, acted in self-defense, they received a reduced sentence. Adams literally saved their lives.

If you are interested in pursuing a career as a criminal defense lawyer, consider getting on the appointment list after law school. You may have the opportunity to help someone in need, develop your skills, and learn much about how the criminal justice system works.

Legal Aid, Legal Services, and Other Nonprofit Organizations

Every community has citizens with unmet legal needs.[78] Legal services organizations, such as those funded by the Legal Services Corporation, strive to provide low-income Americans with access to lawyers and representation for a variety of issues.[79] As a lawyer, you can help these organizations by taking cases or serving in leadership roles for the organization. Not only will you help those in your community, you can deepen your understanding and sharpen your skills in your chosen area of specialty.

Nonprofit organizations may ask you to join their board of directors. Before doing so, be clear about what role you will be serving: director or attorney for the board or organization. Non-lawyers may think you should serve both roles, but this can be an ethically difficult line to walk. Serving in both capacities requires you to switch between roles, and you are ethically bound to advise the board "when you are acting as counsel and when you are acting as a director."[80] This could get complicated. Simply be clear about what role you play. You can help the board by asking the questions it needs to be thinking about and helping it find the right lawyer for the organization's legal needs.

Law Reform Benefiting Low-Income Americans

While serving at the local level or taking a *pro bono* case will directly benefit individuals in your community in a meaningful way, you may want to consider law reform activities that affect everyone in the state or the nation. By engaging in law reform activities, you can identify systematic problems and work on solutions to those problems.

Many landmark Supreme Court cases, such as *Gideon v. Wainwright*[81] which guaranteed the right to appointed counsel, were handled *pro bono*.[82] You can have a broader impact by working on legislative reform to effect change. Each year, access to justice commissions around the country work with their legislatures to enact access to justice solutions. You can get involved with your access to justice commission and lend expertise by either drafting legislation or visiting with legislators. As with the other options noted above, you can use these opportunities to grow your network, build your brand, and learn more about your area of specialty.

HOMETOWN INVOLVEMENT

Getting involved where you live can pay dividends for you and for your community. How you get involved may depend on the size of the town in which you live. Involvement in New York City may take a different approach than involvement in much smaller Laramie, Wyoming. Big cities tend to have a wider array of options for involvement, both in their bar associations and in other legal organizations. In fact, the issue for big cities can be having too many choices. A key to feeling more connected in a big city is to find a smaller group and get involved.

Although smaller cities and towns have some of the same avenues of community involvement that big cities have, the options for lawyers to become involved in the local community are different. You will have opportunities to speak publicly or to make a written contribution to a project whether appearing at the Rotary Club or Career Day at the neighborhood elementary school, speaking to the municipal police force, or drafting your church's employee social media policy. Consider actively supporting local school sports teams by attending such events as high school basketball games. Communicate to the community that you are an active, engaged, and caring member of the community. You will find that you actually enjoy being known as the involved local attorney. Although opportunities in a small city may be more limited, it is much easier to stand out and be recognized.

Leon Jaworski wrote poignantly about practice in a small town. Although he achieved fame and success from his practice in Houston, he missed the life he had led in Waco, Texas:

> There is something about practicing in a small city or in a town that cannot be duplicated in a metropolis. The mad rush is absent — there is usually more camaraderie

among lawyers—outside of the courtroom, to be sure. There is a difference in the practice, and the average client often is friend and neighbor to the lawyer. As I struggled through the maze of complexities in Houston, both in professional and in private life, I more than once took a wistful glance in the direction of Waco.[83]

Rural areas may offer fewer types of involvement than a big city, but you may connect more intimately with and have an active interest in more of the community members' lives. Your community involvement may include membership in local clubs such as Rotary, the local chamber of commerce, and faith-based groups. These activities are effective and vital in establishing a trusted name and building a practice in a rural area.

The key in both small towns and rural areas is that you actually know your neighbors. There is an openness to meeting them and a richness to that involvement. The Covid-19 pandemic will be remembered for tragedy and devastation in many regards, but one positive phenomenon was the reconnection with neighbors in ways not seen in decades. In Italy, neighbors met at their windows in a chorus of singing and dancing to lift their spirits during a nationwide lockdown.[84] New Yorkers joined their neighbors at 7:00 p.m. each evening standing in doorways and hanging out windows cheering for nurses in appreciation as they changed shifts at nearby hospitals.[85] In neighborhoods across the nation, sheltering-in-place families spent more time in the yard, walking the neighborhood and "meeting" neighbors for the first time—all from the expected six-foot distance, of course. Being out and about within your community will serve you well as you build your practice and develop your reputation as a leader.

BROADER IMPACT

Regardless of the type of community in which you choose to practice, consider joining organizations at the state and national levels. Often, this starts with local involvement such as with your local bar association, but you do not have to start locally. Think about what statewide groups to join and select organizations that align with your practice area or your passions and interests. Statewide commitments can be more time-consuming than local as they may involve travel. As with any organization, be sure that if you agree to serve, you are able to serve.

Membership and leadership at the national level can be a career boost given the broad coverage of a national organization. Getting to leadership positions nationally often requires involvement over a longer period of time and a more in-depth commitment to the cause. As with any other position, be sure it is realistic for you to serve before you agree.

BALANCE YOUR WORK AND NON-WORK COMMITMENTS

While it is important to engage with *pro bono* and community opportunities, it is also important to remember that you cannot do it all. Do not join every organization just for the sake of joining or even because a group asks for your help. Be strategic and intentional about what you join and focus on joining those groups that can help your practice. You might also avoid doing too much too soon. Be patient and join additional organizations as permitted by the demands of your schedule. A suggested three-year timeline is as follows:

- Year 1: identify organization and attend meetings;
- Year 2: volunteer for a local, junior-level position within the organization;
- Year 3: escalate involvement by volunteering for additional responsibilities and duties.

Your interest and availability also will change over time as you experience the different seasons of life. If your pets are family members, you may be more interested in animal rights causes. During the season of life devoted to caring for your grandmother or mother who is afflicted with Alzheimer's disease, you may choose to devote your time, talent, and resources in support of a cure. Through each season of life and each new endeavor, remember to care for yourself so that you can continue to contribute to the world in a meaningful manner.

CONCLUSION

Real change, enduring change, happens one step at a time.

Justice Ruth Bader Ginsburg[86]

Your time in law school is the foundation for your career in the law. But the study of law regulations and cases, and practicing legal skills such as advocacy and drafting, are only part of what it takes to be a *complete* lawyer. Besides technical competence or expertise, you will be expected to become wise counselors and trusted advisors as you help clients navigate challenging situations and decisions. With your legal education and the additional skills and professional competencies you accumulate along the way, you will have countless opportunities to serve in leadership positions in organizations and institutions.[87] In each role — technical expert, wise counselor, and effective leader — you must be guided by your ethical duties and professional obligations to society. Together, these four components describe the making of a great lawyer.

Using your resources (time, talent, and treasure) in service to others will help with finding a sense of purpose and meaning in your life when you find an organization or cause that suits your interests. Service in your community also can benefit you professionally. Being dedicated, active, and reliable can increase your standing and reputation in the community, grow your career, and better the world around you. It takes patience; dividends may not come immediately, and sometimes they come in bunches. You must become technically proficient; you must be good at what you do. However, it is just as important to stay personally balanced. Keep your work life appropriately balanced with your personal life, and never let your efforts at growing your practice crowd out your spouse, children, friends, and faith. Above all, be intentional about both your work life and your personal life.

Exercise

Planning Community Involvement

Complete the following chart with at least two activities or causes. We have added a couple of examples to show you what this should look like when completed. Taking the time to create your own will benefit you in the long run.

In the first column, list activities that you enjoy or causes you care about. This may include a cause that was an important factor in motivating you to go to law school, or it might be an activity you enjoy as a hobby.

In the second column, list the skills and/or knowledge you have (or will gain in law school) that could be used to assist with that activity or cause.

In the third column, identify types of organizations that are involved in that activity or cause. This will give you a list of organizations to approach in your community.

In the fourth column, describe how your career might be benefited by your involvement. It's perfectly fine if you choose something that does not have a tangible or intangible link to your career path, but it's something that you should consider.

Activities or Causes	Skills/Knowledge	Organization	Career Benefit
Helping neglected or abused children	Advocacy skills—using the skills I've learned in law school to advocate for children's best interests when they cannot effectively advocate for themselves. Data gathering and assessment—meeting with various people and agencies to help achieve the best interest of the children. Communication skills—collaborating with other professionals; providing written and oral reports.	CASA (Court Appointed Special Advocates)	As a CASA volunteer, by dedicating myself to the work and becoming known as someone who can be trusted and relied on, I will build my reputation as a professional. It may also lead to board service for the organization, which could help me get to know other leaders in the community, which could lead to business development for my firm.

Activities or Causes	Skills/Knowledge	Organization	Career Benefit
Opportunities for youth sports	Teaching young people [a particular sport (baseball, soccer, etc.)]	[Your town's] Little League/ Soccer League/ Pop Warner Football League	As someone engaged in coaching youth sports, I will meet parents and business leaders who sponsor teams. By being dedicated and responsible I will become known and respected in the community, which will help grow my reputation as a professional.

Journal Prompts

1. Describe your progress on the aspects of becoming a complete lawyer.

   a. What skills or competencies are you developing in law school to become technically competent? What progress has been made and what else do you need to learn?

   b. What skills or competencies are you developing in law school to become a wise counselor? What progress has been made and what else do you need to learn?

   c. In your law school classes, how often do you think about the ethical issues related to a course of action? What prompted your inquiry?

2. At this time in your life, what resources (time, talent, and treasure) do you have that can benefit the community through service?

3. Is there a local, state, or national organization that represents people or causes about which you are passionate? Does getting involved with that organization help you achieve your career goals? Identify two to three organizations and groups of various kinds that you should consider joining (both legal and non-legal).

4. Of the organizations you identified in question 3 or the exercise above, pick one you want to join within the first six months of practice.

   a. Why did you pick that one?

   b. List steps or actions you can take within the organization that will likely result in an opportunity to serve in a leadership role.

   c. What is your estimated timeline for taking these steps or actions?

   d. How will you keep yourself accountable for going to meetings and keeping up with your responsibilities?

   e. How will you ensure that you do not over commit yourself?

Endnotes

1. LEON JAWORSKI, THE LAWYER IN SOCIETY 78 (Baylor University Press 2011). Leonidas "Leon" Jaworski was an American attorney and law professor who served as the second special prosecutor during the Watergate scandal. He was the youngest person ever sworn into the Texas Bar in 1925 after his graduation from Baylor Law School.
2. DANIEL CONRAD, YOUTH PARTICIPATION AND EXPERIENTIAL EDUCATION (University of Minnesota 2018).
3. Ben W. Heineman, William F. Lee & David B. Wilkins, *Lawyers as Professionals and as Citizens: Key Roles and Responsibilities in the 21st Century*, CENTER ON THE LEGAL PROFESSION AT HARVARD LAW SCHOOL 9 (Oct. 20, 2014), https://clp.law.harvard.edu/assets/Professionalism-Project-Essay_11.20.14.pdf.
4. *Id.*
5. *Id.* at 11–12.
6. *Id.* at 11.
7. Margaret Mead, QUOTE INVESTIGATOR, https://quoteinvestigator.com/2017/11/12/change-world/ (last visited July 20, 2020).
8. William Shakespeare, BIOGRAPHY.COM, https://www.biography.com/writer/william-shakespeare (last visited July 20, 2020). William Shakespeare, often called England's national poet, is considered the greatest dramatist of all time. His works are loved throughout the world, but Shakespeare's personal life is shrouded in mystery.
9. SAM LEVENSON, IN ONE ERA AND OUT THE OTHER (Open Road Media 2016).
10. MARTIN LUTHER KING, JR. & CORETTA SCOTT KING, THE WORDS OF MARTIN LUTHER KING, JR. (Newmarket Press 1987).
11. Jim Sandman, PENN LAW, https://www.law.upenn.edu/live/profiles/1686-jim-sandman (last visited July 17, 2020).
12. Jim Sandman, *Pro Bono and Public Service: Pillars of Democracy and the Legal Profession*, Association of American Law Schools, Pro Bono and Public Service Opportunities Section (Jan. 4, 2020).
13. David O'Boyle, *Legends in the Law: James J. Sandman*, DC BAR (May 2015), https://www.dcbar.org/bar-resources/publications/washington-lawyer/articles/may-2015-legends-in-the-law.cfm.
14. Carl Rauscher, *LSC President James J. Sandman to Step Down*, LEGAL SERVICES CORPORATION (Jan. 21, 2020), https://www.lsc.gov/media-center/press-releases/2020/lsc-president-james-j-sandman-step-down.
15. Sandman, *supra* note 12.
16. Jim Sandman, LINKEDIN, https://www.linkedin.com/in/jim-sandman-089b0918/ (last visited July 17, 2020).
17. *See* ROBERT K. GREENLEAF, THE POWER OF SERVANT-LEADERSHIP: ESSAYS 18 (Berrett Koehler 1998).
18. Athena Xenikou, *Transformational Leadership, Transactional Contingent Reward, and Organizational Identification: The Mediating Effect of Perceived Innovation and Goal Culture Orientations*, FRONTIERS IN PSYCHOL. 18 (October 2017), https://www.frontiersin.org/articles/10.3389/fpsyg.2017.01754/full; Kevin Kruse, *What Is Authentic Leadership?*, FORBES (May 12, 2013), https://www.forbes.com/sites/kevinkruse/2013/05/12/what-is-authentic-leadership/#6c348681def7; PETER G. NORTHOUSE, LEADERSHIP: THEORY AND PRACTICE 258 (8th ed. 2019).
19. *See* Larry Spears, *Reflections on Robert K. Greenleaf and Servant-Leadership*, 17 LEADERSHIP & ORG. DEV. J. 33 (1996).
20. PETER G. NORTHOUSE, LEADERSHIP: THEORY AND PRACTICE (8th ed. 2019).
21. ROBERT K. GREENLEAF, THE SERVANT AS LEADER 15 (1970).

22. *See, e.g.,* Bruce J. Avolio and William L. Gardner, *Authentic leadership development: Getting to the root of positive forms of leadership,* 16 Leadership Q., no. 3, 315, 331 (2005).

23. Heineman et al., *supra* note 3 at 12. "Although in many circumstances the four ethical responsibilities will be complementary, in others they may be in tension or even conflict. As a result, we recognize that lawyers will sometimes be in the difficult position of choosing which of these responsibilities will take precedence in guiding specific courses of action. Criminal defense lawyers, for example, generally believe that they have, in particular matters, far greater obligations to protect the interests of their clients — and far fewer obligations to protect the rule of law or the public interest — than lawyers who are advising companies on prospective regulatory compliance, where the substantive and procedural context is very different. Even in the criminal defense context, however, we believe that lawyers should consider whether their actions are within a fair interpretation of 'the bounds of the law,' and that those lawyers in any event have an obligation to participate in efforts to reform the legal framework, or society more generally, to better serve the goal of protecting the rights of criminal defendants and the public interest in the fair and efficient administration of justice." *Id. See* Chapter 12 for a more complete discussion of the interplay of integrity and good moral character to navigate the complexities of ethical responsibility.

24. Carol Smith, *The Leadership Theory of Robert K. Greenleaf* 3, Carol Smith (2005), https://www.carolsmith .us/downloads/640greenleaf.pdf.

25. Greenleaf, *supra* note 17.

26. Smith, *supra* note 24.

27. Carmine Gallo, *The Coach Behind the Longest Winning Streak in Sports History Shows How to Build a Championship Business Team,* Forbes (Aug. 19, 2014), https://www.forbes.com/sites/carminegallo/2014/ 08/19/the-coach-behind-the-longest-winning-streak-in-sports-history-shows-how-to-build-a-champion- business-team/#1caf120733a4.

28. *Id.*

29. *Id.*

30. *Id.*

31. *Id.*

32. Model Rules of Prof'l Conduct R. 6.1 (1983).

33. *Id.* at 6.1(a). "In fulfilling this responsibility, the lawyer should: . . . provide a substantial majority of the (50) hours of legal services without fee or expectation of fee to: (1) persons of limited means or (2) charitable, religious, civic, community, governmental and educational organizations in matters that are designed primarily to address the needs of persons of limited means." *Id.*

34. *Id.* at 6.1(b). In fact, the Model Rules specifically highlight the methods in which lawyers can serve: (1) delivery of legal services at no fee or substantially reduced fee to individuals, groups, or organizations seeking to secure or protect civil rights, civil liberties, or public rights, or charitable, religious, civic, community, governmental, and educational organizations in matters in furtherance of their organizational purposes, where the payment of standard legal fees would significantly deplete the organization's economic resources or would be otherwise inappropriate; (2) delivery of legal services at a substantially reduced fee to persons of limited means; or (3) participation in activities for improving the law, the legal system, or the legal profession.

35. Author Stephen L. Rispoli conversation with Matthew L. Czimskey (July 16, 2020).

36. Carmen Symes Dusek, *Lead Attorney for Children of YFZ Ranch Recalls Biggest Child Custody Case in US History,* Go San Angelo (Apr. 2, 2018), https://www.gosanangelo.com/story/news/columnists/2018/04/02/ lead-attorney-children-yfz-ranch-recalls-biggest-child-custody-case-u-s-history/470851002/. Jeffs was later convicted and is serving a life sentence. *Id.*

37. *Id.*

38. *Id.*

39. *Id.*

40. *See, e.g., Over $64,000 Raised for Community Partners of Dallas,* Container Store (Aug. 11, 2017), http:// standfor.containerstore.com/over-64000-raised-for-community-partners-of-dallas; *About Us and Our Grant Making,* The Boone Family Foundation, https://www.theboonefamilyfoundation.org/about-us/ (last visited July 17, 2020).

41. *See, e.g., Foundation FAQ,* Bill and Melinda Gates Foundation, https://www.gatesfoundation.org/Who- We-Are/General-Information/Foundation-FAQ (last visited July 17, 2020).

42. *What We Do,* Bill and Melinda Gates Foundation, https://www.gatesfoundation.org/what-we-do (last visited July 17, 2020).

43. Nicola Crosta, *Think Before You Give: Impact Philanthropy vs. Impulse Philanthropy,* Medium (Oct. 26, 2017), https://medium.com/@Nico_Crost/impact-philanthropy-vs-impulse-philanthropy-7e8f516c2cb6.

44. *See* Chapter 5.

45. Judge Ed Kinkeade, Baylor Academy of the Advocate in St. Andrews (July 30, 2017).
46. *Report on the Future of Legal Services in the United States,* ABA (2016), https://www.americanbar.org/content/dam/aba/images/abanews/2016FLSReport_FNL_WEB.pdf.
47. *Id.* at 8.
48. *Id.*
49. *Id.* at 12.
50. *Id.*; Rebecca L. Sandefur, *What We Know and Need to Know About the Legal Needs of the Public,* 67 S.C. L. Rev. 443, 443 (2016).
51. *Id.* at 444.
52. *Id.* at 443.
53. *Id.* (citing Hazel Genn, Paths to Justice: What People Do and Think About Going to Law 12 (Hart Publishing 1999) (defining "justiciable event")).
54. Jessica K. Steinberg, *Demand Side Reform in the Poor People's Court,* 47 Conn. L. Rev. 741, 749 (2015).
55. *Id.* at 743.
56. *Id.*; *Access to Justice Facts,* Texas Access to Justice Foundation, http://www.teajf.org/news/statistics.aspx (last visited Jan. 1, 2018) ("To qualify for free civil legal services in Texas, an individual must not earn more than $14,850 per year. A family of four must not earn more than $30,375 per year.").
57. *Id.*
58. Steinberg, *supra* note 54, at 743.
59. Sandefur, *supra* note 50, at 448 (citing Rebecca L. Sandefur, *Accessing Justice in the Contemporary USA: Findings from the Community Needs and Services Study* 3 (Aug. 8, 2014)).
60. *Id.*
61. *Id.*
62. For more information, visit the ABA's Access to Justice research and evaluation website: https://www.americanbar.org/groups/legal_aid_indigent_defendants/initiatives/resource_center_for_access_to_justice/atj_commission_self-assessment_materials1/studies.html (last visited July 20, 2020).
63. Elie Mystal, *Earning $250,000 Does Not Make You Rich, Not in My Town,* Above The Law (Sept. 21, 2010), https://abovethelaw.com/2010/09/earning-250000-does-not-make-you-rich-not-in-my-town/; *see also* Michael Zuckerman, *Is There Such a Thing as an Affordable Lawyer?,* The Atlantic (May 30, 2014), https://www.theatlantic.com/business/archive/2014/05/is-there-such-a-thing-as-an-affordable-lawyer/371746/.
64. LegalShield, *The Legal Needs of Small Businesses: A Research Study Conducted by Decision Analyst Commissioned by LegalShield,* Business.com, https://www.business.com/images/content/58a/da0bd2f87b1207f721220/0-0-/ (last visited Jan. 1, 2018).
65. *Id.*
66. *Id.*
67. *New ABA Data Reveals Rise in Number of U.S. Lawyers, 15 Percent Increase Since 2008,* ABA (May 11, 2018), https://www.americanbar.org/news/abanews/aba-news-archives/2018/05/new_aba_data_reveals/#:~:text=May%2011%2C%202018-,New%20ABA%20data%20reveals%20rise%20in%20number%20of%20U.S.%20lawyers,attorneys%20in%20the%20United%20States.
68. Adapted from Loren Eiseley, The Star Thrower (Random House 1978).
69. Lee Dryden, *"Anytime That Lawyers Look Good, It Helps Us,"* Legalnews.com (Nov. 16, 2016), http://legalnews.com/detroit/1433931.
70. Model Rules of Prof'l Conduct R. 6.1(b)(3) (1983).
71. Jaworski, *supra* note 1, at 78.
72. To Kill a Mockingbird (United Artists 1962).
73. A Time to Kill (Warner Bros. 1996).
74. Model Rules of Prof'l Conduct R. 6.2 (1983).
75. *John Adams and the Boston Massacre Trials,* The Constitutional Rights Foundation (2012), https://www.crf-usa.org/images/pdf/JohnAdamsandtheBostonMassacreTrials.pdf.
76. *Id.*
77. Christopher Klein, *Why John Adams Defended British Soldiers in the Boston Massacre Trials,* History.com (Apr. 2, 2020), https://www.history.com/news/boston-massacre-trial-john-adams-dan-abrams.
78. Stephen Rispoli, *Courting Access to Justice,* S. Cal. Rev. L. & Soc. Just. (forthcoming 2020).
79. *See How Legal Aid Works,* Legal Services Corporation (2020), https://www.lsc.gov/.
80. Lucrecia P. Johnson, *The Ethical Pitfalls of Nonprofit Board Service,* A.B.A. J., https://www.americanbar.org/groups/young_lawyers/publications/tyl/topics/ethics/the-ethical-pitfalls-nonprofit-board-service/ (last visited July 17, 2020).
81. *Gideon v. Wainwright,* 372 U.S. 335 (1963).

82. Josh Ashenmiller, *Gideon v. Wainwright*, Britannica (2014), https://www.britannica.com/event/Gideon-v-Wainwright.

83. Jaworski, *supra* note 1, at 75.

84. Matt Clinch, *Italians are Singing Songs from Their Windows to Boost Morale During Coronavirus Lockdown*, CNBC (Mar. 14, 2020), https://www.cnbc.com/2020/03/14/coronavirus-lockdown-italians-are-singing-songs-from-balconies.html.

85. Adam Jeffery, *New Yorkers Stop and Give Daily Thanks and Gratitude for Coronavirus Frontline Workers*, CNBC (Apr. 5, 2020), https://www.cnbc.com/2020/04/05/new-yorkers-stop-and-give-daily-thanks-and-gratitude-for-coronavirus-frontline-workers.html.

86. Irin Carmon, Notorious RBG: The Life and Times of Ruth Bader Ginsburg (Dey Street Books 2015).

87. Heineman et al., *supra* note 3.

Chapter 23

Legacy and Impact

Please think about your legacy because you are writing it every day.

Gary Vaynerchuk[1]

Purpose

Contemplate the legacy of leadership and consider opportunities for impact.

Learning Objectives

At the end of this chapter, you should be able to:

- Discuss the human need for self-actualization and the importance of finding purpose.
- Describe the concept of professional and personal legacy.
- Identify potential areas of service that align with your passion.
- Commit to developing a plan for future impact and influence.

Discussion

INTRODUCTION

The Founders of our nation and the Framers of our Constitution emphasized *justice* as a primary value, recognizing that achieving that goal is the result of a delicate balance.

> Thomas Jefferson said, "The most sacred of the duties of government is to do equal and impartial justice to all its citizens." Alexander Hamilton wrote, "The first duty of society is justice." James Madison in Federalist Number 51 wrote, "Justice is the end of government, it is the end of civil society, never has been, never will be pursued until it be obtained or until liberty be lost in the pursuit." George Washington said, "The due administration of justice is the first pillar of good government."[2]

For the Founders, having spent much of their lives under the undemocratic rule of a distant British monarch, justice was a value literally worth dying for. After nearly 250 years of separation from Britain, however, does justice carry the same weight for us?

The first line of the Constitution reads, "We the people of the United States, in order to form a more perfect union, establish justice. . . ."[3] The Framers combined our solidarity as a country with a need to establish justice. They felt a just country was more important than even the defense of that country. As Jim Sandman noted:

> They recognized that an accessible, well-functioning system of justice is essential to societal stability. It's about the rule of law. You won't long have a nation to defend, or worth defending, without it. This is what Judge Leonard Hand meant, when he said in 1951 speaking to the Legal Aid Society of New York, "If we are to keep our democracy, there must be one commandment. Thou shalt not ration justice."[4]

We all want our lives to count for something. As a lawyer, you have the responsibility to fulfill the promises the Founders made to Americans. Even though the Founders were imperfect, the lofty goals they ascribed to and promulgated were the right goals. Our country will always have to use imperfect humans as the architects and administrators of justice; the fact that our predecessors made mistakes does not detract from the clarity of their vision. Lawyers and law students now become the new guarantors of the need for justice.

President Abraham Lincoln faced this challenge as he attempted to eradicate slavery:[5]

> The Framers, in Lincoln's phrase, made the egalitarian principles of the Declaration of Independence the "apple of gold" of which the Constitution and the Union were merely a "silver picture . . . framed around it." They lacked, however, both the opportunity and the will to get the right fit between the Declaration and the Constitution; the constitutional frame was flawed and imperfect, but unfinished and reinterpretable. Getting

the two texts to fit properly together, in Lincoln's account, was a task the Framers left to future generations, and he called on his generation of citizen-interpreters to spurn the proslavery Constitution of the Court and instead to complete the Founders' "unfinished work" of "Liberty for All."[6]

More recent generations of lawyers continue to fight for more justice nationally and globally, whether in freedom marches in Alabama, pushing for gender equality, or advocating for LGBTQ+ rights. Lawyers must lead the charge to protect the marginalized and the underserved — to close the access to justice gap and ensure equal protection under the law. Lawyers who invest in changing society on a local level can find opportunity to make a larger impact. Consider the impact that Supreme Court Justices Thurgood Marshall and Ruth Bader Ginsburg had in advocating for race and gender equality. While not all lawyers will reach the Supreme Court, countless lawyers contribute to the jurisprudence of our country each year. Each reported opinion lists the lawyers advocating for each side. Adversity makes the law better. By presenting both sides of every argument in a zealous manner, the courts have the ability to craft better law.

Preserving justice requires action on both a micro and a macro scale. Some lawyers achieve justice one client at a time. Whether through litigation or in the transactional world, lawyers can create legacies by giving their clients the best representation they can. Others direct their legacies more systemically by looking at racial or gender discrimination and changing policies at a firm-level, or establishing a nonprofit to create more opportunities for the disadvantaged. As our country tackles issues of race and use of force by police, lawyers are working to facilitate better communication, representing both those who protest and the police, and helping craft legislation to ensure justice for all involved. The combination of individualized effort with broader application can help create a legacy — how each of us works to leave our world a more just place than it was beforehand.

YOUR PERSONAL IMPACT ON THE FUTURE

Your legacy is your personal impact on the future — finding that which gives your life significance. "It means putting a stamp on the future and making a contribution to future generations."[7] People want to leave a legacy because they want to feel that their life mattered to someone. They want to know what difference they made. Thinking about what you want your legacy to be can give your life more meaning and purpose. Beginning to think about legacy as you begin your career can help give you direction and clarify your priorities.

At some level, we desire to be remembered for our contributions so that after we die, the world takes note of the fact we were once in it. That legacy may be satisfied in the family we create or the job we have. For others, the need for legacy takes a broader dimension with a contribution so significant that it changes the world in dramatic and awe-inspiring ways. A more modest legacy does not make the contribution an unimportant one. Think about people who took a chance on you, or teachers who changed your life and led you to believe you could change the world. Whether your legacy is recorded in the history books or just on the hearts of those around you, legacy means you have left a lasting imprint that will be remembered by those whose lives you touched.[8] Every day that we change hearts, minds, and the law, we change the world for the better.

An inscription on the tomb of an Anglican bishop in Westminster Abbey reads:

When I was young and free and my imagination had no limits, I dreamed of changing the world.

As I grew older and wiser I discovered the world would not change — So I shortened my sights somewhat and decided to change only my country, but it too seemed immovable.

As I grew into my twilight years, in one last desperate attempt, I settled for changing only my family, those closest to me, but alas, they would have none of it.

And now I realize as I lie on my deathbed, if I had only changed myself first, then by example I might have changed my family. From their inspiration and encouragement I would then have been able to better my country,

And who knows, I might have even changed the world.[9]

SELF-ACTUALIZATION: THE CATALYST FOR CHANGE

The highest human desire is self-actualization — the realization of one's talents and potential. Until our basic needs are met, there is little room for self-actualization. Once basic needs are fulfilled, though, we can shift away from these external needs such as food, shelter, and sense of belonging, and focus more attention on our internal need for self-growth. We can spend time on what talents we have, how much we can develop them, and how broadly those talents can affect others. Only at this stage can we actualize our innate potential. According to Maslow, growth-motivated individuals seek:

- Ongoing actualization of potentials, capacities, and talents;
- Fulfillment of mission (calling, fate, destiny, vocation);
- Fuller knowledge of, and acceptance of, the person's intrinsic nature; and
- Unceasing trend toward unity, integration, or synergy within the person.[10]

Self-actualization, then, is the engine that drives legacy. The process of striving for and reaching your full potential means aligning your gifts, awakening your passion, and utilizing your talents to pursue opportunities in response to a desire or calling from within that directs your steps. Finding your purpose in life and fulfilling it leads to a peace that transcends the challenges faced along the journey.

The most common regret expressed by dying patients deals with unfulfilled dreams. They wanted to "have had the courage to live a life true to myself, not the life others expected of me." As people face the end of life and see with clarity how theirs was lived, too many see the dreams they left unfulfilled. They regret knowing they did not honor those dreams with the choices they made or did not make.[11]

Your legacy could be using your advocacy skills to prevent further injury, illness, or loss of lives as a result of faulty products. Your legacy might be as a volunteer attorney, helping to protect children from abuse and neglect, or mentoring troubled youth so that they develop the confidence to take control over their destiny. Businesses structured with your help could provide jobs and security for thousands of employees and their families. You might hold political office or help draft legislation that changes the course of history. Other ways of leaving your imprint on society may be through monetary donations as well as service to charitable organizations. For example, each year alumni look for ways to help those who come after them and donate to the dean's excellence or the faculty fund, create a scholarship, or fund an award. Law school is expensive, and each dollar creating access for students to study the law gives greater access for those who would promote justice. As you look around your law school, notice the names of those who gave back and remember the doors they opened for you, your friends, and your colleagues.

For many, the family they create is the greatest legacy, and this is a valuable and important legacy. Being fully present with your family as you act to affect future generations positively reminds you of the impact you can have. Baylor Law Dean Brad Toben often leads students through an exercise to illustrate impact. He asks students to name their grandparents, then their great-grandparents, and if anyone is still responding, to name even one great-great-grandparent. While many of the names are forgotten, the impact on their children and their children's children through their love, attention, teaching, and guidance influences the family for generations.[12]

Leaving a legacy is an important part of one's life work, developed through a life dedicated to self-reflection and purpose. Think about Walt Disney and his legacy. What started with a cartoon mouse revolutionized animation, television, technology, nature and conservation, family entertainment, and more. Each step of his legacy built incrementally on the prior steps but combined to change the world as we know it.

Now it is your turn. Let the journey of self-discovery, expanded by what you have learned about lawyer leadership, guide you toward your legacy. Begin understanding your gifts, finding your passions, and making the most of your talents. A life lived in harmony with your true self produces lasting impact, combined with a sense of peace that you lived the life you were meant to live.

LEGACY: INPUT AND OUTPUT PLUS ATTITUDE

Contemplating how to create impact within your spheres of influence requires that you look at three variables: input, output, and attitude. What do you need to acquire now (input) to produce the desired result (output)? Once you have the necessary input and output, you can adjust your attitude to see the legacy project through to completion.

"Input" includes all that will prepare you for the work you want to do — the knowledge, skills, competencies, and experience. Pursuing the right educational program (such as law school) matters but ultimately is not enough if you do not take the right classes or fully apply yourself to learning the material and understanding the applications. While many schools have a set or core curriculum, no one gives you the life curriculum for achieving your goals. You need to be thoughtful about what knowledge, skills, and competencies you may need for the next job and the next. Once you identify the skills to develop, you will need a plan for how to acquire that which you need. You may learn much of the necessary expertise as you work with other lawyers. Other skills can be gleaned as you do volunteer work or serve as a bar association leader. Still others require additional formal study through a certificate program or advanced degree. Not only will you build a portfolio of talents but you will engage your brain, increase your connections, and be better prepared to lead.

Another aspect of input is human capital. Building a network of people can connect you to resources that help you accomplish your goals and dreams. Intentionally develop relationships with people you meet. People do business with those whom they know, like, and trust. Even buying life insurance becomes more appealing if we like our broker and think she has our best interests at heart. Relationships must be built on trust, managed with integrity, and nurtured so they will grow. The people you involve in your life not only help you grow but allow you to mutually benefit from one another's experience and knowledge. At its most literal sense, you gain input from these multiple sources.

Computer programmers know that the output from a computer program is only as good as the input — more colloquially, "garbage in, garbage out." The same is true here; if you get the input right, the output will flow. The legacy process does not merely come from the accumulation of input, though; having a defined output guides the needed input. In other words, if you are intentional in identifying the desired result of your work, you can be more intentional about the needed input. What problem are you trying to solve? What action will be required to have the desired impact or influence? If you seek to provide a more stable food supply for a community, you must learn about the sources of food, the supply chain, and any available resources. Will they need a better food bank for nonperishable items? Is a community garden for fresh produce an option? Are there more systemic issues involved at the heart of the food shortage, such as unemployment or under-employment? Each issue requires knowledge of how it could be addressed, and what resources can and must be brought to bear; but once you have acquired that input, the output (e.g., a well-provisioned neighborhood) can become a self-sustaining reality.

Having a goal, plans for that goal, and the resources to achieve it are all valuable; but they come to nothing unless your plans are bolstered by the attitude essential for the work. The work of legacy should match your resources (time, talents, treasure) and your heart (your passion). What is needed for the work you choose? Is it compassion, courage, empathy, joy, sincerity, inspiration? What is the commitment — short-term intense focus or long-term perseverance (i.e., a sprint or a marathon)? Does it help the masses broadly or does the work require up-close personal attention? Can you do it alone or must you assemble a multitude of helpers?

Understanding the process — desired output, necessary input, and essential attitude — allows you to begin your work toward achieving a desired goal. You may envision many ideas and accomplish numerous goals in your lifetime, but we encourage you to more intentionally weave together the events of your journey, toward a lasting impact in your professional and personal life.

PLAN FOR FUTURE IMPACT AND INFLUENCE

You likely do not know what your legacy will be, and that is not surprising. You are early in your legal training, and you may not know the community in which you will settle, when you will start a family, or if you will, and what needs your clients will have. Starting to think about legacy now, though, helps you identify what you feel strongly about. You may find areas of law that are a "fit" for you and where you feel you do your best work. You may connect with others in your community who make you aware of needs and opportunities. Knowing that you want to leave a legacy opens the door for you to consider what that legacy might be and how to leverage connections to make it a reality. Some thoughts and suggestions for your consideration at this early stage include the following:

Who Are the People That Are Important to You?

How you spend your time, and with whom, will help define your legacy. "Touching lives and exemplifying a truthful path is paramount to living a joyful and purposeful life. Your legacy will live on."[13] Parents juggling career and family can regret the amount of time they spent away from their young children.[14] They learn too well that the parenting days are long, but the years are short. Time and energy spent with family deserves priority among your important pursuits, even when there is not an easy and immediate measure of the value. Similarly, how many of us lose touch with friends because we are too busy with work or our own families to make time? Too often we become so caught up in our own lives that we let treasured friendships fade. This lack of ongoing connection is a common regret expressed by those in their last days.[15] Many make New Year's resolutions to lose ten pounds or eat more kale. What if you resolved to do something you actually enjoyed: connect with those who were important to you and whom you do not see now? Now that would be a resolution worth keeping.

What Are the Causes About Which You Care Deeply?

That which you are passionate about will garner your energy. When you want to spend time and energy on something, that may tell you that it is a passion. Passions are infectious, with an outpouring of interests and ideas that become a catalyst for action. "Finding and pursing your passion allows you to see your destiny clearly."[16] Life will be more fun and more meaningful when you pursue your passions to the fullest. It can be contagious.[17]

What Brings You Joy?

A common, heartbreaking end-of-life regret is not having chosen to be happier. As Donna Sapolin noted in her book about end-of-life lessons, "Many did not realize until the end that happiness is a choice."[18] Abraham Lincoln had some wisdom about this when he said, "Most folks are about as happy as they make up their minds to be."[19] The sense of comfort from old and familiar habits can rob people of living their best life. Lack of joy and the absence of laughter can adversely affect not only people's mental wellness but their physical bodies as well. "Happiness and good health go hand-in-hand. Indeed, scientific studies have been finding that happiness can make our hearts healthier, our immune systems stronger, and our lives longer."[20]

Happiness is a choice. Choose to seek the silver lining in all that you face. Celebrate positive discoveries, both big and small. Prioritize that which brings glimmers of joy each day. Seek some of the silliness that brought laughter in childhood. Never let joy get buried under the burdens of adulthood. As lawyers, you will have daily opportunities to do as Maya Angelou suggested, "Try to be the rainbow in someone's cloud."[21]

What Keeps You from Being Bold?

BE BOLD! These words of advice from many a commencement speaker or motivational guest lecturer push us to be daring and brave. Boldness can prompt us to climb a mountain so we can look over a cliff, to run for public office, to speak up when we see someone treated unkindly or unfairly, or to act where there is injustice. When you act boldly, you take a risk. You could be risking physical danger, embarrassment, or your reputation.

No one will force you to live a full life, and if you choose inaction, you settle for a mediocre existence. Note how commonly the dying express regret and insight about life unlived. Must you really wait until then to realize the life you want? Not only must you decide to live to your fullest measure, you also need to apply yourself to those dreams. You chose law school and now have the benefit of all the opportunities this marvelous profession has to offer. Be sure to take full advantage of your time in law school and the opportunities for growth that are available.

Even beyond education, many feel as if they have settled for less in their lives. Some choose a career path that is more practical or one that would better support their families financially. Some value keeping peace with others even when conflict might produce a better outcome. Still others feel tied to family expectations. The deathbed question becomes: Which of those paths not taken kept us from becoming all we were capable of becoming? What if those safe choices prevent us from doing that which will be of greater benefit to others?

How Will You Share Yourself, Your Resources, and Your Blessings?

Regardless of your background, you have abundance. As a student in an American law school, you are among the privileged in this world. Lawyers represent less than one-half of one percent of all Americans. Getting into law school is highly competitive. Much will be expected of you when you join the legal profession. Your legal training and a law license create a special status, a privilege, that comes with the responsibility to care for your clients and society. Lawyers have an obligation to serve and to give back. The opportunities will be endless throughout your professional life. Choosing those opportunities that best fit you is the key.

An important part of evaluating your goals and planning your impact is slowing down enough to reassess how you spend your time. Notice your surroundings; "hit 'pause' more often and look deeply."[22] Is your behavior part of a larger pattern of action, or inaction, that you might someday regret?[23] Once you know what you have to give, you can also learn how to guide or mentor others.

> A mentor by definition is a more experienced or more knowledgeable person within an area of expertise. Everyone has some significant truth to impart to others that will guide less experienced people in life. The mentoring/mentee relationship involves personal development and support. This process involves an exchange of knowledge complemented by psychological and/or social support that is crucial to sustaining new mindsets. Sometimes these relationships last a lifetime, even when the mentee has moved on to influence others.[24]

Appreciation, gratitude, and "paying it forward," are also part of a fulfilling legacy. Each of us can and should express more appreciation, love, and respect—in actions and words. Everyone has blessings to share, even if it is a simple smile of acknowledgment, a kind word, or a helping hand. How will you share your abundance with others? What mark will you leave on your loved ones, your colleagues, and your communities—those who are part of your legacy?

How Will You Create a Succession Plan?

Leaders need to know when to hand the reins to someone else and how to do so smoothly. Succession planning acknowledges the need for leadership transition and intentional development of potential leaders in your organization.[25] How can you prepare others to fill your role or take your place? There are several steps an organization can take to plan for succession:

- Develop a mentor network;
- Identify high-potential employees;
- Engage others in leadership development activities;
- Avoid "heir apparent" designations and base succession decisions on a diverse pool of candidates;
- Create opportunities to expose high-potential employees to multiple decision-makers;
- Establish a supportive organizational culture; and
- Evaluate the effectiveness of leadership development.[26]

J. Cary Gray, managing partner of the Gray Reed law firm, notes that the firm engages in long-term planning to ensure that the firm survives each partner's practice.[27] Some law firms do not plan for succession; partners who originate the business intend to keep it until they retire, especially in "eat what you kill" firms whose financial model does not encourage the transition of work over time. By comparison, other firms, especially those built upon principles of servant leadership, look for ways to boost their younger lawyers and put them in a position to lead their practice (or the whole firm) in the future. Likewise, if you are planning to relocate to a small town after graduation, consider looking for a lawyer who is planning to hand over his firm in the future. You can learn a great deal and inherit a practice. Your legacy can also be the lawyers that you trained to replace you. What values do you want them to have? How do you want them to view the practice of law? What do you want them to share with even younger lawyers?

CONCLUSION

No leader sets out to be a leader. People set out to live their lives, expressing themselves fully. When that expression is of value, they become leaders. So the point is not to become a leader. The point is to become yourself, to use yourself completely—all your skills, gifts and energies—in order to make your vision manifest. You must withhold nothing. You must, in sum, become the person you started out to be, and to enjoy the process of becoming.

Warren Bennis[28]

Within our human nature is a desire to find purpose, to be part of something meaningful, and to have our life count for something. The knowledge, skills, and competencies you acquire in law school will equip you to influence people and organizations and to make an impact on causes and communities.

Our Founding Fathers were cognizant of the legacy they were creating as they drafted the Constitution for the new United States of America. No one felt the weight of their decision more than George Washington. As a non-lawyer working with lawyers such as Alexander Hamilton, President Washington "sometimes saw himself as being not up to the job."[29] Yet he knew his duty as first President was to "not only do what was best for the country, but what was best for the country under the Constitution. He was scrupulous about adhering to the Constitution."[30] Acting with deliberation and care, and knowing the importance of their work in those early years, President Washington relied heavily upon the lawyers who served as his advisors.[31] Everything he did set precedent and created a lasting legacy that has stood the test of time.[32]

You may not establish a new government, but you will have opportunities to play significant roles in the lives of others. The questions for you to consider now are: What difference will you make? Who will you help? What cause will you serve that is greater than yourself? Spend time thinking about these questions as you plan for and diligently prepare for your fulfilling life and lasting legacy. Be intentional about how you spend your time. By thoughtfully aligning your time and your abilities with your passions, you will set a direction for your life that will lead to professional satisfaction and achievement, and personal peace and fulfillment. Your path may not be easy, but when that journey is one you choose with thoughtful intentionality and navigate with perseverance and humility, your life will be meaningful, rewarding, and well lived.

Exercise

Write Your Eulogy

Write your eulogy. What would you want the person giving your eulogy to say about you?

Journal Prompts

1. Tim McGraw recorded a song called "Live Like You Were Dying." In the song, a man learns he has terminal cancer. Rather than wait for death, he chose to embrace life and pursue experiences he might never have otherwise. If you were given a similar diagnosis today, how would you change your life? What are the things you would make a priority?

2. Who are the important people in your life right now? Do your current actions communicate your love, admiration, and respect for them? If not, how will you remedy each situation?

3. What brings you joy in life? Are you giving these people or activities enough time while in law school? If not, how will you try to better balance your life and studies? (Remember: We are seeking harmony, not balance. Balance does not always occur

daily, but harmony should occur over some designated and reasonably appropriate window of time.)

4. About what are you passionate? Do your career plans relate to your passions? If not, what is your plan for time and energy spent in pursuit of your passions?

5. In what areas of your life do you need to be bolder? What is one step you can take in that direction?

6. What is your plan to achieve that which you listed in your eulogy?

7. How will you ensure that you review your plans and goals periodically? Will it be every year? Every five years? Or something else?

Endnotes

1. Bill High, *7 Great Quotes on Leaving a Legacy*, BILL HIGH (Aug. 8, 2017) author, and wine critic.
2. Jim Sandman, *Pro Bono and Public Service: Pillars of Democracy and the Legal Profession*, ASSOCIATION OF AMERICAN LAW SCHOOLS, PRO BONO AND PUBLIC SERVICE OPPORTUNITIES SECTION (Jan. 4, 2020).
3. The Constitution, THE WHITE HOUSE, https://www.whitehouse.gov/about-the-white-house/the-constitution/ (last visited July 20, 2020).
4. *Id.*
5. *See* William E. Forbath, *Caste, Class, and Equal Citizenship*, 98 MICH. L. REV. 1, 24 (1999).
6. *Id.* at 24 (internal citations omitted).
7. Dawn Franks, *How to Write a Legacy Statement, the Most Important Gift You Will Leave Behind*, YOUR PHILANTHROPY (Mar. 20, 2018), https://your-philanthropy.com/write-legacy-statement/.
8. Joan Moran, *5 Ways to Leave a Great Legacy*, HUFF. POST (Dec. 6, 2017), https://www.huffpost.com/entry/5-ways-to-leave-a-great-l_b_7148112.
9. *See* Keith Kraft, *The Art of Self Leadership*, KEITH KRAFT (Feb. 17, 2016).
10. Scott Jeffrey, *A Complete Guide to Self-Actualization: 5 Key Steps to Accelerate Growth*, CEOSAGE (2014), https://scottjeffrey.com/self-actualization/.
11. Donna Sapolin, *9 Most Common Regrets of the Living and Dying—and What to Do About Them*, NEXT AVENUE (July 11, 2013), https://www.nextavenue.org/9-most-common-regrets-living-and-dying-and-what-do-about-them/.
12. Leah W. Teague and Stephen L. Rispoli conversation with Bradley J.B. Toben, Dean, Baylor Law School (Nov. 20, 2019).
13. Moran, *supra* note 8.
14. Sapolin, *supra* note 11.
15. *Id.*
16. Moran, *supra* note 8.
17. *Id.*
18. Sapolin, *supra* note 11.
19. Abraham Lincoln quote, BRAINY QUOTE, https://www.brainyquote.com/quotes/abraham_lincoln_100845 (last visited July 20, 2020).
20. Kira M. Newman, *Six Ways Happiness Is Good for Your Health*, GREATER GOOD MAGAZINE (July 28, 2015), https://greatergood.berkeley.edu/article/item/six_ways_happiness_is_good_for_your_health.
21. Maya Angelou quote, BRAINY QUOTE, https://www.brainyquote.com/quotes/maya_angelou_578763 (last visited July 20, 2020).
22. Sapolin, *supra* note 11.
23. *Id.*
24. Moran, *supra* note 8.
25. K.S. Groves, *Integrating Leadership Development and Succession Planning Best Practices*, 26 J. MGMT. DEV. 239–60 (2007), *available at* https://doi.org/10.1108/02621710710732146.

26. *Id.*

27. Leah W. Teague conversation with J. Cary Gray, Baylor Law School (Jan. 6, 2020).

28. *Top 10 Warren Bennis Quotes of All Time*, Paul Sohn, https://paulsohn.org/top-10-warren-bennis-quotes-of-all-time/ (last visited July 9, 2020). Warren Gamaliel Bennis was an American scholar, organizational consultant, and author, widely regarded as a pioneer of the contemporary field of leadership studies.

29. Talmage Boston, Cross-Examining History: A Lawyer Gets Answers from the Experts About Our Presidents (Bright Sky 2016).

30. *Id.*

31. *See* Ron Chernow, Washington: A Life (Penguin 2010).

32. *Id.* The glaring error, though, was Washington's inability to free his slaves during his lifetime. Although he did so through his will when he died, he lacked the courage to do so during his life and face the potential of losing his wealth in the process. While Washington was curating his legacy, he could only go so far and his legacy will forever be tarnished because of it.

Index

441